PALGRAVE LAW MASTERS

Series Editor Marise Cremona

Evidence

Second Edition

Raymond Emson
LLM, Barrister

Series Editor: Marise Cremona
Professor of European Commercial Law
Queen Mary Centre for Commercial Law Studies
University of London

First edition 1999
Second edition 2004
Published by
PALGRAVE MACMILLAN
Houndmills, Basingstoke, Hampshire RG21 6XS
and 175 Fifth Avenue, New York, N.Y. 10010
Companies and representatives throughout the world

ISBN-13 978-0-333-99358-3
ISBN-10 0-333-99358-6

This book is printed on paper suitable for recycling and made from fully managed and sustained forest sources.

A catalogue record for this book is available from the British Library.

10 9 8 7 6 5 4 3 2
13 12 11 10 09 08 07 06 05

Printed and bound in Great Britain by
Creative Print & Design (Wales), Ebbw Vale

Contents

Table of Cases

Metropolitan Railway v. *Jackson* (1877) 3 App Cas 193 (HL) 420
Miller (t/a Waterloo Plan) v. *Crawley* [2002] EWCA Civ 1100 523
Miller v. *Howe* [1969] 1 WLR 1510 (DC) 165
Miller v. *Minister of Pensions* [1947] 2 All ER 372 (KBD) 451, 452, 454
Mills v. *R* [1995] 1 WLR 511 (PC) 182, 183
Mitchell v. *R* [1998] 2 WLR 839 (PC) 234
Montgomery v. *HM Advocate* [2001] 2 WLR 779 (PC) 297
Mood Music Publishing v. *De Wolfe* [1976] 2 WLR 451 (CA) 42
Moore v. *Ransome's Dock Committee* (1898) 14 TLR 539 (CA) 42
Moran v. *CPS* (2000) 164 JP 562 (DC) 376
Mubarak v. *Mubarak* [2001] 1 FLR 698 (CA) 457
Mullen v. *Hackney LBC* [1997] 1 WLR 1103 (CA) 473
Munro, Brice & Co v. *War Risks Association* [1918] 2 KB 78 (KBD) 448
Murdoch v. *Taylor* [1965] 2 WLR 425 (HL) 115, 119, 133, 134, 135, 136
Murray v. *DPP* [1994] 1 WLR 1 (HL) 274
Murray v. *United Kingdom* (1994) 19 EHRR 193 (ECtHR) 434
Murray v. *United Kingdom* (1996) 22 EHRR 29 (ECtHR) 221, 272, 274 275, 276, 277
Mutual Life Insurance Co v. *Hillmon* (1892) 145 US 285 (USSC) 177
Myers v. *DPP* [1964] 3 WLR 145 (HL) 140, 141, 143, 154, 162, 168, 202

Nagy v. *Weston* [1965] 1 All ER 78 (DC) 438
Natta v. *Canham* (1991) 104 ALR 143 (FCA) 513
Neat Holdings v. *Karajan Holdings* (1992) 110 ALR 449 (HCA) 455
Neill v. *North Antrim Magistrates' Court* [1992] 1 WLR 1220 (HL) 196
Nembhard v. *R* [1981] 1 WLR 1515 (PC) 181, 202
Ng Chun Pui v. *Lee Chuen Tat* [1988] RTR 298 (PC) 468
Nicholas v. *Penny* [1950] 2 KB 466 (DC) 467
Nimmo v. *Alexander Cowan & Sons* [1967] 3 WLR 1169 (HL) 441, 442, 444
Noor Mohamed v. *R* [1949] AC 182 (PC) 31, 53, 73
Norbrook Laboratories (GB) v. *Health and Safety Executive* (1998) *The Times* 23.2.98 (DC) 473
Norwich Pharmacal v. *Customs and Excise Commissioners* [1973] 3 WLR 164 (HL) 378
Nottingham City Council v. *Amin* [2000] 1 WLR 1071 (DC) 302, 304
Nye v. *Niblett* [1918] 1 KB 23 (DC) 471

O'Connell v. *Adams* [1973] RTR 150 (DC) 509
O'Rourke v. *Darbishire* [1920] AC 581 (HL) 414
Owen v. *Brown* [2002] EWHC 1135 (QBD) 250
Owen v. *Edwards* (1983) 77 Cr App R 191 (DC) 488
Owen v. *Nicholl* [1948] 1 All ER 707 (CA) 473
Owner v. *Bee Hive Spinning* [1914] 1 KB 105 (DC) 22
Oxley v. *Penwarden* [2001] Lloyd's Rep Med 347 (CA) 362
Oyston v. *United Kingdom* (2002) Application No. 42011/98 (ECtHR) 532

Papakosmas v. *R* (1999) 196 CLR 297 (HCA) 493
Paragon Finance v. *Freshfields* [1999] 1 WLR 1183 (CA) 414
Parker v. *DPP* (2000) 165 JP 213 (DC) 461
Parkes v. *R* [1976] 1 WLR 1251 (PC) 255
Parry v. *Boyle* (1986) 83 Cr App R 310 (DC) 16
Parry-Jones v. *Law Society* [1968] 2 WLR 397 (CA) 412
Patel v. *Comptroller of Customs* [1965] 3 WLR 1221 (PC) 145, 165
Paul v. *DPP* (1989) 90 Cr App R 173 (DC) 472
Perkins v. *Jeffery* [1915] 2 KB 702 (DC) 53
Perry v. *United Kingdom* (2002) Application No. 63737/00 (ECtHR) 323
Pfennig v. *R* (1995) 182 CLR 461 (HCA) 52, 60, 64 73, 74
PG v. *United Kingdom* (2001) Application No. 44787/98 (ECtHR) 229, 284, 392 404
Philcox v. *Carberry* [1960] Crim LR 563 (DC) 439

xx   *Table of Cases*

Table of Statutes

European Convention on Human Rights

xlvi

Table of Rules, Regulations, Codes of Practice and Guidelines

Foreign and Commonwealth Legislation

Acknowledgements

The author and publishers are grateful to the following for permission to reproduce copyright material: AusInfo (Government Information for Australians) for material subject to Commonwealth of Australia copyright; the Council of Law Reporting for Northern Ireland for extracts from the Northern Ireland Law Reports; the Harvard Law Review for material by Julius Stone in vol. 46; Her Majesty's Stationery Office for Crown copyright material; the Incorporated Council of Law Reporting for extracts from the Law Reports; Informa Law for an extract from Lloyd's Law Reports; Jordan Publishing Ltd for an extract from the Family Law Reports; the Jurist Publishing Company Ltd and Round Hall Ltd for an extract from Mr Justice Mackenna's speech published in vol. IX of the *Irish Jurist* (repeated in Patrick Devlin's *The Judge* (OUP, 1979)); Lawbook Co for extracts from the Commonwealth Law Reports and the South Australia State Reports; LexisNexis UK for extracts from the All England Law Reports, Butterworths Company Law Cases and Justice of the Peace Reports; the New Zealand Council of Law Reporting for extracts from the New Zealand Law Reports; Sweet & Maxwell Ltd for extracts from the Criminal Appeal Reports, the Criminal Law Review, Current Law, the European Human Rights Reports, the Road Traffic Reports and the Law Quarterly Review; Sweet & Maxwell Asia for an extract from *Tang Sui Man* v. *HKSAR* (19971998) 1 HKCFA 107; and the Victorian Council of Law Reporting and LexisNexis for extracts from the Victorian Law Reports. Crown copyright material is reproduced with the permission of the Controller of Her Majesty's Stationery Office and the Queen's Printer for Scotland. Extracts from the Commonwealth Law Reports and the South Australia State Reports are reprinted with the expressed permission of the ©Lawbook Co, part of Thomson Legal and Regulatory Limited, www.thomson.com.au. Australian legislation is reproduced by permission but does not purport to be the official or authorised version.

Every effort has been made to contact all copyright-holders, but if any have been inadvertently omitted the publishers will be pleased to make the appropriate arrangement at the earliest opportunity.

The law is as stated on 1 July 2003.

1   Introduction

The law of evidence is a fascinating blend of practical and academic issues. It is practical because it is the law which is applied in the courts every day to determine, *inter alia*, whether evidence ought to be admitted, the use which may be made of evidence once it has been admitted, and the way in which witnesses may be questioned. It is a body of law which must be known and understood thoroughly by any advocate (particularly those who practise in the criminal courts) as he or she may need to make submissions on a question of evidence or related procedure at very short notice. But this does not mean the law of evidence is no more than a body of rules to be learnt by rote. Far from it. The law of evidence is a discipline which *ought* to be studied at an academic level and this is as true for the prospective advocate as it is for any other student of the subject. Much of the law of evidence is indeterminate, and the student or advocate will be able to support his or her submissions on what the law is, or on what it ought to be, only if the principles and considerations of policy which underpin the subject are appreciated. For example, one can comprehend the law of criminal evidence only if something is known of the rights-based theories of jurisprudence, of concepts such as 'logical relevance' and 'proof', and of the weaknesses and prejudices which are an inextricable part of the human psyche.

The law of evidence, criminal evidence in particular, is a dynamic body of flexible discretionary powers and inflexible rules of somewhat uncertain scope which have evolved out of (and continue to be influenced by) considerations of public policy, common sense, logic, psychology, philosophy and legal principle. An important consequence is that, unlike other branches of the law, decided cases do not usually amount to binding precedents to be slavishly followed by judges in subsequent cases. More often than not a case on the law of evidence will provide no more than an *illustration* of how logic and certain well-established principles or considerations of policy have been applied to a particular factual scenario. For example, the fact that a man charged with committing an act of gross indecency on a boy was found to have photographs of naked boys in his home, and that such evidence was held to have been properly admitted at his trial, does not set a precedent to the effect that incriminating articles of this sort are *prima facie* admissible against a man charged with a sexual offence against another male. Nor does a case where indecent photographs in the accused's possession were held to have been wrongly admitted at his trial for indecently assaulting a woman provide any precedent for the inadmissibility of such evidence. To understand decisions of this sort requires an understanding of the *particular* circumstances of the case, the context in which the *logical relevance* and *weight* of the evidence were determined. But it is also necessary to understand the factors which would have militated against the admission of the evidence, the principles and considerations of public policy which would have justified *excluding* the evidence, for it will be seen that much of the law of evidence is concerned with concealing relevant evidence from the jury.

The fact that logically relevant evidence can quite properly be excluded from the trial process in a given case is the practical outcome of a conflict which lies at the heart of the law of evidence – a conflict between the 'principle of free proof' on the one hand and countervailing considerations of public policy on the other (Figure 1.1). The principle of free proof demands the admission of all available evidence which is logically relevant to a disputed issue of fact, for example the accused's guilt or innocence, on the ground that the exclusion of any relevant evidence encourages the jury to determine the issue on a false basis, thereby increasing the possibility that they will reach an erroneous verdict. The problem with this analysis is that it ignores the fallible nature of the human fact-finding tribunal. An item of evidence may well be logically relevant to the determination of a disputed issue of fact, but its admission may distract the jury from other more valuable evidence, or engender in them a feeling of hatred for the accused, or lead them along a path of logical reasoning which would exaggerate the true worth of the evidence. Other evidence may simply be too unreliable to leave to the jury notwithstanding the high value it would have if true. Somewhat paradoxically, then, relevant evidence may be excluded to *reduce* the possibility that the jury will reach the wrong verdict. In practice the exclusionary considerations tend to militate against the admission of prosecution evidence rather than evidence tendered by the accused because of the importance attached to the desirability of acquitting the innocent. The conflict between the principle of free proof and countervailing considerations of policy is often, therefore, a conflict between free proof and the principle that the accused should receive a fair trial.

Great weight is attached to the 'fair trial principle', but it is not the only reason for excluding logically relevant evidence. In other words, the law of evidence is not solely concerned with ensuring that the right decision is reached at the end of the trial. An example is provided by s. 76(2)(*a*) of the Police and Criminal Evidence Act 1984 which renders any confession inadmissible (as a matter of law) if it has been obtained in consequence of oppressive conduct. A confession obtained by oppression is inadmissible even if it is demonstrably true, regardless of the nature of the crime committed. The underlying policy is that the rights and dignity of the suspect must be *protected* if this country is to regard itself as a free and democratic society, even if the result is that the occasional criminal should go unpunished (the 'protective principle').

Logically relevant evidence may be excluded on the ground that it is *unreliable*, for example where the evidence comprises a witness statement made by a proven reprobate who is unwilling to face cross-examination. Conversely, of course, it may be more difficult to justify the exclusion of demonstrably reliable evidence. In other words, the 'reliability principle' may add cogency to the principle of free proof or detract from it. For

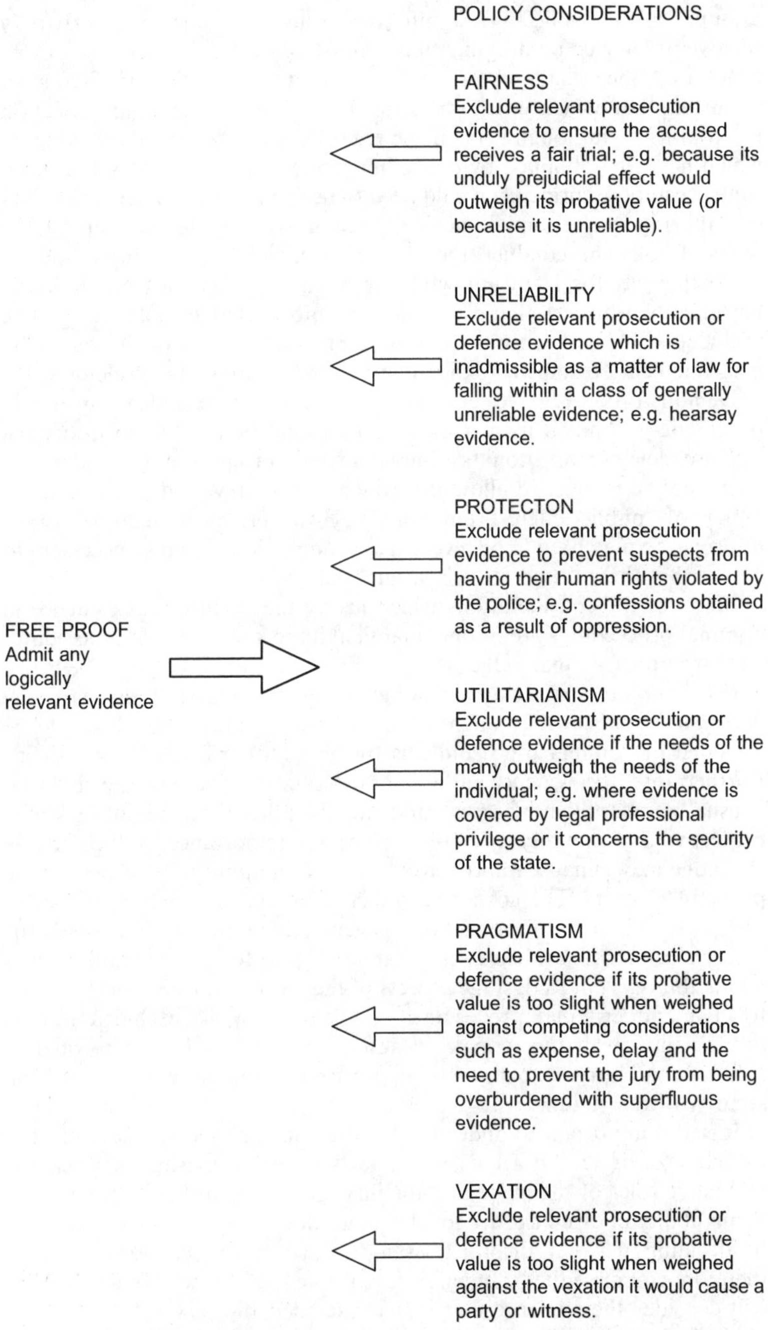

POLICY CONSIDERATIONS

FAIRNESS
Exclude relevant prosecution evidence to ensure the accused receives a fair trial; e.g. because its unduly prejudicial effect would outweigh its probative value (or because it is unreliable).

UNRELIABILITY
Exclude relevant prosecution or defence evidence which is inadmissible as a matter of law for falling within a class of generally unreliable evidence; e.g. hearsay evidence.

PROTECTON
Exclude relevant prosecution evidence to prevent suspects from having their human rights violated by the police; e.g. confessions obtained as a result of oppression.

FREE PROOF
Admit any logically relevant evidence

UTILITARIANISM
Exclude relevant prosecution or defence evidence if the needs of the many outweigh the needs of the individual; e.g. where evidence is covered by legal professional privilege or it concerns the security of the state.

PRAGMATISM
Exclude relevant prosecution or defence evidence if its probative value is too slight when weighed against competing considerations such as expense, delay and the need to prevent the jury from being overburdened with superfluous evidence.

VEXATION
Exclude relevant prosecution or defence evidence if its probative value is too slight when weighed against the vexation it would cause a party or witness.

Figure 1.1   **The law of criminal evidence**

example, if the police break into the accused's home and unlawfully remove a diary containing incriminating statements, the principle of free proof and the reliability principle would work together in favour of admitting that evidence. Its admission would not have an unfair effect on the trial itself, although it might be regarded as unfair to admit evidence which has been obtained by police impropriety. In order to exclude such evidence another principle would need to be found, such as the desirability of not bringing the criminal justice system into disrepute by admitting the fruits of police misconduct (the 'integrity principle') or the importance of protecting citizens from unlawful interference in their private affairs. It has already been seen that even a demonstrably reliable confession will be excluded if it has been obtained by oppression, a case of the reliability principle being trumped by the integrity and/or protective principles.

Demonstrably reliable evidence may also be excluded on purely pragmatic grounds if its probative value would be too low to justify the expense, delay or vexation its admission would bring; or if it would not be in the public interest to allow the evidence to be revealed (the utilitarian policy of 'public interest immunity'). However, even highly sensitive information may need to be revealed if its admission would be necessary to ensure that the accused receives a fair trial.

Many of the considerations which justify the exclusion of evidence in criminal proceedings are of only marginal importance in civil proceedings tried by a professional judge sitting alone. Judges are thought to be better able to assess the reliability and weight of evidence, and to disregard any personal prejudices they might have; so much evidence which would be excluded in criminal proceedings is freely admitted in civil proceedings. Furthermore, the evidence gathering process which precedes the civil trial is usually undertaken by private individuals rather than the police, so the protective and integrity principles are of less importance, particularly as the judge may penalise improper conduct by an appropriate order for the payment of costs. The governing principle in civil proceedings is that of free proof. The risk of unreliability is generally an insufficient reason for the exclusion of evidence: unreliability goes to weight rather than admissibility. That said, some aspects of the law of evidence apply equally to civil and criminal proceedings. Evidence may be excluded if it is insufficiently probative to make its admission worthwhile or if it would be in the public interest to suppress it (for example because it concerns the security of the state).

It is also important to understand that the law of evidence developed in the context of jury trials where there is a sharp division between the respective roles of the judge and the jury. Questions of law, including the admissibility of evidence, are for the judge alone. The jury's role is limited to deciding whether disputed issues of fact have been proved (they therefore comprise the 'tribunal of fact'). The judge ('the tribunal of law') will consider the evidence and if it is excluded the jury will never hear about it. If the evidence is admitted the judge will direct the jury on the limited use which may be made of it, and warn them against impermissible or prejudicial reasoning and/or any factors which might render the evidence unreliable. Accordingly much of the law of evidence is irrelevant to civil proceedings and of only limited significance in proceedings before magistrates, although in theory the law is the same whether the accused is tried summarily or on indictment.

The purpose of the trial is, of course, to give the claimant or prosecution the opportunity to prove an allegation which has been made against the civil defendant or criminal accused. The law of evidence regulates the admission of evidence and the use which may be made of it during the trial, with appropriate directions from the judge in jury trials, but it also establishes who should prove disputed issues of fact and the degree of likelihood which has to be met before a fact can be said to have been 'proved'. In the context of a trial the term 'proof' must be treated with caution, however. Very little, if anything, can be proved with certainty so all that can be hoped for is a sufficiently high probability that the assertion of fact is true or false (as the case may be). As Lord Simon said in *DPP* v. *Shannon* [1974] 3 WLR 155 (HL) (at p. 191):

> 'The law in action is not concerned with absolute truth, but with proof before a fallible human tribunal to a requisite standard of probability in accordance with formal rules of evidence (in particular, rules relating to admissibility of evidence).'

The function of the tribunal of fact – the criminal jury in particular – is therefore somewhat similar to that of the historian, trying to piece together a picture of what happened in the past from fragments of evidence which may be of uncertain (and unascertainable) reliability. The task of the professional historian is arduous enough, but the jury's difficulties are exacerbated by the exclusionary rules which prevent them from seeing much relevant (and even highly probative) evidence, their own 'amateur' composition, and the very nature of the English adversarial system. The evidence presented by each side may have been subjectively selected by the parties to support their respective cases. The defence will withhold anything which undermines the accused's case; the police may intentionally or negligently lose or fail to gather some evidence or perhaps even withhold evidence from the prosecution. Then there is the question of the witnesses' credibility – mistaken observations, misremembered details, confusion, bias, lies, self-interest, self-delusion, self-preservation and so on. All these human failings tend to undermine the jury's search for 'objective truth'. The seemingly credible witness may in reality be a dishonest and skilled hypocrite; the convincing eye-witness may be honestly mistaken or have his own interests to serve; and the jury itself, as a disparate group of individuals, will have their own personal preferences and prejudices.

A case in point, with horrendous consequences for the accused, is that of Mr Mahmoud Mattan. In July 1952, M, a Somali, was tried for the murder of a shopkeeper, V, sentenced to death and executed in September of that year. V had had her throat cut by someone on the evening of 6 March 1952. The case against M depended almost entirely on the identification evidence of one man (W) who claimed that he saw M leave V's shop at 8.15 p.m. on that evening. W's witness statement to the police made on 7 March differed materially from the evidence he gave from the witness box, but it had not been disclosed to the defence. W's statement described the person he had seen as a Somali with a gold tooth, but M had no such tooth and W did not repeat that part of his description during the trial. W's identification evidence was also demonstrably flawed in other respects. Furthermore, W had received a reward from the police, but that fact had not been disclosed. Nor had the defence been informed that four other witnesses who had seen a man near V's shop at or about the time of the murder had failed to pick M out at an identification parade. One witness had even told the police that M was *not* the man she had seen. A witness statement which supported M's alibi was withheld, as was evidence that another suspect, also a Somali, had admitted being near the shop at the time of the murder. That suspect (who had a gold tooth) was subsequently tried for a separate murder by stabbing in 1954 and found not guilty by reason of insanity. M's conviction for the murder of V was quashed in 1998 (*R* v. *Mattan (Deceased)* (1998) *The Times* 5.3.98 (97/6415/S2) (CA)). Rose LJ, having noted that there had been many changes in the law since 1952, said:

> 'The case has a wider significance in that it clearly demonstrates five matters. First, capital punishment was not perhaps a prudent culmination for a criminal justice system which is human and therefore fallible ... Fourthly, no-one associated with the criminal justice system can afford to be complacent. Fifthly, injustices of this kind can only be avoided if all concerned in the investigation of crime, and the preparation and presentation of criminal prosecutions, observe the very highest standards of integrity, conscientiousness and professional skill.'

2 Preliminaries

2.1 Facts in Issue and the Ultimate Probandum

The 'facts in issue' are the disputed issues of fact which the prosecution or claimant must prove in order to succeed, along with the issues of fact which the accused or civil defendant must prove in order to establish his defence. The term 'ultimate probandum' is sometimes used to represent what the prosecution or claimant must *ultimately* prove in order to succeed. The party who is obliged to prove a particular fact in issue is said to bear the 'burden of proof' on that issue (15.1 *post*). The nature and number of the facts in issue depend on the substantive law and what, if anything, has been 'formally admitted' by the parties. The substantive law identifies the facts in issue for the type of case before the court, but once a fact has been formally admitted it ceases to be in issue and need not (indeed cannot) be proved by the adduction of evidence (see 15.6.3 *post*).

Take, for example, a charge of murder. The ultimate probandum is that it was the accused who murdered the person named as the deceased on the indictment. In the absence of any formal admission by the accused, the prosecution must prove the following facts in issue: (i) that the person named on the indictment as the deceased is indeed dead; (ii) that his death was caused by a particular injury; (iii) that the accused caused that injury; and (iv) that the accused had the intention to kill or seriously injure him. The prosecution bear the burden of proof on all these issues and the accused must be acquitted if they are unable to prove any of them (Figure 2.1). If the accused were formally to admit that he killed the deceased it would no longer be necessary for the prosecution to prove the first three of those facts. They would merely need to prove that the accused had the *mens rea* for murder at the time he killed the deceased. If, however, the accused were to raise the partial defence of provocation there would be additional facts in issue to address, that is, the elements of that defence. The prosecution would then have to prove the non-existence of any one of those facts in issue, in addition to the accused's *mens rea*.

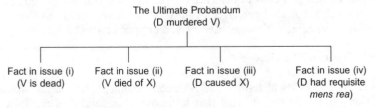

Figure 2.1   **The ultimate probandum**

2.2 Proving Facts in Issue

To prove a fact in issue it is necessary for evidence to be adduced or elicited during the trial. If, for example, the accused is on trial for murder it may be possible to prove his guilt by calling a witness to give oral evidence that he saw him viciously stabbing the deceased to death. Oral evidence which has been given by a witness in court is known as 'testimony' and if, as is usually the case, the witness states what he directly perceived he is said to give 'direct testimony' or 'direct oral evidence' (2.2.1 *post*).

There are, however, some facts in issue which can never be proved by direct testimony, either because there is no available witness or because it is impossible for a person directly to perceive what is in issue. In the latter category would be the accused's state of mind at the time he allegedly committed the *actus reus* of the offence charged. Witnesses cannot give direct testimony of what another man is thinking, so the accused's *mens rea* must be proved in some other way. In the present example the eye-witness to the stabbing would be able to give direct oral evidence that the accused caused the deceased's death, but the prosecution would not be able *directly* to prove the accused's intentions at that time on the basis of that oral evidence. The accused's state of mind would have to be *inferred* from his conduct as proved by the witness's direct oral evidence. The witness's description of the frenzied nature of the attack could allow the jury to infer that the accused intended to kill the deceased. An item of evidence from which a fact in issue may ultimately be inferred is known as an 'evidentiary fact' or a 'fact relevant to a fact in issue' or (more commonly) as 'circumstantial evidence' (2.2.2 *post*). Circumstantial evidence allows a fact in issue to be proved inferentially rather than directly, so it is 'indirect' evidence. An item of circumstantial evidence may be established by direct oral evidence, as in the murder example, or by drawing an inference from other circumstantial evidence. If no-one saw the deceased being stabbed, it would be necessary to infer the accused's *mens rea* from circumstantial evidence, the existence of which would possibly have to be inferred from other, even more remote, circumstantial evidence. For example, it might be possible to infer the accused's *mens rea* from the evidentiary fact that he had a motive to kill the deceased; yet the existence of that evidentiary fact might have to be inferred from even more remote evidentiary facts such as the accused's earlier threat to kill the deceased and a life insurance policy found in his house showing that he would profit from the deceased's death (see Figure 2.2).

Finally, there is a class of evidence – 'real evidence' – which comprises things which are directly perceived by the jury, for example a closed-circuit television recording which has been played in open court (2.2.3 *post*).

2.2.1 Testimonial Evidence

There are two types of testimonial evidence: 'testimony' and 'admissible hearsay'. It will be remembered that testimony is the oral evidence of a witness in court, and if that evidence concerns matters directly perceived

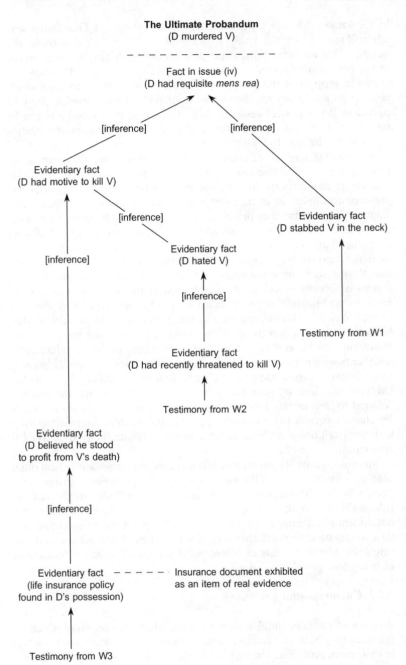

Figure 2.2 **Circumstantial evidence**

by the witness it is direct oral evidence (direct testimony). Oral evidence is admissible to prove the truth of the matters stated by the witness, the weight of the evidence being dependent on the truthfulness and accuracy of the person who provides it. Witnesses give oral evidence ('evidence in chief') in support of the party calling them during their 'examination-in-chief' (16.4 *post*); they are then 'cross-examined' by the opposing party or parties so that any weaknesses in their evidence or their credibility can be revealed, or so that evidence favourable to the cross-examining party's case can be elicited (16.5 *post*).

'Hearsay' is any *out-of-court* statement tendered for the purpose of proving the truth of the matters stated (5.1 *post*). Generally speaking, hearsay is inadmissible in criminal proceedings because witnesses are expected to appear in court to give direct oral evidence and face cross-examination on what they perceived. There are, however, many exceptions to this general exclusionary rule and if a hearsay statement is admissible by virtue of any such exception it is admissible evidence of the truth of the matters stated. In this sense it may be regarded as equivalent to testimony and thus a form of testimonial evidence. If the maker of the hearsay statement directly perceived the matters referred to his evidence is said to be 'first-hand hearsay' (equivalent to direct testimony – the word 'direct' is limited to non-hearsay evidence). The maker may have written down what he saw and subsequently died, in which case his first-hand hearsay statement will be adduced in documentary form, or he may have told another person what he saw, in which case that person will appear in court as a witness to repeat the deceased's oral first-hand hearsay. If the maker (M2) of the hearsay statement did not directly perceive the matters referred to, but merely repeated another hearsay statement made to him by another person (M1) who did perceive the matters referred to, M2's statement is known as 'second-hand hearsay' (while, of course, M1's is first-hand).

An out-of-court statement which is tendered for a relevant reason other than to prove the truth of the matters stated – for example, to prove that a person spoke with an Australian accent – is not excluded by the hearsay rule but is admissible as 'original evidence' (5.4 *post*). Original evidence is not a form of testimonial evidence because the party tendering it does not seek to rely on it to prove the truth of the matters stated. Another type of original evidence consists of out-of-court utterances which are incapable of being true or false (5.5 *post*).

2.2.2 Circumstantial Evidence

An item of circumstantial evidence is an evidentiary fact from which an *inference* may be drawn rendering the existence (or non-existence) of a fact in issue more probable. The fact in issue is not proved by a witness relating what he directly perceived, so circumstantial evidence is 'indirect' evidence. Examples of circumstantial evidence include disposition, motive, knowledge, opportunity, capacity, suspicious behaviour, silence, lies, preparatory acts, and so on. The term covers *any* admissible evidence from which it would be possible to draw an inference going some way towards proving a fact in issue.

The public perception seems to be that circumstantial evidence is in some way an inferior form of evidence. One sometimes hears persons who have been convicted of an offence, or their relatives or solicitors (who should know better), affirm their intention to appeal against a conviction as the evidence was 'only circumstantial'. Students of evidence should disabuse themselves of this myth: 'It is no derogation of evidence to say that it is circumstantial' (*R* v. *Taylor* (1928) 21 Cr App R 20 (CCA)). Circumstantial evidence may be highly probative or even compelling evidence of what happened on a particular occasion. Indeed, so long as the possibility of fabrication can be discounted, circumstantial evidence may be more reliable than direct testimony.

An individual item of circumstantial evidence taken by itself may or may not be particularly probative of the accused's guilt in criminal proceedings. Much depends on the nature of the evidence in question. Some types of circumstantial evidence are inherently cogent, whereas other types may have very little probative value. If the only evidence identifying the accused as the offender is a *single* item of circumstantial evidence then that evidence must of course be sufficiently probative to discount the possibility that any other person could have committed the offence, for example a sufficiently complete fingerprint (11.4 *post*) or a sufficiently sophisticated DNA profile (11.5 *post*). In practice, though, the prosecution are unlikely to base their entire case on a single item of circumstantial evidence. As a general rule the value of circumstantial evidence lies in its *cumulative* effect; that is to say, while a single item of circumstantial evidence may only slightly increase the likelihood that the accused is guilty, several items taken together may carry enough probative force to justify a conviction.

If identity is in issue circumstantial evidence operates by reducing the possibility that anyone else could have committed the offence, and so indirectly identifies the accused. A single item of circumstantial evidence, 'A', will suggest that the offender belongs to a particular group of persons, 'Group A', which is smaller than society as a whole. A further item, 'B', will suggest he belongs to 'Group B' too, and therefore that he also belongs to the even smaller 'Group AB' (that is, those persons who belong to both Groups A and B). Item 'C' will suggest his membership of 'Group C' and therefore the even smaller 'Group ABC', and so on. The more circumstantial evidence there is which identifies the accused as a member of a whole range of groups of person the greater the probability becomes that he, rather than anyone else, is guilty. In *R* v. *Exall* (1866) 4 F & F 922 (Assizes) Pollock CB said of circumstantial evidence (at p. 929):

'It is ... like the case of a rope composed of several cords. One strand of the cord might be insufficient to sustain the weight, but three stranded together may be quite of sufficient strength. Thus it may be in circumstantial evidence – there may be a combination of circumstances, no one of which would raise a reasonable conviction, or more than a mere suspicion; but the whole, taken together, may create a strong conclusion of guilt ... with as much certainty as human affairs can require or admit of.'

Take, for example, a case where a woman has been found raped and murdered. If there is no direct evidence identifying the offender the prosecution will have to rely entirely on circumstantial evidence. This could include a footprint in the mud (*item A*) identifying the offender as a man who wears a particular type of footwear (*Group A*); a tyre print (*item B*) identifying the offender as the driver of a car with particular tyres (*Group B*); a used syringe (*item C*) identifying the offender as a heroin addict (*Group C*); and semen (*item D*) identifying the offender as a man with a particular sexual disease (*Group D1*) and a particular DNA profile (*Group D2*). *Group A* and *Group B* are fairly large so, standing alone, *item A* and *item B* would not be particularly probative; but, taken together, they would have the cumulative effect of narrowing the group of possible offenders to those men who have shoes of that type *and* a car with tyres of that type (*Group AB*). There may still be thousands of such men, but the number of men falling within *Group AB* and within *Group C* is likely to be very small. Only one man (the accused) in *Group ABC* may have the particular sexual disease and so fall within *Group ABCD1*, suggesting, therefore, that *he* is the offender. In other words, the cumulative effect of several items of circumstantial evidence may be great enough to identify the accused, even though each item in isolation would be inherently weak evidence of his guilt. The prosecution case could be further strengthened by other items of circumstantial evidence pertaining to the accused himself. A search of his home might reveal hard core pornographic or 'snuff' videos showing women being raped and murdered (*item E*) or a collection of newspaper clippings relating to the offence in question (*item F*). *Item E* would be probative of the accused's guilt by showing that he is not revolted by the idea of rape. Both the offender and the accused would fall within that group of men (*Group E*) adding weight to the prosecution case. Similarly, both the accused and the offender would fall within that group of men (*Group F*) who are particularly interested in the offence with which the accused has been charged, and this too would suggest his guilt. Again, standing alone, *item F* would have little probative value, but in the factual context of the other circumstantial evidence it would make the case against the accused compelling.

Item D2 deserves separate consideration. If the prosecution manage to obtain a DNA profile of the offender from his semen this will show he belongs to a very small group of men, perhaps just four or five persons in the country. If an analysis of the accused's DNA puts him within that group (*Group D2*) the prosecution would have a highly cogent item of evidence; but, in the absence of any other evidence, it would be insufficient to prove his guilt. The prosecution must prove the accused is guilty beyond reasonable doubt, and the mere fact he is one of the five men in *Group D2* who could have committed the offence is insufficient, for it is a mere 20 per cent possibility. However, *item D2* taken together with any of the other items of circumstantial evidence would almost certainly be enough to narrow that group of five down to one person: the accused (see 11.5 *post*).

Circumstantial evidence may be used not only to identify an offender, but also to prove *mens rea* where identity is not in issue, or even that the *actus reus* of an offence has been committed. An interesting example is provided by the case of *R* v. *Onufrejczyk* [1955] 2 WLR 273 (CCA). The accused in that case was charged with the murder of his business partner, S, who had disappeared without trace on 14 December 1953, the date on which the murder was allegedly committed. The last witness to see him other than the accused was a blacksmith who testified that S had visited his premises to collect a horse on that date. The accused's defence was that on 18 December a large car had driven up to their isolated farmhouse at 7.30 p.m. and three men had kidnapped S at gunpoint. There was no direct evidence that S was dead let alone that he had been killed, but the accused was convicted of his murder as both his death and the fact that the accused had killed him could be inferred cumulatively from several items of circumstantial evidence. First, the accused had had a motive to kill S. He had wanted to obtain S's share in the farm but was in dire need of money, and S had threatened to put the farm up for sale if the accused could not obtain the money to buy him out. (There was also evidence that the accused had made threats against S.) Second, the accused's behaviour after 14 December suggested that he had been aware that S was already dead. On the afternoon of 18 December he had written to an acquaintance explaining that S would be going away for a fortnight and that he, the accused, had already paid him most of the money; and yet, soon after, the accused had gone to London to borrow money from relatives and had got a woman to forge documents purporting to be agreements upon which he had then forged S's signature. The accused had also written a number of letters which suggested that S had gone to Poland and that he would not be returning, and had asked a man to impersonate S at a meeting with his solicitor. Third, S had not taken any of his clothes or possessions away with him. Fourth, the accused had acted in a suspicious manner once the police had begun their investigation into S's disappearance. In particular, he had gone to the blacksmith to bribe him into saying that S had visited him on 17 December. Fifth, minute drops of blood had been found on the walls and ceiling of the farmhouse kitchen.

A further example is provided by *R* v. *Lewis* (1982) 76 Cr App R 33 (CA). The accused in that case faced an allegation that he had indecently touched his partner's daughters. He admitted there had been contact but said in his defence that it had been innocent touching as part of his attempt to be a father figure to the girls. His culpable state of mind could be proved, however, by the presence of magazines and other documents concerning sexual acts with children. Those articles allowed an inference to be drawn that the accused was interested in children as sexual objects, which allowed the further inference to be drawn that he had not acted as a father figure when touching the girls but had groped them for sexual gratification.

Circumstantial evidence may be highly probative of the accused's guilt, but there is always the possibility that it could have been fabricated. Any type of evidence may be fabricated, of course, and one of the reasons for cross-examination is to reveal whether witnesses have been lying on oath during their examination-in-chief. The problem with circumstantial evidence is that its reliability may be unchallengeable. In *Teper* v. *R* [1952] AC 480 (PC) Lord Normand said (at p. 489):

> 'Circumstantial evidence may sometimes be conclusive, but it must always be narrowly examined, if only because evidence of this kind may be fabricated to cast suspicion on another ... It is also necessary before drawing the inference of the accused's guilt from circumstantial evidence to be sure that there are no other co-existing circumstances which would weaken or destroy the inference.'

The final sentence of this dictum is interesting, because it rightly suggests that the accused should not be convicted on the basis of a cumulative inference drawn from circumstantial evidence if an alternative inference could be drawn which would be consistent with a (reasonably possible) theory that the accused is not guilty. A similar point was made in *R* v. *Onufrejczyk* [1955] 2 WLR 273 (CCA) where Lord Goddard CJ said that 'the fact of death, like any other fact, can be proved by circumstantial evidence, that is to say, evidence of facts which lead to one conclusion, provided that the jury are satisfied and are warned that it must lead to one conclusion only'. Accordingly, it was argued before the House of Lords in *McGreevy* v. *DPP* [1973] 1 WLR 276 that where the prosecution case is based wholly or substantially on circumstantial evidence the judge is duty-bound to direct the jury to acquit unless they are satisfied that the evidence is not only consistent with the accused's guilt but also inconsistent with any other reasonable conclusion, in line with the direction given by Alderson B in *R* v. *Hodge* (1838) 2 Lewin 227 (Assizes). The House of Lords rejected this submission, however, being 'averse from laying down more rules binding on judges than are shown to be necessary', and held that the obligation to direct the jury to acquit unless 'satisfied of guilt beyond all reasonable doubt' was a sufficient safeguard which the jury would more readily understand.

2.2.3 Real Evidence

Real evidence is the term used to describe evidence which is directly perceived or inspected by the court itself. This includes tangible items ('exhibits') such as the weapon used in a murder, the goods stolen in a burglary, the handkerchief found at the scene of the crime, the closed-circuit television recording of an offence being committed, a person's physical appearance, and so on. Not every tangible object is automatically admissible on the ground that it is real evidence, however. If a document such as a letter or video-recording is tendered to prove the truth of the matters recorded, it will be admissible only if its contents fall within the scope of an exception to the hearsay rule as the relevance of the document lies solely in its being a conduit for hearsay. The document would be classified as 'documentary evidence' (2.7 *post*) as opposed to 'real evidence'. Of course, if the letter or video tape is relevant for some other reason, because, for example, it bears the accused's bloody fingerprints upon it, it will be admissible as real evidence.

The demeanour and intonation of witnesses is also a form of real evidence, as is a particularly unwieldy object which cannot be brought into court and so has to be viewed *in situ*. In *Buckingham* v. *Daily News* [1956] 3 WLR 375 the plaintiff alleged that he had been injured while cleaning the blades of his employers' rotary press on account of their failure to provide him with a reasonably safe system of work. During the course of the trial the judge, in the presence of counsel, went to the defendant's premises, inspected the machine and observed a demonstration by the plaintiff of how he had cleaned the blades. The Court of Appeal accepted that the judge had been entitled to treat what he had seen as a form of real evidence: it is 'just as much a part of the evidence as if the machine had been brought into the well of the court and the plaintiff had there demonstrated what took place'. Similarly, it may be appropriate for the court to visit a particular location or site. This may be a simple 'view' where the court inspects the place – the '*locus in quo*' – where the road accident occurred or the alleged murder was committed; or the inspection may be combined with a demonstration, where one or more witnesses explain their vantage point and what they saw or heard at the material time.

Although it is clear that an out-of-court demonstration, or the out-of-court inspection of an object which could (in theory) have been seen in the courtroom, is regarded as the observation of admissible real evidence, it has been said that a simple view of the *locus in quo* is strictly speaking nothing more than an opportunity for the tribunal of fact to understand the context of the case so that they can follow the evidence and apply it (*London General Omnibus Co* v. *Lavell* [1901] 1 Ch 135 (CA) at p. 139, *Scott* v. *Numurkah Corporation* (1954) 91 CLR 300 (HCA) at p. 313; see also *Goold* v. *Evans* [1951] 2 TLR 1189 (CA) at p. 1192). It has also been said, however, that a simple view *is* real evidence 'in substitution for or supplemental to plans, photographs and the like' (*Karamat* v. *R* [1956] 2 WLR 412 (PC) at p. 417; see also *Goold* v. *Evans* [1951] 2 TLR 1189 (CA) at p. 1191 and *Tito* v. *Waddell* [1975] 1 WLR 1303 (ChD) at pp. 1307–8). If there is a difference between the status of views and demonstrations, it is a distinction which carries little if any significance in practice.

Recent views of note occurred in *R* v. *Jeffrey Archer* (2001) *The Times* (news report) 21.6.01 (CCC), where the court visited Court 13 at the Royal Courts of Justice, the *locus in quo* of the accused's alleged perjury, and in *R* v. *Stone (No. 2)* (2001) *The Daily Telegraph* (news report) 19.9.01 (CC), where the court observed the secluded copse in Kent where an appalling double-murder was committed in 1996. The most noteworthy demonstration in recent years occurred on 16 February 1999, during the war crimes trial which led to the appeal in *R* v. *Sawoniuk* [2000] 2 Cr App R 220 (CA). In that case the trial court paid a visit to the village of Domachevo (in

Belarus) where the Jewish population were slaughtered by Nazi sympathisers in 1942, and a prosecution eye-witness was permitted to show the jury where he had stood and watched murder being committed (see also Ormerod, 'A Prejudicial View' [2000] Crim LR 452 at pp. 457–60). Because the court is effectively relocating when it inspects a site or object, or observes a demonstration, the judge and jury (if there is one) should attend together, and the parties or their legal representatives should be present (or at least be given the opportunity of being present), save that a judge trying a civil case alone is entitled to conduct a general view of the *locus in quo* by himself if it is a public place (*Goold* v. *Evans* [1951] 2 TLR 1189 (CA) at p. 1191, *Salsbury* v. *Woodland* [1969] 3 WLR 29 (CA)). Similarly, magistrates (including district judges) should not view the scene of the alleged criminal offence unless accompanied by the parties or their representatives, although it would appear that the limited 'general view' exception applies in this context too (*Parry* v. *Boyle* (1986) 83 Cr App R 310 (DC), *Gibbons* v. *DPP* (2000) unreported (CO/1480/2000) (DC)). That said, because some feature of the *locus in quo* may have changed during the period between the relevant incident (for example, the alleged offence) and the trial, or the judge or magistrates may see something of consequence, it is 'undesirable' that even a general view should be conducted in the absence of the parties or their representatives (*Salsbury* v. *Woodland* [1969] 3 WLR 29 (CA), *Parry* v. *Boyle* (1986) 83 Cr App R 310 (DC)). In a case tried on indictment, the judge may need to warn the jurors against visiting the *locus in quo* by themselves (*R* v. *Davis* [2001] 1 Cr App R 115 (CA)).

2.3 *Res Gestae*

Lord Tomlin commented that *res gestae* – which means 'event' or 'transaction' – was 'a phrase adopted to provide a respectable legal cloak for a variety of cases to which no formula of precision can be applied' (*Homes* v. *Newman* [1931] 2 Ch 112 (ChD) at p. 120). Broadly speaking the term now refers to the gate to admissibility through which two types of otherwise inadmissible evidence may be adduced in criminal proceedings, the ground being that the evidence in question is inextricably connected with the circumstances (of the alleged offence), that is, it 'forms part of the *res gestae*'. The first type is evidence of the accused's relevant misconduct during the period surrounding the time when he is alleged to have committed the offence charged, where that misconduct has not given rise to a separate charge in the instant proceedings. It will be seen in Chapter 3 that evidence of the accused's extraneous misconduct is generally inadmissible to prove that he is guilty of the offence charged. There is, however, an exception to this exclusionary rule if the extraneous misconduct can be said to form part of the *res gestae* (see 3.3.9 *post*). The second type of evidence comprises out-of-court statements admissible under one or more common-law exceptions to the exclusionary hearsay rule, the justifications for these exceptions being, first, that statements forming part of the *res gestae* are more likely to be reliable than other out-of-court statements and, second, that there may be no other evidence available to prove what is in issue (see 6.1.1 *post*).

2.4 Collateral Facts

Collateral facts are not directly related to the proof of facts in issue but have an indirect bearing on such proof. The term covers facts which must be proved as a condition precedent to the admissibility of certain evidence (or the competence of a witness to give evidence), but it is primarily used to refer to facts affecting the weight of admissible evidence, especially the credibility of witnesses. Thus, evidence may be adduced to prove a witness has a reputation for dishonesty, is biased or has a defect which might undermine the weight of his testimony (see 16.5.4 *post*).

2.5 Relevance, Probative Value and Admissibility

To be admissible, any item of evidence must be *relevant* to a fact in issue ('relevant to an issue') or a collateral fact such as the credibility of a witness ('relevant to credit') or contribute towards an explanation of the background to the case. Background evidence aside, to be admissible any item of evidence must render more probable or less probable the existence of a fact in issue or a collateral fact (see 3.1 *post*).

The distinction between relevance to an issue and relevance to credit is well established, and underpins one of the exclusionary rules of the law of evidence, but it is not based on logic. Evidence which undermines a witness's credibility will have the knock-on effect of undermining the value of his testimony. If his testimony is relevant to an issue, the evidence undermining his credibility will, by undermining the value of his testimony, also be relevant to an issue, albeit indirectly so. The difference between relevance to an issue (direct relevance to an issue) and relevance to credit (indirect relevance to an issue) is therefore one of degree (see 16.5.2 *post*).

If an item of evidence is relevant it is admissible unless it falls within the scope of an exclusionary rule or a general exclusionary principle, in which case it will be admissible only if it also falls within an exception to that rule or if its probative value is sufficiently high for the exclusionary principle to be overridden by the principle of free proof. The probative value ('cogency' or 'weight') of an item of relevant evidence is the extent to which that evidence affects the probability of the existence of a fact in issue or collateral fact.

2.6 The Discretion to Exclude Admissible Evidence

In criminal proceedings the court (magistrates or judge) has a general discretion at common law to exclude or withdraw admissible prosecution evidence on the ground that its probative value would be outweighed by the undue prejudice its admission would cause the accused, and a more limited common-law discretion to exclude or withdraw confessions and analogous evidence obtained in violation of the accused's privilege against self-incrimination (*R* v. *Sang* [1979] 3 WLR 263 (HL), 10.1 *post*). The general discretion may be applied to exclude manifestly unreliable evidence (*R* v. *Lawson* [1998] Crim LR 883 (CA)) or evidence which would cast the accused in a particularly poor light and encourage the jury to convict him for the wrong reasons (3.3 *post*). The court also has a discretion to exclude prosecution evidence by virtue of s. 78(1) of the Police and Criminal Evidence Act 1984 ('PACE') if its admission 'would have such an adverse effect on the fairness of the proceedings that the court ought not to admit it'. Section 78(1) confers a *duty* upon the trial judge (or magistrates) to consider the exclusion of prosecution evidence, where on the evidence and circumstances it is appropriate, regardless of whether the question has been raised by the defence (*R (Saifi)* v. *Governor of Brixton Prison* [2001] 1 WLR 1134 (DC), *R* v. *Foster* [2003] EWCA Crim 178). Importantly, however, there is no general discretion to exclude admissible evidence tendered by the accused, even if the admission of that evidence would unduly prejudice the defence of a co-accused. Subject to one exception, the accused has an unfettered right to adduce any *admissible* evidence which supports his own defence. This principle was developed by Devlin J in *R* v. *Miller* (1952) 36 Cr App R 169 (Assizes), and has since been applied by the Privy Council and the House of Lords (*Lobban* v. *R* [1995] 1 WLR 877 (PC), *R* v. *Myers* [1997] 3 WLR 552 (HL)). The exception relates to the discretion under s. 25 of the Criminal Justice Act 1988 to exclude hearsay evidence which is *prima facie* admissible under ss. 23 or 24 (6.2.3 *post*).

With regard to the exclusion of prosecution evidence, s. 78(1) of PACE has pretty much supplanted the court's common-law discretion; and, human rights considerations aside, the Court of Appeal or Divisional Court will not interfere with the way the statutory discretion was exercised unless the trial judge or magistrates acted unreasonably in the '*Wednesbury*' sense (from *Associated Provincial Picture Houses* v. *Wednesbury Corporation* [1948] 1 KB 223 (CA) at p. 229). That is to say, so long as all relevant factors were taken into account and all irrelevant factors were disregarded, the ruling will be upheld on appeal unless it was a decision no reasonable judge (or bench of magistrates) could have reached (*R* v. *O'Leary* (1988) 87 Cr App R 387 (CA), *R* v. *Christou* [1992] 3 WLR 228 (CA), *R* v. *Quinn* [1995] 1 Cr App R 480 (CA), *R* v. *Stewart* [1999] Crim LR 746 (98/2314/Y3) (CA)). It has been suggested that the discretion is limited to an assessment of unfairness, and that once it has been concluded that the admission of the evidence 'would have such an adverse effect on the fairness of the proceedings that the court ought not to admit it' the evidence *must* be excluded (*R* v. *Middlebrook* (1994) *The Independent* 7.3.94 (CA), *R* v. *Chalkley* [1998] 3 WLR 146 (CA)). In *R* v. *Dures* [1997] 2 Cr App R 247, however, the Court of Appeal expressed a clear preference for the traditional approach; and in *Thompson* v. *R* [1998] 2 WLR 927 the

Privy Council, having stated that there was no difference between the two approaches, also followed *R* v. *O'Leary* and *R* v. *Christou*. Where, however, it can be shown that the exercise of s. 78(1) during the trial interfered with the human rights of one or more individuals, and the question of proportionality fell to be considered (2.9 *post*), the Court of Appeal (or High Court) will 'assess the balance which the decision maker has struck, not merely whether it is within the range of rational or reasonable decisions' (*R (Daly)* v. *Secretary of State for the Home Department* [2001] 2 WLR 1622 (HL) at p. 1635). Now that the Human Rights Act 1998 is in force, s. 78(1) provides a vital safeguard to ensure that the accused receives a fair trial in accordance with the requirement of Article 6(1) of the European Convention on Human Rights (*R* v. *P* [2001] 2 WLR 463 (HL)).

There is no general common-law discretion to exclude admissible evidence in civil proceedings (*Bradford City Metropolitan Council* v. *K (Minors)* [1990] 2 WLR 532 (FD), *Vernon* v. *Bosley* [1994] PIQR 337 (CA) at p. 339). However, r. 32.1(1) of the Civil Procedure Rules 1998 provides judges with the power to 'control the evidence' by giving directions as to the issues on which evidence is required, the nature of the evidence required and the way in which it is placed before the court; and, by virtue of r. 32.1(2), the court 'may ... exclude evidence that would otherwise be admissible'. This discretion to exclude admissible evidence must, however, be exercised in accordance with the 'overriding objective' (r. 1.1(1)–(2)) to deal with cases justly (*Grobbelaar* v. *Sun Newspapers* (1999) *The Times* 12.8.99 (CA)). This requires the judge to consider not only the case before him but also the wider interests of the administration of justice (*Jones* v. *University of Warwick* [2003] 1 WLR 954 (CA)).

Judges (and magistrates) in any proceedings, civil or criminal, have a general discretion to exclude any logically relevant evidence on the ground that its probative value is too low to justify the problems which would be engendered by its admission. This is not regarded as a discretion to exclude admissible evidence so it does not conflict with the common-law rules recognised in *R* v. *Miller* (1952) 36 Cr App R 169 (Assizes) and *Bradford City Metropolitan Council* v. *K (Minors)* [1990] 2 WLR 532 (FD). Rather, it is a discretion to hold that the evidence is 'irrelevant' and therefore inadmissible as a matter of law (*Vernon* v. *Bosley* [1994] PIQR 337 (CA) at p. 339; see 3.1.3 *post* and Figure 2.3).

Finally, there is no general *inclusionary* discretion in either civil or criminal proceedings. If evidence is inadmissible as a matter of law it cannot be admitted, no matter how reliable or probative it might be (see, for example, *Sparks* v. *R* [1964] 2 WLR 566 (PC), 5.3 *post*). That said, the exercise of a judicial discretion may be the *test* for determining whether evidence is admissible. In criminal proceedings, for example, the judge must apply a discretion to determine whether the accused's bad character is admissible evidence of his guilt (3.3.11 *post*); and in civil proceedings the judge has a discretion with respect to the admissibility of previous consistent statements (s. 6(2) of the Civil Evidence Act 1995).

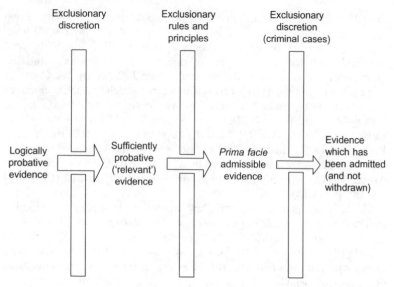

Figure 2.3   **The barriers to the admission of evidence**

2.7 Documentary Evidence and the 'Best Evidence Rule'

Historically a distinction was drawn between the 'best' evidence ('primary evidence') and any other evidence ('secondary evidence'). Only the best evidence that the nature of the case would allow was admissible, so the original of any document had to be produced if it was available and not merely the testimony of someone who had read it, or a copy of it; the original of any object had to be produced if it was available and not merely the testimony of someone who had inspected its condition; and circumstantial evidence was inadmissible if a witness was available to give direct testimony. However, in *Kajala* v. *Noble* (1982) 75 Cr App R 149 (DC) Ackner LJ said (at p. 152):

> 'The old rule, that a party must produce the best evidence that the nature of the case will allow, and that any less good evidence is to be excluded, has gone by the board long ago. The only remaining instance of it is that, if an original document is available in one's hands, one must produce it; that one cannot give secondary evidence by producing a copy. Nowadays we do not confine ourselves to the best evidence. We admit all relevant evidence. The goodness or badness of it goes only to weight and not to admissibility ... In our judgment, the old rule is limited and confined to written documents in the strict sense of the term, and has no relevance to tapes or films.'

In *R* v. *Governor of Pentonville Prison ex parte Osman* (1988) 90 Cr App R 281 (DC) a document was said to be available in one's hands if the party has the original of the document with him in court, or could have it in court 'without any difficulty'.

In *Springsteen* v. *Masquerade Music* [2001] EWCA Civ 563, however, the Court of Appeal refused to recognise the continuing existence in civil proceedings of the 'only remaining instance' of the best evidence rule, holding that there is no *legal* obligation on a party to produce the original of a document in evidence. The true position is that, if the party has the original document available to him, but nonetheless seeks to adduce a copy (or some other secondary evidence) of it, that secondary evidence is *prima facie* admissible but the court will attach no weight to it because of the party's inability to account for the non-production of the original, and will exclude it for that reason. According to the Court (at para. 85):

> '[T]he time has now come when it can be said with confidence that the best evidence rule, long on its deathbed, has finally expired. In every case where a party seeks to adduce secondary evidence of the contents of a document, it is a matter for the court to decide, in the light of all the circumstances of the case, what (if any) weight to attach to that evidence. Where the party seeking to adduce the secondary evidence could readily produce the document, it may be expected that (absent some special circumstances) the court will decline to admit the secondary evidence on the ground that it is worthless. At the other extreme, where the party seeking to adduce the secondary evidence genuinely cannot produce the document, it may be expected that (absent some special circumstances) the court will admit the secondary evidence and attach such weight to it as it considers appropriate in all the circumstances. In cases falling between those two extremes, it is for the court to make a judgment as to whether in all the circumstances any weight should be attached to the secondary evidence.'

The party seeking to adduce secondary evidence of a document need not show that he has conducted an exhaustive, or indeed any, search for the original. The only requirement is that he must provide a reasonable explanation for his non-production of the original 'in the sense that unless he did so the court would almost certainly decline to admit the secondary evidence'; and, in the absence of any allegation of bad faith, the *ex parte Osman* 'without any difficulty' test is an appropriate yardstick.

The remaining instance of the best evidence rule in criminal proceedings applies if a party wishes to rely on the contents of a document, but it relates only to the *method* by which the existence of the contents may be proved. If the party wishes to rely on the contents as evidence of the truth of the matters stated he must first find an exception to the hearsay rule, for only then does the question of how to prove the contents arise. In truth, though, the remaining instance of the rule is of little practical significance because of the common-law and statutory exceptions to it; and if a party is permitted to adduce secondary evidence pursuant to an exception then, as a general rule, 'there are no degrees of secondary evidence': the contents may be proved by any type of secondary evidence, such as a copy of a copy or a witness's testimony as to the contents.

Section 27 of the Criminal Justice Act 1988 now provides that where a statement contained in a document is admissible as evidence in criminal proceedings, it may be proved (*a*) by the production of that document; or (*b*) by the production of a copy of that document (or the material part of it) authenticated in such manner as the court may approve. It is immaterial how many removes there are between a copy and the original. Nor does it matter if the original document is still in existence. Paragraph 5 of Schedule 2 to the Act defines a document as 'anything in which information of any description is recorded', a statement as 'any representation of fact, however made', and a copy as 'anything onto which information recorded in the document has been copied, by whatever means and whether directly or indirectly'. Section 27 is permissive in nature and has not affected the common-law exceptions which generally allow any type of secondary evidence to be given – so oral evidence may still be given if a common-law exception applies (*R* v. *Nazeer* [1998] Crim LR 750 (CA)). Moreover, s. 71 of the Police and Criminal Evidence Act 1984 provides that in criminal proceedings the contents of a document may be proved by the production of an enlargement of a microfilm copy of that document or the material part of it, authenticated in such manner as the court may approve. Again, it does not matter whether the document is still in existence. (Section 8 of the Civil Evidence Act 1995 is almost identical to s. 27 of the 1988 Act and governs the proof of statements contained in documents in civil proceedings. Section 13 of the 1995 Act defines document and copy in the same terms as the 1988 Act; a statement is defined as 'any representation of fact or opinion, however made'.)

There are four common-law exceptions to what remains of the best evidence rule. Any type of secondary evidence is permissible if it is proved (i) the original document has been destroyed or lost and cannot be found after a reasonable search (as in *R* v. *Wayte* (1982) 76 Cr App R 110 (CA)); or (ii) it would be impracticable or unlawful to produce the original (as in *Owner* v. *Bee Hive Spinning* [1914] 1 KB 105 (DC) where a fixed notice was subject to a statutory requirement preventing its removal) or inconvenient (for example, on account of its public nature); or (iii) the original is in the possession of a third party who lawfully refuses to produce it (for example, on the ground of diplomatic immunity, as in *R* v. *Nowaz* [1976] 1 WLR 830 (CA)); or (iv) the original is in the possession of another party who refuses to produce it having been served with a notice to do so.

As a general rule the party who wishes to adduce a document in evidence will also need to prove 'due execution', that is, that the writing or signature on the document has not been forged. This may be done by calling a witness who can give direct testimony in the usual way; or by calling a witness who is familiar with the handwriting of the purported author or signatory to give his opinion; or by a direct comparison of the writing or signature in question with a genuine sample. Section 8 of the Criminal Procedure Act 1865 permits suitably qualified witnesses to give their expert opinion on the similarities and/or dissimilarities between the genuine sample and the writing in dispute. Proof of due execution may occasionally require proof of attestation, that is, proof that the document was executed in the presence of and signed by 'attesting witnesses'. Where proof of attestation is required it is generally no longer necessary for the attesting witnesses to appear in court to give direct testimony. By virtue of s. 3 of the Evidence Act 1938 it is sufficient (in any proceedings) if an attesting witness's signature is proved to be genuine, although an attesting witness should be called (if available) if the document in question is a testamentary document such as a will.

2.8 The Tribunals of Fact and Law

The law of evidence distinguishes between the 'tribunal of law' (which determines all questions of law) and the 'tribunal of fact' (which determines most questions of fact). If the accused is on trial on indictment (in the Crown Court) the judge is the tribunal of law, and the jury collectively comprise the tribunal of fact. It is the judge who decides all questions relating to the substantive criminal law, procedure and the law of evidence. In particular, it is the judge who determines whether evidence is admissible, whether admissible evidence should be excluded under a discretionary power and whether there is sufficient evidence for the case to be considered by the jury. If there *is* a case to answer, the judge will summarise the evidence for the jury at the end of the trial, guide them on matters of weight, and direct them on the law and evidence. It is the jury's role to assess the evidence, in accordance with the judge's directions on the law, to determine whether the facts in issue have been proved and ultimately to decide whether the accused is guilty of the offence charged. All questions of weight and proof at the end of the trial are for the jury alone and the judge must make this clear in his summing-up (see 16.8 *post*).

The judge's fact-finding role during the trial is limited to the determination of any facts which need to be proved as a condition precedent to the admissibility of evidence or the exercise of an exclusionary discretion; and, exceptionally, to the determination of foreign law, which is also a question of fact. For example, a confession is inadmissible as a matter of law if there is a reasonable possibility that it was obtained by oppression, so the judge may have to hear witnesses, at a 'trial-within-a-trial' ('*voir dire*') in the absence of the jury, to determine whether the prosecution are able to prove that the confession was not obtained by oppression. During a *voir dire* the judge is the tribunal of both fact and law. If he decides (as a question of fact) that the prosecution have not been able to prove that the confession was not obtained by oppression, it will be excluded (as a matter of law) and the jury will never hear about it or the judge's ruling. If, however, the judge is satisfied that the confession was not obtained by oppression, the prosecution will be permitted to adduce it (although the judge's ruling will not be mentioned).

Submissions on the law are made to the judge in the absence of the jury so that they will never know about evidence which has been ruled inadmissible or otherwise excluded. One of the principal functions of the law of criminal evidence is to ensure that certain types of relevant evidence are kept from the tribunal of fact, and this object would be defeated if the jury were to remain in the court-room during submissions on whether evidence should be excluded. Most rulings on the law will never be made known to the jury, moreover, because their function is limited to deciding whether the facts in issue have been proved; they need only know the law which relates to their fact-finding role. The judge must explain the substantive criminal law to them, so that they know what the issues are, and direct them on whether it is the prosecution or the accused who bears the burden of proof in respect of those issues, as well as on the 'standard of proof' which has to be met. The jury must also be told what use they are entitled to make of the evidence which has been admitted. For example, if an out-of-court statement has been admitted as 'original evidence', they must be told not to regard it as evidence of the truth of the matters stated; and if the accused's bad character has been revealed solely to undermine his credibility as a witness they must be told not to regard it as evidence of criminal disposition.

In the civil courts the vast majority of trials are now conducted without a jury, so the judge is in all respects the tribunal of both law and fact. This means the judge must exclude from his mind, as the tribunal of fact, any inadmissible evidence he has heard as the tribunal of law. This is not regarded as problematic. First, the reason for excluding much relevant evidence is to ensure that the accused is not wrongly convicted of a criminal offence, and this is not a relevant consideration in civil trials. Second, if the judge does need to disregard evidence, it is generally accepted that his professional experience allows him to do so without too much difficulty. Neither of these justifications applies to criminal proceedings in the magistrates' courts, however. Magistrates are also the triers of both fact and law and are expected to rule on the admissibility of evidence (on the advice of their legally-qualified 'court clerk') and decide whether the facts in issue have been proved at the end of the trial. Magistrates may hear submissions on the admissibility of evidence, exclude it as a matter of law or in the exercise of their discretion, and then carry on and try the case anyway. It is doubtful whether lay magistrates are capable of disregarding all such evidence, particularly if it is of an unduly prejudicial nature (such as the accused's previous convictions), but the present system is justified by its relatively low cost.

It goes without saying that much of the law of evidence cannot be understood without a basic understanding of the context in which it arises, namely the trial. The trial process is covered in some detail in Chapter 16 but, while a full discussion of the topic may safely be left until then, it would be unwise to approach the law of evidence without at least a rudimentary knowledge of the way in which trials are conducted.

The most important type of trial (for students of the law of evidence) is the trial on indictment where the accused is tried before a judge and jury and is usually represented by a defence advocate. The prosecution will open their case by giving a brief speech to the jury summarising the allegation against the accused, and then proceed to call witnesses and tender evidence to prove that allegation. In this context the word 'tender' means no more than to submit that an item of evidence is admissible and that it ought to be placed before the jury. Much prosecution evidence will go unchallenged by the defence, but if they wish to challenge the admissibility of any prosecution evidence as a matter of law, or argue that it ought to be excluded by the judge in the exercise of his discretion, they and the prosecution will make appropriate submissions to the judge in the absence of the jury. If the judge rules that the evidence is admissible, and that he is not going to exclude it in the exercise of his discretion, the prosecution will be entitled to 'adduce' it (that is, place it before the jury for their consideration). Each prosecution witness will be examined in-chief by the prosecution (16.4 *post*). Immediately after each prosecution witness has given his evidence in chief he will be cross-examined by the defence (16.5 *post*). Once the prosecution have adduced all the evidence the judge has permitted them to adduce, and all their witnesses have been examined in-chief and cross-examined, the prosecution case comes to a close.

The next stage of the trial is colloquially known as 'half time' because it is the point between the close of the prosecution case and the start of the defence case. Occasionally the defence will make a submission to the judge that the case against the accused ought to be dismissed on the ground that the prosecution have failed to place before the jury sufficient evidence of his guilt to justify a conviction. A successful 'submission of no case to answer' will result in the judge directing the jury to acquit the accused (16.7 *post*). If the submission of no case to answer fails, or no such submission is made, it is time for the defence case to begin. The procedure is essentially the same as the first stage of the trial. The defence will tender their evidence, there may be submissions on the question of admissibility, and each defence witness (including the accused himself, should he wish to testify) will be examined in-chief by the defence and then cross-examined by the prosecution. At the end of the defence case the prosecution and defence will make their closing speeches to the jury, after which the judge will summarise the evidence and direct the jury on the law (16.8 *post*). Following the summing-up the jury will retire to consider their verdict (16.9 *post*).

2.9 The Right to a Fair Trial

Article 6 of the European Convention for the Protection of Human Rights and Fundamental Freedoms (1950) provides as follows:

(1) In the determination of his civil rights and obligations or of any criminal charge against him, everyone is entitled to a fair and public hearing within a reasonable time by an independent and impartial tribunal established by law. Judgment shall be pronounced publicly but the press and public may be excluded from all or part of the trial in the interest of morals, public order or national security in a democratic society, where the interests of juveniles or

the protection of the private life of the parties so require, or to the extent strictly necessary in the opinion of the court in special circumstances where publicity would prejudice the interest of justice.

(2) Everyone charged with a criminal offence shall be presumed innocent until proved guilty according to law.

(3) Everyone charged with a criminal offence has the following minimum rights:

    (a) to be informed promptly, in a language which he understands and in detail, of the nature and cause of the accusation against him;

    (b) to have adequate time and facilities for the preparation of his defence;

    (c) to defend himself in person or through legal assistance of his own choosing or, if he has not sufficient means to pay for legal assistance, to be given it free when the interests of justice so require;

    (d) to examine or have examined witnesses against him and to obtain the attendance and examination of witnesses on his behalf under the same conditions as witnesses against him;

    (e) to have the free assistance of an interpreter if he cannot understand or speak the language used in court.

Sections 1 to 3 of the Human Rights Act 1998, which came into force on 2 October 2000, provide, *inter alia*, that primary and subordinate legislation must (so far as it is possible to do so) be read and given effect in a way which is compatible with the Convention rights set out in Schedule 1 to the Act, including Article 6, and that any court determining a question which has arisen in connection with a Convention right 'must take into account' any relevant judgment, decision, declaration or advisory opinion of the European Court of Human Rights and any relevant decision or opinion of the (now defunct) European Commission of Human Rights. The lower courts are therefore no longer bound by existing case-law on the interpretation of legislation insofar as the construction of the higher courts would lead to a result which would be incompatible with Article 6. In the words of Lord Slynn: 'long or well entrenched ideas may have to be put aside, [and] sacred cows culled' (*R* v. *Lambert* [2001] 3 WLR 206 (HL) at p. 210). Legislation may therefore have to be 'read down', or additional words 'read in', to ensure that the provisions under consideration are compatible with the Convention. Some common-law rules of evidence may also need to be modified, insofar as their application would lead to a result which would be incompatible with Article 6, by virtue of the obligation on the courts not to act in a way which is incompatible with a Convention right (s. 6(1) and (3) of the 1998 Act).

The Strasbourg jurisprudence on Article 6 does not bind the courts of England and Wales in the sense that there are a number of specific rules of

European law which must be applied in this jurisdiction. The decisions of the European Court of Human Rights (and Commission) are case specific, focusing on the particular facts of the case at hand and whether in all the circumstances, including the pre-trial proceedings and subsequent appeal process, the applicant received a fair hearing. In particular, the European Court of Human Rights has not laid down any rules on the admissibility of evidence, the question being regarded primarily as a matter for regulation under national law. That said, it is possible to elicit from the Strasbourg jurisprudence a number of fundamental *principles* relating to the demands made by the Convention, and by Article 6 in particular, to which the courts in England and Wales are expected to attach great weight. For example, the Convention is a 'living instrument' to be interpreted in the light of present day conditions in a way which will guarantee rights which are 'practical and effective' (as opposed to rights which are merely theoretical or illusory); certain terms in the Convention (for example, the meaning of 'witness' in Article 6(3)(d)) are to be given an 'autonomous' meaning, regardless of the position under national law; and the fact that a particular approach is adopted in a number of contracting states is a relevant consideration when determining whether that 'generally shared approach' accords with the requirements of the Convention.

Although the Article 6(1) right to a fair hearing or trial is absolute (*R* v. *Forbes* [2001] 2 WLR 1 (HL) at p. 13), 'precisely what is comprised in the concept of fairness may be open to a varied analysis' and 'the public interest may be taken into account in deciding what the right to a fair trial requires in a particular context' (*Brown* v. *Stott* [2001] 2 WLR 817 (PC) at pp. 840 and 859). The requirements inherent in the concept of 'fair hearing' are not necessarily the same in civil and criminal proceedings, and contracting states 'have greater latitude when dealing with civil cases ... than they have when dealing with criminal cases' (*Dombo Beheer* v. *Netherlands* (1993) 18 EHRR 213 (ECtHR) at p. 229); but even in criminal proceedings the determination of fairness may require the court to take into account the 'triangulation of interests' of the accused, the complainant and society generally (*R* v. *A (No. 2)* [2001] 2 WLR 1546 (HL) at p. 1560).

The particular rights set out in Article 6(2)–(3) are those of the accused in criminal proceedings, but the list of 'minimum rights' in Article 6(3) is not exhaustive. Other rights are implicit in Article 6(3) as specific aspects of the general right to a fair criminal trial, including the accused's pre-trial privilege against self-incrimination and his related right to remain silent in the face of police interrogation. Several (if not all) of the express and implicit rights in Article 6(2)–(3) are neither absolute nor inflexible (*Brown* v. *Stott* [2001] 2 WLR 817 (PC), *R* v. *Forbes* [2001] 2 WLR 1 (HL), *R* v. *Lambert* [2001] 3 WLR 206 (HL)). A democratic state is entitled to act in a way which *prima facie* infringes those constituent rights if there is a clear and legitimate reason for so acting and the Strasbourg principle of 'proportionality' is satisfied (*Brown* v. *Stott* [2001] 2 WLR 817 (PC), *R* v. *Lambert* [2001] 3 WLR 206 (HL), *R* v. *A (No. 2)* [2001] 2 WLR 1546 (HL) at p. 1577). In other words, a democratic state is entitled to strike a balance between the general interests of the community (including the rights of witnesses, complainants and victims) and the protection of the accused's Article 6(2)–(3) rights, so long as the state does not go beyond what is strictly necessary to accomplish its legitimate objective and, where relevant, any difficulties caused to the defence are sufficiently counter-balanced by safeguards which protect the accused's interests. The European Court of Human Rights has recognised that each contracting state should be permitted a degree of latitude or 'margin of appreciation' in its approach to the way Convention rights are protected, on the basis that national institutions are better placed than the Court to evaluate national needs and conditions, so long as the state's approach does not fall below a minimum standard of acceptability. A domestic version of this doctrine has now been developed in England and Wales to the extent that a degree of deference will be paid on democratic grounds to the considered view of Parliament as to what is in the interest of the community generally (*R* v. *DPP ex parte Kebilene* [1999] 3 WLR 972 (HL) at pp. 993–4, *Brown* v. *Stott* [2001] 2 WLR 817 (PC) at pp. 835 and 842, *R* v. *A (No. 2)* [2001] 2 WLR 1546 (HL) at pp. 1560 and 1567).

The coming into force of the Human Rights Act 1998 has had (and will continue to have) a significant effect on many aspects of the law of evidence. In particular: legislation passed in 1999 to protect complainants in sexual offence cases from being cross-examined on their sexual history was in effect rewritten by the House of Lords to protect the accused's right to a fair trial (17.4 *post*); some statutory provisions which expressly place the burden of proving an issue on the accused have been watered down to impose no more than an 'evidential burden' because they failed the proportionality test (15.2.2.1 *post*); any provision which permits the admission of the accused's self-incriminating answers obtained under compulsion must similarly satisfy the proportionality test to be Convention-compliant (14.1 *post*); in cases where the jury are entitled to draw an adverse inference from the accused's silence during police interrogation they must be given a lengthy and complicated direction to safeguard the accused's interests (9.2.2.4 *post*); a new meaning has been given to the term 'confession' for the purposes of s. 76 of the Police and Criminal Evidence Act 1984 (7.1.1 *post*); and it may be that procedures will have to be introduced to allow the defence to put questions to a witness before the trial if that witness's evidence is to be admitted as a hearsay statement with no opportunity during the trial for cross-examination (6.2.5 *post*).

3 Relevance, Disposition and 'Similar Facts'

3.1 Relevance

To be admissible any item of evidence must be logically relevant to a fact in issue or a collateral fact (or contribute to an explanation of the 'background' so that the issues can be resolved in their proper context). If, as a matter of logic, the evidence is unable to suggest whether an assertion of fact is more or less likely to be true it has no probative value and is inadmissible. This is uncontroversial, but unfortunately judges (and commentators) have sown confusion by using the words 'relevant' and 'irrelevant' in two other ways. First, logically relevant evidence is sometimes said to be 'irrelevant', meaning that it is insufficiently probative to be admissible. In this sense the degree of probative value the evidence has (the 'weight' or 'cogency' of the evidence) is confused with the question whether it has *any* probative value at all. To avoid confusion the two concepts should be kept separate. Probative value is a question of degree, logical relevance is not. Second, the words have also been used as synonyms for 'admissible' and 'inadmissible' respectively. This too should be avoided. Logical relevance is a prerequisite to admissibility, and while evidence which has no probative value can never be admissible, highly cogent evidence may be inadmissible as a matter of law.

3.1.1 Logically Relevant Evidence: the General Rule

Evidence which a party might wish to adduce for consideration by the tribunal of fact will be either logically relevant or logically irrelevant to a matter which needs to be proved: either the evidence will (to any extent) or it will not (at all) affect the probability that some fact in issue or collateral fact can be established. Logically relevant evidence may thus be defined as evidence which, if accepted: 'could rationally affect (directly or indirectly) the assessment of the probability of the existence of a fact in issue' (s. 55 of Australia's Evidence Act 1995) or has 'any tendency to make the existence of any fact that is of consequence to the determination of the action more probable or less probable than it would be without the evidence' (r. 401 of the United States Federal Rules of Evidence). In England and Wales it has been said that evidence is logically relevant if it 'makes the matter which requires proof more or less probable' (*DPP* v. *Kilbourne* [1973] 2 WLR 254 (HL) at pp. 276–7).

If there is a fundamental exclusionary rule of evidence it is that irrelevant evidence is never admissible: 'Nothing is to be received which is not logically probative of some matter requiring to be proved' (Thayer, *A Preliminary Treatise on Evidence* (1898) at p. 530). The corollary of this rule is that for evidence to be admissible it must at the very least be logically relevant to a fact in issue or a collateral fact; and logically relevant evidence *is*, as a *general* rule, admissible. This broad inclusionary rule embodies the principle of free proof (that is, that the tribunal of fact should be permitted to have before them all logically relevant evidence in order to reach the correct decision on the issue before them) but it is subject to a battery of statutory and common-law exceptions, the origins of which lie in considerations of public policy. It is this body of exceptions which comprises much of the law of evidence and the substance of this book.

Whether an item of evidence is *logically* relevant to a matter requiring proof is generally determined by the tribunal of law. Once relevance has been determined, and the evidence has been admitted, it is for the tribunal of fact to determine how cogent it is. Whether an item of evidence is logically relevant is determined by the judicial application of logic, common sense and the conventional wisdom which comes from human experience. General knowledge, experience and inductive reasoning allow for the formulation of broad generalisations (for example, infidelity causes jealousy, alcohol reduces inhibitions and human behaviour tends to repeat itself) which determine whether evidence is logically relevant to a matter which needs to be proved. Adopting syllogistic terminology, with the generalisation (e.g., 'fingerprints are unique') as the major premise and the item of evidence (e.g., 'D's fingerprints were on the safe') as the minor premise, if it is possible for the tribunal of fact to deduce from these two premises an inference as to the likelihood of the matter requiring proof (e.g., 'whether D was the person who ransacked the safe'), then the item of evidence is logically relevant to that matter. Consider a male, D1, who is on trial for raping M, another male. The prosecution might wish to adduce evidence that D1 is a homosexual as circumstantial evidence that he committed the offence, but D1 might argue that his sexual orientation is irrelevant. To determine whether this evidence is logically relevant the judge could construct a syllogism, the major premise being the generalisation that the sort of person who would rape a man is very likely to be a homosexual, the minor premise being the evidence that D1 is a homosexual. The judge would conclude that because the jury could reasonably infer from these premises that the evidence of D1's sexuality contributes to the probability that he is the offender, the evidence is logically relevant. To put it another way, D1's sexuality places him in a smaller group than male society as a whole, and the likelihood is that a person from that smaller group committed the offence. D1's membership of that group – that is, his homosexuality – must logically be relevant to whether he committed the offence. It is of course important to add that the large number of homosexual men in male society means that the evidence is not particularly probative of D1's guilt, but it does have *some* probative value nonetheless. Similarly, if a male, D2, is on trial for raping a female victim, F, then the fact that D2 is heterosexual is logically relevant to whether or not he is the offender. As with the previous example, the evidence of D2's sexuality is logically relevant to the issue of his guilt because the evidence places him in a group of men which is smaller than the entire male population. The difference between the two examples is that D1's sexuality is more probative than D2's because there are fewer homosexuals than heterosexuals in the general male population.

Probative value, unlike logical relevance, is a question of degree. The weight of an item of evidence which is logically relevant to an issue will lie anywhere in the range between 'minimal probative value' (as in the case of D2's sexuality) to 'compelling' (for example where a closed-circuit television recording clearly shows the accused's face as he commits the offence charged). It is important to be aware, however, that the process of inductive reasoning which leads to the formulation of generalisations must be based on a sound factual basis and not on unfounded prejudice or apocryphal stereotypes. Indeed, where it seems that the generalisation has no firm empirical basis it will be open to the opposing party to attack the admissibility of the evidence on the ground that the generalisation itself is invalid and that logical relevance has not been established.

3.1.2 Logical Relevance and 'Relevance' Distinguished

The established statutory and common-law exceptions to the general rule on the admissibility of evidence, together with the judicial discretion to exclude admissible evidence, act as a policy-driven filter to prevent the tribunal of fact from being able to consider certain evidence even if it has *significant* probative value. What is not so clearly recognised, however, principally because of the ambiguities inherent in the terminology used by the judiciary, is that a trial judge may exclude logically relevant evidence and rationalise his decision on the ground that the evidence is 'irrelevant' to any issue in the proceedings. 'The expression logically probative may be understood to include much evidence which English law deems to be irrelevant' (*Noor Mohamed* v. *R* [1949] AC 182 (PC) at p. 194). The same view was expressed by Fisher J in the High Court of New Zealand in *R* v. *Wilson* [1991] 2 NZLR 707 (at p. 711):

> 'For most people a fact is relevant if to even a minute degree its existence would make the fact in issue more or less likely. Whether its effect is strong or weak is more usually referred to as the weight or probative force of the evidence rather than its relevance. However, to understand the authorities it is important to appreciate that relevant is often given the secondary meaning of of significant weight. Weight is a matter of degree. It is concerned with the strength with which the evidence bears upon the likelihood or unlikelihood of a fact in issue.'

In other words, logical relevance is not necessarily enough for evidence to be considered 'relevant' by the trial judge. The evidence may also need to carry enough probative force to make its admission worthwhile in the light of competing considerations. This point was made by the Supreme Court of Victoria in *R* v. *Stephenson* [1976] VR 376 (at pp. 380–1): 'The logical connection between a fact and the issue to be determined may be so slight that the fact is treated as too remote and evidence of it as inadmissible. In some cases, such evidence is described as being irrelevant.'

3.1.3 Probative Value and Admissibility

The principle of free proof may need to give way to policy considerations which militate against the admissibility of insufficiently probative evidence. A vast amount of evidence may be logically relevant while adding little in the way of probative force, and a policy of admitting *any* logically relevant evidence, no matter how slight its probative value, would render the legal system ineffective. Any jurisdiction has a finite number of courts, and human beings live for a finite and relatively short period of time with a limited capacity for digesting information. It is the reality of these constraints, institutional, psychological and physiological, which requires a balancing of probative value against competing policy considerations to determine whether evidence ought to be considered 'relevant'. It is in the public interest that trials should be conducted as expeditiously and inexpensively as possible, and logically relevant evidence of marginal probative value could slow down the proceedings and raise the costs to an unacceptable degree while contributing little to the resolution of the dispute. Indeed some evidence may be superfluous in the context of the other evidence which has been or will be admitted. The desirability of excluding logically relevant evidence for such reasons was recently acknowledged by the Court of Appeal in *R* v. *Carter* (1996) 161 JP 207, but the point was made much earlier by Rolfe B in *Attorney-General* v. *Hitchcock* (1847) 1 Exch 91 (CE) (at p. 105):

'If we lived for a thousand years instead of about sixty or seventy, and every case was of sufficient importance, it might be possible and perhaps proper ... to raise every possible inquiry as to the truth of statements made. But I do not see how that could be ...'

A particularly important consideration is the need to prevent the tribunal of fact from being swamped with evidence. The capacity of the human mind to receive, analyse and remember information is limited, and the admission of too much logically relevant evidence could well be counter-productive. The tribunal of fact could end up becoming confused and distracted, making a correct decision on the facts in issue less likely. The trial judge or magistrates (as the tribunal of law) may also need to consider other factors such as the desirability of avoiding breaches of confidence or unnecessary embarrassment to litigants or third parties (*Vernon* v. *Bosley* [1994] PIQR 337 (CA)), considerations which carry more force now that Article 8 of the European Convention on Human Rights has to be taken into account. Fisher J summarised the common-law position in *R* v. *Wilson* [1991] 2 NZLR 707 (NZHC) (at p. 711):

'[C]ompeting policy considerations can be taken into account. These include the desirability of shortening trials, avoiding emotive distractions of marginal significance, protecting the reputations of those not represented before the Courts and respecting the feelings of a deceased's family. None of these matters would be determinative if the evidence in question were of significant probative value. But if it is not, the proposed evidence can be excluded on the ground of irrelevance ...'

This exclusionary discretion has been expressly incorporated into the United States Federal Rules of Evidence as r. 403:

Although relevant, evidence may be excluded if its probative value is substantially outweighed by the danger of unfair prejudice, confusion of the issues, or misleading the jury, or by considerations of undue delay, waste of time, or needless presentation of cumulative evidence.

An important principle in the law of evidence in both civil and criminal proceedings is that evidence of a party's character ('disposition' or 'propensity'), such as his reputation or his conduct on previous occasions, should not be admitted for the purpose of proving that he acted in a similar way on the occasion which is the subject of the proceedings. The issues should (generally) be determined on the evidence directly pertaining to the incident in question and not on the basis of what happened on other occasions. For example, in civil proceedings: 'It is not legitimate to charge a man with an act of negligence on a day in October and ask a jury to infer that he was negligent on that day because he was negligent on every day in September. The defendant may have mended his ways' (*Hales* v. *Kerr* [1908] 2 KB 601 (DC) at p. 604). Similarly, a party cannot adduce evidence of his general *good* character to *disprove* an allegation against him (*Attorney-General* v. *Bowman* (1791) 2 B & P 532n (CE), *Attorney-General* v. *Radloff* (1854) 10 Ex 84 (CE) at p. 97), although it will be seen that an important concession has been made in this respect for the accused in criminal proceedings (3.4 *post*). However, a party's disposition *will* often be logically relevant to an issue because of the generalisation that human behaviour tends to repeat itself (that is, that people do *not* mend their ways).

In civil cases the judge is likely to exclude evidence of disposition simply on the ground that it is 'irrelevant'. The evidence, while logically relevant, is only indirectly related to the matter under inquiry and may raise a number of collateral matters which will extend the length of the trial, increase costs and lead to further confusion and vexation, particularly if the evidence relates to an allegation of earlier conduct which has neither been proved nor admitted; there is also the risk, at least in civil jury trials, that one of the parties will be unduly prejudiced by its admission.

In *Agassiz* v. *London Tramway* (1872) 21 WR 199 (CE) the plaintiff was injured while travelling as a passenger on the defendant's tram and alleged that the driver had been negligent. The plaintiff sought to adduce evidence that the conductor had told another passenger shortly after the accident that the driver was new, that he had been off the line five or six times that day prior to the accident and that his conduct had already been reported. This evidence was held to be inadmissible on the ground that it would have raised a multiplicity of collateral matters bearing 'no relation to the question before the jury'. The reasoning behind this judgment is not difficult to understand. If such evidence had been admitted the jury would have had to examine the driver's experience with the company, determine whether or not he had previously been off the lines and reported, and would then have had to enter into an inquiry to determine whether he had been at fault on the earlier occasions. Further, even if the conductor's words were true and the evidence did have a degree of probative value with regard to the cause of the accident, the evidence could have unduly prejudiced the jury against the driver – the jury might have attached too much weight to the driver's careless disposition and too little to the possibility that the accident had been caused by something else. The same sort of reasoning explains why evidence of extraneous conduct has been excluded in other civil cases. In *Hollingham* v. *Head* (1858) 27 LJCP 241 (CCP) evidence that a guano dealer had contracted on certain terms with other purchasers of his product was held to be irrelevant to whether he had contracted on such terms with the defendant, even though it was logically relevant to the defendant's case in tending to show the dealer had been promoting his guano on standard terms; in *Holcombe* v. *Hewson* (1810) 2 Camp 391 (KB) evidence that the plaintiff brewer had sold good beer to third parties was not admissible to show he had supplied good beer to the defendant; and in *Edmondson* v. *Amery* (1911) *The Times* 28.1.11 (KBD) the plaintiff, who was pursuing an action in defamation following an allegation that he had been a coward on an occasion during the Boer war, was not permitted to call a witness who would have given evidence of his courageous character. Even a generally brave man may act in a cowardly way on one occasion, and the evidence of the plaintiff's character in the last case, though logically supportive of his claim, would probably have been given more weight by the jury than it deserved, which would have been unfair to the defendant. In *Cooper* v. *Hatton* [2001] EWCA Civ 623 the claimant and defendant had driven their cars in opposite directions along a road with ample space to pass each other, but they nonetheless collided. It had been a dry day with good visibility, there were no skid marks or eye-witnesses, and neither of the drivers could explain the collision. Despite the absence of any such evidence, the trial judge found the defendant entirely to blame, having placed considerable reliance on the evidence of the claimant's employer that the claimant was 'an excellent driver' who was 'calm, assured' and 'never took risks'. The defendant's appeal was allowed because the employer's evidence should not have been taken into consideration; in the words of Parker LJ, it was 'completely worthless'. The Court of Appeal noted that even the best drivers occasionally have lapses of attention of the type which one or other (or both) of the drivers had suffered, and it could not be said on the basis of past record that one driver was more likely than the other to have had such a lapse.

However, where the evidence of a party's disposition is *highly probative*, for example because the similarity between his past conduct and his alleged conduct means the possibility of coincidence can be discounted – the probative value of the evidence being proportional to the unlikelihood of coincidence in such cases – the policy considerations militating against admitting the evidence carry less force. The evidence of disposition may then be regarded as relevant and admissible notwithstanding the collateral matters which can arise as a result. In *Hales* v. *Kerr* [1908] 2 KB 601 (DC), for example, the plaintiff claimed he had contracted a disease ('barber's itch') from the razor and/or towel used by the defendant, a barber, and sought to adduce evidence that two other persons who had visited the defendant's premises at around the same time had contracted the same disorder, having been similarly cut and treated by him. This evidence was held to be admissible to show that a dangerous practice had been carried on in the defendant's establishment.

Generally speaking, in criminal trials evidence of the accused's unpleasant disposition (such as his previous convictions or objectionable interests) cannot be admitted for the purpose of proving that he committed the offence charged. The policy consideration of most significance in this context is the desirability of ensuring that the accused receives a fair trial and is not convicted of an offence he did not commit. The accused should be judged on the evidence directly pertaining to the offence charged and not on what he has done on other occasions. The admission of such evidence would in all likelihood unduly prejudice his defence in the eyes of the jury; so even though his previous misconduct might well increase the probability that he is guilty, the principle of free proof must give way. In short, the undue prejudice generated by the accused's bad character will usually outweigh its probative value.

The fair trial principle also underpins many other aspects of the law of criminal evidence. Indeed judges in criminal trials have a discretion at common law to exclude any relevant evidence tendered by the prosecution if its probative value would be outweighed by the risk of unfairness to the accused (*R* v. *Sang* [1979] 3 WLR 263 (HL)). Alternatively, the risk of unfairness to the accused may be overcome by applying the discretion to exclude any logically probative evidence (from whatever source) on the ground that it is 'irrelevant', an approach exemplified by the way the Court of Appeal has addressed the admissibility of circumstantial evidence of drug-dealing. Take, for example, the situation where the accused is on trial for possessing a controlled drug with intent to supply, the evidence against him having been discovered during a search of his home and comprising a quantity of the drug, a large sum of cash, paraphernalia connected with dealing (such as contaminated scales) and a bank savings book. The prosecution will need to prove that the drug was controlled, that the accused knowingly had it in his possession, and that he intended to supply it to another person. The prosecution will of course adduce evidence that a quantity of the drug was found in the accused's home, but they will also need to adduce evidence from which the jury will be able to infer that he had the requisite intent to supply. If the quantity of the drug is large enough, that alone will allow an inference to be drawn that it was kept for sale and not personal consumption; but suppose in this case the quantity was too small for that inference to be drawn. The prosecution will need to argue that the large sum of cash found in his home is logically relevant evidence of the accused's intent to supply on the ground that dealers tend to work with cash and need a ready sum to buy future supplies. In a number of cases the Court of Appeal has held that the jury are permitted to regard cash as evidence of intent to supply only if they first reject the accused's innocent explanation and conclude, having considered all the other evidence, that it indicates his 'ongoing' (as opposed to entirely past) dealings in the drug. Having concluded that the cash is relevant in this way, the jury are then entitled to infer from it that the accused intended to supply the drugs found in his home. The trial judge is obliged to direct the jury that the cash is *irrelevant* and to be ignored if they conclude that it merely represents the accused's past dealings (*R* v. *Grant* [1996] 1 Cr App R 73 (CA)). Clearly, a large sum of cash is logically relevant to the issue of intent even if it is only evidence of past dealings; but such evidence is not considered sufficiently probative to be admissible given the risk that its admission would unduly prejudice the accused's defence. Evidence of past misconduct is generally inadmissible to prove the accused is guilty of the offence charged, so the cash is deemed to be 'irrelevant' and excluded for that reason. Similarly, the accused's bank books showing considerable savings are unlikely to be considered relevant to the issue of intent as they would at best be evidence of nothing other than past dealings – but if the accused's explanation for having a large sum of cash in his house is that he was nervous about using banks, then the savings books will *become* relevant and admissible to rebut that innocent explanation (*R* v. *Gordon* [1995] 2 Cr App R 61 (CA)).

Although the relevance of cash in the possession of alleged drug dealers has given rise to a large number of appeals, the admissibility of the sort of paraphernalia associated with dealers, such as contaminated scales and lists of debtors, was until recently not so vehemently contested, even though the argument used to exclude cash can equally be relied on to justify the exclusion of such evidence. In *R* v. *Brown* [1995] Crim LR 716 (CA) the point was considered but rejected on the ground that 'different considerations may apply', but more recently the Court of Appeal has accepted that the trial judge should direct the jury not to take such evidence into consideration unless they are sure it is relevant to ongoing and not just past transactions (*R* v. *Lovelock* [1997] Crim LR 821 (CA), *R* v. *Haye* [2002] EWCA Crim 2476).

It had been suggested that evidence of an alleged dealer's lavish lifestyle would rarely be considered relevant to the issue of intent to supply, and never relevant to the issue of possession (*R* v. *Halpin* [1996] Crim LR 112 (CA), *R* v. *Richards* [1997] Crim LR 499 (CA)). However, because the probative value of circumstantial evidence depends on the particular circumstances of the case, it is inappropriate to lay down a blanket ban on the admissibility of such evidence, even if the only issue is possession. This was recognised by the Court of Appeal in *R* v. *Edwards* [1998] Crim LR

207 and it is now clear that cash, paraphernalia and lifestyle evidence may be considered relevant to either or both issues depending on the facts (*R* v. *Guney* [1998] 2 Cr App R 242 (CA), *R* v. *Griffiths* [1998] Crim LR 567 (CA)). In *R* v. *Guney*, Judge LJ said (at pp. 265–7):

> 'The question whether evidence is relevant depends not on abstract legal theory but on the individual circumstances of each particular case ... Accordingly, although evidence of cash and lifestyle may only rarely be relevant where the charge is simple possession, we are unable to accept that as a matter of law such evidence must, automatically, be excluded as irrelevant ... In our judgment where possession with intent is charged, there are numerous sets of circumstances in which cash and lifestyle evidence may be relevant and admissible to the issue of possession itself, not least to the issue of knowledge as an ingredient of possession.'

The facts of that case provide an illustration of how cash or paraphernalia might be relevant to mere possession. G's home was raided by the police and five kilos of heroin were found in his wardrobe along with a loaded handgun and £25,000 in cash. He accepted that the cash was his, but claimed that the drugs and gun had been planted by enemies as part of a 'set-up'. He conceded that the quantity of drugs involved, having a street value of £750,000, meant that if his defence was rejected it could be inferred that he had had the intent to supply and therefore argued, relying on the decision in *R* v. *Halpin* [1996] Crim LR 112 (CA), that the cash was inadmissible as the sole issue was whether he had knowingly been in possession of the drugs. The Court of Appeal rejected this argument. The cash and its close proximity to the drugs and gun, and the way all the items had been poorly concealed, was relevant to whether G had been aware that the drugs were in his wardrobe.

Cash and paraphernalia in cases of this sort, where the accused is charged with possession of drugs with intent to supply, are examples of 'conditionally admissible' evidence. The jury are entitled to take such evidence into consideration at the end of the trial but only if, in the light of the other evidence and a direction from the judge, they are satisfied that it is relevant to a matter which needs to be proved. Conditionally admissible evidence is not therefore an exception to the fundamental rule that irrelevant evidence is inadmissible, but it is an exception to the general rule that the determination of relevance is a question for the judge. In cases where evidence is conditionally admissible it may be necessary for relevance to be determined by the jury acting according to the judge's directions. The need to admit circumstantial evidence before its relevance has been determined is not surprising, given that evidence comes out during the trial by degrees and the relevance of circumstantial evidence may become apparent only when it has been considered in the context of the other admissible evidence. A single item of circumstantial evidence by itself is unlikely to be particularly probative, but the utility of circumstantial evidence lies in the fact that several items of such evidence may have a significant *cumulative* effect resulting in a compelling body of evidence. Thus, if the relevance of a single item of circumstantial evidence were to be determined at the beginning of the trial, before the other evidence has been admitted, it might be excluded on the ground of insufficient probative value, a problem which can be overcome by the evidence being admitted subject to a condition that its relevance will be determined subsequently in its proper context.

Logically relevant evidence may also be excluded on the ground of irrelevance if its admission would provide nothing more than a basis for conjecture as opposed to real belief, even if the evidence could give rise to a reasonable doubt as to the accused's guilt, the underlying rationale being the desirability of preventing indeterminate collateral matters from distracting the jury.

In *R* v. *Woodward* [1995] 1 WLR 375, a case of causing death by dangerous driving, the Court of Appeal held that evidence that the accused had been seen drinking alcohol at a function shortly before the accident was inadmissible as it could do no more than lead the jury to speculate as to the amount of alcohol he had drunk prior to driving. However, it was also felt that if the evidence had been that the accused had drunk enough for it to have adversely affected his driving it would have been relevant to the issue of dangerous driving, and therefore admissible, as the jury would have had a real basis for believing that his ability to drive had been affected (see also *R* v. *Millington* [1995] Crim LR 824 (CA)). A similar approach was adopted by the Supreme Court of Victoria in *R* v. *Stephenson* [1976] VR 376, a case which was also concerned with a fatal road accident. S's vehicle had collided with a Fiat causing the death of three of its four occupants, and following his convictions on three counts of culpable driving causing death he appealed on the ground that he had not been permitted to ascertain whether any or all of the deceased had consumed drugs or alcohol prior to the accident, there having been evidence that one of them had been the driver. The Supreme Court dismissed the appeal for two reasons. First, while the way in which the driver had handled the Fiat at the time of the accident was relevant to the question of S's culpability, and the presence of alcohol or drugs in the blood of the Fiat driver would have been a relevant factor when determining how the Fiat had been driven, in the context of the evidence as a whole the connection of the condition of the Fiat driver with the question of S's guilt was extremely tenuous and, notwithstanding its logical relevance, such evidence might properly be regarded as insufficiently probative and thus 'inadmissible on the ground of remoteness'. Second, as the identity of the driver could not be ascertained, and so any evidence elicited as to the condition of one or more of the deceased could not be linked to the driver, such evidence was in any event irrelevant because the results of the blood tests conducted on the deceased shortly after the accident differed widely.

The leading English authority on conjecture and relevance is the notorious case of *R* v. *Blastland* [1985] 3 WLR 345. B was convicted of buggering and murdering a 12-year-old boy, having admitted that he had attempted to bugger him. B denied killing the boy, claiming that he had abandoned his attempt to bugger, and then left, when he saw another person, M, near by. At his trial B wished to allege that it was M, a homosexual, and not he who had buggered and killed the boy, and sought to adduce evidence that before the boy's body had been found M had stated that a boy had been murdered. The House of Lords held that M's statement had been properly excluded as it was irrelevant to any fact in issue at B's trial. M's statement was relevant only to the state of his own mind, and M had not been on trial. It was felt that M's knowledge of the boy's murder could have come about in a variety of possible ways, only one of which was that M rather than B had committed the offence. To have placed such evidence before the jury would merely have provided them with a basis for speculation as opposed to a rational basis upon which they could logically have drawn an inference that it was M rather than B who had killed the boy. The reasoning of the House of Lords has since been applied by the Court of Appeal. In *R* v. *Akram* [1995] Crim LR 50 the accused had sought to explain that the drugs in his possession belonged to another person, B, who had been near by and in possession of £432, by seeking to cross-examine police officers on the fact that B had given them inconsistent explanations regarding his possession of that cash. The Court of Appeal held that the judge had acted properly in excluding the evidence (see also *R* v. *Kearley* [1992] 2 WLR 656 (HL), 5.6.1.1 *post*).

The strict approach to relevance adopted in *R* v. *Blastland* [1985] 3 WLR 345 (HL) prevented the accused from being able to place before the jury evidence which might well have engendered in their collective mind a reasonable doubt as to his guilt, which might be regarded as wrong in principle; but it is hardly surprising. In many cases there will be not only a body of evidence suggesting the accused's guilt, but evidence implicating one or more third parties too, individuals who for one reason or another came under suspicion but were not charged. The evidence might be that the third party had a motive to commit the offence, or that he shared the offender's disposition, or that he was in the vicinity, or even that he confessed, but there will be a considerably stronger case against the accused. It might be relatively easy for the accused to point to *some* evidence that the offence was committed by a third party, which would distract the jury from the prosecution case and raise an unjustified reasonable doubt as to his guilt. If, for example, the jury hear that a third party has confessed, their natural reaction is likely to be that there *must* be a reasonable doubt; but this could be an unwarranted inference, particularly if the third party has not been subjected to cross-examination on his statement. Confessions are not necessarily reliable, but the jury will almost certainly assume that they are unless shown otherwise in open court. The truth is that some people *do* confess to crimes they did not commit; indeed it is not uncommon for feeble-minded individuals to confess to highly publicised offences because of the notoriety engendered by an association with such criminality (see 7.1.2.1 *post*). It is also quite possible for persons other than the accused to know something about the crime without being a participant in it, and in the absence of cross-examination on that knowledge the jury may well jump to the conclusion that there is a doubt as to the accused's guilt without giving enough consideration to the body of evidence against him.

This does not mean that the accused can never adduce evidence of a third party's guilt; but it does mean that the evidence he wishes to rely on must provide a rational basis for concluding that it was not he who committed the alleged offence. For example, if D is charged with the rape and murder of V it would be permissible to adduce evidence that the rapist's DNA profile, taken from his semen, does not match D's profile; or, if it can be shown from a third party's confession or other statement that he was aware of peculiar facts which no-one other than the murderer could have known, and the possibility of a joint enterprise can be discounted, there would be a rational argument for admitting his statement as evidence of his knowledge (and guilt) regardless of whether he is available for cross-examination (*cf.* M's state of mind in *R* v. *Blastland* [1985] 3 WLR 345 (HL)). This was accepted by the Supreme Court of South Australia in the not dissimilar case of *Re Van Beelen* [1974] 9 SASR 163 (at pp. 229–30):

> 'If the third party's confession did substantially conform to known facts, it could well have been relevant and important, not for its testimonial assertions, but for the esoteric knowledge of details of the *corpus delicti* evidenced by the confession which, in the circumstances, it was unlikely that any but the true offender would have been able to reveal. In those circumstances, the confession (or the material parts of it) could have been admitted ... as evidence of ... the intimate knowledge of the crime possessed by the declarant.'

It is to be noted that Blastland's application to the European Commission of Human Rights, on the basis that he had not received a fair trial, in violation of Article 6(1) of the European Convention, was rejected as manifestly ill-founded in *Blastland* v. *United Kingdom* (1987) 10 EHRR 528.

3.1.4 Legal Relevance

Some writers have propounded a doctrine of 'legal relevance' accepting the view that there has to be something more than a minimum of probative value for admissibility – and to this extent 'legal relevance' could be regarded as nothing more than a convenient label. The logical relevance of an item of evidence is not of itself sufficient for it to be admissible; it must also have sufficient probative value to override competing policy considerations. Unfortunately the term has also been used to represent the view that past decisions on the determination of relevance should act as binding precedents. It is difficult to see how such a doctrine could be of any practical use, however. Evidence, particularly circumstantial evidence, does not carry within it any inherent degree of probative value, so past decisions on what has been held to be relevant are unlikely to be of any assistance to a judge who has to reach a decision on entirely different facts. The probative value of an item of evidence is dependent on the particular issues and on the other admissible evidence before the court – in fact evidence may only become relevant during the course of a trial as other evidence is admitted or new issues arise (see, for example, *R* v. *Bracewell* (1978) 68 Cr App R 44 (CA)). Similarly, the importance to be attached to considerations such as the desirability of avoiding delay, expense and vexation will vary from case to case. Past decisions on relevance can be of only limited importance in respect of certain types of evidence where other considerations render the context immaterial, or where the substantive law has been delineated by the appellate courts to the extent that certain evidence *must* be regarded as relevant (or irrelevant) to a particular issue (for example the accused's characteristics which should, or should not, be taken into consideration when he is relying on the defence of provocation or duress). A doctrine of relevance based on precedent cannot provide a workable theory for the *general* assessment of what is admissible as relevant evidence in the vast majority of factually unique situations which come before the courts. It is also difficult to see how legal relevance could even be defined, and yet the success of the doctrine would depend on a workable definition which judges would be able to apply in practice. The preferable position must be that there is vested in all trial judges a discretion to ensure the proper administration of justice. The judge must weigh the utility of admitting logically probative evidence against competing policy considerations, with past decisions playing only a secondary role by making explicit the policy goals which judges should consider (or, exceptionally, laying down a rule of law in respect of certain types of evidence).

3.2 Similar Fact Evidence – Civil Proceedings

It has been seen that evidence of the disposition of a party to civil proceedings, such as evidence that a party behaved in a particular way on certain occasions in the past, is generally inadmissible if the only reason for admitting it is to show that that party acted in a similar way on the occasion which is the subject of the proceedings. This, it will be remembered, is because its probative value is usually outweighed by competing policy considerations. It follows that evidence of this sort should be admissible if its probative value, in the context of the particular case, is high enough to override such considerations.

Evidence of a party's disposition is invariably (if not somewhat misleadingly) referred to as 'similar fact evidence' because the classic examples involve the use of the defendant's misconduct on other occasions to prove that he acted in a similar way on the occasion which is the subject of the instant proceedings. The term 'similar fact evidence' is misleading for two reasons. First, the evidence of a party's relevant disposition may be something other than that he acted in a similar way on other occasions, for character can be proved in a variety of other ways. Second, the term does not identify whether the evidence is admissible or inadmissible. It is merely a label which has been used for many years, and which will no doubt be used for many more, to indicate that the evidence concerns the character or disposition of a party and that the reason why the opponent wishes to adduce it is to prove that that party acted in a particular way (consistent with his disposition) at the material time.

The principles which underlie the admissibility of similar fact evidence have been developed by the judiciary over the past two centuries. Much of the case law concerns criminal proceedings where the courts have sought to strike a balance between the need to ensure that the jury are not unduly prejudiced against the accused by his past misconduct and the desirability of allowing the jury to determine his guilt or innocence on the basis of an objective appraisal of all the available evidence (see 3.3 *post*). In civil trials, where an experienced professional judge is usually the tribunal of fact, the risk of engendering undue prejudice is not so important a consideration and there is a more relaxed approach to the admissibility of such evidence, the test essentially being one of probative value (*Mood Music Publishing* v. *De Wolfe* [1976] 2 WLR 451 (CA)). In other words, the question of admissibility is governed by the exercise of the judge's preliminary discretion for determining whether evidence is 'relevant' (*Vernon* v. *Bosley* [1994] PIQR 337 (CA) at p. 340). The judge may accept that evidence of a party's previous conduct is logically relevant to an issue, but will need to determine whether that evidence is sufficiently probative to justify the collateral matters, delay, expense and trouble that its admission would be likely to raise. Needless to say, where a civil case is tried before a jury the judge will also have to consider the risk of undue prejudice as in criminal trials (*Thorpe* v. *Chief Constable of Greater Manchester Police* [1989] 1 WLR 665 (CA)). This risk was indeed a consideration which influenced the civil courts in the nineteenth century when jury trials were the norm (*Agassiz* v. *London Tramway* (1872) 21 WR 199 (CE) at p. 200, *Hollingham* v. *Head* (1858) 27 LJCP 241 (CCP) at p. 242).

In determining the probative value of a party's extraneous conduct in relation to the instant proceedings much will depend on the extent to which the possibility of coincidence can be discounted by the judge, and this in turn may depend on the number of examples of extraneous conduct and the peculiar similarities between that conduct and the conduct in issue. In *Mood Music Publishing* v. *De Wolfe* [1976] 2 WLR 451 the defendants raised a defence of coincidence to an allegation that they had been in breach of the plaintiffs' copyright, and the plaintiffs were permitted to adduce evidence that the defendants had been in breach of copyright on other occasions. The Court of Appeal held that while reproducing music which was the subject of copyright could have been a coincidence if done only once, the fact the defendants had done the same thing four times discounted that possibility so the evidence had been properly admitted. Lord Denning MR felt that similar fact evidence was admissible in civil proceedings if the evidence was 'logically probative ... provided that it is not oppressive or unfair to the other side; and also that the other side has fair notice of it' (see also *Berger* v. *Raymond Sun* [1984] 1 WLR 625 (ChD) at p. 632).

In *Moore* v. *Ransome's Dock Committee* (1898) 14 TLR 539 one of the issues was whether the defendants, the proprietors of a dock, had known of its dangerous condition and had therefore been negligent in failing to remedy its defects. The Court of Appeal held that evidence of complaints and drownings on earlier occasions was admissible to demonstrate their knowledge and negligence. In *Joy* v. *Phillips Mills* [1916] 1 KB 849 (CA) a stable boy had been found dying with a halter in his hand next to a horse. Evidence that he had previously teased the horse with a halter was held to be admissible as it tended to prove that the horse had kicked him to death because of his teasing on that occasion, and therefore that he had not died in the course of his employment as alleged by the plaintiff (see also *Hales* v. *Kerr* [1908] 2 KB 601 (DC), 3.1.3 *ante*).

In *Sattin* v. *National Union Bank* [1978] 122 SJ 367 it was alleged that the defendant bank had negligently lost the plaintiff's jewellery. The plaintiff therefore sought to adduce evidence that the bank had lost jewellery belonging to another person on an earlier occasion. The Court of Appeal, stating that the test in civil proceedings was the same as that in criminal trials, held that the evidence should have been admitted as similar fact evidence. However, to say that the test is the same whether the proceedings are civil or criminal is to distort the true position. The risk of undue prejudice will be much lower in civil proceedings and, so long as the similar fact evidence is logically probative, it will be *prima facie* admissible (which is contrary to the general position in criminal proceedings). The judge will then consider his discretion to exclude the evidence on the ground of irrelevance, taking into consideration factors such as oppression, unfairness or surprise (*R* v. *Isleworth Crown Court ex parte Marland* (1997) 162 JP 251 (DC) at pp. 257–8). The key issue should therefore be whether the tribunal of fact is a jury or a professional judge, not the nature of the allegation. However, no doubt mindful of the fact that justice should be *seen* to be done, it seems the criminal rule of *prima facie* inadmissibility will be applied if the civil proceedings are quasi-criminal in nature, even if there is no jury (*Creighton* v. *Creighton* (1997) unreported (CCRTF 97/1212/G) (CA)).

An interesting recent example of evidence of disposition and extraneous misconduct being admitted in civil proceedings is provided by the case of *Irving* v. *Penguin Books and Lipstadt* (2000), reported by Penguin as *The Irving Judgment* (QBD). David Irving, a right-wing historian, sued the two defendants on the ground that he had been libelled by accusations in their book, *Denying the Holocaust*, that he was a Nazi apologist who had distorted facts and manipulated historical documents in support of his right-wing views. The defendants responded with the defence of justification, claiming that Irving had indeed falsified the historical record in relation to what had happened to the Jewish people during the Holocaust. In support of this defence the trial judge permitted the defendants to adduce evidence to suggest that Irving was an anti-Semite and in other respects racist, the argument being that this disposition provided a motive for his deliberate falsification of the historical record. Accordingly, although no allegation of racism or of anti-Semitism was levelled against Irving in *Denying the Holocaust*, evidence was admitted to the effect that Irving had associated with right-wing extremists, made a number of racist comments and composed a racist ditty for his young daughter.

Occasionally it may be necessary to adduce evidence of a third party's character to prove a fact in issue. In *Hurst* v. *Evans* [1917] 1 KB 352 (KBD) the issue was whether one of a shopkeeper's employees had been involved in the theft of jewellery from his shop (as his insurance policy did not cover inside jobs). The underwriters were allowed to call evidence that one of the employees, Mason, had been in earnest conversation with three highly-skilled safe-breakers two days before the assured's safe was blown. Mason's association with such persons of ill repute was evidence of a dishonest character and allowed an inference to be drawn that he may have been involved in the theft. Lush J said (at p. 355):

> 'I doubt whether the evidence would have been admissible in a criminal prosecution, not because it was irrelevant, but because in a criminal case evidence is frequently rejected which tends to prejudice the defendant and prevent a fair trial. I admitted the evidence because, although taken by itself its weight is slight, I cannot say that it is irrelevant in this case, where the whole question is whether Mason was acting dishonestly and in complicity with the actual thieves.'

3.3 Similar Fact Evidence – Criminal Proceedings

In criminal proceedings the term 'similar fact evidence' is generally taken to mean evidence of the accused's unpleasant disposition (that is, evidence of his general propensity to act or think in a particular unpleasant way) which is *directly* relevant to whether he committed the crime with which he is charged (as opposed to having an indirect bearing on his guilt, in the sense that it undermines his credibility as a witness). The unpleasantness may be evidenced by criminal conduct on extraneous occasions (occasions unrelated to the alleged offence), or by morally culpable conduct at the fringes of criminality or by lawful conduct which many people might nonetheless find morally reprehensible; but it might just as easily be demonstrated by the accused's possession of certain articles, such as child pornography or a book on cracking safes, or by the accused's criminal associations or even by his own admission. Thus, similar fact evidence may not in fact be 'similar' to anything else, but (if admitted) it will have a direct bearing on whether the accused is guilty of the offence charged. The general rule is that evidence of the accused's extraneous misconduct or bad character is admissible evidence of his guilt only if its probative value is so great that it would be just to admit it, bearing in mind the unduly prejudicial effect its admission might have on the jury.

3.3.1 The Probative Value of Similar Fact Evidence

Evidence of the accused's disposition may be logically relevant to an issue in the proceedings because of the general tendency for human behaviour to repeat itself or the general tendency for people with particular beliefs to behave in accordance with them. Where the identity of the offender is in issue but it can be surmised that he has a peculiar disposition which the accused shares, that disposition must be logically probative of the accused's guilt. He and the offender share a peculiar character trait and that means he is more likely to be guilty than otherwise. In this sense the evidence of disposition can help to identify an unknown offender by placing both the offender and the accused within the same sub-group of society as a whole. If the accused's disposition is relied on to identify him as the unknown offender then, in the absence of any other evidence implicating him, the probative value of his disposition will depend on its peculiarity, that is, on the unlikelihood of coincidence. In isolation, a commonplace character trait will have little probative value because of the large number of other persons sharing it who might just as easily have committed the offence. So, for example, it would not be possible to convict D of burglary merely on the basis that he has previous convictions for the same offence – the sub-group comprising burglars is too large to discount the possibility that the offender was someone else. A bizarre or strikingly peculiar character trait will be far more probative because of the smaller number of persons falling within the particular sub-group of people sharing it. The more peculiar the character trait, the fewer the number of persons there will be in the sub-group and the greater will be the probative value of the similar fact evidence as evidence identifying the accused as the offender. In an extreme case the disposition might be so rare that it will place the offender and the accused in a sub-group of just a few persons. By itself this would be insufficient to convict the accused, but with some other circumstantial evidence identifying him as the offender the overall effect could be compelling (see *R* v. *Straffen* [1952] 2 QB 911 (CCA), 3.3.4 *post*). Of course where there is additional circumstantial evidence identifying the accused as the offender the probative value of his disposition will depend on the strength of the other evidence and may have considerable probative force in the absence of any striking peculiarity. If, for example, a sexual offence was committed by a male offender on a boy on Friday and the offender arranged to meet that boy at an isolated spot on the following Monday, evidence of the accused's enjoyment of pederasty would be only slightly probative of his guilt in the absence of other evidence; but that same evidence would be highly probative of his guilt if he happened to turn up at the rendezvous on Monday (see *Thompson* v. *R* [1918] AC 221 (HL), 3.3.4 *post*).

Where identity is not in issue the evidence of the accused's disposition may still be relevant, but in a different way. It might establish that the accused had the *mens rea* for the offence charged, if his conduct could be construed as either innocent or criminal depending on his frame of mind at the time; or it might show that the *actus reus* of the alleged offence occurred if this is disputed. If it has been established that the accused committed the *actus reus* of an offence but his defence is absence of *mens rea*, the probative value of his disposition will depend on how closely related it is to the state of mind which the law requires for guilt. Intimate physical contact between a man and his child may be accidental or an indecent assault depending on the man's state of mind; and evidence of articles such as child pornography in his possession, suggesting an interest in children as sexual objects, would be highly probative of his having the requisite *mens rea* and being guilty of the offence (see *R* v. *Lewis* (1982) 76 Cr App R 33 (CA) and *R* v. *Downes* [1981] Crim LR 174 (CA)). A motorist who kills a female cyclist on the highway may have committed an offence or may simply have been involved in a road accident; but evidence that the accused had knocked down two other female cyclists the day before and assaulted them, and knocked down another female cyclist a few hours after the fatal collision and stolen her handbag, would suggest it was probably not just an unfortunate accident but a deliberate assault (see *R* v. *Mortimer* (1936) 25 Cr App R 150 (CCA)). The accused may have an innocent explanation for being in a garage in possession of skeleton keys, but evidence that a week earlier he had entered into a criminal conspiracy with other persons to use skeleton keys to burgle an office would indicate that his explanation is unlikely to be true (see *R* v. *Hodges* (1957) 41 Cr App R 218 (CCA)). Similarly, the accused charged with attempted burglary with intent to rape may have been walking round a secluded house late at night genuinely looking for directions, notwithstanding his possession of a knife, glove and condom, but previous convictions for rape where he managed to enter the victims' homes after asking for directions, and then used a knife to procure the victims' submission, would militate against any such innocent explanation (*R* v. *Toothill* (1998) unreported (97/06019/W3) (CA)). If the accused denies that the *actus reus* of the offence has been committed, evidence of similar occurrences connected with him on other occasions will logically undermine the possibility of accident. The accused's wife may have died in her bath following an epileptic fit or because she was murdered by him, but the possibility that it was murder as opposed to natural causes becomes much higher if his other wives have died in similar circumstances (see *R* v. *Smith* (1915) 11 Cr App R 229 (CCA), 3.3.4 *post*). In all these examples the possibility of coincidence is too remote to be given credence, and it is for this reason that the disposition evidence is so highly probative of the accused's guilt.

Occasionally the accused's extraneous misconduct may be relevant in a way which does not depend to any extent on his having a disposition to commit crimes of the type charged, and there may be no possibility of the jury's reasoning from disposition to guilt. For example the accused's fingerprints at the scene of a burglary committed at 7 Acacia Avenue on Saturday night could not be admitted to prove that he was guilty of murder on the basis that a person with a burglarious disposition is more likely to commit the more serious offence. But if there is other circumstantial evidence that he is the murderer, and the murder was committed at 9 Acacia Avenue on Saturday night, it becomes apparent that the evidence of his having committed burglary is relevant to whether he also committed the murder, if only because it shows he was in the vicinity at the time. Such evidence is not usually regarded as similar fact evidence, and would appear to be *prima facie* admissible simply on the ground that it has significant probative value (although a further justification for its admissibility – that it is evidence forming part of the *res gestae* – could be provided in respect of this example). Not all such evidence of extraneous misconduct forms part of the *res gestae*, however, so it would be wrong to classify it as such; for example the evidence might consist of the accused's attempts to pervert the course of justice by bribing witnesses some weeks or months after the alleged offence occurred. If such evidence is to be excluded it cannot be because of the risk that the jury might reason from disposition to guilt, so it can only be because of the 'moral prejudice' which might be engendered by the jury's becoming aware that the accused is guilty of misconduct (3.3.2 *post*).

If, however, evidence of extraneous misconduct is tendered to prove guilt in a way which does not depend on disposition, but that evidence might logically lead the jury to reason from disposition to guilt, it should fall within the general category of evidence governed by the law on the admissibility of similar fact evidence. *R* v. *Lovegrove* [1920] 3 KB 643 (CCA) provides an example of this sort of case. L was on trial for causing the death of Mrs P by performing an unlawful abortion on her. Mr P gave evidence that Mrs T had given him L's address and he had gone there and arranged with L to perform an abortion on Mrs P. It was put to Mr P in cross-examination that there had been no such conversation, and that Mr P had visited L's house to look for accommodation. The prosecution were allowed to call Mrs T to give evidence that L had performed an abortion on her and that she had given L's address to Mr P. The reason for admitting Mrs T's evidence was to show that Mr P was not lying as alleged, and not for the purpose of allowing the jury to reason from disposition to guilt, but there was clearly a danger that the jury would have applied the evidence in the latter sense (see also *R* v. *Da Silva* [1990] 1 WLR 31 (CA)).

Another type of evidence of extraneous misconduct which is *prima facie* admissible (again, falling outside the scope of the law governing the admissibility of similar fact evidence generally) is 'background evidence'. This sort of evidence is admissible to ensure that the jury will have before them a continuous and intelligible account of the relationship between the accused and the complainant or victim of the alleged criminal offence (see 3.3.9 *post*).

The probative value of similar fact evidence, like any other logically relevant circumstantial evidence, is very much a question of degree depending on a multitude of variables including the other admissible evidence and the accused's purported defence. Indeed, as can be seen from the above examples (and it is important to note that they are no more than examples) the nature of the prospective defence may be the key element which gives the similar fact evidence its cogency. This was recognised in *R* v. *Lunt* (1986) 85 Cr App R 241 (CA) where Neill LJ said (at p. 245):

'In order to decide whether the evidence is positively probative in regard to the crime charged it is first necessary to identify the issue to which the evidence is directed. Thus the evidence may be put forward, for example, to support an identification ... or to prove intention or to rebut a possible defence of accident or innocent association.'

Two final points need to be borne in mind. First, while the probative value of disposition evidence may depend on similarities, it may also depend on the absence of dissimilarities. In *R* v. *Johnson* [1995] 2 Cr App R 41 (CA) the trial judge had failed to take into account the nature and quality of the demonstrable disparities when assessing the probative value of the evidence, giving too much weight instead to the similarities, and for this reason the convictions were quashed (see also *R* v. *West* [1996] 2 Cr App R 374 (CA) at pp. 390–1). Second, although admissible disposition evidence is directly relevant to whether the accused committed the offence charged, it will also be logically relevant to the accused's credibility should he decide to testify, and will for this reason also have an indirect bearing on whether the accused is guilty. The obvious example would be where the accused is charged with having committed perjury and there is evidence that he has previous convictions for the same offence. A disposition to lie on oath demonstrated by the previous convictions would be regarded as directly relevant to whether he committed perjury on the occasion in question, but it would also be relevant to whether the accused should be believed when giving evidence in his own defence. It should be noted, however, that *any* evidence of extraneous misconduct might be regarded as having a bearing on whether the accused should be believed, on the ground that a disposition to act in an immoral or unlawful way suggests that the accused is not the sort of person to be trusted or believed, regardless of whether his previous convictions are for dishonesty offences.

3.3.2 The Unduly Prejudicial Effect of Similar Fact Evidence

As with any other logically relevant circumstantial evidence, similar fact evidence must be sufficiently probative to be admissible when weighed against competing policy considerations. In criminal proceedings the principal consideration militating against the admission of such evidence is the risk of unduly prejudicing the accused in the eyes of the jury to the extent that he would be denied a fair trial. This risk arises because the similar fact evidence will comprise evidence of extraneous behaviour (usually criminal conduct) and/or a disposition which many jurors will find unpalatable. Research suggests that if during the trial the jury (or magistrates) become aware of the accused's similar misconduct on previous occasions or his unappealing disposition, that information may weigh heavily on their minds, and their verdict may be reached without sufficient regard to the non-extraneous evidence before them (see Appendix D of the Law Commission's Consultation Paper No. 141 (1996), and Appendix A of the Commission's Report, Law Com No. 273 (2001)). Such findings would seem to be confirmed by what happened in the case of *R* v. *Bills* [1995] 2 Cr App R 643. The jury had convicted B of an offence contrary to s. 20 of the Offences Against the Person Act 1861, rather than the more serious s. 18 offence, and while still sitting in the jury box they heard the prosecution inform the judge about B's several previous convictions for violent conduct. The jury then sought to change their verdict and to convict him of the s. 18 offence. Surprisingly, the judge acceded to their request, but the Court of Appeal restored the original s. 20 conviction as it was quite possible that the jury had been influenced by the revelation of his previous misconduct in their presence (see also *R* v. *Boyes* [1991] Crim LR 717 (CA) and *R* v. *Newton* (1912) 7 Cr App R 214 (CCA)).

The problem with similar fact evidence is that when its probative value in tending to show the accused's guilt is high there is often a concomitant increase in the likelihood that the jury will convict him for the wrong reasons and therefore that the accused may be convicted of a crime he did not commit. By its very nature all prosecution evidence will prejudice the accused by making his conviction more likely, but the admission of similar fact evidence is hazardous because it is likely to cause him *undue* prejudice. The jury (or magistrates) may judge him more on the basis of his past misconduct ('he's done it before, he must be guilty') or distasteful disposition ('what an odious man; let's send him down') than upon a disinterested appraisal of the evidence relating directly to the offence charged. The Law Commission has referred to these two distinct types of undue prejudice as 'reasoning prejudice' and 'moral prejudice' (Consultation Paper No. 141 (1996) at pp. 122–6). Reasoning prejudice suggests that the jury or magistrates may reason that because the accused has committed similar offences before or is of a particular disposition he is guilty of the offence charged (a logical chain of reasoning given the tendency for offenders to re-offend and for individuals to act in accordance with their disposition) but attribute to it far more probative value than it deserves and fail to give sufficient consideration to other possibilities, for example that the accused may have changed his ways, or that he may have been the focus of police attention and charged partly because of his previous convictions, or that there might be many other persons who could equally have committed the offence. If the accused has a long record showing he has committed numerous offences of the same type the prejudice will be more severe because of the cumulative effect caused by the disclosure of so many convictions. Moral prejudice, on the other hand, suggests that the jury may convict the accused for a reason other than by a process of logical reasoning. The jury may find the accused's character so distasteful that the non-extraneous evidence becomes of secondary importance and the conviction is based more on fear or hatred: a desire to punish such a dissolute character for what he is, or what he has done in the past, and to prevent him from behaving in a similar way in the future. Even when due consideration is given to the non-extraneous evidence, the knowledge of the accused's disposition may deprive him of the benefit of the reasonable doubt he is entitled to. The undue prejudice which comes with knowledge of the accused's disposition therefore undermines a cardinal principle of criminal justice: the presumption that the accused is innocent until his guilt has been proved beyond reasonable doubt. Indeed, the undue prejudice created by an awareness of the accused's disposition may lead the jury to approach the case with a presumption of *guilt*. These prejudicial effects are likely to be particularly severe if the offence charged is of the most heinous kind, such as a sexual offence against a young child:

> 'Nothing can so certainly be counted upon to make a prejudice against an accused upon his trial as the disclosure to the jury of other misconduct of a kind similar to that which is the subject of the indictment, and, indeed, when the crime alleged is one of a revolting character ... and the hearer is a person who has not been trained to think judicially, the prejudice must sometimes be almost insurmountable.' (*R* v. *Bond* [1906] 2 KB 389 (CCCR) at p. 398)

Thus, while evidence of the accused's bad character may be logically relevant to whether he committed the offence in question, and therefore ought to be admissible by virtue of the principle of free proof, the risk that the evidence may be used inappropriately by the tribunal of fact may justify its exclusion. In short, the process of determining guilt or innocence may be more distorted by the admission of such evidence than by its exclusion. Similar fact evidence tendered by the prosecution is therefore generally inadmissible 'because its logically probative significance is grossly outweighed by its prejudice to the accused, so that a fair trial is endangered if it is admitted' (*DPP* v. *Kilbourne* [1973] 2 WLR 254 (HL) at p. 277), or the court may simply hold such evidence to be 'irrelevant' (3.3.7 *post*). Similar fact evidence tendered by the prosecution is therefore *prima facie* inadmissible unless its probative value is so great that the risk of the accused being unfairly prejudiced by its admission can be disregarded or eliminated by an adequate direction from the judge. The rule is based on the way jurors are understood to be influenced by such evidence, so where the tribunal of fact is a judge sitting alone, and the risk of undue prejudice can be ameliorated, the focus should be on probative value with a *prima facie* rule of admissibility subject to the general discretion to exclude evidence on the ground of 'irrelevance' (*Attorney-General of Hong Kong* v. *Siu Yuk-Shing* [1989] 1 WLR 236 (PC) at p. 241). That said, there is nothing to suggest that this approach is adopted by professional magistrates (district judges) – presumably because justice must not only be done but be seen to be done.

3.3.3 Determining Admissibility

The law governing the admissibility of similar fact evidence represents the judiciary's attempt to reconcile two competing principles: that unduly prejudicial evidence should be excluded while probative evidence of the accused's guilt should be admitted. But reconciling these principles requires finding a solution to a paradox. The more probative a piece of similar fact evidence is (and consequently the greater the force of the inclusionary free proof principle) the more unduly prejudicial it is also likely to be (and consequently the greater the force of the exclusionary fair trial principle). There are good reasons for excluding such evidence where the risk of undue prejudice is greater than the probative value provided by admitting the evidence, but, as in civil proceedings, some similar fact evidence will occasionally be so probative that as a matter of common sense the inclusionary principle should weigh more heavily than the exclusionary principle. The similar fact evidence will be *so* probative, either standing alone or in conjunction with other admissible evidence, that the jury would be *compelled* to find the accused guilty, in which case the question of undue prejudice effectively disappears. The law now recognises that a test along these lines is the only practicable way of resolving the paradox (*DPP* v. *P* [1991] 3 WLR 161 (HL), 3.3.6 *post*), yet there are obvious difficulties involved in its practical application.

The trial judge not only has to ascertain what the individuals on the jury are likely to think but also has to compare two incomparable considerations with little practical assistance from any other source. Just as past decisions on what is sufficiently probative to be considered 'relevant' evidence cannot be binding precedents for other factually unique cases, any assessment of the probative value and undue prejudice of similar fact evidence, and the point at which the probative value becomes the paramount consideration, has to be made without recourse to decided cases. The large number of variables involved and the fact that 'probative value' and 'prejudicial effect' are questions of degree dependent on the factual matrix of the case means that the trial judge is only able to come to a decision on admissibility by applying the underlying principles. Much will depend on the type of offence, the accused's defence, the facts of the case, the nature of the accused's disposition, his age, the locality, the values and concerns of the people from whom the jury are drawn and, of course, the shrewdness of the judge who has to make the decision.

Past decisions should be regarded as *illustrations* of when similar fact evidence has been admitted or excluded, but no more than that. In recent years this has indeed been recognised, and there are now only a few decisions which can properly be regarded as binding precedents. But this was not always the case. Until the decision of the House of Lords in *DPP* v. *Boardman* [1974] 3 WLR 673 undue emphasis was placed on previous cases and too little on the underlying principles, which led to considerable confusion and an absurd approach to admissibility which was dependent on finding a specific 'category of relevance' into which the evidence could be pigeon-holed while paying scant regard to the question of trial fairness. It is an unfortunate fact, however, that while this former approach has been discredited by the House of Lords, the Court of Appeal still occasionally reverts to it when determining whether similar fact evidence ought to have been admitted (3.3.16 *post*). For this reason it is still necessary to understand the historical background to the modern law.

3.3.4 The Evolution of the Law

The judiciary's approach to the admissibility of similar fact evidence developed during the nineteenth century and crystallised in *Makin* v.

Attorney-General for New South Wales [1894] AC 57. John and Sarah
Makin received a baby, Horace, from its mother following representations
by them that they would adopt him, and for this they were paid a small
sum of money. Horace's body was subsequently found buried in the
garden of the premises formerly occupied by them, and their defence to a
charge of murder was that Horace had been adopted in good faith and
had died accidentally. The trial judge allowed the prosecution to rebut that
defence by adducing evidence that the bodies of nine other infants had
been discovered in the garden where Horace's body had been found and in
the grounds of other premises occupied by the Makins, and that five
women had similarly given their infants over to the Makins for adoption
having paid a small sum of money to them. The Makins were convicted of
Horace's murder and appealed unsuccessfully to the Privy Council on the
ground that such evidence was inadmissible. Lord Herschell set out a two-
limbed test for determining the admissibility of similar fact evidence (at
p. 65):

> 'It is undoubtedly not competent for the prosecution to adduce evidence
> tending to show that the accused has been guilty of criminal acts, other
> than those covered by the indictment, for the purpose of leading to the
> conclusion that the accused is a person likely from his criminal conduct
> or character to have committed the offence for which he is being tried.
> On the other hand, the mere fact that the evidence adduced tends to
> show the commission of other crimes does not render it inadmissible if it
> be relevant to an issue before the jury ...'

The prosecution evidence (the testimony of the other women and the
discovery of the other bodies) was relevant to the issue of guilt as it
suggested that the Makins had not adopted Horace in good faith and that
his death had not been accidental. It was therefore held that the evidence
had been properly admitted. Lord Herschell gave two examples of when
previous misconduct could be relevant to an issue before the jury for the
second limb of the test: (i) if it showed 'whether the acts alleged to
constitute the crime charged in the indictment were designed or
accidental', and (ii) if it was able 'to rebut a defence which would
otherwise be open to the accused'. The prosecution had not adduced the
similar fact evidence to prove that the Makins had a disposition to murder
young children and that they were therefore guilty of Horace's death –
indeed the Makins had not been convicted of any offences in relation to
the other bodies – so the evidence was not excluded by the first limb of
Lord Herschell's test. The evidence was relevant in another way, and
therefore admissible by virtue of the second limb of the test, as the jury
could properly infer from it that the defence of accident was false. It would
have been an affront to common sense to believe that Horace had died of
natural causes given the large number of other dead infants discovered.
Perhaps two accidental deaths would have been a reasonable possibility
(that is, no more than an unfortunate coincidence) but the existence of
nine other bodies meant that coincidence could be discounted. As
McHugh J said in *Pfennig* v. *R* (1995) 182 CLR 461 (HCA) (at p. 531):

'The propensity of the accused to kill the babies was only established by the conclusion that it was probable to the point of certainty that so many babies including [Horace] could not have died by accident ... It was the verdict that established the accused's propensity.'

In subsequent cases the focus moved away from a consideration of the *principles* underlying the *Makin* formula – the need to avoid unduly prejudicing the accused and the desirability of admitting probative evidence of the accused's guilt – and instead turned to whether the facts of a particular case could be brought within one of the *Makin* categories of relevance (or an analogous category) and thus be automatically admissible (see, for example, *Perkins* v. *Jeffery* [1915] 2 KB 702 (DC)). A corollary of the *Makin* test, as subsequently interpreted and applied, was that if the accused indicated he would not raise an affirmative defence the similar fact evidence would be inadmissible; so where the defence was simply a bare denial of the allegation, evidence of the accused's disposition or extraneous misconduct could not be adduced (*R* v. *Cole* (1941) 28 Cr App R 43 (CCA), *R* v. *Flack* [1969] 1 WLR 937 (CA)).

That this artificially mechanistic approach to both admission and exclusion should have developed is not particularly surprising given the ease with which the test could be applied by judges, for similar fact evidence was automatically admissible so long as it could undermine a defence which was reasonably open to the accused (*R* v. *Boyle* [1914] 3 KB 339 (CCA), *Harris* v. *DPP* [1952] AC 694 (HL)). However, this interpretation of the second limb of the *Makin* test allowed for the possibility that unduly prejudicial evidence could be admissible without sufficient consideration being given to the actual probative value of the evidence or the extent of its unduly prejudicial effect, and effectively gave the prosecution the right to adduce evidence of disposition simply by finding an appropriate category of relevance: 'relevance for that purpose is being used as a peg upon which to hang the dirty linen of the accused, so the jury may determine what sort of man it is upon whose acts they are to render a verdict' (*per* Julius Stone, (1932) 46 Harvard Law Review 954 at p. 983). Stone argued that the *Makin* test did not provide adequate protection for the accused, and that an additional safeguard was required: 'that the trial judge should be recognised to have a discretion to decide whether the probative weight of proffered evidence outweighs its ... prejudice.' An exclusionary discretion was indeed expressly recognised in later cases on similar fact evidence (*Noor Mohamed* v. *R* [1949] AC 182 (PC) at p. 192, *Harris* v. *DPP* [1952] AC 694 (HL) at p. 707) and was subsequently held by the House of Lords to be of general application in relation to *any* admissible prosecution evidence in *R* v. *Sang* [1979] 3 WLR 263. The absence of a recognised exclusionary discretion in the decades following *Makin* does not mean that the cases during this period were incorrectly decided, though, because the similar fact evidence held to be admissible on appeal was, despite the post-*Makin* test of categorisation, very often so probative when compared with the risk of undue prejudice that it would have been admissible even applying the modern test:

'a tribute to the power of common sense over the forms of legal reasoning' (*per* Hoffmann, (1975) 91 LQR 193 at p. 204). A case in point is the *cause célèbre R* v. *Smith* (1915) 11 Cr App R 229 – the 'Brides in the Bath Case'. S was charged with the murder of his recent bride, Bessie Munday, who had drowned in her bath in 1912, and he raised the defence that she had died of natural causes following a fit. The prosecution were allowed to adduce evidence that, subsequent to the death of Bessie Munday, another two of his recent brides had similarly died while having a bath, and that in all three cases: (i) S had warned his doctor that the woman suffered from epilepsy, (ii) the woman had died in a bath after apparently suffering a fit, (iii) the bathroom door could not be locked from the inside, (iv) S stood to profit from the woman's death, and (v) S had claimed he had been out shopping for groceries at the time. The Court of Criminal Appeal held that the evidence had been properly admitted to rebut S's defence of accidental death. There was such a large aggregation of similarities that any possibility of coincidence could be discounted, and while the evidence was held to be admissible because of the second limb of the *Makin* test, there can be no doubt that the same decision would have been reached if the modern test had been applied. Much the same can be said of other decisions where the *Makin* test was applied to admit similar fact evidence. Indeed a number of decisions *prior* to *Makin* would be decided the same way today (see, for example, *R* v. *Gray* (1866) 4 F & F 1102 (Assizes)).

The *Makin* test was unsatisfactory in an additional respect, however. Its first limb seemed to comprise an absolute ban on the admissibility of similar fact evidence if its relevance was entirely dependent on a process of reasoning from disposition to guilt; yet evidence which is relevant only in this way may occasionally be highly probative or even compelling evidence of the accused's guilt. This is exemplified by several cases following *Makin* where the first limb was in effect disregarded. In *R* v. *Ball* [1911] AC 47 a brother and sister were charged with committing incest in 1910, the non-extraneous evidence against them being that there was only one furnished bedroom in their house and that they had shared a double bed during that year. The prosecution were permitted to adduce evidence that the couple had had a prior sexual relationship, when incest was not yet an offence and during which time they had lived as husband and wife, and that they had had a child in 1908. The House of Lords, while expressly approving the *Makin* test, held the evidence to have been properly admitted to show their 'guilty passion' for each other and that their sleeping arrangements in 1910 were not innocent. However, the evidence of their earlier conduct was relevant to the 1910 proceedings only by way of an argument from disposition to guilt. The earlier relationship demonstrated their mutual sexual attraction and from this, together with their sleeping arrangements, it could be inferred that they were still sexually active as a couple in 1910. The House of Lords could justify its decision in terms of the second *Makin* principle permitting the admission of similar fact evidence which could 'rebut a defence which would otherwise be open to the accused' (in this case the defence of innocent cohabitation), but the decision shows that the first limb of the *Makin* test, insofar as it represented a blanket ban on reasoning from disposition, could not be regarded as a correct statement of the law (see also *R* v. *Marsh* (1949) 33 Cr App R 185 (CCA)).

Thompson v. *R* [1918] AC 221, another *cause célèbre*, provides a further illustration. T was charged with committing acts of gross indecency on two boys on 16 March 1917 in the urinal near Turnham Green railway station in west London. On 19 March the police observed him near the same place at about the same time of day. The boys stated that he was the same man who had committed the offences against them three days earlier and who had on that occasion asked them to meet him at the same time and place on 19 March 'to do it again'. In his defence T claimed he had been mistakenly identified, that he had never seen the boys before and that he had only spoken to them on 19 March to discourage them from following him. The trial judge allowed the prosecution to adduce evidence that powder puffs were found on T when he was arrested (powder puffs apparently being 'things with which persons who commit abominable and indecent crimes with males furnish themselves') and that several photographs of naked boys had been discovered in his lodgings. The House of Lords dismissed T's appeal and held that the incriminating articles were admissible as they were relevant to rebut his defence of mistaken identity and to prove that he was the offender on 16 March. But, as in *R* v. *Ball* [1911] AC 47 (HL), the relevance depended entirely on reasoning from disposition to guilt. Unfortunately, for many years *Thompson* v. *R* was seen as laying down a binding precedent for the admissibility of articles showing a homosexual disposition (this is no longer the law: *R* v. *Horwood* [1969] 3 WLR 964 (CA), *DPP* v. *Boardman* [1974] 3 WLR 673 (HL)); yet the case is still a very useful illustration of why previous decisions on similar fact evidence should not be treated as precedents. The probative value of similar fact evidence depends on the unique factual context of the particular case being tried, and in *Thompson* v. *R* this depended on the unlikelihood that an innocent man with exactly the same tendencies as the offender of 16 March should coincidentally have turned up at a rendezvous arranged by that offender equipped for buggery: 'It would be strange, indeed, if one man should commit with the boys the offence charged on the 16th, and make an assignation with them to commit it again upon the 19th, that another man should, with an intent to do the same, take up and fulfil the first man's engagement' (at p. 229). The probative value of the articles would have been significantly reduced if the facts had been a little different – if, for example, the lavatory in question had been a common meeting ground for homosexuals, particularly at that time of the day, for then the possibility that T's presence was a mere coincidence could not so easily have been discounted. The circumstances which give rise to the high probative value of incriminating articles in one case may be entirely absent in another case. Thus in *R* v. *Bartlett* [1959] Crim LR 285 (CCA) it was held that an obscene photograph found in the accused's possession soon after an alleged indecent assault by him on a woman should not have been admitted at his trial.

Perhaps the most striking example of similar fact evidence being admitted when its relevance depended entirely on reasoning from disposition to guilt is the case of *R* v. *Straffen* [1952] 2 QB 911. S was charged with murdering a young girl, Linda Bowyer, who had been found strangled in a village but who had not been sexually molested or concealed. S had escaped from Broadmoor (a mental hospital) and was on the run at the time of Linda's murder. He admitted he had been in the village and seen Linda but claimed he had not killed her – although news of her death had not at that stage been released – and this was admitted in evidence at his trial. Further, although his defence was one of bare denial the prosecution were permitted to adduce evidence of S's murderous propensity: the fact that he had been incarcerated in Broadmoor for killing two young girls in a similar way a year earlier. The Court of Criminal Appeal held that the similar fact evidence had been properly admitted as S's abnormal propensity to strangle young girls identified him as the murderer.

Evidence of disposition was admitted in the foregoing cases to prove guilt, notwithstanding the prohibition in the first limb of the *Makin* test and even though the accused had raised no defence other than that of 'bare denial'. That such evidence *should* occasionally be admitted, even in the absence of an affirmative defence, is clearly illustrated by the facts of *R* v. *Straffen* [1952] 2 QB 911 (CCA), which is perhaps the best illustration of the inadequacy of both limbs of the *Makin* test. There are many other examples where evidence of disposition has been admitted to prove the accused's guilt and it is now clear that there is no barrier to the admissibility of such evidence just because it is relevant only in this way. In *R* v. *Thrussell* (1981) [1997] Crim LR 501n (CA), for example, a copy of *The Cocaine Consumer's Handbook* found at the accused's home was admitted to prove his involvement in smuggling cocaine. He and his co-accused had travelled together in Peru but they had returned to England separately, and only the co-accused had been found in possession of the cocaine. The book was therefore admissible to prove that he had been party to a joint enterprise. Despite its unequivocal wording, the first limb of the *Makin* test should therefore be regarded as no more than an expression of the principle requiring the exclusion of unduly prejudicial evidence, and as such it may be outweighed by the competing principle that highly probative evidence should be admitted, even where the relevance of such evidence depends entirely on drawing an inference of guilt from the accused's disposition.

Where the inference from disposition is not very strong – which will usually be the case if the disposition is not particularly unusual – the similar fact evidence will now be inadmissible because the undue prejudice caused by its admission will outweigh its limited probative value. The same result was reached in the decades following *Makin* by the application of the first limb of Lord Herschell's test. Thus in *R* v. *Brown* (1963) 47 Cr App R 204 (CCA), where S and others had been charged with breaking into a shop at lunch-time with a skeleton key, it was held that the prosecution should not have been permitted to adduce evidence that S had used a skeleton key to break into a shop 20 miles away at lunch-time five days earlier. The evidence merely demonstrated his propensity to break into shops at that time of day. Given the relatively large number of persons sharing his disposition it was not particularly probative of his guilt, but it would have been unduly prejudicial (certainly in the reasoning sense). Similarly, in *R* v. *Taylor* (1923) 17 Cr App R 109 (CCA), where evidence that a jemmy had been found at the accused's house was adduced at his trial for breaking into a shop (even though no jemmy had actually been used to commit the offence), it was held that the evidence should not have been admitted (see also *R* v. *Manning* (1923) 17 Cr App R 85 (CCA)).

Where, however, an incriminating article found in the accused's possession is particularly probative in the factual context of the case it may be admissible even though it is not directly connected to the offence charged (as in *Thompson* v. *R* [1918] AC 221 (HL)). In *R* v. *Reading* (1965) 50 Cr App R 98 several co-accused were charged with hijacking a lorry and the trial judge admitted evidence that walkie-talkie sets had been found in their cars and that number plates and a police-type uniform had been found in the house of one of the co-accused, although none of this evidence had been used in the offence charged. The Court of Criminal Appeal held that the articles had been properly admitted as the evidence was of 'powerful probative value in relation to the vital issue as to the identification of these accused people'. Rather curiously, in *R* v. *Mustafa* (1976) 65 Cr App R 26 the Court of Appeal felt that the decision in *R* v. *Reading* provided a quite separate ground for admitting incriminating articles outside the ambit of the law on similar fact evidence, but this is clearly incorrect as the same principles must apply whether the accused's criminal disposition is inferred from extraneous misconduct or incriminating articles found in his possession. In *R* v. *Clarke* [1995] 2 Cr App R 425 the Court of Appeal expressly recognised that the admissibility of such evidence is governed by the (modern) similar facts test, and held that a 'robber's kit' found in the accused's car on 20 June 1992 had been properly admitted as circumstantial evidence identifying him as the man who had committed a robbery in Essex on 21 April 1992, even though the robber's kit had not been used to commit that offence.

In short, the *Makin* test failed to make explicit the true rationale governing the admissibility of similar fact evidence. Its first limb expressly excluded any evidence which was relevant only by reasoning from disposition to guilt, whereas in reality such evidence could be admitted when it had sufficient probative value; and the second limb focused on categories of relevance without any consideration of the probative value of the similar fact evidence in question or the undue prejudice which could be engendered by its admission. If the first limb of the test is understood to represent the *principle* that unduly prejudicial evidence should be excluded, with the second limb representing the competing free proof *principle* that highly probative evidence of the accused's guilt should be admitted, then the *Makin* formula could indeed be said to have laid down the correct approach for assessing the admissibility of similar fact evidence. Read literally, though, Lord Herschell's test obscured the correct approach. The key to the admissibility of similar fact evidence depends on which of the two competing principles should outweigh the other in the context of the particular case being tried, and this, as has since been recognised, must depend on probative value.

3.3.5 *DPP* v. *Boardman*

The House of Lords took the opportunity offered to it in *DPP* v. *Boardman* [1974] 3 WLR 673 to restate the principles governing the admissibility of similar fact evidence in terms of probative value and undue prejudice. B (the headmaster of a language school) was charged with attempted buggery with one boy (S) and of incitement of another boy (H) to commit buggery. He was tried for the two separate offences during the one trial, and the evidence of each offence was held by the trial judge to be admissible similar fact evidence in respect of the other offence (3.3.13 *post*) on the ground that there were peculiar similarities between the offences: S and H were both pupils at B's school; both had been aroused from their sleep by B and invited to his sitting room; and B had wished to adopt the passive sexual role in each case. B appealed unsuccessfully to both the Court of Appeal and the House of Lords. The question of law which had been certified by the Court of Appeal required an answer to the question whether there was a particular category of relevance for evidence of homosexual activities which took a particular form. The House of Lords unanimously rejected the post-*Makin* 'categories of relevance' approach and instead sought to explain admissibility by reference to the underlying principles.

The test according to Lords Wilberforce and Cross was whether the similar fact evidence was sufficiently probative to justify its admission despite the risk of undue prejudice: 'The basic principle must be that the admission of similar fact evidence ... is exceptional and requires a strong degree of probative force' (*per* Lord Wilberforce at p. 690); 'The question must always be whether the similar fact evidence taken together with the other evidence would do no more than raise or strengthen a suspicion that the accused committed the offence with which he is charged or would point so strongly to his guilt that only an ultra-cautious jury, if they accepted it as true, would acquit in the face of it' (*per* Lord Cross at p. 702). Somewhat paradoxically, however, three members of the House of Lords (Lords Hailsham, Morris and Salmon), while emphasising the importance of probative value, expressly approved the *Makin* formula, with Lord Hailsham stating (at p. 698): 'I do not know that the matter can be better stated than it was by Lord Herschell'. Interestingly Lords Cross and Wilberforce failed to refer to *Makin* at all. The House of Lords also expressed various opinions on the degree of probative value which ought to be necessary for the admissibility of similar fact evidence, the consensus being that admissibility depended on there being a 'striking similarity' between the facts of the separate incidents, inexplicable on the basis of coincidence, so that exclusion would be an affront to common sense. In the words of Lord Hailsham (at pp. 699–700):

'For instance, whilst it would certainly not be enough to identify the culprit in a series of burglaries that he climbed in through a ground floor window, the fact that he left the same humorous limerick on the walls of the sitting room, or an esoteric symbol written in lipstick on the mirror might well be enough. In a sex case ... whilst a repeated homosexual act by itself might be quite insufficient to admit the evidence as confirmatory of identity or design, the fact that it was alleged to have been performed wearing the ceremonial head-dress of an Indian chief or other eccentric garb might well in appropriate circumstances suffice.'

However, the term 'striking similarity' is misleading as a general standard for the admission of similar fact evidence for two reasons. First, many offences committed by different persons may be very similar simply because of the common way certain offences are often committed (see, for example, *R* v. *Brown* (1963) 47 Cr App R 204 (CCA), 3.3.4 *ante*). The accused's *modus operandi* for burglary, such as entering through a ground floor window, may be identical to that used by thousands of other burglars, and therefore its probative value would be minimal when weighed against the risk of undue prejudice notwithstanding its 'striking similarity' to the method used in respect of the instant charge. It is the *peculiarity* of the incidents rather than the similarity which needs to be considered for the determination of probative value. Second, evidence of disposition may be highly probative notwithstanding the complete absence of any striking similarity when compared with the facts of the offence charged. It has already been seen that the probative force of an item of circumstantial evidence depends on the other admissible evidence, and this is as true for similar fact evidence as it is for any other such evidence. To explain the requisite degree of cogency in terms of 'striking similarity' is an impracticable formula for determining admissibility, and detracts from the logical assessment of probative value which is required. The evidence of homosexuality in *Thompson* v. *R* [1918] AC 221 (HL) was admissible not because of any 'striking similarity', but simply because in the context of the other evidence it had a high degree of probative value; the evidence of powder puffs and photographs would not have been nearly so probative if the lavatory had been a popular meeting ground for homosexual men. Similarly, the evidence of past intercourse in *R* v. *Ball* [1911] AC 47 (HL) would not have been so probative if the brother and sister had merely been cohabiting but sleeping separately in 1910. Even the evidence of murderous propensity in *R* v. *Straffen* [1952] 2 QB 911 (CCA) would have lost much of its probative value if S had not admitted to being in the area at around the time Linda Bowyer was strangled.

Where a man has committed a sexual offence on another male the accused's homosexuality will always be logically relevant, but whether it will be probative enough to be admissible will depend on the other evidence. Compare, for example, the facts of *R* v. *King* [1967] 2 WLR 612 (CA), where such evidence was admissible (albeit with a judicial warning against undue prejudice), with *R* v. *Horwood* [1969] 3 WLR 964 (CA) where it was inadmissible. In *R* v. *King* the accused admitted he had shared a bed with one of the boys in question, whereas in *R* v. *Horwood* there was no such evidence of intimacy, allowing *R* v. *King* to be distinguished as an 'exceptional case'. 'The slightest movement of the kaleidoscope of facts creates a new pattern which must be examined afresh' (*per* Hoffmann, (1975) 91 LQR 193 at p. 204). In *R* v. *King* it is easy to see why the evidence of homosexuality was admitted, but there were no 'striking similarities' involved: the similar fact evidence was merely K's admission under cross-examination that he was a homosexual, and this was felt to be sufficiently probative given the allegation against him and his admission that he had slept with one of the boys in question. In *R* v. *Morgan* [1993] Crim LR 56 (CA) evidence that the accused had associated with people who used cocaine was admissible at her trial for smuggling that drug into the UK from Jamaica. Her defence was that she had been an innocent dupe on whom the drugs had been planted, so her disposition was relevant in that it made her defence of ignorance less credible. The probative value of the evidence did not depend on any striking similarities but simply on the unlikelihood of coincidence. Similarly, in *Attorney-General of Hong Kong* v. *Siu Yuk-Shing* [1989] 1 WLR 236 (PC) the fact that the accused had been convicted of being a member of the 14K Triad Society in 1975 was held to have been rightly admitted against him at his trial for being a member of the same society in 1986 and for possession of Triad insignia and writings. There was no question of any striking similarities, given that the similar fact evidence was the bare fact of his membership of 14K a decade earlier, and the similar fact evidence was not adduced for the purpose of inviting the tribunal of fact to reason from disposition to guilt. The accused had been found in possession of a number of articles used by 14K members in their Triad rituals. The evidence of his previous membership established that he knew the 14K rituals and that the items in his possession were Triad related.

Another telling example is provided by the Australian case of *Pfennig* v. *R* (1995) 182 CLR 461 (HCA). A 10-year-old boy, Michael Black, disappeared from the Sturt Reserve in South Australia on 18 January 1989 and his bicycle was subsequently found by a river at the nearby Thiele Reserve, suggesting he might have gone swimming and drowned. However, he had gone to Sturt Reserve with a fishing rod, had not taken any swimming clothes or towel, was a competent swimmer, did not like Thiele Reserve and his body was never recovered, rendering it almost certain that he had been abducted from Sturt Reserve and murdered. P had been in Sturt Reserve with his van and had spoken to Michael Black around the time he disappeared. Almost a year later, on 30 December 1989, P abducted a 13-year-old boy ('H') by inveigling him into his van. He then left H's bicycle at the top of a cliff before taking him to his house where he was sexually abused. H managed to escape, and P was convicted of having abducted and raped him. P was subsequently put on trial for the murder of Michael Black and convicted. The evidence against P comprised his presence with his van at the Sturt Reserve at around the time Michael

Black had disappeared, his contact with that boy and his violent and sexual disposition as established by his conduct in relation to H (and his admission to his then wife that he had been thinking about abducting a boy). Once the possibility of an accidental drowning had been discounted, the probative value of the extraneous (in this case subsequent) misconduct evidence lay not in any striking similarities but in the unlikelihood that two persons with exactly the same violent and sexual disposition would have been in exactly the same area at the same time on 18 January 1989, in conversation with Michael Black, and with the means with which to abduct him. Given the very small sub-group of individuals to which both P and the abductor belonged, it would have been an affront to common sense to accept the existence of such a coincidence. The similarity in the way the abductor in each case had sought to lay a false trail by depositing the boy's bicycle by a river or near a cliff provided the evidence with a degree of additional probative value, but in the context of the case as a whole it was superfluous. The evidence relating to H would have been sufficiently cogent without that similarity in the *modus operandi*.

Unfortunately, in the cases following *DPP* v. *Boardman* the 'striking similarity' test was seen as something of a panacea for determining admissibility and too little regard was paid to the underlying principles referred to in the speeches of Lords Wilberforce and Cross. 'Striking similarity' or a similar phrase had found unanimous approval in the House of Lords, giving the impression of a straightforward test when it in fact clouded significant differences between their Lordships' approaches to admissibility; and although in some notable judgments the Court of Appeal recognised that this test was not of universal application and that it should be regarded as no more than a 'label' for the general requirement of high probative value (*R* v. *Rance* (1975) 62 Cr App R 118, *R* v. *Scarrott* (1977) 65 Cr App R 125) the need to find a striking similarity became in effect the test for admissibility (see *R* v. *Clarke* (1977) 67 Cr App R 398 (CA), *Lanford* v. *General Medical Council* [1989] 3 WLR 665 (PC) at p. 671 and *R* v. *Brooks* (1990) 92 Cr App R 36 (CA)). Thus, in *R* v. *Butler* (1986) 84 Cr App R 12 (CA) evidence of consensual oral sex by B's former girlfriend in his car was held to be strikingly similar to acts the rapist had forced his victims to perform in his car, so it was admissible to identify B as that rapist. However, there was nothing strikingly peculiar about the sexual act in question, at least not in the sense envisaged by Lord Hailsham in *DPP* v. *Boardman*. There was some highly probative circumstantial evidence that B was the offender (transferred fibres, one victim's ear-ring and another victim's hair in his car, matching tyre impressions, lack of sperm in the offender's and B's semen) and the evidence of B's sexual disposition was indeed highly probative in the context of this other evidence to rule out the possibility of coincidence. Yet the failure to assess admissibility in accordance with the underlying principles, and the perceived need to identify a striking similarity, exemplifies the general approach of the Court of Appeal in the years following *DPP* v. *Boardman*. Moreover, the perceived need to find 'striking similarity' in evidence which was highly probative for a reason other than striking similarity resulted in the courts accepting a very low standard in order to satisfy the *Boardman* test. In *R* v. *Shore* (1988) 89 Cr App R 32 (CA), for example, a striking similarity was found in the way a headmaster had tickled and touched his young pupils; and in *R* v. *Mustafa* (1976) 65 Cr App R 26 (CA) a striking similarity was found in the accused's loading a trolley with frozen meat in a frozen-food supermarket together with his possession of a stolen credit card.

Even more worrying was the reversion to the *Makin* formula in some cases, suggesting a misunderstanding of the underlying principles. In *R* v. *Seaman* (1978) 67 Cr App R 234 the Court of Appeal relied entirely on the *Makin* test (and made no reference to *DPP* v. *Boardman*) to uphold the trial judge's decision to admit similar fact evidence. S was charged with theft, having been seen placing bacon into his shopping bag before going to the supermarket check-out. Evidence that he had been seen on earlier occasions to place bacon into his shopping basket, only for it to have disappeared by the time he arrived at the check-out, was held to be admissible to rebut his defence of accident. In *R* v. *Lewis* (1982) 76 Cr App R 33, L was charged with indecently assaulting his partner's daughters and with offences of indecency which did not involve physical contact (an admitted incident when he waved his penis at the girls, and an allegation that he had masturbated in front of them). In his defence he claimed he had only waved his penis in fun, and the touching was an innocent attempt to become a father figure to them; he denied the alleged masturbation incident. Magazines, documents and posters which showed that L had a sexual interest in children were admitted at the trial, and he was convicted. The Court of Appeal referred to *DPP* v. *Boardman* but, astonishingly, felt it did not apply as it had been 'concerned solely with similar fact evidence and that is not this case'. Applying the *Makin* test, the Court held that the evidence had been properly admitted to rebut L's defence of accident or innocent explanation in respect of the counts where he had admitted the incident but claimed he was acting innocently. The Court further held, however, that the evidence should not have been admitted in respect of the masturbation count as L had denied that incident and no question of accident or innocent explanation arose (see 3.3.4 *ante*).

In a commentary on *DPP* v. *Boardman*, Hoffmann presciently stated that 'at least one more excursion to the House of Lords will probably be necessary before the law can be said to be established on a simple and rational basis ... to consolidate what *Boardman* has achieved' ('Similar Facts After *Boardman*' (1975) 91 LQR 193 at p. 193).

3.3.6 *DPP* v. *P*

P was charged with rape and incest in respect of his two daughters, B and S, and the evidence of each daughter was admitted as similar fact evidence to prove the separate offences against the other. The Court of Appeal quashed P's conviction on the ground that the girls' accounts of P's behaviour towards them had not shown any striking similarities and should not have been admitted. The prosecution successfully appealed to the House of Lords (*DPP* v. *P* [1991] 3 WLR 161) and Lord Mackay, in a speech (at pp. 170–2) with which the rest of the House agreed, took the opportunity to restate the underlying principles as the test for admissibility in what is now the leading case on similar fact evidence:

> 'From all that was said by the House in *R* v. *Boardman* I would deduce the essential feature of evidence which is to be admitted is that its probative force in support of the allegation that an accused person committed a crime is sufficiently great to make it just to admit the evidence, notwithstanding that it is prejudicial to the accused in tending to show that he was guilty of another crime. Such probative force may be derived from striking similarities in the evidence ... But restricting the circumstances in which there is some striking similarity between them is to restrict the operation of the principle in a way which gives too much effect to a particular manner of stating it, and is not justified in principle ... Where the identity of the perpetrator is in issue, and evidence of this kind is important in that connection, obviously something in the nature of what has been called ... a signature or other special feature will be necessary.'

The girls' evidence had been sufficiently probative to be admissible given that in each case there had been domination and threats against them by P, and P had also paid for abortions for both girls. Thus there was, according to the House of Lords, a single test for the admissibility of similar fact evidence. The trial judge must assess the probative value and the prejudicial effect of the evidence and admit it only if the probative value is so great that it would be just to admit it in spite of the prejudicial effect. This test not only expresses the principles which have always underpinned the law but has had the effect of consolidating the law on the admissibility of similar fact evidence with the general theory on the admissibility of relevant evidence (3.1.3 *ante*) and (to all intents and purposes) the trial judge's common-law discretion to exclude any unduly prejudicial evidence tendered by the prosecution (*R* v. *Sang* [1979] 3 WLR 263 (HL)). One qualification was added by the House of Lords, however: if the identity of the offender is in issue the judge will need to identify a striking peculiarity or 'signature' method as a prerequisite to admissibility (see 3.3.14 *post*).

It should be noted that in a number of European jurisdictions evidence of extraneous misconduct is routinely admitted as evidence against the accused, even before lay tribunals of fact, and there is nothing in the jurisprudence of the European Court of Human Rights to suggest that this is regarded as unfair (see Law Com No. 273 (2001) at p. 40). The test developed in *DPP* v. *P* exists to ensure that the accused receives a fair trial, and the Court of Appeal has now stated that if the accused's extraneous misconduct is admissible at common law it cannot be said to breach Article 6(1) of the European Convention on Human Rights (*R* v. *Singh* [2001] EWCA Crim 2884). In most cases similar fact evidence will be *inadmissible* on account of its low probative value, and where it is ruled to be admissible it will be because the probative value is so high that any undue prejudice can be disregarded (or eliminated by an adequate direction from the judge). The test might therefore be regarded as an *additional* safeguard over and above what is required for Article 6(1) compatibility. Indeed, similar fact evidence which, when considered in the context of all the other evidence, would present a compelling case against the accused will be excluded if the additional probative value is insufficient to justify the risk of undue prejudice. Consider, for instance, the trial which led to the conviction of the paedophile Roy Whiting for the kidnap and murder of an eight-year-old girl, Sarah Payne, in the summer of 2000. There was a considerable body of evidence linking him to the murder, including eye-witness testimony that a person with a similar appearance had driven away from the scene in a white van, his possession of a white van (which was equipped with rope, hand ties, a knife, a cushion, masking tape and baby oil), the presence of one of Sarah's hairs on his clothing, and fibres from items in the van on one of Sarah's shoes, but evidence that he had been convicted in 1995 for kidnapping and molesting a nine-year-old girl was ruled inadmissible by the trial judge (*R* v. *Whiting* (2001) *The Times* 13.12.01 (news report) (CC)). Whiting's sexual disposition did not *add* sufficient probative value to justify the reasoning and moral prejudice it might have engendered, and to ensure he received a fair trial it was excluded (*cf. Pfennig* v. *R* (1995) 182 CLR 461 (HCA) and *R* v. *Black* [1995] Crim LR 640 (CA)).

The application of the modern test can be illustrated by reference to the decision in *R* v. *Sokialiois* [1993] Crim LR 872. The accused was charged with importing cocaine which he had sought to collect from a postal depot, yet he claimed not to have any involvement with drugs when interviewed by Customs officers. The prosecution were allowed to adduce evidence that his holdall had been discovered in a hotel and that it contained cocaine of similar purity to the cocaine which was the subject of the charge. The Court of Appeal, applying *DPP* v. *P*, held that the cocaine in the holdall had been properly admitted as its probative value, in the context of the accused's replies in his interview and his defence of having been framed, was high compared with its unduly prejudicial effect. Discounting the possibility that the cocaine could have been planted in the hotel room (and the jury were directed to disregard it if they felt it had been planted) it would have been a bizarre coincidence that the accused, who denied any involvement with drugs, should have a holdall of cocaine in his room if he was innocent (see also *R* v. *Groves* [1998] Crim LR 200 (CA), *R* v. *Yalman* [1998] 2 Cr App R 269 (CA) and *R* v. *Clark* [2000] All ER (D) 1219 (CA)).

In *R* v. *Caceres-Moreira* [1995] Crim LR 489 the accused was charged with being concerned in the importation of cocaine. The drug had been posted to L, and he and P had then taken the package to a meeting with the accused at a pub. P and the accused were arrested as they went to his car. The accused denied any involvement and claimed that he had simply been invited for a drink by P and was going to give him a lift. The prosecution were allowed to adduce evidence that in 1990 a greetings card addressed to the accused's wife had contained cocaine, and that shortly after its delivery it had been passed on to the accused. The Court of Appeal held that the evidence had been admissible similar fact evidence demonstrating the accused's knowledge that P's package contained cocaine. It was irrelevant that the charge in 1990 had been thrown out at the committal stage and that the accused had never been convicted of any charge arising out of that incident. In other words, the admissibility of any prosecution evidence suggesting that the accused has a disposition to commit the offence charged should be considered in the light of the principles which underlie the similar facts test. It does not matter that the accused's extraneous conduct is not *per se* unlawful (*R* v. *Butler* (1986) 84 Cr App R 12 (CA)); nor does it matter, if it *is* unlawful, that the accused has not been convicted of an offence in relation to it. If the jury might be unduly prejudiced against the accused on account of the admission of evidence of his disposition, then there will need to be an assessment of probative value and the risk of undue prejudice in order to determine admissibility, although it will be seen below that a different test applies for certain types of evidence of extraneous misconduct (3.3.8–10 *post*).

In *R* v. *Z* [2000] 3 WLR 117 the House of Lords held that it was permissible for the prosecution to adduce similar fact evidence relating to other incidents in respect of which the accused had already been tried and *acquitted*, the reasoning being that as he was not being tried again for those other alleged offences there was no infringement of the rule against double jeopardy (see also *R* v. *Ollis* [1900] 2 QB 758 (CCCR)). The appeal in *R* v. *Z* arose out a preliminary ruling by the judge at the trial of one Nicholas Edwards for raping a woman in 1998. Following the decision of the House of Lords the prosecution were able to call the complainants who had alleged that he had raped them on other occasions, even though he had been acquitted of those charges. He had endeared himself to each of the women, taken them out on a date, and then turned violent and allegedly raped them when his advances were spurned. Each woman's testimony was admissible similar fact evidence in relation to the fresh 1998 allegation, of which he was subsequently found guilty (*R* v. *Edwards* (2000) *The Times* 22.9.00 (news report) (CCC)).

3.3.7 Similar Fact Evidence and Relevance

The generally accepted view is that evidence of the accused's disposition or conduct on other occasions is logically relevant to the issue of his guilt but usually too prejudicial for it to be admitted (see, for example, *R* v. *Clarke* [1995] 2 Cr App R 425 (CA)). There is an alternative analysis, however. In *DPP* v. *Boardman* [1974] 3 WLR 673 (HL) Lord Hailsham recognised that there were two theories for the exclusionary principle in the *Makin* test (at p. 697):

> '[S]uch evidence is simply irrelevant ... According to this theory, similar fact evidence excluded under Lord Herschell LC's first sentence has no probative value ... The second theory is that the prejudice created by the admission of such evidence outweighs any probative value it may have ...'

In *R* v. *Miller* (1952) 36 Cr App R 169 (Assizes), Devlin J said (at p. 171):

'The fundamental principle ... is that it is not normally relevant to inquire into a prisoner's previous character, and, particularly, to ask questions which tend to show that he has previously committed some criminal offence. It is not relevant because the fact that he has committed an offence on one occasion does not in any way show that he is likely to commit an offence on any subsequent occasion. Accordingly, such questions are, in general, inadmissible, not primarily for the reason that they are prejudicial, but because they are irrelevant.'

The express application of the irrelevance theory for excluding similar fact evidence can be found in several cases. In *R* v. *Rodley* [1913] 3 KB 468 (CCA), for example, evidence that the accused had entered C's house by its chimney at about 2 a.m. and had then had consensual intercourse with C was held to be irrelevant to the question whether one or two hours earlier he had broken into V's premises through the back door with the intent to rape her. Similarly, in *R* v. *Holloway* [1980] 1 NZLR 315 (NZSC), a rape trial, evidence that several other women had been forced to have sex with the accused at his home was held to be irrelevant to whether the complainant had consented to an admitted act of sexual intercourse (see also *R* v. *Bradley* (1979) 70 Cr App R 200 (CA) and *R* v. *Knutton* (1992) 97 Cr App R 115 (CA)). The most recent application of this theory to evidence of disposition can be found in the older cases dealing with the admissibility of cash and drug-dealing paraphernalia in the possession of alleged dealers (3.1.3 *ante*), although more recently the Court of Appeal has expressly applied similar fact reasoning to such evidence (*R* v. *Guney* [1998] 2 Cr App R 242, *R* v. *Yalman* [1998] 2 Cr App R 269).

However, once it is remembered that the word 'irrelevant' can be used to mean that evidence is insufficiently probative to be admitted, given the weight of the countervailing policy considerations, it is apparent that the two theories identified by Lord Hailsham are in fact different ways of stating the same thing.

3.3.8 'Moral Prejudice Evidence'

Historically, the courts have focused on 'reasoning prejudice' rather than 'moral prejudice' when considering the admissibility of similar fact evidence. This is clear from the first limb of the *Makin* test (3.3.4 *ante*) which refers to 'the conclusion that the accused is a person likely from his criminal conduct or character to have committed the offence for which he is being tried'. Thus, when the *Makin* test was applied, relevant evidence of the accused's extraneous misconduct which was fundamentally different from the conduct associated with the alleged offence (giving rise to no possibility of reasoning prejudice) was automatically admissible under the second limb of the test.

A man charged with the murder of a young girl in a village may have visited his sister-in-law in London and asked her to give false testimony that he was staying with her on the night the offence was committed. The prosecution would be able to call the sister-in-law to testify that the accused had attempted to pervert the course of justice, as circumstantial evidence of his guilt, even though that evidence would suggest a separate crime has been committed by him. If the accused instead gives as his false alibi that he was with a prostitute whose name he does not know, it would be permissible for the prosecution to show that his fingerprints were found at the scene of a burglary in the girl's village on the night of her murder to prove he was in the vicinity around the time she was killed. In *Jones* v. *DPP* [1962] 2 WLR 575 (HL) (at p. 597) Lord Denning felt that such evidence was *prima facie* admissible on the ground that it fell within the second limb of the *Makin* test. A further example is provided by *R* v. *Onufrejczyk* [1955] 2 WLR 273 (CCA) where the fact that the accused, on trial for murder, had tried to bribe a blacksmith to lie about the date the deceased had collected a horse was admissible notwithstanding the obvious inference that the accused had committed a separate (but dissimilar) offence.

Bad-character evidence of this sort could be called 'moral prejudice evidence' on the ground that moral prejudice is the only type of undue prejudice the evidence might give rise to in the jury's collective mind. As noted above, such evidence was *prima facie* admissible under the second limb of the *Makin* test, and it would appear to have been *prima facie* admissible (for the same reason) during the period when *DPP* v. *Boardman* [1974] 3 WLR 673 (HL) was the leading case on similar fact evidence. In *R* v. *Anderson* [1988] 2 WLR 1017 the accused was charged with conspiracy to cause explosions, and her defence was that the evidence against her (false papers and cash) was evidence of her involvement in a separate conspiracy to smuggle escaped prisoners from Ireland to continental Europe. She claimed that she would have accompanied male escapees to hoodwink immigration officials into thinking they were an innocent couple on holiday. The prosecution elicited evidence that she was 'wanted' by the police in Northern Ireland, and the Court of Appeal took the view that it could properly have been admitted under the second limb of the *Makin* test to rebut her defence. The probative value of the evidence lay in demonstrating that the accused would not have been selected for the role of accompanying escaped prisoners, for her presence would have increased rather than reduced the possibility of the police noticing them. In other words, the evidence was *prima facie* admissible because it was relevant and there was no possibility of reasoning prejudice.

Notwithstanding the modern test for the admissibility of similar fact evidence established in *DPP* v. *P* [1991] 3 WLR 161 (HL), it may well be that 'moral prejudice evidence' remains *prima facie* admissible, along with background evidence and *res gestae* evidence of bad character (3.3.9 *post*). If evidence of this sort is indeed *prima facie* admissible, the judge will have to consider whether it ought to be *excluded* at common law or under s. 78(1) of the Police and Criminal Evidence Act 1984 on the ground that, despite any direction he might give the jury, the moral prejudice generated by its admission would deny the accused a fair trial.

3.3.9 Background Evidence and *Res Gestae*

Evidence of extraneous misconduct may be highly probative if it comprises an integral part of the *history* of the instant offence or sets out the *context* in which the offence was committed; and, again, such probative value will not necessarily depend on any striking similarity. Carter ((1985) 48 MLR 29 at p. 30) gives the example of D being on trial for stealing from V's safe and the prosecution wishing to adduce evidence that D had stolen V's diary on an earlier occasion. D's earlier theft would be highly probative evidence that he was aware of the combination to V's safe if the combination had been recorded in the diary.

In *R* v. *Ball* [1911] AC 47 (HL) (at p. 68) Lord Atkinson felt that if the accused stands trial for murder, evidence of his past enmity to the deceased would be admissible to prove his motive and that he had killed the deceased with the requisite *mens rea* (see *R* v. *Buckley* (1873) 13 Cox CC 293 (Assizes)). Lord Atkinson's dictum was approved in *R* v. *Williams* (1986) 84 Cr App R 299 where the Court of Appeal held that evidence of the accused's previous history of assaulting the victim was admissible to prove that he had intended his words to be taken seriously when he had threatened to kill her. Further support was obtained from the decision in *R* v. *Pettman* (1985) unreported (5048/C/82), now the leading authority on what has become known as 'background evidence', where, giving the judgment of the Court of Appeal, Purchas LJ said:

'[W]here it is necessary to place before the jury evidence of part of a continual background or history relevant to the offence charged in the indictment, and without the totality of which the account placed before the jury would be incomplete or incomprehensible, then the fact that the whole account involves including evidence establishing the commission of an offence with which the accused is not charged is not of itself a ground for excluding the evidence.'

In both *R* v. *Williams* (1986) 84 Cr App R 299 and *R* v. *Pettman* the Court of Appeal was of the view that background evidence is *prima facie* admissible by virtue of the second limb of the *Makin* test, a point reaffirmed in *R* v. *Fulcher* [1995] 2 Cr App R 251 where the Court of Appeal concluded that such evidence is not covered by the similar fact rule of *prima facie* inadmissibility (see also *R* v. *Bond* [1906] 2 KB 389 (CCCR) at p. 400). Background evidence is therefore admissible so long as it can be shown to be relevant to an issue in the proceedings, save that (as with 'moral prejudice evidence') it may be excluded by the judge at common law or under s. 78(1) of the Police and Criminal Evidence Act 1984.

There is, however, a difference between 'moral prejudice evidence' and 'background evidence'. The former is (by definition) evidence which cannot possibly give rise to any reasoning prejudice, but the same cannot be said about the latter. Background evidence will often disclose extraneous misconduct which is similar in nature to the offence charged, and may therefore engender the same sorts of prejudice which underlie the general rule of *prima facie* inadmissibility. In her commentary on the case of *R* v. *Stevens* [1995] Crim LR 649 (at p. 651) Professor Di Birch drew a distinction between similar fact evidence and background evidence which has been cited with approval by the Court of Appeal (*R* v. *M(T)* [2000] 1 WLR 421 at pp. 426–7). Background evidence was said to be admitted in order to put the jury in the general picture about characters involved in the action and the run-up to the alleged offence, and 'may or may not involve prior offences'. This is of course correct, and would justify the rule of *prima facie* admissibility at a *general* level, but it can hardly justify the application of that rule when extraneous misconduct of a similar nature to the offence charged *is* disclosed as part of the background. The general rule of *prima facie* inadmissibility should apply – at least in cases where the misconduct cannot properly be said to form part of the *res gestae* in its narrowest sense – lest similar fact evidence of insufficient probative value be admitted too readily. Be that as it may, the rule of *prima facie* admissibility has been reaffirmed on a number of occasions. In *R* v. *Clarke* [2002] EWCA Crim 2948 the prosecution were permitted to adduce evidence that the accused and the deceased victim (V) of an east London shooting had previously been arrested in respect of a serious assault, that V had on that occasion 'grassed' on the accused, and that, having found out, the accused had subsequently threatened to use violence on him. Holding that the evidence of extraneous misconduct had been properly admitted, the Court of Appeal stated that the 'true principles to be applied are whether the evidence is relevant to an issue in the case and if so, whether its prejudicial effect is such that, despite its probative value, it should be excluded as a matter of discretion'. Similarly, in *R* v. *Phillips* [2003] EWCA Crim 1379, where the accused's threats to kill his wife were admitted at his trial for her murder, the Court of Appeal stated that relevant background evidence 'is admissible unless, in the exercise of its discretion, the court decides that fairness requires it to be excluded'.

The problem with a test of *prima facie* admissibility for any type of background evidence is evident from the Australian case of *R* v. *O'Leary* (1946) 73 CLR 566. The deceased had been violently attacked around the head and face with a bottle at the workers' camp adjacent to a secluded timber mill in the early hours of Sunday morning, the inference being that the murderer was one of the workers resident at the camp. OL was one such worker, and evidence was admitted that during the preceding Saturday afternoon and evening he had made a number of unprovoked drunken assaults on other workers, with injuries being caused to the head, throat or face in each case. The majority of the High Court of Australia concluded that the evidence of the assaults on the other workers was *prima facie* admissible, and had been properly admitted, as evidence which established the context of what had happened immediately prior to the attack on the deceased. The 'drunken orgy' and subsequent attack on the deceased comprised a connected series of events which could properly be regarded as a single transaction – that is, the extraneous misconduct formed part of the *res gestae* – and the evidence of what had happened during the orgy made it possible for the jury to obtain a real appreciation of the events at the camp prior to the murder: if that evidence had not been admitted the jury would have been presented with an 'unreal and not very intelligible event'. However, given the paucity of other evidence linking OL to the attack (OL's pullover being found nearby and evidence that OL had been in possession of a bottle shortly before the discovery of the deceased) the prosecution case was almost entirely dependent on this evidence of extraneous misconduct; and to justify the admission of the evidence on the ground that it set the murder in its proper context is to pay scant regard to the principles which are supposed to ensure that the accused receives a fair trial. The correct approach would have been to apply the similar facts test, assessing the probative value of the evidence by reference to the unlikelihood of coincidence. The murderer was almost certainly a worker at the timber mill and, given the manner of the brutal attack around the deceased's head and face and the inoffensive nature of the deceased, he was also an individual who was capable of inflicting appalling injuries without provocation while remaining oblivious to any sense of pity. OL fell into this very small category of individuals at the time in question, and was present in the camp, so the evidence of his previous misconduct was extremely probative. It was highly improbable that there was more than one person in the vicinity who would have murdered the deceased in such a brutal fashion, and the evidence of OL's disposition with the other two items of circumstantial evidence established a compelling case against him. Interestingly the trial judge would seem to have reasoned along these lines when ruling that the evidence was admissible similar fact evidence.

Background evidence must therefore be 'approached with particular care when it is being relied upon as part of the prosecution case' (*R* v. *R* [2001] 1 WLR 1314 (CA) at p. 1319; see also *R* v. *Dolan* [2003] 1 Cr App R 281 (CA)). The judge should consider both reasoning prejudice and moral prejudice when deciding whether to *exclude* evidence of this sort in the exercise of his discretion, so the discretion to admit similar fact evidence has in effect become a discretion to exclude background evidence, the two tests being to all intents and purposes the same (a point which seems to have been acknowledged in *R* v. *Underwood* [1999] Crim LR 227 (CA) and *R* v. *PR* [2001] Crim LR 314 (CA), and which is exemplified by the way in which the trial judge in *R* v. *Sawoniuk* [2000] 2 Cr App R 220 (CA) approached the question of admissibility). That said, the *prima facie* rule of admissibility which governs background evidence may lead to this sort of evidence being admitted more readily, with a lower threshold of probative value being applied. This is what seems to have happened in *R* v. *Butler* [1999] Crim LR 835 (CA), where evidence of the accused's violent conduct against the deceased three years prior to the fatal incident was held to have been wrongly admitted by the trial judge.

The case of *R* v. *Sawoniuk* [2000] 2 Cr App R 220 is of particular interest. S was charged under the War Crimes Act 1991 with the murder of a number of Jewish people in the east European town of Domachevo during the Second World War. The allegation was that, as a member of the local police force in collaboration with the German occupation forces, he had personally killed four individuals during the hunt for survivors following the German massacre of the Jewish population in Domachevo on 20 September 1942, although a successful submission of no case to answer meant verdicts were required on only two of the murders. The direct evidence comprised eye-witness testimony that S had perpetrated those murders within the few weeks following the massacre. S's defence was that, though he had been a member of the local police, he had not been in Domachevo at the time the massacre had taken place, he had not seen any Jewish persons in Domachevo following his return to the town and there had been no police search and kill operation during that period after the massacre. The prosecution were permitted to call further witnesses who provided evidence of extraneous misconduct, the trial judge having ruled that it was relevant in showing that S had been actively involved in search and kill operations and that it ought not to be excluded in the exercise of his discretion as the probative value of the evidence outweighed its prejudicial effect. One of these witnesses, IB, testified that in the days following the massacre he had seen S commit a 'heavy assault' on a Jewish woman and lead a Jewish family to the site of the massacre (none of whom IB ever saw again). Another witness, EM, testified that about 10 days after the massacre he had seen S and other policemen herding a group of Jewish people towards what had been the Jewish ghetto and that he never saw any of that group again. On appeal it was argued that the evidence of IB and EM should have been excluded as inadmissible similar fact evidence, but this submission was rejected by the Court of Appeal. First, it was held that the evidence was relevant in showing S's involvement in search and kill operations and that he was a member of the group of individuals to which the murderer belonged. The evidence was not adduced for the purpose of inviting the jury to reason from disposition to guilt, so it was not covered by the similar fact rule of *prima facie* inadmissibility – a peculiar conclusion as it implies that the test in *DPP* v. *P* [1991] 3 WLR 161 (HL) (3.3.6 *ante*) does not apply *unless* the prosecution tender the extraneous misconduct evidence for that specific purpose. Second, applying *R* v. *Pettman* (1985) unreported (5048/C/82) (CA), it was held that the evidence was in any event properly admitted on the 'broader basis' that criminal charges cannot be fairly judged in a factual vacuum and 'in order to make a rational assessment of evidence directly relating to a charge it may often be necessary for a jury to receive evidence describing, perhaps in some detail, the context and circumstances in which the offences are said to have been committed'. Applying this test, it was held to be 'necessary and appropriate' for the prosecution to prove that S, as a locally recruited policeman, played a leading and notorious role in enforcing Nazi policies against the Jewish population in Domachevo and that, following the massacre, he had been involved in the operation to hunt down and kill any Jewish survivors. Accordingly the evidence was 'probative and admissible' for 'had these gruesome events not been set in their factual context, the jury would have been understandably bewildered'.

Finally, although it has been suggested above that the general test for admitting similar fact evidence should apply to background evidence which might give rise to reasoning prejudice, an exception would be justified when the extraneous misconduct is *inextricably* linked in time and space with the commission of the offence charged, so that it might properly be regarded as part of the *res gestae* (in the sense that it is truly part and parcel of the instant allegation). As McHugh J said in *Harriman v. R* (1989) 167 CLR 590 (HCA) (at p. 633):

> 'If evidence which discloses other criminal conduct is characterized as part of the transaction which embraces the crime charged, it is not subject to any further condition of admissibility. Evidence which directly relates to the facts in issue is so fundamental to the proceedings that its admissibility as a matter of law cannot depend upon a condition that its probative force transcends its prejudicial effect ... Consequently, it is a matter of great importance whether the evidence is classified as part of the *res gestae* ...'

Three points need to be noted about the *res gestae* justification. First, if the misconduct in question is charged as a separate count on the indictment then evidence in relation to it is admissible: it is not evidence of extraneous misconduct but of additional misconduct in respect of which the accused is on trial. Second, if there is no possibility of reasoning prejudice it may in any event be *prima facie* admissible for reasons which have already been given (3.3.8 *ante*); an example would be where criminal damage is committed in order to break into a house, but only the burglary is charged on the indictment. Third, the duration of the *res gestae* should be construed narrowly to ensure that the term is not simply used as a mechanism for admitting similar fact evidence 'through the back door' without a proper assessment of its probative value and unduly prejudicial effect (*R v. O'Leary* (1946) 73 CLR 566 (HCA), above; and see *R v. Rearden* (1864) 4 F & F 76 (Assizes)).

3.3.10 The Scope of the Similar Facts Rule

The general exclusionary rule would appear to apply only to prosecution evidence of the accused's extraneous misconduct or disposition when it is tendered (i) to prove that the accused is guilty *because* of his disposition or (ii) to prove that the accused is guilty on some other logical basis but which *might* incidentally lead the jury to reason from disposition to guilt on account of the nature of the evidence and the offence charged. Prosecution evidence which falls into either of these categories is *prima facie* inadmissible *unless* it can properly be categorised as background (or *res gestae*) evidence or there is a statutory exception which disapplies the exclusionary rule. These types of evidence, along with (it seems) 'moral prejudice evidence', are governed by a rule of *prima facie* admissibility, but may be excluded by the application of the common-law *Sang* discretion or s. 78(1) of the Police and Criminal Evidence Act 1984.

3.3.11 Similar Fact Evidence: Discretion or Rule of Law?

The test for determining the admissibility of similar fact evidence in criminal proceedings is a particular application of the general test in any proceedings for determining whether evidence should be considered 'relevant' and *prima facie* admissible. Each test involves the weighing of probative value against competing factors underpinned by considerations of policy. It follows that, just as there can be no doctrine of 'legal relevance' with judges bound by past decisions (3.1.4 *ante*), it is unrealistic to regard the application of the principles governing the admissibility of similar fact evidence as anything other than the exercise of a judicial discretion. This was explicitly recognised by the Court of Appeal in *R* v. *Sokialiois* [1993] Crim LR 872 and *R* v. *Kidd* [1995] Crim LR 406, but it is implicit in a number of earlier judgments (see, for example, *R* v. *Robinson* (1953) 37 Cr App R 95 (CCA) at p. 103, *R* v. *Scarrott* (1977) 65 Cr App R 125 (CA) at p. 130 and *R* v. *Butler* (1986) 84 Cr App R 12 (CA) at p. 16). The same point was made by the Supreme Court of Canada in *R* v. *B(CR)* [1990] 1 SCR 717.

The trial judge's decision will be based on his personal assessment of the psychology of the jury: how the jury will approach the evidence, the weight they are likely to give it in the context of the other evidence and admissions, the extent to which the accused might be prejudiced in their collective mind and any other relevant considerations (such as whether the jury might be distracted from the central issues which have to be decided). The trial judge must 'make a value judgment, not a mathematical calculation' (*Pfennig* v. *R* (1995) 182 CLR 461 (HCA) at p. 529) and 'it may often be very difficult to draw the line and to decide whether a particular piece of evidence is on the one side or the other' (*Makin* v. *Attorney-General for New South Wales* [1894] AC 57 (PC) at p. 65). It is therefore quite possible that different judges will reach a different view on the same facts, but this does not mean that there is no rule of law. The rule is that there is, in effect, an inclusionary discretion, but once the trial judge concludes that the evidence is so probative that it ought to be admitted, notwithstanding the risk or certainty of undue prejudice, it *is* admissible.

The pre-*Boardman* test of *automatic* admissibility was a much less flexible rule. If the similar fact evidence was admissible by virtue of its falling within a category of relevance it was *ipso facto* admissible, save that the judge could apply his exclusionary discretion if its admission would unduly prejudice the accused (*Noor Mohamed* v. *R* [1949] AC 182 (PC) at p. 192, *R* v. *Straffen* [1952] 2 QB 911 (CCA) at p. 917, *Harris* v. *DPP* [1952] AC 694 (HL) at p. 707, *DPP* v. *Boardman* [1974] 3 WLR 673 (HL) at p. 699). The continuing relevance of the exclusionary discretion was acknowledged by the Court of Appeal in a number of post-*Boardman* cases (for example, *R* v. *Mustafa* (1976) 65 Cr App R 26, *R* v. *Lewis* (1982) 76 Cr App R 33, *R* v. *Lunt* (1986) 85 Cr App R 241 and *R* v. *Butler* (1986) 84 Cr App R 12); but if the rule governing admissibility is in effect an *inclusionary* discretion, it is difficult to accept the argument that an independent *exclusionary* discretion may be applied to exclude otherwise admissible similar fact evidence, for the common-law *Sang* discretion to exclude admissible prosecution evidence itself requires a consideration of probative value and undue prejudice.

One way of rationalising an additional exclusionary discretion would be to hold that the initial test for admissibility requires, as a matter of law, an analysis of *reasoning* prejudice and probative value, with *moral* prejudice being brought into the equation, along with any other relevant factors, for the subsequent exercise of the trial judge's common-law and/or statutory discretion. After all, when determining the admissibility of similar fact evidence the courts have traditionally been concerned with reasoning prejudice – avoiding the 'forbidden chain of reasoning' – and there would appear to be a rule of *prima facie* admissibility for 'moral prejudice evidence' (3.3.8 *ante*).

However, there has been no explicit recognition that reasoning and moral prejudice are to be decoupled by the judge when considering whether to admit similar fact evidence; and it is highly unlikely that trial judges divide up the species of undue prejudice in this way (in cases where both types of prejudice are possible). In *R* v. *B(CR)* [1990] 1 SCR 717 the majority of the Supreme Court of Canada, having accepted that the admissibility of similar fact evidence depends on 'whether the probative value of the proposed evidence outweighs its prejudicial effect', went on to state that 'where the similar fact evidence sought to be adduced is prosecution evidence of a morally repugnant act committed by the accused, the potential prejudice is great and the probative value of the evidence must be high indeed to permit its reception', implying that moral as well as reasoning prejudice must be considered at the admissibility stage (see also *R* v. *Bond* [1906] 2 KB 389 (CCCR) at p. 398, 3.3.2 *ante*). And in *Pfennig* v. *R* (1995) 182 CLR 461 (HCA) McHugh J said (at p. 515) that 'once it is accepted that the prejudicial effect of the evidence is a matter going to admissibility, no scope remains for the exercise of the discretion to reject probative evidence in criminal trials on the ground that it is unduly prejudicial to the accused'.

3.3.12 Directing the Jury

If evidence of the accused's bad character is admitted as similar fact evidence, the trial judge will need to consider whether it is necessary to direct the jury on the use which may be made of it, to minimise the risk of undue prejudice. In extreme factual situations, where the evidence of disposition is so compelling that it comprises the entire prosecution case, any warning on the need to avoid giving too much weight to the evidence would be otiose because the jury are actually being invited to reason that the accused is guilty on the basis of his highly unusual disposition (as in *R* v. *Straffen* [1952] 2 QB 911 (CCA)). However, in some cases it might still be appropriate to warn the jury against the risk of moral prejudice.

In other cases the risk of both moral and reasoning prejudice may need to be explained to the jury, but much will depend on the facts of the case and the reason for admitting the evidence. In *DPP* v. *Boardman* [1974] 3 WLR 673 (HL) Lord Hailsham expressed the view (at p. 699) that a judge should always direct the jury not to reason from propensity to guilt –

'a warning from the judge that the jury must eschew the forbidden reasoning' – but his analysis was based on the first limb of the *Makin* formula, which excluded similar fact evidence if it was relevant only via an argument from disposition to guilt. It is apparent that similar fact evidence is admissible even if its relevance is entirely dependent on 'forbidden' reasoning, and clearly a blanket warning of the sort envisaged by Lord Hailsham would be absurd in such cases, as indeed was recognised by the Court of Appeal in *R* v. *Sokialiois* [1993] Crim LR 872 (see also *R* v. *Roy* [1992] Crim LR 185 (CA) and *R* v. *Whitehouse* [1996] Crim LR 50 (CA)).

However, in other cases a warning from the judge is likely to be the best way of reducing the risk of undue prejudice. Thus, while a warning is not a mandatory requirement in all cases (*R* v. *Rance* (1975) 62 Cr App R 118 (CA)) a direction of some kind *will* be necessary if the relevance of the accused's previous misconduct is not based on reasoning from disposition to guilt or the accused's disposition is particularly unpleasant. If the accused is charged with the manslaughter of a child he has beaten on several occasions in the past, and the prosecution case is that his attempts to beat the child again caused him to run away and fall down the stairs, the accused's previous ill-treatment of the child would be admissible 'background evidence' (*R* v. *Mackie* (1973) 57 Cr App R 453 (CA)). The reason for admitting the evidence would be to show that the child was afraid of being beaten again, and that it is reasonable to expect that he would rush down the stairs to escape from the accused. The accused's past misconduct would be relevant to the issue of causation, but its relevance would not depend on reasoning from disposition to guilt. As such, it would be necessary for the judge to give an appropriate direction to the jury on the limited use which could be made of the evidence (a point made in *R* v. *PR* [2001] Crim LR 314 (00/2431/Y3) (CA)). *R* v. *Singh* [2001] EWCA Crim 2884 provides another useful example. In that case the accused's previous conviction for unlawfully wounding a French student at 42 Oakridge Road in 1998 was admitted at his trial for blackmailing a number of students living at 44 Oakridge Road in 1999. The conviction supported the students' visual identification of the accused as the blackmailer, as he had told them during the course of his 'protection racket' that he had stabbed a French student in their house or a nearby house a year earlier. In other words, the conviction was admitted not for the purpose of proving that the accused was guilty on the basis of his disposition, but to prove that the accused had been correctly identified by the students as the blackmailer. However, because the conviction also showed that he was a violent person, and the blackmailer had backed up his demands with threats of violence, the trial judge quite properly directed the jury not to treat the conviction as evidence of disposition.

Finally, a warning on the weight to be attached to admissible similar fact evidence will be necessary in cases where there is a risk of collusion between complainants (*R* v. *H* [1995] 2 WLR 737 (HL), 3.3.13 *post*) or there are dissimilarities which ought to be brought to the jury's attention (*R* v. *Tricoglus* (1976) 65 Cr App R 16 (CA)).

3.3.13 Joinder of Counts and Cross-Admissibility

Section 4 of the Indictments Act 1915 and r. 9 of the Indictment Rules 1971 provide that charges relating to separate offences may be joined as several counts on a single indictment if the offences are 'founded on the same facts or form part of a series of offences of the same or a similar character'. The trial judge has a statutory discretion to order separate trials if the accused might be prejudiced or if it is otherwise desirable (s. 5(3) of the 1915 Act). If the prosecution allege that the accused has committed a series of similar offences, the separate charges will initially be joined as counts on a single indictment and, following submissions from prosecution and defence counsel on probative value, prejudice and convenience, there will be one or more of three possible outcomes:

(i)   The judge may hold the prosecution evidence to be 'cross-admissible' as similar fact evidence. The charges will be tried together as separate counts on a single indictment, and the judge will direct the jury that the prosecution evidence on each count may be considered relevant evidence tending to prove the accused's guilt in respect of the other counts.

(ii) The judge may hold that the evidence is not cross-admissible (as the probative value is not high enough to amount to admissible similar fact evidence) but still allow the counts to be tried together on the ground of expediency. The jury will be directed not to regard the evidence on one count as relevant to any other count. This option is a natural consequence of *Ludlow* v. *Metropolitan Police Commissioner* [1970] 2 WLR 521 where the House of Lords held that for counts to be joined on an indictment all that is needed is a loose nexus between the offences so that they can be described as a series – cross-admissibility is not a prerequisite to joinder. In fact the judge may decide that the evidence is cross-admissible at the beginning of the trial (option (i)) and change his mind as the true probative value of the evidence materialises; the judge will then direct the jury not to consider the evidence to be cross-admissible, or he may discharge the jury if the undue prejudice generated cannot be removed by any such direction (option (iii) below). Conversely, the judge is free to decide that the evidence is cross-admissible during the trial notwithstanding a contrary decision at the outset.

(iii) The judge may hold that it would be too prejudicial for the charges to be tried together. The charges will be tried separately before different juries who will be kept in the dark about the other charges against the accused.

Option (ii) is far from satisfactory as the jury will hear unduly prejudicial evidence and may regard it as relevant to the other counts no matter what the judge says. If the accused is charged with having committed separate similar offences and the judge decides the evidence is not cross-admissible one might think, as a matter of principle, that separate trials should be ordered to ensure he receives a fair trial. However, s. 5(3) of the Indictments Act 1915 gives the judge a broad discretion and the Court of Appeal will generally not interfere with the judge's view unless he has 'failed to exercise the discretion upon the usual and proper principles' which requires fairness to the accused, the prosecution and other persons involved in the proceedings (*R* v. *Cannan* (1990) 92 Cr App R 16 (CA) at p. 23, *R* v. *Christou* [1996] 2 WLR 620 (HL) at pp. 629–30).

If the accused faces several separate charges of sexual abuse against young persons known to each other (such as class-mates or siblings) the probative value of their testimony will turn on the possibility that they have either conspired with each other to bring similar false allegations or been innocently infected by other persons (or media reports). The judge must come to a decision at the beginning of the trial on the issue of joinder, and it is clear from *R* v. *Christou* [1996] 2 WLR 620 (HL) that no special rules apply just because it is alleged that the accused has sexually abused children. The judge will also need to reach a provisional decision on the issue of cross-admissibility, and this will be based on the available witnesses' statements and the extent to which the jury are likely to be unduly prejudiced against the accused. At the pre-trial stage the possibility of conspiracy or innocent infection is likely to be no more than speculation, so generally the judge should not take it into account when assessing the probative value of the complainants' evidence: their evidence is to be presumed true at this stage (*R* v. *H* [1995] 2 WLR 737 (HL)). Assessing the risk of conspiracy or innocent infection is a matter for the jury, although the judge will need to give them an appropriate warning and, it seems, direct them to disregard the complainants' evidence if they are not satisfied that their evidence is free from conspiracy. (If the risk is one of innocent infection it seems the judge need only direct the jury to take that risk into consideration when assessing the weight of the evidence.) If the judge decides that no reasonable jury could be sure the complainants' evidence is free from conspiracy he will have to order separate trials, so it may exceptionally be necessary to hold a *voir dire* to determine the extent of this risk at the pre-trial stage.

3.3.14 Identification and Striking Similarity

In *DPP* v. *P* [1991] 3 WLR 161 (HL) Lord Mackay felt that where the identity of the offender is in issue 'something in the nature of ... a signature or other special feature will be necessary' in the similar fact evidence for it to be admissible (see also *R* v. *West* [1996] 2 Cr App R 374 (CA) at pp. 390–1). It is difficult to see why this should be a rule of general application, however. The probative value of similar fact evidence depends on the other admissible evidence and the suggestion that there must be a 'signature' (that is, some form of striking peculiarity) in all identification cases fails to appreciate this. If the prosecution case depends entirely or primarily on similar fact evidence to identify the accused as the offender, then it is correct to say that the similar fact evidence must demonstrate some form of 'signature' – and the absence of any significant disparities (*R* v. *Johnson* [1995] 2 Cr App R 41 (CA)). Yet more often than not one would expect there to be other evidence identifying the accused, and in such cases no striking peculiarity ought to be necessary. In *Thompson* v. *R* [1918] AC 221 (HL) (3.3.4 *ante*) the issue was whether the accused was the person who had committed an offence on 16 March, but the evidence of his sexual appetite could not be described as an identifying 'signature'. Lewd photographs and powder puffs would appear to have been the standard accoutrements of any pederast of that era. The probative value of that evidence depended not on any need for striking peculiarities but on the fact that the accused turned up at the rendezvous with a predilection for young boys, equipped for buggery. The Court of Appeal has since recognised that a striking similarity is not always necessary for identification cases (*R* v. *Wharton* [1998] 2 Cr App R 289; see also *R* v. *Downey* [1995] 1 Cr App R 547 (CA) at pp. 550–51, *R* v. *Ruiz* [1995] Crim LR 151 (CA) and *R* v. *Lee* [1996] Crim LR 825 (CA)).

3.3.14.1 Two Approaches to Identification Evidence

It is not uncommon for several offences to be committed in a similar way, suggesting a single offender, but with the evidence identifying the offender on each occasion being in some way unsatisfactory. The question is whether, and if so in what circumstances, the separate weak identifications should be regarded as mutually supportive to provide sufficiently probative evidence identifying the offender. In *R* v. *McGranaghan* [1995] 1 Cr App R 559 the accused was tried on a single indictment containing 17 different counts arising out of three separate aggravated burglaries in which women were woken up in the middle of the night and grossly abused and/or raped. The evidence of each attack was held to be cross-admissible similar fact evidence to prove the other attacks. In each case the victims were able to identify the offender as about 5' 10" tall with, *inter alia*, dark hair and either a Scottish or Irish accent; and the offender told all of his victims to turn their eyes away from him during the assaults. The sole issue was the identity of the offender, but the victims had only been able to glance at his face in dark conditions and there was no circumstantial evidence linking the accused to the offences. The Court of Appeal laid down a general rule that where an accused is charged with more than one offence and the facts of each offence are similar enough for the evidence in relation to one offence to be admissible in support of the identification of the accused as the perpetrator of another, the judge must direct the jury that they should first disregard the similar fact evidence and be sure from the other evidence that the accused committed at least one of the offences. Only then would it be permissible for the jury to use the similar fact evidence to decide whether the accused committed the other offences too: 'The similar facts go to show that the same man committed both offences not that the defendant was that man. There must be some evidence to make the jury sure that on at least one offence the defendant was that man' (at p. 573). The Court of Appeal seemed to feel that there could be no circumstances where cumulative evidence of identification could be relied on, but the error in this reasoning has been demonstrated by a number of subsequent cases.

If there is clear evidence that the same offender committed all the offences charged, then there is no logical reason why a number of separate identifications should not be considered cumulatively to identify that offender. This was recognised in *R* v. *Downey* [1995] 1 Cr App R 547 where the accused was charged with two robberies which had been committed at petrol stations separated by three miles within 15 minutes of each other. In each case the offender had been white and of similar build, and had worn a black stocking mask, threatened a member of staff with a gun and grabbed money from the till. There was also a photograph of the offender at the first petrol station. The trial judge directed the jury that if they were sure that the same person had committed both robberies, then they were entitled to look at the cumulative effect of all the identification evidence to see whether that person was the accused. This direction was upheld on appeal as there was a clear nexus between the two robberies entitling the jury to adopt such an approach. The Court of Appeal went on to explain that there were two different 'aspects' to the similar fact situation; these may be summarised as follows.

First, there is the sequential (*McGranaghan*-type) situation where the jury are invited to reason that because the accused committed offence B he was also the unidentified person who committed offence A. To prove the accused committed offence A requires proof that he actually committed offence B, and also evidence of peculiar characteristics ('striking similarities') relating to the surrounding circumstances or the commission of both offences A and B. The clearest example is *R* v. *Straffen* [1952] 2 QB 911 (CCA) (3.3.4 *ante*) where the accused's confession as to the way he had previously strangled two other girls was admitted to demonstrate the strikingly peculiar way in which all three girls had been killed, tending to prove that the same person had been responsible for all these offences (see also *R* v. *Black* [1995] Crim LR 640 (CA)). By contrast, in *Harris* v. *DPP* [1952] AC 694 (HL) the accused faced eight counts of burglary but the only evidence connecting him with seven of the burglaries was evidence of opportunity, although there was some other circumstantial evidence that he had committed the eighth burglary. The House of Lords held that the evidence of the first seven counts should not have been admitted to show he had committed the eighth burglary as the prosecution had not proved that the accused had committed any of those seven burglaries or indeed that the same person had been responsible for all eight offences.

Second, there is the type of case exemplified by *R* v. *Downey* [1995] 1 Cr App R 547, where the circumstances clearly show that the same offender committed offences A and B, because of the way the offences are 'welded together', but the identification evidence falls short of proving that that person is the accused in either case taken alone. The Court of Appeal felt a cumulative approach to be appropriate in such cases and that the trial judge's direction had therefore been correct. It should be noted that striking peculiarities are unnecessary in cases of this type because the prosecution are not heavily dependent on the similar fact evidence. In *R* v.

Downey it was primarily the close proximity in time and space between the separate offences which lent force to the theory that the same offender had committed both offences; the similar fact evidence merely needed to show that there were sufficient similarities in appearance and *modus operandi* on each occasion to prevent any suggestion that the robberies had not been the work of the same person. The cumulative approach has been followed by the Court of Appeal in a number of other cases. In *R* v. *Barnes* [1995] 2 Cr App R 491, for example, the fact that a number of sexual offences had all been commenced in a similar way in the same month in the same part of north London by a young black man with acne provided the nexus which allowed the jury to be directed along the lines approved in *R* v. *Downey* (see also *R* v. *Grant* [1996] 2 Cr App R 272).

3.3.14.2 Identification Evidence and Gangs

Where the issue is whether several offences were committed by the same gang, it is necessary to adopt a two-stage approach requiring a consideration of (i) whether the same gang was actually responsible on each occasion and, if so, (ii) whether the gang comprised the same members on each occasion. If the sequential approach is used it must first be proved that the gang committed one offence. The similarities between the offences must then be assessed to see whether the same gang committed the other offence, and once this has been proved the individuals themselves must be the focus of attention to see whether they were members of the gang on both occasions. The cumulative approach will require proof that the same gang committed both offences (for example because of the close relationship between the offences in space and time), with the evidence linking an individual to one offence then being admissible to link him with the other offence.

In cases of group identification the sequential approach is more likely to be appropriate because there is always a danger that the gang's composition might have changed between offences, particularly where the offences are not sufficiently 'welded together'. In *R* v. *Lee* [1996] Crim LR 825 four accused were charged with two counts of burglary relating to separate incidents. The trial judge ruled that the evidence in respect of count 1 (the first burglary) was admissible similar fact evidence in relation to count 2 (the second burglary) because similarities in the way the offences had been committed indicated that the same gang had been responsible on both occasions. However, as already noted, while a gang may have a particular signature method this does not necessarily mean that it comprised exactly the same members during the commission of each offence. Lee's conviction for the second burglary was quashed by the Court of Appeal for, while there was sufficient evidence linking him with the first burglary, the evidence linking him to the second had little probative value.

R v. *Lee* [1996] Crim LR 825 was a case where the sequential approach was thought appropriate, but in *R* v. *Brown* [1997] Crim LR 502 the Court of Appeal applied the cumulative approach on the ground that the similarities between the separate robberies, in each case relating to grocery shops in the same chain, showed the same gang to have been involved. The offences occurred on 20 February and 4 April 1994 in west and north London respectively, and in each case the same shotgun and similar cable ties had been used by the offenders. The identification evidence of the offenders was weak, so the trial judge allowed the jury to adopt the cumulative approach once they were satisfied that the same gang had committed both offences. This approach was approved by the Court of Appeal: once the jury had concluded that the same gang had been involved on both occasions they were entitled to pool all the admissible evidence to determine the involvement of each individual. It was emphasised, however, that the totality of the admissible evidence must make the jury sure of each individual's involvement both as a gang member *and* as a participant in the particular offences.

3.3.15 Section 27(3) of the Theft Act 1968

Since the nineteenth century there has been, in respect of allegations of handling stolen property, a statutory provision allowing the prosecution to adduce evidence of the accused's conduct on other occasions as evidence that he had the *mens rea* for handling (that is, that he knew or believed the property was stolen). The justification for this departure from the general rule governing the admissibility of similar fact evidence seems to lie in the difficulty of proving the *mens rea* for handling in cases where the accused has been found in possession of stolen goods. The latest incarnation of this provision is s. 27(3) of the Theft Act 1968 which provides as follows:

> Where a person is being proceeded against for handling stolen goods . . . then at any stage of the proceedings, if evidence has been given of his having or arranging to have in his possession the goods the subject of the charge, or of his undertaking or assisting in, or arranging to undertake or assist in, their retention, removal, disposal or realisation, the following evidence shall be admissible for the purpose of proving that he knew or believed the goods to be stolen goods –
>
> (*a*) evidence that he has had in his possession, or has undertaken or assisted in the retention, removal, disposal or realisation of, stolen goods from any theft taking place not earlier than twelve months before the offence charged; and
>
> (*b*) (provided that seven days' notice in writing has been given to him of the intention to prove the conviction) evidence that he has within the five years preceding the date of the offence charged been convicted of theft or of handling stolen goods.

Once the *actus reus* of handling the subject matter of the proceedings has been proved, evidence which supposedly shows the accused to have a disposition to handle stolen goods (within the preceding year) and evidence of his convictions over the preceding five years for handling and/ or theft is admissible. But s. 27(3) allows the prosecution to adduce such evidence only where knowledge or belief that the goods were stolen is in issue; the evidence cannot be adduced for any other reason such as to show dishonesty (*R* v. *Duffus* (1993) 158 JP 224 (CA)). The judge must therefore give the jury a careful direction on the use which may be made of the evidence if the accused is charged with several counts of handling on the same indictment, and knowledge or belief is in issue for some counts but not others (*R* v. *Wilkins* (1975) 60 Cr App R 300 (CA)).

3.3.15.1 Section 27(3)(*a*)

In *R* v. *Bradley* (1979) 70 Cr App R 200 the accused had been found in possession of a stolen ring and the judge allowed the prosecution to adduce evidence that he had been in possession of another ring (which had been stolen within the preceding 12 months) and also evidence of that other theft and how the accused had come to be in possession of that ring. The Court of Appeal held that s. 27(3)(*a*) was to be strictly construed and that it did not empower the prosecution to adduce 'details of the very transactions as a result of which that earlier property had come into the possession of the accused'. Only the fact of possession of stolen property on an earlier occasion should have been admitted. Similarly, in *R* v. *Wood* (1987) 85 Cr App R 287 (CA) it was held that s. 27(3)(*a*) did not allow evidence of the circumstances in which the stolen goods were found or statements made in explanation of possession.

The reason for admitting evidence under s. 27(3)(*a*) is to allow the jury to reason from disposition to guilt (a single possession apparently being sufficient evidence of disposition for this purpose). Yet s. 27(3)(*a*) allows the prosecution to adduce evidence of just the bare fact of any other possession even though that other possession may have been entirely innocent. The probative value of evidence admissible under s. 27(3)(*a*) is rarely going to be particularly high, and would seem to have no function other than to make admissible what would ordinarily be regarded as irrelevant. To be able to reason from another possession to guilt must depend on the improbability of a person on trial for handling being innocent if he has been found in possession of stolen goods on another recent occasion. But that chain of reasoning is generally going to be unsound when there is a reliance on s. 27(3)(*a*) as there will usually remain a real risk of coincidence.

Section 27(3)(*a*) would make some sense if it had been drafted to allow the prosecution to adduce evidence that the accused had the *mens rea* for handling on the other occasions, in which case its probative value would be much greater; or if the provision had been interpreted to allow the prosecution to adduce evidence of the circumstances surrounding the other possession, for any probative value the fact of possession has will depend on those circumstances and on the accused's explanation. Indeed, the Court of Criminal Appeal in *R* v. *Smith* (1918) 13 Cr App R 151 interpreted an earlier version of s. 27(3)(*a*) (s. 43(1)(*a*) of the Larceny Act 1916) so as to permit the adduction of evidence of circumstances, but in *R* v. *Bradley* (1979) 70 Cr App R 200 the Court of Appeal declined to accept that *R* v. *Smith* had established a precedent, holding instead that s. 27(3)(*a*) had to be interpreted restrictively to protect the accused. The prosecution therefore have the right to adduce the fact of a possession but nothing which would enable the jury to assess its probative value.

3.3.15.2 Section 27(3)(*b*)

Section 27(3)(*b*) was also interpreted restrictively in *R* v. *Fowler* (1987) 86 Cr App R 219 (CA), precluding the admission of any details of the previous offence bar the fact of the conviction. However, that decision was disapproved by the House of Lords in *R* v. *Hacker* [1994] 1 WLR 1659 on the ground that s. 73(2)(*a*) of the Police and Criminal Evidence Act 1984 allows the 'substance and effect' of an admissible previous conviction to be adduced.

3.3.15.3 The Exclusionary Discretion

It was held by Roskill J in *R* v. *List* (1965) 50 Cr App R 81 (Assizes), a decision approved in *R* v. *Herron* (1966) 50 Cr App R 132 (CCA), that the trial judge had an overriding common-law discretion to exclude prosecution evidence tendered pursuant to s. 43(1) of the Larceny Act 1916 if its prejudicial effect would outweigh its probative value. The discretion applies equally to s. 27(3) of the Theft Act 1968 (*R* v. *Knott* [1973] Crim LR 36 (CA), *R* v. *Perry* [1984] Crim LR 680 (CA)), although it must now be regarded as no more than one facet of the more general discretion recognised in *R* v. *Sang* [1979] 3 WLR 263 (HL) to exclude any admissible prosecution evidence.

3.3.16 The Ghost of *Makin*

In *R* v. *Burrage* [1997] 2 Cr App R 88 it was alleged that B had indecently assaulted his grandsons. B denied the allegations and the trial judge allowed the prosecution to adduce evidence of his collection of pornographic magazines depicting heterosexual and homosexual adults in action. The Court of Appeal quite properly quashed his convictions as the magazines clearly indicated nothing more than an interest in adult pornography and were of very little probative value in the context of the offence charged. What is worrying is that the Court expressly based its decision on *Makin* v. *Attorney-General for New South Wales* [1894] AC 57 (PC) and applied *R* v. *Wright* (1989) 90 Cr App R 325 (CA), a throw-back to the post-*Makin* 'categories of relevance' approach to admissibility. B had not raised any of the recognised defences which brought into play the automatic admissibility of similar fact evidence (his defence was a bare denial of the allegation) and therefore the evidence of his disposition was held to be inadmissible (see also *R* v. *Lewis* (1982) 76 Cr App R 33 (CA)). *DPP* v. *P* [1991] 3 WLR 161 (HL) was mentioned only in passing, and *DPP* v. *Boardman* [1974] 3 WLR 673 (HL) was not mentioned at all, demonstrating that the ghost of *Makin* lives on notwithstanding two attempts by the House of Lords to exorcise it. Indeed, both *R* v. *Burrage* and *R* v. *Wright* were relied on as *precedents* in *R* v. *Alowi* (1999) unreported (97/08493/W3) (CA), which is absurd. Reverting to categories of relevance is to be deprecated as illogical and wrong in principle. Why should child pornography be admissible if the accused admits contact but claims it was innocent (the post-*Makin* category of 'innocent association') and yet be inadmissible if his defence is a bare denial of any contact? It is true that where contact has been admitted the context may increase the probative value of such evidence, but that does not mean the evidence will never be so probative in the absence of such an admission. A young child may accuse his stepfather of specific indecent acts, and the accused may have, locked away in some secret hiding place, pornographic photographs of the very same acts by adult men against young boys. It would be an affront to common sense if the photographs could not be admitted on the ground that the accused's defence was one of bare denial.

Another problem is that, even when the modern (*DPP* v. *P*) test is expressly applied, the Court of Appeal occasionally speaks in the language of the *Makin* test, with reference to 'whether the acts alleged to constitute the crime charged were designed or accidental' and 'to rebut a defence which would otherwise be open to the accused' (see, for example, *R* v. *Kidd* [1995] Crim LR 406 (CA)). While it is necessary to identify the context which gives similar fact evidence its probative value, it would be better if this assessment could be made without reference to the post-*Makin* categories.

3.3.17 Similar Fact Evidence Adduced by a Co-accused

If D1 and D2 are tried together for committing the same offence as a joint enterprise, they may each pursue a 'cut-throat' defence, denying personal involvement and blaming each other. In such circumstances D2 may wish to adduce evidence of D1's extraneous misconduct or disposition to show that D1 is more likely than D2 to have committed the offence. So long as such evidence is relevant to D2's defence, the judge has no discretion to exclude it just because it would unduly prejudice D1. Similarly, if D2 raises the defence of duress, and claims that he committed the offence charged because D1 had threatened him with violence, it would be permissible for D2 to adduce evidence of an extraneous act of violence by D1 against him regardless of whether it occurred before or after the offence charged, and regardless of any undue prejudice engendered against D1 by its admission (*R* v. *Nethercott* [2002] 2 Cr App R 117 (CA)). This is an application of the principle established in *R* v. *Miller* (1952) 36 Cr App R 169 (Assizes) which allows an accused to adduce any admissible evidence supportive of his own defence no matter how prejudicial it would be to his co-accused. It is not enough, however, that the evidence of D1's disposition makes it more likely that D1 committed the offence if it has no probative value in relation to D2's defence. In *R* v. *Knutton* (1992) 97 Cr App R 115 (CA) D1's 'formidable list of previous convictions' for offences of violence was held to be irrelevant to the question whether D2 had also been involved in an aggravated burglary with D1 or had been elsewhere.

In practice, though, the trial judge does have a limited discretion to exclude evidence of D1's extraneous misconduct even if it is logically relevant to D2's defence. This is a consequence of the theory which justifies the exclusion of any logically probative evidence on the ground of 'irrelevance' (3.3.7 *ante*). No party may adduce evidence which is deemed to be irrelevant to an issue or collateral fact, and it has been seen that logically relevant evidence may be excluded on the ground of irrelevance if it is expedient to do so (3.1.3 *ante*). Thus in *R* v. *Neale* (1977) 65 Cr App R 304, where D1 and D2 were jointly charged with arson and manslaughter and it was D2's defence that he had not been present, evidence that D1 had a propensity to commit arson by himself was excluded as irrelevant to the question whether or not D2 had been involved with him on the occasion in question. D1's disposition to act alone had a degree of probative value with regard to D2's defence, but the Court of Appeal dismissed this argument as a *non sequitur*. A different approach was adopted in *R* v. *Kracher* [1995] Crim LR 819, however. The prosecution in that case alleged that two bouncers, D1 and D2, had assaulted V as a joint enterprise, and D2 raised the defence that he had merely been holding V to protect him from D1's attack. The Court of Appeal held that D2's evidence of D1's propensity to sudden unprovoked violence was relevant to his defence and should have been admitted. Perhaps the evidence was admissible because there was no risk of unduly prejudicing D1, who had already pleaded guilty (unlike the situation in *R* v. *Neale* where both D1 and D2 had pleaded not guilty).

In *R* v. *Thompson* [1995] 2 Cr App R 589 the Court of Appeal left open the question whether it could ever be appropriate to balance probative value and undue prejudice where the accused seeks to adduce evidence of his co-accused's disposition. The prosecution case was that three men had been involved in burglary, arson and manslaughter as part of a joint enterprise. Before the trial, all three admitted involvement in the burglary and that a fire had been started, but D1 and D3 blamed D2 for the fire while D2 blamed the other two. During his interview with the police D2 mentioned that D1 had told him in the presence of D3 that they always 'torched their jobs' to cover their tracks and that they had burgled and set fire to a housing office a week earlier. The whole of D2's interview was admitted in evidence at the trial without objection. The trial judge also allowed D2's counsel to cross-examine witnesses called by the prosecution to elicit evidence that D1 and D3 had been seen by them at the scene of a fire at a housing office a week before the instant offence. The Court of Appeal held that D2's counsel had been entitled to do this, notwithstanding the undue prejudice caused to D1 and D3, as the evidence elicited was relevant to the consistency and credibility of D2's defence. It was also held that even if an exclusionary discretion did exist it would have been exercised in D2's favour.

The co-accused's adverse disposition will be relevant to the accused's defence and therefore admissible if they blame each other and the co-accused claims to be of a disposition which makes him less likely to be guilty. In *R* v. *Bracewell* (1978) 68 Cr App R 44, D1 and D2 were jointly charged with the violent murder of an elderly man during the course of their admitted burglary of his home, with each of them blaming the other for the killing. The Court of Appeal held that while evidence of D1's violent disposition was not originally relevant to whether D2 had also been involved, it became relevant, and therefore admissible, when D1 claimed that he was a non-violent professional burglar and that D2 was inexperienced and excitable. D2 should therefore have been able to cross-examine D1 on his violent disposition and call evidence to rebut his denial if necessary (see also *R* v. *Douglass* (1989) 89 Cr App R 264 (CA), 3.4.5 *post*). A similar decision had been reached in *Lowery* v. *R* [1973] 3 WLR 235 where two men were jointly charged with the sadistic murder of a 15-year-old girl. Each blamed the other for the offence, although they both admitted they had been at the scene. The Privy Council upheld the trial judge's decision to allow D2 to adduce expert opinion evidence of D1's aggressive personality disorder and of D2's own weak personality. The scientific evidence 'could point to the probability that the perpetrator was the one rather than the other'. It was D2's defence that only D1 had been involved in the murder and evidence of their respective personalities was therefore relevant to his defence. The Court of Appeal has recently confirmed that, where D1 and D2 are jointly charged with an offence of violence, and evidence of D1's violent disposition is adduced or elicited by D2 pursuant to a cut-throat defence, D1's bad-character is admissible not only to demonstrate that D1 is not worthy of belief as a witness but also (as similar fact evidence) to show that D1 is more likely than D2 to have committed the offence charged (*R* v. *Randall* [2003] EWCA Crim 436).

3.3.18 Special Cases

Occasionally it will be necessary for the prosecution to adduce evidence that the accused has (or may have) committed an offence before, either because the commission of a prior offence is a necessary element of the offence charged or because the nature of the charge means it would be impossible to withhold the evidence. For example, to prove a charge of driving while disqualified, contrary to s. 103(1)(*b*) of the Road Traffic Act 1988, it is necessary to prove that the accused was disqualified (following a conviction) at the relevant time; and to prove a charge of absconding on bail contrary to s. 6(1) of the Bail Act 1976 it is impossible to withhold the fact that the accused was on bail for an alleged offence.

3.3.19 The Disposition of Persons other than the Accused

If the accused is charged with an offence involving a third party, the accused may wish to cast the blame on to him in order to exculpate himself. The obvious example would be where the accused admits he killed another person but raises self-defence. Evidence of the deceased's own violent disposition would be logically relevant to his defence and therefore admissible. Similarly, if the accused is charged with the murder of his wife, and he claims that she committed suicide, he would be able to give evidence of her previous attempts to kill herself (as in *R* v. *Kavanagh* [2002] EWCA Crim 904); and in a case where the accused relies on the defence of duress, he would be able to adduce evidence of the violent disposition of the third party who allegedly threatened him. Once the judge has concluded that the evidence is relevant to the accused's defence, and is therefore *prima facie* admissible, there is no further discretion to exclude it. The case of *R* v. *Murray* [1995] RTR 239 provides a useful illustration. M was charged with reckless driving, his defence being that his car had been deliberately forced off the road by the driver of another car, a Golf, and in a frightened state he had driven off at speed pursued by the Golf. The driver of the Golf, McM, did not turn up at the trial and the prosecution relied instead on the evidence of his passenger. M had wished to cross-examine a police officer on McM's previous convictions but the trial judge ruled against that submission on the ground that the convictions were irrelevant. McM was not a witness so his credibility was not in issue; and his convictions were for dishonesty and firearms offences rather than driving offences or offences of violence. The Court of Appeal took a different view, however, and quashed M's conviction for reckless driving. McM had a long record of anti-social conduct stretching over 10 years and his convictions had been relevant to M's credibility and defence as they suggested that McM was the sort of man who would have acted in the way M had described.

When determining whether to exclude logically probative evidence of this sort on the ground of 'irrelevance', the risk of undue prejudice to the accused now operates as a justification for *admitting* the evidence, against which must be weighed competing considerations such as vexation to the third party or his family, delay, cost, the number of collateral matters which would be raised, the risk of overburdening the jury and so on. Such a balancing exercise was conducted by Fisher J in the New Zealand case of *R* v. *Wilson* [1991] 2 NZLR 707 (NZHC) where an alleged murderer wished to adduce evidence of the deceased's previous convictions to support his defence that he had acted in self-defence. Fisher J allowed the accused to adduce evidence of the deceased's violent disposition but not his past use of drugs.

Given the importance attached by the law of criminal evidence to the accused's right to defend himself, one could be forgiven for assuming that policy considerations would rarely prevent the accused from adducing evidence which logically supports his defence. And yet, bizarrely, the Court of Appeal has come to the conclusion in a number of cases that evidence of a prosecution witness's disposition is not admissible to prove that he acted in accordance with his character on a particular occasion. In *R* v. *Irish* [1995] Crim LR 145 the accused was charged with having wounded J with intent to cause him grievous bodily harm, and it seems his defence was that he had acted in self-defence. J was called to give evidence for the prosecution and the accused cross-examined him on his recent conviction for an assault on another person, S. Cross-examining a witness on his previous convictions is a standard way of attacking his credibility (16.5 *post*), but the accused wished to go further than that. He sought leave to call S to explain the circumstances of that assault on the ground that it would show that J could not resist using violence. The judge ruled against this request and the accused was convicted. The Court of Appeal rejected the argument based on similar facts as 'misconceived', adopting the view of Lord Lane CJ in *R* v. *Edwards* [1991] 1 WLR 207 (CA), a case on the evidential value of police misconduct.

Logically, if there is evidence that a police officer has a tendency to fabricate evidence and lie on oath (for example, because his evidence has been demonstrably disbelieved by juries on past occasions, or by a judge in civil proceedings, or he has been found guilty of perjury or perverting the course of justice) it should be regarded as evidence of his disposition which would support a defence that he has fabricated his evidence against the accused in the instant proceedings. Notwithstanding the logic of this argument, and the absence of the principal considerations which justify excluding evidence of the accused's extraneous misconduct, the Court of Appeal in *R* v. *Edwards* [1991] 1 WLR 207 made it quite clear that such evidence is to be considered relevant only to the question of the officer's *credibility* as a witness for the prosecution (see also *R* v. *Clancy* [1997] Crim LR 290 (CA), *R* v. *Edwards (Maxine)* [1996] 2 Cr App R 345 (CA) and *R* v. *Malik* [2000] 2 Cr App R 8 (CA)). A police officer may be cross-examined on relevant proven misconduct, or on an implicit finding of perjury by a jury's decision to acquit in a previous trial, to show that the officer is not worthy of belief; but it is not permissible to adduce evidence of such extraneous misconduct as 'reverse similar fact evidence' to prove perjury in the instant proceedings or, where the allegation is that the officer fabricated evidence in a particular way prior to the trial, to prove his misconduct with evidence that he behaved in a similar way on other occasions in relation to other suspects. Moreover, because the evidence is regarded as relevant to nothing more than credit, the rule on the 'finality of answers on collateral matters' (16.5.2 *post*) means that it is not possible to adduce evidence to contradict the answers given during cross-examination unless the limited 'bias' exception applies (16.5.4.2 *post*) or the officer's credibility can be said to be inextricably linked with an issue.

If there is one case more than any other which exemplifies the desirability of admitting police officers' extraneous misconduct as 'reverse similar fact evidence', at least in some cases, it is *R* v. *Twitchell* [2000] 1 Cr App R 373. T was convicted in February 1982 of manslaughter and robbery, and while there was some circumstantial evidence implicating him, the heart of the prosecution case comprised the confessions he had made when interviewed in November 1980 by police officers of the notoriously corrupt (and now disbanded) West Midlands Serious Crime Squad, including one DS Brown. It was T's contention that he had been denied access to a solicitor and that the first of his admissions had been forced out of him by torture, in that he had been hand-cuffed to a chair and deprived of oxygen by having a plastic bag held over his head. He had reported what had happened to his solicitor at the earliest opportunity and raised the issue at the trial, but he was nonetheless convicted and served 11 years in prison. However, in a civil claim brought by another man, Tr, against the Chief Constable of the West Midlands in the 1990s, it was found that he (Tr) had been denied access to a solicitor, handcuffed and 'bagged' in April 1982 in a similar way to that alleged by T at his trial, and that he too had signed a confession as a result. The trial judge in Tr's civil proceedings not only found that Tr had indeed been 'bagged' as claimed but also that one of the officers involved was none other than DS Brown, who was expressly found to be a dishonest witness. Tr's conviction was quashed as a result in 1996, which led to T's own case being referred to the Court of Appeal by the Criminal Cases Review Commission. Needless to say T's conviction was quashed too, but the basis of the decision was that the *credibility* of DS Brown (and other officers involved in T's interrogation) had been seriously damaged. There was no suggestion that Tr's account could be regarded as directly relevant (in the similar fact sense) to the question whether T was tortured as claimed, even though the similarities between his and Tr's accounts were strikingly peculiar. Assuming collusion or contamination can be discounted, there would seem to be no sound reason for limiting the relevance of such extraneous misconduct to credibility. Indeed s. 41(3)(*c*) of the Youth Justice and Criminal Evidence Act 1999, in relation to extraneous sexual conduct by the complainant in proceedings for a sexual offence (17.4 *post*), demonstrates that the reverse similar facts argument is far from 'misconceived'.

The foregoing analysis has focused on evidence of bad character, but it is now clear that a third party's *good* character may be adduced in a criminal trial, in some circumstances at least, to prove that he would not have acted in a contrary fashion. In particular, if the accused is charged with a sexual offence, and the issue is consent, the prosecution may adduce evidence of the complainant's chaste or respectful disposition to prove that she would not have consented in the circumstances of the alleged offence (*R* v. *Amado-Taylor (No. 2)* [2001] EWCA Crim 1898, *R* v. *Tobin* [2003] Crim LR 408 (CA); 16.4.2 *post*). Moreover, in *R* v. *Amado-Taylor (No. 2)* it was accepted that in a case where the accused relies on self-defence against an allegation of violence, the non-violent disposition of the complainant would be logically relevant to that defence, and that, because the accused may adduce evidence of his own good character (3.4 *post*), 'it would seem anomalous if the complainant were not able to seek to establish his non-violent disposition', the implication being that such evidence would be admissible at the behest of the prosecution. A question of this sort arose in *R* v. *G(R)* [2003] Crim LR 43, a case of alleged murder where the accused's case was that he had disarmed the deceased of his knife and stabbed him in self-defence. The prosecution witnesses were permitted to state that, to their knowledge, the deceased had not habitually carried a knife; but the judge refused to allow the prosecution to elicit evidence of the deceased's non-violent disposition. The Court of Appeal quashed the murder conviction because the witnesses' answers to the question 'have you ever known [the deceased] to carry a knife?' had minimal probative value in the factual context of the case – but the Court was willing to assume that the witnesses' answers to that question were *prima facie* admissible.

3.3.20 Reform

In its report, 'Evidence of Bad Character in Criminal Proceedings' (Law Com No. 273 (2001)), the Law Commission has reaffirmed the view expressed in its consultation paper ((CP No. 141 (1996)) that the law governing similar fact evidence should be codified to bring 'greater clarity, certainty and accessibility'. According to the proposed scheme, prosecution evidence of the accused's extraneous misconduct or disposition would be admissible, as evidence tending to prove the accused's guilt of the instant charge, only if the evidence has 'substantial probative value' in relation to a matter in issue (other than whether the accused has a propensity to be untruthful) which is 'of substantial importance in the context of the case as a whole' and the interests of justice require it to be admitted, taking into account its potentially prejudicial effect. The judge would be required to consider the risk of both moral and reasoning prejudice, and to take into account a non-exhaustive list of factors when determining probative value. The Commission has also suggested that 'background evidence' which shows the accused's extraneous misconduct should be *prima facie* admissible only if it is inextricably linked to the facts relating to the offence charged 'by reason of its close connection with them in time and space' (that is, it forms part of the 'narrative' or the *res gestae*), the reason being that it would 'be very strange if evidence of an assault committed in the course of a rape, but not separately charged, were to be treated as *prima facie* inadmissible'. Other types of background evidence ('explanatory evidence') revealing the accused's extraneous misconduct would be *prima facie* inadmissible, requiring the judge to weigh the importance of the evidence against the undue prejudice its admission might engender. Evidence of the accused's disposition or extraneous misconduct tendered by his co-accused would be admissible only if the evidence has 'substantial probative value' in relation to a matter in issue between them 'of substantial importance in the context of the case as a whole', the judge again being guided by the non-exhaustive list of factors when determining probative value. In each case the probative value of the evidence would be assessed on the assumption that it is true (unless the jury or magistrates could not reasonably find it to be true), reflecting the decision of the House of Lords in *R* v. *H* [1995] 2 WLR 737.

Other recommendations include a test of 'substantial probative value in relation to a matter in issue which is itself of substantial importance in the context of the case as a whole' for evidence of disposition or extraneous misconduct relating to a person other than the accused (with reference being made to the non-exhaustive list of factors); an amendment to s. 5 of the Indictments Act 1915 to ensure the accused receives a fair trial; and the repeal of s. 27(3) of the Theft Act 1968 on the ground that it is 'neither justified nor useful'.

3.4 The Accused's Law-abiding Disposition: Good-character Evidence

Just as the accused's peculiar, criminal or anti-social disposition may be logically probative of his guilt, and exceptionally admissible against him as similar fact evidence, the accused's law-abiding disposition may be logically *disprobative* of his guilt therefore admissible as evidence of his innocence. If the accused has led a blameless and positively altruistic life he is less likely to have broken the criminal law than if has committed similar (or even dissimilar) offences in the past; and he is also less likely to commit perjury in the witness box. This would appear to be common sense, but it is a view of enduring human nature which is based on little more than the assumption that certain people behave in a way which is consistently 'good', regardless of the context in which they find themselves – an assumption which has been thrown into doubt in recent years by empirical research (see *Melbourne* v. *R* (1999) 198 CLR 1 (HCA) at pp. 40–2). If the assumption is incorrect the admissibility of such evidence can only be justified as an illogical 'indulgence granted to the accused which continues to be maintained for historical reasons', the basis of which is the 'policy and humanity' of the common law (*Melbourne* v. *R* at p. 20).

Whether or not the assumption is correct, proving that a person has a good character is hardly a straightforward task. It is the accused's inherent nature which is assumed to have probative value, but a person's 'goodness' can only be established by evidence of past positive acts directly perceived by persons who know him well (and know that he has not committed any disreputable acts). In theory the best evidence of good character, insofar as it is relevant to innocence, would be testimony from disinterested witnesses that the accused has consistently behaved in a way which is dissimilar to the particular allegation against him, but for obvious reasons evidence of this sort will rarely be available. Evidence of positive deeds at a more general level, combined with the absence of any convictions or cautions, is more likely to be forthcoming, and will have some probative value; but occasional acts of altruism or honesty do not necessarily mean that a person is inherently or consistently good, and it will be seen below that such evidence has been held to be inadmissible for this reason. Furthermore, there is a distinction between a person's inherent nature and the reputation he has amongst those who know him, and this distinction can be disregarded only when the character witnesses have sufficient knowledge of the accused's conduct and behaviour over a sufficiently long period. As Lord Denning said in *Plato Films* v. *Speidel* [1961] 2 WLR 470 (HL) (at p. 487):

> 'A man's character ... is *what he in fact is*, whereas his reputation is *what other people think he is*. ... But there is another sense in which the word character is used, and quite properly used, when it overlaps the word reputation. ... In short, his character is the esteem in which he is held by others who know him and are in a position to judge his worth.'

Needless to say, in most cases the only objective and admissible evidence of the accused's good character is likely to be the fact that he has *not* previously been convicted or cautioned in respect of other offences, but there is a real difficulty with this proposition. The absence of any proven bad character does not necessarily mean the presence of a good character; it is neutral rather than positive evidence of innocence. Nevertheless, the accused who has no record is regarded as having a positively good character, and the jury or magistrates must take it into consideration as evidence of his innocence and (where relevant) his credibility. There is no judicial discretion to exclude evidence tendered by the accused in support of his innocence unless its probative value is so slight that it can be considered 'irrelevant', and as a concession to the accused the absence of a criminal record is regarded as sufficiently probative to be admissible.

Evidence of the accused's good character may be adduced or elicited in a number of different ways: (i) it may be put to prosecution witnesses in cross-examination as part of the accused's case (as in *R* v. *Wood* [1920] 2 KB 179 (CCA)); (ii) it may be given on oath by defence witnesses called for this purpose (as in *R* v. *Winfield* (1939) 27 Cr App R 139 (CCA)); or (iii) the accused himself may wish to give an account of his good character as part of his own testimony (as in *R* v. *Powell* [1985] 1 WLR 1364 (CA)). It will be seen below that the law governing the admissibility of such evidence was developed at common law for the first two situations and that, rather inappropriately, this has been extended to cover the third situation. If evidence of the accused's good character is admitted in any of these ways, the prosecution are entitled to adduce evidence of his bad character in rebuttal. If the accused fails to testify, the admissibility of his bad character for the purpose of rebutting his purported good character is governed by the common law (3.4.5 *post*). If the accused testifies, the admissibility of his bad character will usually arise during his cross-examination (4.4 *post*).

3.4.1 The Meaning and Admissibility of the Accused's Good Character

Evidence of the accused's past meritorious conduct, his positive reputation amongst those who know him and the absence of a criminal record have all been permitted on occasion to show that he has a good character, but, as a matter of law – at least in cases where the accused refuses to testify – only reputation evidence and the absence of a (relevant) criminal record are admissible for this purpose (the latter situation being the 'usual case': *R* v. *Aziz* [1995] 3 WLR 53 (HL) at p. 60). This rule, that it is not permissible to call or adduce evidence of the accused's past meritorious conduct, or even extraneous conduct of a more neutral nature which might undermine the allegation against him, was laid down in the case of *R* v. *Rowton* (1865) Le & Ca 520 where the majority of the Court for Crown Cases Reserved held, first, that if the accused wishes to call or elicit evidence of his good character that evidence must be limited to his 'general reputation in the neighbourhood in which he lives' and should not include evidence of particular facts; second, that the accused's good-character witnesses must not give their own personal opinion of his character (although they must actually have a good opinion of him to be competent as a good-character witness); and, third, that it is permissible for any such witness to say that he has never heard anything bad about the accused. The rule that good-character evidence is limited to the accused's general reputation was justified on the grounds of academic authority and pragmatism. It was felt that good-character evidence went to the issue of the accused's general disposition against committing the offence charged and, according to Cockburn CJ, such disposition could only be ascertained from the accused's general reputation in his community. Similarly, Willes J felt that evidence of particular facts had to be excluded 'because a robber may do acts of generosity, and the proof of such acts is therefore irrelevant to the question whether he was likely to have committed a particular act of robbery'.

In *R* v. *Samuel* (1956) 40 Cr App R 8 (CCA) the accused was charged with having stolen a camera he had found in the grounds of a museum and had kept for five weeks, and was permitted to testify that he had, on specific previous occasions, handed in other property he had found as evidence of his honest disposition. The admissibility of this evidence was not queried on appeal, suggesting that the *Rowton* test for admissibility might have become more flexible following the enactment of the Criminal Evidence Act 1898 and with it the accused's right to testify in his own defence. In *R* v. *Redgrave* (1981) 74 Cr App R 10, however, the *Rowton* test was reaffirmed by the Court of Appeal. R was charged with having solicited in a public place for immoral (homosexual) purposes in that he had openly masturbated in the presence of male undercover police officers in a public lavatory, staring at them while doing so. His defence was that he had merely been satisfying his lust in the absence of his girlfriend, and he sought to adduce evidence of his heterosexual disposition in the form of letters from girls, suggesting that he had been sexually involved with them, and photographs showing his friendly relationships with girls generally. The trial judge excluded the evidence, and the Court of Appeal upheld R's conviction, applying *R* v. *Rowton* (1865) Le & Ca 520, on the ground that the accused 'is not allowed, by reference to particular facts, to call evidence that he is of a disposition which makes it unlikely that he would have committed the offence charged'. R could, therefore, only have called evidence that he did not have a reputation for the type of conduct alleged by the prosecution, a decision justified on two grounds: first, the accused could easily fabricate the sort of evidence which R had sought to adduce; and, second, it would not be in the public interest to allow the accused to compel women to testify as to their sexual relations with him. While these are no doubt commendable policy objectives, the decision is nonetheless fundamentally flawed. *R* v. *Rowton* represented the common-law position at a time when the accused was not competent to testify and was therefore unable to give oral evidence of his own good character, whereas in *R* v. *Redgrave* the accused not only had the right to give evidence but wished to exercise that right to explain his own character. It is difficult to see how an individual can be expected to give evidence of his reputation amongst those who know him, and a different test must surely apply when it is the accused himself who wishes to testify as to his good character. Arguably, then, the accused should be permitted to give evidence of particular meritorious acts so long as that evidence is sufficiently probative of his disposition. If the evidence has little probative value and would cause undue distress to witnesses compelled by him to attend, it would always be open to the judge to exclude it on the ground of 'irrelevance'. The Court of Appeal did recognise, however, that the common-law rule was no longer as rigid as it had been in 1865, and suggested that it could have been acceptable for the accused to give evidence of a stable and satisfactory heterosexual relationship with his wife or girlfriend as an 'indulgence' on the part of the court. The problem with this approach is that any such 'indulgence' would amount to an inclusionary discretion to admit inadmissible evidence, which cannot be right. The better view is that a more flexible approach to admissibility exists by virtue of the accused's right (since 1898) to testify in his own defence. This would explain not only why the accused in *R* v. *Samuel* (1956) 40 Cr App R 8 (CCA) was permitted to testify as to his previous conduct but also the numerous other instances where the rule in *R* v. *Rowton* has been ignored. For example in *R* v. *Scranage* [2001] EWCA Crim 1171 the accused's colleagues were permitted to give evidence of his honesty and the way he conducted himself at work; and in *R* v. *Sabahat* [2001] EWCA Crim 2588 the accused's character witnesses were permitted to testify as to his 'generous, kind, naïve, trustworthy, very honest, very nice and ... good character' (see also *R* v. *Douglass* (1989) 89 Cr App R 264 (CA) and 4.4 *post*).

3.4.2 The Evidential Value of the Accused's Good Character

If the accused testifies in his own defence, or is able to rely on an admissible hearsay statement made by him before the trial, admissible evidence of his good character will be relevant in two senses. First of all it will show his law-abiding propensity (that is, his disposition); in this sense it goes *directly* to the issue of his innocence or guilt. Second, it will be relevant to whether his testimony (or admissible hearsay statement) ought to be believed; in this sense it goes to the collateral question of his credibility as a witness and therefore *indirectly* to the issue of his innocence or guilt. If the accused refuses to testify, and has made no admissible hearsay statement which supports his defence, his good character will of course be relevant only in the first sense. Although this chapter is primarily concerned with evidence of disposition which is directly relevant to a fact in issue, it is convenient to consider here the evidential value of the accused's good character in both its senses. (Evidence of the accused's *bad* character elicited or adduced to undermine his credibility as a witness is covered in Chapter 4.)

In *R* v. *Rowton* (1865) Le & Ca 520 (CCCR) Cockburn CJ and Erle CJ were of the view that the accused's good character gives rise to a presumption that he is incapable of committing the crime charged, Cockburn CJ recognising that this was 'an anomalous exception to the general rule' excluding evidence of extraneous matters which 'had arisen from the fairness of our laws' (see also *R* v. *Stannard* (1837) 7 C & P 673 (CCC) at pp. 674–5 and *Attorney-General* v. *Radloff* (1854) 10 Ex 84 (CE) at p. 97). The value of the accused's good character as evidence tending to bolster his credibility was not addressed in *R* v. *Rowton* because it was not then possible for the accused to testify in his own defence; but once the accused became generally competent to testify (by virtue of s. 1 of the Criminal Evidence Act 1898) the relevance of such evidence to credibility was not only acknowledged but also considered – until relatively recently – to be of greater significance. The relevance of the accused's good character to both innocence and credibility is now firmly established and the judge is obliged to give the jury a direction on its evidential value as part of his summing-up at the end of the trial (*cf.* the earlier discretionary approach in *R* v. *Smith* [1971] Crim LR 531 (CA)).

The law was settled by the Court of Appeal in *R* v. *Vye, R* v. *Wise, R* v. *Stephenson* [1993] 1 WLR 471 (hereafter '*R* v. *Vye*') and by the House of Lords in *R* v. *Aziz* [1995] 3 WLR 53. The good-character direction has therefore come to be known as the '*Vye* direction'. V, a 50-year-old man with no previous convictions, appealed on the ground that the judge had failed properly to direct the jury on his good character. W, a 35-year-old man with no previous convictions, appealed on the basis that while the judge had directed the jury on the relevance of his good character to his credibility, he should also have given a direction on its relevance to the unlikelihood that he had committed the offence charged (the trial judge, following *R* v. *Berrada* (1989) 91 Cr App R 131 (CA), had felt that the propensity direction was optional). Both V and W had their convictions quashed, and the Court of Appeal laid down clear guidance for trial judges when giving directions on the accused's good character, removing the uncertainty over when a propensity direction should be given: first, it is obligatory for the judge to give a direction on the relevance of the accused's good character to his credibility if he has testified and/or made an admissible pre-trial exculpatory statement (*the credibility direction*); second, it is in all cases obligatory for the judge to give a direction on the relevance of the accused's good character to the likelihood of his having committed the offence charged (*the propensity direction*). The Court went on to state, however, that the trial judge retains a discretion as to how the good-character direction should be tailored to the particular circumstances of the case and the judge 'would probably wish to indicate ... that good character cannot amount to a defence'. Where the judge rules that the accused is of 'good character', but no *Vye* direction is given, an appeal will be successful if that failure can be said to have threatened the safety of the conviction (*R* v. *Micallef* (1993) *The Times* 26.11.93 (CA), *R* v. *Durbin* [1995] 2 Cr App R 84 (CA), *R* v. *Fulcher* [1995] 2 Cr App R 251 (CA), *R* v. *Howell* [2001] EWCA Crim 2862).

So long as the two limbs of the direction are given, it is not necessary for the judge to use any particular form of words (*R* v. *Miah* [1997] 2 Cr App R 12 (CA)), save that the direction is not to be given as a series of rhetorical questions but in the form of a clear affirmative statement and it is necessary to explain to the jury that the accused's good character is something which they *should* take into consideration (*R* v. *Lloyd* [2000] 2 Cr App R 355 (CA), *R* v. *Scranage* [2001] EWCA Crim 1171). However, the *Vye* direction should not be qualified with a suggestion that the accused's good character might carry less weight where the allegation is one of spontaneous conduct, particularly if the accused has been working (and kept his good character) in a job where spontaneous incidents are common (*R* v. *Fitton* [2001] EWCA Crim 215).

In *R* v. *Aziz* [1995] 3 WLR 53 (HL) it was made clear that the reference in *R* v. *Vye* to pre-trial exculpatory statements was a reference to statements admissible as an exception to the hearsay rule as a form of testimonial evidence – that is, the exculpatory parts of a 'mixed statement' (7.1.1 *post*). In other words, it is mandatory to give the two limbs of the *Vye* direction if the accused is of good character and has testified in court or made a pre-trial mixed statement which has been adduced by the prosecution. The three co-accused in that case were nominally of good character in the sense of having no (or no relevant) convictions, but evidence came out during their trial of misconduct on the part of two of them: Y and T had both admitted making false mortgage applications and had respectively admitted lying to Customs officers and failing to declare income to the Inland Revenue. The House of Lords held that while a two-limbed *Vye* direction should be given if an accused is of good character in the sense of having no (or no relevant) convictions, the judge would need to qualify that direction to take into account any disclosed criminal conduct to ensure the jury are given a 'fair and balanced picture', save that the trial judge retains a limited discretion to dispense with the *Vye* direction altogether (that is, to hold that the accused is not a person of good character) if the revealed criminal conduct would make any such direction an 'insult to common sense'. In other cases where the accused has a blemished character the judge must treat the accused as a person of good character and give a qualified direction.

It follows that if the accused has admitted his guilt and been cautioned in respect of other misconduct, his absence of previous convictions will not necessarily entitle him to a full *Vye* direction. In *R* v. *Martin* [2000] 2 Cr App R 42 (CA), for example, it was held that the accused's two cautions for possessing an offensive weapon justified the judge's decision to give a direction without the propensity limb. The accused had been on trial for two robberies (during which he had been armed with a hammer) and it would have been 'absurd' and 'misleading' to direct the jury on propensity. By contrast, in *R* v. *Sanchez* [2003] EWCA Crim 735, a case of drug smuggling, it was held that the judge had been entitled to give only the propensity direction in respect of the accused's lack of previous convictions, on the basis that her caution for shoplifting had been relevant to her credibility as a witness. In *R* v. *S* [2000] All ER (D) 1482 the Court of Appeal stated that it would only exceptionally interfere with the way the judge had exercised his discretion in cases such as this, and listed four factors to be taken into consideration: (i) whether the offence for which the accused has been cautioned affects his veracity as a witness; (ii) the similarity of that offence to the offence charged; (iii) the seriousness of that offence; and (iv) the time which has passed between the caution and the trial. *R* v. *Clarius* [2000] All ER (D) 951 is one such exceptional case. The 20-year-old accused, on trial for unlawful wounding, had no previous convictions but had been cautioned six years earlier for stealing an umbrella. The trial judge limited the good-character direction to the credibility limb, making no reference to the accused's lack of propensity to commit the sort of offence charged. The Court of Appeal allowed the appeal because the claim to good character had not been spurious and the theft was wholly irrelevant to the question of propensity. Both limbs of the *Vye* direction should have been given.

Needless to say, if the judge rules that the accused is not of good character then neither limb of the *Vye* direction should be given, even though the accused has no previous convictions. In *R* v. *Zoppola-Barraza* [1994] Crim LR 833 the accused (who had no convictions) was charged with smuggling cocaine but only a credibility direction was given, as he had admitted smuggling gold and jewellery into the UK on previous occasions. It was conceded by the prosecution on appeal that if he was to be regarded as a man of previous good character a propensity direction ought to have been given too. The Court of Appeal dismissed the appeal, however, as it would have been 'an affront to common sense' to direct the jury on either the propensity limb or the credibility limb given the gravity of the blemish to his character. ZB had not been a person of previous good character, no direction had been necessary and the direction on credibility the judge had given had been an undeserved bonus for him (*R* v. *Durbin* [1995] 2 Cr App R 84 (CA) at p. 89).

3.4.3 Qualifying the *Vye* Direction

In both *R* v. *Vye* [1993] 1 WLR 471 (CA) and *R* v. *Aziz* [1995] 3 WLR 53 (HL) it was accepted that the mere absence of convictions could amount to 'good character'; but it was also felt that the accused could be entitled to this label, and therefore a two-limbed direction, even though he had been convicted of some misconduct in the past or had committed some past or recent criminal conduct for which he had not been convicted, save that in such cases the direction would need to be qualified by additional words.

It is perhaps understandable that the absence of criminal convictions, as opposed to positive evidence of good character, should be regarded as relevant to credibility and law-abiding propensity, but it is difficult to understand why the accused should be regarded as a person of good character when there is actual evidence before the jury that he is not. Nevertheless, in *R* v. *Aziz* the House of Lords held that both Y and T were of 'good character', and so entitled to the two limbs of a (qualified) *Vye* direction, notwithstanding their admitted criminal conduct and the fact that neither of them had been able to adduce any positive evidence of good character. This sort of reasoning is likely to lead to some very bizarre directions. Consider, for example, *R* v. *Anderson* [1990] Crim LR 862 where the accused was a police officer charged with raping a woman in his patrol car. He had no previous convictions and asserted that the complainant had consented to sex with him. His evidence was not believed, he was convicted and he appealed on the basis of an inadequate direction on his 'good character'. His conviction was quashed by the

Court of Appeal because it was felt he had been entitled to a direction on the relevance of his character to his credibility and to his law-abiding disposition. He was of 'good character' even though he had admitted having sex with a woman in his patrol car while on duty as a uniformed officer. In *R* v. *Durbin* [1995] 2 Cr App R 84 (CA) the accused, a truck driver charged with importing cannabis, was held to be of 'good character' even though he had previous convictions for offences of dishonesty (albeit spent), had lied to prosecution witnesses, and had admitted smuggling computer parts across Europe for reward at the time of the alleged offence. He was therefore entitled to a qualified *Vye* direction, regardless of the fact that the evidence suggested he was of bad character. The case of *R* v. *Soukala-Cacace* [1999] All ER (D) 1120 (99/335/Z4) provides a more recent but equally bizarre example. The accused was convicted of a number of dishonesty offences (relating to false statements in her applications for charge cards and a hire purchase agreement in 1997) and appealed on the ground that, having no previous convictions, the judge should have given the jury a good-character direction on both propensity and credibility (rather than just the former). The fact is, however, that she was not of good character. She had falsely claimed to be a doctor when changing her driving licence and applying for a bank account in 1994, and had falsely claimed to be unemployed in a county court application form. Nevertheless, the Court of Appeal held that 'there was no justification for departing from the conventional direction' and 'if any tailoring was called for, it should have been in [her] favour'. She had been entitled to an unqualified two-limbed direction because her defence of marital duress had depended heavily on the jury's assessment of her credibility.

Assuming for the sake of argument that there is some logic in holding a blemished accused to be of good character, there is considerable uncertainty over how blemished an accused's character needs to be before he loses that status and the right to the *Vye* direction. Durbin was of good character, but Zoppola-Barraza was not (a distinction justified by the Court of Appeal in *R* v. *Durbin* on the ground that Durbin's lies and smuggling related to the circumstances of his alleged drug smuggling, while Zoppola-Barraza's misconduct had not been so connected). In *R* v. *Akram* [1995] Crim LR 50 (CA) the accused's admission that he had used heroin in the past disentitled him from being regarded as a person of good character when on trial for drugs offences, whereas in *R* v. *Anderson* [1990] Crim LR 862 the police officer's serious misconduct did not disentitle him from that status. Soukala-Cacace was a person of good character even though the evidence suggested she had a disposition to commit the type of offence with which she had been charged.

A further problem the courts have had to address is whether a person charged with more than one offence arising out of the same incident is entitled to be regarded as a person of good character when he has no previous convictions but has pleaded guilty to one of the less serious charges on the indictment. In *R* v. *Teasdale* (1993) 99 Cr App R 80 the accused was charged with, and pleaded not guilty to, causing grievous bodily harm with intent but pleaded guilty to an alternative charge of assault occasioning actual bodily harm (which was not revealed to the jury). The trial judge recognised that the outcome of the trial depended on the jury's assessment of the conflicting testimony of the accused and the victim, and therefore the credibility of these two witnesses, but he made no reference to the accused's character, even though she had no previous convictions, on the ground that she had admitted the lesser assault. The Court of Appeal held that she had still been a person of good character and so entitled to a *Vye* direction (see also *R* v. *Richens* [1993] 4 All ER 877 (CA)). *R* v. *Teasdale* was distinguished in *R* v. *Challenger* [1994] Crim LR 202, however. In that case the accused, who had no previous convictions, pleaded guilty to simple possession of cannabis but not guilty to the more serious alternative charge of possession with intent to supply and to the charge of possession of an offensive weapon. The trial judge refused to give any character direction and the accused appealed. The Court of Appeal held that the decision in *R* v. *Teasdale* applied only to situations where the accused pleaded guilty to a less serious alternative charge, and not in a case such as this where there was an offence which stood independently. The accused had ceased to be a person of unblemished character as soon as he had pleaded guilty to possession and a *Vye* direction was therefore no longer obligatory (see also *R* v. *Shepherd* [1995] Crim LR 153 (CA)).

Where the accused has previous convictions which are spent under the Rehabilitation of Offenders Act 1974 (16.5.4.1 *post*) the judge has a discretion to rule that he is a person of good character. According to the Court of Appeal in *R* v. *Nye* (1982) 75 Cr App R 247 (at p. 250):

'It may well be that the past spent conviction happened when the defendant being tried was a juvenile, for instance for stealing apples, a conviction of many years before. In those circumstances quite plainly a trial judge would rule that such a person ought to be permitted to present himself as a man of good character. At the other end of the scale, if a defendant is a man who has been convicted of some offence of violence and his conviction has only just been spent and the offence for which he is then standing trial involves some violence, then it would be plain that a trial judge would rule that it would not be right for such a person to present himself as a man of good character. The essence of this matter is that the jury must not be misled and no lie must be told to them about this matter.'

In *R* v. *H* [1994] Crim LR 205 the accused was charged with rape and indecent assault. As his only previous conviction was a spent one for possession of an airgun 12 years earlier, the Court of Appeal felt that he was a man of good character. The same approach was adopted in *R* v. *Burnham* [1995] Crim LR 491 (CA) where the accused, on trial for affray, had one spent conviction for criminal damage, and in *R* v. *Davis* [2003] EWCA Crim 402 where the accused, on trial for handling stolen goods, had spent convictions for criminal damage and threatening behaviour (see also *R* v. *Heath* (1994) *The Times* 10.2.94 (CA)). So long as the judge exercises his discretion properly the Court of Appeal will not interfere, even if other judges would have taken a different view (*R* v. *Bailey* [1989] Crim LR 723 (CA), *R* v. *Bett* [1999] 1 Cr App R 361 (CA)).

The Court of Appeal's decision in *R* v. *Nye* (1982) 75 Cr App R 247 makes it quite clear that even if a blemished accused has been ruled to be a person of good character the jury must not be misled. In particular, they must not be told that the accused has no convictions (*R* v. *O'Shea* (1993) *The Times* 8.6.93 (CA)). It seems, however, that when giving the *Vye* direction in such cases it may not always be necessary to reveal the fact of his spent convictions to the jury (*R* v. *Durbin* [1995] 2 Cr App R 84 (CA) at p. 92). If the accused has recent convictions which, though not spent, are felt to be irrelevant to the present charge, it is still permissible for the judge to rule that he is of good character. For example in *R* v. *Timson* [1993] Crim LR 58 (CA) a solicitor on trial for legal aid fraud was felt to be of good character when his only blemish was a recent drink-driving conviction.

How the words of the *Vye* direction should be modified in cases where the accused has a blemished character has not been explained by the Court of Appeal, so it is left entirely to the ingenuity of the trial judge. As Munday notes ([1997] Crim LR 247 at pp. 251–2), this is likely to be difficult for the judge and perhaps even more difficult for the jury to understand considering the contradictions involved. In fact the accused might be better off not having a good-character direction given at all as the jury would have their attention expressly drawn to his previous misconduct (a point recently acknowledged by the Privy Council in *Shaw* v. *R* [2001] 1 WLR 1519). The difficulties inherent in the English approach to the accused's character have deterred other common-law jurisdictions from following *R* v. *Vye* [1993] 1 WLR 471 (CA) and *R* v. *Aziz* [1995] 3 WLR 53 (HL). The majority of the New Zealand Court of Appeal in *R* v. *Falealili* [1996] 3 NZLR 664 declined to hold that the mere absence of previous convictions warrants a good-character direction (reflecting the approach adopted in the pre-*Vye* case of *R* v. *Buzalek* [1991] Crim LR 116 (CA)). The accused in New Zealand who has a good character will usually be entitled to the two-limbed direction, but there must be *positive* evidence that he has a good character. In the words of Henry J (at p. 667):

'We think there are logical difficulties with the proposition that an absence of previous convictions is in itself evidence establishing a person's good character. It may be a factor in assessing good character, but standing on its own it is generally neutral. A person of bad repute may well have no convictions. We do not think it necessary for directions to be given merely because absence of previous convictions has been elicited.'

The problems which have arisen in England and Wales in recent years are therefore unlikely to arise in New Zealand: if a person has no convictions but has committed some criminal conduct prior to or at the same time as the alleged offence, or even if his only evidence of bad character comprises spent convictions, then he will not be entitled to a good-character direction (unless there is positive evidence of good character) and the jury will not have to try to make sense of the qualified *Vye* direction. Thomas J went further, suggesting in dissent that a good-character direction should not be mandatory, even if there is positive evidence of good character, as every criminal trial is factually unique and it should lie within the judge's discretion whether a direction is or is not appropriate. It is this approach which was adopted by the majority of the High Court of Australia in *Melbourne* v. *R* (1999) 198 CLR 1 (reaffirming the test established in *Simic* v. *R* (1980) 144 CLR 319 (HCA)). McHugh J summarised the position (at p. 14):

'The ... trial judge must retain a discretion as to whether to direct the jury on evidence of good character after evaluating its probative significance in relation to both (a) the accused's propensity to commit the crime charged; and (b) the accused's credibility. The judge may conclude that the good character evidence adduced is of probative significance in relation to (a) only, (b) only, both (a) and (b) or neither (a) nor (b), and can direct (or not direct) the jury accordingly ... Two considerations lead me to this conclusion. First, the difference between the use of good character evidence and the use of bad character evidence in a criminal trial is logically anomalous and, while that difference is too deeply rooted in the law to be removed by judicial decision, it should not be widened. Second, in cases where good character evidence has no logical connection with the elements of the offence, a mandatory direction is likely to divert the jury from properly evaluating evidence which more directly and logically bears upon the guilt of the accused ...'

Whether the House of Lords will revert to the former position, where any direction was discretionary, remains to be seen, but at present it seems unlikely. The Privy Council applied *R* v. *Aziz* [1995] 3 WLR 53 (HL) to the Caribbean states accepting its jurisdiction in *Barrow* v. *R* [1998] 2 WLR 957, but it is to be noted that the Court of Appeal has indicated a degree of dissatisfaction with the present approach:

'Ever since the law started to lay down what a jury must be told as to the effect of good character nearly 30 years ago in *Bellis* [1966] 1 WLR 234 there has been trouble. Could the jury perhaps be allowed to work it out for themselves? We are, however, bound by the case of *Vye* ...' (*R* v. *Wood* [1996] 1 Cr App R 207 at p. 218)

The Hong Kong Court of Final Appeal has also adopted a more flexible approach, based on the exercise of judicial discretion to ensure a fair and balanced summing-up:

'The *Vye* rules, applied in practice, might be highly artificial. They might amount to no more than the incantation of a well-worn formula. The need to heavily qualify the direction, to avoid an affront to common sense, might make the words virtually meaningless. This is liable to induce cynicism and despair on the part of trial judges, and lower the standing of the law in the eyes of juries. It might also confuse the jury.' (*Tang Sui Man* v. *HKSAR* (1997–1998) 1 HKCFA 107 at p. 130)

3.4.4 The Relevance of a Bad Co-accused

In *R* v. *Vye* [1993] 1 WLR 471 the Court of Appeal also had to consider the position where there are several co-accused of whom only some are of good character. S, a man with previous convictions, had been tried with his co-accused, H, who had no convictions apart from one 'peccadillo' when he was 16. The judge had directed the jury in respect of H's good character, and S appealed on the basis that his own (undisclosed) bad character had been highlighted as a consequence. The Court held that H had been entitled to a good-character direction notwithstanding having S as a co-accused; and while it was recognised that the judge has a discretion to comment on the co-accused's bad character and may, for example, warn the jury not to speculate about his character, there is no obligation to give any such direction (see also *R* v. *Houlden* (1993) 99 Cr App R 245 (CA) and *R* v. *Durbin* [1995] 2 Cr App R 84 (CA)). In *R* v. *Cain* (1993) 99 Cr App R 208 there were two co-accused: H, of good character, and C, of bad character. The Court of Appeal confirmed that H had been entitled to both the credibility and propensity limbs of the *Vye* direction and this was so even though C's previous convictions had been revealed during the trial (at his own request). It was also held, however, that the trial judge should have told the jury that C's bad character was relevant only to his credibility, for otherwise the jury might have assumed (quite logically) that C's convictions were evidence of a criminal propensity in the same way that H's good character was relevant evidence of her law-abiding propensity.

This rule, that the 'good' accused is entitled to a *Vye* direction notwithstanding the adverse effect it may have on his 'bad' co-accused, is a further manifestation of the general principle established in *R* v. *Miller* (1952) 36 Cr App R 169 (Assizes) that the judge retains no discretion to exclude admissible evidence adduced or elicited by the accused just because it would unduly prejudice his co-accused's defence.

3.4.5 Rebutting the Accused's Good-character Evidence at Common Law

Evidence of the accused's bad character may be adduced by the prosecution at common law to rebut the accused's evidence of his good character. In *R* v. *Rowton* (1865) Le & Ca 520, R, on trial for indecently assaulting a 14-year-old boy, had called witnesses to give evidence of his good character as a 'moral and well-conducted man' and the prosecution witness called to rebut this evidence gave his opinion that R was 'a man capable of the grossest indecency and the most flagrant immorality'. R was convicted of indecent assault and appealed. The Court for Crown Cases Reserved held that if the accused has adduced admissible evidence of his good reputation the prosecution are entitled to rebut that evidence by adducing evidence of his bad reputation, but not specific examples or individual opinions of the accused's bad character. The witness's opinion should not have been admitted and R's conviction was therefore quashed. R did not give evidence himself because the accused was not then competent to testify. If the accused puts his good character in issue and testifies he may be cross-examined on his bad character (including his previous convictions) under s. 1(3)(ii) of the Criminal Evidence Act 1898 to undermine his credibility as a witness (see 4.4 *post*).

Where the evidence of the accused's good reputation has been given by a defence witness called for that purpose the prosecution may cross-examine that witness on whether he is aware of the accused's bad reputation in order to show that he is mistaken and that his testimony should not be relied on. Further, the witness may also be cross-examined by the prosecution on whether he is aware of the accused's previous convictions (*R* v. *Redd* [1923] 1 KB 104 (CCA), *R* v. *Winfield* (1939) 27 Cr App R 139 (CCA)). If the witness denies any such knowledge it would appear that the convictions can be proved (*R* v. *Redd*). If it is permissible to adduce evidence of the accused's convictions it can only be for the purpose of rebutting the good-character evidence (of reputation) which has been given; the evidence would be inadmissible if tendered merely to show the witness's understanding is wrong, because of the rule on the finality of answers on collateral matters (16.5.2 *post*). The common law on the admissibility of bad-character evidence governs two other possible situations where the accused has failed to testify: first, where the accused or his counsel has cross-examined a witness called by his co-accused or the prosecution to elicit evidence of his good character; and, second, where a defence witness called to give evidence relating to the case has volunteered evidence of the accused's good character. In *R* v. *Redd* the Court of Criminal Appeal held that in the latter type of case the defence witness should not be cross-examined by the prosecution on the accused's previous convictions.

The prosecution cannot adduce evidence of the accused's bad character in rebuttal at common law unless the accused has put his character in issue. If the accused refuses to testify and, instead of adducing or eliciting evidence of his good character, he or his counsel simply attacks the character of a prosecution witness, the accused does not run the risk of having his bad character admitted (*R* v. *Butterwasser* [1948] 1 KB 4 (CCA)) – although he does run the risk of having an adverse inference drawn from his failure to testify (9.3.2 *post*). If the accused testifies he may be cross-examined on his bad character by virtue of the Criminal Evidence Act 1898 (4.5–7 *post*).

In *R* v. *Rowton* (1865) Le & Ca 520 (CCCR) (at p. 531) it was said that bad-character evidence adduced in rebuttal by the prosecution must be 'of the same character and confined within the same limits' as the accused's good-character evidence: 'as the prisoner can only give evidence of general good character, so the evidence called to rebut it must be evidence of the same general description, sh[o]wing that the evidence which has been given in favour of the prisoner is not true, but that the man's general reputation is bad'. There is, however, authority to suggest that the accused puts the whole of his character in issue once he has adduced or elicited evidence of his good reputation. The accused's character is said to be 'indivisible'. By adducing evidence to show that one aspect of his character is 'good' he allows the prosecution to adduce evidence in rebuttal of an entirely different aspect of his character which is 'bad'. In *R* v. *Winfield* (1939) 27 Cr App R 139 (CCA) the accused was on trial for indecently assaulting a woman and he called a character witness who gave evidence of his 'exemplary' behaviour with regard to women. It was held that the prosecution had been entitled to cross-examine that witness on the accused's previous convictions for offences of dishonesty: 'If a prisoner chooses to put his character in issue, he must take the consequences'. Unfortunately it is not clear whether *R* v. *Winfield* is authority for the position at common law as there is a conflict between the two reports of this case. In *R* v. *Winfield* (1939) 27 Cr App R 139 it seems the accused did not himself testify (although p. 141 suggests he possibly did) while *R* v. *Winfield* [1939] 4 All ER 164 reports that the accused was himself cross-examined, suggesting that the case is authority for the position under the Criminal Evidence Act 1898 Act (4.4 *post*). Given the conflict between *R* v. *Rowton* and *R* v. *Winfield* the latter case, if indeed it is a decision under the common law, would seem to have been incorrectly decided. Nonetheless, given that the accused's character is indivisible under the 1898 Act, it may safely be assumed that the same rule now operates in cases where the accused fails to testify.

The common-law rule is of interest because it permits the admission of the accused's bad character to rebut a defence assertion of good character even though the question of the accused's credibility has not arisen. The evidence may have a bearing on the credibility of the accused's defence, insofar as an affirmative defence manifests itself during the cross-examination of prosecution witnesses, but the justification for admitting this sort of evidence is to *rebut* his good-character evidence. In other words, it is adduced to show the accused does not have the claimed law-abiding propensity. Given that this evidence is unlikely to be regarded as merely neutralising the good-character evidence, it would seem to have evidential value suggesting the accused has a criminal propensity and for that reason is more likely to be guilty. If this is correct, the rule is in effect an exception to the general rule of *prima facie* inadmissibility which governs similar fact evidence tendered by the prosecution.

The accused may adduce evidence to rebut his co-accused's good-character evidence, whether or not the co-accused testifies, so long as the co-accused's bad character is relevant to the accused's defence (3.3.17 *ante*). In *R* v. *Douglass* (1989) 89 Cr App R 264, D1 and D2 were charged with causing death by reckless driving on the basis that one or both of them must have been responsible. D1 did not give evidence but the defence put by his counsel was that D2 had been drinking and was solely responsible. D1's counsel also cross-examined a prosecution witness to elicit good-character evidence that D1 had not drunk alcohol in the two years she had known him, implying that he, unlike D2, had not been affected by alcohol at the time of the crash and that D2 was more likely to have been responsible. D2 wished to elicit evidence of D1's convictions for serious motoring offences and offences of violence, dishonesty and drink-driving, but the trial judge refused this application and D2 was convicted. The Court of Appeal held that as D1 had put his own character in issue, suggesting a propensity for non-reckless driving, D2 had been entitled to elicit evidence of D1's bad character to show his propensity for reckless driving as it had been relevant to his defence.

Chapter Summary

- To be admissible an item of evidence must be 'relevant' to an issue or a collateral fact (or an explanation of the background). However, logically relevant evidence may be considered 'irrelevant', given its relatively low probative value, if its admission cannot be justified in the light of countervailing considerations such as the need to minimise undue prejudice, speculation, delay, expense, vexation and the proliferation of collateral matters.
- The test for determining the admissibility of evidence of a party's extraneous misconduct or disposition ('similar fact evidence') to prove an issue is but one aspect of the general discretion to exclude logically relevant evidence on the ground that it is 'irrelevant'. In criminal proceedings the judge will explicitly 'balance' the probative value of the (logically relevant) bad-character evidence against the risk of causing the accused undue prejudice. However, some evidence of extraneous misconduct may be *prima facie* admissible in criminal proceedings on the ground that there is no risk that the jury will reason from disposition to guilt, or because the evidence explains the 'background' to the case or forms part of the *res gestae*.
- Evidence of a party's positive extraneous conduct is generally inadmissible to demonstrate that he acted in the same way on a particular occasion. However, in criminal proceedings the accused's good character is admissible evidence that he did not commit the alleged offence (and, where relevant, that he is a credible witness). The positive disposition of a complainant who alleges that she was sexually assaulted by the accused is also admissible to show that she did not consent.

Further Reading

Stone, 'The Rule of Exclusion of Similar Fact Evidence: England' (1932) 46 Harvard LR 954

James, 'Relevancy, Probability and the Law' (1941) 29 California LR 689

Trautman, 'Logical or Legal Relevancy – A Conflict in Theory' (1952) 5 Vanderbilt LR 385

Hoffmann, 'Similar Facts After *Boardman*' (1975) 91 LQR 193

Carter, 'Forbidden Reasoning Permissible' (1985) 48 MLR 29

Allan, 'Similar Fact Evidence and Disposition' (1985) 48 MLR 253

Munday, 'What Constitutes Good Character?' [1997] Crim LR 247

Redmayne, 'The Relevance of Bad Character' (2002) CLJ 684

Law Commission Consultation Paper No. 141 (1996)

Law Commission Report, Law Com No. 273 (2001)

Criminal Justice Bill (2003), Part 11, Chapter 1 and Explanatory Note (www.publications.parliament.uk)

4 The Criminal Evidence Act 1898

It has been seen that the accused's good character is admissible for the purpose of bolstering his credibility as a witness and to show he has a law-abiding propensity (3.4 *ante*). It has also been seen that evidence of the accused's propensity in other respects (that is, similar fact evidence of his bad character) is inadmissible unless its probative value is sufficiently high to justify its admission despite the risk of any undue prejudice (3.3 *ante*). Section 1 of the Criminal Evidence Act 1898 governs the extent to which the accused may be cross-examined on his bad character to undermine his credibility as a witness. Unlike admissible similar fact evidence, which is directly relevant to whether the accused is guilty of the offence charged, such cross-examination is only *indirectly* relevant to his guilt. It is intended to show that because of his dissolute character his testimony, and therefore his defence, should not be believed.

One of the reasons for cross-examining a witness is to undermine his credibility, and an effective way of doing this is to question him on his past illegal or immoral conduct. By bringing out the witness's moral failings the tribunal of fact is encouraged to think less kindly of him as a person and therefore to attach less weight to his testimony. A witness who has been guilty of misconduct in the past is represented as a person who cannot be trusted to tell the truth on oath. Moreover, evidence of the witness's previous convictions (or evidence showing bias or a dishonest reputation) may be adduced if he refuses to accept the truth of the allegations made against him (16.5.4 *post*). However, if the prosecution or a co-accused were entitled to cross-examine *the accused* on his bad character as of right, there would be a real danger that he would not get the fair trial to which he is entitled at common law (even if the trial would be regarded as fair by the European Court of Human Rights). This would have the knock-on effect of deterring accused persons from testifying in their own defence. The accused has therefore been given a degree of protection – a 'shield' – from cross-examination on his bad character which he will lose only in certain circumstances. Both the shield itself, and the circumstances in which he runs the risk of losing it, are set out in s. 1 of the 1898 Act.

If the accused does not testify there is of course no possibility of his being cross-examined as to credit, and the admissibility of his bad character is governed by the common law (3.3–4 *ante*). If, however, the accused gives evidence in chief which results in the loss of his shield, but he then refuses to allow himself to be cross-examined, the prosecution may still adduce evidence of his bad character to undermine his credibility (*R* v. *Forbes* [1999] 2 Cr App R 501 (CA)).

4.1 The Compromise

There was, until the mid-nineteenth century, a general prohibition on interested parties being able to give sworn evidence, whether in civil or criminal proceedings, and although a number of statutes prior to 1898 allowed the accused to testify in his own defence in certain situations, it was not until s. 1 of the Criminal Evidence Act 1898 Act came into force that this right (now found in s. 53(1) of the Youth Justice and Criminal Evidence Act 1999) was extended to cover all criminal proceedings.

With Parliament's decision to allow the accused to testify in his own defence, it was necessary to address the issue of his being cross-examined. In 1898 witnesses could already be cross-examined as to their credit on, for example, their previous convictions and if they denied having any such convictions, evidence to the contrary could be proved in rebuttal (16.5.4.1 *post*). But other witnesses are in a different league from the accused. If a witness (who is not a party) has his bad character elicited in cross-examination the personal consequences for him are generally bearable. It is the party relying on the witness who suffers so far as the trial is concerned. The situation is very different for the accused – if his previous misconduct is raised in cross-examination there is a real danger that he and his defence will be unduly prejudiced. To bring out the accused's previous convictions in cross-examination is likely to create in the minds of the jurors or magistrates not only a feeling that he is less credible as a witness but also a degree of moral and/or reasoning prejudice against him, with the real possibility that he will be judged not so much on the admissible evidence but on his doubtful moral standing (see 3.3.2 *ante*). Accordingly, Parliament had to introduce special measures to ensure that any accused who took advantage of his right to testify would receive a fair trial, for otherwise no accused with any sizeable record would give evidence in his own defence. However, to have given the accused absolute immunity from cross-examination on his character would have been unfair to the prosecution and any co-accused. Evidence considered relevant to his credibility as a witness would have been kept from the jury, and yet he would have retained his own right to cross-examine the witnesses called by any co-accused or the prosecution on their previous convictions.

To overcome these problems Parliament effected a compromise by including in s. 1 of the Act two important provisions governing the cross-examination of the accused. The first (formerly s. 1(*e*), now s. 1(2)) exposes the accused to cross-examination on his alleged involvement in the offence charged, removing his common-law privilege against self-incrimination in respect of that offence (*Maxwell* v. *DPP* [1935] AC 309 (HL) at p. 318). The second (formerly s. 1(*f*), now s. 1(3)) gives the accused a degree of protection (his 'shield') from cross-examination on his bad character. But s. 1(3) is qualified by three exceptions which allow the accused's shield to be lost in certain circumstances. Sections 1(*e*) and 1(*f*) became ss. 1(2) and 1(3) respectively with effect from 24 July 2002 by virtue of Schedule 4 to the Youth Justice and Criminal Evidence Act 1999 (and SI 2002 No. 1739).

Section 1 of the Criminal Evidence Act 1898 now provides as follows:

(2) A person charged in criminal proceedings who is called as a witness in the proceedings may be asked any question in cross-examination notwithstanding that it would tend to criminate him as to any offence with which he is charged in the proceedings.

(3) A person charged in criminal proceedings who is called as a witness in the proceedings shall not be asked, and if asked shall not be required to answer, any question tending to show that he has committed or been convicted of or been charged with any offence other than one with which he is then charged, or is of bad character, unless –

  (i) the proof that he has committed or been convicted of such other offence is admissible evidence to show that he is guilty of an offence with which he is then charged; or

  (ii) he has personally or by his advocate asked questions of the witnesses for the prosecution with a view to establish his own good character, or has given evidence of his good character, or the nature or conduct of the defence is such as to involve imputations on the character of the prosecutor or the witnesses for the prosecution or the deceased victim of the alleged crime; or

  (iii) he has given evidence against any other person charged in the same proceedings.

In s. 1(3) the term 'character' has a broader meaning than at common law (*R* v. *Dunkley* [1927] 1 KB 323 (CCA) at p. 329; see also *Stirland* v. *DPP* [1944] AC 315 (HL) at p. 325 and *Selvey* v. *DPP* [1968] 2 WLR 1494 (HL) at p. 1514; *cf. Jones* v. *DPP* [1962] 2 WLR 575 (HL) at p. 623). If the accused's bad character can be revealed by virtue of one of the exceptions, for example because he claims to be of good character, the prosecution and/or co-accused need not limit their cross-examination to evidence of his bad reputation. Evidence of specific incidents (such as previous convictions) may be revealed. Similarly, the accused may put his good character in issue for the purposes of the first limb of s. 1(3)(ii) by referring to his own specific meritorious acts (as, for example, in *R* v. *Samuel* (1956) 40 Cr App R 8 (CCA)) and may be cross-examined under the second limb of s. 1(3)(ii) on his bad character if he casts specific imputations on the character of a prosecution witness. This approach was reaffirmed by the Court of Appeal in *R* v. *Carter* (1996) 161 JP 207 where it was held that 'bad character' in s. 1(3) encompasses not only the accused's criminal record but also reputation and disposition, and that cross-examination on the accused's discreditable behaviour in relation to a civil claim fell within the scope of the subsection. This broad interpretation makes sense. If character were limited to general reputation the accused would find it difficult to give evidence of his own good character, whereas s. 1(3)(ii) recognises his right to do so; and if 'imputations' covered nothing other than allegations of bad reputation, the accused would be able to maintain his shield even after alleging that prosecution witnesses had committed serious acts of misconduct.

The two subsections apply to any accused who gives evidence, even if he does not give evidence in support of his own defence but merely supports a co-accused (*R* v. *Rowland* (1909) 3 Cr App R 277 (CCA)). The phrase 'charged with any offence' in s. 1(3) has been interpreted to mean 'accused before a court' (*Stirland* v. *DPP* [1944] AC 315 (HL) at p. 323). But, though it is not necessary for there to have been a conviction, an acquittal must satisfy the paramount test of relevance to justify its being raised in cross-examination. In *Maxwell* v. *DPP* [1935] AC 309 the accused was alleged to have unlawfully killed a woman upon whom it was said he had performed an illegal abortion. He gave evidence of his good character and the prosecution cross-examined him pursuant to s. 1(3)(ii) of the Act on his previous acquittal following a similar charge. The House of Lords held that this charge should not have been raised as the mere fact that he had been acquitted of an offence was relevant neither to any issue at the trial nor to the accused's credibility as a witness. This does not mean that an acquittal will always be irrelevant, however, for otherwise the inclusion of 'charged with any offence' in s. 1(3) would be otiose. In *Maxwell* v. *DPP* Viscount Sankey LC gave the example of the accused having given evidence at an earlier trial, following which he was acquitted, which contradicts the evidence given by him during the subsequent trial. Cross-examination on the inconsistencies would be relevant to his credibility at the later trial. Conversely, the accused's credibility may be undermined by his having advanced the same or a similar defence on another occasion. In *R* v. *Williamson* [2003] EWCA Crim 544, a trial for possession of cannabis with intent to supply, the co-accused was permitted to cross-examine the accused under s. 1(3)(iii) in respect of a similar charge of possession with intent for which a prosecution was *pending*. The accused's defence in the instant case and the defence disclosed in the other case were similar, insofar as they each comprised a claim that the drugs had come into the accused's immediate vicinity without his being aware of the fact, and this was relevant to his credibility. Furthermore, where evidence of other alleged criminal conduct has been given against the accused at earlier trials (for that conduct) but the trials resulted in his being acquitted, and that evidence is nonetheless sufficiently probative to be admitted in the instant trial as similar fact evidence of his guilt on the basis that he *did* commit those other offences (*R* v. *Z* [2000] 3 WLR 117 (HL), 3.3.6 *ante*), it should be possible for the evidence of the allegations to be elicited in cross-examination under an exception to s. 1(3) if it has not already been adduced.

4.2 The Relationship Between Subsections (2) and (3)

The meaning of and relationship between the two subsections have been described as a 'nightmare of construction' (*R* v. *Anderson* [1988] 2 WLR 1017 (CA) at p. 1023). Subsection (2) permits 'any question' notwithstanding that it would tend to criminate the accused as to any offence with which he is charged. Subsection (3) prohibits 'any question' tending to show that the accused has committed or been convicted of or been charged with any other offence or is of bad character. And yet questions prohibited by subsection (3) will often tend to criminate the accused as to the offence charged and therefore seem to be permitted by subsection (2). Moreover, subsection (3) is qualified by exception (i) which permits questions otherwise prohibited if proof that the accused has committed or been convicted of the other offence is 'admissible evidence to show that he is guilty of an offence with which he is then charged'.

In short, subsection (3) sets out the general prohibition on questions which might be called 'indirectly incriminating', that is questions on *extraneous* matters which suggest that the accused is of bad character. As a general rule no question may be asked about the accused's bad character whether such evidence be directly relevant to the question of guilt (that is, similar fact evidence) or indirectly relevant to his guilt (that is, evidence suggesting that his testimony ought not to be believed). Subsection (2) allows questions which might be called 'directly incriminating', that is any questions which are logically relevant to an issue or the accused's credibility as a witness other than questions which suggest the accused is guilty or lacking in credibility on account of his bad character. The prohibition in subsection (3) is subject to three important exceptions. Exception (i) allows questions relating to other offences the accused has committed to prove he is guilty of the offence charged. Such questions might be described as 'indirectly incriminating', as they relate to other offences, but the evidence thereby elicited is directly relevant to whether or not the accused is guilty as charged. This is because the exception covers offences committed by the accused which are admissible as similar fact evidence at common law (or pursuant to a statutory provision) to prove the accused's *guilt* (see 3.3 *ante*). Exceptions (ii) and (iii) also allow 'indirectly incriminating' questions to be asked in certain circumstances, but only for the limited purpose of undermining the accused's *credibility*. Thus, unlike similar fact evidence, bad-character evidence elicited under these two exceptions is only indirectly relevant to whether the accused is guilty.

Some questions may be aimed at eliciting evidence which is directly relevant to an issue in the proceedings while giving rise to an *incidental* reference to the accused's bad character. The problem the courts have had to grapple with is whether such questions may be asked under subsection (2), notwithstanding the prohibition in subsection (3). This depends on which subsection is paramount.

If subsection (3) is paramount no question which suggests previous misconduct or immorality may be asked unless an exception applies. This *exclusionary* interpretation would have the effect of preventing key questions from being asked on matters which are directly relevant to an issue if, incidentally, such questions would also reveal a bad-character trait. For example, if the accused is on trial for handling stolen goods and his defence is that he did not know or believe the goods were stolen, the exclusionary interpretation would prevent the prosecution from being able to question him on his close friendship with the notorious burglar from whom he bought the goods (see Cross, 'The Criminal Evidence Act 1898' (1962) 78 LQR 407 at p. 411). Although the questions would be directly relevant to the issue of *mens rea*, they would incidentally suggest that the accused has criminal associations and is therefore of bad character. Similarly, if the accused raises an alibi which is exactly the same as the alibi he raised at a previous trial, it would not be possible for the prosecution to cross-examine him on the previous alibi as it would fall foul of subsection (3), even though the questions would be directly relevant to an issue, that is the truth or falsity of the accused's defence. If subsection (2) is paramount then any question which is directly relevant to an issue may be asked even if it would incidentally suggest previous misconduct or immorality. This *inclusionary* interpretation would broaden the scope of permissible questioning under subsection (2) and narrow the scope of the prohibition in subsection (3). The alleged handler could then be cross-examined on his close friendship with the miscreant from whom he bought the stolen goods; and the accused who has relied on a similar alibi at an earlier trial could be cross-examined on those similarities. The practical effect of this interpretation would be to render any question permissible so long as it was relevant to an issue in the proceedings; and subsection (3) would be limited to excluding questions on the accused's bad character which are relevant to nothing other than the collateral question of his credibility. The problem with the inclusionary interpretation is that it would render exception (i) otiose. Admissible similar fact evidence is directly relevant to an issue and not just credibility. If questions on such evidence were permissible under subsection (2) there would be no need for exception (i). For this reason the exclusionary interpretation, whereby subsection (2) is subservient to subsection (3), must be the correct approach, although this was not the interpretation originally adopted.

In *R* v. *Chitson* [1909] 2 KB 945 the accused was charged with having had unlawful intercourse with a 14-year-old girl, K. K gave evidence for the prosecution and said that shortly after their act of intercourse the accused told her he had previously done the same thing with another girl, H. The prosecution were allowed to cross-examine the accused on whether he had made that statement to K and whether he had actually had an immoral relationship with H, who the prosecution suggested had been under the age of 16 at the time. The accused replied that H had been over 16. Clearly the cross-examination suggested that the accused was of bad character (that is, sexually immoral) and also that he might have committed a criminal offence with H; but the questions were relevant to an issue because his answers corroborated K's testimony that it was the accused who had been sexually involved with her. The Court of Criminal Appeal adopted an inclusionary interpretation of the exceptions and held that the questions had been properly put notwithstanding the incidental suggestion of bad character. The Court did not explain whether the questioning had been permissible under s. 1(2) or 1(3)(i) – the head-note states s. 1(3)(i) – but since no evidence was adduced to prove that H had been under 16 at the time of her involvement with the accused s. 1(3)(i) could not have been relevant and it must be seen as a decision under s. 1(2). An exclusionary interpretation of the exceptions would have prevented the accused from being asked the questions about the statement to K and his relationship with H as the s. 1(3) prohibition would have overridden s. 1(2) (see also *R* v. *Kennaway* [1917] 1 KB 25 (CCA)). In *R* v. *Kurasch* [1915] 2 KB 749 the accused and four other co-accused were charged with conspiring to defraud (by holding a mock auction) and the accused testified that he was merely the employee of a Mrs D who controlled the auction business. An exclusionary interpretation of the exceptions would have prevented the prosecution from cross-examining the accused on the fact that he and Mrs D were cohabiting as man and wife because of the necessary implication of immorality, even though the questions on their relationship would have been relevant to the question whether his defence was true. Again the Court of Criminal Appeal held that the questions had been properly put, suggesting an inclusionary interpretation.

The meaning of the two subsections and the relationship between them was addressed by the House of Lords in *Jones* v. *DPP* [1962] 2 WLR 575. J was charged with the murder of a girl guide and at his trial he explained that he had given a false alibi to the police as he had been 'in trouble' before. His true alibi, he said, was that he had been with a prostitute, and he gave evidence that his wife had reacted stormily to his late return home and that they had had conversations about a report of the girl's disappearance in their newspaper. The prosecution sought leave to cross-examine him on his testimony in a trial a year earlier (for the rape of a different girl guide, which had occurred a month before the murder) during which he had raised a strikingly similar defence. The prosecution submitted that the fact J had raised an identical defence on two occasions would reveal to the jury how unlikely it was that he was telling the truth in the present case. The judge allowed the cross-examination and, though no mention was made of the nature of the earlier offence or his conviction, other than references to his 'explanation' on 'another occasion' relating to an 'incident' which had been reported in their newspaper, J was convicted. He appealed on the ground that he had done nothing to lose his s. 1(3) shield and yet had been asked questions 'tending to show that he has committed or been convicted of or been charged with any offence'.

The question the House of Lords had to answer was whether it had been permissible for the prosecution to question J on his earlier explanation when that cross-examination had certainly implied he had been charged with another offence. The majority (Lords Simonds, Reid and Morris) felt that the questioning would not have been possible under s. 1(2) if s. 1(3) had applied. However, the words 'tending to show' in s. 1(3) had to be interpreted to mean 'tending to reveal' to the jury *for the first time*, and as J had already mentioned he had been 'in trouble' s. 1(3) could no longer prevent the prosecution's questions. This was so even though the questions went beyond the vague admission J had made. The majority view amounted to an *exclusionary* interpretation of the exceptions: s. 1(2) sets out the questions which the accused may be asked, but this is *subject to* s. 1(3) which sets out the questions the accused may never be asked unless one of its exceptions applies. The majority accepted that s. 1(2) could be interpreted in two ways: a broad (inclusionary) interpretation would allow any question tending to persuade the jury of the accused's guilt, but this would result in a conflict between the two subsections; a narrower (exclusionary) interpretation would restrict the class of questions to those which did nothing other than directly connect the accused with the commission of the offence charged (questions 'directly relevant to the charge') and avoid any such conflict. The majority approved the interpretation of Viscount Sankey LC in *Maxwell v. DPP* [1935] AC 309 (HL) (at p. 319) that s. 1(3) was 'universal and absolute' unless one of its exceptions applied. In the words of Lord Morris (at p. 608):

> 'All questions put to witnesses must satisfy the test of relevance and this applies to questions put in cross-examination to an accused. If, however, questions are proposed which can be regarded as relevant, but which tend to show that he has committed or been convicted of or has been charged with some offence other than that wherewith he is then charged or is of bad character, such questions can only be put and can only be allowed if they qualify within the permitting provisions of [s. 1(3)] ... This means that even if the questions are relevant and have to do with the issue before the court they cannot be asked unless covered by the permitting provisions of [s. 1(3)].'

It was fortunate for the prosecution that J had mentioned he had been 'in trouble' before, for otherwise he would have been immune to cross-examination on his previous explanation despite its direct relevance to the issue of his defence and the murderer's identity. Lord Reid explained that *R v. Chitson* [1909] 2 KB 945 (CCA) (and *R v. Kennaway* [1917] 1 KB 25 (CCA)) had been correctly decided but for the wrong reasons: the cross-examination in those cases could be justified on the ground that the accused's misconduct had already been revealed to the jury.

The minority (Lords Denning and Devlin) adopted an inclusionary interpretation: the questions had been properly allowed under s. 1(2) which, it was felt, permitted any questions which were 'directly relevant to the offence charged' or 'relevant to the issue' even if such questions *incidentally* showed the accused had been charged with another offence. J had given a detailed alibi and it was of direct relevance for the prosecution to have shown his explanation was false and that he could be identified as the murderer.

By virtue of the majority view, so long as the s. 1(3) prohibition remains in place no question may be asked which would 'indirectly incriminate' the accused unless an exception applies. Only 'directly incriminating' questions may be asked under s. 1(2). This means that questions which are directly relevant to an issue cannot be asked if they would incidentally suggest misbehaviour by the accused on another occasion. If the s. 1(3) prohibition disappears then (subject to any other prohibition) any question may be asked whether it is 'directly incriminating' or 'indirectly incriminating'.

The accused benefits from the House of Lords' interpretation as s. 1(3) absolutely prohibits any cross-examination which would tend to show the accused's bad character unless one of the exceptions is triggered. In practice, however, the strength of the accused's protective shield has been significantly undermined by the majority view that s. 1(3) ceases to have any role to play if the accused's character has been revealed to the jury before his cross-examination. Indeed, the facts of *Jones* v. *DPP* [1962] 2 WLR 575 (HL) and Lord Reid's interpretation of *R* v. *Chitson* [1909] 2 KB 945 (CCA) suggest that any mention that the accused has been in trouble previously, even if made by a prosecution witness, could lose him his shield. In *R* v. *Anderson* [1988] 2 WLR 1017 the accused, a member of the IRA, was charged with conspiring to cause explosions in southern England. Her 'ambush' defence was that her role as a member of the IRA had been limited to acting as an escort to help escaped prisoners make their way to continental Europe, and that the incriminating articles found in her possession had been to assist her in that lesser conspiracy. The prosecution were permitted to cross-examine her on the fact that she was 'wanted' by the police in Northern Ireland and that she would therefore not have been given such an overt role by the IRA or wish to have accepted it. The Court of Appeal held that because she had already revealed her involvement in criminal activities with the IRA when giving her evidence in chief s. 1(3) no longer applied, and the prosecution had been able to cross-examine her on the fact that she was 'wanted' in Northern Ireland. It would therefore seem that the accused's s. 1(3) shield will be lost in respect of any other misconduct if its prejudicial effect would be no greater than the misconduct which has already been revealed.

4.3 Exception (i)

Under the first exception to s. 1(3) the accused may be cross-examined on other offences he has *committed* or *been convicted of* where such offences amount to 'admissible evidence to show that he is guilty of an offence with which he is then charged'. This exception covers evidence of other offences admissible at common law or pursuant to a statutory provision to prove the accused's guilt of the instant charge. The most obvious example is similar fact evidence of the accused's earlier offences. It is important to note, however, that while the exception permits cross-examination only on offences the accused has 'committed or been convicted of', if the prosecution are permitted to adduce in chief (that is, as part of their case) similar fact evidence of a different kind, such as disreputable behaviour not amounting to an offence, the evidence will already have been revealed to the jury before the accused faces cross-examination, and, by virtue of the decision of the House of Lords in *Jones* v. *DPP* [1962] 2 WLR 575 (4.2 *ante*), s. 1(3) will not provide the accused with any protection against cross-examination on it.

In the light of *R* v. *Z* [2000] 3 WLR 117 (HL) (3.3.6 *ante*) it is apparent that the accused may be cross-examined on admissible similar fact evidence which suggests that he 'committed' other offences even if he has already been acquitted of them, whether or not the evidence has already been adduced by the prosecution as part of their case. However, evidence of an acquittal which is insufficiently probative to be adduced in chief at common law, and which is not relied on in the instant trial on the basis that the accused was in fact guilty of the offence he was acquitted of, cannot be elicited under this exception. In *R* v. *Cokar* [1960] 2 WLR 836 the accused's defence to a charge of burglary was that he had merely entered the house for warmth and shelter. The prosecution were allowed to cross-examine him on his acquittal following a similar charge, not on the basis that he was guilty of that offence but to show that he had become aware that he could not be found guilty in such circumstances. The Court of Criminal Appeal quashed the conviction as s. 1(3) amounted to an absolute prohibition on questions about the accused's previous charges, and exception (i) did not apply (see also *R* v. *Pommell* [1999] Crim LR 576 (CA)).

4.4 Exception (ii) – The First Limb

The first limb of exception (ii) allows the prosecution – and possibly a co-accused (*Murdoch* v. *Taylor* [1965] 2 WLR 425 (HL) at p. 437) – to cross-examine the accused on his bad character in response to a defence assertion of good character. The accused may wish to adduce evidence of his good character as evidence that he is unlikely to have committed the offence charged and that he is more worthy of belief (3.4.2 *ante*), so it is quite logical that the prosecution should be permitted to cross-examine the accused to show the falsity of his assertion and that he is willing to mislead the court.

A literal interpretation of the first limb would suggest that the prosecution's right to cross-examine the accused on his bad character can arise only if the accused's good character has been put in issue in one of the specified ways ('personally or by his advocate asked questions of the witnesses for the prosecution with a view to establish his own good character, or has given evidence of his good character'), that is, that the accused's shield is not lost if he calls a witness to testify as to his good character. It has been held, however, that even if it is not the accused himself who gives evidence of his good character he may still lose his shield and face cross-examination on his bad character (*R* v. *Ellis* [1910] 2 KB 746 (CCA), *R* v. *Waldman* (1934) 24 Cr App R 204 (CCA), *R* v. *Winfield* [1939] 4 All ER 164 (CCA)). That said, if a witness is called for a reason unconnected with giving good-character evidence and he *volunteers* such evidence without the accused's authority, the shield will not be lost (*R* v. *Redd* [1923] 1 KB 104 (CCA)). *R* v. *Winfield* [1939] 4 All ER 164 reports that the accused, on trial for indecently assaulting a woman, was cross-examined on his convictions for dishonesty offences, even though it was his good-character witness who had given evidence of his sexual morality. This case is therefore authority for the indivisibility of the accused's character should he face cross-examination under exception (ii) (see also *Stirland* v. *DPP* [1944] AC 315 (HL) at p. 326 and *R* v. *Buzalek* [1991] Crim LR 116 (CA)).

In *R* v. *Ellis* [1910] 2 KB 746 (at pp. 762–3) the Court of Criminal Appeal addressed the policy behind the first limb of the exception in the following terms:

'It was intended to apply to cases where witnesses to character were called, or where evidence of the good character of the prisoner was sought to be elicited from the witnesses for the prosecution. In civil actions evidence of good character is not, as a rule, admissible. It is admissible in criminal cases, and it is to this class of evidence that the statute refers, not to mere assertions of innocence or repudiation of guilt on the part of the prisoner, nor to reasons given by him for such assertion or repudiation.'

Importantly, then, the accused will not trigger exception (ii) if he gives evidence on matters relating to the offence charged which incidentally casts him in a good light. Thus in *Malindi* v. *R* [1966] 3 WLR 913 (PC) it was held that the accused, on trial for conspiring to commit arson at a meeting in 1962, had not put his good character in issue by testifying that the meeting had broken up because he had expressed his disapproval of violence.

In other situations the case-law demonstrates that the accused runs the risk of losing his shield even if the assertions of good character are relatively commonplace. Moreover, it is not necessary for the good-character evidence to be evidence of general reputation for the accused to lose his shield. In other words, the courts have focused on whether it was right to have allowed the prosecution to cross-examine the accused under exception (ii) following an assertion of good character, regardless of whether his evidence of good character was technically admissible (in accordance with the decision in *R* v. *Redgrave* (1981) 74 Cr App R 10 (CA), 3.4.1 *ante*).

It is important to bear in mind that 'good character' is very much a question of degree, and the judge's ruling will in practice depend as much on the factual context of the case as on the nature of the assertion made (see *R* v. *Parker* (1924) 18 Cr App R 14 (CCA) at p. 17). In *R* v. *Coulman* (1927) 20 Cr App R 106 (CCA), for example, it was felt that the accused, charged with indecently assaulting boys, could have put his good character in issue merely by stating that he was married with a family; and in *R* v. *Baker* (1912) 7 Cr App R 252 (CCA) an assertion by the accused that he had been 'earning an honest living' for several years was enough to lose him his shield when charged with possessing a mould for counterfeiting coins. More recently, in *R* v. *Davison-Jenkins* [1997] Crim LR 816 (CA) the accused, who was charged with shoplifting, lost her shield by testifying as to her job as a manageress, her university education and to her having a wealthy partner (see also *R* v. *Powell* [1985] 1 WLR 1364 (CA)). An accused charged with an offence of dishonesty can expect to lose his shield if he gives evidence of specific incidents of honest conduct in the past (*R* v. *Samuel* (1956) 40 Cr App R 8 (CCA)); and claiming to be a practising Catholic for many years would be an assertion of good character if charged with stealing from a Catholic church (*R* v. *Ferguson* (1909) 2 Cr App R 250 (CCA)). Similarly, a purported reluctance to drive at high speeds when charged with high-speed motor manslaughter could amount to an assertion of good character (*R* v. *Beecham* [1921] 3 KB 464 (CCA)). The accused will also put his good character in issue by stating he has no previous convictions. This happened in *R* v. *Marsh* [1994] Crim LR 52 (CA) where the prosecution were allowed to cross-examine the accused on his disciplinary record of violent play on the rugby field.

A line has to be drawn somewhere, however, for otherwise the mere wearing of a smart suit for the trial, or the assertion of being employed, could be construed as an implied assertion of good character. In *R* v. *Stronach* [1988] Crim LR 48 (CA) it was accepted, in the factual context of the case, that evidence of the accused's employment with London Transport and his being married was insufficient to trigger the exception (although in reality this seems to have been a *Malindi*-type situation); and the mere wearing of a regimental blazer was held not to be an assertion of good character in *R* v. *Hamilton* [1969] Crim LR 486 (CA). In *R* v. *Robinson* [2001] Crim LR 478 the Court of Appeal held that holding or waving a small Bible while giving evidence could not amount to an implied assertion of good character. As the accused does not suggest he is of good character (for the purposes of the exception) by taking the oath, he cannot put his character in issue by reminding the jury of that fact or by waving a Bible during the course of his testimony.

If the accused has mentioned only one of his several previous convictions – for example, to explain his conduct at the scene of the crime, such as running away when spotted by a police officer – he will not have asserted his good character unless he has also expressly or impliedly understated his criminal record and thereby represented that his character is better than it really is (*R* v. *Thompson* (1965) 50 Cr App R 91 (CCA); see also *R* v. *Mauricia* [2002] 2 Cr App R 377 (CA)). Nor is it generally an assertion of good character to attack the character of another person (*R* v. *Lee* [1976] 1 WLR 71 (CA)).

If it is ruled that the accused has adduced evidence of his good character, the judge retains a discretion as to whether the prosecution should be allowed to cross-examine him on his bad character (*R* v. *Thompson* (1965) 50 Cr App R 91 (CCA)); but if such cross-examination is permitted the questions must relate to actual bad character as opposed to mere suspicion of bad character. In other words, the questions must satisfy the general requirement of relevance. In *Maxwell* v. *DPP* [1935] AC 309 the accused gave evidence that he had 'lived a good, clean, moral life' and thereby lost his shield, but the House of Lords held that his acquittal following an earlier trial should not have been raised by the prosecution. It had been a mere 'misfortune' which was of no relevance to his credibility. *Maxwell* v. *DPP* was distinguished in *R* v. *Waldman* (1934) 24 Cr App R

204, however. The accused in that case, on trial for receiving stolen goods, called a witness to testify that he bore 'a good reputation for honesty'. The prosecution subsequently recalled the accused and cross-examined him on his prior conviction and acquittal for receiving, having already cross-examined the good-character witness on the same matters. The Court of Criminal Appeal felt that a charge of receiving could justify cross-examination on a previous acquittal for the same offence by analogy with what is now s. 27(3) of the Theft Act 1968 (3.3.12 *ante*).

Because evidence of good character is relevant both to law-abiding propensity and to credibility, evidence of bad character raised in rebuttal pursuant to the first limb of exception (ii) might logically be regarded as relevant in the same ways on the ground that such questions are asked 'to show the contrary' (*Maxwell* v. *DPP* [1935] AC 309 (HL) at p. 319). It might be argued, moreover, that there would be no injustice in adducing bad-character evidence for this purpose (insofar as the evidence is in fact logically probative of the accused's guilt and the jury are properly directed) if the accused has deliberately sought to deceive the court by adducing false evidence of law-abiding propensity. However, because it is thought to be undesirable in principle to admit the accused's bad character for the purpose of proving guilt unless it is sufficiently probative to be admissible as similar fact evidence, the courts have recognised on several occasions that bad-character evidence brought out under the first limb of s. 1(3)(ii) is to be considered relevant only to the accused's credibility (see, for example, *R* v. *Richardson* [1968] 3 WLR 15 (CA)). The courts have also recognised, however, that this distinction is likely to be lost on a jury. In *R* v. *Samuel* (1956) 40 Cr App R 8 (CCA) the accused was tried for the theft of a camera he said he had found. He gave evidence of handing in lost property on previous occasions to show he would eventually have got round to handing the camera in, and this caused him to lose his shield. Lord Goddard CJ said (at p. 12):

'It is very difficult to see how if it is permissible to cross-examine a prisoner with regard to convictions, for instance, if he is a thief and he is cross-examined on previous convictions of larceny, the jury is not, in effect, being asked to say: "The prisoner is just the sort of man who will commit these crimes and therefore it is highly probable he did." In theory, at any rate, what the jury is being asked to do is to reject the prisoner's evidence when he says: "I acted honestly in this case ... I always intended to hand back that camera to the police when I had a reasonable opportunity." By putting these questions to him the prosecution were in fact trying to destroy his credibility ...'

In practice, because good-character evidence goes to propensity, there may be a greater willingness to admit evidence which is suggestive of a bad propensity under this limb than under the second limb of the exception. In *R* v. *Marsh* [1994] Crim LR 52 it was felt that the accused's record of violent conduct during rugby matches could have been raised against him on a charge of inflicting grievous bodily harm on another rugby player during a match, even though it would have suggested a violent disposition.

Interestingly, the Court of Appeal accepted that the evidence might not have been admissible if the second limb rather than the first limb had been triggered.

If the accused loses his shield, and faces cross-examination under this limb, the prosecution may bring out his convictions whether they are for offences committed before or after the offence for which he is on trial (*R* v. *Wood* [1920] 2 KB 179 (CCA)).

4.5 Exception (ii) – The Second Limb

The second limb of exception (ii) allows the accused to be cross-examined on his bad character by the prosecution – and possibly by a co-accused (*Murdoch* v. *Taylor* [1965] 2 WLR 425 (HL) at p. 437; *R* v. *Lovett* [1973] 1 WLR 241 (CA) at p. 245) – if the 'nature or conduct of the defence' is such as to involve imputations on the character of the prosecutor, a witness for the prosecution or the deceased victim of the alleged crime. If the prosecution adduce a witness statement under an exception to the hearsay rule, the maker of that statement is deemed to be a prosecution witness for the purposes of this limb (*R* v. *Miller* [1997] 2 Cr App R 178 (CA)). The accused may be able to avoid losing his shield if the imputations were made in reply to prosecution questions, so as not to have been part of 'the nature or conduct of the defence' (*R* v. *Jones* (1910) 3 Cr App R 67 (CCA)). This is not an absolute rule, however, for there are cases where the exception was triggered by imputations made by the accused during cross-examination (for example *R* v. *Rappolt* (1911) 6 Cr App R 156 (CCA) and *R* v. *Stone* [2001] EWCA Crim 2379). In *R* v. *Bartholomew* [2002] EWCA Crim 1312 the Court of Appeal accepted that the accused could say something in the course of his being cross-examined which might trigger the exception, but went on to state that, as a general rule, the trial judge should warn the accused of the consequences of his making an imputation against a prosecution witness.

Bad-character evidence brought out pursuant to the second limb is relevant to the accused's credibility but not his guilt (*R* v. *Inder* (1977) 67 Cr App R 143 (CA), *R* v. *McLeod* [1995] 1 Cr App R 591 (CA), *R* v. *Barratt* [2000] Crim LR 847 (CA)). For this reason, it has been held that if the bad-character evidence includes previous convictions the prosecution should limit their questioning to the bare facts of the offences and not bring out any specific details (*R* v. *Khan* [1991] Crim LR 51 (CA)). More recently, however, the Court of Appeal has accepted that it may be permissible to bring out further details of the offences to demonstrate that a similar defence was raised by the accused and disbelieved on a previous occasion, even if a collateral effect of such questioning would be to suggest propensity, so long as the prosecution do not go 'too far' (*R* v. *Barsoum* [1994] Crim LR 194, *R* v. *McLeod* [1995] 1 Cr App R 591). The prosecution may bring out convictions for offences committed before or after the offence for which the accused is on trial (*R* v. *Coltress* (1978) 68 Cr App R 193 (CA)).

The second limb, based on the retaliatory policy of 'tit for tat', prevents the accused from being able to undermine the credibility of prosecution witnesses without having his own credibility as a witness, or the credibility of his defence, brought into question. If the accused is going to impugn the credibility of those who testify against him:

> 'it is only fair that the jury should have before them material on which they can form their judgment whether the accused person is any more worthy to be believed than those he has attacked. It is obviously unfair that the jury should be left in the dark about an accused person's character if the conduct of his defence has attacked the character of ... the witnesses for the prosecution ...' (*R* v. *Jenkins* (1945) 31 Cr App R 1 (CCA) at p. 15)

One justification for the second limb is the desirability of equipping the jury (or magistrates) with information which would help them to compare the veracity and therefore testimony of opposing witnesses, but this cannot be the sole rationale. The accused's bad character may now be revealed if he attacks the character of a deceased victim who is not the author of any testimonial evidence. In such cases there is no need for any comparison of conflicting testimony. The essence of the second limb, much like the first limb, is to ensure that the tribunal of fact is not misled by the accused's tactics. If the accused tries to tilt the balance of the proceedings in his own favour by raising character, it is essential that the balance should be restored if the tribunal of fact would otherwise be misled. It would be repugnant to common sense to allow an accused with numerous previous convictions to make imputations against prosecution witnesses for the purpose of showing them to be morally bankrupt, and therefore less worthy of belief, if at the same time he would be completely immune to a similar attack by the prosecution. The tribunal of fact would be left with a poorer image of the prosecution witnesses and have no reason to doubt the veracity of the accused. The same must be true if the accused has killed the deceased, raised self-defence, and attacked the violent character of the deceased as a way of supporting his version of events. If the accused also has a history of violent conduct his defence is likely to be less credible, so his bad character should be revealed to the jury to help them come to the correct decision at the end of the trial.

As with the first limb, the accused's character is indivisible. The accused may bring out any immoral conduct of prosecution witnesses to show that their general moral character (their 'moral credibility') is such that no conviction should be based on their evidence. Similarly, the prosecution may adduce any evidence of the accused's immorality to show that he (and his defence) ought not to be believed. The rationale is that one who is generally immoral is less likely to be truthful in court, and for this reason the evidence of bad character need not be evidence of past dishonesty. Some types of past misconduct will of course be far more disprobative of truthfulness than others. In the self-defence example, the fact the accused has a violent disposition or convictions for perjury would make his testimony and defence less credible than convictions for drink-driving or theft. The problem is that where bad-character evidence is highly disprobative of truthfulness, and therefore indirectly probative of guilt, the tribunal of fact may mistakenly regard it as evidence of propensity directly suggesting guilt and end up convicting on an erroneous basis.

One further justification for the second limb is that it acts as a deterrent, preventing gratuitous attacks on the character of prosecution witnesses. If there were no inhibitory rule prospective witnesses might be reluctant to come forward as there would be little to stop the accused from casting aspersions on their character. This justification is undermined, however, by the fact that the accused can refuse to testify and instruct his counsel to make any such imputations on his behalf (*R* v. *Butterwasser* [1948] 1 KB 4 (CCA), 3.4.5 *ante*).

Although there is something to be said for the tit-for-tat rule, its application will often be far from fair in practice. First, the undue prejudice which is likely to result from the accused's misconduct being revealed will in many cases outweigh any damage caused to the prosecution case by the accused's imputations. The accused is on trial; the prosecution witnesses are not. Although the jury will be told that the accused's bad character is relevant only to his credibility, there will always be a risk of moral prejudice, and a high risk of reasoning prejudice whenever his past misconduct is similar to the charge he now faces (see 3.3.2 *ante*). Second, the accused will often have no choice but to cast imputations on prosecution witnesses as part of his defence, and yet a literal reading of the second limb of the exception means he may still lose his shield despite the necessity of adopting such tactics. It will be seen below that the literal interpretation has indeed been accepted as the correct approach. Even if the accused alleges that evidence against him has been fabricated, or he simply brings out a prosecution witness's conviction for perjury, he faces the prospect of having all his own misconduct revealed; and as there is no rule which obliges the prosecution to reveal their own witnesses' convictions during the trial (*R* v. *Carey* (1968) 52 Cr App R 305 (CA)) the accused's advocate may have no choice but to elicit their convictions during cross-examination. Third, although defence counsel has to tread carefully to ensure that the accused's shield is not lost, there is no such deterrent influencing the prosecution. The prosecution are free to attack the character of defence witnesses safe in the knowledge that if the defence retaliates in kind the accused will run the risk of losing his shield. The consequence is that prosecution witnesses may be left appearing entirely credible even though the accused's witnesses have been thoroughly discredited. Fourth, the second limb encourages police malpractice. A corrupt officer can fabricate evidence against a suspect with previous convictions in the knowledge that if he alleges such malpractice in court his convictions will be revealed. Of course the accused always has the option of not testifying so that he can discredit the prosecution witnesses without having his own bad character revealed, but this approach now permits an inference to be drawn in support of the case against him (*R* v. *Cowan* [1995] 3 WLR 818 (CA), 9.3.2 *post*; see also *R* v. *Taylor* [1999] Crim LR 77 (CA)).

The judiciary began to recognise the problems associated with the application of the second limb soon after the 1898 Act came into force and have, to some extent at least, sought to prevent it from being applied too harshly (although, as noted above, one problem stems from the literal way in which the exception has been interpreted). First, it has been held that a mere 'emphatic denial of the charge' will not lose the accused his shield, notwithstanding the implied suggestion that prosecution witnesses are lying; nor, generally, will the accused lose his shield by expressly calling prosecution witnesses liars. This is not a particularly surprising interpretation of the exception, for any other approach would have rendered the accused's right to testify devoid of all substance, at least in cases where there can be no possibility of mistake. A mere plea of 'not guilty' will often be an implied assertion that prosecution witnesses are willing to commit perjury to see the accused convicted. For example, if D faces a charge of indecently assaulting C, D's defence of consent will not only suggest that C was quite happy to be sexually molested, but also that C was willing to lie on oath to secure an innocent person's conviction. Similarly, D's plea of self-defence to a charge of battery will necessarily involve a suggestion that C is the sort of person who is willing to start a fight and then perjure himself. Second, the trial judge has been recognised to have an exclusionary discretion to ensure a fair trial, and this discretion can be applied to prevent cross-examination of the accused on his bad character even though he has fallen squarely within the scope of the second limb (see 4.6 *post*). Third, the Court of Appeal has recognised that the convictions of an accomplice who has pleaded guilty and decided to turn Queen's evidence should be revealed by the prosecution at the beginning of the trial (*R* v. *Taylor* [1999] 2 Cr App R 163).

Nevertheless, despite these concessions the accused still runs the risk of losing his shield even though casting imputations on the character of prosecution witnesses is a necessary part of his defence, and the indivisibility of his character means that any evidence of his bad character can, subject to the application of the judge's exclusionary discretion, be raised in cross-examination. It is true that bad-character evidence is admissible under the second limb of the exception solely for the purpose of demonstrating the accused's lack of credibility, but, as noted already, the practical effect of the evidence will often be to lead the jury along a forbidden chain of reasoning from disposition to guilt (*R* v. *Samuel* (1956) 40 Cr App R 8 (CCA), 4.4 *ante*). This undermines the principle that the jury or magistrates should decide whether the accused is guilty of the particular offence charged and not simply judge him on his past misconduct or unappealing character.

The decision of the House of Lords in *Selvey* v. *DPP* [1968] 2 WLR 1494, the leading case on the second limb of exception (ii), illustrates some of the problems an accused may face when his defence necessitates an attack on a prosecution witness. M had gone to the police claiming that D had buggered him, and medical evidence showed that he had indeed recently been buggered. In his defence D testified to the effect that he had not buggered M, and that M had told him he had been buggered by someone else earlier that day for £1. D also gave evidence that M had offered himself to D for £1 too, an offer D said he had declined and which had resulted in M bringing his false allegation. The trial judge ruled that D had thrown away his shield and allowed the prosecution to cross-examine him on his previous convictions for indecently assaulting young boys and importuning male persons. D appealed on the ground that, because the imputations against M had been a necessary part of his defence, the prosecution should not have been allowed to cross-examine him on his convictions. The House of Lords confirmed the existence of the trial judge's discretion to prevent cross-examination under the exception, but, approving *R* v. *Hudson* [1912] 2 KB 464 (CCA), dismissed D's appeal, holding that there was no rule disapplying the exception or obliging the trial judge to exercise his discretion in the accused's favour just because the nature of his defence necessarily involved casting aspersions on a prosecution witness's character. The House of Lords also confirmed, however, that if an imputation in reality amounts to no more than a denial of the offence charged, even if expressed in emphatic language, it should not be regarded as triggering the second limb. (*Cf. R* v. *Britzman* [1983] 1 WLR 350 (CA) (at p. 355) where it was felt that a mere denial could amount to an imputation save that cross-examination was to be prevented in such cases by the mandatory application of the exclusionary 'discretion'.)

An emphatic denial of guilt will very often carry with it an implied imputation, but this is not enough to lose the accused his shield. The difficulty lies in trying to determine in advance how far the accused can develop his denial before it becomes an imputation likely to trigger the exception. Decided cases offer some guidance, but should not be regarded as precedents because of the unique factual context of each case (though it will be seen that there is a precedent for rape trials). Furthermore, before the judicial discretion to prevent cross-examination was recognised, it is quite possible that judges sometimes regarded an attack on the character of a prosecution witness as a mere 'denial of guilt' if it was thought the accused should not be cross-examined on his character. The same situation today is more likely to lead to a ruling that there actually has been an imputation, with the discretion being applied in the accused's favour.

Generally speaking, to call a prosecution witness a liar will not lose the accused his shield on the ground that it is no more than an emphatic denial of guilt (*R* v. *Rouse* [1904] 1 KB 184 (CCCR), *Selvey* v. *DPP* [1968] 2 WLR 1494 (HL)). If, however, the accused goes beyond merely calling a witness a liar he will trigger the application of the exception. In *R* v. *Rappolt* (1911) 6 Cr App R 156 (CCA), for example, the accused lost his shield after asserting that the prosecution witness was a 'horrible liar'; and in *R* v. *Lasseur* [1991] Crim LR 53 (CA) the accused lost his shield by asserting that his former accomplice (who had pleaded guilty and testified for the prosecution) was lying in order to get a lighter sentence. In *R* v. *Wignall* [1993] Crim LR 62 the Court of Appeal felt that the accused might have crossed the line when his counsel accused a prosecution witness of 'making up her evidence as she went along to bolster her case', but accepted that the allegation had added little to the suggestion that the witness's evidence was untrue and that defence counsel 'had to be allowed a certain latitude'. It was also felt that if the line had been crossed the judge in his discretion should not have allowed the prosecution to bring out the accused's convictions (see also *R* v. *Desmond* [1999] Crim LR 313 (CA)). One conclusion which can be drawn from the cases is that there will be an imputation once the accused or his counsel has suggested an offensive reason for the witness's alleged dishonesty, even though the reason gives credence to the accused's denial. Thus, in *R* v. *Dunkley* [1927] 1 KB 323 (CCA) the accused lost his shield not because he had called the prosecution witness a liar, but because he added that her lies were actuated by malice; and in *R* v. *McLean* (1926) 19 Cr App R 104 (CCA) the accused lost his shield by alleging that the complainant had lied to obtain money from her relatives. In *R* v. *Manley* (1962) 126 JP 316 (CCA) it was alleged that the witness had been lying because he wanted to keep the accused away from his (the witness's) wife. This had not suggested any impropriety on the part of the witness; it had merely brought out the fact that his marriage was on the rocks. Lord Parker CJ said (at p. 318):

'[T]he mere suggestion of a reason for the lie does not change the position at all unless the reason itself imputes some bad character or previous conviction to the witness. Here, however disagreeable it may have been for [the prosecution witness] to have his private life referred to in public, it was in no way suggesting that he ... had been guilty of any disgraceful or criminal conduct.'

It is now well established that if the accused is charged with rape and he asserts that the complainant consented, his shield is not lost. In *R* v. *Turner* [1944] KB 463 (CCA) the accused stated not only that the complainant had consented but also that she had initiated intercourse by handling his penis (conduct amounting, in the words of the trial judge, to an imputation that she was a 'filthy, nasty woman, utterly filthy, who would commit an indecent assault upon that man'). It was held on appeal, however, that this additional assertion was no more than a description of the complainant's conduct showing that she had consented and did not cause the accused's testimony to amount to an imputation. Consent to sexual intercourse should not be regarded as an imputation because the issue is central to the definition of rape. In other words, because it is for the prosecution to prove the absence of consent, to raise consent is no more than a denial of rape. However, in *Selvey* v. *DPP* [1968] 2 WLR 1494 (HL) it was suggested (at pp. 1512 and 1520) that an assertion of consent in a rape case is an imputation on the character of the complainant, save that there is a special rule that the judge is obliged to exercise his 'discretion' in the accused's favour in such cases.

Logically one might think that any defence which comprises no more than a denial of an ingredient of the offence, such as self-defence, should similarly prevent the application of s. 1(3)(ii), but this view has not been accepted. A recent example is provided by *R* v. *Stone* [2001] EWCA Crim

2379, where the accused triggered the exception by his assertion that he had acted in self-defence against a knife attack by the complainant. The necessity of casting an imputation is not of itself a ground for preventing the application of the second limb of s. 1(3)(ii), and it would seem that rape is the only exception (*R* v. *Cook* [1959] 2 WLR 616 (CCA), *Selvey* v. *DPP* [1968] 2 WLR 1494 (HL)).

Whether an assertion amounts to an imputation in other types of case is governed by an objective test. It does not matter that the accused did not intend to make the imputation and that he only wished to explain his defence. He will be held to have made an imputation if a reasonable person would regard it as such (*R* v. *Bishop* [1974] 3 WLR 308 (CA) at p. 312). The judge must therefore place himself in the role of the reasonable person and decide whether, according to the moral standards of the day, the allegation is serious enough to amount to an attack on the moral credibility of the witness. If the judge comes to the conclusion that it is, then *prima facie* the accused's bad character is admissible to be weighed in the balance by the jury when they come to decide which version of events to believe. If the allegation is so trivial and commonplace that the reasonable person would not regard it as an imputation then s. 1(3)(ii) will not be triggered.

A mere allegation that a prosecution witness was drunk and foul-mouthed on one or more occasions is likely to be regarded as too trivial to count as an imputation (*R* v. *McLean* [1978] Crim LR 430 (CA), *R* v. *Morris* [2002] EWCA Crim 2968) as, it would seem, is an allegation that a prosecution witness is an habitual drunkard (*R* v. *Westfall* (1912) 7 Cr App R 176 (CCA)). However, to accuse a prosecution witness of being an offensive drink-driver *is* likely to be an imputation (*R* v. *Brown* (1960) 44 Cr App R 181 (CCA)) as is an allegation of corruption such as bribery (*R* v. *Wright* (1910) 5 Cr App R 131 (CCA)) or involvement in the offence charged (*R* v. *Hudson* [1912] 2 KB 464 (CCA)) or theft and unlawful sexual intercourse (*R* v. *Morris* (1959) 43 Cr App R 206 (CCA)). It is hardly surprising that allegations of criminality should be regarded as imputations triggering s. 1(3)(ii), but even an allegation of non-criminal behaviour will amount to an imputation if the judge feels most people would disapprove of it. In *R* v. *Jenkins* (1945) 31 Cr App R 1 (CCA), for instance, the accused was charged with receiving stolen property and he alleged that the complainant, a married woman, had been sexually involved with him and had allowed him to take photographs of her in the nude; this amounted to an imputation (see also *R* v. *Morris* (1959) 43 Cr App R 206 (CCA)). In *R* v. *Bishop* [1974] 3 WLR 308 (CA) the accused sought to explain his fingerprints in a prosecution witness's room by saying that he had been having a homosexual relationship with him. He was held to have lost his shield. In other words, so long as it is thought that reasonable people regard homosexual relations as immoral an allegation of this sort will amount to an imputation.

The theoretical distinction between a mere emphatic denial of guilt and an imputation remains even if the prosecution witness is a police officer, although the distinction becomes even more contrived in this context – it is 'one thing ... to deny that he had made the confession; but it is another thing to say that the whole thing was a deliberate and elaborate concoction on the part of the inspector; that seems to be an attack on the character of the witness' (*R* v. *Jones* (1923) 17 Cr App R 117 (CCA) at p. 120; see also *R* v. *Clark* [1955] 3 WLR 313 (CCA)). An analysis of the case-law suggests that merely to call an officer a liar will not trigger s. 1(3)(ii) so long as the sole imputation cast upon that witness is one of perjury. However, if the defence case goes beyond that, either expressly or impliedly suggesting additional misconduct, then s. 1(3)(ii) will be triggered. In *R* v. *Jones* (1923) 17 Cr App R 117 (CCA), for example, it was an imputation to allege that a confession had been fabricated by a police officer. The line between an allegation of perjury and additional misconduct is clearly a fine one, and for this reason the Court of Appeal has laid down guidelines for judges on how they should exercise their discretion in such cases (*R* v. *Britzman* [1983] 1 WLR 350 (CA), 4.6 *post*). An imputation will also be made if it is alleged that a confession was improperly induced. This occurred in *R* v. *Cook* [1959] 2 WLR 616 (CCA), where the accused claimed he had only confessed because of the threats made by a police officer to charge his wife, and in *R* v. *Wright* (1910) 5 Cr App R 131 (CCA) where it was alleged that a police officer had persuaded the accused to confess by offering him tobacco and matches. An allegation that two or more officers have conspired to commit perjury will also trigger s. 1(3)(ii). In *R* v. *Clark* [1955] 3 WLR 313 (CCA) Lord Goddard CJ said (at p. 320):

> 'I do not believe that any judge would allow a roving cross-examination into the prisoner's past merely because he said, "The police constable is a liar", or "The police constable is not telling the truth"; for all he is doing is pleading not guilty with emphasis ... It is quite another thing to make the suggestion against police officers that they have been conspiring together to defeat the ends of justice.'

An imputation may be made in such cases either expressly or impliedly; that is to say, it is the *substance* of the defence case as opposed to its form which determines whether s. 1(3)(ii) has been triggered. In *R* v. *Tanner* (1977) 66 Cr App R 56 (CA) the accused's counsel put to police officers that their testimony was 'wishful thinking', although it was not expressly put to them that they were lying, and the accused simply denied having made the confession attributed to him. Browne LJ said (at p. 64) that 'the appellant was saying impliedly that the police officers had made up a substantial and vital part of their evidence and ... had conspired together to do so'. The implied suggestion that the officers had conspired to commit perjury was therefore an imputation.

It has been suggested that in many if not most cases it is desirable that the trial judge should give a warning to defence counsel if it is felt an imputation is being made against a prosecution witness (see, for example, *Selvey* v. *DPP* [1968] 2 WLR 1494 (HL) and *R* v. *Stanton* [1994] Crim LR 834 (CA)). However, there is no rule of law which makes such a warning obligatory (*R* v. *McGee* (1979) 70 Cr App R 247 (CA)). Nor is there any rule requiring the judge to state in advance how he would exercise his exclusionary discretion in the event that an imputation is made by the accused (*R* v. *Dempster* [2001] Crim LR 567 (CA)).

The final words 'or the deceased victim of the alleged crime' in s. 1(3)(ii) were added by s. 31 of the Criminal Justice and Public Order Act 1994. This amendment demonstrates that the rationale for the second limb cannot solely be the desirability of furnishing the tribunal of fact with sufficient information for a comparative assessment of opposing witnesses' testimony, unless the deceased was the author of an admissible hearsay statement incriminating the accused. The amendment was relied on in *R* v. *Wainwright* [1998] Crim LR 665 (CA) where the accused, on trial for the murder of T, lost his shield under both limbs of the exception by adducing evidence of T's violent disposition and his own 'friendly and soft' disposition. The accused had raised self-defence and it was therefore necessary for the success of his defence to show the difference in their respective characters. This did not, of course, prevent the operation of s. 1(3)(ii) and his convictions for dishonesty offences and 'a grave offence of violence' were brought out in cross-examination. It did not matter that the allegations made against the deceased victim were true and not in dispute. If what is alleged amounts to an imputation according to the standard of ordinary people then s. 1(3)(ii) is triggered.

4.6 Judicial Control Over Exception (ii) Cross-examination

It has been seen that the trial judge has a discretion to prevent cross-examination under both the first limb (*R* v. *Thompson* (1965) 50 Cr App R 91 (CCA)) and the second limb (*Selvey* v. *DPP* [1968] 2 WLR 1494 (HL)) of s. 1(3)(ii). The prosecution must therefore seek the judge's leave before commencing cross-examination pursuant to this exception (*R* v. *Carter* (1996) 161 JP 207 (CA); *cf. Fearon* v. *DPP* (1995) 159 JP 649 (DC)).

The judge's exclusionary discretion is simply one facet of the judge's general common-law discretion in criminal trials to exclude prosecution evidence which would unduly prejudice the accused and adversely affect the fairness of his trial. If the probative value of the previous convictions in undermining the accused's credibility would be outweighed by the unduly prejudicial effect that evidence would have on him and his defence then the judge should not allow (or should limit the extent of) the cross-examination. In *Maxwell* v. *DPP* [1935] AC 309 (HL) Viscount Sankey said (at p. 321):

> '[T]he question whether a man has been convicted, charged or acquitted ought not to be admitted, even if it goes to credibility, if there is any risk of the jury being misled into thinking that it goes not to credibility but to the probability of his having committed the offence of which he is charged.'

This sound guiding principle has often been ignored in practice, however. The fact that the accused's previous convictions are for offences similar to the offence charged will not necessarily be enough to persuade the judge to exercise his discretion in the accused's favour, as recently illustrated by *R* v. *Stone* [2001] EWCA Crim 2379 where the accused, on trial for wounding with intent, was cross-examined on his convictions for a number of offences involving violence. In *Selvey* v. *DPP* [1968] 2 WLR 1494, where the accused was on trial for buggering a young man, the trial judge allowed the prosecution to cross-examine the accused on his convictions for indecently assaulting young boys and importuning male persons, but did not allow cross-examination on the accused's convictions for dishonesty offences. Curiously the House of Lords did not address the nature of the convictions which had been revealed, although it was felt that the judge had not exercised his discretion improperly. The accused's homosexual propensity was therefore regarded as relevant to his credibility, and admissible solely for that purpose, while his history of dishonest conduct was not. A homosexual disposition of itself has no bearing on the question of veracity at a general level, but in the context of the case the accused's disposition certainly undermined the credibility of his testimony and defence. The problem with this reasoning is that, while it is quite logical, it is also analogous to the justification for admitting past misconduct as similar fact evidence to prove *guilt*.

In *Maxwell* v. *DPP* [1935] AC 309 the House of Lords held that the questions which had been put to the accused in cross-examination about a previous acquittal should have been prevented on the ground of irrelevance. This is the starting point for determining the permissibility of any question which the prosecution would wish to ask pursuant to s. 1(3)(ii). If the bad character is not logically relevant to the question of the accused's credibility then the questions should not be asked. If, however, the accused's bad character logically has something to say about the likelihood of his testimony and/or his defence being untruthful then the judge should balance that probative value against the risk of undue prejudice to ensure the accused receives a fair trial.

Bad-character evidence can be relevant to the veracity of the accused or the credibility of his defence in a number of ways. Before looking at some examples, though, it should be noted that the accused's veracity is not irrelevant just because he has failed to testify. Even if the accused has failed to give evidence, his veracity is relevant to the extent that the defence run by his counsel is based on the version of events put forward by the accused in conference before the trial. Apart from the (it is hoped) rare cases where a corrupt advocate has fabricated a defence for his client, any defence run during the trial must be based on what the accused has actually told his lawyers. His advocate acts as his mouthpiece, putting forward the defence he has been instructed to run. It follows that the accused's veracity is always relevant once he has pleaded not guilty and proceeded to trial with an affirmative defence.

Some types of bad character will always be specifically disprobative of the accused's truthfulness, for example convictions for perjury or perverting the course of justice. Perhaps one could even extend this argument by holding that any conviction following a trial in which the accused has testified is logically probative of perjury, but given that a conviction does not always mean the accused was disbelieved this would be an untenable inference to draw in the absence of sufficient information about the earlier trial. (The tribunal of fact might have believed the accused's testimony but concluded that it was not sufficient to justify an acquittal.) Convictions for offences of dishonesty other than perjury (and related offences) will always be logically disprobative of truthfulness to the extent that such convictions demonstrate the accused's willingness to be deceitful in *some* circumstances, but with such convictions there is a danger the jury will reason that dishonesty in an entirely different context necessarily means the accused is lying on oath. Paradoxically, then, evidence of out-of-court dishonesty could be unduly prejudicial when compared with its probative value as evidence of perjury. Perhaps this is what influenced the trial judge in *Selvey* v. *DPP* [1968] 2 WLR 1494 (HL) when he disallowed cross-examination on such convictions.

In isolation, a conviction for a violent or sexual offence might seem to have no probative value on the question of veracity, but this does not mean such evidence is actually irrelevant to the credibility of the accused and his defence. It has been seen that whether or not the accused testifies, his bad character may undermine the likelihood that his defence is true if his convictions are for offences similar to the one he now faces, although this is where the risk of reasoning prejudice is so high that the judge ought to consider excluding the evidence (unless it would be admissible as similar fact evidence). Moreover, general immorality would seem to have some logical relevance to the likelihood of the accused's lying on oath no matter what the offence charged, even though the convictions have no dishonesty ingredient. If one were to accept that any out-of-court dishonesty is logically probative of testimonial dishonesty while an offence against the person is not, it would follow that a convicted rapist is more likely to tell the truth on oath than a petty thief, which is surely repugnant to common sense.

The courts have therefore taken a pragmatic approach and held that the accused's character is indivisible, and that any bad-character trait ought to be regarded as relevant to the accused's '*general* credibility' (*R* v. *Richardson* [1968] 3 WLR 15 (CA) at p. 24). When a judge directs a jury that the accused's bad character is relevant only to his credibility this would seem to mean that the jury may use it in any way they wish, so long as they do not follow a forbidden chain of reasoning and directly infer guilt from that evidence or convict just because of the sort of person the accused is. It can be used to compare the moral character of the accused with the moral character of the prosecution witnesses, and this can then be applied as a tool for the comparative assessment of the veracity and therefore the weight of the opposing witnesses' evidence. Alternatively, if the person impugned is the deceased alleged victim, there can be no comparison of truthfulness and the relevance of the accused's bad character on the question of credibility lies in its preventing the jury from being misled by a distorted picture of the accused. This will adversely affect the tribunal of fact's assessment of the accused's veracity and therefore the weight of his testimony. Accordingly, there can be no justification for allowing a non-testifying accused to impugn the character of prosecution witnesses or the deceased with impunity. The rule in *R* v. *Butterwasser* [1948] 1 KB 4 (CCA) (3.4.5 *ante*) ought to be abolished, with the non-testifying accused being brought within the scope of the second limb of s. 1(3)(ii). The law at present allows a distorted picture to be painted of the relative moral credibility of the accused and prosecution witnesses (or the deceased) with the likelihood that the jury will be misled.

The Court of Appeal has on occasion implied that it is logically fallacious to infer a willingness to lie on oath from non-dishonest misconduct. In *R* v. *Watts* (1983) 77 Cr App R 126 the accused was charged with indecent assault and lost his shield after alleging that police officers had fabricated evidence against him. He was subsequently cross-examined on his convictions for sexually assaulting his young nieces, and appealed on the ground that the judge should not have allowed such cross-examination given the nature of the offence charged and his criminal record. The Court of Appeal quashed his conviction for the following reason (at pp. 129–30):

'There are numerous decisions of this Court and of the House of Lords to the effect that the only relevance of the previous convictions of the defendant, admitted by virtue of [s. 1(3)(ii)], is as to the credibility of the prisoner, and that the jury must not be asked to infer guilt from such convictions. This in many cases requires the jury to perform difficult feats of intellectual acrobatics ... The prejudice which the appellant must have suffered in the eyes of the jury when it was disclosed that he had previous convictions for offences against young children could hardly have been greater. The probative value of the convictions, on the sole issue upon which they were admissible, was, at best, slight. The previous offences did not involve dishonesty ... In short, their prejudicial effect far outweighed their probative value.'

In *R* v. *Powell* [1985] 1 WLR 1364, however, the Court of Appeal suggested that as the House of Lords in *Selvey* v. *DPP* [1968] 2 WLR 1494 had not criticised the trial judge's ruling it could be taken that the Court of Appeal must have fallen into error in *R* v. *Watts*. The correct position was summarised as follows (at p. 1370):

'In short, if there is a deliberate attack being made upon the conduct of a prosecution witness calculated to discredit him wholly, if there is a real issue about the conduct of an important witness which the jury will have to settle in order to reach their verdict, the judge is entitled to let the jury know the previous convictions of the man who is making the attack. The fact that the defendant's convictions are not for offences of dishonesty, the fact that they are for offences bearing a close resemblance to the offences charged, are matters for the judge to take into consideration, but they certainly do not oblige the judge to disallow the proposed cross-examination.'

This approach has been reaffirmed by the Court of Appeal on a number of occasions (see, for example, *R* v. *Owen* (1985) 83 Cr App R 100 and *R* v. *McLeod* [1995] 1 Cr App R 591). Any evidence of past misconduct is therefore *prima facie* relevant to the question of credibility with its probative value to be left to the jury, save that the judge should prevent cross-examination under s. 1(3)(ii) where the nature of the bad-character evidence would unduly prejudice the accused. The judge will also prevent bad-character evidence from being raised in cross-examination if it is so trivial and stale that any probative value it might have is minimal (*R* v. *Nye* (1982) 75 Cr App R 247 (CA), *R* v. *Barratt* [2000] Crim LR 847 (CA)), or where an imputation which triggers the second limb of s. 1(3)(ii) relates to only one of several counts on the indictment and his previous convictions would, if revealed, prejudice his defence in respect of the other counts (*R* v. *Curbishley* [1963] Crim LR 778 (CCA)).

In *R* v. *McLeod* [1995] 1 Cr App R 591 the Court of Appeal reviewed the authorities and expressed its view on the general principles which ought to govern the exercise of the judge's discretion to disallow cross-examination under s. 1(3)(ii). First, the 'primary purpose' of cross-examination of the accused on his bad character is to show that he is not worthy of belief and not to show that he has a disposition to commit the type of offence with which he is charged; but the mere fact that the offences are of a similar type to that charged or because of their number and type have the incidental effect of suggesting a disposition to commit the offence charged will not make them improper. Second, it is undesirable that there should be prolonged or extensive cross-examination in relation to previous offences, and the prosecution should not seek to probe or emphasise similarities between the underlying facts of previous offences and the instant offence. Third, similarities of defences which have been rejected by juries on previous occasions, for example false alibis or the defence that an incriminating substance has been planted and whether or not the accused pleaded guilty, or was disbelieved having given evidence on oath, may be a legitimate matter for questions as they are relevant to credibility. Fourth, underlying facts which show a particularly bad character are not necessarily to be excluded, although the judge must be careful to balance the attack on the prosecution witness with the degree of prejudice to the accused. Fifth, defence objections to the line of cross-examination adopted ought to be made as soon as it seems the prosecution are going too far. Sixth, the Court of Appeal will not interfere with the exercise of the judge's discretion save on well-established principles. Seventh, the judge must direct the jury that the purpose of the questioning goes only to credit and they should not consider that it shows a propensity to commit the offence they are considering. With regard to the fourth point, in *R* v. *Taylor* [1999] 2 Cr App R 163 the Court of Appeal stated that where the accused has a particularly bad or damaging record then the judge is likely to admit it only if the imputations made against the prosecution witness are correspondingly grave.

In *R* v. *McLeod* the Court of Appeal also pointed out that details of sexual offences against children are likely to be particularly prejudicial to the accused. So if the accused has been convicted of a particularly heinous offence the judge is more likely to prevent the prosecution from raising it, as in *R* v. *Watts* (1983) 77 Cr App R 126 (CA); or, if such questioning *is* allowed, the details of those convictions may be withheld. Such offences will inevitably give rise to severe moral prejudice no matter what the instant allegation against the accused. It may also be appropriate to exclude any mention of less serious offences, notwithstanding the low risk of moral prejudice, if there is a high risk of reasoning prejudice. In *R* v. *Showers* [1996] Crim LR 739 the accused faced a charge of possessing a flick-knife. He denied possession of the knife and made imputations against the police witness, triggering s. 1(3)(ii), and the judge gave the prosecution leave to cross-examine him on his convictions for possessing offensive weapons. The Court of Appeal quashed his conviction on the ground, *inter alia*, that the judge had 'failed expressly to weigh up the very prejudicial effect on the defendant of admitting evidence of his particular convictions'. In *R* v. *Davison-Jenkins* [1997] Crim LR 816 the accused triggered s. 1(3)(ii) during her trial for shoplifting cosmetics by giving evidence of her good character, and the prosecution were allowed to cross-examine her on her previous convictions, referring specifically to a conviction for shoplifting cosmetics. The Court of Appeal quashed her conviction as it had been 'effectively impossible for the jury to disregard propensity once they had been given the information about the previous offence of shoplifting'. Moreover, the judge's satisfactory direction on the evidential value of her convictions had not negated that 'overwhelming prejudice'. The prosecution ought not to have gone into the specific details of the earlier offences but should merely have referred to the bare facts of her convictions for other forms of dishonesty. In *R* v. *Wignall* [1993] Crim LR 62 the Court of Appeal felt that the judge should have exercised his discretion in favour of the accused, on trial for theft, to prevent the prosecution from revealing his numerous convictions which included several for theft. The combination of moral prejudice arising from the accused's large number of convictions and the reasoning prejudice caused by his convictions for similar offences justified this approach. The Court of Appeal has also laid down guidelines for the exercise of the judge's discretion in cases where the accused has alleged that evidence given by police witnesses has been fabricated by them or that they are mistaken:

'Firstly, [the discretion] should be used if there is nothing more than a denial, however emphatic or offensively made, of an act or even a short series of acts amounting to one incident or in what was said to have been a short interview ... The position would be different however if there were a denial of evidence of a long period of detailed observation extending over hours ... Secondly, cross-examination should only be allowed if the judge is sure that there is no possibility of mistake, misunderstanding or confusion and that the jury will inevitably have to decide whether the prosecution witnesses have fabricated evidence. Defendants sometimes make wild allegations when giving evidence. Allowance should be made for the strain of being in the witness box and the exaggerated use of language which sometimes results from such strain or lack of education or mental instability ... Finally, there is no need for the prosecution to rely upon section [1(3)(ii)] if the evidence against a defendant is overwhelming.' (*R* v. *Britzman* [1983] 1 WLR 350 at p. 355)

Now that police interviews are routinely recorded, allegations of false confessions are less common, but as there is still scope for fabricating confessions en route to the police station, or planting incriminating evidence, the guidelines continue to be of importance.

Although the judge's role usually becomes relevant only once the prosecution have submitted that s. 1(3)(ii) has been triggered, or where the judge of his own volition has decided to warn defence counsel about a dangerous line of cross-examination, his duty is not only to ensure a fair trial for the accused but also to ensure fairness for prosecution witnesses. The Court of Appeal has therefore recognised the judge's right to initiate an application to cross-examine under s. 1(3)(ii) if the prosecution fail to do so (*R* v. *Chinn* (1996) 160 JP 765; *cf. R* v. *Goodwin* (1993) *The Times* 26.11.93 (CA)).

4.7 Exception (iii) – The 'Cut-Throat' Defence

If the accused is adjudged to have 'given evidence' against a co-accused 'charged in the same proceedings' the co-accused is entitled to cross-examine the accused on his bad character. The purpose of the provision is to provide a mechanism by which a co-accused is able to undermine the credibility of the accused, who has sought to lay the blame for the offence on him while testifying in his own defence, and thereby show that the accused's testimony should not be relied on. As with s. 1(3)(ii), there is an assumption that general bad character is evidence of testimonial dishonesty. It is important to note that s. 1(3)(iii) applies so long as two or more persons are tried together; they do not need to be charged with the same offence.

While s. 1(3)(iii) is fair to the extent that it allows a co-accused to defend himself by revealing the character of the person who has testified against him (as if he were a prosecution witness), the exception provides a real dilemma for the innocent accused with a bad record who wishes to clear himself by revealing to the court that it was the co-accused and not he who committed the offence. His bad character will be revealed and, if the co-accused is of good character, the jury are unlikely to give the accused's testimony much credence. If the accused blames his co-accused, the co-accused will inevitably retaliate and blame the accused, so by refusing to order separate trials and allowing them to 'cut each other's throats' the prosecution's task is facilitated (*R* v. *Varley* (1982) 75 Cr App R 242 (CA) at p. 246).

The leading case on s. 1(3)(iii) is *Murdoch* v. *Taylor* [1965] 2 WLR 425. M and L were jointly charged with receiving stolen cameras knowing them to be stolen. M had several previous convictions, whereas L was of good character. During cross-examination by L's counsel M claimed that the transaction in question, when they had tried to sell the cameras to a third party, had been L's responsibility and that he had not known what was in L's box. L's counsel then cross-examined M pursuant to s. 1(3)(iii) and M was convicted. His appeal was dismissed by the House of Lords on the ground that he had 'given evidence against' L even though he had made his comments during cross-examination, had not borne any hostile intent against L (the test is objective) and his answers had been given in reply to specific questions put by L's counsel. The test for whether an accused has given evidence against a co-accused is whether his evidence 'supports the prosecution's case in a material respect or . . . undermines the defence of the co-accused'. The majority of the House of Lords further held that the judge has no discretion to exclude cross-examination by a co-accused as to credit once s. 1(3)(iii) has been triggered, but Lord Morris pointed out that whether or not the exception has been triggered is itself a question for the judge and he can always prevent irrelevant cross-examination.

The freedom given to a co-accused to cross-examine an accused who has given evidence against him is an application of the general principle established in *R* v. *Miller* (1952) 36 Cr App R 169 (Assizes) that the trial judge has no discretion to prevent an accused from adducing or eliciting admissible evidence relevant to his defence just because it would unduly prejudice a co-accused's defence. By contrast, while it is permissible for the prosecution to cross-examine an accused as to his bad character pursuant to s. 1(3)(iii) (*R* v. *Seigley* (1911) 6 Cr App R 106 (CCA)) they must first seek leave, for in this respect the judge does retain a discretion to prevent cross-examination.

Although the test for having 'given evidence against' is objective, not every contradiction between the evidence of the accused and his co-accused will trigger s. 1(3)(iii). In *R* v. *Bruce* [1975] 1 WLR 1252 eight youths were charged with robbery and the judge ruled that B had given evidence against McG by contradicting the latter's evidence that there had been a plan to rob. B's convictions were brought out in cross-examination and he was convicted. The Court of Appeal held that while B's contradiction had undermined part of McG's defence, and damaged his credibility, it had not undermined his evidence that he had not taken part in the robbery, and in fact had undermined the prosecution case. B's evidence had made it less rather than more likely that McG would be convicted and he had not therefore given evidence against him. According to the Court (at p. 1259): 'evidence cannot be said to be given against . . . if its effect, if believed, is to result not in his conviction but in his acquittal' (see also *R* v. *Kirkpatrick* [1998] Crim LR 63 (CA)).

A mere denial by the accused can amount to evidence against his co-accused if it necessarily implies that the co-accused is guilty of the offence. In *R* v. *Davis* [1975] 1 WLR 345, D and O faced an allegation of stealing, *inter alia*, a gold cross on a chain. D denied the charge but when cross-examined by O's counsel he said: 'I am not suggesting [O] took the cross and chain. As I never, and it is missing, he must have done it, but I am not saying he did ... I never saw him steal it. I have got no idea.' The Court of Appeal held that D had given evidence against O. As only D or O (or both of them) could have stolen the cross and chain, his denial that he had done so necessarily meant that O had. A similar conclusion was reached in *R* v. *Varley* (1982) 75 Cr App R 242, where V's denial of any participation in an alleged joint enterprise, a robbery, with D, contradicting D's account that V had forced him to commit the robbery, necessarily amounted to an assertion that D had voluntarily committed the robbery on his own and not acted under duress. As such V was held to have given evidence against D and been properly cross-examined on his convictions. The Court of Appeal felt, first, that merely to deny participation in a joint enterprise would not of itself be sufficient to rank as evidence against a co-accused unless the denial 'must lead to the conclusion' that if the accused did not participate then it must have been the co-accused who did; and, second, that s. 1(3)(iii) could also be triggered if the accused asserted a view of the joint enterprise which was directly contradicted by the co-accused. V had fallen within the ambit of both these propositions. In *R* v. *Crawford* [1997] 1 WLR 1329, C and A were alleged to have robbed a woman of her handbag in a restaurant lavatory with the assistance of another accomplice (L) who had not been traced. A claimed to have been a mere bystander in the lavatory and blamed C and L. C's evidence was that she had no longer been present in the lavatory when A and L entered and that she saw them leave shortly after the victim had cried out. The Court of Appeal held that C's evidence regarding A's presence at the time of the robbery had not amounted to evidence against her because A's presence had not been in issue: it had not supported the prosecution's case 'in a material respect'. However, as C's evidence that she had not been in the lavatory herself, if believed, would have jeopardised A's credibility and made her version of events less likely, it had amounted to evidence against A for those (alternative) reasons and C had been properly cross-examined on her convictions. Counsel for C had argued that this was not a case where two persons were alleged to have been involved and that C's evidence was not such that it 'must lead to the conclusion' that A was guilty. The Court of Appeal rejected this interpretation of what was said in *R* v. *Varley* – it is sufficient if the accused's evidence 'may' lead to the conclusion that the co-accused is guilty (a point reaffirmed by the Court of Appeal in *R* v. *Rigot* (2000) unreported (99/2892/Y4)).

Although there is no judicial discretion to prevent cross-examination of an accused by a co-accused pursuant to s. 1(3)(iii) once the exception has been triggered – even if the accused's convictions are spent (*R* v. *Corelli* [2001] Crim LR 913 (CA)) – in *R* v. *Varley* (1982) 75 Cr App R 242 the Court of Appeal recognised that care must be taken to see that the accused's evidence 'clearly undermines' the co-accused's defence. This suggests a *de minimis* principle echoing Lord Morris's view in *Murdoch* v. *Taylor* [1965] 2 WLR 425 (HL) (at p. 428) that 'anything trivial or casual' ought to be disregarded when deciding whether s. 1(3)(iii) has been triggered. The same point was made in *R* v. *Crawford* [1997] 1 WLR 1329, where the Court of Appeal felt that s. 1(3)(iii) would be triggered only if the accused's evidence, if accepted, 'damaged in a significant way' the co-accused's defence.

If bad-character evidence is elicited by a co-accused and/or the prosecution pursuant to s. 1(3)(iii) the value of such evidence is limited to showing that the accused's 'testimony is not worthy of belief' (*Murdoch* v. *Taylor* [1965] 2 WLR 425 (HL) at p. 435). That said, according to the Court of Appeal in *R* v. *Reid* [1989] Crim LR 719, if s. 1(3)(iii) is relied on by a co-accused the cross-examination 'must be allowed to the full extent desired, subject only to the test of relevance' to credibility, even though highly prejudicial facts suggesting propensity may be brought out in the process. In that case, R and three other men were jointly charged with the robbery of a taxi driver, and R claimed that he had got into the car only after the robbery had occurred. He also said that one of the co-accused had held a knife to the taxi driver's throat, which led to R's being cross-examined on his previous conviction for robbing a taxi driver where his defence had been that he had left the taxi before the robbery occurred. The Court of Appeal dismissed R's appeal as the facts relating to the earlier offence had been relevant to his credibility by suggesting his defence was untrue and that he was willing falsely to incriminate others.

4.8 Proposals for Reform

The problems with s. 1 of the 1898 Act are catalogued in the Law Commission's report, Law Com No. 273 (2001) (at pp. 56–74). Section 1(3)(i) is defective because it excludes misconduct falling short of crime. Section 1(3)(ii) is open to criticism on at least nine grounds. First, psychological research does not support the notion that a person's character is indivisible (see also Consultation Paper No. 141 (1996) at pp. 101–4). Second, evidence of the accused's bad character is relevant only to credibility whereas evidence of his good character is relevant to his credibility and propensity, but it may be difficult in practice for the jury to draw this distinction when his bad character is elicited. Third, it is unclear what kinds of assertion will be regarded as a claim to good character and trigger the first limb. Fourth, there is no exception under the second limb for *necessary* imputations. This may deter the accused from giving oral evidence in support of a legitimate defence. Fifth, there is over-reliance on the trial judge's exclusionary discretion, which means that defence advocates may find it difficult to predict whether the accused's shield will be lost. (The defence is not entitled to an advance ruling as to how the discretion will be exercised: *R* v. *Dempster* [2001] Crim LR 567 (CA).) Sixth, the justifications for admitting the accused's bad character under the second limb are unsound. The accused's previous misconduct may have little if any probative value in relation to his credibility as a witness; there is no fairness in penalising the accused for daring to dispute and contradict the evidence against him; and there are better ways of protecting prosecution witnesses from irrelevant and unfair cross-examination. Further, in cases where there are two co-accused, D1 (with a bad record) and D2 (with no record), it is possible for D2 to attack prosecution witnesses for the benefit of both co-accused and thereby avoid having D1's record elicited under the second limb. Seventh, the non-testifying accused cannot lose his shield under the second limb of the exception, even though his previous misconduct may have a bearing on the credibility of the defence put forward on his behalf by his advocate. Eighth, investigating officers may be tempted to fabricate evidence against the accused, on the ground that if he alleges fabrication at his trial he is likely to lose his shield. Ninth, it is unclear what sort of allegation will be regarded as an imputation, or whether a co-accused can cross-examine the accused on his bad character pursuant to the second limb. With regard to s. 1(3)(iii), there is no exclusionary discretion to prevent the cross-examination of one co-accused (D1) on his bad character by another (D2), giving precedence to the interests of D2 over the interests of D1. Second, a co-accused may be inhibited in his defence as he will be aware that, if he gives evidence against the other co-accused, he will have his bad character revealed.

The Criminal Law Revision Committee's Eleventh Report (Cmnd 4991 (1972) at pp. 71–85) contained a number of proposals for reforming the 1898 Act. However, while there was a clear preference for the minority view in *Jones* v. *DPP* [1962] 2 WLR 575 (HL) (4.2 *ante*), a reform which would allow cross-examination on an issue even if matters prohibited by s. 1(3) were incidentally referred to, the Committee were deeply divided over how the second limb of exception (ii) should be reformed. The view which prevailed was that the second limb should be triggered only if the main purpose of the cross-examination of a prosecution witness was to undermine that witness's credibility. If the imputation was necessary for the accused's defence as a matter relevant to an issue and not just the witness's credibility the shield would not be lost. This concession was somewhat undermined, however, by the suggestion that the accused would lose his shield by making an imputation on the character of a witness called by a co-accused. The Royal Commission on Criminal Justice (Cm 2263 (1993) at p. 127) agreed with the suggestion that s. 1(3)(ii) should not be triggered if the imputation was 'central' to the accused's defence, as opposed to being mere gratuitous disparagement, but further suggested that the rule in *R* v. *Butterwasser* [1948] 1 KB 4 (CCA) (3.4.5 *ante*) ought to be abolished. In reality this rule has lost much of its practical significance since s. 35 of the Criminal Justice and Public Order Act 1994 came into force (9.3.2 *post*).

In Law Com No. 273 the Law Commission recommended that the 1898 Act be repealed and replaced by a new scheme which would apply whether or not the accused gave evidence in his own defence. The Commission's view was that relevant imputations of bad character relating to the events which are the subject of the trial or their investigation or prosecution ('the central set of facts'), whether made by the prosecution or the defence, should be *prima facie* admissible. However, it would not be possible to adduce or elicit evidence of the accused's bad character (outside the central set of facts) unless the court's leave was first obtained or the accused consented.

Evidence of the accused's bad character (outside the central set of facts) would be admissible at the behest of the prosecution in only two situations, but in each case the evidence would have to have substantial (that is, more than trivial) probative value and it would have to be shown that the interests of justice require that it should be admitted on account of its importance and probative value, notwithstanding the reasoning and/or moral prejudice which might be engendered by its admission. Under the 'corrective exception' evidence of the accused's bad character would be adduced or elicited by the prosecution to correct a false or misleading impression for which the accused was responsible. In other words, sufficiently probative bad-character evidence would be admissible to rebut the accused's false or misleading evidence of good character. Under the 'credibility exception' sufficiently probative evidence of the accused's propensity to be untruthful would be adduced or elicited by the prosecution if the accused's credibility was in issue and he had (with the court's leave) introduced evidence showing that another person – most obviously a prosecution witness – had a propensity to be untruthful. This exception would ensure that the jury were not left with a misleading impression of the accused's propensity to be untruthful in comparison with that of the other person.

The Commission also recommended that one co-accused (D1) should be able to introduce sufficiently probative evidence of another co-accused's (D2's) bad character (outside the central set of facts) to show that D2 has a propensity to be untruthful, but only if D2 has undermined D1's own defence. While it would be necessary for D1 to obtain the leave of the court before introducing D2's bad character under this 'co-defendant exception', he would not need to satisfy the additional 'interests of justice' test.

Bad-character evidence admitted under the 'corrective exception' could be considered relevant to the accused's credibility and to whether or not he was guilty of the offence charged. Bad-character evidence adduced or elicited by the prosecution under the 'credibility exception' or by a co-accused under the 'co-defendant exception' would be admitted in order to shed light on the accused's credibility. The Commission suggested, however, that in cases where the bad-character evidence would also suggest that the accused has a propensity to commit offences of the type he is on trial for, the judge should explain to the jury why the evidence was not being introduced for that purpose and warn them that they should not attach undue weight to it. For example the judge might explain that it can be very dangerous to reason that the accused is guilty merely because he has done something similar in the past.

Chapter Summary

- The accused may be cross-examined under s. 1(2) of the Criminal Evidence Act 1898 about his involvement in the offence he is on trial for, so long as the questions do not expressly or impliedly suggest he has been involved in some other offence or is in other respects of bad character. Section 1(3) sets out an *absolute* prohibition on such questioning, although this barrier to admissibility disappears once the jury have become aware that the accused is of bad character.
- If s. 1(3) applies, the accused may be cross-examined in a way which expressly or impliedly suggests he is of bad character *only if* one of its exceptions applies. However, if one of the exceptions applies the judge may prevent or limit cross-examination by the prosecution to ensure that the accused receives a fair trial.
- Exception (i) permits cross-examination on 'similar fact evidence' of offences the accused has committed. Exception (ii) permits cross-examination on the accused's bad character to rebut evidence of his purported good character or because the defence has impugned the character of a prosecution witness or the deceased 'victim'. Exception (iii) permits cross-examination on the accused's bad character if he has given evidence which undermines the defence of a co-accused or supports the prosecution case against him.
- Bad-character evidence elicited under exceptions (ii) and (iii) is admissible for the limited purpose of showing that the accused (and his testimony) is not worthy of belief. Bad-character evidence elicited under exception (i) is admissible evidence that the accused (and his testimony) is not worthy of belief *and* that he is guilty of the alleged offence.

Further Reading

Gooderson, 'Is the Prisoner's Character Indivisible?' [1953] CLJ 377

Cross, 'The Criminal Evidence Act 1898' (1962) 78 LQR 407

Tapper, 'The Meaning of Section 1(*f*)(i)' in *Crime, Proof and Punishment – Essays in Memory of Sir Rupert Cross* (London, 1981) p. 296

Pattenden, The Purpose of Cross-Examination Under Section 1(*f*) [1982] Crim LR 707

Dennis, 'Evidence Against a Co-Accused' (1983) 36 CLP 177

Munday, 'Reflections on the Criminal Evidence Act 1898' [1985] CLJ 62

Munday, 'Stepping Beyond the Bounds of Credibility' [1986] Crim LR 511

Seabrooke, 'Closing the Credibility Gap' [1987] Crim LR 231

Mirfield, 'The Argument from Consistency for Overruling *Selvey*' [1991] CLJ 490

Elliott, 'Cut Throat Tactics' [1991] Crim LR 5

Law Commission Consultation Paper No. 141 (1996)

Law Commission Report, Law Com No. 273 (2001)

Criminal Justice Bill (2003), Part 11, Chapter 1
and Explanatory Note (www.publications.parliament.uk)

5 The Scope of the Hearsay Rule

5.1 Hearsay Defined

In *R* v. *Sharp* [1988] 1 WLR 7 (HL) Lord Havers said (at p. 11):

> 'I accept the definition of the hearsay rule in Cross on Evidence, 6th ed. (1985), p. 38: "an assertion other than one made by a person while giving oral evidence in the proceedings is inadmissible as evidence of any fact asserted."'

Hearsay is defined in the Civil Evidence Act 1995 as 'a statement made otherwise than by a person while giving oral evidence in the proceedings which is tendered as evidence of the matters stated' (s. 1(2)(*a*)), but for ease of exposition it might equally be described as 'any out-of-court statement tendered for the purpose of proving the truth of the matters stated'. In this context 'out-of-court' is no more than a convenient way of describing a statement made otherwise than by a witness on oath during the instant proceedings. A statement made on oath in earlier proceedings is hearsay for the purposes of any subsequent proceedings if it is tendered to prove the truth of the matters stated (see *R* v. *Lockley* [1995] 2 Cr App R 554 (CA)). The exclusionary hearsay rule referred to in *R* v. *Sharp* [1988] 1 WLR 7 (HL) no longer applies in civil proceedings (8.1 *post*), but still operates with full effect in criminal trials and has been described, justifiably, as 'inflexible and sometimes absurdly technical' (*R (McCann)* v. *Crown Court at Manchester* [2002] 3 WLR 1313 (HL) at pp. 1323–4). That said, there are numerous statutory and common-law exceptions to the rule which allow hearsay to be admitted as a form of testimonial evidence in certain circumstances; but, in the absence of any such exception, hearsay evidence is absolutely prohibited no matter how reliable or important it may be (*Myers* v. *DPP* [1964] 3 WLR 145 (HL), 5.8 *post*). The exceptions to the hearsay rule are explained in Chapters 6 and 7.

It is crucial to understand at the outset that the exclusionary rule applies only to 'statements' ('assertions') which actually have a descriptive content capable of being true and which are tendered to prove the truth of that content. Any out-of-court, non-descriptive utterance which is incapable of being either true or false cannot fall (directly) within the scope of the hearsay rule and may, if relevant, be admissible as 'original evidence'. Nor does the hearsay rule apply if an out-of-court statement, having a content which *is* capable of being true, is tendered for a reason other than to prove the truth of that content; such statements may similarly be admissible as original evidence:

'Evidence of a statement made to a witness by a person who is not himself called as a witness may or may not be hearsay. It is hearsay and inadmissible when the object of the evidence is to establish the truth of what is contained in the statement. It is not hearsay and is admissible when it is proposed to establish by the evidence, not the truth of the statement, but the fact that it was made.' (*Subramaniam* v. *Public Prosecutor* [1956] 1 WLR 965 (PC) at p. 970)

'A question of hearsay only arises when the words spoken are relied on testimonially ... establishing some fact narrated by the words.' (*Ratten* v. *R* [1971] 3 WLR 930 (PC) at pp. 933–4)

5.2 Justifications for the Hearsay Rule

In *Teper* v. *R* [1952] AC 480 (PC) Lord Normand said (at p. 486):

'The rule against the admission of hearsay evidence is fundamental. It is not the best evidence and it is not delivered on oath. The truthfulness and accuracy of the person whose words are spoken to by another witness cannot be tested by cross-examination, and the light which his demeanour would throw on his testimony is lost.'

In *R* v. *Sharp* [1988] 1 WLR 7 (HL) Lord Havers said of the rule (at p. 11):

'I suspect that the principal reason that led the judges to adopt it many years ago was the fear that juries might give undue weight to evidence the truth of which could not be tested by cross-examination, and possibly also the risk of an account becoming distorted as it was passed from one person to another.'

Accordingly, the rationale for the rule is: (i) that it is not the best evidence; (ii) that it is not delivered on oath; (iii) that inaccuracy may have arisen through repetition; (iv) that the demeanour of the maker cannot be seen; (v) that the veracity of the maker cannot be tested in cross-examination; and (vi) that the accuracy of the maker cannot be tested in cross-examination.

The first two points are hardly compelling reasons for excluding hearsay. Hearsay (in particular certain types of documentary hearsay) may in fact be better evidence than direct testimony, but in the absence of a recognised exception to the exclusionary rule it will still be inadmissible (as in *Myers* v. *DPP* [1964] 3 WLR 145 (HL), 5.8 *post*); and even if it is less satisfactory than direct testimony it may be the best *available* evidence. The fact that hearsay is not given on oath is perhaps of no more than historical interest, and certainly fails to explain why testimony given on oath is inadmissible in subsequent proceedings. The third reason is sound insofar as it applies to multiple oral hearsay, but it can hardly justify first-hand hearsay or hearsay transferred from one document to another in circumstances where the risk of error can be discounted. The fourth reason is inextricably linked with the fifth and sixth, but standing alone it is a weak justification given the unreliability of demeanour as an indicator of witness reliability. Thus, the principal reason for excluding hearsay is a compendium of the last two points:

> 'The rationale of excluding it ... is a recognition of the great difficulty ... of assessing what, if any, weight can properly be given to a statement by a person whom the jury have not seen or heard and which has not been subject to any test of reliability by cross-examination.' (*R* v. *Blastland* [1985] 3 WLR 345 (HL) at p. 350)

The maker could have fabricated the evidence or been mistaken and yet he is unavailable for cross-examination on his statement; and where the statement is heard and passed on by someone who is himself unavailable for cross-examination the problem is multiplied. In particular, if the prosecution were to be permitted to adduce any hearsay statement as part of their case, the accused would often be unable effectively to challenge the veracity or reliability of the maker, and if that person is his accuser it is immediately obvious that the adduction of such evidence might prevent him from being able to defend himself in any meaningful sense, violating a fundamental tenet of natural justice. It is for this reason that Article 6(3)(d) of the European Convention on Human Rights expressly recognises as an integral component of the right to a fair trial the accused's right 'to examine or have examined witnesses against him'. A related component of the Article 6(1) right to a fair trial is the accused's right to *participate* (a right which manifests itself on a number of occasions in Article 6(3)). Justice demands that the accused should be able to defend himself effectively by challenging the evidence against him and that he should be able to participate fully in the proceedings. The 'minimum rights' of Article 6(3) ensure not only that the accused will be fairly tried, but that his trial will be seen to be fair and that a finding of guilt against him will be legitimate in terms of both factual accuracy and public perception.

The exclusionary rule prohibiting the adduction of hearsay therefore accords with Article 6(3)(d) of the European Convention insofar as it prevents the prosecution from adducing such evidence as part of their case. In this context the possibility of a breach of Article 6 of the Convention will arise only if the prosecution are permitted to rely on an exception to the rule (see 6.2.5 *post*). However, the exclusionary rule works both ways, and may therefore operate so as to prevent the accused from adducing evidence which supports his defence. Whether the exclusion of hearsay evidence would deny the accused a fair trial depends on how reliable that evidence is and how important it would be to his defence; but the purpose of the hearsay rule is legitimate and the rule is not in principle contrary to Article 6(1) of the European Convention where it operates against the accused (*Blastland* v. *United Kingdom* (1987) 10 EHRR 528 (ECmHR) at p. 531).

The justification based on the inability to cross-examine and challenge prosecution evidence is somewhat flawed as a rationale for the very broad scope of the common-law rule. Certain types of documentary hearsay may be inherently reliable and, in any event, cross-examination is not necessarily a useful forensic tool for testing such evidence. For example, records made in the course of a business many years before the trial are likely to be accurate and reliable, and the witnesses who compiled them are unlikely to remember anything of significance so long after the event. Nevertheless, even reliable business records are inadmissible at common law (*Myers* v. *DPP* [1964] 3 WLR 145 (HL)). That said, the scope of the hearsay rule cannot properly be considered in isolation from the numerous common-law and statutory exceptions to it. It will be seen that certain categories of hearsay evidence which are likely to be reliable (such as business records) – and in respect of which the right to challenge becomes less important – *are* admissible.

5.3 Statements Excluded as Hearsay

The hearsay rule applies to *any* statement (whether made orally, in a document or by way of a gesture) if it is tendered for the purpose of proving the truth of the matters stated. It is an absolute and indiscriminate exclusionary rule subject to specific statutory and common-law exceptions. The trial judge has no discretion to admit such evidence merely because it seems to be reliable and highly probative.

Decided cases provide useful illustrations of how the rule has been applied in practice and the potential for injustice. Perhaps the most notorious case is that of *Sparks* v. *R* [1964] 2 WLR 566 (PC). The accused in that case, a white male, was charged with having indecently assaulted a three-year-old child. The child, who did not give evidence, had told her mother soon after the assault that the offender had been 'a coloured boy' and the accused sought to have that statement admitted as evidence that he was not the offender. The judge ruled that the statement was inadmissible hearsay, a ruling subsequently upheld by the Privy Council on the ground that there is 'no rule which permits the giving of hearsay evidence merely because it relates to identity'.

In *R* v. *Turner* (1975) 61 Cr App R 67 one of the co-accused, B, was convicted of robbery following the trial judge's refusal to allow him to adduce evidence that a third party, S, who was not called as a witness, had confessed to the offence. The Court of Appeal held (at p. 87) that S's confession was inadmissible hearsay and the judge had been right to exclude it. A similar view was adopted by the House of Lords in *R* v. *Blastland* [1985] 3 WLR 345. B was charged with buggering and murdering a 12-year-old boy and sought (i) to adduce evidence that a third party, M, had confessed to those crimes, (ii) to adduce evidence that M had made statements showing he had known the murder had been committed before the body was found and (iii) to compel M's attendance as a defence witness so that he could be treated as 'hostile' and cross-examined on what he had said and known. The trial judge refused the applications and B was convicted on both counts. He sought leave to appeal to the House of Lords on two grounds: first, that M's confession had been wrongly excluded; and, second, that other comments made by M ought to have been admitted as evidence of his knowledge that a murder had been committed (3.1.3 *ante*). The House of Lords refused leave on the first of the two points as such evidence was hearsay which did not fall into any recognised exception to the exclusionary rule. In the words of Lord Bridge (at p. 349):

> 'To admit in criminal trials statements confessing to the crime for which the defendant is being tried made by third parties not called as witnesses would be to create a very significant and, many might think, a dangerous new exception.'

Lord Bridge did not explain why an exception for third-party confessions would be dangerous, but the question was addressed in some detail by the Supreme Court of South Australia in *Re Van Beelen* [1974] 9 SASR 163 (at p. 205):

> 'The mere knowledge that an extra-judicial confession of crime could, in favourable circumstances, be received to exculpate an alleged offender, would ... tempt the less scrupulous members of our community to undertake clandestine operations of self-help. All that would be required by a guilty accused person would be the services of two or three accomplices and a person, known to all, who had died after the date of the alleged offence and who, theoretically, could have committed it. The accomplices, when called as witnesses, could then simply attribute a confession to the deceased man, and the confession could be given artistic verisimilitude by inserting in it evidence of esoteric knowledge that had, in fact, come from the best of all sources – the offender. If there were not at hand a deceased person into whose mouth the confession could conveniently be put, the unavailability of a living person could, no doubt, be arranged by any one of a number of irregular methods – direct or indirect. Where serious crime was alleged, the motive for making such arrangements would be strong ... Perjurious or lying defences would thus become dangerously easy to fabricate, and correspondingly difficult to expose.'

Following the House of Lords' dismissal of Blastland's appeal he applied to the European Commission of Human Rights on the ground that the exclusion of M's confession and the evidence of his state of mind had prevented him from receiving a fair trial, given that the prosecution had been permitted to adduce his own admissions to the police. The Commission rejected this 'equality of arms' argument because M could have been called by the defence (although it was acknowledged that M would not have been obliged to provide any self-incriminating answers), B had been afforded full facilities to challenge the hearsay ruling and the case against him, and some other evidence relating to M had been placed before the jury (see *Blastland* v. *United Kingdom* (1987) 10 EHRR 528).

It should be noted, however, that so long as the criterion of relevance can be established it may be possible for the accused to adduce a third party's confession by virtue of one of the statutory or common-law exceptions to the hearsay rule. In particular, if the confession is in a document it would be possible to rely on ss. 23 and/or 24 of the Criminal Justice Act 1988, subject to the judge's discretion to exclude the evidence under ss. 25 or 26 (see *R* v. *Iqbal* (1990) 91 Cr App R 193 (CA)). But if no such exception is available, and the third party's confession appears to be reliable and is supported by extraneous evidence which also tends to exculpate the accused, the accused may be denied a fair trial if he is prevented from relying on that evidence (see, for example, *Chambers* v. *Mississippi* (1973) 410 US 284 (USSC)).

The exclusionary hearsay rule applies with equal force to statements in writing or communicated in any other manner. In *Patel* v. *Comptroller of Customs* [1965] 3 WLR 1221 (PC) the accused was charged with making a false declaration in a customs import form. The allegation was that he had described the provenance of his imported bags of Moroccan coriander seed as India, and the prosecution were allowed to rely on a statement on the bags which read 'produce of Morocco'. It was held that the statements were inadmissible hearsay, and as there had been no other evidence that the seeds had come from Morocco the conviction was quashed. A similar approach was adopted in *R* v. *Brown* [1991] Crim LR 835. The accused in that case was charged with obtaining property by deception in that he had overcharged for surgical appliances he had supplied to a number of patients. The prosecution called an expert witness who testified that he had examined the appliances and identified the patients to whom they had been supplied on the basis of the name on a shoe, what he had been told by third parties and an invoice. The Court of Appeal held that all the identification evidence was inadmissible hearsay.

A number of cases involve inadmissible hearsay statements which were made to police officers and recorded in writing. The officer is not permitted to read out the note from his pocket book or refresh his memory from it; nor can he tell the court what he remembers having been told. *Ahmed* v. *DPP* [1998] RTR 90 provides a recent example. A motorist spoke to a police officer informing him that a Nissan Primera car was being driven dangerously along the M27 motorway and reported the registration number as 'M911 SJB'. The officer made enquiries through the police national computer and established that a car of that number had been rented to D and that it was a Nissan Primera. At the trial the officer could not give evidence of the registration number which had been reported to him as it was hearsay, but the magistrates convicted D on the basis that the officer's enquiries established a nexus between the car seen on the M27 and D's car. The Divisional Court quashed D's conviction because the magistrates had heard no admissible evidence connecting his car M911 SJB with the car which had been driven dangerously (see also *R* v. *Eleftheriou* [1993] Crim LR 947 (CA), *Jones* v. *Metcalfe* [1967] 1 WLR 1286 (DC), *R* v. *McLean* (1967) 52 Cr App R 80 (CA) and 16.4.1 *post*).

An out-of-court statement made entirely by way of a physical gesture is similarly covered by the hearsay rule. In *Chandrasekera* v. *R* [1937] AC 220 a woman who had had her throat cut could respond to questions put to her only by nodding her head and making other signs. She died before the trial, so the prosecution were obliged to call evidence of her physical responses to prove that the accused had been responsible for her fatal injury. The accused was convicted and appealed on the ground that such evidence ought not to have been admitted. The Privy Council held that the deceased's nod of assent to a question put to her amounted to a hearsay statement (which had been properly admitted by virtue of a statutory exception to the exclusionary rule). In *R* v. *Gibson* [1887] 18 QBD 537 (CCCR) the accused's conviction for malicious wounding was quashed on the ground that the complainant had been permitted to give evidence that a passer-by had pointed to the door of the accused's house and said, 'The person who threw the stone went in there.' The spoken words *and* the gesture were inadmissible.

A witness's testimony based not on his own personal knowledge but on inadmissible hearsay which has been related to him is equally inadmissible if such testimony is given for the purpose of proving the truth of the hearsay statement. Such testimony is nothing more than a repetition of the hearsay and therefore equally worthless as evidence. In *R* v. *Rothwell* (1993) 99 Cr App R 388 the accused was charged with supplying heroin to third parties and a police officer gave evidence that he had observed the accused passing small packets to persons he knew to be heroin users. The Court of Appeal held that the witness should not have been permitted to give evidence that the third parties had been heroin users as his knowledge had been based on what he had been told by other persons as opposed to his own direct perception of, for example, hypodermic needle marks on their arms. The prosecution should have adduced evidence of the third parties' convictions for possession of heroin pursuant to s. 74(1) of the Police and Criminal Evidence Act 1984 (*R* v. *Warner* (1992) 96 Cr App R 324 (CA)). Alternatively, the police officer could have testified that the third parties were heroin users if he had known of their relevant convictions (*R* v. *Rothwell* (1993) 99 Cr App R 388).

An admission made by the accused which is based on inadmissible hearsay is also inadmissible if the prosecution seek to rely on the admission to prove the truth of the hearsay statement. In *R* v. *Marshall* [1977] Crim LR 106 (CC) the accused, on trial for receiving stolen goods, admitted that when purchasing the goods he had been told by the seller that they were stolen. His admission was inadmissible for the purpose of proving the goods were stolen. Similarly, in *Comptroller of Customs* v. *Western Lectric* [1965] 3 WLR 1229 (PC) the accused's admission regarding the provenance of goods he had imported was based entirely on the hearsay statements in the labels attached to the goods, so his admission was of no evidential value and inadmissible.

5.4 Out-of-court Statements Admissible as Original Evidence

Any out-of-court statement which is tendered not to prove the truth of the matters stated but for another relevant reason is admissible as 'original evidence'. In such cases it is the mere fact the statement has been made, not that its content is true, which is relevant.

If the accused is charged with an offence and he raises the defence of duress he will need to adduce or elicit evidence that he was threatened with death or serious injury and that he reasonably believed the threat would be carried out. Whether the person making the threat truly intended to carry it out is irrelevant. The question for the jury is the accused's state of mind (his belief) and this depends on whether or not the threat was actually made. Thus in *Subramaniam* v. *Public Prosecutor* [1956] 1 WLR 965, where the accused raised the defence of duress to a charge of having been in unlawful possession of ammunition, the Privy Council held that he should have been allowed to give evidence of the threat to show he had *believed* he would be murdered unless he committed the offence. An out-of-court statement may also be relevant to the accused's state of mind in other situations, such as where he has raised the partial defence of provocation and needs to give evidence of the 'things said' which caused him to lose his self-control (s. 3 of the Homicide Act 1957), or where he is charged with theft and his defence is that he was told by a third party that he could have the goods as they were his to give away.

Conversely, the prosecution may adduce an out-of-court statement as original evidence to prove that the accused had the *mens rea* for the offence charged. If the charge is one of handling stolen goods it will be permissible to adduce the accused's admission that the person from whom he bought the goods had told him they were stolen. The statement is relevant to whether the accused had *believed* the goods were stolen when handling them (*R* v. *Hulbert* (1979) 69 Cr App R 243 (CA); *cf. R* v. *Marshall* [1977] Crim LR 106 (CC), 5.3 *ante*). Similarly, evidence of a statement made by a third party to the accused, regardless of its truth, could be relevant in showing the accused had a motive for committing the offence charged. For example, the third party might have insulted the accused, providing evidence of the accused's reciprocated enmity towards him; or the third party might have written a letter explaining that the accused's wife was having an affair, suggesting that the accused had a motive for murdering her. The prosecution may also adduce an out-of-court statement to show its *falsity* if it is relevant to an issue in the trial. In *Mawaz Khan* v. *R* [1966] 3 WLR 1275 (PC) the accused's purported alibi, provided before the trial, was admissible for the purpose of proving that he had lied, allowing an inference to be drawn that he had been conscious of his guilt.

If the accused submits that an adverse inference should not be drawn from his failure to mention in his police interview facts he has relied on in his defence at trial, on the ground that he was advised to remain silent by his solicitor, it may be necessary for him to give evidence of what his solicitor said to him (9.2.2.5 *post*). This is permissible so long as he does not infringe the hearsay rule. If the mere fact that the statement was made explains the accused's state of mind at that time, and therefore his reason for remaining silent, the evidence is admissible as original evidence. But if the accused wishes to repeat the out-of-court statement to prove the truth of something his solicitor said the evidence will be inadmissible. The judge should be informed in advance, in the absence of the jury, what the evidence is going to be and the purpose for giving it so that a ruling can be made on admissibility (*R* v. *Davis* [1998] Crim LR 659 (CA)).

The state of mind of a person other than the accused may be relevant and therefore justify the admission of an out-of-court statement as original evidence. For example, in *R* v. *KL* [2002] EWCA Crim 2171, a rape case, the prosecution adduced a video recording of an interview with the mentally-handicapped complainant, not because they were relying on the substance of what she was saying, but to prove her child-like mental state and inability to consent to sexual intercourse. In *Ratten* v. *R* [1971] 3 WLR 930 (PC) the accused was charged with the murder of his wife and his defence was that he had accidentally shot her while cleaning his gun. A telephonist was allowed to give evidence of the deceased's hysterical and fearful request for the police ('Get me the police please!') a few minutes before the fatal shooting. The call itself was relevant in that it rebutted the accused's denial that any call had been made, and the deceased's hysterical request for the police was also admissible 'to explain and complete the fact of the call being made'. *Ratten* v. *R* was distinguished by the House of Lords in *R* v. *Blastland* [1985] 3 WLR 345 (5.3 *ante*) on the ground that while the comments made by the third party, M, indicated his awareness that the murder had been committed, his state of mind was not actually relevant to any issue in the trial. The evidence had therefore been properly excluded (see also 3.1.3 *ante*).

One class of out-of-court words usually considered in the context of original evidence is that of 'operative words', that is, words which have a legal effect irrespective of the intention of the person who wrote or spoke them. Such words have often been regarded as statements in that they may be said to carry a content capable of being true. However, the truth (or falsity) of that content is deemed to be irrelevant to the effect of the statement as a matter of law. Operative words are regarded, objectively, as having a legal effect just because they have been made. An example is the offer and acceptance which give rise to a valid contract. If O has made an offer and A has accepted it, both parties are bound by their agreement even if O or A had been joking or deceitful and had not intended to be bound. If Oliver says, 'I offer to sell you my computer for £500,' the truth or falsity of what he has stated is irrelevant; he is deemed to have made an offer. If Alex replies, 'I accept your offer and will pay you £500,' the truth or falsity of what he says is also irrelevant; he too is bound by the contract irrespective of his real intention.

This reasoning explains the decision in *Woodhouse* v. *Hall* (1980) 72 Cr App R 39. The accused was charged with having been involved in the management of a brothel contrary to s. 33 of the Sexual Offences Act 1956, but the magistrates prevented the police officers called by the prosecution from giving evidence that they had been offered 'hand relief' and 'topless hand relief' by ladies working there. The prosecution appealed by way of case stated to the Divisional Court where it was held that as a brothel was 'an establishment at which two or more women were *offering* sexual services' the police officers had been entitled to give evidence that a sexual service (in this case masturbation) had been offered. The evidence was not hearsay. Donaldson LJ said (at p. 42):

'I suspect that the justices ... may have thought that they had to be satisfied as to the truth of what the ladies said or were alleged to have said in the sense they had to satisfy themselves that the words were not a joke but were meant seriously and something of that sort. But this is not a matter of truth or falsity. It is a matter of what was really said – the quality of the words, the message being transmitted.'

To reason that a brothel is an establishment where sexual services are offered, whether or not such offers are intended to be taken seriously, is to accept a broad interpretation of the substantive criminal law to justify the admission of what would otherwise be inadmissible evidence. The same sort of approach was adopted by the Court of Appeal in the earlier case of *R* v. *Chapman* [1969] 2 WLR 1004, where a police officer was permitted to give evidence that when a breath test was administered to the accused in the casualty department of a hospital following a road accident the doctor had 'made no objection'. On appeal it was submitted that this evidence was hearsay and inadmissible. The Court of Appeal held that as s. 2(2)(*b*) of the Road Safety Act 1967 prohibited the taking of samples if 'the medical practitioner ... objects to the provision of a specimen' the question was simply whether or not there had been an objection. Consequently the evidence was held to have been properly admitted.

5.5 'Performative Words' as Original Evidence

Many out-of-court utterances do not amount to (descriptive) statements in that the words carry no content capable of being true. Utterances such as 'Hello!' or 'What is your favourite colour?' or 'Gosh!' do not fall within the scope of the hearsay rule as nothing capable of being considered true has been stated. Operative words (5.4 *ante*) will often carry a descriptive content capable of being true or false, and such words have traditionally been admitted on the ground that the sincerity of the maker (and so the truth of the matters stated) is irrelevant. However, in addition to the descriptive content, operative words have a *performative* function. Indeed the real significance of operative words lies in this function, with the descriptive content existing as an unintended and incidental side-effect which can be disregarded. As such, operative words could be described as 'performatives' as their function is, in the appropriate context, intended to be performative as opposed to descriptive.

Words such as 'I marry you' or 'I'm sorry' or 'I bet you £5 Arsenal will beat Spurs' or 'I offer you my computer for £500' or 'Would you like topless hand relief?' or 'I do not object to your taking a specimen from my patient' or 'Get me the police please' or 'Look after this ammunition or I'll kill you' are not primarily descriptive statements; nor are they intended to be. The descriptive element is incidental to the performative function of

the words, and the person who utters them does so, in the appropriate
context, for the purpose of performing that intended function, whether it
be to marry, or apologise, or place a bet, or make an offer of sale, or offer
a sexual service, or authorise an act, or request a service or make a threat.
In each case the person is doing something over and above merely saying
something. Once it is appreciated that the descriptive factor is incidental to
the performative function of such words a more appropriate rationale for
their admissibility as non-hearsay materialises.

Operative words give the appearance of a descriptive content but their
intended function is the non-descriptive (non-narrative) performance of an
act. For this reason, operative words (and their non-verbal equivalents)
should not be regarded as descriptive statements at all for the purposes of
the hearsay rule. They are examples of performative non-statements and
should be considered *prima facie* admissible for that reason. This
approach has the advantage of dispensing with the somewhat artificial
approach adopted in cases such as *Woodhouse* v. *Hall* (1980) 72 Cr App R
39 (DC) (an offer) while also justifying the admissibility of performative
words in other cases such as *Subramaniam* v. *Public Prosecutor* [1956] 1
WLR 965 (PC) (a threat) without the need to question the maker's
sincerity. Similarly, when the deceased in *Ratten* v. *R* [1971] 3 WLR 930
(PC) asked for the police she was not intending to make a descriptive
statement but simply making a request; her words were primarily
performative and the admissibility of her request could also be justified
on this basis.

5.6 The Problem of 'Implied Assertions'

The hearsay rule clearly applies to statements which are intended by the
maker to be descriptive of some matter ('express assertions') whether the
maker's method of communicating that statement is oral, written, or
otherwise. The question is whether the hearsay rule, as currently defined in
England and Wales, also applies to unintended but logically *inferable*
statements, that is, where a person has conducted himself and/or spoken in
a way which, in the circumstances, allows an inference logically to be
drawn as to his belief in (or knowledge of) the existence of a fact and
therefore that the fact actually exists. If Anthony asks Paul to pass the salt
one may logically infer that Paul and not Anthony has the salt. The
request 'Pass the salt please, Paul' allows the statement 'Paul has the salt'
to be inferred. Such an inferred statement (more commonly – but
incorrectly – referred to as an 'implied assertion') would seem, logically, to
be covered by the hearsay rule as defined in *R* v. *Sharp* [1988] 1 WLR 7
(HL) (5.1 *ante*) if tendered to prove that Paul did indeed possess the salt at
the time the request was made.

5.6.1 Does the Hearsay Rule Extend to 'Implied Assertions'?

A witness's statement such as 'the doctor told me David was dead' is a
statement of fact. It is possible for the matter stated to be true (or false):

either David was dead or he was alive. An express out-of-court assertion such as this would therefore fall within the scope of the hearsay rule and, in the absence of an exception, would not be admissible in a criminal trial to prove David's death. However, if the witness had not been spoken to by the doctor but instead had *seen* the doctor cover David's face with a blanket, would the witness be allowed to state in court that David had died? The traditional view is that he would. Any witness is allowed to give his opinion if it is no more than a compendious way of summarising a number of observations and the inferences drawn from them (12.1 *post*). As the witness would have directly perceived an incident and logically inferred death he should be able to testify to that effect. Unfortunately there is a body of case law which throws doubt on the admissibility of such evidence on the ground that it would amount to an 'implied assertion' covered by the hearsay rule. It is now well established that a statement which can be inferred from spoken or written words is covered by the hearsay rule, and it is therefore possible (although there is no clear authority on the point) that any statement which can be inferred from conduct will also fall foul of the rule.

5.6.1.1 Statements Inferred from Spoken or Written Words

The starting point for any discussion on the admissibility of statements which can be inferred from spoken or written words is the case of *Wright* v. *Tatham* (1837) 7 Ad & El 313. The issue in that case was whether a testator, John Marsden, had been sane at the time he made his will. The party wishing to uphold the will sought to adduce letters written to Marsden by third parties who had been well-acquainted with him but who had also died before the trial. The reasoning was that as the persons who had written to Marsden had done so in respectful terms which demonstrated their opinion of his good health and sound mind, it could be inferred that he had been sane when his will was drawn up and that it was therefore valid. The Court of Exchequer Chamber held that the letters had been properly excluded as 'mere hearsay evidence', and Parke B gave examples of other types of correspondence which would fall foul of the hearsay rule for the same reason: a letter demanding the payment of a debt to prove the debt was due, and a note congratulating a person on his high state of bodily vigour to prove he was in good health.

An example of an 'implied assertion' being held to be inadmissible hearsay is provided by the case of *Teper* v. *R* [1952] AC 480. T was charged with setting fire to the shop where he conducted his business in order to claim on insurance policies, and his defence was that he had been elsewhere. At his trial a police officer was allowed to give evidence that he had seen a motorist resembling T driving away from the fire after he had heard an unidentified woman shouting, 'Your place burning and you going away from the fire!' The Privy Council quashed T's conviction because what the police officer had heard was hearsay evidence. The sole relevance of the woman's words lay in the inference that she had identified T fleeing the scene, and this 'implied assertion' fell within the scope of the exclusionary rule. Similarly, in *Walton* v. *R* (1989) 166 CLR 283 it was held by the majority of the High Court of Australia that a three-year-old child's greeting of 'Hello Daddy' to someone on the phone was an 'implied assertion' identifying the caller as 'Daddy' and therefore inadmissible; and in *R* v. *West* [1999] All ER (D) 1005 (99/04541/W3) the Court of Appeal accepted that the words 'Fuck off, Adrian!' amounted to a hearsay statement of identification (*cf. R* v. *Sawoniuk* [2000] 2 Cr App R 220 (CA) at p. 229).

The question of 'implied assertions' also arose in the case of *R* v. *Blastland* [1985] 3 WLR 345. It has been seen already (3.1.3 *ante*) that comments made by a third party, M, to the effect that the deceased had been murdered, were excluded even though M's words amounted to evidence from which the jury might have inferred M's involvement and therefore B's innocence. The reason for the judge's ruling was that the defence wished to rely on the comments as an implied admission by M that he had known about the crime and therefore an implied admission of his involvement. Although the House of Lords dismissed B's appeal on the ground that M's state of mind had not been relevant to any issue in the trial, Lord Bridge approved the judge's approach, stating (at p. 350) that a contrary decision would have led to 'the very odd result that the inference that Mark may have himself committed the murder may be supported indirectly by what Mark said, though if he had directly acknowledged guilt this would have been excluded'.

The case of *Ratten* v. *R* [1971] 3 WLR 930 (PC) (5.4 *ante*) raised similar problems. If the evidence was simply that a telephone call had been made by a woman from the accused's house the question of hearsay would not have arisen. The mere fact of the call would have rebutted the accused's denial of a call having been made. However, the telephonist was also permitted to give evidence that the deceased had been hysterical and sobbing and that she had requested the police ('Get me the police please!'). The Privy Council justified the admission of this evidence of the deceased's emotional state as it explained her reason for making the call, and the request for the police indicated the nature of her emotional state. Such evidence was relevant as it tended to rebut the accused's defence of a peaceful lunch-time which was shattered by an unfortunate accident, but the evidence would also appear to have infringed the hearsay rule. The request for the police together with her highly-charged emotional state allowed a statement to be inferred from the deceased that she was in desperate need of help from the police, that is, that she was in imminent danger from someone or something.

Ratten v. *R* [1971] 3 WLR 930 exemplifies the important point that where out-of-court words give rise to an 'implied assertion', that inference will not prevent the words from being admissible if they are otherwise relevant to an issue in the trial for a reason unconnected with the hearsay element. The deceased's request had 'double relevance'. It was relevant as original evidence for the purpose of rebutting the accused's denial that a call had been made and showing the deceased's emotional state, thereby undermining his defence of accident; but it was *additionally* relevant in that a (hearsay) inference could be drawn from the request and the deceased's emotional state that she believed her life was in danger from the accused. Because the prosecution had relied on the original evidence aspect and not on the hearsay aspect the conviction was upheld. If the prosecution had relied on the hearsay aspect the conviction would have been quashed in the absence of a recognised exception to the hearsay rule. As it was, the Privy Council felt that even if the hearsay aspect had been relied on it would have been admissible under one of the *res gestae* exceptions to the exclusionary rule (6.1.1.1 *post*). Thus, where a party wishes to rely on words as original evidence an incidental hearsay inference will not prevent the admissibility of the words if the party is not relying on that inference. For example, if a party wishes to rely on a witness's out-of-court statement to demonstrate the witness's consistency and credibility (by virtue of an exception to the rule prohibiting reliance on previous consistent statements) the possibility that the jury might erroneously rely on the forbidden hearsay element will not prevent the non-hearsay aspect from being admissible (see 16.4.2 *post*).

In giving the judgment of the Privy Council in *Ratten* v. *R* [1971] 3 WLR 930, Lord Wilberforce made a fleeting reference to *McGregor* v. *Stokes* [1952] VLR 347 in which the ruling of Salmond J in *Davidson* v. *Quirke* [1923] NZLR 552 (NZSC) was approved by the Supreme Court of Victoria. These are but two examples of the many 'betting cases' which have come before the courts of Australia, New Zealand and the United States of America, the question in each case being whether police officers could give evidence that a large number of telephone calls had been made to certain establishments, for the purpose of placing bets, to prove those premises had been used by the occupiers for illegal gambling. In *Davidson* v. *Quirke* [1923] NZLR 552 (at pp. 555–7) Salmond J held that the telephone calls and their content were admissible:

'Such a practice does not arise by accident or mistake, and points logically to the inference that such use of the telephone by outsiders has its source in the agreement and purpose of the occupier himself ... I am of the opinion that, notwithstanding the general rule which excludes evidence of statements, the contents of those telephone messages as received and testified to by the police officers are legally admissible in evidence. This is an illustration of the principle that, notwithstanding the rule against hearsay, where the purpose or meaning of an act done is relevant, evidence of contemporaneous declarations accompanying and explaining the act is admissible in proof of such purpose and meaning ... The position is the same as if those persons had resorted to the appellant's premises in person and had there offered to make bets with a police officer in the belief that he was the occupier. In such a case evidence would have been admissible not merely of the fact of such visits, but of contemporaneous statements made by the visitors as to their motives and purposes.'

An offer to place a bet is a performative utterance comprising a verbal method of effecting an act. It is not intended to be descriptive or narrative.

Such words do not therefore directly infringe the rule against hearsay, but they do allow a descriptive statement to be *inferred* (that is, the words give rise to an 'implied assertion'). The words allow an inference to be drawn that the caller knows or believes that gambling occurs in his interlocutor's premises, which gives rise to the further inference that gambling does indeed take place there. If the only relevance the words have is based on a process of reasoning which depends on the truth of the 'implied assertion' (that is, there is no 'double relevance') then, according to the decision in *Wright* v. *Tatham* (1837) 7 Ad & El 313 (CEC), the words are inadmissible unless there is a recognised hearsay exception which can be relied on. To say that the content of such a conversation is admissible to explain the purpose of the caller in making the call is to ignore the fact that the only probative value the calls have in such cases is to prove a belief that the premises were being used for gambling. This belief is then relied on as evidence that the premises were actually being used for gambling. This was recognised in the leading English case on 'implied assertions', *R* v. *Kearley* [1992] 2 WLR 656, where the majority of the House of Lords refused to follow the Commonwealth betting cases. Before considering the facts of *R* v. *Kearley*, though, it should be noted that the principle referred to by Salmond J, and regarded as a way of admitting original evidence in *McGregor* v. *Stokes* [1952] VLR 347 (VSC) and *Ratten* v. *R* [1971] 3 WLR 930 (PC), is in truth the application of a common-law exception to the hearsay rule (6.1.1.4 *post*).

Alan 'Chippie' Kearley, was charged with possession of amphetamine with intent to supply contrary to s. 5(3) of the Misuse of Drugs Act 1971. 17.4 grammes of the drug were found in a rabbit hutch at his home, but that quantity was not of itself sufficient to permit a proper inference that he had intended to supply it to other persons. Following K's arrest, and while he was being kept out of the way, police officers remained at his home and received a number of telephone calls and personal callers. Ten of the telephone callers asked for 'Chippie' and for drugs. Seven of the personal callers indicated that they wanted to purchase drugs and some of them were carrying cash in their hands. At the trial the prosecution called the police officers, and the judge allowed them to give evidence of those calls to prove K's intent to supply. K was convicted and the Court of Appeal dismissed his appeal, relying on the case of *Woodhouse* v. *Hall* (1980) 72 Cr App R 39 (DC) (5.4 *ante*) as authority for the proposition that the offer to buy drugs was admissible original evidence to prove that the premises were being used to supply drugs, which was evidence that K himself was the supplier, the two issues being inextricably linked.

The majority of the House of Lords (Lords Bridge, Ackner and Oliver) allowed K's appeal. Lord Ackner simply held the evidence to be inadmissible on the ground of irrelevance; the requests for drugs did not amount to factual assertions (that is, they were performative words) and while those words indicated the state of mind of the callers (namely their belief that K was a supplier) they had no bearing on the state of mind of K himself. However, his Lordship did suggest that if the words could be said to have given rise to an 'implied assertion' that K was a supplier, that assertion was inadmissible hearsay. Lords Bridge and Oliver agreed that the state of mind of any caller was not of itself relevant to any issue, but accepted that the words spoken had given rise to an 'implied assertion' as to the callers' belief that K was a supplier and that this in turn gave rise to an 'implied assertion' that he was in fact a supplier. While this latter assertion was relevant to the question of K's state of mind it was inadmissible hearsay on account of the rule in *Wright* v. *Tatham* (1837) 7 Ad & El 313 (CEC). This was not a case of 'double relevance' so K's conviction could not stand; and the fact that there had been such a large number of 'implied assertions' made no difference. Relying on the decision of the House of Lords in *Myers* v. *DPP* [1964] 3 WLR 145, Lord Oliver said (at pp. 696–7):

'The multiplicity of calls can go only to indicating that a shared belief is more likely to be true than a belief held by a single person or a few people. That, however, goes to weight or reliability, not to admissibility and it cannot in itself make admissible that which is inadmissible ... I cannot, for my part, see any logical difference between evidence of a positive assertion and evidence of an assertion expressed as a question from which the positive assertion is to be inferred. In both cases the opinion or belief of the maker is unsworn and untested by cross-examination and is equally prejudicial. To admit such statements as evidence of the fact would, in my opinion, not only entail ... the overruling of a case of high authority which has stood unchallenged for a century and a half but would involve embarking upon a process of judicial legislation.'

The majority agreed that the Commonwealth betting cases could not be reconciled with English authorities. Lord Bridge said (at p. 669):

'While the admissibility of words which accompany an action may be derived from the relevance of the action itself, if an action considered apart from any accompanying words is not of any relevance, the action will be of no assistance in establishing the admissibility of the accompanying words. Moreover, if the words and action considered together amount to no more than an implied assertion of a fact which, if asserted directly by the speaker, would be excluded as hearsay, they clearly fall within the exclusionary principle ...'

While Lords Oliver and Bridge were clearly unhappy to be bound by *Wright* v. *Tatham*, given the high probative value of the hearsay evidence (on account of the plurality of calls) their Lordships accepted that any reform must come from Parliament. The minority (Lords Griffiths and Browne-Wilkinson) felt they could find 'double relevance' by applying the reasoning of Salmond J in *Davidson* v. *Quirke* [1923] NZLR 552 (NZSC), arguing that the reference to his ruling in *Ratten* v. *R* [1971] 3 WLR 930 meant the Privy Council had approved the Commonwealth betting cases. On this view the large number of calls, explained by the callers' state of mind as revealed by their contemporaneous words, were relevant in that they showed a potential market was available for the purchase of drugs from K, and this opportunity for K to supply drugs allowed an inference to be drawn that K had an intention to supply drugs. While this evidence was also capable of giving rise to an impermissible secondary inference (that the callers believed K supplied drugs) this could not preclude its admissibility for the purpose of showing an available market. The minority accepted the irrelevance of the callers' belief in K's state of mind, but the calls and the words spoken had, on this view, additional relevance in that they demonstrated an available market. Not surprisingly, Lords Griffiths and Browne-Wilkinson shared the view of Lords Oliver and Bridge that the hearsay rule was in need of reform. The majority judgment led to a result which is contrary to common sense, so it is not surprising that the minority should have tried to find an additional aspect of relevance by which to admit the evidence. The large number of callers and their requests for drugs were of course relevant to the question of whether K was a supplier, but that relevance was based on the 'implied assertion' that K was a supplier, and the majority were not willing to accept the argument advanced by the minority. As Lord Oliver asked (at p. 691):

'What is it about the existence of a potential customer or of a body of customers, whether substantial or not, that tends to render it more or less likely that a given individual intends to supply their requirements?'

The prosecution might, however, have tried to have the evidence admitted by an alternative route. The *collective* belief amongst the callers that K supplied drugs was logically relevant to whether he had the intention to supply the drugs in his possession. The large number of callers and their belief demonstrated his general reputation in the local community as a dealer, which was relevant to his state of mind if only on the ground that a notorious reputation is usually deserved. If a person's belief is relevant to an issue in the trial, his out-of-court statement is admissible to prove it (6.1.1.2 *post*), so the numerous requests might have been tendered *together* on this ground to prove K's reputation for supplying drugs in his immediate community. On this analysis the question of admissibility should have been one of 'similar facts': was the evidence of K's disposition to deal in drugs (inferable from his general reputation) sufficiently probative in the context of the other admissible evidence that it could be admitted to prove *mens rea* notwithstanding the risk that his defence might be unduly prejudiced?

The rule that 'implied assertions' are covered by the hearsay rule can operate just as much against the accused as it can work in his favour. In *R* v. *Harry* (1986) 86 Cr App R 105 cocaine and drug-dealing paraphernalia were found in a flat used by H and his co-accused 'Sacha'. After they had been arrested, the police intercepted a number of telephone calls to the flat during which the callers asked for 'Sacha' and whether drugs were for sale. H was not allowed to cross-examine the police officers for the purpose of eliciting this evidence and showing that it was his co-accused and not he who had been the dealer. This ruling was upheld by the Court of Appeal on the ground that the evidence had been inadmissible hearsay.

R v. *Kearley* [1992] 2 WLR 656 (HL) was recently applied in *R* v. *O'Connell* [2003] EWCA Crim 502; but it was distinguished in *R* v. *Warner* (1992) 96 Cr App R 324 (CA). In the latter case the two co-accused were charged with supplying heroin. The prosecution were allowed to adduce evidence, pursuant to s. 74(1) of the Police and Criminal Evidence Act 1984 (12.3.2 *post*), that a large number of persons had been seen by the police to pay very short visits to the co-accused's house and that eight of the visitors had previous convictions for the possession or supply of heroin. The Court of Appeal held that the evidence showed the character of the persons visiting their house and that the question of hearsay did not even arise. The defence which had been raised was that the callers had been paying social visits, and the callers' bad character was therefore relevant (albeit weak) circumstantial evidence from which it could be inferred that the sale of heroin had been taking place, confirming the 'primary evidence' of the witnesses who had given direct testimony that the two co-accused had been dealing in heroin. The prosecution had not relied on anything said by the callers so there was no question of any 'implied assertion' (from words). The evidence had been relevant and *prima facie* admissible subject to the judge's discretion to exclude it if its probative value was outweighed by its unduly prejudicial effect.

5.6.1.2 Statements Inferred from Conduct

In *Wright* v. *Tatham* (1837) 7 Ad & El 313 (CEC) Parke B went on to consider some examples of statements which could be inferred from conduct and would therefore be inadmissible as hearsay: (i) the payment of a wager to prove the outcome of the event in respect of which the wager had been made; (ii) the payment to third parties by underwriters under an insurance policy to prove the subject-matter insured had been lost; (iii) the conduct of the family of a testator, taking the same precautions in his absence as if he were a lunatic to prove that he was one, or electing him in his absence to some responsible office to prove he was competent to hold that office; (iv) the conduct of a doctor who permitted a will to be executed by a sick testator to prove that the testator was competent to make the will; and (v) the conduct of a deceased captain on a question of seaworthiness, who, after examining every part of the vessel, embarked in it with his family.

If this is a correct statement of the hearsay rule its scope is far wider than most practitioners would appreciate. If it is impermissible to give evidence that a doctor permitted a will to be executed by a patient, on the ground that this would imply a statement that the testator was competent, so it cannot be permissible to give evidence that a doctor covered a patient's face to prove that the patient was dead. Indeed, in the New York case of *Thompson* v. *Manhattan Railway Co* (1896) 11 ADR 182 (NYSC) it was not possible for the plaintiff to elicit from a witness that she had been cauterised on the back by a doctor to prove that she had suffered a spinal injury. Such proof was held to be in the nature of hearsay. Similarly, in the Australian case of *Holloway* v. *MacFeeters* (1956) 94 CLR 470 (HCA) it

was felt by Dixon CJ and Kitto J that the conduct of a motorist in running
away after a road accident in which he had been involved would amount
to an 'implied assertion' of culpability covered by the hearsay rule. Such
evidence would therefore be admissible as an implied *admission* of liability
(an exception to the hearsay rule) if the driver was a party to the
proceedings, but not otherwise. The same must be true for criminal
proceedings, save that the admissibility of the accused's implied admission
of guilt is subject to s. 76(2) of the Police and Criminal Evidence Act 1984
(7.1.3 *post*). The reasoning in *Holloway* v. *MacFeeters* provides an
alternative explanation for the decision in *Mawaz Khan* v. *R* [1966] 3 WLR
1275 (5.4 *ante*). The accused's false statement in that case was in effect an
'implied assertion' of culpability and hearsay, save that it was admissible
by virtue of the confessions exception. Following *R* v. *Kearley* [1992] 2
WLR 656 (HL), an out-of-court statement made by the accused and
tendered by the prosecution to prove its falsity should have to satisfy the
requirements of s. 76(2) of PACE. This has now been brought about,
albeit by a different route, as a result of the decision of the Court of
Appeal in *R* v. *Z* [2003] 1 WLR 1489 (7.1.1 *post*).

There is no binding authority in English law that assertions inferred
from conduct are covered by the hearsay rule, although the reliance placed
on *Wright* v. *Tatham* (1837) 7 Ad & El 313 (CEC) in *R* v. *Kearley* [1992] 2
WLR 656 (HL) supports the argument that they are. In *Manchester
Brewery* v. *Coombs* (1901) 82 LT 347 (ChD) it was felt, *obiter*, that
evidence that customers in a public house had tasted beer and left it or
thrown it away would be admissible to prove the beer was bad; but that
decision could also be explained as the application of an exception to the
hearsay rule to otherwise inadmissible 'implied assertions' (6.1.1.4 *post*).

5.6.2 Should the Hearsay Rule Cover 'Implied Assertions'?

The scope of the exclusionary hearsay rule should be no wider than its
rationale demands. If the rule fails to serve the interests of justice or
otherwise adversely affects the admissibility of evidence which generally
ought to be admitted then its scope should be redefined by Parliament.
Whether the hearsay rule should cover 'implied assertions' depends
primarily on whether the justifications for excluding express assertions
apply with equal force to inferred statements.

It has been seen that the principal justification for the hearsay rule is to
exclude evidence of unascertainable reliability. The person who made the
out-of-court statement, assuming he exists, may have been lying or
mistaken about the matters he was purporting to narrate (or misinterpreted by a nonetheless convincing witness); and yet the maker is
unavailable for cross-examination. However, where a statement has been
inferred from words or conduct, the likelihood that the maker intended to
mislead the reporter will often be low. As a general rule people do not
request drugs from a person on the off-chance that someone is listening
who will infer that that person is a dealer, or go through the charade of
covering a patient's face to mislead an observer into thinking he has died,

or call an establishment to place a bet hoping the call will be intercepted by the police.

In those examples the risk of deception is probably low enough to be discounted, but it is quite possible to envisage other situations where the risk of deception cannot so easily be ignored. If a house is raided by the police and D1 and D2 are charged with possession of heroin with intent to supply, is it really too far-fetched to imagine that D1 would arrange to have several calls made to the house asking for drugs from D2? Can it be taken for granted that a letter written in a respectful way reflects the author's true feelings about the recipient? In *Wright* v. *Tatham* (1837) 7 Ad & El 313 (CEC) (5.6.1.1 *ante*) there was evidence that the testator, Marsden, had actually been insane; and it is therefore quite possible that the persons who wrote to him were acting in accordance with the social conventions of the early nineteenth century and that their letters did not reflect their true opinion of his state of mind, particularly if they had been aware that their correspondence would be dealt with by a sane person acting on Marsden's behalf.

Furthermore, even if deception can be discounted there is still the possibility of unreliability from mistake on the part of the maker, whose powers of perception and memory cannot be tested in cross-examination. *Teper* v. *R* [1952] AC 480 (PC) (5.6.1.1 *ante*) is a case in point. If the hearsay rule had not been applicable the absent woman's shout of 'Your place burning and you going away from the fire!' would have been *prima facie* admissible notwithstanding her unavailability for cross-examination on what she had said and the circumstances of her visual identification. There is also the possibility of an erroneous inference being drawn by the jury from what has been seen or heard by the witness, particularly in cases where there is a degree of ambiguity in the maker's words or conduct. In Parke B's example of the ship's captain (5.6.1.2 *ante*), the mere fact that he was seen walking round his vessel could lead to any number of inferences as to his state of mind or competence, even though deliberate deception would have been unlikely. He could, for example, have been exercising or checking the paintwork or looking for something he had lost; and if he was indeed inspecting the vessel for seaworthiness it would be necessary to consider the collateral question of whether he actually knew what he was doing. If evidence such as this were to be admitted to prove that the ship was seaworthy it is difficult to see how the tribunal of fact would properly be able to evaluate its reliability and weight. The reasoning process would be predicated on little more than speculation, and it has already been seen that this is not an acceptable basis for resolving issues of fact (*R* v. *Blastland* [1985] 3 WLR 345 (HL), 3.1.3 *ante*).

On the other hand, there can be little doubt that a hearsay rule which would exclude any statement which is inferable from words or conduct is far too wide to be acceptable. A rule along these lines would, subject to any exception, prohibit probative and reliable evidence which is now admitted as a matter of course. Most if not all human conduct gives rise to an inference about the actor's state of mind such as his belief or intention and it would be absurd if all such evidence were to be excluded, subject to the availability of a suitable exception, on the ground that it is inherently unreliable.

If the above examples illustrate anything it is that an absolute exclusionary rule is out of place in the law of evidence where each case turns on its own facts. Some form of guided discretion is needed for hearsay evidence and, drawing on the law governing the admissibility of the accused's extraneous misconduct for an analogy (3.3.11 *ante*), a solution would be to have a *prima facie* rule of inadmissibility (subject to an inclusionary discretion) for express assertions (6.4 *post*) and a rule of *prima facie* admissibility (subject to an exclusionary discretion) for 'implied assertions'.

Rule 801 of the United States Federal Rules of Evidence provides as follows:

> A 'statement' is (1) an oral or written assertion or (2) non-verbal conduct of a person, if it is intended by the person as an assertion ... 'Hearsay' is a statement, other than one made by the declarant while testifying at the trial or hearing, offered in evidence to prove the truth of the matter asserted.

Although it is first necessary to eliminate the possibility that the inferred statement was intended by the maker, this rule has the merit of making (unintended) statements of fact which have been inferred from words or conduct *prima facie* admissible on account of the absence or the unlikelihood of deception. The Law Commission (Law Com No. 245 (1997) at pp. 85–90) has accepted this approach as its preferred option for reform:

> '(1) ... in criminal proceedings a statement not made in oral evidence in the proceedings should not be admissible as evidence of any matter stated, and (2) a matter should be regarded as stated in a statement if (and only if) the purpose, or one of the purposes, of the person making the statement appears to the court to have been (a) to cause another person to believe the matter, or (b) to cause another person to act, or a machine to operate, on the basis that the matter is as stated.'

The risk of mistake remains, but this can be effectively ameliorated. If either party wishes to adduce an 'implied assertion' any such risk can be taken into account when the judge determines the question of relevance. If, for example, the probative value of the evidence is dependent on speculation, or a proper assessment of its probative value would require the jury to resolve a number of extraneous collateral questions, it might be appropriate to exclude the evidence on the ground that it is 'irrelevant' (3.1.3 *ante*). Of course if the evidence is tendered by the prosecution the judge would be able to take the risk of mistake and fabrication into account when exercising his common-law or statutory discretion to exclude it.

Taking Parke B's example again, the various inferences which might be drawn from the conduct of the ship's captain would necessitate a process of reasoning which would depend on speculation. To avoid such speculation it would be necessary to resolve the collateral matter of what the captain was actually doing, which would mean that evidence (and no doubt counter-evidence) would need to be adduced, leading to lengthier and costlier proceedings. And even if it could be inferred that the captain was indeed inspecting his ship for seaworthiness, an enquiry into whether he was mistaken in his conclusion would depend on an assessment of his experience, qualifications and competence, which would necessitate the resolution of a further collateral matter. Accordingly, there would be a sound basis for excluding the evidence on the ground that it is 'irrelevant'.

5.7 Hearsay and Mechanically-generated Documents

The hearsay rule applies to out-of-court statements which have emanated from a *human* source. If there is no human involvement the question of hearsay does not arise. Thus, where a machine, instrument or computer has produced a statement in the absence of any human input between the act of measuring or calculating and the production of the statement, the sole question is whether the machine, instrument or computer is reliable and not whether an exception to the hearsay rule applies. Such mechanically-generated statements are admissible as real evidence.

Television footage is admissible real evidence (*Kajala* v. *Noble* (1982) 75 Cr App R 149 (DC)) as are still photographs and audio recordings (*R* v. *Maqsud Ali* [1965] 3 WLR 229 (CCA)). In *Taylor* v. *Chief Constable of Cheshire* [1986] 1 WLR 1479 (DC) it was held that witnesses could give evidence of what they had seen on a video recording if the tape was no longer available at the time of the trial. In *The Statue of Liberty* [1968] 1 WLR 739 (PD) it was held that radar recordings were admissible; Simon P said (at p. 740):

'Similarly, if evidence of weather conditions were relevant, the law would affront common sense if it were to say that those could be proved by a person who looked at a barometer from time to time, but not by producing a barograph record. So, too, with other types of dial recordings. Again, cards from clocking-in-and-out machines are frequently admitted in accident cases. The law is now bound to take cognizance of the fact that mechanical means replace human effort.'

Other examples of real evidence include print-outs from Intoximeter breath-test machines (*Castle* v. *Cross* [1984] 1 WLR 1372 (DC)), from weighing machines and spectrometers (*R* v. *Wood* (1982) 76 Cr App R 23 (CA)) and from computerised machines which automatically record that telephone calls have been made (*R* v. *Spiby* (1990) 91 Cr App R 186 (CA)). In *R* v. *Wood* (1982) 76 Cr App R 23 (CA) a print-out from a computer which had performed nothing more than calculations in respect of data produced by an X-ray spectrometer was held to be admissible real evidence (although the evidence would not have been admissible if the chemists had not given oral evidence of the data which had been entered into the computer). In *R* v. *Pettigrew* (1980) 71 Cr App R 39 (CA), however, it was assumed that the print-out of a computer in the Bank of England's automatic sorting machine was hearsay. This cannot be right as there was no human input at all (see *R* v. *Governor of Brixton Prison ex parte Levin* [1997] 3 WLR 117 (HL) at p. 121).

Where there is a degree of human involvement which has influenced the final statement the hearsay rule *does* apply. Thus in *R* v. *Coventry Justices ex parte Bullard* (1992) 95 Cr App R 175 (DC) a computer print-out stating that the accused was in arrears with his poll tax payments was inadmissible hearsay because it was based on information entered into the computer by a person and that information had not been properly proved (*cf. R* v. *Wood* (1982) 76 Cr App R 23 (CA)); and in *R* v. *Shephard* (1991) 93 Cr App R 139 the Court of Appeal felt that as the information recorded on till rolls had been supplied by cashiers it was hearsay. The Law Commission (Law Com No. 245 (1997) at p. 92) has made the following recommendation in line with *R* v. *Coventry Justices ex parte Bullard*:

'Where a representation of any fact is made otherwise than by a person, but depends for its accuracy on information supplied by a person, it should not be admissible as evidence of the fact unless it is proved that the information was accurate.'

5.8 Circumventing the Hearsay Rule

In *Myers* v. *DPP* [1964] 3 WLR 145 the accused faced several charges of receiving stolen cars. The prosecution case was that wrecked cars and their log books had been bought at a very low price and then cars of the same type had been stolen, passed off and sold as the legitimately bought cars. The prosecution were allowed to establish that the cars were stolen by calling employees of the car manufacturers, and those witnesses produced microfilm records (photographs of the written record compiled by anonymous workmen on the production line) purporting to show the cylinder block numbers which had been indelibly stamped on the engines and contemporaneously recorded during the manufacturing process. The majority of the House of Lords held that the evidence had been wrongly admitted on the ground that the hearsay rule was absolute unless an exception applied. The list of common-law exceptions was closed, and the mere fact that hearsay evidence was highly reliable could not justify its admission in the absence of an established exception.

The technical nature of the hearsay rule has created difficulties for the courts. If highly reliable and probative evidence falls within the scope of the exclusionary rule it is inadmissible unless a statutory or established common-law exception can be found to justify its admission. In the absence of any such exception the courts must either exclude the evidence or find a way of side-stepping the hearsay rule. This side-stepping has been effected in two ways. First, the courts have been willing to redefine evidence so that it is not caught by the exclusionary rule at all, and this has led to anomalous cases where what appears to be hearsay has been classified as something else. Second, where it has been thought inappropriate to redefine an item of obvious hearsay evidence as non-hearsay the courts have ignored the hearsay problem altogether or broadened an existing exception so that the evidence can be brought within its scope.

A written entry in a record which a party relies on for the purpose of proving the truth of the matter recorded falls within the scope of the hearsay rule, and logically the same should be true for the absence of an entry if it too amounts to an assertion of fact. If a teacher places a tick next to the name of any students who are present and makes no mark next to the names of absent students, the absence of a tick amounts to an assertion of fact ('this student was absent on this date') just as much as the tick ('this student was present on this date') and as such both should be covered by the hearsay rule. This is not the approach the Court of Appeal has adopted, however. In *R* v. *Patel* (1981) 73 Cr App R 117, P faced a charge of assisting the illegal entry into the UK of a third party, A, and the prosecution called an immigration officer to prove that A was an illegal entrant. The immigration officer was allowed to rely on Home Office records he had previously examined and gave evidence that A's name was not recorded as a person entitled to a certificate of registration in the UK. Although P's conviction was quashed on appeal, on account of the immigration officer's reliance on hearsay evidence, the Court of Appeal went on to intimate that it would have been permissible for the officer responsible for the compilation and custody of the records to give evidence that the method of compilation and custody was such that if A's name was not there he must be an illegal entrant. The Court of Appeal did not explain why the evidence would not be hearsay merely because it was given by one type of officer rather than another, but the dictum was considered with approval in *R* v. *Shone* (1982) 76 Cr App R 72. The accused in that case was charged with handling stolen vehicle springs which had been identified as coming from a particular wholesaler. The wholesaler's stock clerk and parts sales manager were called and they gave evidence that while the receipt and the sale or use of all spare parts were recorded on cards, there was no record of the sale or use of the material springs, even though those springs had been received and found to be missing from their stock. The Court of Appeal held that the absence of any mark indicating the sale or use of the springs, as related to the court by the witnesses, was not hearsay but direct evidence from which the jury had been entitled to draw the inference that the springs were stolen. It would seem to be permissible, therefore, to relate hearsay evidence in court, thereby converting it into admissible direct testimony, so long as the hearsay relied on is the absence of a record rather than a positive entry. It is a sensible result, but it is also a new common-law exception to the hearsay rule.

The hearsay rule was simply ignored in *R* v. *Muir* (1983) 79 Cr App R 153. The accused in that case was charged with stealing a video recorder he had hired from Granada Television Rentals, his defence being that two men had called round to collect the video, and his wife, presuming they were employees of Granada, had allowed them to take the video away.

The prosecution were allowed to call Granada's district manager to give evidence that he had been told by his head office that no repossession order had been made in respect of the accused's video. The Court of Appeal held that as this was not a case where a document was relied on, and there was no document in existence (*cf. R* v. *Shone* (1982) 76 Cr App R 72 (CA)), the question for the jury was simply whether or not the video had been repossessed by Granada as the accused had claimed. The district manager as 'the best person to give the relevant evidence' had therefore been entitled to say that he had been informed by his head office that the video had not been repossessed.

A number of decisions concerning identification evidence exemplify the pragmatic approach adopted by the Court of Appeal to the admissibility of hearsay evidence. The hearsay rule was ignored in *R* v. *Osbourne* [1973] 2 WLR 209 (CA), a common-law exception was widened in *R* v. *McCay* [1990] 1 WLR 645 (CA) (6.1.1.4 *post*), and in *R* v. *Cook* [1987] 2 WLR 775 (CA) hearsay evidence was held to be admissible on the ground that the evidence in question (photofits and sketches) was *sui generis* and not hearsay at all (see generally 16.4.2.5 *post*). More recently, in *R* v. *Ward* [2001] Crim LR 316 the Court of Appeal held that if a person identifies himself with reference to a name and the date of birth and address of the person bearing that name this may be regarded as an admission of identification (and therefore presence) for the purposes of the statutory exception to the hearsay rule which governs confessions – even though the statement is being tendered to prove the identity of the maker of the statement (and the exception to the hearsay rule can be relevant only if the identity of the maker as the accused is first established by other evidence). The consequence is that if person X knows the name, address and date of birth of person Y he can, if asked by a police officer to identify himself, give those details; and if Y is subsequently charged with the offence committed by X the evidence of the purported self-identification will be admissible against Y as an admission of his presence at the time the statement was made. The Court of Appeal justified its approach on the ground that evidence that a person has provided a name along with a corresponding address and date of birth is compelling evidence of a self-identification, although it was recognised that the jury should be given a (somewhat circular) direction not to rely on such evidence as an admission of presence by the accused unless they are first sure from the contents of the statement and any other evidence that it was indeed the accused identifying himself. A more appropriate way of justifying the admission of this sort of evidence is addressed in Chapter 6 (6.1.1.2 *post*).

Hearsay evidence may also be relied on by expert witnesses (*R* v. *Abadom* [1983] 1 WLR 126 (CA), 12.2.3 *post*), and the House of Lords in *R* v. *Sharp* [1988] 1 WLR 7 (HL) created a new common-law exception by recognising that the exculpatory parts of a 'mixed' statement were admissible as evidence of the truth of the matters stated (7.1.1 *post*). It should also be noted that the common law allows hearsay evidence to be admitted 'through the back door' in two other ways: a witness who relies on his earlier statement to 'refresh his memory' in respect of an event which he has entirely forgotten is in effect relating hearsay to the court (16.4.1 *post*); and hearsay may also become admissible if a document containing it is given to a witness to read during cross-examination and he accepts the truth of the matters stated therein (16.5.1 *post*).

A case which has given rise to much academic discussion is *R* v. *Rice* [1963] 2 WLR 585. Rice and his several co-accused, including Moore and Hoather, were charged with two counts of conspiracy. The prosecution were allowed to adduce a used airline ticket for two seats with the names 'Rice' and 'Moore' as evidence from which it could be inferred that Rice had travelled from London to Manchester with Hoather (who had admitted using Moore's booking and travelling with Rice). The ticket was produced by a representative of the airline who had custody of tickets returned after use. The Court of Criminal Appeal held that the ticket had been properly admitted as real evidence, although its evidential value was said to be limited to allowing the jury to draw an inference that 'probably two people had flown on the particular flight and that it might or might not seem to them by applying their common knowledge of such matters that the passengers bore the surnames which were written on the ticket'. (It was accepted that the latter inference was not one to be readily drawn given the suggestion that Moore had not taken the flight.) The Court drew an analogy with passports: just as a passport is likely to be in the possession of the person to whom it has been issued, so an airline ticket which has been used on a particular flight and which has a name on it is likely to have been used by a person of that name (or by one of two men whose names are on it). However, the ticket was inadmissible for the purpose of 'speaking its contents' as this would be hearsay. A passport could not be adduced to say 'my bearer is X' and equally an airline ticket could not be adduced to say 'I was issued to Y'. According to this reasoning the document was not admissible as an assertion ('this ticket was issued to Rice') but it was nonetheless admissible for the purpose of linking Rice to it on that flight. This decision has been criticised as an example of hearsay being improperly admitted, on the ground that the probative value of the ticket depended on an 'implied assertion' of possession ('this ticket was used by Rice') like the expressly assertive labels in *Patel* v. *Comptroller of Customs* [1965] 3 WLR 1221 (PC) and *R* v. *Brown* [1991] Crim LR 835 (CA) (5.3 *ante*).

The decision in *R* v. *Rice* can be justified, however, if it is seen as an example of evidence having 'double relevance' (5.6.1.1 *ante*). If the word 'Rice' on the ticket is regarded as an identifying mark, rather like a fingerprint, it has additional probative value based on the unlikelihood of a coincidence. Identifying marks which are not intended to be assertive do not fall directly within the scope of the hearsay rule (see *Miller* v. *Howe* [1969] 1 WLR 1510 (DC)). It is true that such a mark can give rise to an 'implied assertion' of possession (or presence at the place where the object was found), but the evidence is not relied on for that purpose. Its evidential value depends not on an acceptance of the truth of any 'implied assertion' but on the unlikelihood that a person other than the accused was also in possession of something with such a distinctive mark upon it.

If a rare, intricately-embroidered handkerchief is found at the scene of a crime, the fact the accused was in possession of a similar handkerchief, now lost, would be probative of his presence there. The same would be true if the handkerchief was uncommon for a more prosaic reason, for example because it bore the accused's initials upon it. The initials would give rise to an 'implied assertion', but the evidence would not be adduced for the purpose of proving the truth of that assertion. The evidential value relied on would be the fact that the accused belongs to the class of persons who have such a mark on their handkerchiefs. Taking this one step further, the same must be true if the handkerchief was marked with a surname. If a handkerchief bearing the name 'Rice' is found at the scene of a crime this is admissible circumstantial evidence that a person who is likely to have handkerchiefs decorated with that name (that is, a person called Rice) was there. In *R* v. *Rice* the ticket had been returned to the airline by the passenger at the end of the flight so it amounted to an item of circumstantial evidence directly connecting a person called Rice to that particular flight to Manchester. Just as a handkerchief marked 'Rice' is likely to have been used by a person called Rice, an airline ticket marked 'Rice' and handed in immediately after a flight is likely to have been used on that flight by a person called Rice. The probative value depends on this degree of likelihood and not on the truth of an 'implied assertion' such as 'this ticket was issued to Rice' or 'Rice travelled on this flight'. If the ticket had been found in any other place it would not have had probative value as circumstantial, real evidence; its only relevance would have lain in the 'implied assertion' that the ticket had been issued to and used by a person called Rice, which would have been inadmissible hearsay. Strictly speaking, of course, the evidence was tainted by hearsay to the extent that usually a name is printed on a ticket, or a monogram is printed on a handkerchief, because the person requesting the item has expressly or impliedly represented that a person with those initials or that name will be using it. However, when it is understood that much evidence is dependent upon hearsay to *some* extent (after all, how does anyone know his name or age or where he lives?) this can be disregarded as a *de minimis* taint, and *R* v. *Rice* would seem to have been correctly decided. In this respect it is worth noting the recent decision in *R* v. *Clarke* [2003] EWCA Crim 718, where it was held, in effect, that the hearsay rule is indeed subject to a *de minimis* limitation. V had identified two of her assailants as girls who had been at the same school as her, whose names she had come to know over a period of four years, although she had never spoken to them or heard either of them acknowledge their names. The Court of Appeal held that this was a case of recognition as opposed to mere identification, and that the argument that V's evidence was tainted by hearsay (and so either inadmissible or unreliable) lacked 'practical realism'. According to the Court, over a period of several years schoolchildren, or others in comparable institutions, get to know who their fellows are, often because they are named by persons who know them and there is nothing to suggest the contrary. Accordingly, 'what once may have been hearsay to start with, after much uncontradicted repetition over a period of time becomes repute and common knowledge', and to hold otherwise would be 'an affront to common sense'.

Another case of 'double relevance' which is in some respects similar to *R* v. *Rice* [1963] 2 WLR 585 (CCA) is that of *R* v. *Lydon* (1986) 85 Cr App R 221. The accused, Sean Lydon, was charged with robbery and the prosecution sought to identify him as one of the offenders by adducing, *inter alia*, a gun, which had been found along the route used by the getaway car, and pieces of paper bearing the words 'Sean rules' and 'Sean rules 85' which had been found near the gun. Scientific analysis showed that smears of ink on the gun matched the ink on the pieces of paper. Lydon appealed on the ground that the evidence linking him to the gun (the references to Sean) was hearsay and ought not to have been admitted. The Court of Appeal held that the evidence had been properly admitted because it was 'no more than a statement of fact involving no assertion as to the truth of the contents of the document'. The notes had not been relied on by the prosecution for the purpose of proving the truth of any express or 'implied assertion'. The relevance of the note, as in *R* v. *Rice*, lay simply in the likelihood that the person who would write such notes would be called Sean. As such, the evidence was not hearsay at all but circumstantial evidence from which the jury had been entitled to draw an inference that Lydon had disposed of the gun and been involved in the robbery (see also *R* v. *Orrell* [1972] RTR 14 (CA)).

In *R* v. *McIntosh* [1992] Crim LR 651 (CA) the accused was charged with being concerned in the importation of cocaine and the prosecution were permitted to adduce a piece of paper of unknown authorship bearing calculations of the price and weight of a quantity of drugs. The piece of paper had been found concealed in the chimney of the house where the accused had been living prior to his arrest, and was held to be admissible real evidence which did not infringe the hearsay rule. The document was adduced not for the purpose of proving the truth of the matters stated but simply to show the accused had an interest in the information it contained. Similarly, in *R* v. *Snowden* [2002] EWCA Crim 923 it was held that the accused's retention of a humorous birthday card with the words 'Keep on the grass man' and 'Get mown away! It's your birthday!' had been properly admitted as real evidence that he was treating the cultivation of cannabis as a joke, and that he had not therefore been forced to do it under duress as he had claimed. The same sort of reasoning applies to items such as a book which reveals the accused's interest in a particular branch of knowledge or type of news. In *R* v. *George* [2002] EWCA Crim 1923, for example, the prosecution were entitled to rely on the fact that magazine articles relating to the murder G had allegedly committed were found in his flat, along with articles about (and photographs of) the deceased, to show his fascination with her (and other television personalities) and to rebut his assertion when interviewed that he had never heard of her. Similarly, if the accused is charged with being involved in a joint enterprise to import cocaine, the mere fact he has a book entitled *The Cocaine Consumer's Handbook* would be relevant circumstantial evidence of his involvement (*R* v. *Thrussell* (1981) [1997] Crim LR 501n

(CA)). The book would not be relied on as evidence of the truth of the matters stated so the hearsay rule would not apply. However, because a book on cocaine consumption would suggest a criminal disposition the evidence would have to satisfy the 'similar facts' test before it could be admitted.

5.9 Reforming the Hearsay Rule

A sure indicator that the hearsay rule is in need of reform is the way the courts have tried to circumvent the decision of the House of Lords in *Myers* v. *DPP* [1964] 3 WLR 145 (5.8 *ante*). This is not surprising. The exclusionary rule is absolute unless one of the well-established exceptions applies, regardless of how reliable or probative the evidence might be. The rule can prevent the prosecution from relying on cogent and reliable evidence of the accused's guilt; and it is quite possible to envisage situations where the absence of a suitable exception will prevent the accused from being able to defend himself with cogent evidence of his innocence (as, for example, in *Sparks* v. *R* [1964] 2 WLR 566 (PC)). The latter eventuality could well result in a violation of Article 6(1) of the European Convention on Human Rights.

The Law Commission (Law Com No. 245 (1997) at pp. 69–80) considered six options: (i) the free-admissibility approach; (ii) the best-available-evidence approach; (iii) an exclusionary rule with a general inclusionary discretion; (iv) adding an inclusionary discretion to the present scheme; (v) categories of automatically admissible evidence; and (vi) an exclusionary rule with categories of automatic admissibility and a 'safety-valve' inclusionary discretion.

The free-admissibility approach (that is, the complete abolition of the hearsay rule) was rejected for the traditional reasons (5.2 *ante*), including the possibility of infringing Article 6(3)(d) of the European Convention on Human Rights, and because of the likelihood that much superfluous evidence would be rendered admissible. The best-available-evidence approach (which would allow hearsay to be admissible when direct testimony was unavailable) was also rejected because of the possibility that the parties would not respect their obligations to produce witnesses and the difficulty magistrates would face in applying the test. The third option was rejected because of the potential for uncertainty and inconsistency and, again, the fear that magistrates would be unable to apply the test. The fourth option was rejected because of the uncertainty which would result and the Commission's desire for other reforms. The fifth option, which would require a number of exceptions allowing in hearsay where it was likely to be reliable and/or where direct testimony was unavailable, was rejected because of the possibility that unforeseen situations would arise and cogent evidence would still end up being excluded.

This left the sixth option, which would entail reforming the exclusionary rule and its exceptions and providing judges (and magistrates) with a 'very limited discretion' to ensure highly reliable hearsay would not be excluded.

The Scope of the Hearsay Rule 169

This option was described as one striking the right balance between certainty and flexibility: 'a general rule against hearsay, subject to specified exceptions, plus a limited inclusionary discretion.' The discretion would be exercised in favour of admitting the evidence where the circumstances surrounding the making of the statement indicated that it could be treated as reliable (see 6.4 *post*).

Chapter Summary

- The common-law rule against hearsay prohibits the admission of any out-of-court statement if it is tendered to prove the *truth* of the matters stated, unless a statutory or common-law exception applies. In the absence of any such exception the courts must exclude the evidence, no matter how reliable or cogent it might be, unless a way can be found to 'side-step' the rule.
- The rule does not prohibit the admission of any statement which has been automatically generated by a machine without the benefit of human intervention.
- The rule against hearsay does not prevent the admission of an out-of-court statement if it is tendered as 'original evidence' to prove that the statement was *made* (if that is relevant). Nor does the rule prohibit the admission of a descriptive statement (e.g., a book) which is tendered not to prove the truth of the matters described but as (real) circumstantial evidence from which it can be inferred that the person in whose possession it was found had a particular interest or from which it can be inferred that a particular person had it in his possession.
- The rule against hearsay does not directly prevent the admission of words or 'utterances' which do not carry any (or any relevant) descriptive content, but it does prohibit the admission of statements of truth which can be *inferred* from such words or 'utterances'.
- It is unclear whether statements of truth which can be inferred from human conduct are similarly inadmissible, but what limited authority there is suggests that such statements are indeed encompassed by the rule.

Further Reading

Guest, 'The Scope of the Hearsay Rule' (1985) 101 LQR 385
Ashworth and Pattenden, 'Reliability, Hearsay and the Criminal Trial' (1986) 102 LQR 292
Birch, 'Hearsay-logic and Hearsay-fiddles' in *Essays in Honour of JC Smith* (1987) 24
Carter, 'Hearsay, Relevance and Admissibility' (1987) 103 LQR 106
Guest, 'Hearsay Revisited' (1988) 41 CLP 33
Carter, 'Hearsay: Whether and Whither?' (1993) 109 LQR 573
Pattenden, 'Conceptual versus Pragmatic Approaches to Hearsay' (1993) 56 MLR 138
Rein, 'The Scope of Hearsay' (1994) 110 LQR 431
Ormerod, ''Reform of Implied Assertions' (1996) 60 JCL 201
Zuckerman, 'The Futility of Hearsay' [1996] Crim LR 4

Law Commission Consultation Paper No. 138 (1995)
Law Commission Report, Law Com No. 245 (1997)

Criminal Justice Bill (2003), Part 11, Chapter 2 (on 'statements' and 'matters stated')
and Explanatory Note (www.publications.parliament.uk)

6 Exceptions to the Hearsay Rule

In civil proceedings s. 1 of the Civil Evidence Act 1995 provides that evidence is no longer inadmissible merely on the ground that it is hearsay, although as a rule certain notice conditions have to be complied with to ensure that the judge does not attach insufficient weight to the evidence (8.1 *post*). The notice provisions are unnecessary if the evidence is adduced pursuant to a separate statutory exception (8.2 *post*) or one of the few common-law exceptions preserved by the Act (8.3 *post*).

In criminal proceedings the position is more complicated. The general exclusionary rule remains absolute in nature subject to a number of statutory and well-established common-law exceptions, the former applying only to hearsay evidence in documentary form. Although only a few common-law exceptions are still of any relevance in civil proceedings, they all apply in criminal proceedings; indeed it is only by relying on a common-law exception that the prosecution (or the accused) may adduce oral hearsay evidence. If the hearsay evidence is in documentary form it may be possible to admit it at common law or pursuant to a statutory exception (or both). Confessions were formerly admissible at common law but the exception governing such statements has now been replaced by an important statutory regime which deserves separate treatment (7.1 *post*). This chapter is concerned with the other statutory exceptions which may be relied on in criminal proceedings together with the remaining common-law exceptions.

6.1 The Common-law Exceptions

Several exceptions to the hearsay rule have evolved at common law on account of the supposed reliability of statements made in certain circumstances and/or because of the unlikelihood of any non-hearsay evidence being available to prove the issue in dispute. Unless otherwise stated these exceptions have been superseded in civil proceedings by the provisions of the Civil Evidence Act 1995.

6.1.1 Statements Forming Part of the *Res Gestae*

A 'statement forming part of the *res gestae*' is one which can be said to be inextricably linked in time and space with an event or state of affairs. The expression is most often used in relation to spontaneous statements ('excited utterances') made approximately contemporaneously with a dramatic incident, usually the commission of a criminal offence, the assumption being that such circumstances provide some guarantee against the risk of unreliability from fabrication by the declarant. However, statements made approximately contemporaneously with the declarant's state of mind or health or conduct are also admissible to prove his state of mind or health at that time or to explain his conduct. These exceptions are also grouped under the general *res gestae* heading but the risk of fabrication cannot so easily be discounted in such cases, and the rationale underlying them is less certain. Although the requirement of contemporaneity may provide something of a safeguard against the risk of fabrication and mistake on the part of the declarant, it would seem the principal reason for admitting such evidence is necessity.

6.1.1.1 'Excited Utterances'

A statement made during or soon after an overwhelmingly dramatic event (or just prior to an imminent event of this sort) which can be said to have been made spontaneously and in response to (or in immediate anticipation of) that event, is admissible as evidence of the truth of the matters stated. The high degree of spontaneity involved means that the risk of fabrication can be discounted, and it is this reduced risk of unreliability which justifies the admission of such evidence. In the context of criminal proceedings it used to be thought that the dramatic event (the *res gestae*) must be the commission of the offence itself, but it now seems that this is not a requirement.

Until relatively recently the exception was construed rather strictly, with almost exact contemporaneity being required before an excited utterance could be admitted as part of the *res gestae*. There is no better illustration of this than the old case of *R* v. *Bedingfield* (1879) 14 Cox CC 341 (Assizes). Henry Bedingfield was charged with the murder of a woman, the facts being that she and Bedingfield had been in a house together when she suddenly came out with her throat severely cut saying, 'See what Harry has done!' She died 10 minutes later. This statement was ruled inadmissible on the ground that because it had not been something said *while* her throat was being cut it had not formed part of the *res gestae*. Similarly, the lack of contemporaneity (and physical proximity) meant that the exception could not be relied on in *Teper* v. *R* [1952] AC 480 (PC) (5.6.1.1 *ante*) where a woman was heard to identify the accused ('Your place burning and you going away from the fire!') 26 minutes after the relevant fire had started and some 200 metres away from it.

The excited utterance exception was reformulated in the seminal case of *Ratten* v. *R* [1971] 3 WLR 930 (5.6.1.1 *ante*). It will be remembered that the deceased's emotional telephone call to the local operator, and her words ('Get me the police please!') about five minutes before her death, were held to be admissible on the ground that the call itself was relevant, as it rebutted the accused's denial that any such call had been made, while her words and sobbing explained her reason for making the call. According to the Privy Council the deceased's words and emotional state had been properly admitted as original evidence. (In fact it is an exception to the hearsay rule; see 6.1.1.4 *post*.) Of more importance in the present context is that the Privy Council went on to consider the question of admissibility on the basis that the deceased's words had 'impliedly asserted' that she was in imminent danger from the accused, concluding (*obiter*) that her request for the police would have been admissible as part of the *res gestae*. The test to be applied was simply whether, on account of the statement having been made 'in circumstances of spontaneity or involvement in the event', the possibility of concoction could be disregarded. It was not necessary for the words to be exactly contemporaneous with the event, and as the deceased's words had been closely associated in time and space with the shooting, and had clearly been forced from her by the overwhelming pressure of the surrounding circumstances, the test had been satisfied. The inflexible criterion of exact contemporaneity was thus discarded in favour of a common-sense test based on sincerity.

The *Ratten* test was subsequently applied on a number of occasions by the Court of Appeal (see for example *R* v. *Nye* (1977) 66 Cr App R 252 and *R* v. *Turnbull* (1984) 80 Cr App R 104) but received its most authoritative stamp of approval when the House of Lords considered it in *R* v. *Andrews* [1987] 2 WLR 413. In that case, a drunken man was stabbed and mortally wounded by two men who had called at his flat, but within a few minutes of the attack he had been able to make his way to a neighbour's flat on the floor below. The police arrived a few minutes later and while administering emergency first aid asked the victim if he could identify who had stabbed him. The victim replied that one of the assailants was known to him as 'Donald' or 'Donavon' and the prosecution sought to have this evidence admitted at Donald Andrews' trial for murder. The trial judge applied the *Ratten* test and held that the statement of identification was admissible as part of the *res gestae*, a decision upheld by the House of Lords. Lord Ackner, in a speech with which all their Lordships agreed, overruled *R* v. *Bedingfield* (1879) 14 Cox CC 341 (Assizes) and laid down fresh guidelines (at pp. 422–3):

'1. The primary question which the judge must ask himself is – can the possibility of concoction or distortion be disregarded? 2. To answer that question the judge must first consider the circumstances in which the particular statement was made, in order to satisfy himself that the event was so unusual or startling or dramatic as to dominate the thoughts of the [declarant], so that his utterance was an instinctive reaction to that event, thus giving no real opportunity for reasoned reflection. In such a situation the judge would be entitled to conclude that the involvement or the pressure of the event would exclude the possibility of concoction or distortion, providing that the statement was made in conditions of approximate but not exact contemporaneity. 3. In order for the statement to be sufficiently 'spontaneous' it must be so closely associated with the event which has excited the statement that it can be fairly stated that the mind of the declarant was still dominated by the event ... The fact that the statement was made in answer to a question is but one factor to consider under this heading.'

Lord Ackner further stated that any other 'special features' in the case, such as alleged malice on the part of the declarant, had to be taken into consideration when deciding whether the possibility of concoction or distortion could be discounted. With regard to the possibility of error, it was felt that while the ordinary weaknesses of human recollection went merely to weight and not to the admissibility of the statement, where there were 'special features' giving rise to the possibility of error, such as the drunken state or defective eyesight of the declarant, or where the declarant's statement of identification was made in circumstances of poor visibility, the trial judge would have to consider those features when determining whether the possibility of error could be excluded. If the judge decided to allow the evidence to be adduced he was still obliged to give the jury an appropriate direction on the possibility of concoction, distortion or mistake and to point out to them any special features relevant to that possibility.

The approval of the flexible approach adopted in *Ratten* v. *R* [1971] 3 WLR 930 (PC) means that a trial judge's ruling on the admissibility of an excited utterance will not be interfered with on appeal so long as he properly directed himself and there was material entitling him to reach his conclusion. The test is one of reliability, based on the assumption that the effect of dramatic circumstances on the mind of a declarant considerably reduces the possibility of his having lied or distorted the truth (if not the possibility of error). Furthermore, even a fairly lengthy interval between the event in question (generally the commission of the offence) and the making of the declarant's statement may be an insufficient basis for refusing to admit that evidence under the *Andrews* test. A case in point is *R* v. *Carnall* [1995] Crim LR 944 where the severely injured victim of a violent attack took about an hour to crawl for help before making a statement identifying the accused. The Court of Appeal held that his statement had been correctly admitted as part of the *res gestae* (see also *R* v. *Gilfoyle* [1996] 1 Cr App R 303 (CA), 6.1.1.2 *post*).

However, if the possibility of error or concoction cannot be discounted the evidence will be inadmissible. In *R* v. *Harris* [2002] EWCA Crim 1597, for example, it was held that an eight-year-old witness's declaration on the telephone to the police should not have been admitted as she had spoken to a number of individuals before making her call and might therefore have been intentionally or inadvertently influenced by them; and in *Furbert* v. *R* [2000] 1 WLR 1716 (PC) a declaration by V as to who had shot him, made shortly after he was mortally wounded, was inadmissible because his location meant that he would not have been able to see his assailant.

It has been noted that an impending emergency, such as the circumstances immediately preceding the commission of an offence, may be sufficiently dramatic to justify the admission of a statement as part of the *res gestae*. This is clear from the facts of *Ratten* v. *R* [1971] 3 WLR 930 (PC) where the deceased's statement was made possibly several minutes before her death, in response to the imminent attempt on her life. But not every statement made in the run up to the commission of an offence will be admissible as an excited utterance. In *R* v. *Newport* [1998] Crim LR 581 the deceased had made a telephone call to her friend about 20 minutes before she was fatally stabbed, and that friend was allowed to give evidence that the deceased had sounded agitated and had asked whether she could stay at her house in the event of her having to flee her husband (the accused) at short notice. The Court of Appeal held that the deceased's statement should not have been admitted as it had not been a spontaneous and unconsidered reaction to an impending emergency.

In *Teper* v. *R* [1952] AC 480 the Privy Council felt that a statement prompted by the sight of a person leaving the scene of an offence, rather than by the offence itself, would not justify its admission, so the accused's apparent flight from his burning business was not regarded as the *res gestae*. The *Andrews* test fails to draw any such distinction, however, and there would seem to be no good reason why some other type of sufficiently dramatic event should not be regarded as the *res gestae*, so long as the criteria of that test are satisfied. Indeed the Court of Appeal has recently suggested (albeit *obiter*) that being asked to write suicide notes might amount to a sufficiently dramatic event to justify the admission of a statement made the next day, even though the alleged offence (murder) occurred some two months later (*R* v. *Gilfoyle* [1996] 1 Cr App R 303 (CA), 6.1.1.2 *post*). Conversely, the mere fact that the event is an offence is not of itself enough to make it a *res gestae* event – it must be a *dramatic* offence. This is exemplified by *Tobi* v. *Nicholas* (1987) 86 Cr App R 323 (DC) where a statement made by the driver of a coach damaged in a traffic accident about 20 minutes after the accident was held to be inadmissible on the ground that 'there is a world of difference between such an unfortunately commonplace situation and the thoughts of somebody who has been assaulted or stabbed'. In *R* v. *West* [1999] All ER (D) 1005 (99/ 04541/W3) (CA) the circumstances of an assault on the complainant were sufficiently dramatic for her 'implied assertion' of identification ('Fuck off, Adrian!') to be admissible as an excited utterance.

It was stressed in *R* v. *Andrews* [1987] 2 WLR 413 (HL) that if the declarant was available as a witness the *res gestae* doctrine should not be used as a device to avoid calling him. However, this does not mean that witness unavailability is a precondition for an excited utterance to be admissible. According to the Court of Appeal in *Attorney-General's Reference (No. 1 of 2003)* [2003] EWCA Crim 1286, a declaration satisfying the *Andrews* criteria is *prima facie* admissible, and the availability of the declarant is a factor for the judge to take into consideration when deciding whether the hearsay statement (tendered by the prosecution) should be excluded under s. 78(1) of the Police and Criminal Evidence Act 1984. In that case, V, having made an excited utterance at the time of the attack on her, refused to testify against her son, the accused, and the prosecution had no choice but to rely on her hearsay statements. The Court of Appeal accepted that the prosecution had not relied on the *res gestae* exception as a device to avoid calling their witness, so it is to be presumed that in cases where the exception *is* used as such a device the evidence will be ruled inadmissible, particularly as s. 78(1) cannot be relied on to exclude *res gestae* evidence tendered by the accused.

Finally, although it is often the case that the excited utterance was made by the victim or complainant this is by no means a requirement of the

Andrews test. In *R* v. *Glover* [1991] Crim LR 48 (CA) the assailant himself was so excited following his assault on V that his self-identifying boast ('I am David Glover ... we will not think twice of shooting you and your kids') was held to be admissible as a statement forming part of the *res gestae* (see also *R* v. *Harris* [2002] EWCA Crim 1597, above).

6.1.1.2 Statements Relating to the Declarant's State of Mind

An out-of-court statement may be admissible to prove the contemporaneous state of mind of the declarant:

> 'What a person said or heard said may well be the best and most direct evidence of that person's state of mind. This principle can only apply, however, when the state of mind evidenced by the statement is either itself directly in issue at the trial or of direct and immediate relevance to an issue which arises at the trial.' (*R* v. *Blastland* [1985] 3 WLR 345 (HL) at p. 351)

A recent example is provided by *R* v. *Gregson* [2003] EWCA Crim 1099, where it was held that the accused's friends should have been allowed to give evidence of what he had said to them in anxious terms about the large number of ecstasy tablets which had inadvertently come into his possession, to the effect that he had believed he was buying fewer tablets (for his own use) and had wanted to know what to do with the excess. The evidence was relevant to the issue whether he had intended to supply them as a dealer. In *R* v. *Gilfoyle* [1996] 1 Cr App R 303 the central issue was whether the deceased had committed suicide or been murdered. She had been found hanging and had left a number of suicide notes suggesting that she had taken her own life and not been murdered by her husband as the prosecution alleged. The Court of Appeal held that statements made by the deceased to her friends the day after she had written the suicide notes, to the effect that she had been asked to write them by her husband to help him with a suicide course at his place of work, could have been admitted to show that she had not been in a suicidal frame of mind when writing them. The Court was of the view that as the deceased's state of mind had been one of the principal issues at the trial such evidence was admissible as original evidence (citing *Subramaniam* v. *Public Prosecutor* [1956] 1 WLR 965 (PC), 5.4 *ante*) or under this *res gestae* exception, to rebut the inference which might otherwise be drawn from her notes. However, it is difficult to understand how the deceased's statements could have been admitted as original evidence unless the *manner* in which she made them demonstrated a non-suicidal state of mind at that time. The content of a statement made by a declarant will have probative value as evidence of his own state of mind only if it reflects what the declarant is actually thinking. If a person is heard to state that he is cheerful, the content of that statement can be evidence of his cheerful frame of mind only if it is accepted that he is speaking the truth. This must be contrasted with the situation where one person's declaration is heard by *another* person and adduced to prove the latter's state of mind, as in *Subramaniam* v. *Public Prosecutor*. The truth or falsity of the declaration in such cases is irrelevant and therefore admissible as original evidence. Similarly, a statement made by a declarant may be admissible as original evidence to prove his state of mind if it is not the content of the statement which is being relied on but the way in which it was made (for example, in a cheerful or non-suicidal manner).

Statements falling within this hearsay exception are not admissible to prove the cause of the declarant's state of mind, and in *R* v. *Gilfoyle* [1996] 1 Cr App R 303 (CA) it was accepted that the deceased's statements could only show that, when writing the suicide notes, she had *believed* she was assisting her husband in a course at work and had not been suicidal. (The Court of Appeal did, however, go on to consider whether the statements could have been admitted by virtue of the separate *Andrews* test (6.1.1.1 *ante*) as evidence that her husband had asked her to write the notes. It was accepted that as her mind had still been dominated by the note-making event when making her statements the next day those statements had been sufficiently spontaneous to discount the possibility of invention or unreliability.)

It is well established that a statement which is admissible to show the declarant's belief about a past or present matter is not admissible to show that what was believed was *actually* true (*Thomas* v. *Connell* (1838) 4 M & W 267 (CEC)). The rule against hearsay excludes 'what a stranger to the cause has said ... if it is offered to prove his knowledge of some fact and thus the existence of that fact' (*Martin* v. *Osborne* (1936) 55 CLR 367 (HCA) at p. 375). This is quite logical. If the exception could be used to prove the existence of the matter referred to, the hearsay rule would be otiose. It would seem, however, that a declarant's statement that he *intended* to do a certain future act is admissible not only to prove his state of mind (the intention itself) but also to prove that the act was actually done by him in accordance with his declared intention. In *R* v. *Moghal* (1977) 65 Cr App R 56 the Court of Appeal was of the opinion (albeit *obiter*) that a tape recording by the accused's mistress, in which she had expressed an intention to kill the deceased six months before he was murdered, could have been admitted at the accused's trial for that murder to support his defence that it had been the mistress and not he who had been responsible. This decision was doubted by the House of Lords in *R* v. *Blastland* [1985] 3 WLR 345 on the ground that the mistress's state of mind had not been relevant to the issue whether the accused had been involved in the murder, but their Lordships did not reject the possibility that a declarant's statement of intention could be admissible to prove it was carried out by him if the test of relevance was satisfied. In *R* v. *Buckley* (1873) 13 Cox CC 293 (Assizes) a statement by a police officer to his inspector that he was setting out to watch the accused's movements was admitted to prove that he had carried out his intention. The officer had been found dead some distance from the accused's cottage and the inspector was permitted to give evidence of what the officer had said as additional circumstantial evidence supporting the prosecution case that the accused had murdered him. Similarly, in *R* v. *Hart* (1932) 23 Cr App R 202 (CCA) the accused's stated intention to harm a prison warder – 'I'll do you for this; I've got a gang outside that will fix you up' – was admissible to identify him as one of the men who attacked the warder a few days later. These decisions accord with the approach taken in a number of civil cases. In *Sugden* v. *Lord St Leonards* (1876) 1 PD 154 (CA) it was held that a testator's pre-testamentary declaration of intention as to the content of his prospective will was admissible evidence from which the content of his missing will could be inferred; and in *Lloyd* v. *Powell Duffryn Steam Coal Co* [1914] AC 733 the House of Lords held that statements by a man to the effect that he would marry the infant plaintiff's mother before the child was born were admissible to show his intention to marry her, which in turn allowed an inference to be drawn that he would have supported the child (see *R* v. *Blastland* [1985] 3 WLR 345 (HL) at pp. 352–3). Similarly, in *Marshall* v. *Owners of SS Wild Rose* [1910] AC 486 (HL) evidence that the engineer on board a steam trawler had remarked to his companion that he intended to go on deck for fresh air was admitted without objection to show he had gone on deck.

That said, there are also a number of criminal cases where statements of intention have been ruled inadmissible when tendered to prove the intention was carried out. In *R* v. *Wainwright* (1875) 13 Cox CC 171 (CCC) a statement by the deceased that she was going to visit the accused's premises was ruled inadmissible on the ground 'that it was only a statement of intention which might or might not have been carried out'. A similar view was taken in the earlier case of *R* v. *Pook* (1871) 13 Cox CC 172n (CCC); and in *R* v. *Thomson* [1912] 3 KB 19 (CCA) it was held that a statement by the deceased that she intended to perform an abortion on herself had been properly excluded at the accused's trial for performing that operation on her.

The admissibility of statements of intention in criminal proceedings was considered by the High Court of Australia in *Walton* v. *R* (1989) 166 CLR 283. The prosecution case was that the accused had lured the deceased to the town centre of Elizabeth in South Australia and thereafter driven her into the country and killed her to claim on an insurance policy in his favour. In support of the prosecution case, several witnesses were called to testify that the deceased had stated her intention to meet the accused in the town centre the following evening, evidence which the Court held had been properly admitted as original evidence of her state of mind from which an inference could be drawn that she had actually gone to that location to meet him. The United States Supreme Court had adopted a similar approach in *Mutual Life Insurance Co* v. *Hillmon* (1892) 145 US 285 in holding that letters sent by a man, W, in which he had stated his intention to travel with H, were admissible original evidence of that intention from which it could be inferred that he had indeed travelled with him (see also *R* v. *Smith* [1992] 2 SCR 915 (SCC)).

If statements of intention are generally admissible in England and Wales for this purpose (and the weight of authority suggests that they are) it should be seen as an application of the present exception to the hearsay rule, notwithstanding the commonly stated view that such evidence is 'original evidence' of a state of mind from which an inference may be drawn. As noted above, the statement is adduced for the purpose of proving the intention was honestly held by the declarant. Indeed, it is only upon that basis that a circumstantial inference *can* be drawn that the intention was subsequently put into effect. Whether any such inference should be drawn depends on whether the declarant was the sort of person who carried out his intentions, or whether a valid generalisation can be established to the effect that people generally do what they say they intend to do and that the declarant was one such person. Presumably the trial judge would have to direct the jury on all the relevant circumstances of the case, such as any evidence that the declarant had made statements of intention in the past and acted upon them (or not acted upon them as the case may be), the interval between the statement of intention and the incident, and the nature of the act intended.

A statement of intention may also be admissible to prove that the accused still had that state of mind when he committed a particular act on a subsequent occasion. The probative value of any such statement depends on the time interval between the statement and the act, that is, on the strength of the presumption of continuance (15.5.1 *post*). Such a statement of intention was admissible in *R* v. *Valentine* [1996] 2 Cr App R 213, a rape case in which the accused was alleged to have said to the persons giving him a lift into town, 'I am going to get a ride tonight one way or the other.' He had sexual intercourse with a woman in the middle of a playing field later that night and was charged with her rape, his defence being that she had consented. The Court of Appeal held that the accused's statement of intention was admissible as it was relevant to whether he had had the *mens rea* for the offence when intercourse took place some hours later.

The presumption of continuance explains why statements relating to the declarant's state of mind (or indeed physical sensation, 6.1.1.3 *post*) need not be exactly contemporaneous with the mental (or physical) state which is in issue. In *R* v. *Gilfoyle* [1996] 1 Cr App R 303 (CA) the deceased's statements to her friends were made some time after the suicide notes had been written, but logically a person who is not suicidal on one day is unlikely to have been suicidal on the previous day (although the converse may not be true). The strength of the presumption of continuance is a question of fact dependent on the type of state of mind (or physical condition) in issue and the interval between the time of its (purported) existence and the time when the statement was made.

Finally, it should be noted that this *res gestae* exception provides an explanation for the admissibility of the statement in *R* v. *Ward* [2001] Crim LR 316 (5.8 *ante*) which does not depend on the circular reasoning relied on by the Court of Appeal. If a person identifies himself with reference to a person's name and personal details (such as his address and date of birth) that statement of identification would be admissible to show an awareness on the part of the declarant (X) that the person bearing that name (Y) has such details. This would then allow a circumstantial inference to be drawn that X and Y are the same person, the strength of which inference would depend on the nature of the personal details known. The more X knows about the personal details of Y the more likely it is that X and Y are the same person, particularly if those details are unlikely to be known by anyone other than Y. Accordingly, X's knowledge of Y's name, address and date of birth would place X in the small class of individuals (including Y) who are aware of those details and this would be some evidence that X is Y. One might expect several other individuals of the same sex to know those details, however, and that knowledge would therefore be insufficiently peculiar to justify the inference of self-identification unless supported by some other evidence. If, however, X were to state facts such as Y's blood group and mother's maiden name, demonstrating a unique awareness of Y's personal details, it would be possible to assume that the class of individuals into which X and Y fall comprises no more than one person, and that X is indeed Y.

6.1.1.3 Statements Relating to the Declarant's Physical Sensations

Just as a declarant's statement may be the best, indeed only, evidence of his state of mind, such evidence is admissible to prove his contemporaneous physical sensations, although it is not admissible to prove how he came to be in that condition. Thus, in *Gilbey* v. *Great Western Railway Co* (1910) 102 LT 202 (CA) the deceased's statement to the effect that he was in pain due to an injury caused while carrying a side of beef as a porter was admissible to prove his painful condition, but not for the purpose of showing it had been caused by an accident in the course of his employment. Other examples are provided by *R* v. *Conde* (1868) 10 Cox CC 547 (CCC), where evidence that a deceased boy had complained of hunger and begged for bread was admissible for the purpose of proving his state of health, and *Aveson* v. *Lord Kinnaird* (1805) 6 East 188 (KB) where a woman's declaration about the poor state of her health both then and a few days earlier in Manchester was admissible to prove that she had been ill on that earlier occasion. (See also *R* v. *Nicholas* (1846) 2 C & K 246 (Assizes) and *R* v. *Gloster* (1888) 16 Cox CC 471 (CCC) at p. 473.)

The decision in *Aveson* v. *Lord Kinnaird* (1805) 6 East 188 (KB) was relied on in *Tickle* v. *Tickle* [1968] 1 WLR 937 where the Divisional Court held that what a psychiatrist had told a patient about the latter's state of health was admissible to prove what the patient himself had believed about his mental health. This had been relevant to whether the patient had intended to bring cohabitation with his wife permanently to an end and was therefore admissible even though the patient was not the declarant. It should be noted, however, that because it was the patient's belief rather than his actual physical condition which was relevant, the psychiatrist's statement could have been admitted as original evidence (5.4 *ante*).

6.1.1.4 Statements Relating to the Declarant's Performance of a Relevant Act

A statement made by the declarant while performing a relevant act is admissible to explain the act and his reason for so acting. The justification appears to be that many acts would be inexplicable or erroneously interpreted in the absence of an explanation by the person performing it, and the requisite degree of contemporaneity between the statement and the act affords some protection against unreliability. Thus, in *R* v.

Edwards (1872) 12 Cox CC 230 (Assizes), where the accused faced a charge of having murdered his wife, evidence was admitted that the deceased had left a carving knife and an axe with her neighbour a week before her death, stating that as her husband was always threatening her with those implements she would feel safer if they were out of the way. In *R* v. *Wainwright* (1875) 13 Cox CC 171 (CCC) (6.1.1.2 *ante*) it was submitted by the prosecution that the declarant's statement upon leaving her house that she intended to go to the accused's premises was admissible as a statement explaining her act of departure. Lord Cockburn CJ refused to accept this argument on the ground that it had been an incidental remark and no part of the act of leaving. (*Cf. Thomas* v. *Connell* (1838) 4 M & W 267 (CEC) where Parke B was of the opinion that a statement explaining a person's absence from home was admissible if made just before or during his act of departure. If this is correct it provides an alternative explanation for *Marshall* v. *Owners of SS Wild Rose* [1910] AC 486 (HL), 6.1.1.2 *ante*.)

This exception has recently been applied by the Court of Appeal to justify the admission of a statement of identification made by a witness at an identification parade (*R* v. *McCay* [1990] 1 WLR 645). At the parade the witness had identified the accused by saying, 'It is number 8' but could not remember that number at the time of the trial. The trial judge allowed a police officer to give evidence of what the witness had said at the parade, a ruling which was upheld on appeal on the ground that it had been a statement by the witness 'explaining his physical and intellectual activity in making the identification at the material time'.

Other common-law jurisdictions have relied on this *res gestae* exception to justify the admission of bets placed by telephone for the purpose of proving illegal gambling (for example, *Davidson* v. *Quirke* [1923] NZLR 552 (NZSC) and *Lenthall* v. *Mitchell* [1933] SASR 231 (SASC)). In *Ratten* v. *R* [1971] 3 WLR 930 (5.6.1.1 *ante*) the Privy Council preferred to interpret this ground of admissibility in terms of original evidence (see also *McGregor* v. *Stokes* [1952] VLR 347 (VSC)).

6.1.1.5 The Relationship Between the *Res Gestae* Exceptions

While excited utterances are admissible because of the reduced possibility of fabrication by the declarant, the other *res gestae* exceptions are primarily based on necessity, although the common requirement of approximate contemporaneity does act to reduce the possibility of fabrication and/or error to some extent. In *R* v. *Callender* [1998] Crim LR 337, however, the Court of Appeal felt that the test for excited utterances (6.1.1.1 *ante*) governs the admissibility of any evidence tendered pursuant to one of the *res gestae* exceptions. This novel attempt to reconcile the different grounds of admissibility cannot be regarded as a correct statement of the law, although it is perhaps an unsurprising development given the trial judge's duty to ensure that the adduction of hearsay evidence by the prosecution does not contravene Article 6 of the European Convention on Human Rights (as to which, see 6.2.5 *post*). The decision in *R* v. *Callender* should therefore be interpreted to mean nothing more than that the judge should take into consideration the question of mistake and (in particular) fabrication when deciding whether to allow hearsay evidence to be admitted under one of the *res gestae* exceptions.

6.1.1.6 The Future of the *Res Gestae* Exceptions

The Law Commission has recommended that the four *res gestae* exceptions be codified to cover the following: (a) any statement made by a person so emotionally overpowered by an event that the possibility of concoction or distortion can be disregarded; (b) any statement accompanying an act which can be properly evaluated as evidence only if considered in conjunction with that statement; and (c) any statement relating to a physical sensation or a mental state (see Law Com No. 245 (1997) at pp. 123–8).

6.1.2 Statements Made by Persons now Deceased

Several exceptions to the hearsay rule have been recognised to ensure that the knowledge possessed by persons who have died prior to the trial should not be lost, but this is not the sole criterion of admissibility. The exceptions are circumscribed by further considerations which have traditionally been seen as a guarantee against insincerity on the part of the declarant. The upshot is that the mere fact the declarant has died is insufficient to justify the admission of his statement at common law, although by virtue of s. 23 of the Criminal Justice Act 1988 (6.2.1 *post*) the fact of death may be enough for the evidence to be admitted if his statement was made in a document. Moreover, it is only death which justifies the admission of the declarant's hearsay statement at common law. If the declarant is unavailable for any other reason, or no longer able to testify on the ground of his poor physical or mental health, his statement is inadmissible (*cf.* s. 23 of the 1988 Act).

6.1.2.1 Dying Declarations

If the accused has been charged with the murder or manslaughter of the declarant, the declarant's oral or written statement as to the cause of his death is admissible to prove those circumstances, so long as he had a settled hopeless expectation that he would die within a short time when his statement was made (*R* v. *Perry* [1909] 2 KB 697 (CCA), *R* v. *Austin* (1912) 8 Cr App R 27 (CCA)). However, a dying declaration which is incomplete is inadmissible on the ground that it is impossible to tell what the declarant would have added to his statement. In *Waugh* v. *R* [1950] AC 203 (PC) the deceased started to make a statement but slipped into a coma (from which he never recovered) just as he was about to explain why the accused bore him a grudge. It was held that the statement ought not to have been admitted. If a dying declaration is admitted it is incumbent upon the judge to remind the jury that it has not been tested by cross-examination and that it ought to be scrutinised with care, but there is no requirement that the jury should be directed that it would be dangerous for them to convict on that evidence alone (*Nembhard* v. *R* [1981] 1 WLR 1515 (PC)).

A recent example is provided by the case of *R* v. *Lawson* [1998] Crim LR 883. The deceased had been found badly burnt and unconscious at the scene of a fire following an argument with her husband, the accused. On the way to hospital she began to regain consciousness and said, 'You have really got me now.' At the hospital she managed to dislodge her oxygen mask to say 'Murder, murder!' She died the next afternoon. The Court of Appeal held that her words were *prima facie* admissible as dying declarations, subject to the judge's inherent discretion to exclude the evidence if it was so unreliable or ambiguous that it would be unfair to invite the jury to consider it. (It was noted that the words were also admissible under the 'excited utterance' *res gestae* exception.)

In addition to the necessity of admitting dying declarations to ensure justice is done, the rationale underlying this exception has traditionally been based on the assumption that a person is highly unlikely to lie about the cause of his death once he has realised that his involvement in worldly affairs is soon to end (*R* v. *Woodcock* (1789) 1 Leach 500 (CCC)). It is for this reason that the law requires a settled hopeless expectation of death within a short time. However, although it has been said that the declarant's sincerity can be assumed from his realisation that he would soon be in the 'presence of his Maker' (*R* v. *Osman* (1881) 15 Cox CC 1 (Assizes)) it is no longer necessary to prove that the declarant had any particular religious belief for his declaration to be admissible; indeed in *Mills* v. *R* [1995] 1 WLR 511 the Privy Council expressly rejected the rationale based on religious belief. Despite this trend it may still be the law that if the declarant could not possibly have been able to understand the meaning of death on account of his tender years or mental condition his statement will be inadmissible. In *R* v. *Pike* (1829) 3 C & P 598 (Assizes) a four-year-old girl's dying declaration was ruled inadmissible on this ground.

It is the declarant's belief at the time his statement was made which is relevant, so if he believed he would die from his injuries, and subsequently regained hope of recovery before dying, his declaration will still be admissible (*R* v. *Austin* (1912) 8 Cr App R 27 (CCA)). Indeed, dying declarations have been admitted even though the declarants died some considerable time after making their statements; in *R* v. *Bernadotti* (1869) 11 Cox CC 316 (Assizes) the intervening period between the declaration ('Be quick, or I shall die') and death was nearly three weeks. Conversely, if there was some hope of survival at the time the statement was made it will be inadmissible. In *R* v. *Jenkins* (1869) LR1 CCR 187 (CCCR) the deceased had the original words 'with no hope of my recovery' in her written statement amended to read 'with no hope at present of my recovery.' This indication of some slight hope rendered her statement inadmissible (see also *R* v. *Gloster* (1888) 16 Cox CC 471 (CCC)).

Evidence of what the declarant was told at the time by the persons around him, or what he himself said, is admissible to show his state of mind on the ground that it is either original evidence or hearsay forming part of the *res gestae*, but in the absence of such evidence appropriate inferences will need to be drawn from the circumstances to prove the declarant's state of mind. In *R* v. *Woodcock* (1789) 1 Leach 500 (CCC) the deceased's statement was left to the jury even though the only evidence of her belief that she was soon to die was the inference which could be drawn from her awareness of the severity of her wounds. However, other cases suggest a reluctance to draw such an inference. In *R* v. *Bedingfield* (1879) 14 Cox CC 341 (Assizes), for instance, the judge refused to admit the deceased's statement as a dying declaration even though her throat had been severely cut and she died just 10 minutes later (see also *R* v. *Cleary* (1862) 2 F & F 850 (Assizes) and *R* v. *Morgan* (1875) 14 Cox CC 337 (Assizes)).

The dying declaration exception is of limited use in practice. It allows a deceased's statement to be admitted at the trial for his murder or manslaughter only if he believed that he was soon to die and if the statement relates to the circumstances of his death. Thus, if a dying declaration relates to the commission of another offence against the declarant, or to the murder or manslaughter of another person, it is inadmissible despite the assumed sincerity of the declarant at that time. Moreover, the rule is based entirely on the supposed sincerity of those who believe in divine retribution. The rule prevents the admission of a declarant's statement, no matter how probative it is of the accused's guilt (or innocence), unless the declarant was completely convinced he would soon die; and the very real possibility of the declarant's being mistaken or confused is disregarded for the purposes of determining admissibility. In *Mills* v. *R* [1995] 1 WLR 511 the Privy Council favoured a more flexible test, based on probative value, so that other statements made by deceased persons could be admitted.

6.1.2.2 Statements Against the Declarant's Pecuniary or Proprietary Interest

An oral or written statement by a person now deceased which was, at the time he made it and to his personal knowledge, against his pecuniary or proprietary interest is admissible to prove the truth of the facts stated, the reason being that a person can be presumed not to make such an adverse statement unless it is true (*R* v. *Rogers* [1995] 1 Cr App R 374 (CA)). Thus, an acknowledgement by the deceased of a debt owed by him to another person would be admissible to prove the fact of that debt. The exception also applies to any incidental fact mentioned in the statement against interest so long as the fact was within the declarant's personal knowledge and explains the nature of the transaction in question. Thus, in *Higham* v. *Ridgway* (1808) 10 East 109 (KB) the statement of a deceased male midwife, recording that he had been paid for delivering a child on a certain date, was admissible to prove the child's date of birth.

In *R* v. *Rogers* [1995] 1 Cr App R 374 the accused sought to adduce a statement by a deceased third party, L, to the effect that he was being pursued for money relating to heroin the police had found. It was argued that this statement had been against L's pecuniary interest and that the incidental facts he had mentioned, namely that the accused had been unaware of the heroin store or the presence of a gun, were admissible to show the accused had not been in possession of heroin with intent to supply or possession of a firearm as alleged. The judge's ruling that the evidence was inadmissible was upheld by the Court of Appeal on two grounds. First, L's statement that he was being pursued for money had not amounted to an acknowledgement of a debt owed by him, so it had not been a statement against his pecuniary interest. Secondly, even if L's statement had been against his pecuniary interest the incidental facts were not necessary to explain the nature of the transaction to which they related. The Court also reaffirmed that the fact an obligation to pay a sum of money is not legally enforceable, for example because it relates to an illegal drugs transaction, will not prevent a declaration in respect of that obligation from being admissible (see also *Coward* v. *Motor Insurers' Bureau* [1962] 2 WLR 663 (CA)).

In the *Sussex Peerage Case* (1844) 11 Cl & F 85 the House of Lords held that the exception does not extend to a statement against the declarant's *penal* interest, a somewhat anomalous proviso given that criminal liability may bring with it a financial penalty such as a fine, a compensation order or an order for costs. An important practical consequence of this decision is that a deceased third party's confession to the offence the accused is charged with is not admissible at common law to establish the accused's innocence (5.3 *ante*). The United States and Canada have departed from the English approach and now accept that statements against penal interest fall within the scope of this common-law exception to the hearsay rule, at least in relation to third-party confessions tendered by the accused. In *Chambers* v. *Mississippi* (1973) 410 US 284 the US Supreme Court held that such evidence is admissible if the surrounding circumstances provide 'considerable assurances of [its] reliability' (regardless of whether the declarant is dead). In *R* v. *O'Brien* [1978] 1 SCR 591 the Supreme Court of Canada extended the common-law exception to third-party confessions so long as the declarant was aware that his self-incriminating statement might well be used against him; but the exception cannot be relied on by the prosecution to incriminate the accused (*R* v. *Lucier* [1982] 1 SCR 28 (SCC)). In *Bannon* v. *R* (1995) 185 CLR 1 the High Court of Australia considered the possibility of including statements against penal interest within the scope of this common-law exception but left the question open. A third party's confession in documentary form may now be admissible in England and Wales by virtue of ss. 23 and/or 24 of the Criminal Justice Act 1988 (6.2.1–2 *post*; *cf.* s. 65(2)(*d*) of the Australian Evidence Act 1995 and r. 804(*b*)(3) of the US Federal Rules of Evidence).

6.1.2.3 Statements Made During the Course of a Duty
An oral or written statement of fact by a person now deceased while acting under a duty to another to record or report his performance of an act is admissible at common law to prove the truth of the part of the statement which it was his duty to make. This exception to the hearsay rule may be justified on the ground that a person acting under a duty is likely to record or report his own acts accurately and truthfully and because of the necessity of admitting such evidence (*R* v. *McGuire* (1985) 81 Cr App R

323 (CA)). Given that such records are usually made in documentary form and may now be admissible in criminal proceedings by virtue of ss. 23 and/or 24 of the Criminal Justice Act 1988 (6.2.1–2 *post*) this exception is no longer of much practical importance.

Before hearsay evidence can be admitted under this exception it must be proved not only that the declarant is dead and that he was acting under a duty but also that the statement was made approximately contemporaneously with the act in question and that it deals with the declarant's own acts. Further, a statement of this sort will be inadmissible if it can be proved that the declarant had a motive to misrepresent the facts stated. In *The Henry Coxon* (1878) 3 PD 156 (PD) a written record in a ship's log of the circumstances of a collision with another vessel was held to be inadmissible on three grounds. First, the record had not been made sufficiently contemporaneously with the collision as there had been a two-day delay; second, it was impossible to disentangle the parts of the entry relating to what had been done by the vessel on board which the log had been kept from entries relating to the acts of third parties on board the other vessel; and third, the ship's mate had had a motive to misrepresent the facts so as to cast the blame for the collision on the bad navigation of the other vessel.

Unlike the exception governing the admissibility of statements against interest (6.1.2.2 *ante*), the present exception does not render admissible incidental facts mentioned in the statement which the declarant was under no duty to record (*Chambers* v. *Bernasconi* (1834) 3 LJ Ex 373 (CEC)).

6.1.2.4 Statements as to Pedigree

The oral or written statement of a relative now deceased regarding a matter of family pedigree (such as consanguinity or affinity) is admissible to prove the truth of the facts stated, so long as the statement was made before any dispute about the matter arose and the deceased was either a blood relative of the family or married to a person so related. It does not matter whether the declarant had personal knowledge of the matter stated (in other words, multiple hearsay evidence of family tradition or reputation suffices). This exception, which can be justified on the grounds of necessity and presumed sincerity, has been preserved for civil proceedings by s. 7(3)(*b*) of the Civil Evidence Act 1995.

6.1.2.5 Statements as to Public or General Rights

The oral or written statement of a person now deceased regarding the reputed existence of an ancient right relating to the entire population (a public right) or to a particular section of the population (a general right) is admissible to prove the existence of that right so long as the statement was made before any dispute about it arose and, in the case of general rights, the deceased had sufficient knowledge to speak competently about the matter. This exception (which has been preserved for civil proceedings by s. 7(3)(*b*) of the Civil Evidence Act 1995) can be justified on the ground of necessity and the likelihood that such statements are true, having been discussed in public and not contradicted.

6.1.2.6 Witnesses who Die Before the Accused's Retrial
If a witness who gave evidence at the accused's trial is unable to attend the
retrial on account of his death the transcript of his testimony is admissible
at common law to prove the truth of the matters stated therein (*R* v. *Hall*
[1972] 3 WLR 974 (CA)). The exception has also been held to apply to
witnesses who are unable to attend because of illness or incapacity to be
called (*R* v. *Thompson* [1982] 2 WLR 603 (CA)). Such statements are now
also admissible by virtue of ss. 23 or 24 of the Criminal Justice Act 1988
(*R* v. *Lockley* [1995] 2 Cr App R 554 (CA)) or Schedule 2 to the Criminal
Appeal Act 1968.

6.1.3 Statements Made by Parties to a Common Enterprise

A statement made by one party to a common enterprise (such as a
criminal conspiracy) is admissible at common law against any other party
to the enterprise so long as it was made in the course or furtherance of the
enterprise and there is independent evidence of both the enterprise and the
other party's involvement in it (*R* v. *Murray* [1997] 2 Cr App R 136 (CA)
at pp. 147–9; *R* v. *Smart* [2002] EWCA Crim 772, *R* v. *Williams* [2002]
EWCA Crim 2208). Thus in *R* v. *Jones* [1997] 2 Cr App R 119 (CA) it was
held that a recording of telephone conversations between parties to a
common enterprise to import cannabis and third parties, during which the
involvement of B (a co-accused) had been mentioned, was admissible
evidence of B's guilt. Until recently it was necessary to prove that the
statement had been made in the course and furtherance of the enterprise,
but the trend has been to admit statements which merely record the
progress of the enterprise without actually furthering it (as, for example, in
R v. *Ilyas* [1996] Crim LR 810 (CA) where a record of the receipt of stolen
car parts was held to be admissible under this exception).

6.1.4 Statements in Public Documents

A document prepared by a public official acting pursuant to a legal duty
to prepare and keep the same as a record or register for the public to use
and refer to is admissible at common law to prove the truth of its contents
(*Sturla* v. *Freccia* (1880) 5 App Cas 623 (HL) at p. 643), save that if the
official did not himself have personal knowledge of the information
recorded (or did not inquire into the accuracy of the information pursuant
to a legal duty to satisfy himself of its truth) the person providing it must
have had such knowledge and been acting under a legal duty to provide it
(*R* v. *Halpin* [1975] 3 WLR 260 (CA)). This exception is now of limited
importance in criminal proceedings on account of s. 24 of the Criminal
Justice Act 1988 (6.2.2 *post*). Section 7(2)(*b*) of the Civil Evidence Act 1995
preserves the common-law exception for civil proceedings (with s. 7(2)(*c*)
preserving the exception governing the admissibility of documents such as
treaties and court records).

6.1.5 Works of Reference

Published works of reference dealing with matters of a public nature (such as maps, dictionaries and scientific reports) are admissible at common law to prove the facts stated therein. This exception has been preserved for civil proceedings by s. 7(2)(*a*) of the Civil Evidence Act 1995.

6.1.6 Evidence of Reputation

In criminal proceedings the accused's good or bad character may be proved by his general reputation amongst those who know him in his community (*R* v. *Rowton* (1865) Le & Ca 520 (CCCR)). Thus, a witness may give evidence that the accused has a good or bad character based on what he has heard said by persons to whom the accused is known. This is, in effect, an extension of the *res gestae* exception relating to the state of mind of the declarant. The witness has heard the accused's neighbours or colleagues express a view on the accused's character, the inference being that that their views have been expressed sincerely and reflect their true opinion of him. If those views tally, the witness is permitted to relay to the court the nature of that collective belief as evidence that the accused is good or bad (as the case may be).

Evidence of reputation is also admissible in civil and criminal proceedings to prove a witness's dishonesty and, where such evidence has been adduced, to re-establish his status as an honest witness (16.5.4.3 *post*). Section 7(3)(*a*) of the Civil Evidence Act 1995 provides that the common-law rule which permits evidence of reputation to be adduced to prove good or bad character is preserved for civil proceedings.

6.2 Statutory Exceptions (and Supplementary Provisions) in Criminal Proceedings

While most of the common-law exceptions apply to any type of hearsay statement tendered in criminal proceedings, whether made orally or in a document or by way of a gesture, the statutory exceptions, justified on the grounds of necessity and reliability, apply only to statements in documentary form. The principal statutory exceptions are found in ss. 23 and 24 of the Criminal Justice Act 1988, but even if the conditions of admissibility set out in either or both of these sections have been satisfied the judge may still exclude the evidence under ss. 25 or 26 if its admission would not be in the interests of justice. If the party tendering the evidence manages to overcome these hurdles the opposing party is still entitled to attack the credibility of the absent witness by virtue of provisions contained in Schedule 2 to the Act. Section 28(1)(*a*) of the Act provides that no other hearsay exceptions are prejudiced by ss. 23 to 26, so it will often be the case that documentary hearsay is admissible under more than one exception.

Section 27 of the 1988 Act provides that a statement contained in a document which is admissible in criminal proceedings may be proved by the production of an authenticated copy of that document. Paragraph 5 of Schedule 2 to the Act gives definitions of some of the key words used in ss. 23 to 27: a document is 'anything in which information of any description is recorded'; a statement is 'any representation of fact, however made'; and a copy is 'anything onto which information recorded in the document has been copied, by whatever means and whether directly or indirectly'. So, for example, an oral statement recorded by the maker on to an audio tape would be a statement in a document; and, for the purposes of s. 27, an authenticated transcript of that recording would be a copy.

6.2.1 Section 23 of the Criminal Justice Act 1988

Section 23(1) provides that 'a statement made by a person in a document shall be admissible in criminal proceedings as evidence of any fact of which direct oral evidence by him would be admissible' if: 'the person who made the statement' is dead or by reason of his bodily or mental condition unfit to attend as a witness (s. 23(2)(*a*)); or he is outside the United Kingdom and it is not reasonably practicable to secure his attendance (s. 23(2)(*b*)); or all reasonable steps have been taken to find him but he cannot be found (s. 23(2)(*c*)); or the statement was made to a police officer or some other person charged with the duty of investigating offences or charging offenders and the person who made the statement does not give oral evidence 'through fear or because he is kept out of the way' (s. 23(3)). The party tendering a statement under s. 23 must prove with admissible evidence one of the four reasons for the unavailability of its maker. The standard of proof depends on whether it is the defence or prosecution who wish to adduce the evidence (*R* v. *Mattey* [1995] 2 Cr App R 409 (CA), *R* v. *Medway* (1999) unreported (98/7579/Y3) (CA)). As a general rule, the defence are entitled to cross-examine the witnesses called by the prosecution to establish the reason relied on (*R* v. *Wood* [1998] Crim LR 213 (CA), *R* v. *Elliott* [2003] EWCA Crim 1695).

Section 23 allows a hearsay statement to be admitted only if the person who made it ('the maker') would have been able to give oral evidence of the facts stated. There are two points to note about this restriction. First, according to the Court of Appeal in *R* v. *D* [2002] 3 WLR 997, it is doubtful whether this means that a preliminary ruling must be made on whether the maker of the statement would actually be competent to give oral evidence. The question whether the requirements of s. 53(3) of the Youth Justice and Criminal Evidence Act 1999 (16.3.3 *post*) are satisfied should be a matter for the judge to consider at the stage when he decides whether to exclude the evidence under ss. 25 or 26 of the Act. Second, although, as a general rule, only first-hand documentary hearsay is admissible under this section (that is, statements containing facts which the maker himself directly perceived), if the maker directly perceived another person's out-of-court statement of fact admissible at common law, and included it in his documentary statement, his evidence should still be admissible. If, for example, M opened his front door to find V bleeding to death from severe wounds and V stated that he had just been stabbed by D, M would be able to give oral evidence of V's identifying statement under the 'excited utterance' *res gestae* exception (6.1.1.1 *ante*). If M later records what V told him in a document but M himself is subsequently unable to give oral evidence for one of the four s. 23 reasons, his written statement, including V's statement, should still be admissible even though M did not personally see V being stabbed by D. This interpretation of s. 23 is supported by the decision in *R* v. *Lockley* [1995] 2 Cr App R 554 (CA) where it was felt that a documentary hearsay statement made by an absent witness, to the effect that one of the accused had made an oral confession to her, was *prima facie* admissible under s. 23 to prove the truth of the confession.

To be admissible the statement must have been 'made by a person in a document'. Thus, the maker's own written statement, or one dictated and verified by him, or a statement which he knowingly allows to be recorded on audio tape (or by a court stenographer) or one which he types up on a computer will all fall within the scope of this expression. In *R* v. *McGillivray* (1992) 97 Cr App R 232 the victim of an attack had been set on fire and was therefore unable to write because of the severity of his burns, but he was able to dictate a statement to a police officer who wrote it down and read it back to him in the presence of a nurse. The victim could not sign his name but he was able to say that the statement had been correctly recorded. The Court of Appeal held the statement to be admissible under s. 23 (following the victim's death) as his oral verification of its content meant it had been made by him in a document even though he had not signed it.

A statement other than one 'made by a person in a document' is not admissible under s. 23. In *Re D (a Minor)* [1986] 2 FLR 189 (FD), a case on Part I of the Civil Evidence Act 1968 (which has now been repealed), it was held that the notes taken by a solicitor during an interview with the deceased did not amount to a statement made by the deceased as she had not verified or even seen what the solicitor had written. In *Ventouris* v. *Mountain (No. 2)* [1992] 1 WLR 887 (CA), another case on Part I of the Civil Evidence Act 1968, it was held that a surreptitiously made audio recording of an oral statement was not a statement made in a document as the maker had not intended his conversation to be recorded. Furthermore, a statement cannot be admitted under s. 23 if it is so ambiguous that it is impossible to determine whether the maker, if available, would have been able to give oral evidence of the matters stated, that is, it is unclear whether or not the maker was referring to matters which he had directly perceived (*R* v. *JP* [1999] Crim LR 401 (CA)).

The first ground for admitting hearsay evidence under this provision (s. 23(2)(*a*)) is self-explanatory, covering not only persons who are physically unable to get to court but also those who would not have the capacity to give evidence in accordance with their earlier statement (*R* v. *Setz-Dempsey* (1993) 98 Cr App R 23 (CA)). The second ground (s. 23(2)(*b*)) requires proof that it is not reasonably practicable to secure the attendance of the maker, the question of reasonableness being governed by a cost-benefit analysis. In *R* v. *Castillo* [1996] 1 Cr App R 438 the Court of Appeal set out certain considerations for the judge to take into account: (i) the importance of the maker's evidence, (ii) the expense and inconvenience involved in securing his attendance from overseas and (iii) the reasons put forward to explain why it was not reasonably practicable for him to attend. With regard to the third point, the judge should consider the extent to which the party tendering the statement has actually taken steps to secure the maker's attendance (*R* v. *Bray* (1988) 88 Cr App R 354 (CA)). Although it must be proved that it was not reasonably practicable to secure the maker's attendance, there is no bar to the use of another person's admissible hearsay statement for this purpose. In *R* v. *Castillo* the prosecution wished to adduce the written statement of a travel agent, M, based in Venezuela. To do this a British customs officer gave oral evidence on the *voir dire* that it was not reasonably practicable to secure the attendance of a customs liaison officer, T, also based in Venezuela. T's written statement explaining why it was not reasonably practicable to secure the attendance of M was therefore admitted under s. 23 for the purpose of having M's statement admitted under the same provision. The third ground (s. 23(2)(*c*)) also includes a criterion of reasonableness, in respect of which it has been held that the importance of the witness and the resources of the police are relevant factors, but the seriousness of the offence is not (*R* v. *Coughlan* (1999) unreported (98/05345/Y3) (CA)).

The fourth ground (s. 23(3)) actually comprises two alternative grounds, although in each case the statement must be one which was made to a police officer or similar such person. A witness's statement may be admitted on the ground of 'fear' or because 'he is kept out of the way', but neither ground is qualified by a requirement of reasonableness or any causal link with the offence charged or its consequences. In *R* v. *Martin* [1996] Crim LR 589 the Court of Appeal stated that s. 23(3) had been introduced to combat the problem of witness intimidation and held that there was no reason why its words should be qualified in any way. Protection for the accused is provided by the leave requirement of s. 26 (6.2.3 *post*). The obligation to comply with Article 6(1) and 6(3)(d) of the European Convention on Human Rights militates against allowing witnesses to avoid cross-examination simply on the basis of 'fear', at least in cases where the witness has not been intimidated; and it may be that a pre-trial procedure which would allow the defence to put questions to the witness will need to be established if the requirements of the Strasbourg jurisprudence are to be complied with in cases where s. 23(3) is relied on (see 6.2.5 *post*). In *R* v. *H* [2001] Crim LR 815 (CA) it was said that when considering the admissibility of evidence under s. 23(3) there should be evidence before the court to prove the witness's fear at the time of the trial, an explanation (preferably from the witness himself) as to his reason for being afraid, and an explanation of the steps taken to persuade him to attend or to alleviate his fears (for example by an offer of screens at court). The last two factors are not relevant to s. 23(3) itself but will be taken into account when s. 26 is considered.

The common-law *res gestae* exception which allows the maker's oral or written statement as to his contemporaneous state of mind to be admitted for the purpose of proving the truth of the matters stated can be relied on to satisfy the 'fear' requirement imposed by s. 23(3) (see 6.1.1.2 *ante*). Thus if a police officer hears from the maker and other officers that the maker is too frightened to testify, that officer may give evidence of what he was told by the maker himself but not what he was told by those other officers (*R* v. *Wood* [1998] Crim LR 213 (CA)). Alternatively, the maker may explain his state of mind in a written statement which can be put before the court (*R* v. *Fairfax* [1995] Crim LR 949 (CA)); or he may attend court to explain his fear to the judge or magistrates in person, in which case he need not be sworn (*R* v. *Greer* [1998] Crim LR 572 (CA)). In *R* v. *H* [2001] Crim LR 815 the Court of Appeal suggested that, where possible, the witness should provide an explanation for his fear in person or by video link or tape recording.

Section 23 may also be relied on where the maker has attended court to give oral evidence, been sworn and started to testify, so long as his refusal to give the additional evidence expected of him (or his claim to have 'forgotten' it) is due to fear (*R* v. *Ashford Justices ex parte Hilden* [1993] 2 WLR 529 (DC), *R* v. *Waters* (1997) 161 JP 249 (CA)). The fact of the maker's fear can be established from his testimony, or by an inference drawn from his demeanour in the witness box (as in *R* v. *Ashford Justices ex parte Hilden*), or by the adduction of earlier statements made by him regarding his state of his mind.

The Law Commission has recommended a wider statutory exception based on the unavailability of the maker which would also allow oral hearsay to be admitted, so long as the maker could be identified and he would have been competent to give oral evidence at the time the statement was made. The grounds of unavailability match those in s. 23, save that the leave of the court would be required if the reason relied on was that of fear; and the 'kept out of the way' exception would be abolished (see Law Com No. 245 (1997) at pp. 94–112).

6.2.2 Section 24 of the Criminal Justice Act 1988

Section 24(1) provides that a statement in a document shall be admissible in criminal proceedings as evidence of any fact of which direct oral evidence would be admissible if: (i) the document was created or received by a person in the course of a trade, business, profession or other occupation or as the holder of a paid or unpaid office; and (ii) the information contained in the document was supplied by a person (whether or not the maker of the statement) who had, or who may reasonably be supposed to have had, personal knowledge of the matters dealt with.

It does not matter whether the information contained in the document was supplied directly or indirectly through intermediaries, save that if it was supplied indirectly each person through whom it was supplied must have received it in the course of a trade, business, profession or other occupation, or as the holder of a paid or unpaid office (s. 24(2)). However, if the statement was prepared for the purposes of pending or contemplated criminal proceedings or a criminal investigation it is not admissible by virtue of s. 24(1) unless one of the four s. 23 grounds of admissibility has been satisfied or 'the person who made the statement' cannot reasonably be expected (having regard to the time which has elapsed since he made the statement and to all the circumstances) to have any recollection of the matters dealt with in the statement (s. 24(4)).

Section 24 differs from s. 23 in several ways. It is limited to certain types of document which are assumed to be more reliable than documents generally, and allows multiple hearsay to be admissible, no matter how many times removed the final statement is from the person who directly perceived the events, so long as each intermediary through whom the information was passed was acting in the course of an occupation or as the holder of some office. It is not necessary that the person who perceived the events or any other person should be unavailable for a documentary statement to be admissible under s. 24 (unless the statement was prepared for pending or contemplated criminal proceedings or a criminal investigation). And while s. 23 is concerned with only one person – the person who made the statement in the document – s. 24 refers to three types of person: the person reasonably supposed to have had personal knowledge of the events who supplied the information; the person who created or received the document in the course of a trade (etc.); and the person who made the statement.

Consider the following example. Sam, a university librarian, tells David's tutor that he has seen David tearing pages out of library books. The tutor later informs the head of department who makes a written note of it, intending to pass it on to the discipline officer. Having ascertained the extent of the damage, the head of department decides it is a matter for the police and calls them in several months later. The police charge David with criminal damage but are unable to find Sam as he has emigrated to Australia. The written note would be admissible under s. 24 as the document was created by a person (the head of department) in the course of his profession, and the information in the document was supplied by a person (Sam) who may reasonably be supposed to have had personal knowledge of the matters dealt with. It does not matter that the information was supplied through an intermediary (the tutor) as he received it in the course of his profession, although the statement would presumably be inadmissible if the intermediary had been a student.

The statement in this example was made for the purposes of contemplated disciplinary proceedings, but if the head of department had written his note in the contemplation of criminal proceedings one of the s. 24(4) grounds of admissibility would need to be satisfied. The prosecution would then need to prove that the 'person who made the statement' (i) was dead or unfit to attend, (ii) was outside the country and that it was not reasonably practicable to secure his attendance, (iii) could not be found, (iv) would not give oral evidence through fear or because of his being kept out of the way (if the statement had been made to a police officer etc.) or (v) that he could not reasonably be expected to have any recollection of the matters dealt with in the statement. Logically, then, the 'person who made the statement' should be the person who directly perceived the event and supplied the information (that is, Sam), but s. 24(1) envisages situations where the maker of the statement and the supplier of the information are different persons ('supplied by a person (whether or not the maker of the statement)'), suggesting that the maker of the statement is the person who wrote (or otherwise placed) the statement into the document (that is, the head of department). A literal interpretation of s. 24 would therefore lead to the absurd result that it is the absence or the recollection of the person who wrote the statement in the document which is relevant for s. 24(4) as opposed to the person who perceived the matters dealt with in the statement. This interpretation was adopted in a number of cases (*Brown* v. *Secretary of State for Social Security* (1994) *The Times* 7.12.94 (DC), *R* v. *Carrington* (1993) 99 Cr App R 376 (CA), *R* v. *Hogan* [1997] Crim LR 349 (CA)) and would mean Sam's absence would not satisfy s. 24(4). The evidence would be inadmissible unless the head of department could be placed within one of the five s. 24(4) categories.

To overcome this absurdity there are two options. First, it might be possible to interpret s. 24 purposively rather than literally, an approach which is implicit in the judgment of the Court of Appeal in *R* v. *Lockley* [1995] 2 Cr App R 554, where it was held that the transcript of a witness's testimony was admissible at the accused's retrial under s. 24 (as well as under s. 23). The witness had supplied information to the court (at the first trial) and this had been put into documentary form by the court's stenographer acting in the course of that profession. As the transcript was made during the course of criminal proceedings it was held to fall within the expression 'prepared for the purposes of contemplated criminal proceedings', requiring a s. 24(4) condition to be satisfied. The Court of Appeal assumed that the s. 23(2)(*c*) condition had been met by the fact the witness had absconded from prison, even though she had been the supplier of the information and not the person who had placed the statement in the document. A more authoritative decision, though, is the case of *R* v. *Derodra* [2000] 1 Cr App R 41, where the problem was confronted head-on. D was charged with obtaining a pecuniary advantage by deception, the allegation being that he had taken out an insurance policy following a burglary and then claimed under the policy for goods stolen. Central to the prosecution case was the fact that D's tenant had reported the burglary (and the goods stolen) on a particular date, which report had been received by one PC Gable and entered into the computer to form a computerised record of incident ('the CRIS report'). The tenant could not be found, however, and the prosecution sought to have the CRIS report admitted under s. 24(1) on the basis that s. 24(4) was satisfied (by virtue of the tenant's unavailability and s. 23(2)(*c*)). D appealed on the ground that it was not the tenant but PC Gable who was 'the person who made the statement', and PC Gable did not fulfil any of the criteria in s. 24(4). Recognising that the literal interpretation of s. 24 adopted in *Brown* v. *Secretary of State for Social Security* (1994) *The Times* 7.12.94 (DC) was 'a construction that produces absurdity', the Court of Appeal held that the person who made the statement is 'the person testifying to the facts represented by the statement', in other words, 'the person who makes or vouches for the representation of fact that the statement consists of', and who that person is would depend on the circumstances of the particular case. The tenant was the person who had made the statement, as he had 'made the representation of fact of which the evidence consisted' and it was his veracity and reliability which should have been in issue. The CRIS report had therefore been properly admitted.

The second (and more appropriate) alternative would be to rectify the defect by amending s. 24(1) to read: 'supplied by a person (whether or not the creator of the document)'; and the Law Commission has recently recommended that s. 24 be amended so that it would be the supplier of the information who is unavailable or unable to remember the matters dealt with (Law Com No. 245 (1997) at pp. 115–16). Parliament could also take the opportunity to clarify the meaning of 'received by a person in the course of a trade' in s. 24(1) as it seems to make just about any documentary hearsay admissible so long as it has been received by someone in the course of his employment, which surely cannot be what was intended. The mere receipt of a statement in a document would seem to provide no guarantee of reliability at all.

Finally, whether a document falls within the scope of s. 24(1) will often be inferable from the document itself, and extraneous evidence to prove compliance with the subsection will generally be unnecessary (*R* v. *Foxley* [1995] 2 Cr App R 523 (CA), *R* v. *Ilyas* [1996] Crim LR 810 (CA)).

6.2.3 Sections 25 and 26 of the Criminal Justice Act 1988

A statement in a document which is *prima facie* admissible by virtue of ss. 23 or 24 may nevertheless be excluded by the trial judge if its admission would not be in the interests of justice. Section 25 provides the judge with an exclusionary discretion with regard to any statement tendered under ss. 23 or 24. Section 26 is narrower in scope as it applies only to statements which were prepared for pending or contemplated criminal proceedings or a criminal investigation; yet it is also more potent than s. 25, providing that no such evidence may be admitted without the judge's leave. These provisions do not in any way affect the judge's more general common-law and statutory discretions to exclude any evidence tendered by the prosecution (s. 28(1)(*b*)), but it is important to note that ss. 25 and 26 are not limited to prosecution evidence and may be applied to exclude documentary hearsay tendered by the defence too.

Both sections list a number of factors the judge is obliged to take into consideration before exercising his discretion or granting leave. For the purposes of s. 25 the judge must take into account 'all the circumstances' (s. 25(1)) having particular regard to four factors listed in s. 25(2): (*a*) the nature and source of the document and its likely authenticity; (*b*) the extent to which the statement supplies evidence which would otherwise not be readily available; (*c*) the relevance (that is, probative value) of the evidence; and (*d*) any risk, having regard in particular to whether it is likely to be possible to controvert the statement, that the admission or exclusion of the evidence will result in unfairness to the accused. This last consideration is repeated in s. 26, along with two others: the content of the statement and any other circumstances which appear to be relevant. If the judge permits the hearsay evidence to be adduced reasons should be given to explain why the ss. 25 or 26 discretion was exercised in favour of the party tendering it (*R* v. *Denton* [2001] 1 Cr App R 227 (CA)).

The relationship between ss. 25 and 26 was considered by the Court of Appeal in the leading case of *R* v. *Cole* [1990] 1 WLR 866, the conclusion being that where s. 26 applies there is a presumption in favour of exclusion so it is for the party tendering the evidence to persuade the judge to grant leave; but where s. 26 is inapplicable the presumption is that the evidence ought to be admitted and it is for the opposing party to persuade the judge to exclude it under s. 25. The Court of Appeal emphasised the importance to be attached to the quality of the hearsay evidence and rejected an argument that a statement tendered by the prosecution could be controverted only by cross-examination. Controvert was said to have the same meaning as contradict and as such it was always open to the accused to give evidence himself or to call other witnesses to dispute the hearsay evidence. It was also felt that the judge should consider the extent to which any unfairness arising from the accused's inability to cross-examine on a hearsay statement could be counter-balanced by an effective warning and explanation to the jury as part of his summing-up (see also 6.3 *post*).

When considering the application of ss. 25 or 26 the judge must take into account all the circumstances and undertake 'a complex balancing exercise' (*R* v. *Cole* [1990] 1 WLR 866 (CA) at p. 876) to ensure not only that the accused receives a fair trial but also that the prosecution can properly present their case. The judge has a duty to be fair and even-handed to both sides (*R* v. *Patel* (1992) 97 Cr App R 294 (CA), *R* v. *Gokal* [1997] 2 Cr App R 266 (CA), *R* v. *W* [1997] Crim LR 678 (CA)). Each case will of course turn on its own facts. For this reason decided cases should not be regarded as precedents, but they do provide useful illustrations of how these provisions have been applied in practice and give an indication of the factors which are considered to be particularly important. One factor which ought not to be over-emphasised, though, is the importance of the evidence to the prosecution case, for as a consideration it cuts both ways. To exclude such evidence might result in the prosecution case collapsing, and might therefore be considered a reason for admitting it (*R* v. *Batt* [1995] Crim LR 240 (CA)); but to admit the evidence might prevent the accused from being able to challenge the substance of the case against him, justifying a decision to exclude it, for the accused 'cannot conduct an argument with, nor ask questions of, a piece of paper' (*R* v. *Radak* [1999] 1 Cr App R 187 (CA) at p. 200).

Where there is reason to doubt the credibility of the absent witness and that witness's evidence is central to the prosecution case, the absence of any opportunity to cross-examine militates strongly against the admission of the statement. In *R* v. *Lockley* [1995] 2 Cr App R 554 (CA), for example, it was felt that while the absent witness's evidence was *prima facie* admissible under both ss. 23 and 24 it ought to have been excluded under s. 26 because of her bad and dishonest character. She had openly boasted of her ability to deceive the staff at large stores when out shoplifting and her evidence concerned a purported confession to her by one of the accused while they had been a sharing a cell in the absence of any other witnesses. It was felt to be of great importance that the jury should have been able to assess her credibility for themselves, and as she had absconded from prison and could not be found her evidence ought to have been excluded.

It has also been said that courts 'will be cautious about admitting ... documentary evidence of identification ... where this is the principal element in the prosecution's case' (*Neill* v. *North Antrim Magistrates' Court* [1992] 1 WLR 1220 (HL) at p. 1229), but this dictum should not be seen as an exclusionary presumption to be applied inflexibly in all cases where identification evidence is tendered. The question of admissibility must turn on the quality of the identification evidence, and if its quality is high it may be possible to justify admitting it so long as the accused's interests are protected by an adequate direction to the jury. A good example is provided by *R* v. *Dragic* [1996] 2 Cr App R 232 (CA), a case in which a pub landlord had found three men burgling his premises and recognised D, one of his regular customers, following an observation which lasted for between five and ten seconds in a well-lit room. D was subsequently identified by the landlord at a confrontation and charged with burglary, his defence being one of alibi. The landlord made a written statement for the police and, as he was taken ill prior to the trial, the prosecution were given leave to adduce it pursuant to ss. 23 and 26 of the 1988 Act. D was convicted and appealed on the ground that it had not been in the interests of justice for the landlord's statement to be admitted since it was identification evidence and the prosecution case depended almost entirely on it. The Court of Appeal dismissed his appeal as the landlord's evidence had not been weak, D had been able to controvert it with his own alibi evidence, and the judge had properly exercised his discretion under s. 26.

A relevant consideration for the purposes of s. 26, where the prosecution wish to rely on the 'fear' requirement of s. 23(3), is whether the accused has directly or indirectly intimidated the witness. In *R* v. *Harvey* (1998) unreported (98/00885/Y4) the Court of Appeal stated that it 'does not lie in the mouth of a defendant to complain that a witness is not available for cross-examination when he himself has been instrumental in bringing that situation about', but accepted that if the accused gave credible evidence on the *voir dire* that he neither knew nor approved of such intimidation that would be a relevant factor in the exercise of the judge's discretion. This approach was approved in *R* v. *Montgomery* [2002] EWCA Crim 1655 and *R* v. *M(KJ)* [2003] 2 Cr App R 322 (CA).

6.2.4 Schedule 2 to the Criminal Justice Act 1988

Once the party tendering a statement under ss. 23 or 24 of the 1988 Act has satisfied the conditions of admissibility in either of those sections, and the judge has exercised his discretion under s. 25 or given leave under s. 26 in favour of that party, allowing the evidence to be adduced, the opposing party (usually the accused) is entitled to adduce evidence of his own to impeach the absent witness's credibility and undermine the probative value of the statement. The relevant provisions are to be found in paragraph 1 of Schedule 2 to the 1988 Act, which supplement ss. 23 to 28 (s. 28(2)). These provisions are intended to compensate the opposing party for his inability to cross-examine the absent witness as to credit (as to which, see 16.5 *post*). The opposing party may therefore adduce any evidence relevant to the absent witness's credibility which would have been admissible had that witness been called to give oral evidence (paragraph 1(*a*); 16.5.4 *post*), but he may also apply to the judge to waive the rule on the finality of answers on collateral matters (16.5.2 *post*) in order that he be allowed to adduce evidence relevant to credibility which would not have been admissible had the witness been called (paragraph 1(*b*)). Any previous inconsistent statement made by the absent witness is admissible for the purpose of showing he has contradicted himself (paragraph 1(*c*); see 16.5.3 *post*). It is important to note, however, that if these provisions are relied on by the accused to attack the credibility of an absent prosecution witness he runs the risk of losing his shield against cross-examination on his own bad character (if any) should he decide to testify (*R* v. *Miller* [1997] 2 Cr App R 178 (CA), 4.5 *ante*).

6.2.5 Hearsay and the European Convention on Human Rights

Article 6(3)(d) of the European Convention expressly provides that the accused has the right 'to examine or have examined witnesses against him' as one of the facets of his more general right to a fair trial under Article 6(1). It is therefore necessary to consider whether the adduction of hearsay evidence incriminating the accused is compatible with the Convention, bearing in mind that the rights in Article 6(3) are not absolute and may be qualified so long as any qualification is directed towards a legitimate objective (such as convicting those who have committed crimes) and is a proportionate way of achieving that objective (2.9 *ante*).

The earlier relevant judgments of the European Court of Human Rights include *Kostovski* v. *Netherlands* (1989) 12 EHRR 434, *Unterpertinger* v. *Austria* (1986) 13 EHRR 175, *Windisch* v. *Austria* (1990) 13 EHRR 281, *Delta* v. *France* (1990) 16 EHRR 574, *Asch* v. *Austria* (1991) 15 EHRR 597, *Ludi* v. *Switzerland* (1992) 15 EHRR 173, *Saidi* v. *France* (1993) 17 EHRR 251, *Doorson* v. *Netherlands* (1996) 22 EHRR 330 and *Van Mechelen* v. *Netherlands* (1997) 25 EHRR 647. Although each case before the Strasbourg court is decided on its own facts, a number of principles may be derived from these cases in relation to whether, and in what circumstances, it is permissible for the prosecution to adduce hearsay evidence. First, the maker of a hearsay statement admitted against the accused is a 'witness' for the purpose of Article 6(3)(d). Second, complainants and witnesses in criminal proceedings also have rights under the Convention, and in appropriate cases their interests may have to be balanced against the interests of the defence. Third, whether a hearsay statement has been properly admitted as evidence is a question for the domestic courts to decide – the task of the Strasbourg Court is not to hold in the abstract whether oral evidence given on oath should always be relied on in preference to a hearsay statement made by that witness; rather, it is to ascertain (retrospectively, and in relation to the particular applicant before the Court) whether the proceedings as a whole, including the way in which the evidence was taken, were fair. Fourth, the use of statements obtained before the trial is not in itself inconsistent with Article 6(1) taken together with Article 6(3)(d) so long as the rights of the defence have been respected, which requires, as a general rule, that the accused be given an adequate and proper opportunity to challenge and question the maker of that statement. Fifth, any measures restricting the rights of the defence should be strictly necessary. Sixth, there is no violation of Article 6(1) taken together with Article 6(3)(d) if it can be shown that the handicaps under which the defence laboured were sufficiently counterbalanced by procedures which allowed the accused effectively to challenge the evidence. Seventh, relevant factors are whether there was any evidence against the accused in addition to the hearsay statement and whether the accused was able to adduce evidence which would put the credibility of the maker of the statement in doubt. Eighth, a conviction should not be based solely or to a decisive extent on anonymous witness statements.

However, a number of more recent cases suggest that the principle that a conviction should not be based solely or to a decisive extent on anonymous witness statements and the principle that, as a general rule, the accused should have an adequate and proper opportunity to challenge and question the maker of a hearsay statement have been merged, and in the process altered, to become a broader principle to the effect that 'where a conviction is based solely or to a decisive degree on [witness statements] that have been made by a person whom the accused has had no opportunity to examine or to have examined, whether during the investigation or at the trial, the rights of the defence are restricted to an extent that is incompatible with the guarantees provided by Article 6' (*Luca* v. *Italy* (2001) Application No. 33354/96 (ECtHR), *PS* v. *Germany* (2001) 36 EHRR 1139 (ECtHR)). This principle would certainly appear to prohibit the use by the prosecution of the complainant's witness statement in a *sexual* offence case, where the complainant's credibility is central to the truth of her allegation, there is no other independent evidence of the accused's guilt and the defence have been given no opportunity to challenge her evidence (*AM* v. *Italy* (1999) Application No. 37019/97 (ECtHR), *PS* v. *Germany* (2001) 26 EHRR 1139 (ECtHR)).

However, *Luca* v. *Italy* (2001) Application No. 33354/96 (ECtHR) should not be taken to have established an inflexible requirement of 'opportunity to examine or to have examined' for *any* case where the prosecution case is 'based solely or to a decisive degree' on the witness statements of one or more absent witnesses. In some cases it will be impossible to question the sole prosecution witness during the pre-trial proceedings or the course of the trial itself (for example, where the witness has died or is seriously ill, as in *Ferrantelli* v. *Italy* (1996) 23 EHRR 288 (ECtHR)) and, if there is no reason to doubt that witness's reliability, it would hardly be in the interests of justice if a mandatory rule of law prohibited a conviction just because there has been no pre-trial examination. The ultimate question is whether the *particular* accused can receive a fair trial in the *particular* circumstances of his case, and it may be that a fair trial is possible so long there is some other mechanism which can allow the defence effectively to challenge the absent witness's evidence.

Where, however, the witness *is* available (but afraid to testify) it may now be necessary to consider alternatives to ss. 23–26 of the Criminal Justice Act 1988, on the basis that any measures restricting the rights of the defence should be *strictly* necessary. If a less restrictive measure would suffice then that measure should be used instead (*Van Mechelen* v. *Netherlands* (1997) 25 EHRR 647 (ECtHR)). Procedures such as those set out in Chapter I of Part II of the Youth Justice and Criminal Evidence Act 1999 (16.4.4 *post*), where the witness may be cross-examined via a live television link, or in advance of the trial, would be less restrictive for the accused than the alternative under the Criminal Justice Act 1988, and it may be that in cases where the witness is available (and still capable of giving coherent evidence) measures of this sort should be used instead of the 1988 Act. Alternatively, there might need to be some form of challenge before or during the trial, where questions are put to the prosecution witness through the accused's legal representative or an intermediary, to *supplement* the hearsay evidence adduced under the Act, particularly if the prosecution case is based solely or to a decisive extent on that witness's evidence (see *SN* v. *Sweden* (2002) Application No. 34209/96 (ECtHR), 16.4.4 *post*).

The issue of Article 6(1) and (3)(d) compatibility has been addressed by the Court of Appeal on a number of occasions, the conclusion being that, despite the absence of any mechanism for challenging an absent witness's evidence in advance of the trial, there is no conflict between ss. 23 and 24 of the Criminal Justice Act 1988 and Article 6 because the judge's exclusionary powers in ss. 25 and 26 and the credibility provisions in Schedule 2 operate to ensure that the accused will receive a fair trial (*R* v. *Gokal* [1997] 2 Cr App R 266, *R* v. *Thomas* [1998] Crim LR 887, *R* v. *D* [2002] 3 WLR 997, *R* v. *M(KJ)* [2003] 2 Cr App R 322). The obligation on the trial judge to direct the jury on any weaknesses in the witness's evidence and on the fact that it was not tested by cross-examination provides an additional safeguard for the accused (6.3 *post*).

In *R* v. *M(KJ)* [2003] 2 Cr App R 322, a case relating to a fatal stabbing, the Court of Appeal strongly deprecated the view that ss. 23 and 26 should never be relied on in a case where the essential or only witness for the prosecution is afraid to testify (although it is to be noted that the Court did not consider any alternative mechanisms for protecting frightened witnesses):

'That would seem to us an intolerable result as a general proposition and could only lead to an encouragement of criminals to indulge in the very kind of intimidation which the sections are designed to defeat. Certainly, decisions of this court before the passage of the Human Rights Act 1998, as well as common sense, suggest that no invariable rule to that effect should be either propounded or followed ... [W]e would not subscribe to any formulation of the approach to be adopted which states without qualification that a conviction based solely or mainly on the impugned statement of an absent witness necessarily violates the right to a fair trial under Article 6.'

There will be a violation of Article 6, however, if the prosecution case depends wholly or mainly on the hearsay statement of a witness whose credibility is in real doubt, where the defence would be significantly handicapped by the inability to cross-examine. Such a state of affairs led to a successful appeal in *R* v. *M(KJ)*, where it was held that the trial judge had wrongly allowed the statement of the sole prosecution witness to be read under s. 23. The witness had himself been a suspect in the murder inquiry; he had refused to co-operate with the police; his change of heart had come at a time when he was on bail in respect of a charge of robbery, when the offer of a reward for information relating to the murder had come to his attention; and he had considerably 'improved' his evidence with the passage of time. There was thus 'every reason to question his motive and his veracity in pinning the murder on the defendant, a person with the mind of a child who ... could have no realistic opportunity of going into the witness box and defending himself'.

The decision of the European Commission of Human Rights in *Trivedi* v. *United Kingdom* (1997) EHRLR 521 (Application No. 31700/96) provides support for the view that ss. 23–26 of the 1988 Act are compatible with the requirements of Article 6 in cases where the witness is unavailable and there is additional evidence of the accused's guilt. T was convicted of false accounting on the basis of, *inter alia*, two hearsay statements made by C. These statements were adduced by the prosecution pursuant to ss. 23 and 26 of the 1988 Act on account of C's poor mental condition at the time of the trial. T complained to the Commission on the ground that there had been no opportunity for him to question C or challenge his evidence. The Commission rejected the application as manifestly ill-founded as T's rights had been respected. First, in order to assess the quality of C's evidence, and before deciding to grant the prosecution leave to adduce the same under s. 26 of the Act, the trial judge had received evidence in the absence of the jury on C's mental condition and memory when the statements were made and had heard oral submissions on the issue. Second, there was other evidence of T's guilt. Third, T had been able to give evidence which stood uncontroverted because of C's absence. Fourth, T's counsel had been given a full opportunity to comment on C's evidence with a view to impugning his credibility and reliability. Fifth, the judge had expressly directed the jury during his summing-up to attach less weight to C's evidence as it had not been tested by cross-examination.

Insofar as ss. 23–26 of the Criminal Justice Act 1988 are compatible with the European convention, it follows that, where the prosecution seek to rely on a hearsay statement which is *prima facie* admissible at common law, the judge should adopt an approach similar to that laid down in ss. 25 and 26 when determining whether the evidence should be excluded under s. 78(1) of the Police and Criminal Evidence Act 1984, with particular emphasis on whether the evidence is sufficiently reliable to be placed before the jury. The decision of the Court of Appeal in *R* v. *Callender* [1998] Crim LR 337 (6.1.1.5 *ante*) might be seen as an attempt to achieve the same result by a different route.

6.2.6 Schedule 2 to the Criminal Procedure and Investigations Act 1996

Written statements which have been admitted at committal proceedings in the magistrates' court prior to trial on indictment are now admissible in the Crown Court trial by virtue of s. 68 of the Criminal Procedure and Investigations Act 1996 and paragraph 1(2) of Schedule 2 to the Act, the only safeguards being the judge's discretion not to allow such evidence to be admitted (paragraph 1(3)(*b*)) and an 'interests of justice' test which must be applied when a party to the proceedings (that is, the accused) objects (paragraph 1(4)). This is an alarmingly wide exception to the rule against hearsay, as prosecution statements tendered at committal proceedings are now admitted in those proceedings as a matter of course (ss. 5A and 5B of the Magistrates' Courts Act 1980) and there are no safeguards in Schedule 2 such as those connected with the admissibility of evidence tendered pursuant to ss. 23 and 24 of the Criminal Justice Act 1988 (although no doubt judges will turn to ss. 25 and 26 of the 1988 Act for guidance in practice). Paragraph 2 of Schedule 2 makes similar provision for the admissibility at trial of certain written depositions admitted at committal proceedings pursuant to s. 97A of the Magistrates' Courts Act 1980. The Law Commission, noting that Schedule 2 may contravene Article 6 of the European Convention on Human Rights, has recommended the repeal of paragraphs 1(4) and 2(2) (see Law Com No. 245 (1997) at pp. 122–3). This would have the effect of preventing the admission of evidence if an objection has been raised by the accused.

6.2.7 Other Significant Statutory Exceptions

A video-recording of an interview with a vulnerable witness (other than the accused) may be admitted to stand in place of his evidence in chief under Chapter I of Part II of the Youth Justice and Criminal Evidence Act 1999 (see 16.4.4 *post*). Section 30 of the Criminal Justice Act 1988 provides that an expert's written report is admissible evidence of any fact or opinion stated therein if the expert would have been competent to give such evidence if called as a witness. The court's leave is required before such evidence can be admitted unless the expert is called to testify. Section 9 of the Criminal Justice Act 1967 allows any party in criminal proceedings to adduce a witness's written statement instead of calling him so long as no other party objects within seven days of being notified. Section 3 of the Bankers' Books Evidence Act 1879 allows copies of entries in bankers' books to be admissible in any proceedings (subject to certain conditions in s. 4 being satisfied). Schedule 2 to the Criminal Appeal Act 1968 permits the adduction at a retrial of the record of a witness's evidence given at the previous trial.

6.3 Directing the Jury

If a party is permitted to adduce an absent witness's hearsay statement in criminal proceedings the judge should give an appropriate direction to the jury, warning them to have regard to the lack of cross-examination when evaluating its probative value (*Scott* v. *R* [1989] 2 WLR 924 (PC), *R* v. *Curry* (1998) *The Times* 23.3.98 (CA)) and directing them to consider any specific weaknesses in the evidence (*R* v. *Kennedy* [1994] Crim LR 50 (CA)). In *R* v. *McCoy* (1999) unreported (99/01674/W4) the Court of Appeal stated that where the hearsay evidence is that of a critical prosecution witness it is incumbent on the judge to ensure that the jury realise the drawbacks imposed on the defence and that they might feel quite unable to attach anything like as much weight to the evidence because that witness has not been cross-examined. This is not a hard and fast rule, though, for more recently it has been said that the judge has a discretion as to the direction which should be given, appropriate to the circumstances of the case (*R* v. *Hardwick* [2001] EWCA Crim 369).

Where the hearsay statement is related to the court by another witness, for example a bystander who overheard the deceased's oral 'excited utterance' or dying declaration, it is most important that the jury should be directed to scrutinise the hearsay evidence with care as they have the additional task of deciding whether the witness before them can be relied on (*Nembhard* v. *R* [1981] 1 WLR 1515 (PC)). In *R* v. *Andrews* [1987] 2 WLR 413, the leading case on excited utterances, Lord Ackner said (at p. 424):

'Of course, having ruled the statement admissible the judge must ... make it clear to the jury that it is for them to decide what was said and to be sure that the witnesses were not mistaken in what they believed had been said to them. Further, they must be satisfied that the declarant did not concoct or distort to his advantage or the disadvantage of the accused the statement relied upon and where there is material to raise the issue, that he was not activated by any malice or ill-will. Further, where there are special features that bear on the possibility of mistake then the [jury's] attention must be invited to those matters.'

However, it seems the judge's failure to give a warning on the need for caution when assessing an excited utterance untested by cross-examination will not prove fatal so long as the jury have had their attention drawn to all the relevant matters. In *R* v. *Carnall* [1995] Crim LR 944 the Court of Appeal rejected an argument to the contrary on the ground that 'it was obvious that someone who had died could not be cross-examined'.

6.4 An Inclusionary Discretion?

The common-law exceptions evolved in a piecemeal fashion to allow for the admission of out-of-court statements made in a variety of situations on the ground that the peculiar nature of those situations could be assumed to enhance the *reliability* of the hearsay evidence, and the absence of any other evidence on the disputed issue *necessitated* an exception. These twin grounds of necessity and reliability also underpin ss. 23 and 24 of the Criminal Justice Act 1988. The problem is that, as the law stands, it is impossible to adduce reliable hearsay evidence which does not fall within a recognised exception even though there may be no other available evidence on the disputed issue. In the absence of any recognised exception the exclusionary hearsay rule is absolute which means the prosecution may be prevented from adducing cogent evidence of the accused's guilt and the accused may be unable to adduce cogent evidence of his innocence. It was decided in *Myers* v. *DPP* [1964] 3 WLR 145 (HL) that it is no longer possible for the courts to create new exceptions to the hearsay rule, so unless an existing exception such as the *Andrews* test for excited utterances (6.1.1.1 *ante*) is enlarged to be of general application any reform must come from Parliament.

The most obvious reform would be to give trial judges an inclusionary discretion so that hearsay evidence falling outside the recognised common-law and statutory exceptions could be admitted if it was in the interests of justice to do so. It has already been suggested (5.6.2 *ante*) that the rule of *prima facie* inadmissibility should be limited to express assertions and qualified by an inclusionary discretion, but it would not be necessary for any such discretion to replace the existing exceptions. Rather, a residual discretion could be introduced to *supplement* the common-law and statutory exceptions. This would strike the right balance between the desirability of maintaining certainty in the law and the necessity of serving the interests of justice. The judge would take into consideration a range of factors when deciding whether to admit the hearsay, particularly the twin considerations of necessity and reliability. The criterion of necessity would be satisfied if the maker of the statement was unavailable for a good reason (as with s. 23 of the Criminal Justice Act 1988) or was, for example, a very young child who could no longer remember his earlier statement. Reliability would depend on the risk of deception and mistake in the light of all the circumstances in which the statement was made. In other words, the judge would determine whether cross-examination could safely be dispensed with. This test would be similar to that applied by the judge when considering whether a confession should be admitted when it has been challenged under s. 76(2)(*b*) of the Police and Criminal Evidence Act

1984 (7.1.3.2 *post*), in the sense that the judge would not determine reliability itself (as that would usurp the function of the jury) but whether the statement is *apparently* reliable and therefore safe for the jury to consider despite the absence of any cross-examination.

A residual inclusionary discretion would make the law more logical, ensure fairness for the prosecution and the accused and obviate the need to create new quasi-exceptions (5.8 *ante*). A common-law discretion of this sort has now been recognised in New Zealand (*R* v. *Manase* [2001] 2 NZLR 197 (NZCA)). Canada too has a principled common-law discretion to admit hearsay evidence based on 'necessity and reliability', although it is considerably broader than the New Zealand exception. Indeed it has recently been held that the 'necessity and reliability' test is applicable in *all* cases, with the traditional exceptions to the hearsay rule comprising nothing more than 'practical manifestations of the principled approach' raising a strong presumption in favour of admitting the evidence (*R* v. *Starr* [2000] 2 SCR 144 (SCC)). The High Court of Australia has yet to recognise a common-law inclusionary discretion, but there are dicta to the effect that a discretion of this sort may exist, or that exceptions to the hearsay rule will be developed if reliability can be guaranteed (*Walton* v. *R* (1989) 166 CLR 283, *R* v. *Benz* (1989) 168 CLR 110, *Pollitt* v. *R* (1992) 174 CLR 558, *Bannon* v. *R* (1995) 185 CLR 1).

The Law Commission has recommended a statutory 'safety-valve' inclusionary discretion, which would be available to both the prosecution and the accused, to prevent potential injustice in exceptional circumstances (see Law Com No. 245 (1997) at pp. 129–34). The test to be applied by the court would be one of potential reliability based on the circumstances in which the statement was made and whether its admission could be justified in the interests of justice. Rule 807 of the United States Federal Rules of Evidence sets out a residual exception of this sort for hearsay evidence which does not fall within any of the other exceptions in the Rules, where the evidence has 'equivalent circumstantial guarantees of trustworthiness' and ought to be admitted in the interests of justice.

Chapter Summary

- A number of common-law and statutory exceptions to the hearsay rule have been recognised or created, the underlying principles being reliability and necessity.
- The most important common-law exceptions for criminal proceedings allow oral as well as documentary hearsay evidence to be admitted. These are the *res gestae* exceptions and (for trials involving joint enterprises and conspiracies) the exception for statements made by parties to a common enterprise.
- Most hearsay evidence in criminal proceedings is now admitted in documentary form pursuant to a statutory exception. Agreed statements may be admitted under s. 9 of the Criminal Justice Act 1967 ('section 9 statements'), but contested evidence must satisfy the requirements of ss. 23 or 24 of the Criminal Justice Act 1988, and overcome the hurdle of the leave requirement in ss. 25 or 26. If documentary hearsay evidence is admitted under ss. 23 or 24 the credibility of the absent witness may be challenged under Schedule 2 to the Act.

- If hearsay evidence is admitted pursuant to a common-law exception or under ss. 23 or 24 of the Criminal Justice Act 1988, the judge should give the jury an appropriate direction on any weaknesses in the absent witness's evidence and the disadvantage caused to the opposing party (usually the accused) by the unavailability of the witness for cross-examination.
- The provisions of the Criminal Justice Act 1988 have been held to comply with the requirements of Article 6 of the European Convention on Human Rights, but additional powers may need to be introduced to ensure that the accused's interests are sufficiently safeguarded if the prosecution case is heavily dependent on an available witness who does not wish to testify through fear.

Further Reading

Tapper, '*Hillmon* Rediscovered and *Lord St Leonards* Resurrected' (1990) 106 LQR 441
Smith, 'Sections 23 and 24 of the Criminal Justice Act 1988' [1994] Crim LR 426
Spencer, 'Orality and the Evidence of Absent Witnesses' [1994] Crim LR 628
Ormerod, 'The Hearsay Exceptions' [1996] Crim LR 16
Spencer, 'Hearsay Reform: A Bridge Not Far Enough' [1996] Crim LR 29
Murphy, 'Practising Safe Hearsay' (1997) 1(3) E&P 105
Ormerod, 'Redundant *Res Gestae*?' [1998] Crim LR 301

Law Commission Consultation Paper No. 138 (1995)
Law Commission Report, Law Com No. 245 (1997)

Criminal Justice Bill (2003), Part 11, Chapters 2 and 3
and Explanatory Note (www.publications.parliament.uk)

7   Admissions

A party's *informal admission* (or, in criminal proceedings, the accused's *confession*) is an out-of-court statement made by that party which is adverse to his case. Such admissions have long been recognised as an exception to the exclusionary hearsay rule and are thus admissible to prove the truth of the matters stated. Confessions tendered by the prosecution are now governed by s. 76 of the Police and Criminal Evidence Act 1984 ('PACE'), whereas in civil proceedings informal admissions are admissible by virtue of s. 1(1) of the Civil Evidence Act 1995. A confession or an informal admission is not conclusive evidence of any fact admitted, however; the party who made it may adduce other evidence at the trial to show why it should not be relied on. By contrast, a party's *formal admission* is conclusive evidence of any fact admitted; the effect of any such admission is to obviate the need for the opposing party to prove the admitted fact, thereby reducing the length and cost of the trial (see 15.6.3 *post*). It is with confessions (and, to a lesser extent, informal admissions in civil proceedings) that this chapter is concerned.

7.1 Criminal Proceedings: *Confessions*

In England and Wales a confession may be relied on as sufficient proof of guilt even if it is unsupported by any other evidence (*R* v. *Sykes* (1913) 8 Cr App R 233 (CCA)). This is a natural consequence of the traditional justification for the admissibility of confessions: 'A free and voluntary confession is deserving of the highest credit, because it is presumed to flow from the strongest sense of guilt, and therefore it is admitted as proof of the crime to which it refers' (*R* v. *Warickshall* (1783) 1 Leach 263 (CCC) at p. 263). More recently, in *Western* v. *DPP* [1997] 1 Cr App R 474 (DC) Butterfield J said (at p. 481):

> 'This exception [to the hearsay rule] is based on the assumption that what a person says against his or her own interests is likely to be true, although the reliability of this assumption has long been doubted.'

There are two points to note about this dictum. First, to say that the admissibility of confessions is predicated upon the likelihood of their being true does not satisfactorily explain the decisions in *R* v. *Turner* (1975) 61 Cr App R 67 (CA) and *R* v. *Blastland* [1985] 3 WLR 345 (HL) (5.3 *ante*) where it was held that a third party's confession to the offence charged is inadmissible at common law. The better view is that confessions are admissible for a combination of two reasons. The principal objection to the admissibility of hearsay evidence – that the declarant is unavailable for cross-examination – does not apply if an out-of-court statement has been made by a party to the proceedings; after all, a party who has volunteered an admission can hardly complain that he is unavailable for cross-examination. Then there is the traditional justification: the common-sense view that a statement which is inculpatory is more likely to be truthful than one which is exculpatory. The second noteworthy point about the dictum is that, by recognising that the traditional assumption 'has long been doubted', Butterfield J was suggesting that the accused may have falsely confessed to his guilt. The possibility of false confessions has long been recognised – as indeed it was in *R* v. *Warickshall* (1783) 1 Leach 263 (CCC) – and at common law the accused's confession was admissible against him only if it was free and voluntary. If the confession was elicited by oppression or 'by fear of prejudice or hope of advantage excited or held out by a person in authority' it was inadmissible (*DPP* v. *Ping Lin* [1975] 3 WLR 419 (HL) at p. 439, *R* v. *Rennie* [1982] 1 WLR 64 (CA) at p. 70). The common law on confessions has now almost entirely been supplanted by s. 76(1)–(2) of PACE.

7.1.1 Confessions as an Exception to the Rule Against Hearsay

Any out-of-court inculpatory statement made by the accused – that is, an admission that he committed the offence charged or an admission of some fact which goes towards proving he committed the offence charged – is admissible against him at his trial to prove the truth of the matters admitted:

> In any proceedings a confession made by an accused person may be given in evidence against him in so far as it is relevant to any matter in issue in the proceedings and is not excluded by the court in pursuance of this section. (s. 76(1) of PACE)

> In this Part of this Act – 'confession' includes any statement wholly or partly adverse to the person who made it, whether made to a person in authority or not and whether made in words or otherwise. (s. 82(1) of PACE)

Before the Human Rights Act 1998 came into force, it was said that, for the purposes of s. 82(1) of PACE, a statement made by the accused was a confession only if it was adverse to him at the time he actually made it (*R* v. *Sat-Bhambra* (1988) 88 Cr App R 55 (CA), *R* v. *Park* (1993) 99 Cr App R 270 (CA)). Accordingly, if the accused made a wholly exculpatory statement before the trial (for example, 'I was elsewhere, playing golf') which subsequently became adverse to him because it was shown to be false, that admissible non-hearsay statement (5.4 *ante*) would not directly fall within the meaning of s. 82(1) and the prosecution would not need to satisfy the conditions of s. 76(2) of PACE (7.1.3 *post*). The position was recently reconsidered in *R* v. *Z* [2003] 1 WLR 1489 (CA), however, where it was held that, in the light of *Saunders* v. *United Kingdom* (1996) 23 EHRR 313 (ECtHR) (14.1 *post*), Article 6 of the European Convention on Human Rights demands that an out-of-court statement be regarded as a confession if it is self-incriminating *at the time of the trial*, even if the accused intended it to be exculpatory when he made it (although the Court queried whether the statement 'I did not do it' could amount to a confession). Thus, if the prosecution wish to support their case against the accused with an out-of-court statement made by him which was intended to be exculpatory, but can now be shown to be a lie, that false statement will be admissible at the behest of the prosecution only if they are able to discharge the burden(s) imposed upon them by s. 76(2). This is a sensible return to the position at common law (*R* v. *Wattam* (1952) 36 Cr App R 72 (CCA)). Given the rationales which underpin s. 76(2), it would be absurd if, for example, a false statement elicited from the accused by torture could be *prima facie* admissible against him.

An out-of-court statement made by the accused which is (and continues to be) wholly exculpatory in relation to the offence charged is not admissible at his trial for that offence under s. 76(1) to prove the truth of the matters stated (see, for example, *R* v. *Squire* [1990] Crim LR 341 (CA)). Nor is such a statement admissible to show the accused's consistency as a witness (*R* v. *Roberts* (1942) 28 Cr App R 102 (CCA), 16.4.2 *post*). A statement of this sort will be admissible only by virtue of a separate exception to the rule against hearsay; or under an exception to the 'rule against narrative' to show the accused's consistency and reaction when taxed with incriminating facts (16.4.2.4 *post*). If, however, the accused has made a 'mixed statement' in response to an allegation, that is, a statement which is partly inculpatory and partly exculpatory, the whole statement is *prima facie* admissible as evidence of the truth of the matters stated under s. 76(1), save that the jury ought to be directed that the inculpatory parts are more likely to be true (*R* v. *Sharp* [1988] 1 WLR 7 (HL)). There are limits to this exception, however. In *R* v. *Aziz* [1995] 3 WLR 53 (HL) it was felt that a mixed statement could be admissible only at the behest of the prosecution; and in *Western* v. *DPP* [1997] 1 Cr App R 474 the Divisional Court felt that where there was no other evidence in support of the exculpatory part of a mixed statement its weight was likely to be minimal. Moreover, not every exculpatory comment will be admissible hearsay just because the accused also made a trivial admission. The admission must be significant in the sense that it is 'capable of adding some degree of weight to the prosecution case on an issue which [is] relevant to guilt' (*R* v. *Garrod* [1997] Crim LR 445 (CA)).

A confession made by the accused which inculpates his co-accused, and which does not fall within any other exception to the hearsay rule, is no evidence of the co-accused's guilt unless he accepts its truth; and the jury must be directed to this effect (*R* v. *Gunewardene* [1951] 2 KB 600 (CCA)). To ensure that the co-accused's defence is not prejudiced by the admission of such a confession, it may be appropriate for the prosecution to edit out the references to him (or substitute a letter for the co-accused's name), but this is not an absolute rule. If the accused objects to such editing because the references to the co-accused comprise the exculpatory part of his mixed statement the judge has no power to prevent the confession from being admitted in its unedited form (*Lobban* v. *R* [1995] 1 WLR 877 (PC)).

Like any other statement, a confession may be made orally, in writing or by way of a gesture or action. In *Li Shu-Ling* v. *R* [1988] 3 WLR 671 (PC), for example, it was held that a video recording of the accused's demonstration of how he had strangled his victim had been properly admitted as an admission that he had indeed killed her in that way (see also *Lam Chi-Ming* v. *R* [1991] 2 WLR 1082 (PC) and *Timothy* v. *The State* [2000] 1 WLR 485 (PC)). In certain circumstances it may be possible to infer an admission of guilt from the accused's reaction or demeanour or silence in the face of an allegation made against him in his presence and hearing (9.2.1 *post*) or from his fleeing from the authorities or (as noted above) from his lying when interrogated, so long as there is no realistic possibility of an innocent explanation for his conduct (11.6 *post*). In *R* v. *Stubbs* [2002] EWCA Crim 2254 it was held that an intercepted hand-written letter in which the author identified himself as the offender in two attached photographs (taken from closed-circuit television footage of two robberies) had been properly admitted as a confession by the accused of his involvement in those robberies, as the author could not conceivably have been anyone other than the accused.

It is also possible for an admission to be made on the accused's behalf by his agent. So long as the agent was duly authorised by the accused to speak on his behalf and the admission was made within the scope of that authority it will be *prima facie* admissible against the accused as a confession. Thus in *R* v. *Turner* (1975) 61 Cr App R 67 (CA) the accused, S, was bound by the incriminating comments his barrister had made when speaking on his behalf during a speech in mitigation in earlier proceedings. The Privy Council has indicated, however, that admissions made in mitigation should not subsequently be held against the accused as it is often unrealistic for the advocate to continue to assert his client's innocence following a conviction (*Wu Chun-Piu* v. *R* [1996] 1 WLR 1113). In *R* v. *Turner* the barrister acting for S was assumed to have been acting within the scope of his authority, but generally it will be necessary to prove that the agent was authorised to speak on the accused's behalf. In *R* v. *Evans* [1981] Crim LR 699 (CA) a statement made by a solicitor's clerk was not admissible against his client as there was no admissible evidence to prove the clerk had been given such authority. If admissions made by an authorised agent are not admissible by virtue of s. 76(1) of PACE (which covers confessions 'made by an accused person') they presumably remain admissible at common law.

7.1.2 The Reliability of Confessions

A truthful confession may be the best evidence for the prosecution, and in some cases the only evidence against the accused. It is not unknown for suspects, or even individuals who have not fallen under suspicion, to confess to their crimes because they are overcome with the stress associated with having a guilty conscience and/or the fear of detection. Confessing to an offence may provide cathartic relief for the offender in addition to the obvious evidential benefit for the prosecution, so it should not be surprising that confessions are admissible. This is of course dependent on the confession being truthful. It is true to say that people rarely make false confessions in ordinary circumstances; but most confessions are made in the face of questioning by agents of the state in an alien and potentially hostile environment. In the context of a formal interrogation a suspect may indeed falsely incriminate himself for a variety of possible reasons, and it is only when those possibilities have been sufficiently reduced or eliminated that a confession should be left to the jury. The law must therefore ensure that confessions are not made in circumstances which might cast doubt on their reliability as truthful assertions of fact. This requires, first, a body of rules governing the conduct of interviews generally, to minimise the potential for unreliability; and, second, rules to prevent the admission of any confession made in circumstances where the risk of unreliability is too great for it to be safe to allow the jury to consider it. This is not to say that reliability is the sole consideration governing the admissibility of confessions, however. Even a demonstrably reliable confession may be excluded if it has been obtained with scant regard for the accused's privilege against self-incrimination, for example by physical abuse (see *Lam Chi-Ming* v. *R* [1991] 2 WLR 1082 (PC) and 10.2.3 *post*). In addition to the question of the truth or falsity of a confession which has been provided by the accused, there is the separate question of 'verballing' where the accused denies that he made the statement which has been attributed to him. Whether a confession has been concocted by a corrupt interrogator or some other person with an axe to grind is ultimately a question of fact for the jury (or magistrates), but it is essential that the law should minimise the scope for fabrication and the risk that the accused will be able to make a false allegation of fabrication at his trial. Any body of rules governing the interrogation of suspects must therefore include provisions to minimise the possibility of verballing.

Thus, whenever the prosecution wish to adduce a confession purportedly made by the accused two questions may need to be considered. First, did the accused actually make the confession or was it fabricated by the witness for the prosecution? Second, if the accused *did* confess as alleged, are the matters to which he confessed true or false? False confessions are most likely to be made during the course of a formal interrogation, and it is this risk which is discussed below (7.1.2.1 *post*); but it should always be remembered that even in a less formal context the accused's inculpatory remarks might have been mistakenly overheard, or misinterpreted, or deliberately taken out of context and misrepresented by the witness.

7.1.2.1 False Confessions Made by the Accused

A suspect may falsely confess to an offence he did not commit or overstate his involvement in an offence for a number of reasons. One such reason can generally be discounted, though, on the ground that it is rare and the confession can usually be shown to be false. This is where a person voluntarily confesses to a notorious offence as a way of basking in reflected notoriety. The example usually referred to in this context is that of the large number of persons who falsely confessed to having kidnapped the American aviator Charles Lindbergh's baby in 1932. In *R* v. *Sykes* (1913) 8 Cr App R 233 (CCA), a case concerning the murder of an 11-year-old girl, Ridley J accepted that: 'the murder was the talk of the countryside, and it might well be that a man under the influence of insanity or a morbid desire for notoriety would accuse himself of such a crime'. Needless to say, a voluntary confession of this sort is likely to be made by a confessor who is suffering from a mental illness or personality disorder, following the commission of a highly-publicised offence. In 1974 Judith Ward, an IRA sympathiser, confessed to a number of IRA bombings including the destruction of a coach in which 12 persons were killed. One of the reasons why her conviction was subsequently quashed was the availability of fresh evidence suggesting that in 1974 she had been suffering from a severe mental disorder which had caused her to fantasise about being involved with members of the IRA (*R* v. *Ward* [1993] 1 WLR 619 (CA)). A more recent example is provided by the case of Peter Fell, a fantasist who had his convictions for two murders quashed in 2001, having spent 17 years in prison (*R* v. *Fell* [2001] EWCA Crim 696). Fell, who had a history of making up stories about himself, made a series of anonymous telephone calls in 1982 and 1983 naming himself as the culprit and subsequently admitted being involved in an attack on the victims. Apart from his personality disorder, it appears that one of the reasons for his confession was that he was trying to give the police the impression that he should be charged with manslaughter, having become convinced that he would soon be charged with murder.

Less severe psychological conditions may also cause a suspect to volunteer a false confession. The suspect may be particularly susceptible to suggestions put to him (as in *R* v. *Raghip* (1991) *The Times* 6.12.91 (CA) and *R* v. *King* [2000] 2 Cr App R 391 (CA)) or feel an overwhelming need to get the interview over and done with (as in *R* v. *Delaney* (1988) 88 Cr App R 338 (CA)) or confess on account of a child-like desire to protect a loved one (as in *R* v. *Harvey* [1988] Crim LR 241 (CCC)) or because of a sense of guilt over some other real or imagined misconduct in the past. A simple-minded suspect, not realising the long-term implications of any admissions, may confess as the quickest and easiest way of getting home, or accept suggestions put by those in authority that he may have committed the offence while he was suffering from a black-out (as in *R* v. *Paris* (1992) 97 Cr App R 99 (CA)). For similar reasons, even quite normal suspects may falsely confess, particularly if the stress of the interview has become intolerable. The combination of constant questioning and the sterile environment of the interview-room is likely to cause any sane person's resistance to drop eventually and this may lead to a false confession as a way of escape – the immediate prospect of freedom outweighing the obvious long-term consequences. Alternatively, the suspect may be a mother who wishes to get home to look after her children (a point raised unsuccessfully in *R* v. *Tyrer* (1989) 90 Cr App R 446 (CA)) or be suffering from the effects of a prescribed drug (as in *R* v. *Sat-Bhambra* (1988) 88 Cr App R 55 (CA)) or wish to get out of custody in order to obtain a 'fix' of a drug to which he is addicted (as in *R* v. *Goldenberg* (1988) 88 Cr App R 285 (CA)).

Police trickery or impropriety may also induce false confessions. The suspect may be deceived about the evidence against him or have had evidence planted on him and realise he has little chance of being believed by a jury. The reduction in sentence the accused can expect on account of his confessing at an early stage in the proceedings is an added incentive to make a false confession in such circumstances. The suspect may falsely confess to a lesser offence following threats that he (or perhaps members of his family) will otherwise be charged with a more serious offence. The police may promise bail (as in *R* v. *Barry* (1991) 95 Cr App R 384 (CA)) or threaten custody, or promise to drop other charges (or threaten to add more charges), or understate the seriousness of the offence (as in *R* v. *Delaney* (1988) 88 Cr App R 338 (CA) and *R* v. *Kirk* [2000] 1 WLR 567 (CA)), or even promise not to proceed with any prosecution at all (as in *R* v. *Mathias* (1989) *The Times* 24.8.89 (CA)). In *R* v. *Clark* [1999] Crim LR 573 (CA) a conviction was quashed because fresh evidence suggested that the police might have left heroin in the suspect's cell and that he had confessed after smoking it.

The most serious form of police misconduct is oppression, whether it amounts to threats, physical abuse or something more insidious such as sleep deprivation. It would appear, for example, that four members of the 'Birmingham Six' signed false confessions to mass murder in 1974 in consequence of police brutality (*R* v. *McIlkenny* (1991) 93 Cr App R 287 (CA)), 7.1.2.2 *post*) and that Keith Twitchell confessed to his involvement in an armed robbery in 1980 only after members of the notorious West Midlands Serious Crime Squad had suffocated him by placing a plastic bag over his head (*R* v. *Twitchell* [2000] 1 Cr App R 373 (CA), 3.3.19 *ante*). It may be that prolonged oppression or torture will eventually cause *any* person to confess to *any* offence, no matter how serious the allegation may be.

7.1.2.2 Oral Confessions Fabricated by Interrogators

It is not only the risk of false confessions actually made by the accused which needs to be considered. The accused may assert that the confession was *fabricated* by the prosecution witness. An obvious example is so-called 'noble-cause corruption', where a police officer feels the need to construct evidence against the person he genuinely believes committed the offence, but against whom he is unable to gather sufficient evidence.

In 1975 the 'Birmingham Six' were convicted of terrorist outrages which killed 21 people the year before. Two of the six were alleged to have made oral confessions (which they denied) while the other four admitted signing written confessions but asserted that they were false and had been elicited by force (see Mullin, *Error of Judgment* (1986, Chatto & Windus) at pp. 57–103). The prosecution case was based on these confessions, corroborated by expert scientific evidence suggesting that two of the six men had been handling the explosive nitroglycerine. The convictions were quashed in 1991 on the ground that the scientific evidence could no longer be regarded as reliable and that police witnesses had lied on oath (*R* v. *McIlkenny* (1991) 93 Cr App R 287 (CA)). Interestingly, the psychologist Dr Gudjonsson applied his 'suggestibility and compliance' test to the six men in 1987 and found that the two who failed to sign written confessions registered very low scores, one possible conclusion being that while brutality was enough to force the other four to sign false confessions the remaining two held out, compelling the police to fabricate oral confessions instead (Gudjonsson, *The Psychology of Interrogations, Confessions and Testimony* (1992, John Wiley), at pp. 270–2; see generally Dennis, 'Miscarriages of Justice and the Law of Confessions' (1993) PL 291). Similarly, the conviction of Winston Silcott for the murder of PC Blakelock during a riot in north London in 1985 was quashed on the ground that evidence of his purported oral admission had been severely undermined. The only evidence against Silcott was that he had made oral admissions to a Detective Chief Superintendent during his interview, but in the light of expert evidence demonstrating that that officer had been guilty of 'misbehaviour' (altering his interview notes) the prosecution evidence was rendered worthless and Silcott's conviction could not be allowed to stand (*R* v. *Silcott* (1991) *The Times* 6.12.91 (CA)).

7.1.2.3 Ensuring the Reliability of Confession Evidence

Section 76(2) of PACE was enacted to ensure that potentially unreliable (that is, potentially false) confessions would be excluded as a matter of law. The subsection prevents the admission of confessions (even if they are true) if they have been obtained as a consequence of oppression or anything said or done which was likely in the circumstances to render unreliable any such confession made by the accused.

A confession which has been made in consequence of oppression is inadmissible for a number of reasons. First, as a matter of common sense any confession obtained by oppression is highly likely to be unreliable (the 'reliability principle', 10.2.1 *post*). Second, an exclusionary rule of this sort reflects the need in a civilised society to protect the rights of any suspect being questioned by agents of the state (the 'protective principle', 10.2.3 *post*), in particular the suspect's right not to incriminate himself and his right to be treated in a way which is neither degrading nor oppressive. To torture or in some other way maltreat a suspect in order to elicit a confession from him is unacceptable, and one way in which the law can prevent such behaviour is to exclude any confession so obtained. Closely allied to the protective principle is the 'disciplinary principle', which acts to deter police misconduct by excluding the fruits of their impropriety. However, because it has been said on a number of occasions that it is not the function of the Court of Appeal to discipline the police, the true rationale would (in theory) seem to be protective rather than disciplinary (see 10.2.2 *post*). Finally there is the 'integrity principle'. This demands that the moral integrity of the criminal justice system, and the moral soundness of a verdict of guilt at the end of the trial, should not be undermined by evidence obtained in consequence of police misconduct (10.2.4 *post*).

Oppression aside, admissibility under s. 76(2) turns on the question of reliability, but this does not mean reliability in the sense that the confession is *actually* a truthful assertion by the accused, for that is a question of fact for the jury; it is *apparent* reliability in the sense that the confession can safely be placed before the jury so that they can decide whether or not it is true. Section 76(2)(*b*) therefore excludes the accused's confession if it was made in consequence of anything said or done which was likely, in the circumstances, to render unreliable *any* (such) confession which the accused might have made in consequence thereof. If the thing said or done was such that any (such) confession made by the accused in consequence is likely to be unreliable, the accused's confession can be placed before the jury only if it is first proved that it was not so obtained (7.1.3.2 *post*). For the purposes of this admissibility test the *actual* truth or falsity of the confession is irrelevant; so in *R* v. *Cox* [1991] Crim LR 276 (CA) it was held that the judge should have disregarded the accused's admission on the *voir dire* that his confession was true (see also *R* v. *McGovern* (1990) 92 Cr App R 228 (CA)). But if a confession can be ruled inadmissible under s. 76(2)(*b*) notwithstanding its actual reliability it follows that, as with s. 76(2)(*a*), there must be some other policy consideration at work. Given that most confessions are made in response to questions put by agents of the state, such as police or customs officers, reliability (in both senses of the word) is best ensured by the elimination of any factors during the interview process as a whole, including any periods of detention, which might cause a suspect to make a false confession; and one way of achieving this is to impose certain obligations on those who investigate offences. The purpose of s. 76(2)(*b*) (and the Codes of Practice issued under ss. 60 and 66) is to ensure, first, that suspects are not treated in a way which would cast doubt on the reliability of their confessions and, second, that their human rights are respected and protected at a more general level, beyond the specific prohibition on oppressive interviewing techniques imposed by s. 76(2)(*a*).

7.1.3 Confessions Tendered by the Prosecution

There are five ways in which a confession tendered by the prosecution may be challenged, to prevent the jury from considering it at the end of the trial. Two of these are found in s. 76(2) of PACE, requiring the exclusion of a confession as a matter of law if the prosecution are unable to prove it was not obtained as a result of oppression (s. 76(2)(*a*)) or anything said or done which renders it potentially unreliable (s. 76(2)(*b*)). If the confession falls to be excluded under s. 76(2) the judge has no discretion to allow it to be admitted (*R* v. *Paris* (1992) 97 Cr App R 99 (CA)). If a confession is not excluded under s. 76(2) it is *prima facie* admissible, but may be excluded by the judge in the exercise of his statutory discretion to exclude any prosecution evidence which would adversely affect the fairness of the proceedings (s. 78(1) of PACE). The judge also has a broad common-law discretion to exclude (or withdraw) any prosecution evidence which would be unduly prejudicial to the accused, and a narrower common-law discretion to exclude (or withdraw) any confession tendered (or adduced) by the prosecution if it was obtained in violation of the accused's right not to incriminate himself (*R* v. *Sang* [1979] 3 WLR 263 (HL), 10.1 *post*).

When deciding whether to exclude a confession the judge will take into consideration any breaches of PACE, such as s. 56 (the right to have someone informed) and s. 58 (the right to legal advice), and the latest (2003) version of its Codes of Practice, particularly Codes C and E. Section 67(11) provides that if any provision of the Codes appears to be relevant to any question arising in the trial it '*shall* be taken into account'. Code C contains provisions relating to, *inter alia*, the right not to be held incommunicado (C-5 and Annex B); the right to legal advice (C-6 and Annex B); the conditions of detention for suspects (C-8); the treatment of detained suspects (C-9); the cautioning of suspects (C-10); interviews – including special rules governing the interviewing of juveniles and the mentally-handicapped – (C-11, C-12, Annexes C and E), written statements under caution (Annex D), interpreters (C-13), special restrictions on questioning (C-14), reviews and extensions of detention (C-15) and charging (C-16). Codes E and F respectively govern the audio and 'visual' recording of interviews (although Code F, issued under s. 60A of PACE, currently applies only to certain areas of England and Wales as part of a pilot study). These Codes of Practice bind all persons 'charged with the duty of investigating offences' (s. 67(9)) such as police officers, customs officers and even commercial investigators (*R* v. *Twaites* (1990) 92 Cr App R 106 (CA)) and private store detectives (*R* v. *Bayliss* (1993) 98 Cr App R 235 (CA)).

7.1.3.1 Section 76(2)(*a*) of PACE: *Oppression*

> If, in any proceedings where the prosecution proposes to give in evidence a confession made by an accused person, it is represented to the court that the confession was or may have been obtained – (*a*) by oppression of the person who made it ... the court shall not allow the confession to be given in evidence against him except in so far as the prosecution proves to the court beyond reasonable doubt that the confession (notwithstanding that it may be true) was not obtained as aforesaid.

Section 76(8) provides that 'oppression' includes torture, inhuman or degrading treatment, and the use or threat of violence (whether or not amounting to torture), reflecting the substance of Article 3 of the European Convention on Human Rights. Code C-11.5 complements s. 76(2)(*a*) by prohibiting investigating officers from trying to obtain answers or elicit a statement by oppression. If the accused does not raise the issue, the court itself may require proof that a confession was not obtained by oppression (s. 76(3)).

The meaning of oppression was considered by the Court of Appeal in *R* v. *Fulling* [1987] 2 WLR 923. The accused claimed she had been told by a police officer that her lover had a mistress who was being kept in the adjoining cell. This, it was claimed, had so distressed her that she had confessed simply to get out, and it was argued on appeal that the police officer's conduct had amounted to oppression. The Court of Appeal rejected this submission, holding that oppression was to be given its ordinary dictionary meaning – the 'exercise of authority or power in a burdensome, harsh or wrongful manner; unjust or cruel treatment of subjects, inferiors, etc.; the imposition of unreasonable or unjust burdens' – and that for conduct to amount to oppression there would generally have to be impropriety on the part of the interrogator. According to Lord Lane CJ, the word 'oppression' connotes 'detestable wickedness', so it should not be surprising that rude and discourteous questioning has been held not to amount to oppression (*R* v. *Emmerson* (1990) 92 Cr App R 284 (CA)). Where the questioning is more aggressive and intimidating, however, it may enter the realm of oppression and justify the exclusion of a confession under s. 76(2)(*a*). In *R* v. *Paris* (1992) 97 Cr App R 99 (CA) the fact that the accused ('M') had made his first inculpatory comment within an hour of having been continuously bullied and shouted at by interviewing police officers resulted in his conviction being quashed. The 'force and menace' of the officers' technique amounted to oppression, and this was not altered by the fact that his solicitor had been with him and failed to intervene. M, who was of low intelligence, had been continuously hectored during the interrogation, even though he denied any involvement in the alleged offence over and over again, and had been crying and sobbing for extended periods.

At common law the particular character of the accused was deemed to be relevant to the question of oppression, so the hardened criminal was expected to put up with a more vigorous style of interrogation. This would still seem to be the position under s. 76(2)(*a*). The mental state of the accused was thought to be relevant in *R* v. *Paris* (where it was felt the questioning would have been oppressive even for a suspect of normal intelligence) and in *R* v. *Spens* [1992] 1 WLR 148 (CA) the 'intelligent and sophisticated' personality of the accused was considered relevant to whether he had been questioned oppressively.

7.1.3.2 Section 76(2)(*b*) of PACE: *Unreliability*

If, in any proceedings where the prosecution proposes to give in evidence a confession made by an accused person, it is represented to the court that the confession was or may have been obtained ... (*b*) in consequence of anything said or done which was likely, in the circumstances existing at the time, to render unreliable any confession which might be made by him in consequence thereof, the court shall not allow the confession to be given in evidence against him except in so far as the prosecution proves to the court beyond reasonable doubt that the confession (notwithstanding that it may be true) was not obtained as aforesaid.

Code C-11.5 prohibits police officers from indicating, except in answer to a direct question, what action the police will take in the event that the suspect answers questions or makes a statement or refuses to do either.

Section 76(3) of PACE provides that the court itself may require the prosecution to prove that a confession was not obtained in consequence of anything said or done which was likely to render it unreliable.

There will inevitably be an overlap between the two limbs of s. 76(2) if it is oppressive behaviour which has led to the potential unreliability of the confession (as in *R* v. *Paris* (1992) 97 Cr App R 99 (CA); see also *R* v. *Beales* [1991] Crim LR 118 (CC)). But the test in s. 76(2)(*b*) is broader in scope than s. 76(2)(*a*). The phrase 'anything said or done' covers not only threats but also favourable inducements such as a promise to grant bail or an assurance that the accused's family members will not be charged. It also covers words or behaviour emanating from another source which would render the accused's confession unreliable; for example, where the accused heard her lover confess and wished to protect her by taking the blame upon herself (as in *R* v. *Harvey* [1988] Crim LR 241 (CCC)) or where, during the interview, the accused's solicitor behaved like an incredulous and hostile police officer (as in *R* v. *M* (2000) unreported (99/4259/X4) (CA)). Unlike s. 76(2)(*a*), however, there need be no impropriety on the part of interviewing officers for a confession to fall foul of s. 76(2)(*b*) (*R* v. *Fulling* [1987] 2 WLR 923 (CA), *R* v. *Walker* [1998] Crim LR 211 (CA)).

The test for admissibility was broken down by the Court of Appeal in *R* v. *Barry* (1991) 95 Cr App R 384 in the following way: (i) Was there 'anything said or done'? (ii) If so, was the thing said or done likely in the circumstances to render unreliable 'any confession' which might have been made by the accused as a consequence? (iii) If so, did the thing said or done actually cause the accused to make his particular confession? Sensibly, the reference to 'any confession' in s. 76(2)(*b*) has been interpreted to mean 'any such' or 'such a' confession as the one the accused made, as opposed to any entirely different confession (*R* v. *Bow Street Magistrates' Court ex parte Proulx* [2001] 1 All ER 57 (DC) at p. 77).

The accused merely needs to represent to the judge (or magistrates) that his confession may have been obtained in consequence of anything said or done which was likely, in the circumstances existing at the time, to render unreliable any (such) confession. It is then for the prosecution to prove beyond reasonable doubt that the accused's particular confession was not obtained in consequence of the thing said or done. This is a test of causation. The test is not whether the particular confession is actually unreliable, but whether any (such) confession which might have been made by the (particular) accused in those circumstances, as a result of the thing said or done, is likely to be unreliable. If the accused's particular confession was actually made in consequence of that thing said or done, in those circumstances, it is inadmissible as a matter of law. Every case will turn on its own facts, but consideration will be given to the nature of what was said or done, the personality of the accused, the nature of the offence in question, the accused's experience of the criminal justice system, the accused's mental or physical health, the nature and extent of the confession and indeed any other relevant circumstances existing at the time. The underlying policy is to ensure that a confession should be made available to the jury only when it is safe to do so – whether the confession is actually reliable, in the sense of being true, is a question of fact for them.

In *R* v. *Goldenberg* (1988) 88 Cr App R 285 the Court of Appeal held that 'anything said or done' was limited to extraneous matters and did not apply to anything emanating from the accused himself, in that case the accused's purported craving for heroin during his interview which, it was suggested, had caused him to confess in the hope of obtaining police bail. The same point was made in *R* v. *Lovell* (1999) unreported (99/3783/Y3) (CA) in respect of the accused's mental state as described by a psychologist. In *R* v. *Crampton* (1990) 92 Cr App R 369 the Court of Appeal doubted whether holding an interview while the accused was suffering from withdrawal symptoms was something done within the meaning of s. 76(2)(*b*). The question whether a drug addict was fit to be interviewed was said to be a matter for the officers and the police doctor who had been there at the time of the interview; but, even if it was to be accepted that holding an interview while the accused was suffering from withdrawal symptoms could amount to a thing done, as the officers and doctor had considered the accused fit to be interviewed the judge had been entitled to admit the confession. The Court went on to approve the dictum of Lord Lane CJ in *R* v. *Rennie* [1982] 1 WLR 64 (CA) (at p. 69):

> 'Very few confessions are inspired solely by remorse. Often the motives of an accused person are mixed and include a hope that an early admission may lead to an earlier release or a lighter sentence. If it were the law that the mere presence of such a motive, even if prompted by something said or done by a person in authority, led inexorably to the exclusion of a confession, nearly every confession would be rendered inadmissible. That is not the law. In some cases the hope may be self-generated. If so, it is irrelevant, even if it provides the dominant motive for making the confession. In such a case the confession will not have been obtained by anything said or done ...'

Given the purpose of s. 76(2)(*b*) it would be absurd if the effects of drugs or withdrawal symptoms were to be entirely disregarded, but it may be that such effects can be taken into account as a relevant circumstance just as the accused's mental or physical weaknesses may be taken into consideration. In *R* v. *McGovern* (1990) 92 Cr App R 228 (CA), for example, it was felt the accused's pregnancy and the fact she had been vomiting prior to the interview ought to have been taken into consideration by the judge.

In *R* v. *Everett* [1988] Crim LR 826 (CA) the accused's confession was held to be inadmissible because, although he was 42 years old, he had an IQ of 61 and a mental age of an eight-year-old. A similar approach was taken in *R* v. *Raghip* (1991) *The Times* 6.12.91 (CA) where it was held the 19-year-old accused's IQ of 74, his mental age of nine and his susceptibility ought to have been taken into consideration, supported by appropriate medical evidence (see also 12.2.1 *post*). A further example is provided by *R* v. *Delaney* (1988) 88 Cr App R 338 (CA), a case in which the 17-year-old accused's IQ of 80 and his emotional personality meant he might have confessed to get the interview over with as quickly as possible. These mental characteristics, together with the fact the interviewing officers had played down the gravity of the offence (an indecent assault on a young girl) and had failed to record what precisely was said to him, meant his confession should have been excluded.

In *R* v. *Walker* [1998] Crim LR 211 expert psychiatric evidence suggested that the accused suffered from a personality disorder which might have led her to elaborate inaccurately on events without understanding the implications of what she was saying, particularly as she was a user of crack cocaine. The Court of Appeal held that any mental or personality abnormalities may be of relevance and this included the accused's personality disorder. As such, it should have been taken into consideration by the trial judge when deciding the question of admissibility under s. 76(2)(*b*), and her conviction was therefore quashed (see also *R* v. *Ward* [1993] 1 WLR 619 (CA)). The Court of Appeal did not feel the need to consider fresh evidence suggesting that she had been under the influence of drugs at the time of the interview, although in principle it is difficult to see why the effect of drugs should not also be regarded as a relevant circumstance. Some authority for this proposition can be found in *R* v. *Sat-Bhambra* (1988) 88 Cr App R 55 (CA) where the trial judge excluded a confession made while the accused was under the influence of Valium (although as this drug had been prescribed by the police doctor it could have been considered a 'thing done') and was possibly also under the influence of the medication he had taken for his diabetes. Moreover, in *R* v. *Barry* (1991) 95 Cr App R 384 (CA) it was accepted that the accused's 'urgent desire for bail' (so that he would not lose custody of his young son) could amount to a circumstance. There would seem to be no reason why a craving for heroin should not also be taken into consideration.

A thing said or done will justify exclusion under s. 76(2)(*b*) only if the prosecution are unable to prove that it did not cause the accused's confession to be made. In other words, a confession will be admissible if was not caused by the thing said or done. Thus, in *R* v. *Tyrer* (1989) 90 Cr App R 446 (CA) although the police had done something by bringing in a blanket and a mattress, implying that the accused would have to stay in the cells overnight away from her children and kittens, the judge decided as a question of fact that it was not that conduct which had caused her to confess. Rather, she had confessed because the interviewing officer had exposed her story as nonsense. In *R* v. *Weeks* [1995] Crim LR 52 (CA) the accused made a confession following a police officer's comments suggesting that if a confession was not forthcoming he would remain in custody. Although there was a 'clear risk' that the comments might have caused the accused to admit more than his true involvement, the accused's astute personality, experience of being interviewed by the police and denial of other allegations meant that causation could be disproved.

An omission to do something the police are under a duty to do, for example non-compliance with provisions of the PACE Codes of Practice, may amount to a thing said or done for the purposes of s. 76(2)(*b*) (*R* v. *Doolan* [1988] Crim LR 747 (CA)). A breach of Code C may therefore lead to the exclusion of a confession under s. 76(2) (or s. 78(1)) but, again, there must be causation. In *R* v. *Alladice* (1988) 87 Cr App R 380 (CA) the accused confessed to his part in a robbery after the police had refused him access to a solicitor (in breach of Code C and s. 58 of PACE). This breach, though a thing done, had not caused the accused to confess. The accused had understood the caution, had admitted that he was well able to cope with interviews and had been aware of his rights, including his (then) right to remain silent.

In some circumstances even a technical breach of Code C may lead to the exclusion of a confession under s. 76(2)(*b*) if it has given rise to potential unreliability. In *DPP* v. *Blake* [1989] 1 WLR 432 the accused, a 16-year-old juvenile who refused to have anything to do with her parents, was interviewed with her father present as the 'appropriate adult' required under (what is now) C-11.15. The police had tried to obtain a social worker but no-one was willing to attend if a parent was available. The police therefore had no choice but to go ahead with the father, even though the absence of any empathy between him and his daughter meant he could not adequately perform the advisory function required of an appropriate adult (see C-11.17). The magistrates excluded her confession under s. 76(2)(*b*), a decision upheld by the Divisional Court on the ground that the accused had not benefited from the presence of an appropriate adult. Breaches of Code C were also relevant in *R* v. *Chung* (1990) 92 Cr App R 314 (CA) where the accused's oral admission at his flat regarding stolen motor insurance notes was held to be inadmissible under s. 76(2)(*b*). He had been refused legal advice in breach of s. 58 of PACE and there had been a number of breaches of Code C: no contemporaneous record had been kept of the alleged conversation, the eventual note of the conversation had not been shown to the accused and his solicitor had not been informed of the conversation. This does not mean that any breach of Code C will justify exclusion under s. 76(2)(*b*), however, as the Divisional Court made clear in *DPP* v. *Blake* [1989] 1 WLR 432. The question is always whether the breach renders the confession potentially unreliable.

Finally, it has been held that advice properly given to the accused by his solicitor will not normally provide a basis for excluding a subsequent confession under s. 76(2)(*b*), but the position might be different if the accused was particularly vulnerable (*R* v. *Wahab* [2003] 1 Cr App R 232 (CA)).

7.1.3.3 Section 78(1) of PACE: *Unfairness*
Section 78(1) provides the trial judge (or magistrates) with a discretion to exclude evidence on which the prosecution propose to rely if, having regard to all the circumstances, including the circumstances in which the evidence was obtained, its admission would have 'such an adverse effect on the fairness of the proceedings' that it ought not to be admitted. In *R* v. *Mason* [1988] 1 WLR 139 (CA) it was held that s. 78(1) could also be applied to exclude confessions. A confession *prima facie* admissible under s. 76(1) of PACE may therefore be excluded by the judge under s. 78(1)

where, for example, there has been a significant breach of PACE and/or its Codes of Practice prior to or during the interrogation, so long as that breach is such that the proceedings would be rendered sufficiently unfair if the confession were admitted.

Section 78(1) is a statutory *discretion*, and ultimately every case will turn on its own facts, but it seems that there is a presumption in favour of excluding confessions where the police have been guilty of deliberate misconduct. In *R* v. *Alladice* (1988) 87 Cr App R 380 (CA), a case concerning a breach of s. 58 of PACE, the Court of Appeal said (at p. 386):

'If the police have acted in bad faith, the court will have little difficulty in ruling any confession inadmissible under section 78, if not under s. 76. If the police, albeit in good faith, have nevertheless fallen foul of section 58, it is still necessary for the court to decide whether to admit the evidence would adversely affect the fairness of the proceedings, and would do so to such an extent that the confession ought to be excluded.'

Section 58(1) provides that a suspect who is under arrest and being questioned in custody is entitled to consult a solicitor in private, save that access may be delayed for up to 36 hours in certain circumstances (see s. 58(5)–(11)). A breach of s. 58 of PACE (and/or Code C-6 and Annex B) may result in a confession being excluded under ss. 76(2)(*b*) or 78(1), albeit for different reasons. Section 58 does not apply to persons detained under the Terrorism Act 2000 (see s. 58(12) of PACE and Schedule 8 to the 2000 Act, allowing a delay of up to 48 hours).

The suspect's right to legal advice is 'one of the most important and fundamental rights of a citizen' (*R* v. *Samuel* [1988] 2 WLR 920 (CA) at p. 934) – *a fortiori* if the suspect is mentally ill (*R* v. *Aspinall* [1999] 2 Cr App R 115 (CA) at p. 122) – and the European Court of Human Rights has accepted that this right is implicit in Article 6(3)(c) of the European Convention, exemplifying the fact that pre-trial irregularities may have a bearing on whether there has been a breach of Article 6(1) (*Murray* v. *United Kingdom* (1996) 22 EHRR 29 at pp. 64–7, *Magee* v. *United Kingdom* (2000) 31 EHRR 822 at pp. 831–5, *Averill* v. *United Kingdom* (2000) 31 EHRR 839 at pp. 855–7). As with the subsidiary rights expressly set out in Article 6, however, this implicit pre-trial right to legal advice is not absolute. In *Magee* v. *United Kingdom* (2000) 31 EHRR 822 the European Court of Human Rights said (at p. 834) that although Article 6 normally requires that the accused be allowed to benefit from the assistance of a lawyer at the initial stages of police interrogation: 'this right ... may be subject to restrictions for good cause', the question in each case being 'whether the restriction, in the light of the entirety of the proceedings, has deprived the accused of a fair hearing'. In that case, the accused was arrested early in the morning of 16 December 1988 in connection with an attempted terrorist offence and interrogated for extended periods by alternating pairs of detectives until the end of the following day. While in detention he was held incommunicado in austere conditions and prevented from contacting a solicitor and, on 17 December, he finally made oral admissions during his sixth interview (09:30 to 13:00) and signed a lengthy statement explaining his involvement later that afternoon (14:00 to 16:20), which statement subsequently formed the basis of the prosecution case against him. It was only after that statement had been signed that he was allowed to consult with his solicitor. The Strasbourg Court concluded that the austerity of the conditions of his detention and his exclusion from outside contact were intended by the police to be psychologically coercive and conducive to breaking down any resolve he may have manifested at the beginning of his detention to remain silent. The Court held that, in the light of those circumstances, the accused should have been given access to a solicitor at the initial stages of the interrogation 'as a counterweight to the intimidating atmosphere specifically devised to sap his will and make him confide in his interrogators'. Even though the accused had not been ill-treated during his detention, the offence was one of alleged terrorism and the confession had been given voluntarily it was held that there had been a violation of Article 6(1) in conjunction with Article 6(3)(c). According to the Court (at p. 835), 'to deny access to a lawyer for such a long period and in a situation where the rights of the defence were irretrievably prejudiced is – whatever the justification for such denial – incompatible with the rights of the accused under Article 6'.

The accused's conviction may be quashed, therefore, if there has been a breach of s. 58 and the sole ground of appeal is that the trial judge refused to exclude his confession under s. 78(1). In *R* v. *Walsh* (1989) 91 Cr App R 161 (CA) Saville J said (at p. 163):

'The main object of section 58 of the Act and indeed of the Codes of Practice is to achieve fairness ... To our minds it follows that if there are significant and substantial breaches of section 58 or the provisions of the Code, then prima facie at least the standards of fairness set by Parliament have not been met. So far as a defendant is concerned, it seems to us also to follow that to admit evidence against him which has been obtained in circumstances where these standards have not been met, cannot but have an adverse effect on the fairness of the proceedings. This does not mean, of course, that in every case of a significant or substantial breach of section 58 or the Code of Practice the evidence concerned will automatically be excluded. Section 78 does not so provide. The task of the court is not merely to consider whether there would be an adverse effect on the fairness of the proceedings, but such an adverse effect that justice requires the evidence to be excluded ... However, although bad faith may make substantial or significant that which might not otherwise be so, the contrary does not follow. Breaches which are in themselves significant and substantial are not rendered otherwise by the good faith of the officers concerned.'

It should always be remembered, however, that s. 78(1) gives the judge a discretion and any appeal on the ground of its misapplication is unlikely to be successful unless it can be shown that he acted perversely in the sense of being '*Wednesbury* unreasonable' (*R* v. *O'Leary* (1988) 87 Cr App R 387 (CA)). In other words, the appeal will fail unless it can be shown that the judge failed to take into consideration relevant matters (such as breaches of the Codes of Practice) or took into consideration irrelevant matters or his decision was one which no reasonable judge could have reached. In *R* v. *Jelen* (1989) 90 Cr App R 456 (CA) Auld J said (at pp. 464–5):

> '[T]he decision of a judge whether or not to exclude evidence under section 78 of the 1984 Act is made as a result of the exercise by him of a discretion based upon the particular circumstances of the case and upon his assessment of the adverse effect, if any, it would have on the fairness of the proceedings. The circumstances of each case are almost always different, and judges may well take different views in the proper exercise of their discretion even where the circumstances are similar. This is not an apt field for hard case law and well-founded distinctions between cases.'

The question of causation is as relevant to the determination of fairness under s. 78(1) as it is to the question of admissibility under s. 76(2). If it can be shown that the breach of s. 58 or any other provision in PACE or the Codes of Practice would have made no difference to how the accused conducted himself then, in the absence of bad faith on the part of the police, an application to exclude a confession under s. 78(1) is unlikely to succeed. In *R* v. *Dunford* (1990) 91 Cr App R 150 (CA) the police had refused the accused access to his solicitor in breach of s. 58, but his experience of having been arrested and detained (as exemplified by his previous convictions) and his awareness of his rights entitled the judge to conclude that a solicitor's advice would probably have caused him to behave no differently. There had been no bad faith and his admissions during the interview had been properly relied on at his trial. Similarly, in *R* v. *Oliphant* [1992] Crim LR 40 (CA) it was held that the accused had confessed because that was what he had wanted to do. The breach of s. 58 and Code C had made no difference as the accused had been aware of his rights. Conversely, it has been said that where the accused *was* given the opportunity to consult with his solicitor, but the solicitor acted wholly improperly by, for example, persuading the accused to confess in order that he, the solicitor, could obtain a bribe from a police officer or some advantage for another client, s. 78(1) 'would provide an ample basis for exclusion, notwithstanding that the reliability of the confession was not in doubt' (*R* v. *Wahab* [2003] 1 Cr App R 232 (CA) at p. 242).

The dictum of Saville J in *R* v. *Walsh* (1989) 91 Cr App R 161 (CA) (above) sets out another principle which may determine how s. 78(1) is applied. If the breach of PACE or the Codes is of a technical or *de minimis* nature not involving any bad faith on the part of the police (that is, a breach which is not 'significant and substantial') there will be insufficient unfairness to justify the exclusion of the accused's confession (see also *R* v. *Keenan* [1989] 3 WLR 1193 (CA) at p. 1206).

One particular breach of Code C which *is* likely to be considered significant and substantial is a failure to caution the accused before questioning him about the alleged offence, as required by C-10.1 (*R* v. *Pall*

[1992] Crim LR 126 (CA)). The caution is given to ensure that the suspect is aware of his privilege against self-incrimination. Code C-10.1 provides that if there are grounds to suspect a person has committed an offence he must be cautioned (in accordance with C-10.5) before any questions are put to him regarding his involvement or suspected involvement in that offence. The provision goes on to state that a caution need not be given if the questions are put to a person for 'other necessary purposes' such as to establish his identity or his ownership of any vehicle. The test set out in C-10.1 is an objective one: the caution need be given only where there are 'grounds to suspect', first, that an offence has been committed and, second, that the person being questioned committed that offence. If the officer is merely acting on a subjective hunch there is no need to give the caution prior to questioning (*R* v. *Shah* [1994] Crim LR 125 (CA)). In other words, 'grounds to suspect' means 'reasonable grounds for suspicion' (*R* v. *James* [1996] Crim LR 650 (CA)). It is to be noted that, in determining whether a police officer had reasonable grounds for suspicion, the judge is entitled to consider evidence which is protected from disclosure by public interest immunity (*R* v. *Smith* [2001] 1 WLR 1031 (CA)). Furthermore, the suspect should be told the true nature of the investigation being conducted, in line with the purport of C-10.1 and Article 5(2) of the European Convention on Human Rights, so that he can give proper weight to that factor when deciding whether to seek legal advice and/or respond to the questions put to him. In *R* v. *Kirk* [2000] 1 WLR 567 the police questioned the accused about the theft of a bag, which had been snatched from an elderly lady in the street, without telling him that the lady had fallen over and subsequently died. The accused admitted that he had snatched a bag in the vicinity without knowing the true gravity of the situation, and his confession was adduced by the prosecution at his trial for robbery and manslaughter. The Court of Appeal quashed his convictions on the ground that in normal circumstances s. 78(1) should be applied to exclude a confession which has been given by the accused in ignorance of the offence being investigated and which might not have been given if he had been aware of the true nature of the investigation. Code C-11.1A now provides that the interviewee must be informed of the 'nature of the offence, or further offence'.

A clear example of the application of s. 78(1) where there has been a failure to caution is *R* v. *Hunt* [1992] Crim LR 582. A police officer saw the accused putting a flick-knife into his pocket and he was searched. Without cautioning him the officer asked him what the knife was for, to which the accused responded that it was his and he would carry it if he wanted. The Court of Appeal quashed his conviction for possessing an offensive weapon on the ground, *inter alia*, that the conversation ought to have been excluded under s. 78(1) (see also *Batley* v. *DPP* (1998) *The Times* 5.3.98 (DC)). In *R* v. *Okafor* (1993) 99 Cr App R 97 (CA) uniformed customs officers at Gatwick Airport found that a bag of stewed snails in the accused's luggage contained packages of cocaine, but without giving the caution they asked him questions about the snails and he admitted that he had bought them and that they were his. It was held that his admission of ownership ought to have been excluded. The extent to which customs officers can question a suspect about his luggage before cautioning him arose again in *R* v. *Nelson* [1998] 2 Cr App R 399. Two sisters, N and R, entered the UK from Jamaica with cocaine secreted in their luggage. By the time N was questioned the customs officer had already developed a suspicion that she was carrying drugs because he had seen that the metal stiffeners on her suitcase were thicker than usual, and this was a known method by which to smuggle drugs. He should not therefore have asked her questions about her luggage until he had cautioned her, even though he had not at that stage conducted a field test for drugs. (The Court of Appeal conceded that a simple question tying her to the suitcase such as 'This is your suitcase is it?' would not need to have been preceded by a caution.) As a caution should have been given before N was questioned the whole of her interview ought to have been excluded under s. 78(1). By contrast, the objective ground for suspecting R's involvement, the new riveting and thick stiffeners on her suitcase, was noticed by the officer only *after* R had been questioned. There had therefore been no breach of C-10.1 in her case and her interview had been properly admitted. More prosaically, in *McNamara* v. *Television Licensing Region* [2002] EWHC 2798 Admin (QBD) it was held that, because an offence under s. 1(1) of the Wireless Telegraphy Act 1949 is committed only if a television is *used* without a licence, an enquiry officer may ask a householder whether he has a television set and whether he has a licence without first cautioning him. The questions are asked to establish 'primary facts' rather than self-incriminating answers.

A breach of C-10.1 will not lead to the exclusion of a confession, however, unless its admission would have a sufficiently adverse effect on the fairness of the proceedings. In *R* v. *Hoyte* [1994] Crim LR 215 (CA), for example, although a caution should have been given to the accused following an overheard conversation between him and his co-accused which suggested their involvement in a conspiracy, the judge's decision to allow his subsequent confession to be admitted was upheld on appeal. The police had acted in good faith and there had been no unfairness to the accused. Similarly, in *R* v. *Doyle* [2002] EWCA Crim 1176, a case of alleged benefit fraud where D had telephoned the local authority's investigator with a view to exculpating himself following a request to make contact, but had not been cautioned at the outset of the call, it was held that even if a caution had been required the judge had been entitled to admit the record of D's incriminating comments. D (a senior police officer) had been aware of his right not to incriminate himself; he had known to whom he was talking and the reason for his having been contacted; he had not been placed under any pressure to make the telephone call or incriminate himself; and the investigator had not acted in bad faith.

Formal interviews in police stations relating to indictable offences are now contemporaneously recorded on audio tape, in accordance with Code E, but there is still the risk of 'verballing' in other contexts. Many of the provisions in Code C-11 were introduced to minimise the risk of confessions being fabricated or inaccurately recorded in such circumstances and have therefore come to be known as the 'verballing provisions'. They have three purposes: first, to eliminate the possibility of fabricated confessions; second, to ensure that what the accused said was accurately recorded; and third, to ensure that the accused will not be able to make a false allegation of police impropriety (see *R* v. *Ward* (1993) 98 Cr App R 337 (CA) at pp. 340–1 and *R* v. *Canale* (1989) 91 Cr App R 1 (CA) at p. 5). Briefly, an accurate record must be made at the same time as the interview or as soon afterwards as is practicable (C-11.7 to 11.9); this record must be shown to the suspect for him to indicate whether or not he agrees with it (C-11.11) and to his solicitor or appropriate adult if any such person is present (C-11.12); and a record should be made of the suspect's comments outside the context of the interview, which should also be shown to him for his approval (C-11.13). Code C-11.1A defines an interview as 'the questioning of a person regarding [his] involvement or suspected involvement in a criminal offence or offences', and it is now clear that even a single question may amount to an interview for this purpose. In *R* v. *Miller* [1998] Crim LR 209 the accused was arrested and cautioned, and upon arrival at the police station was seen to drop a package on to the floor. The officer who saw this said that she had asked him whether the package contained ecstasy tablets and he had replied in the affirmative. The Court of Appeal held that this exchange amounted to an interview.

Although bad faith on the part of the police may lead to the exclusion of a confession, surreptitious methods of criminal investigation will not fall foul of s. 78(1) so long as the undercover tactics were legitimate and not employed simply to avoid the application of PACE and the Codes of Practice. In 1990 the police established a mock jewellery shop ('Stardust Jewellers') for three months in north London for the purpose of apprehending criminals wishing to dispose of stolen goods. Video cameras and audio equipment were installed to record those who entered and what they said, and the shop was staffed by undercover officers purporting to be dishonest jewellers. The officers entered into friendly banter with their customers, and in order to maintain their cover asked the sort of questions shady jewellers would be expected to ask, such as questions about the parts of London where it would be unwise to try to resell the goods. Everything was contemporaneously recorded by the equipment concealed for that purpose. The operation resulted in many persons being charged, including two men who eventually pleaded guilty to handling following a failed application to have the evidence of their conversations excluded. Nevertheless they appealed on the ground that as they had been tricked into incriminating themselves in informal interviews, and the police officers had not cautioned them beforehand in accordance with C-10.1, the evidence ought to have been excluded under s. 78(1) or at common law (*R* v. *Christou* [1992] 3 WLR 228). The Court of Appeal dismissed their appeals holding, first, that they had voluntarily applied themselves to the trick and had done nothing which they would not have done anyway; and, second, Code C did not apply to undercover operations of this kind where the police officer and suspect were on 'equal terms'. The Code was intended to protect suspects who were vulnerable to abuse or pressure from police officers perceived to be in a position of authority. The situation in Stardust Jewellers was quite different as the police officers had not been overtly acting as such. Moreover, the undercover officers had not been asking questions 'about' the offence (C-10.1) but had merely asked the sort of questions to be expected of a shady jeweller in order to maintain their cover. However, the Court of Appeal did add the important caveat that it would be wrong for police officers to adopt covert techniques for the purpose of circumventing the Code.

The absence of independent evidence (such as a tape recording) supporting the undercover officer's version of events will militate against the admission of any incriminating remarks made by a suspect. The absence of such evidence certainly influenced the Court of Appeal in *R* v. *Bryce* (1992) 95 Cr App R 320. In that case, the accused was alleged to have made incriminating comments while negotiating the sale of a stolen car. The officer had called the accused on his mobile phone and asked him 'how warm' the car was, to which the accused had replied that it was a 'couple of days old'. The two men met the next afternoon and the officer expressly asked, 'How long has it been nicked?' to which the accused replied, 'Two to three days.' The accused was convicted of handling stolen goods and appealed on the ground that those conversations ought to have been excluded under s. 78(1). Although it was accepted that Code C did not apply to undercover officers acting on equal terms with a suspect, the Court of Appeal held that the incriminating remarks should have been excluded for two reasons. First, the questions asked by the officer had gone directly to the issue of *mens rea* – they had not been oblique in nature or necessary for the officer's cover. Second, the accused had denied giving the answers he was alleged to have made and yet there was no contemporaneous record to support the officer's version of what had happened. The risk of concoction could not therefore be eliminated.

In *R* v. *Kosten* [1993] Crim LR 687 there was a ruse which provided the accused (K) with an opportunity to incriminate himself but he was not compelled to do so, as in *R* v. *Christou* [1992] 3 WLR 228 (CA). Customs officers had tricked K into thinking he was dealing with the car salvage operator who had taken control of his courier's car and drugs, and during telephone conversations with an officer he disclosed incriminating information which was tantamount to a confession and subsequently admitted at his trial. The Court of Appeal held that the evidence had been properly admitted. K had initiated contact with his courier's relatives to find out where the car was being kept, he had freely volunteered the incriminating information to the undercover officer, he and the customs officer had been speaking on equal terms and their telephone conversations had been contemporaneously recorded on audio tape (see also *R* v. *Lin* [1995] Crim LR 817 (CA) and *R* v. *Edwards* [1997] Crim LR 348 (CA)).

A surreptitious recording of an undercover operation will reduce the scope for a successful submission that admissions obtained as a result ought to be excluded under s. 78(1); and if the presence of a police officer might cause the suspect to incriminate himself, as in *R* v. *Bryce* (1992) 95 Cr App R 320 (CA), it would seem to make sense, at least from the point of view of law enforcement, to remove that human factor from the equation and rely entirely on a hidden microphone. In *R* v. *Ali* (1991) *The Times* 19.2.91 (CA) a recording of inculpatory comments made by the accused in conversation with his family the day after he had been charged with murder, while they were together in a bugged interview room, was held to be admissible as a matter of law and the judge had been entitled not to exclude it under s. 78(1). In *R* v. *Bailey* (1993) 97 Cr App R 365 the police bugged a cell and induced the two co-accused to share it, having pretended that this was contrary to the wishes of the investigating officers to allay their suspicions. Duly duped, and despite a warning from a solicitor, the two co-accused made a number of damaging admissions to each other which were recorded and subsequently adduced at their trial by the prosecution. The Court of Appeal held that the judge had properly exercised his discretion not to exclude the evidence as it had been lawfully obtained notwithstanding the measure of trickery employed (see also *R* v. *Parker* [1995] Crim LR 233 (CA)).

In *R* v. *Roberts* [1997] 1 Cr App R 217, 'C', a suspect who had agreed with the police to stay in the accused's bugged cell to elicit admissions from him, caused the accused to make admissions which were recorded. The Court of Appeal held that it was not the function of Code C to protect one suspect in relation to questioning by another suspect, and though there had been breaches of Code C in respect of what had passed between the police officers and 'C' those breaches had been 'insignificant' as they had not caused the accused's admissions. The Court added that the trial judge was given a 'wide margin of discretion' under s. 78(1) which would be disturbed on appeal only if it could be shown that he had erred in principle or was plainly wrong. It seems that it was 'C' who initiated his agreement with the police, but if the police had approached him the result would probably have been no different. Such a chain of events occurred in *R* v. *Jelen* (1989) 90 Cr App R 456 (CA) where the trial judge allowed a recorded conversation to be admitted notwithstanding the fact that the police had asked another suspect, 'D', to record the accused's comments with the aid of a concealed tape recorder (though it should be noted that the accused was not under arrest at the time). The ruling was upheld on appeal as the judge had been entitled to conclude that the tactics used had not had such an adverse effect on the fairness of the proceedings to warrant the exclusion of the evidence.

The foregoing cases were decided prior to the quasi-incorporation into English law of the European Convention on Human Rights, Article 8(1) of which provides that everyone has the right to respect for his private life (subject to permissible interference 'in accordance with the law' by virtue of Article 8(2)). Nevertheless it is clear that a breach of Article 8 does *not* compel the judge to apply s. 78(1) in the accused's favour. The test for the application of s. 78(1) remains the same, and if the breach has not resulted in the requisite degree of unfairness to justify exclusion the confession will be admitted.

In *R* v. *Khan* [1996] 3 WLR 162 police officers placed a listening device on the outside wall of a suspect's flat, trespassing on and damaging his property in the process. A recording of the inculpatory comments made by the accused, a visitor at the flat who was suspected of being involved in an importation of heroin a few months earlier, was ruled admissible and not excluded under s. 78(1). The House of Lords upheld this ruling on the ground that the gravity of the offence (the large-scale importation of heroin) outweighed the invasion of privacy, the civil trespass and the possible breach of Article 8 of the European Convention. The case was considered by the European Court of Human Rights in *Khan* v. *United Kingdom* (2000) 31 EHRR 1016, the conclusion being that while there had been a violation of Article 8 there had been no violation of Article 6(1). It was conceded by the Crown that there had been a breach of Article 8(1) but it was argued that Article 8 as a whole had not been infringed because the conduct of the police had been justified by virtue of Article 8(2). This submission was rejected because at the time of the operation there was no statutory system in place to regulate the use of covert listening devices (see also *PG* v. *United Kingdom* (2001) Application No. 44787/98 (ECtHR)). According to the European Court of Human Rights in *Khan* v. *United Kingdom* (at pp. 1026–7):

> '[T]he admissions made by the applicant ... were made voluntarily ... the applicant being under no inducement to make such admissions. The unlawfulness of which complaint is made ... relates exclusively to the fact that there was no statutory authority for the interference with the applicant's right to respect for private life ... [T]he applicant had ample opportunity to challenge both the authenticity and the use of the recording ... The Court would add that it is clear that, had the domestic courts been of the view that the admission of the evidence would have given rise to substantive unfairness, they would have had a discretion to exclude it under section 78 of PACE.'

Police surveillance operations which do not involve covert entry upon or interference with property (or interference with wireless telegraphy), such as surveillance operations in police cells or the recording of a telephone conversation by one of the parties to the call, are now governed by Part II of the Regulation of Investigatory Powers Act 2000 and the Codes of Practice issued under s. 71: the *Covert Surveillance Code of Practice* and the *Covert Human Intelligence Sources Code of Practice*. Surveillance operations involving interference with property (or wireless telegraphy), such as the operation undertaken in *R* v. *Khan* [1996] 3 WLR 162 (HL), are now governed by Part III of the Police Act 1997 and the *Covert Surveillance Code of Practice*.

Thus, if for some reason the accused's confession was obtained by the police in breach of Article 8 of the European Convention, or indeed some other rule of law, he is not (as a general rule) entitled to have that evidence excluded. What he *is* entitled to is an opportunity to challenge its use and admission in evidence and a judicial assessment of the effect of its admission upon the fairness of the trial as provided for by s. 78(1) (*R* v. *P* [2001] 2 WLR 463 (HL) at p. 474, *R* v. *Bailey* [2001] EWCA Crim 733, *R* v. *Wright* [2001] EWCA Crim 1394). In *R* v. *Mason* [2002] 2 Cr App R 628 three suspected robbers and gang members were placed in a bugged cell resulting in a number of conversations and admissions being covertly recorded, but the decision to undertake this surveillance operation was not in strict accordance with the (then) non-statutory guidelines. Having assumed for the sake of argument that the Human Rights Act 1998 applied (even though the trials took place before the Act came into force) the Court of Appeal held that the confessions had been properly admitted. There had been proper grounds for the arrests, the police had acted in good faith, and if there had been a breach of the guidelines it was of no significance. It was accepted that there had been a violation of Article 8 of the European Convention, and that this was a matter which the trial judge was required to take into consideration when exercising his discretion under s. 78(1), but it was nonetheless recognised that such a breach should not mean that evidence must automatically be excluded. There were other remedies available to the accused, including a finding that there had been a breach or an award of compensation. To insist on the exclusion of evidence could lead to greater injustice to the public than the infringement of Article 8 had created for the accused. Nor, it was felt, had the accused's right to remain silent or privilege against self-incrimination been breached, for the police had done no more than arrange a situation which was likely to result in a confession being *volunteered*. (The Court of Appeal did recognise, however, that a covert surveillance operation undertaken in bad faith might lead to a different result.) The same approach was adopted in *R* v. *McLeod* [2002] EWCA Crim 989, where it was held that the trial judge had been entitled to admit a covertly recorded confession made by the accused to one of his associates in the back of a police van, notwithstanding the 'probable breach of Article 8'. Authority for the surveillance had been granted in accordance with the non-statutory guidelines then in force, in respect of an alleged murder; there had been no illegality in the gathering of the evidence; the accused had not been tricked or pressurised into making his comments; there was an accurate record of what he had said; and the offences he had been charged with were very serious.

Each case will turn on its own facts, so where the police or their civilian stooges exceed what the trial judge considers to be acceptable practice there will always be a real risk that any confession obtained in consequence will be excluded (or that the proceedings will be stayed as an abuse of process) even if a contemporaneous recording of the confession was made and the charge is serious. An important consideration is whether the conduct of the police violated the accused's right not to incriminate himself by *inducing* him to say something he would not otherwise have said. In the context of s. 78(1), if the police play a trick which affects the mind of the suspect and so causes him to incriminate himself his inculpatory remarks are likely to be excluded, as in *R* v. *Bryce* (1992) 95 Cr App R 320 (CA)). In *R* v. *Hall* (1994) *The Times* 11.3.94 (news report) (CC) an undercover female police officer seduced the accused in a car and managed to elicit a statement from him that he had strangled his wife and incinerated her body. Waterhouse J excluded the confession under s. 78(1) (as well as s. 76(2)(*b*)) even though it had been contemporaneously recorded and the charge was murder, because the seduction had in effect amounted to an interview and the accused had neither been cautioned nor given the opportunity to have a solicitor present (see also Sharpe, 'Covert Police Operations and the Discretionary Exclusion of Evidence' [1994] Crim LR 793 at p. 801).

If the police employ a civilian *agent* instead, the risk of exclusion will be just as real. In *R* v. *H* [1987] Crim LR 47 (CC) the complainant in a rape case had been asked to telephone her alleged rapist (her erstwhile boyfriend) and record their conversation in order to elicit a confession from him. The accused made inculpatory comments having been told by the complainant that the call was not being recorded. That evidence was excluded. In *R* v. *Allan* (1999) unreported (98/1754/Y2) the Court of Appeal refused D's application to appeal against his conviction, where he had made admissions during his incarceration to an informant (H) being handled by the police with a view to eliciting such admissions, and the prosecution had been permitted to rely on those admissions at D's trial for murder. D had refused to co-operate with the police, availing himself of his pre-trial right of silence, so H had been coached by the police 'to push him for what you can get' following lengthy police interrogations which, it seems, were designed to unsettle D into being more talkative and vulnerable to H's questioning when they were alone together in their cell. However, the European Court of Human Rights in *Allan* v. *United Kingdom* (2002) Application No. 48539/99 held that there had been a breach of Article 6 of the European Convention because the essence of D's privilege against self-incrimination had been extinguished. The persistent questioning of D by H pursuant to the police's instructions, channelling their conversations into discussions of the murder, could be regarded 'as the functional equivalent of interrogation, without any of the safeguards which would attach to a formal police interview, including the attendance of a solicitor and the issuing of the usual caution'; and D 'would have been subject to psychological pressures which impugned on the voluntariness of the disclosures'. The Strasbourg Court therefore held that the evidence had been 'obtained in defiance of the will of the applicant' and its use by the prosecution had 'impinged on the applicant's right to silence and privilege against self-incrimination'.

The above cases should be contrasted with *R* v. *Cadette* [1995] Crim LR 229 (CA). A drugs courier intercepted at Heathrow Airport was asked to telephone C, who was expecting a call in relation to those drugs, and to pretend that she had not been arrested. The call was made and their conversation was recorded and admitted at C's trial. Although the courier had in effect been an agent of Customs at the time the call was made it was held that their subterfuge did not mean that the evidence obtained as a result had to be excluded. This is not surprising. C had been expecting the telephone call and the only difference between what had been expected and what had happened was that her conversation with the courier was being recorded.

Undercover operations must be distinguished from deliberate malpractice during the formal interview which could result in any confession made in consequence being excluded under ss. 76(2) and/or 78(1) of PACE. A good example is provided by *R* v. *Mason* [1988] 1 WLR 139. Someone had set fire to the car, and M fell under suspicion because of the hostility between him and the owner and his obvious motive. M was questioned but denied any involvement and, as there was no other evidence against him, the police decided to pretend that his fingerprints had been found on fragments of glass recovered from the petrol bomb, hoping that this would elicit a confession. The same lie was told to M's solicitor and consequently he advised M to admit his involvement. The Court of Appeal had no hesitation in quashing M's conviction on the ground that the judge should have excluded the evidence under s. 78(1). Watkins LJ said (at p.144):

> '[The judge] omitted a vital factor from his consideration, namely, the deceit practised upon the appellant's solicitor … [W]e hope never again to hear of deceit such as this being practised upon an accused person, and more particularly possibly on a solicitor whose duty it is to advise him unfettered by false information from the police.'

That said, the police may use inadmissible evidence during the interrogation process as a means by which to encourage the suspect to confess. If, for example, D1 and D2 are both questioned about a crime, D2's statement blaming D1 may be read to D1 during his interview in the hope that D1 will confess, even though that statement would be inadmissible against D1 at his subsequent trial. In *R* v. *Sargent* [2001] 3 WLR 992 (HL) the accused was charged with conspiracy to commit arson on the basis of a confession he had given to the police. The confession had been elicited by the revelation that an inculpatory conversation between the accused and his lover had been surreptitiously recorded by the victim, a telephone engineer, who had unlawfully tapped the lover's telephone line. Although the fact of the interception, and the recording and transcript of what was said during the telephone conversation, should not have been admitted, by virtue of a prohibition in the (then) Interception of Communications Act 1985, the confession to the police was *prima facie* admissible, so long as any references to the inadmissible evidence were removed.

Finally, it should be noted that where the police impropriety in obtaining the accused's confession is so grave that it would be inappropriate even to allow the trial to continue the judge may stay the proceedings as an abuse of process rather than exclude the confession under s. 78(1). This was the approach adopted in the Crown Court by Newman J in *R* v. *Sutherland* (2002) *The Times* (news report) 30.1.02 (T/2002/7203) when it was discovered that the police had surreptitiously recorded the privileged conversations between the five co-accused and their solicitors and thereby obtained confidential information (albeit not necessarily admissions). Given the importance attached by the law to the privilege between lawyers and their clients and the statutory right to consult a solicitor privately this is not a surprising decision. Indeed the European Court of Human Rights has acknowledged that, in the absence of a compelling countervailing consideration, the accused's implicit Article 6(3)(c) right to legal advice before his trial requires that there should be no surveillance (*Brennan* v. *United Kingdom* (2001) 34 EHRR 507, *Lanz* v. *Austria* (2002) Application No. 24430/94).

7.1.3.4 The Judge's Common-law Exclusionary Discretion
The judge may also exclude a confession tendered or already adduced by the prosecution at common law to ensure the accused receives a fair trial, or because the accused's privilege against self-incrimination has been violated. These two discretions were recognised by the House of Lords in *R* v. *Sang* [1979] 3 WLR 263 (10.1 *post*) and have been preserved by s. 82(3) of PACE. One can quite clearly see the application of the principles underlying the common-law discretions in the way the judiciary have applied s. 78(1), which has effectively supplanted the common law in this field. That said, the *Sang* discretions are of continuing importance as they may be applied to *withdraw* a confession which has been erroneously placed before the jury. Sections 76(2) and 78(1) of PACE may be utilised only to exclude confessions which have not yet been adduced. If the judge decides that a confession ought not to have been admitted he may withdraw the confession from the jury's consideration (with an appropriate direction) or, if that would not be an effective remedy, he may discharge the jury from reaching a verdict and order a re-trial (*R* v. *Sat-Bhambra* (1988) 88 Cr App R 55 (CA)).

7.1.3.5 The Role of the Judge and Jury
If the question of admissibility under s. 76(2) of PACE arises it will be decided by the judge following a hearing on the *voir dire* in the absence of the jury. (A similar procedure is adopted in magistrates' courts: *R* v. *Liverpool Juvenile Court ex parte R* [1987] 3 WLR 224 (DC).) The judge will also take advantage of this opportunity to consider the application of s. 78(1). Witnesses, including the accused, may be called to give evidence of the circumstances surrounding the confession to enable the judge to ascertain whether the prosecution have proved beyond reasonable doubt that the confession was not obtained in one of the ways set out in s. 76(2). The question of admissibility under s. 76(2) does not arise if the sole question is whether the accused actually made the confession, which is a question of fact for the jury (*Ajodha* v. *The State* [1981] 3 WLR 1 (PC)). If, however, the accused denies he made the confession *and* also alleges that he was ill-treated prior to or at the time the purported confession was made, the judge should still determine the question of admissibility under s. 76(2). If the confession is ruled admissible it will be adduced in evidence

for the jury to decide whether it was actually made by the accused and, if so, whether it is true (*Thongjai* v. *R* [1997] 3 WLR 667 (PC), *Timothy* v. *The State* [2000] 1 WLR 485 (PC)). If the sole ground for arguing that a confession should be excluded turns on the application of the judge's exclusionary discretion, a *voir dire* will need to be held if there is a disagreement as to what occurred (although in summary proceedings this will not always be necessary: *Halawa* v. *Federation Against Copyright Theft* [1995] 1 Cr App R 21 (DC)). In the absence of any such disagreement it will be sufficient for the judge to hear submissions on unfairness in the absence of the jury.

It is for the judge to decide the question of admissibility and, if the confession is admitted, for the jury to decide whether or not the confession is true. Thus, if the accused raises the question of unreliability under s. 76(2)(*b*) of PACE the judge is not to decide whether the confession is reliable in the sense of actually being true, for that would be to usurp the jury's role. The judge should therefore disregard any admission by the accused on the *voir dire* that the confession is true (*R* v. *Cox* [1991] Crim LR 276 (CA)). If the confession is admitted the judge will direct the jury on the factors which they ought to take into consideration when evaluating its reliability in the sense of being true. This division of functions has been held to comply with the requirements of Article 6 of the European Convention on Human Rights, as the accused is able to present his objections to the evidence being admitted without being inhibited by the presence of the jury, and the judge must give a reasoned judgment which may be scrutinised by the Court of Appeal (*R* v. *Mushtaq* [2002] EWCA Crim 1943). The judge's decision on the admissibility of a confession following a *voir dire* should not be revealed to the jury for they might be influenced by his findings of fact (*Mitchell* v. *R* [1998] 2 WLR 839 (PC)).

At common law it was held that whatever the accused said on the *voir dire* could not be raised by the prosecution during the trial, save that if the confession was ruled *admissible* the accused could be cross-examined during the trial on any inconsistent statement he had made on the *voir dire* (*Wong Kam-Ming* v. *R* [1979] 2 WLR 81 (PC)). There was also a dictum to the effect that a 'boast' by the accused on the *voir dire* that he had committed the alleged crime would be admissible in the trial as evidence of his guilt (*R* v. *Brophy* [1981] 3 WLR 103 (HL) at p. 107). An admission by the accused on the *voir dire* that the confession is true would now be *prima facie* admissible under s. 76(1) as it is unlikely s. 76(2) could be applied to exclude it, but the judge would be entitled to apply s. 78(1) or his common-law discretion to prevent its admission in an appropriate case. In *Wong Kam-Ming* v. *R* [1979] 2 WLR 81 it was also thought that the accused should not be asked on the *voir dire* whether his confession was true, concluding in the process that the decision of the Court of Criminal Appeal to the contrary in *R* v. *Hammond* (1941) 28 Cr App R 84 was wrong. Recent dicta suggest that the Privy Council's view will be followed should the question arise again (*R* v. *Liverpool Juvenile Court ex parte R* [1987] 3 WLR 224 (DC), *R* v. *Davis* [1990] Crim LR 860 (CA)).

7.1.3.6 The Tainting Principle

In *R* v. *McGovern* (1990) 92 Cr App R 228 the accused was aged 19, six months' pregnant, physically ill and of limited intelligence. In breach of s. 58 of PACE and Code C she was denied access to a solicitor during an emotional interview in which she confessed to being involved in the killing of another young woman. In further breach of Code C no contemporaneous record was made of the interview. The next day she was interviewed again, in the presence of her solicitor, and again she made admissions, although this time they were more coherent and there were no further breaches of the Code. The trial judge refused to exclude the confession evidence and she was convicted of manslaughter. The Court of Appeal quashed her conviction on the ground that the breach of s. 58 and the Code during the first interview meant that her first confession was likely to be unreliable, and therefore inadmissible under s. 76(2)(*b*); this in turn had 'tainted' her subsequent confession which was therefore also inadmissible under s. 76(2)(*b*). Importantly, the solicitor at the second interview had not been told the accused had confessed during her first interview. If the solicitor had been aware of the earlier breach there can be little doubt that she would have prevented the subsequent interview from taking place. The Court of Appeal emphasised that the very fact that the accused's first confession had been made was likely to have had an adverse effect upon her during the course of her second interview. In other words, once the accused had already confessed she would have felt there was little if anything to lose by repeating her admission. According to the Court (at p. 234):

'One cannot refrain from emphasising that when an accused person has made a series of admissions as to his or her complicity in a crime at a first interview, the very fact that those admissions have been made [is] likely to have an effect upon her during the course of the second interview.'

At common law a different approach was taken. A subsequent confession would be admissible so long as the threat or inducement which rendered the first confession involuntary (and therefore inadmissible) was no longer operating on the accused at the time of his subsequent confession. So in *R* v. *Smith* [1959] 2 WLR 623 (C-MAC) the mere fact the accused had had his earlier confession put to him at the start of his second interview did not prevent his subsequent confession from being voluntary; the inducement or threat which had elicited his first confession the day before had by then dissipated.

In *R* v. *Glaves* [1993] Crim LR 685 the 16-year-old accused's first confession, excluded at his trial under s. 76(2) of PACE on account of the manner of the interrogation (in the absence of an appropriate adult), was made over a week before his subsequent confession to different officers. The Court of Appeal held that the second confession should also have been excluded, but the reasoning is far from clear. The judgment itself suggests that the conduct which had caused the first confession to be inadmissible had still been operating on him at the time of his second interview, and in this sense the test is similar to that which was applied at common law. However, given the duration of the intervening period a more plausible explanation is that the accused felt he had nothing to lose by repeating what he had said earlier, particularly as he had not consulted a solicitor prior to his second interview.

Where an act of oppression or 'anything said or done' renders an earlier confession inadmissible under s. 76(2) of PACE, any subsequent confession is likely to be regarded as tainted and similarly inadmissible for one or more reasons. It has already been mentioned that the accused may feel he has nothing to lose by repeating himself, particularly if he has not benefited from informed legal advice prior to the second interview (as in *R* v. *McGovern* (1990) 92 Cr App R 228 and *R* v. *Glaves* [1993] Crim LR 685), so the second confession should be considered as unreliable as the first. To commence the second interview with a recapitulation by the interviewing officers of what was admitted in the first interview is likely to reinforce this taint, and this was accepted by the Court of Appeal in *R* v. *Wood* [1994] Crim LR 222. (Code C-11.4 requires the interviewing officer to put any previously made 'significant statement' to the suspect at the beginning of an interview.) Second, a subsequent confession may be tainted on account of the interview during which it was made and its surrounding circumstances being inextricably connected with the improper circumstances of the first interview. (In *R* v. *Glaves* [1993] Crim LR 685 the accused's answers in an interview, in the presence of his father, conducted soon after the first interview were also excluded at his trial.) Third, the earlier taint may remain operative on the mind of the accused during his subsequent interview. This represents the approach adopted at common law, and it is no less valid today. Fourth, the courts may refuse to allow a subsequent confession to be adduced on the ground that any alternative approach would allow police officers to circumvent s. 76(2) with impunity, safe in the knowledge that any misconduct applied to elicit an initial confession would not prevent a subsequent confession from being admitted (see *R* v. *Ismail* [1990] Crim LR 109 (CA)).

In *R* v. *Canale* (1989) 91 Cr App R 1 it was alleged that the accused had confessed during interviews which had not been contemporaneously recorded in compliance with Code C and that he had subsequently repeated his confessions at properly recorded interviews. The accused admitted making his earlier oral admissions but asserted they were false and had been made in consequence of certain promises. Because of the police officers' cynical disregard for the rules and the breaches of Code C the Court of Appeal held that the unrecorded interviews had been 'fatally flawed'. The breaches had 'affected the whole series of purported admissions', so s. 78(1) should have been applied to exclude them all. The Court would seem to have been influenced by two separate considerations: the need to ensure future compliance with Code C and, secondly, the possibility that promises may indeed have been made to the accused (the nature of which could not be ascertained because of the failure to record what had happened in the earlier interviews) and that such promises had still been operating on the accused's mind during the recorded interviews. Similarly, in *R* v. *Kirk* [2000] 1 WLR 567 (CA) (7.1.3.3 *ante*) it was held that s. 78(1) should have been applied to the accused's subsequent confession, which (unlike his initial confession) had been made when he was in full possession of the facts, as his position had by then been 'hopelessly compromised' and it was impossible to say what (if any) admission would have been made if he had been made aware of the gravity of the situation from the outset.

Section 78(1) gives the trial judge a discretion, so 'there can be no universal rule that whenever the Code has been breached in one or more interviews, all subsequent interviews must be tainted and therefore should be excluded' (*R* v. *Gillard* (1990) 92 Cr App R 61 (CA) at p. 65). Where the initial confession is tainted by breaches of Code C justifying its exclusion under s. 78(1), the judge retains a discretion as to whether any subsequent confession ought to be excluded too, and how his discretion is exercised will depend on all the circumstances of the case. In *Y* v. *DPP* [1991] Crim LR 917, for example, the accused made a spontaneous confession before being cautioned and subsequently, having been cautioned, confessed again, although no contemporaneous note was made. A formal interview was eventually held in compliance with Code C and the accused confessed again. The Divisional Court upheld the magistrates' decision to admit the final confession despite their having excluded the earlier confessions under s. 78(1). The magistrates had been entitled to take into account the spontaneous nature of the first confession and the absence of bad faith on the part of the police officers involved. In *R* v. *Neil* [1994] Crim LR 441 the Court of Appeal reviewed the authorities and held that where a first interview has been excluded under s. 78(1) the question whether a later interview should also be excluded was a matter of fact and degree:

> 'It is likely to depend on a consideration of whether the objections leading to the exclusion of the first interview were of a fundamental and continuing nature, and, if so, if the arrangements for the subsequent interview gave the accused a sufficient opportunity to exercise an informed and independent choice as to whether he should repeat or retract what he said in the excluded interview ...'

In *R* v. *Nelson* [1998] 2 Cr App R 399 (CA) (7.1.3.3 *ante*) it was felt the mere fact the accused had been reminded of what she had said in her first interview, which should have been excluded under s. 78(1) because of the breach of Code C-10.1, was not sufficient to justify the exclusion of the subsequent properly conducted interview under s. 78(1). This is not surprising. Code C-11.4 obliges interviewing officers to remind their suspects of inculpatory remarks made at an earlier occasion. If compliance with C-11.4 were enough to demand the exclusion of the subsequent interview the judge would have no discretion to exercise.

7.1.3.7 The Fruit of Inadmissible Confessions
Section 76 of PACE provides as follows:

(4) The fact that a confession is wholly or partly excluded in pursuance
     of this section shall not affect the admissibility in evidence (*a*) of
     any facts discovered as a result of the confession; or (*b*) where the
     confession is relevant as showing that the accused speaks, writes or
     expresses himself in a particular way, of so much of the confession
     as is necessary to show that he does so.

(5) Evidence that a fact ... was discovered as a result of a statement
     made by an accused person shall not be admissible unless evidence
     of how it was discovered is given by him or on his behalf.

(6) Subsection (5) above applies (*a*) to any fact discovered as a result of
     a confession which is wholly excluded in pursuance of this section;
     and (*b*) to any fact discovered as a result of a confession which is
     partly so excluded, if the fact is discovered as a result of the
     excluded part of the confession.

The mere fact that the accused's confession has been ruled inadmissible
under s. 76(2) does not prevent the prosecution from adducing non-
confessional evidence of facts discovered as a result of that confession, but
only the accused or his agent may reveal to the court how such evidence
came to be discovered. Section 76(4)(*a*) represents the pre-PACE position
at common law. In *R* v. *Warickshall* (1783) 1 Leach 263 (CCC) the accused
was induced to confess to a charge of receiving stolen goods by assurances
given to her, but as her confession had not been made voluntarily it was
ruled inadmissible. This did not preclude the prosecution from adducing
evidence that the stolen goods had been found hidden in her bed, so long
as it was not revealed that the evidence had been discovered as a result of
her inadmissible confession. Although the reliability of the confession was
in doubt, the reliability of any tangible evidence discovered as a result was
unaffected 'for a fact, if it exist at all, must exist invariably in the same
manner, whether the confession from which it is derived be in other
respects true or false'.

Similarly, in *R* v. *Berriman* (1854) 6 Cox CC 388 (Assizes), a case in
which the accused faced a charge of concealing the birth of her child, it
was permissible for the prosecution to elicit evidence from their witness
that an infant's corpse had been found, but the witness was not allowed to
reveal that the corpse had been found in consequence of the accused's
inadmissible confession. In *Lam Chi-Ming* v. *R* [1991] 2 WLR 1082 the
three co-accused had confessed to murder, but at their trial the confessions
were ruled inadmissible as the prosecution could not prove they had not
been extracted by force. The Privy Council held that evidence should not
have been given of how they had subsequently led the police to the place
where the murder weapon was found. Evidence of their conduct, taking
the police to the water-front and then gesturing to show how the weapon
had been disposed of, amounted to an extension of the inadmissible
confessions and was equally inadmissible. The fact that the murder
weapon was later discovered off the water-front was *prima facie*

admissible, but not how the police came to find it there. Interestingly, as the weapon bore no identifying marks linking any of the accused to it, it had no inherent probative value and could have been ruled inadmissible on the ground of irrelevance. The extremely high probative value of the weapon lay in the fact that the accused had shown the police where they had disposed of it, and yet the conduct which gave the weapon that value was inadmissible. Moreover, the conduct of the accused in taking the police to where the knife had been disposed of demonstrated the reliability of their inadmissible confessions; but nonetheless their confessions remained inadmissible. As the Privy Council conceded, the decision can only be justified if it is accepted there is a reason other than the risk of unreliability which justifies the exclusion of involuntary confessions. This, it was said, is the desirability of preventing the police from subjecting persons in their custody to ill treatment or improper pressure in order to extract confessions from them, the privilege against self-incrimination and 'fairness' (see also *Wong Kam-Ming* v. *R* [1979] 2 WLR 81 (PC) and *R* v. *Sang* [1979] 3 WLR 263 (HL)). This application of the 'protective' principle justified the exclusion of highly probative and reliable evidence identifying the persons who had committed a most brutal murder. At face value the exclusion of such evidence is an affront to common sense: if the police use brutal measures against the accused and thereby elicit a *demonstrably* reliable confession, justice would be best served by allowing the evidence to be admitted and prosecuting the police officers involved for their own criminal conduct. The flaw in this analysis is the failure to recognise how difficult it can be to prove police impropriety beyond reasonable doubt. Other considerations are the importance of ensuring that the police do not act oppressively in the belief that the end justifies the means and the desirability of maintaining the moral integrity of the trial process and the final verdict.

Section 76(4)(*b*) reaffirms the position at common law that an inculpatory statement may still be admissible as original evidence even if it is held to be inadmissible hearsay (by the application of s. 76(2)). A useful illustration of how the written word may be admissible as original evidence is provided by *R* v. *Voisin* [1918] 1 KB 531 (CCA). The headless trunk of a woman's body had been found in a parcel with a piece of paper bearing the words 'Bladie Belgiam' enclosed with it. The accused was interviewed, without having been cautioned, during which he wrote 'Bladie Belgiam' upon being asked to write out 'Bloody Belgian'. This writing was held to have been properly admitted against him at the trial as evidence of his handwriting and spelling. This evidence, together with the fact the deceased's head and hands had been found in the accused's cellar, identified him as the murderer.

If a confession tendered by the prosecution has been ruled inadmissible under s. 76(2) of PACE or otherwise excluded by the judge in the exercise of his discretion, the prosecution cannot cross-examine the accused on it; in fact 'nothing more ought to be heard of it' as between the prosecution and the accused (*R* v. *Treacy* [1944] 2 All ER 229 (CCA), *Lui Mei-Lin* v. *R* [1989] 2 WLR 175 (PC)).

7.1.4 Confessions Tendered by the Accused

In *R* v. *Myers* [1997] 3 WLR 552 the House of Lords held that the accused
is entitled to adduce in support of his defence his co-accused's confession,
to prove the truth of the matters stated, even if it would have been
excluded by virtue of s. 78(1) of PACE if tendered by the prosecution, so
long as it is relevant to his defence and was voluntarily made by the
co-accused (in the sense that it was not made in consequence of oppression
or anything said or done which was likely in the circumstances to render it
unreliable).

Since the case of *R* v. *Miller* (1952) 36 Cr App R 169 (Assizes) it has
been accepted that the accused has an absolute right to elicit or adduce
admissible evidence which is relevant to his defence even though such
evidence might unduly prejudice his co-accused. This general principle was
reaffirmed by the Privy Council in *Lobban* v. *R* [1995] 1 WLR 877, and the
decision in *R* v. *Myers* [1997] 3 WLR 552 (HL) is a further application of
it. Q and M were tried together for the murder of a mini-cab driver who
had died from a single stab wound to the heart, an application for separate
trials having been made to and rejected by the trial judge. M had told the
police prior to being cautioned that it was she who had stabbed the
deceased, but at the trial M blamed Q who in turn blamed M. Because of
the breach of Code C-10.1 (7.1.3.3 *ante*) the prosecution did not even seek
to adduce evidence of M's confession as it would inevitably have been
excluded under s. 78(1) of PACE. However, the trial judge allowed Q to
elicit the confession during his counsel's cross-examination of the police
officers to whom it had been made. Consequently M was convicted of
murder and Q was convicted of manslaughter. The House of Lords
dismissed M's appeal, and Lord Slynn said (at p. 564):

> 'For Myers to deny the confession in evidence would have allowed the
> police officers to be called by Quartey pursuant to s. 4 of [the Criminal
> Procedure Act 1865]. It seems to me that it was also relevant and
> admissible for the police officers ... to be asked about the confession on
> behalf of Quartey. It was not suggested that the confessions were
> obtained in the circumstances referred to in section 76(2) of the Act of
> 1984, and the fact that the prosecution was not able to introduce the
> evidence because of breaches of the police Code did not preclude
> Quartey's counsel from doing so.'

Lord Slynn's speech was approved by Lords Steyn and Hutton and as
such must be accepted as the law. M had been a party to the proceedings
and her confession was therefore *prima facie* admissible by way of the
confessions exception to the rule against hearsay. While there is nothing to
suggest that a co-accused's confession should not be admitted by the
accused under s. 76(1) of PACE, Lord Slynn refused to decide whether the
subsection could be relied on by the accused or whether the confession was
admissible at common law. M's confession had been made voluntarily (in
the sense of there having been no breach of requirements analogous to

those found in s. 76(2)) and was relevant to Q's defence. As the trial judge had no discretion to prevent him from adducing it either at common law or under s. 78(1) (which applies only to evidence tendered by the prosecution) it was admissible at his behest. Although Lord Slynn was deliberately circumspect and did not expressly say that the old common-law test of voluntariness applied, the fact that s. 76(2) was inapplicable leads to no other conclusion. In any event this is a distinction without a difference as the common-law test (if that is what it is) would now seem to be the same as that found in s. 76(2). The Law Commission had already recommended that the admissibility of a co-accused's confession tendered by the accused should be governed by provisions similar to s. 76(2) (Law Com No. 245 (1997) at p. 118) and Lord Slynn was mindful of that. Accordingly, so long as the accused can prove on the balance of probabilities that considerations analogous to those in s. 76(2) do not apply, and so long as the confession is relevant to his own defence, he has an absolute right to adduce it or to elicit it in cross-examination of the persons to whom it was made. He can of course also cross-examine the co-accused on it if he decides to testify.

Lord Hope (with whom Lord Mustill concurred) agreed with the majority view that Q had been entitled to adduce M's confession in support of his own defence. However, rather than suggesting a common-law test of admissibility analogous to s. 76(2) (and no doubt aware that such a test could be said to conflict with the principle reaffirmed in *Lobban* v. *R* [1995] 1 WLR 877 (PC)) he preferred to rely on the trial judge's common-law discretion to exclude any evidence of insufficient probative value (3.1.3 *ante*). According to this view, a confession which has been made in consequence of oppression or anything said or done which was likely in the circumstances to render it unreliable (that is, in breach of the requirements set out in s. 76(2)) is likely to be so lacking in probative value as to be 'worthless' and therefore inadmissible. Notwithstanding the view of the Privy Council in *Lobban* v. *R* that there is no discretion to exclude admissible evidence tendered by an accused, this must be read in the light of the judge's discretion to exclude any evidence, no matter by whom it is tendered, if it is deemed to be 'irrelevant'. This itself is not controversial, and was actually recognised by the Privy Council in *Lobban* v. *R* where it was said that the accused's absolute right to deploy his case asserting his innocence was 'subject to considerations of relevance'. Unfortunately, Lord Hope's approach does not provide a satisfactory test. A confession made by a co-accused in circumstances such as to be excluded under s. 76(2) may be both true and highly probative evidence in support of the accused's defence; indeed this is expressly recognised in s. 76(2) which states that 'the court shall not allow the confession to be given in evidence ... notwithstanding that it may be true'.

The decision of the House of Lords in *R* v. *Myers* [1997] 3 WLR 552, while establishing that a co-accused's confession may be adduced by the accused, fails to explain how such confessions fall to be admitted. It is not even clear whether they are admissible by virtue of s. 76(1), which does not refer to the prosecution, or at common law. The test for admissibility is found in s. 76(2), but as this subsection applies only to evidence tendered by the prosecution the test would seem to be the common-law test of voluntariness, reinterpreted to mean the same as the statutory test. It should also be noted that if M and Q had been tried separately M's confession would not have been admissible at Q's behest as M would not have been a party to the proceedings. The absurd consequence is that where joint trials are ordered and a co-accused has made a confession following a significant breach of Code C that confession will be admissible against her. If, however, they are tried separately the jury will never hear about the confession.

R v. *Myers* was concerned with a co-accused's confession which would have been excluded under s. 78(1) of PACE. If the co-accused's confession had been (or would have been) ruled inadmissible under s. 76(2) it would not have been admissible as evidence of the truth of the matters stated at the behest of the accused. Yet even exclusion under s. 76(2) will not prevent the accused from relying on a co-accused's confession for all purposes. In *Lui Mei-Lin* v. *R* [1989] 2 WLR 175 the Privy Council held that so long as a co-accused's confession is relevant to the accused's own defence the accused may cross-examine him on it, as a previous inconsistent statement, even though it is inadmissible on the ground of having been made involuntarily (see also *R* v. *Rowson* [1985] 3 WLR 99 (CA)). In such a case the judge must explain to the jury why the confession was originally excluded and warn them that the confession is not evidence of the truth of the matters stated but is relevant only to the co-accused's credibility as a witness. The Court of Appeal has recently confirmed that these principles have not been affected by the decision of the House of Lords in *R* v. *Myers* (*R* v. *Corelli* [2001] Crim LR 913).

7.1.5 Reform

In the context of formal interviews the risk of fabricated or otherwise untrue confessions being considered by the jury has been significantly reduced by the introduction of PACE and its Codes of Practice. This is particularly so now that Code E-3 requires interviews relating to any indictable offence to be recorded on audio tape if the machinery is working and it is possible a prosecution will ensue (save that the audio recording of interviews under the Terrorism Act 2000 is governed by a separate code). However, despite these reforms it is still possible that some false confessions will slip through the net and be admitted. In particular, it remains the case that no audio recording is required if the interview relates to a summary offence; such interviews are governed by the manual recording requirements of Code C-11. Nor does Code E apply in other contexts, such as where an admission is purported to have been made on the way to the police station or during an informal conversation. The potential for unreliability is greatest in these situations and an obvious further safeguard would be to extend the application of Code E to cover them. After all, there is no good reason why all formal interviews should not be contemporaneously recorded on audio tape (and on video tape for that matter); and, given the portability of pocket cassette recorders, it should be possible to record informal interviews too.

To eliminate the possibility of fabrication, it should be a prerequisite to admissibility that any confession made outside the formal environment of the interview room should be repeated and recorded on tape as soon as possible thereafter. If the accused fails to repeat his confession on tape it should be inadmissible unless there is some other independent evidence of his having made it, such as the testimony of a disinterested third party. In fact the Court of Appeal has already held that the trial judge is entitled to take into consideration the presence of other safeguards or supporting evidence when deciding whether or not breaches of Code C justify the exclusion of a confession under s. 78(1) of PACE. In *R* v. *Dunn* (1990) 91 Cr App R 237 (CA) clear breaches of the Code C 'verballing' provisions could not justify the exclusion of the confession, which the accused denied having made, because his solicitor's clerk had been present throughout his interview. It has also been seen that independent evidence is an important consideration for the purpose of s. 78(1) where a confession is alleged to have been made to an undercover police officer in a situation not covered by the Codes of Practice (*R* v. *Bryce* (1992) 95 Cr App R 320 (CA), 7.1.3.3 *ante*).

However, while the existence of independent confirmation that a purported confession was made may be a relevant consideration for determining whether it should be excluded under s. 78(1), once a confession has been admitted the accused may be convicted despite the absence of any independent evidence tending to show the confession is true. One suggestion for reform which has been mooted is that there should always be some other supporting evidence independent of the confession suggesting not only that the confession was made by the accused but also that it is true. A corroboration requirement of sorts exists in some other jurisdictions, for example in Scotland and the USA, and it has been argued that a requirement of supporting evidence would act as a further safeguard against miscarriages of justice in England and Wales. Unfortunately, it is questionable whether any such reform would really provide an effective safeguard. The supporting evidence itself could be unreliable and its existence may in fact have the effect of bolstering an otherwise unreliable confession. The 'Birmingham Six' were convicted on the basis of their confessions to murder supported by what seemed to be incontrovertible scientific evidence that two of them had been in contact with nitroglycerine, but their convictions were subsequently quashed because of doubts about the reliability of their confessions *and* the scientific evidence in support (*R* v. *McIlkenny* (1991) 93 Cr App R 287 (CA)). The scientific evidence in that case was unreliable on account of the fallibility of the test used for detecting nitroglycerine, but it is not difficult to envisage corrupt police officers manufacturing supporting evidence. There is also a danger that a requirement of supporting evidence independent of the confession would suggest a general disbelief in police testimony, undermining public confidence in the police force. Perhaps the strongest argument against any such reform lies in the fact that it would allow offenders to walk free despite their having made voluntary confessions in the presence of independent witnesses and in circumstances where the likelihood of falsity could be discounted. Nor should one be overly influenced by the existence of a corroboration requirement in other jurisdictions. In the USA a confession may generally be corroborated by mere evidence that the crime has actually been committed, while in Scotland the requirement has almost disappeared in practice. The Royal Commission on Criminal Justice (1993) Cm 2263 (at pp. 49–68) rejected a supporting evidence requirement for England and Wales, proposing instead that there should be a judicial warning similar to that which has been introduced for visual-identification evidence (11.1.1 *post*). In other words, there should be a mandatory direction to the jury of the special need for caution before convicting solely on the basis of the accused's confession, supplemented by a direction on the reasons why the accused might have falsely confessed. As the law stands the judge is not obliged to warn the jury of any need for caution – although such a warning may occasionally be required if the accused is mentally handicapped (s. 77(1) of PACE, 11.9 *post*) or the person to whom the confession was purportedly made is an unreliable witness (11.8 *post*); but there is nothing to prevent the judge giving a warning in the exercise of his discretion. The question is whether a warning should be mandatory in all cases where the prosecution case depends wholly or substantially on the accused's confession.

Given the possible reasons for making a false confession there is some force in the analogy with visual-identification evidence. In each case the evidence may be false but there is a risk that the jury will accept it at face value and treat it as compelling evidence of guilt unless warned of the reasons why it might be unreliable. The likelihood of false confessions is clearly high for certain types of vulnerable individual such as the mentally ill and juveniles and such persons ought to be brought within the scope of s. 77(1) of PACE. However, the risk of falsity may be very low in other situations and a direction in all cases might lead to the sort of absurd directions judges were obliged to give prior to the abolition of mandatory corroboration warnings. In the final analysis the best approach would seem to be for the judge to give a warning whenever there is a significant possibility that the accused might have falsely confessed. If, taking all the circumstances into account, such a risk cannot be discounted the judge ought to warn the jury of the possibility of falsity, explaining why a person might confess to a crime he has not committed and pointing out the factors in the instant case (such as the character of the accused and the method by which he was interrogated) which might have caused the accused falsely to confess. There should be no such warning or direction if the risk of falsity can be entirely discounted.

7.2 Civil Proceedings: *Informal Admissions*

The admissibility of informal admissions (out-of-court statements made by a party to the proceedings which are adverse to his case) is now governed by the Civil Evidence Act 1995 (ss. 1(1) and 7(1), see generally 8.1 *post*). Informal admissions are therefore *prima facie* admissible in civil proceedings (so long as the maker was competent as a witness when the statement was made) and the tribunal of fact will take into consideration any relevant circumstances, including the particular factors specified in s. 4(2) of the Act, when determining how much weight the admission should be given.

For the purposes of the 1995 Act, a statement is defined in s. 13 as 'any representation of fact or opinion, however made', which would seem to cover admissions which may properly be inferred from conduct, such as a motorist's act of running away from the scene of the road accident in which he has just been involved (*Holloway* v. *MacFeeters* (1956) 94 CLR 470 (HCA), 5.6.1.2 *ante*) or a failure to respond to an allegation in a business letter (*Wiedemann* v. *Walpole* [1891] 2 QB 534 (CA), 9.2.1 *post*).

At common law an informal admission could be made directly by the party himself or vicariously by someone in privity with him (such as someone who shared a common interest with the party or acted as his agent). As hearsay is now generally admissible in civil proceedings a relevant out-of-court statement adverse to a party is *prima facie* admissible no matter who the maker is.

Chapter Summary

- A confession is an out-of-court statement made by the accused which is self-incriminating (at the time of the trial). A confession made by the accused is admissible against him at the behest of the prosecution under s. 76(1) of PACE (an exception to the rule against hearsay) so long as the prosecution have been able to discharge their burden of proof in respect of the oppression and reliability provisions of s. 76(2).
- If the prosecution are able to prove that s. 76(2) does not render the confession inadmissible, the judge may nonetheless exclude it in the exercise of his discretion under s. 78(1) or at common law. The judge will take into consideration all relevant circumstances when determining whether the confession is inadmissible or ought to be excluded, including breaches of PACE and significant breaches of Code C of the PACE Codes of Practice. Particularly important considerations are whether the police cautioned the accused before he made his confession, whether the police acted in bad faith and whether the police tricked the accused into confessing in violation of his privilege against self-incrimination.
- If a confession is ruled inadmissible under s. 76(2) a subsequent confession is likely to be ruled inadmissible on the ground that it is 'tainted'. If a confession is excluded under s. 78(1) a subsequent confession may be excluded depending on the circumstances.
- The fact that a confession is inadmissible under s. 76(2) does not prevent the prosecution from adducing real evidence found as a result of the confession, save

that they may not disclose to the jury how that evidence came to be discovered. An inadmissible confession may also be admitted as original evidence to show how the accused expresses himself.

- The accused may adduce a co-accused's voluntarily made confession (as admissible hearsay) if it is relevant to his defence, even if the prosecution could not adduce it by virtue of the application of s. 78(1) of PACE. The accused may also cross-examine the co-accused on his involuntarily made confession to undermine his credibility (if it is relevant to the accused's defence).

Further Reading

Criminal Law Revision Committee, 11th Report (1972) Cmnd 4991, pp. 34–47
Pattenden, 'Should Confessions be Corroborated?' (1991) 107 LQR 317
Dennis, 'Miscarriages of Justice and the Law of Confessions' [1993] PL 291
The Royal Commission on Criminal Justice Report (1993) Cm 2263, Chapter 4
Smith, 'Exculpatory Statements and Confessions' [1995] Crim LR 280
Mirfield, 'Successive Confessions and the Poisonous Tree' [1996] Crim LR 554
Hirst, 'Confessions as Proof of Innocence' [1998] CLJ 146

Criminal Justice Bill (2003), Part 11, Chapter 2 (on confessions)
and Explanatory Note (www.publications.parliament.uk)

8 Hearsay in Civil Proceedings

In *Ventouris* v. *Mountain (No. 2)* [1992] 1 WLR 887 (CA) Balcombe LJ said (at p. 899):

> 'The modern tendency in civil proceedings is to admit all relevant evidence, and the judge should be trusted to give only proper weight to evidence which is not the best evidence ...'

There has been a general trend in favour of the principle of free proof in civil proceedings, and this is exemplified by Parliament's approach to the admissibility of hearsay evidence. Judges sitting alone as the tribunal of fact are, on account of their experience, regarded as better able to assess the probative value of hearsay evidence than their lay counterparts in criminal proceedings. Part I of the Civil Evidence Act 1968 first provided for the admissibility of much hearsay evidence in civil proceedings, subject to compliance with complicated procedural rules, but this statutory scheme was considered unsatisfactory and has now been repealed and replaced by the simpler but more comprehensive Civil Evidence Act 1995 in line with recommendations made by the Law Commission in 1993 (Law Com No. 216). The provisions of the 1995 Act are complemented by Part 33 of the Civil Procedure Rules 1998 (or, in the case of magistrates' courts, by the Magistrates' Courts (Hearsay Evidence in Civil Proceedings) Rules 1999 (SI 1999 No. 681)).

By virtue of s. 1(1) of the Civil Evidence Act 1995, the exclusionary rule no longer applies to hearsay evidence tendered in civil proceedings which falls within the scope of the definition in s. 1(2); and although there are still some pre-trial procedural requirements, non-compliance goes to weight rather than admissibility. If hearsay evidence is admissible by virtue of some other statutory or retained common-law exception the notice requirements and safeguards in ss. 2 to 6 of the Act do not need to be complied with (s. 1(4)). Should a hearsay statement not fall within the scope of s. 1(2) of the Act it will remain inadmissible – the common-law exclusionary rule applies in civil as well as criminal proceedings (*Bradford City Metropolitan Council* v. *K (Minors)* [1990] 2 WLR 532 (FD)).

8.1 The Civil Evidence Act 1995

Section 1 of the Act provides as follows:

(1) In civil proceedings evidence shall not be excluded on the ground that it is hearsay.
(2) In this Act –
    (a) "hearsay" means a statement made otherwise than by a person while giving oral evidence in the proceedings which is tendered as evidence of the matters stated; and
    (b) references to hearsay include hearsay of whatever degree.

The definition of hearsay in s. 1(2)(*a*) is similar to that accepted by the House of Lords in *R* v. *Sharp* [1988] 1 WLR 7 (5.1 *ante*). Given that inferred ('implied') assertions are more likely to be reliable than express assertions, and that the Law Commission has recently recommended that implied assertions should be admissible in criminal proceedings (5.6.2 *ante*), the statutory definition will presumably be interpreted to accommodate such evidence. Indeed, although in Law Com No. 216 (at p. 34) the Law Commission left open the question whether 'implied assertions' should be admissible in civil proceedings, 'statement' is defined in s. 13 to mean 'any representation of fact or opinion, however made'. Hearsay evidence falling within the scope of s. 1(2) is admissible in civil proceedings before magistrates as well as in the county courts and the High Court (s. 11).

Subject to the provision governing exclusion or waiver in s. 2(3) of the Act, and the limited exceptions set out in r. 33.3 of the Civil Procedure Rules 1998, any party wishing to adduce evidence at the trial pursuant to s. 1(1) is under an obligation, first, to identify the evidence as hearsay and, second, to give the other party or parties notice of that fact and (if requested) provide 'such particulars of or relating to the evidence, as is reasonable and practicable in the circumstances for the purpose of enabling him or them to deal with any matter arising from its being hearsay' (s. 2(1)). This prevents the other party or parties being taken by surprise at the trial and provides them with the opportunity to demand the particulars they require to be able to make a proper assessment of the weight of the evidence (see Law Com No. 216 at p. 26). The notice requirements are set out in r. 33.2 of the Civil Procedure Rules 1998.

Importantly, a failure to comply with the requirements of s. 2(1) or the relevant procedural rules does not affect the admissibility of the evidence but, *inter alia*, 'may be taken into account by the court ... as a matter adversely affecting the weight to be given to the evidence in accordance with section 4' (s. 2(4)(*b*)). It should be borne in mind, however, that r. 32.1(2) of the Civil Procedure Rules 1998 provides the judge with a general discretion to exclude any admissible evidence, including hearsay evidence admissible by virtue of s. 1(1) of the Act.

Section 4(1) obliges the judge to take into account 'any circumstances from which any inference can reasonably be drawn as to the reliability or otherwise of the evidence' when estimating the weight (if any) to be attached to an item of hearsay evidence admissible under s. 1(1). Section 4(2) provides a list of six factors the judge should take into consideration when assessing the weight of the evidence: (*a*) whether it would have been reasonable and practicable for the party by whom the evidence was adduced to have produced the maker of the original statement as a witness; (*b*) whether the original statement was made contemporaneously with the occurrence or existence of the matters stated; (*c*) whether the evidence involves multiple hearsay; (*d*) whether any person involved had any motive to conceal or misrepresent matters; (*e*) whether the original statement was an edited account, or was made in collaboration with another or for a particular purpose; and (*f*) whether the circumstances in which the evidence is adduced as hearsay are such as to suggest an attempt to prevent proper evaluation of its weight. Needless to say, the safeguards in s. 4 of the Act ensure that the party against whom the hearsay is admitted has a fair hearing in the determination of his civil rights and obligations for the purposes of Article 6(1) of the European Convention on Human Rights (a point noted by Lord Hutton in *R (McCann)* v. *Crown Court at Manchester* [2002] 3 WLR 1313 (HL) at p. 1352).

Rule 32.5(5) of the Civil Procedure Rules 1998 provides that where a party has served a witness statement on the other parties in advance of the trial, but that party neither calls the witness to give oral evidence nor adduces the witness statement as hearsay evidence, any other party may adduce that statement as hearsay evidence. This provision has not affected the rule of evidence which prohibits a party from impeaching his own witness (16.4.3 *post*), so if C has a witness statement served on him in advance of the trial by D, but ultimately D decides not to call that witness or adduce the statement as hearsay evidence, it is open to C to adduce that statement as hearsay evidence on his own behalf, but he cannot then assert that much of what is said in the statement is untrue (*McPhilemy* v. *Times Newspapers (No. 2)* [2000] 1 WLR 1732 (CA)). Rule 33.4(1) provides that where a party proposes to rely on a hearsay statement, and does not propose to call the person who made that statement to give oral evidence, any other party may apply to call that person to be cross-examined on the contents of his statement. Rules 32.5(5) and 33.4(1) may be read together, so, for example, if D adduces a witness statement served on him by C under r. 32.5(5) as hearsay evidence, it is open to C to apply for that absent witness to be called for cross-examination on his statement (*Douglas* v. *Hello!* [2003] EWCA Civ 332).

If an absent witness is not called for cross-examination, and a hearsay statement made or reported by him has been adduced in evidence, this usual forensic tool for undermining a witness's credibility is unavailable. Section 5(2)(*a*) therefore allows the opposing party to adduce any admissible evidence which would undermine that person's credibility, and, in particular, the opposing party may call evidence to prove that he has made a statement inconsistent with his hearsay statement (s. 5(2)(*b*)). The opposing party must, however, give notice of his intention to attack the credibility of an absent person (CPR 1998 r. 33.5), and the rule on the finality of answers on collateral matters (16.5.2 *post*) continues to apply (s. 5(2)). Section 5(2)(*a*) also allows the party adducing the hearsay statement to adduce admissible evidence to support his absent witness's credibility (see 16.4.2.1–6 *post*).

Hearsay evidence is inadmissible to the extent that it consists of (or needs to be proved by means of) a statement made by a person who at the time he made the statement was not competent as a witness (s. 5(1)). A child is competent if he satisfies the test in s. 96 of the Children Act 1989 (16.3.3 *post*). Section 6 of the 1995 Act governs the admissibility and evidential value of admissible previous statements made by a person who has given evidence as a witness in the proceedings.

If a hearsay statement is contained in a document, the statement may be proved by the production of the document (s. 8(1)(*a*)) or the production of an authenticated copy of the document, whether or not the document is still in existence (s. 8(1)(*b*)). It is immaterial how many removes there are between a copy and the original (s. 8(2)). Section 13 of the Act provides that a 'document' is 'anything in which information of any description is recorded', and a 'copy' is 'anything onto which information recorded in the document has been copied, by whatever means and whether directly or indirectly'. Section 9 governs the proof of documents (as opposed to statements contained therein) which form part of the records of a business or public authority (see also r. 33.6 of the CPR 1998).

In short, hearsay evidence is not inadmissible merely because it is hearsay, but the judge will take into consideration the factors which justified the common-law exclusionary rule when he determines how much weight, if any, the evidence should be given. Accordingly, s. 1(1) of the Act will be relied on primarily where the hearsay evidence is relatively uncontroversial, and is likely to be given sufficient weight notwithstanding the absence of the (available) witness, or in cases where it is impossible or impracticable to call the witness but his evidence is likely to be accepted as reliable. If the hearsay evidence is inherently unreliable it may be given no weight at all, meaning in effect (if not in theory) that it remains inadmissible despite s. 1(1) of the Act. A recent example is provided by *Owen* v. *Brown* [2002] EWHC 1135 (QBD) where a faxed letter from 'Fish Insurance' offering the claimant insurance for driving a vehicle, was given no weight. First, the letter did not address the concerns raised by a medical expert as to whether the claimant would be able to maintain the necessary level of concentration for safe driving; second, there was no evidence of the experience or authority of the person who wrote the letter; third, there was no evidence as to whether it would have been practicable and reasonable to have called the writer to give oral evidence; fourth, the claimant had not revealed to Fish Insurance the nature of his disability; and, fifth, the writer appeared to be under the (probably erroneous) impression that the claimant had already disclosed his condition to the licensing authority (the DVLA). Suggesting that similar reasoning must apply to the application of the 1995 Act, the trial judge (Silber J) referred with approval to the dictum of Brandon J in *The Ferdinand Retzlaff* [1972] 2 Lloyd's Rep 120 (QBD) (at p. 127):

'I cannot think that the Civil Evidence Act 1968 was intended, in general, to change the long-established system by which seriously disputed central issues in civil cases are tried on oral evidence, given on oath and capable of being tested by cross-examination, and to substitute for it a system of trial on unsworn documents brought into existence by parties to the proceedings *post litem mortam*, and I do not think the Act should be used, or rather abused, so as to produce such a result.'

Support for this view may also be found in the Civil Procedure Rules 1998, r. 32.2(1) of which provides, as a general rule, that where any fact needs to be proved during a trial by the evidence of witnesses, they should give their evidence orally.

Another recent case where hearsay evidence admissible under s. 1(1) of the Act was disregarded is *Brownsville Holdings* v. *Adamjee Insurance* [2000] 2 All ER (Comm) 803 (QBD). The informal admission purportedly made by the owner of a yacht to a witness called by the insurers, to the effect that the owner had ordered that the ship be scuttled in order to recover the insurance proceeds, was given no weight at all on account of the witness's evident motive not to tell the truth, her unreliability in other respects and the inherent improbability that the owner would have confessed to her in the circumstances existing at that time.

8.2 Other Statutory Exceptions

The Children (Admissibility of Hearsay Evidence) Order 1993 (SI 1993 No. 621) made under s. 96(3) of the Children Act 1989 permits the admission of hearsay evidence in the High Court, county courts and magistrates' courts if the case is concerned with the upbringing, maintenance or welfare of a child. A number of other statutory provisions provide for the admissibility of more specific types of hearsay in civil (and criminal) proceedings. For example, s. 34(6) of the Births and Deaths Registration Act 1953 provides, *inter alia*, that a certified copy of an entry in the register of births or deaths is admissible to prove the occurrence of a birth or death, so long as certain conditions have been satisfied; s. 65(3) of the Marriage Act 1949 provides that a sealed or stamped certified copy of an entry in the register of marriages is admissible to prove the marriage, and under s. 3 of the Bankers' Books Evidence Act 1879 a copy of an entry in a bankers' book is evidence of the matters recorded therein (so long as certain conditions set out in s. 4 are satisfied). It should also be noted that where a witness is called to give oral evidence in civil proceedings, his out-of-court witness statement will generally stand as his evidence in chief (see r. 32.5(2) of the CPR 1998).

8.3 Common-law Exceptions

Section 7 of the Civil Evidence Act 1995 preserves certain common-law exceptions, but expressly provides that the admissibility of informal admissions is now governed by the general provisions of the Act (s. 7(1)). An informal admission may be made expressly or be inferred from a party's words, conduct or silence (so-called 'implied' admissions). Express admissions are clearly covered by s. 1(1); presumably s. 1(2)(*a*) covers 'implied' admissions too.

Three common-law exceptions to the hearsay rule are preserved by s. 7(2): (*a*) published works dealing with matters of a public nature (such as histories, scientific works, dictionaries and maps); (*b*) public documents (such as public registers); and (*c*) records (such as records of courts and treaties). Evidence of reputation is still admissible at common law for the purpose of proving good or bad character (s. 7(3)(*a*)); and evidence of reputation or family tradition is admissible (i) for the purpose of proving or disproving pedigree or the existence of a marriage and/or (ii) for the purpose of proving or disproving the existence of any public or general right or of identifying any person or thing (s. 7(3)(*b*)).

9   Inferences from Silence

9.1 **The Relevance of Silence**

A party's silence in the face of an allegation or question may be of evidential significance if a response could reasonably have been expected in the circumstances. The party's failure to respond may amount to a tacit acceptance of an allegation made against him or demonstrate his consciousness of guilt, or it may simply undermine the credibility of a defence raised for the first time by him at the trial. In the absence of a credible alternative explanation, the party's silence (or rather the inference drawn from it) may be significant enough to amount to a confession, or it may support his opponent's case as just another item of circumstantial evidence. Subject to any legal restriction on the nature of the inference which may properly be drawn, the tribunal of fact must rely on its experience of human nature to determine whether any inference should be drawn and, if so, its nature and cogency, taking into consideration all relevant factors such as the silent party's personality, his innocent explanation, the context in which the question or allegation was put and the seriousness of the occasion. Silence is generally an unreliable source from which to draw inferences because an individual may remain silent in the face of questioning for any of a wide range of reasons, so extreme caution needs to be exercised before any such inference is drawn, particularly in criminal proceedings:

> 'While it may no doubt be expected in most cases that innocent persons would be willing to co-operate with the police in explaining that they were not involved in any suspected crime, there may be reasons why in a specific case an innocent person would not be prepared to do so. In particular, an innocent person may not wish to make any statement before he has had the opportunity to consult a lawyer.' (*Averill* v. *United Kingdom* (2000) 31 EHRR 839 (ECtHR) at p. 853)

9.2 **Silence Before the Trial**

The admissibility and evidential value of a party's pre-trial silence, when some response could reasonably have been expected, is governed by the common law and legislation.

9.2.1 **The Position at Common Law**

A person's statement (for example, an allegation) made in the presence and hearing of a party to civil or criminal proceedings is admissible against that party as evidence of the facts stated (or alleged) if, by his demeanour, conduct or words, he can reasonably be taken to have accepted the truth of those facts (*R* v. *Christie* [1914] AC 545 (HL)). In *R* v. *Christie* it was also held that a denial by the party would not render the statement inadmissible in law, for the manner of the denial could constitute evidence from which an acknowledgement could be inferred, save that in criminal proceedings the trial judge would be expected to exercise his discretion and exclude an accusation denied by the accused as its evidential value would generally be outweighed by its unduly prejudicial effect. Where in criminal proceedings the accused has accepted the truth of an accusation made against him, that acceptance will fall within the definition of a confession (7.1.1 *ante*) and be capable of corroborating other evidence against him (*R* v. *Cramp* (1880) 14 Cox CC 390 (Assizes)).

Whether a party can be taken to have accepted the truth of an accusation by his silence will depend on whether it would have been reasonable to expect a denial from him in the circumstances. In *R* v. *Mitchell* (1892) 17 Cox CC 503 (Assizes) Cave J said (at p. 508):

'Now the whole admissibility of statements of this kind rests upon the consideration that if a charge is made against a person in that person's presence it is reasonable to expect that he or she will immediately deny it, and that the absence of such a denial is some evidence of an admission on the part of the person charged, and of the truth of the charge. Undoubtedly, when persons are speaking on even terms and a charge is made, and the person charged says nothing, and expresses no indignation, and does nothing to repel the charge, that is some evidence to show that he admits the charge to be true.'

It is for the tribunal of fact to determine whether the party has accepted the truth of an accusation in whole or in part, the test being one of common sense based on logic and human experience. The status of the accused and the accuser (that is, that they should be on equal terms) is a relevant factor, but all the circumstances should be taken into consideration when determining whether it would have been reasonable to expect some form of denial. A particularly taciturn person is less likely to react than most people in any circumstances, and even the most reasonable person is unlikely to respond to an allegation made by a drunken, obnoxious or hysterical accuser. The test is therefore a subjective one: whether it would have been reasonable for *that* accused to respond to *that* accuser in the circumstances then present.

In *R* v. *Mitchell* (1892) 17 Cox CC 503 a woman lying on her death bed was having her evidence formally taken in the presence of a number of persons including the accused and her solicitor. In such circumstances it was not unreasonable that the accused should have remained silent, so the allegation and the accused's silence were inadmissible. In the Australian case of *Thatcher* v. *Charles* (1961) 104 CLR 57 (HCA) the infant plaintiff was injured when the defendant reversed his car into her. Immediately after the accident the child's mother alleged that the defendant generally drove too fast, but that statement and the defendant's silence were not admissible as evidence of his negligence. The defendant had been very upset following the accident and would naturally have been most unwilling to enter into an argument with the injured girl's distraught mother. (Moreover, the accusation related to the defendant's general driving and not to the incident in question.) Those two cases should be contrasted with *Parkes* v. *R* [1976] 1 WLR 1251. A mother found her daughter bleeding from stab wounds and went up to the accused, who lived in the same house as her daughter, and asked him why he had stabbed her. The accused, holding a closed flick-knife, remained silent and when the mother seized him, saying she would hold him until the police came, he opened the knife and tried to stab her. The Privy Council concluded that in those circumstances, with the mother and accused speaking on equal terms, the jury had been entitled to take into account both the accused's silence and his subsequent attempt to stab the mother as evidence that he had stabbed and murdered her daughter (see also *R* v. *Cramp* (1880) 14 Cox CC 390 (Assizes)). Similarly, in *Bessela* v. *Stern* (1877) 2 CPD 265 (CA), a civil action for breach of promise of marriage, evidence was admissible to show that the defendant had made no denial when scolded by the plaintiff for having repeatedly promised to marry her and then failing to do so. In *Wiedemann* v. *Walpole* [1891] 2 QB 534 (CA) it was felt that a failure to respond to a letter on a matter of business could be regarded as evidence that the truth of its content had been accepted by the recipient, but that, in other contexts, a failure to respond to a letter alleging 'some offence or meanness' would not allow any such inference to be drawn as it was the ordinary practice of mankind not to answer such letters.

More recently, in *Freemantle* v. *R* [1994] 1 WLR 1437 (PC) a man's failure to deny a statement identifying him as 'Freemantle' allowed an inference to be drawn that he had accepted the truth of that identification. The accused was charged with the murder of a woman who had been shot while watching a film. His defence was that he had been elsewhere, but a prosecution witness testified that he had recognised the gunman as he was making off and had shouted, 'Freemantle, me see you!' The gunman's retort ('Go suck your mumma!') was felt to be capable of amounting to 'an implied acknowledgement by the defendant that he had been correctly identified by way of recognition and as an expression of the defendant's resentment of [the witness's] public disclosure of the identification'.

If, in criminal proceedings, the allegation against the accused was made by a person on equal terms with him, the mere presence of a police officer at the scene is a factor to be weighed in the balance as part of the circumstances (*R* v. *Christie* [1914] AC 545 (HL), *R* v. *Horne* [1990] Crim LR 188 (CA)); but if the allegation was made *by* a police officer or some other agent of the state there is authority for the view that his silence should not be regarded as an acceptance by him of the charge because an officer of the law is not on equal terms with a suspect (*Hall* v. *R* [1971] 1 WLR 298 (PC)). In *R* v. *Chandler* [1976] 1 WLR 585, however, the Court of Appeal refused to accept that this was an absolute rule, holding that silence in such circumstances could amount to an acceptance of the allegation if made prior to the caution being given and in circumstances where the police officer and accused could in fact be said to have been on equal terms, such as where the accused was in the presence of his solicitor. This decision has not been applied, however, because the police are obliged to caution a suspect *before* he is interrogated (see 7.1.3.3 *ante*).

In *R* v. *Christie* [1914] AC 545 (HL) Lord Reading added (at pp. 565–6) that a statement made in the presence of the accused could be admissible for the prosecution, even if his response (if any) did *not* amount to an acknowledgment of its truth, in order 'to prove the conduct and demeanour of the accused when hearing the statement'. The accused's exculpatory response to an allegation is admissible evidence of his consistency and reaction (16.4.2.4 *post*), but Lord Reading had in mind evidence of the accused's conduct and demeanour being admissible to show he was conscious of his guilt at the time he heard the statement. The accused's silence in the face of an allegation may therefore be evidence of his admission of guilt (if he can be deemed to have accepted the truth of the allegation) and/or evidence of his conscious awareness of guilt.

If the accused was found in possession of recently stolen goods and failed to give any (or any plausible) explanation prior to his being cautioned as to how he came to have those goods, it is permissible for the jury to infer, as a matter of common sense, that he was handling the goods knowing or believing them to be stolen (*R* v. *Ball* [1983] 1 WLR 801 (CA)) or that he had stolen the goods himself (*R* v. *Seymour* [1954] 1 WLR 678 (CCA)). It is the failure to offer a plausible explanation in a situation where an explanation is clearly called for that logically allows an inference to be drawn. For similar reasons the common law also recognises that a person found in a compromising position should explain himself or suffer the risk of an adverse inference being drawn from his silence. In *R* v. *Wood* (1911) 7 Cr App R 56 (CCA) the accused had been found in the front hall of a house by the householder's chauffeur. The jury were therefore entitled to infer an intent to commit a felony on account of his failure to give a satisfactory explanation to the chauffeur for his being there. It has also been held that an adverse inference may be drawn from the accused's pre-trial refusal to stand in an identification parade, so long as the evidence is presented to the jury in a fair way (*R* v. *Doyle* [2001] EWCA Crim 2883).

At common law a suspected offender was recognised to have the right to remain silent in the face of an interrogation by an agent of the State. In other words, a suspect could not be compelled to speak to the investigating authority (usually the police) and his silence under caution could not subsequently be regarded as evidence against him (as the accused) or be adversely commented upon by the trial judge (see, for example, *R* v. *Gilbert* (1977) 66 Cr App R 237 (CA) and *R* v. *Alladice* (1988) 87 Cr App R 380 (CA)). The second limb has now been curtailed by s. 34 and ss. 36–37 of the Criminal Justice and Public Order Act 1994, but even before those provisions came into force it was clear that this aspect of the 'right of silence' represented a general rather than an absolute prohibition. The accused who had answered some but not other questions under caution ran the risk of having his whole interview admitted (*R* v.

Mann (1972) 56 Cr App R 750 (CA)); and even a limited degree of judicial comment on the accused's silence was permissible. In *R* v. *Gerard* (1948) 32 Cr App R 132 (CCA), where the accused (as a suspect) had stated that he would reserve his comments for the court, it was held that the judge had been entitled to comment that it was perhaps 'a little odd' for him to have made that comment before being charged (see also *R* v. *Tune* (1944) 29 Cr App R 162 (CCA)). The trial judge also had a limited discretion to comment on the accused's failure to disclose his defence during the pre-trial proceedings, thereby preventing the police from being able to investigate it, as a factor affecting the weight of his evidence in support of that defence (*R* v. *Littleboy* [1934] 2 KB 408 (CCA)). In *R* v. *Ryan* (1964) 50 Cr App R 144 (CCA) this principle was extended to a situation where there could have been no police investigation, although the reasoning was subsequently criticised by the Court of Appeal in *R* v. *Gilbert* (1977) 66 Cr App R 237 where it was felt that a trial judge's discretion was limited to commenting that the accused's defence had been put forward for the first time at the trial. (*R* v. *Littleboy* was not mentioned in *R* v. *Gilbert*, however, and, since it can be distinguished from *R* v. *Ryan*, it was probably still good law when the 1994 Act came into force.)

9.2.2 Section 34 of the Criminal Justice and Public Order Act 1994

This provision, like s. 35 of the 1994 Act (9.3.2 *post*), has its origins in the Criminal Law Revision Committee's Eleventh Report (Cmnd 4991 (1972) at pp. 16–34). In short, it provides the prosecution with an additional evidential factor in support of their case if the accused failed to mention his defence when interrogated by the police; that is to say, the jury or magistrates are entitled to draw an adverse inference from the accused's silence when questioned by the police under caution if his defence could reasonably have been mentioned during that interview. Section 34 applies whether the accused is interviewed (charged or informed) by police officers or other persons charged with the duty of investigating offences such as customs officers (s. 34(4)). The caution now reads: 'You do not have to say anything. But it may harm your defence if you do not mention when questioned something which you later rely on in court. Anything you do say may be given in evidence.'

Although s. 34 has curtailed the accused's pre-trial right of silence, the right has *not* been abolished (see 9.5 *post*). Subject to any legitimate statutory interference with the privilege against self-incrimination, a suspect cannot be compelled to answer any questions put to him; and it is not silence *per se* which allows an adverse inference to be drawn under this provision.

Section 34 provides, *inter alia*, that where evidence is given that the accused 'failed to mention any fact relied on in his defence' when questioned under caution before he was charged with the offence (or on being charged with the offence or officially informed that he might be prosecuted for the offence) and the fact was one 'which in the circumstances existing at the time the accused could reasonably have been expected to mention when so questioned, charged or informed, as the case may be', then the tribunal of fact 'may draw such inferences from the failure as appear proper' in determining whether the accused is guilty of the offence (s. 34(1) and 34(2)(*d*)). However, it is not permissible to convict the accused solely on the basis of any such inference (s. 38(3)).

With regard to the pre-trial stage, if a suspect has not had the opportunity to give his own version of events, it is permissible for the police to question him notwithstanding the belief of the custody officer or the officer in charge of the investigation that, in the absence of an exculpatory explanation from the suspect, there is already sufficient evidence for a prosecution to succeed, for the suspect may give an exculpatory account which reduces or extinguishes the prospects of a successful conviction (Code C-11.6, following a line of cases from *R* v. *McGuinness* [1999] Crim LR 318 (CA) to *R* v. *Elliott* [2002] EWCA Crim 931 (C-MAC)). It has also been held that, if the accused was silent during his police interview but the interview record is excluded under s. 78(1) of the Police and Criminal Evidence Act 1984 because of breaches of Code C of the PACE Codes of Practice – preventing any inference from being drawn from *that* silence – it may nevertheless be possible to allow an inference to be drawn from the accused's subsequent silence at the time he was charged, so long as this would not have the effect of nullifying the safeguards contained in the 1984 Act and its Codes (*R* v. *Dervish* [2002] 2 Cr App R 105 (CA)).

An adverse inference may be drawn at the trial only if a 'fact' has been 'relied on' by the accused in his defence, so no such inference may be drawn from the accused's failure to admit part of the case *against* him if he subsequently makes a bare admission at his trial (*R* v. *Betts* [2001] 2 Cr App R 257 (CA)). It is important to note, however, that a fact may be 'relied on' by the accused even if he does not give oral evidence. A fact relied on may be established 'by the accused himself in evidence, by a witness called on his behalf, or by a prosecution witness' (*R* v. *Bowers* (1998) 163 JP 33 (CA)) or where 'a co-accused gives evidence and his evidence is adopted in counsel's closing speech or where ... suggestions are put to witnesses albeit that they are not accepted' (*R* v. *Webber* [2002] EWCA Crim 2782).

The word 'fact' has been interpreted to mean not only 'an actual deed or thing done', but also 'something that is actually the case ... as opposed to ... a conjecture'; so it is wide enough to encompass a previously undisclosed explanation for aspects of the prosecution case which are not in dispute at the trial, such as the defence of 'innocent association' (*R* v. *Milford* [2001] Crim LR 330 (CA)). In *R* v. *Nickolson* [1999] Crim LR 61 (CA) it was held that the accused's conjectural explanation in the witness box as to how his step-daughter's night-dress might have come to be stained with semen could not be construed as a 'fact'. However, in *R* v. *B(MT)* [2000] Crim LR 181 the Court of Appeal acknowledged that a suggested explanation cannot always be divorced from 'facts'. If the accused's explanation at trial was in his mind when interviewed, and was based on a specific incident of which he was also then aware, then both his explanation and the preceding incident could be 'facts', and an adverse inference would be permissible if he could reasonably have been expected to mention them to the police.

In *R* v. *Ali* [2001] EWCA Crim 863 it was held that, if the accused provided 'no comment' responses to the questions put to him by the police during his interview, but he did (at that time) provide the police with a prepared statement which disclosed the essential facts of his defence, then it was not permissible to draw an adverse inference under s. 34. It would seem, moreover, that no inference will be drawn where there has been unequivocal pre-interview disclosure of the 'fact' relied on by the accused (see *R* v. *O(A)* [2000] Crim LR 617 (CA)).

In *R* v. *Mountford* [1999] Crim LR 575 (CA) and *R* v. *Gill* [2001] 1 Cr App R 160 (CA) it was held that where the fact relied on is so central to the accused's defence that its rejection would inevitably lead to a verdict of guilty, and the s. 34 issue cannot therefore be resolved as an independent issue, no adverse inference should be drawn. This approach (for which no support can be found in the Act) has now been rejected, for if it were to be applied generally to cover the range of cases in which innocent explanations are belatedly advanced at trial, the very purpose of the provision would be defeated (*R* v. *Hearne* (2000) unreported (99/4240/Z4) (CA), *R* v. *Milford* [2001] Crim LR 330 (CA) (99/07176/Y4), *R* v. *Gowland-Wynn* [2002] 1 Cr App R 569 (CA), *R* v. *Daly* [2002] 2 Cr App R 201 (CA), *R* v. *Chenia* [2003] 2 Cr App R 83 (CA)).

9.2.2.1 The Propriety of Drawing an Inference

Section 34(1) expressly provides that an inference may be drawn only if the fact relied on by the accused in his defence, but not mentioned in his police interview, is one 'which in the circumstances existing at the time the accused could reasonably have been expected to mention'. A suspect cannot reasonably be expected to mention a fact of which he is unaware, so where the accused was charged with a sexual offence, and at the time of his interview neither the police nor he knew of the seminal staining on the complainant's clothes, his failure to explain the stain to the police could not permit an adverse inference to be drawn (*R* v. *Nickolson* [1999] Crim LR 61 (CA)). Similarly, in *R* v. *Stocker* [2001] EWCA Crim 1334 no adverse inference could be drawn from the accused's failure to explain the presence of his fingerprints at the scene of two burglaries, as it had not been proved that he knew his fingerprints had been found by the police (see also *R* v. *B(MT)* [2000] Crim LR 181 (CA)). It would not be reasonable to expect a suspect to mention a specific fact which he was aware of if he was unaware of its significance and the police did not expressly ask him about it; but this does not mean that a *specific* question pertaining to the fact must always be put during the interview. If it can be proved that the accused knew of the fact and its significance, and he could reasonably have been expected to mention it during the interview, an adverse inference may be drawn if that fact was subsequently relied on in his defence. Thus, in *R* v. *Flynn* [2001] EWCA Crim 1633 an adverse inference could be drawn from the accused's failure to mention his defence that, at the time of the fatal road accident caused by his driving, he had not been affected by alcohol, because the police had begun his (first) interview by setting out what he had said at the scene and explaining that his roadside breath test had proved positive.

The most important question in practical terms is the extent to which a suspect may rely on his solicitor's advice not to answer police questions as a reason in support of a submission that the judge should direct the jury not to draw an adverse inference. This question first arose in *R* v. *Condron* [1997] 1 WLR 827, where the Court of Appeal held that the key issue was not so much the advice given by the solicitor as the reason why the accused had chosen to remain silent, which was generally a question for the jury. The fact that the accused had acted on his solicitor's advice could be put forward as an argument to dissuade the jury from drawing an adverse inference, but this would usually require the reason for that advice to be revealed too. It was recognised, however, that it would be possible to have a 'no comment' interview excluded (following a *voir dire* if necessary) if there had been significant breaches of the Police and Criminal Evidence Act 1984 Codes of Practice, justifying the application of s. 78(1) of that Act, or where it 'would be perverse of a jury to draw an adverse inference', such as where the accused was 'of very low intelligence and understanding and [had] been advised by his solicitor to say nothing'. In other cases a submission that the jury should be directed not to draw an adverse inference would have to be made at the end of the defence case, although it was thought that 'the judge is likely to consider that the question why the defendant did not answer is one for the jury'.

In *R* v. *Argent* [1997] 2 Cr App R 27 the accused was questioned by the police as to whether he had been involved in the death by stabbing of a man outside a London nightclub. The interview followed an identification parade at which he had been positively identified, but his solicitor felt that as the police had failed to make full disclosure of their case he would be well-advised to remain silent, this advice being in line with the Law Society's guidelines. The accused gave a 'no comment' interview, but testified at trial that he had not been involved in any act of violence after leaving the nightclub. The judge therefore directed the jury that they were entitled to draw an adverse inference from his pre-trial silence, and the accused was convicted of manslaughter. Dismissing his appeal, the Court of Appeal reiterated its position that, as a general rule, the question of drawing inferences under s. 34 should be left to the jury with a careful direction from the judge. The jury would be directed to take account of all the relevant circumstances existing at the time of the interview, and the advice given to the accused by his solicitor was only one factor amongst many others. Lord Bingham CJ usefully summarised the correct approach (at p. 33):

'The courts should not construe the expression "in the circumstances" restrictively: matters such as time of day, the defendant's age, experience, mental capacity, state of health, sobriety, tiredness, knowledge, personality and legal advice are all part of the relevant circumstances; and those are only examples of things which may be relevant. When reference is made to 'the accused' attention is directed not to some hypothetical, reasonable accused of ordinary phlegm and fortitude but to the actual accused with such qualities, apprehensions, knowledge and advice as he is shown to have had at the time. It is for the jury to decide whether the fact (or facts) which the defendant has relied on in his defence in the criminal trial, but which he had not mentioned when questioned under caution ... is (or are) a fact (or facts) which in the circumstances as they actually existed the actual defendant could reasonably have been expected to mention. Like so many other questions in criminal trials this is a question to be resolved by the jury in the exercise of their collective common-sense, experience and understanding of human nature. Sometimes they may conclude that it was reasonable for the defendant to have held his peace for a host of reasons, such as that he was tired, ill, frightened, drunk, drugged, unable to understand what was going on, suspicious of the police, afraid that his answer would not be fairly recorded, worried at committing himself without legal advice, acting on legal advice, or some other reason accepted by the jury. In other cases the jury may conclude, after hearing all that the defendant and his witnesses may have to say about the reasons for failing to mention the fact or facts in issue, that he could reasonably have been expected to do so. This is an issue on which the judge may, and usually should, give appropriate directions. But he should ordinarily leave the issue to the jury to decide. Only rarely would it be right for the judge to direct the jury that they should, or should not, draw the appropriate inference.'

Accordingly, the jury are not concerned with the correctness of the solicitor's advice to remain silent, nor with whether the advice complied with the Law Society's guidelines. The question they need to answer is simply whether the accused's decision to remain silent was reasonable in all the circumstances. Neither the allegation against Argent nor his defence was particularly complex, so it would have been reasonable for him to give his account notwithstanding the inadequate disclosure by the police, particularly as he already knew the main thrust of the case against him and that he had been positively identified. In different circumstances, though, a refusal to comment following legal advice on the basis of inadequate police disclosure may well persuade the jury that the accused's silence was reasonable. In *R* v. *Roble* [1997] Crim LR 449 (CA) Rose LJ commented that it could be reasonable to remain silent where 'the interviewing officer has disclosed to the solicitor little or nothing of the nature of the case against the defendant, so that the solicitor cannot usefully advise his client, or where the nature of the offence or the material in the hands of the police is so complex, or relates to matters so long ago, that no sensible immediate response is feasible'. However, in *R* v. *Beard* [2002] Crim LR 684 the Court of Appeal held that it had been appropriate to allow the jury to draw an adverse inference from B's 'no comment' interviews, even though his solicitor had not understood the nature or relevance of the seized documents which had been disclosed and had advised B to remain silent. Most of the disclosed documents had been recovered from B himself, so he could have explained to his solicitor what each of them meant; and the majority of the unanswered questions did not even relate to the disclosed documents. (Another reason for the solicitor's advice was that the police should not be given an opportunity to link the instant allegation with a separate allegation the accused faced, but as there was nothing to suggest that any of the questions put to B were irrelevant to the instant allegation that argument for not drawing an inference was also rejected.)

In *Condron* v. *United Kingdom* (2000) 31 EHRR 1 (at p. 21) the European Court of Human Rights said: '[T]he very fact that an accused is advised by his lawyer to maintain his silence must . . . be given appropriate weight by the domestic court. There may be good reason why such advice may be given.' The same point was made in *Averill* v. *United Kingdom* (2000) 31 EHRR 839 (at p. 854), where the Court said that 'due regard' must be given to whether the accused's silence is based on *bona fide* advice received from his lawyer; and in *Beckles* v. *United Kingdom* (2002) Application No. 44652/98 the Court held that the trial judge's direction to the jury had failed to give appropriate weight to the accused's explanation that he had remained silent on the advice of his solicitor and the background matters which made that explanation plausible. Following the decision in *Condron* v. *United Kingdom*, the Court of Appeal concluded in *R* v. *Betts* [2001] 2 Cr App R 257 that no adverse inference should be drawn from the accused's silence under s. 34 if 'it is a plausible explanation that the reason for not mentioning facts is that [he] acted on the advice of his solicitor and not because he had no, or no satisfactory, answer to give'.

However, in *R* v. *Howell* [2003] EWCA Crim 1, a case where the allegation was that the accused had seriously assaulted the complainant, the Court of Appeal noted that the European Court of Human Rights had referred to remaining silent for 'good reason', and rejected the view that adverse comment is disallowed merely because it is shown that a solicitor's advice (of whatever quality) had genuinely been relied on. Giving the judgment of the Court, Laws LJ said (at para. 24):

'[T]he public interest that inheres in reasonable disclosure by a suspected person of what he has to say when faced with a set of facts which accuse him is thwarted if currency is given to the belief that if a suspect remains silent on legal advice he may systematically avoid adverse comment at his trial. And it may encourage solicitors to advise silence for other than good objective reasons. . . . What is reasonable depends on all the circumstances. We venture to say, recalling the circumstances of this present case, that we do not consider the absence of a written statement from the complainant to be good reason for silence (if adequate oral disclosure of the complaint has been given), and it does not become good reason merely because a solicitor has so advised. Nor is the possibility that the complainant may not pursue his complaint good reason, nor a belief by the solicitor that the suspect will be charged in any event whatever he says. The kind of circumstance which may most likely justify silence will be such matters as the suspect's condition (ill-health, in particular mental disability; confusion; intoxication; shock and so forth ...), or his inability genuinely to recollect events without reference to documents which are not to hand, or communication with other persons who may be able to assist his recollection. There must always be soundly based objective reasons for silence, sufficiently cogent and telling to weigh in the balance against the clear public interest in an account being given by the suspect to the police. Solicitors bearing the important responsibility of giving advice to suspects at police stations must always have that in mind.'

It follows that, regardless of any legal advice he has received, a suspect may be obliged to provide a response to a bare allegation, even if it is unsubstantiated by any other evidence and there is a risk that it has been concocted or embellished by the complainant.

9.2.2.2 The Nature of the Inference Drawn

No guidance is given in the Act as to what amounts to a 'proper' inference under s. 34, but, as noted in *R* v. *Self* (1999) unreported (98/6128/W2) (CA), it would not assist the jury to speak generally of inferences without indicating what those inferences might be. Silence in response to police questioning followed by an explanation at trial is most likely to lead to an inference that the explanation was subsequently fabricated, allowing the jury to infer that the accused has no true defence and, therefore, that he is more likely to have committed the offence charged. It now seems to be established, however, that post-interview fabrication is not the only permissible inference which may be drawn (notwithstanding the contrary view expressed in *R* v. *Samuel* (1997) unreported (97/1143/Z2) (CA)). It is also permissible for the jury to infer that the accused had already prepared his false account by the time of the interview, knowing that it was one which would not withstand scrutiny if revealed in advance of the trial (*R* v. *Randall* (1998) unreported (97/05960/X4) (CA)). In *R* v. *Daniel* [1998] 2 Cr App R 373 the Court of Appeal stated that in appropriate cases the jury would be entitled to conclude that the accused's silence could only sensibly be attributed to his unwillingness to be subjected to further questioning when in a compromising position or to his having no innocent explanation when questioned or to his not having thought out all the facts (see also *R* v. *Argent* [1997] 2 Cr App R 27 (CA) at p. 34 and *R* v. *Beckles* [1999] Crim LR 148 (CA)). In *R* v. *Milford* [2001] Crim LR 330 (99/07176/Y4) the Court of Appeal reviewed the authorities and approved the broader approach, stating (at para. 33) that the inference which may be drawn is not limited to one of recent fabrication, but 'extends to a fact or explanation tailored to fit the prosecution case or which the defendant believed would not stand up to scrutiny at the time'.

9.2.2.3 Establishing a Case to Answer

Inferences from the accused's failure 'to mention any fact relied on in his defence' may also be drawn by the judge (or magistrates) at 'half time' to see whether the prosecution have established a case to answer (s. 34(2)(*c*)), although it is not permissible to rely solely on any such inference (s. 38(3)). Because the defence case is not heard prior to a submission of no case to answer, there will be few opportunities for the courts to rely on s. 34(2)(*c*); but this does not mean the provision is otiose. In *R* v. *McLernon* [1992] NI 168 (NICA) it was accepted that an inference could be drawn (under an equivalent provision) where 'defence counsel suggested a fact, which assisted the accused, to a prosecution witness in the course of cross-examination and the witness accepted it'. In *R* v. *Bowers* (1998) 163 JP 33 the Court of Appeal was of the view that a fact relied on may be established by a prosecution witness in evidence in chief or in cross-examination; and in *R* v. *Webber* [2002] EWCA Crim 2782 it was held that a fact relied on could be a suggestion put to a prosecution witness in cross-examination whether or not that witness accepted it. In *R* v. *Hart* [1998] CLY 374 (97/03362/W4) the Court of Appeal envisaged that s. 34(2)(*c*) could also be triggered where the accused 'has chosen to refuse to answer questions when initially interviewed but some time later, after consulting his solicitor, has produced a prepared statement or has given later answers'. In *R* v. *McLernon* [1992] NI 168 the accused had refused to answer police questions for several days but subsequently prepared an exculpatory written statement prior to his trial. The Northern Ireland Court of Appeal held that the judge had been entitled to draw a half-time adverse inference from the accused's refusal to speak when interviewed as his exculpatory statement contained facts he was relying on in his defence which he could reasonably have been expected to mention in the course of his interviews. At the trial defence counsel had expressly conceded that the accused was relying on the facts in the exculpatory statement as part of his defence, and for this reason it was felt an inference could be drawn even though the statement had been adduced by the prosecution as part of their case. Arguably, though, it should not be possible to draw a 'proper' inference if the prosecution have adduced an exculpatory or mixed statement and there has been no such concession from the defence. For one thing, a purely exculpatory statement would be admissible only as evidence of the accused's reaction and not as evidence of any facts stated (16.4.2.4 *post*); and the exculpatory part of a mixed statement, though admissible hearsay, has 'minimal' weight in the absence of other supporting evidence (*Western* v. *DPP* [1997] 1 Cr App R 474 (DC)).

If the accused manages to get to half time without triggering s. 34(2)(*c*), but the judge rules that there is a case to answer, the accused may decide to 'put the prosecution to proof' by refusing to testify and adducing no evidence. If the accused does this it will not be permissible for the jury to draw an inference under s. 34(2)(*d*) as he will not have relied on any facts in his defence (*R* v. *Moshaid* [1998] Crim LR 420 (CA)); but his failure to testify may allow an adverse inference to be drawn under s. 35 of the Act (9.3.2 *post*). The situation may be different, however, if the accused is tried with a co-accused who adopts a more active line of defence. If the judge rules that the accused has relied on facts relied on by his co-accused, it is possible that s. 34(2)(*d*) will be triggered and an adverse inference drawn from his pre-trial silence, notwithstanding his own refusal to testify (*R* v. *Reader* (1998) unreported (97/06342/W2) (CA)).

9.2.2.4 Directing the Jury

Guidelines for directing the jury on s. 34 were first established in *R* v. *Condron* [1997] 1 WLR 827 (CA), where it was held that the judge should explain the basis for drawing an inference under s. 34; that the burden of proof remains with the prosecution; that the accused was entitled to remain silent during his interview (or when charged); that the jury are entitled but not obliged to draw an adverse inference from his silence; and that, if an adverse inference is drawn, it cannot of itself prove the accused's guilt but may be taken into account as some additional support for the prosecution case (in line with s. 38(3) of the Act). The Court of Appeal also thought it would be 'desirable' for the judge to explain to the jury that an adverse inference may be drawn only once they have concluded that the accused's silence 'can only sensibly be attributed to [his] having no answer, or none that would stand up to cross-examination'. In *Condron* v. *United Kingdom* (2000) 31 EHRR 1, however, the European Court of Human Rights held that this last direction was more than merely desirable. Indeed, the absence of this additional restriction on the jury's discretion to draw an adverse inference had been incompatible with the exercise by the applicants of their right to silence at the police station, meaning that there had been a violation of their Article 6(1) right to a fair trial. Accordingly, the Court of Appeal has now held that the trial judge must also direct the jury that, before they are able to draw an adverse inference under s. 34, they must be satisfied that the real reason for the accused's silence is that he had no innocent explanation to offer (*R* v. *Milford* [2001] Crim LR 330, *R* v. *Morgan* [2001] EWCA Crim 445, *R* v. *Chenia* [2003] 2 Cr App R 83 (CA)); or, to put it another way, the jury must be satisfied that the only sensible explanation for the accused's silence is that he had no answer to the charge or none that would stand up to questioning and investigation (*R* v. *Betts* [2001] 2 Cr App R 257 (CA), *R* v. *Daly* [2002] 2 Cr App R 201 (CA), *R* v. *Chenia* [2003] 2 Cr App R 83 (CA)).

The jury must be referred to any fact which the accused has relied on in his defence but which was not mentioned during his interview or when charged (see, for example, *R* v. *Gill* [2001] 1 Cr App R 160 (CA)). A direction must also be given, in line with the guidance provided in *R* v. *Argent* [1997] 2 Cr App R 27 (CA) and subsequent cases (9.2.2.1 *ante*), that an inference may be drawn only if the jury are satisfied that the fact relied on is one which, in the circumstances existing at the time, the accused could reasonably have been expected to mention; and the jury must be told that appropriate weight is to be given to the accused's explanation that he remained silent on the advice of his solicitor. Where the jury are being asked to infer that the accused has lied, it may also be appropriate to supplement the s. 34 direction with a *Lucas* direction (*R* v. *O(A)* [2000] Crim LR 617 (CA); see also 11.6 *post*).

As noted above, the jury must be told that an adverse inference from silence cannot of itself prove the accused's guilt; but the jury should also be directed that an inference may be drawn only if they are first satisfied that there is a *prima facie* case against the accused on the basis of other evidence (*R* v. *Milford* [2001] Crim LR 330, *R* v. *Morgan* [2001] EWCA Crim 445, *R* v. *Gill* [2001] 1 Cr App R 160 (CA)). This further safeguard reflects the view of the European Court of Human Rights that the extent to which adverse inferences may be drawn from the accused's failure to respond to police questioning 'must be necessarily limited' (*Averill* v. *United Kingdom* (2000) 31 EHRR 839 at p. 853). In effect, though, it is no more than a restatement of the requirement that an adverse inference should provide no more than 'some additional support' for the prosecution case, ensuring that a conviction will not be based only *or even mainly* on the accused's pre-trial silence (*R* v. *Everson* [2001] EWCA Crim 896).

Where there are inconsistencies between the accused's version of events at trial and the version given by him during his interview, the trial judge has a discretion to give a direction on the relevance of those inconsistencies to the accused's credibility rather than a s. 34 direction (*R* v. *McCaffrey* [2003] EWCA Crim 970). Where, however, the requirements in s. 34(1) have not been satisfied, and no inference may therefore be drawn under s. 34(2)(*d*), it is incumbent on the trial judge to direct the jury not to draw an adverse inference from the accused's pre-trial silence (*R* v. *McGarry* [1999] 1 Cr App R 377 (CA)). That said, a failure to give such a 'counterweight direction' is unlikely to affect the safety of the conviction if the accused refused to say anything before the trial and refused to testify in his own defence (*R* v. *La Rose* [2003] EWCA Crim 1471). The Court of Appeal has also said that 'it may well be that in many cases where the guilt or innocence of two or more defendants stands or falls together' it 'will generally be desirable' to direct the jury that an adverse inference drawn from the silence of one should not be held against the other (*R* v. *McClean* (1999) unreported (98/01354/R2)).

9.2.2.5 Privilege and Waiver

If the accused's reason for remaining silent in the face of police interrogation is that he followed his solicitor's advice and it was reasonable for him to do so, his assertion will need to be supported by admissible evidence. The accused and/or his solicitor will therefore need to give evidence of what passed between them; but by giving such evidence the accused will be deemed to have waived his legal professional privilege (14.2.3 *post*) and he (and his solicitor, if called) will face cross-examination on all aspects of the advice which was given, including any tactical reasons for giving it. In *R* v. *Bowden* [1999] 1 WLR 823 the Court of Appeal held that legal professional privilege could be waived whether the explanation was given by the accused or his solicitor, regardless of whether it was given during the interview or at the trial, save that a 'simple statement' at the trial to the effect that the accused did not answer questions following legal advice (or a statement at the interview to the same effect) would not amount to waiver. Where the accused makes such a 'simple statement' during cross-examination, the privileged nature of the matter means that it should not be pursued by the prosecution or the judge; it is for defence counsel to decide whether to question the accused during re-examination on the advice he was given (*R* v. *Wood* [2002] EWCA Crim 2474).

In *R* v. *Fitzgerald* (1998) unreported (97/2011/W5) F's solicitor made a statement at the start of the police interview to explain why F would remain silent. He said that he had spoken to F and was concerned 'that the possible involvement of other parties ... may prevent him from putting his defence fully and frankly'. At his trial for robbery F gave evidence that he had simply been in the area by chance to meet friends in a local public house and had not been involved in the offence. The Court of Appeal held that the prosecution had been entitled to adduce in evidence the solicitor's statement as it was relevant to whether an adverse inference should be drawn under s. 34 and it had been made in the presence and hearing of F. F had therefore impliedly accepted the truth of his solicitor's statement by not dissenting from it (see 9.2.1 *ante*). Moreover, by making that statement to the police the solicitor had waived the privilege which had hitherto attached to what F had told him in confidence.

9.2.3 Sections 36 and 37 of the Criminal Justice and Public Order Act 1994

Section 36 of the 1994 Act provides that where at the time of the accused's arrest there was an object, substance or mark (or a mark on any such object) (i) on his person or (ii) in or on his clothing or footwear or (iii) otherwise in his possession or (iv) in any place in which he was at the time of his arrest, which the arresting officer or another investigating officer reasonably believed might be attributable to his participation in the commission of a specified offence, then so long as he was told of the officer's belief, asked to account for the presence of the object (etc.) and warned of the consequences of his failing or refusing to comply with the request, evidence of his failure or refusal to comply will allow the tribunal of fact to draw such inferences as appear proper in determining whether he is guilty of the specified offence (s. 36(2)(*d*)). Section 36 inferences may also be drawn by the court in determining whether there is a case to answer (s. 36(2)(*c*)). However, it is not permissible to determine that there is a case to answer, or find the accused guilty, solely on the basis of any such inference (s. 38(3)). Section 36 applies equally to the condition of clothing or footwear as it applies to any substance or mark thereon (s. 36(3)).

The drawing of adverse inferences under s. 36 was recently considered in *R* v. *Compton* [2002] EWCA Crim 2835, where the Court of Appeal came to the following conclusions. First, it is sufficient if the accused was informed by the officer of the 'offence-context' ('drug-trafficking') even if he was not informed of the particular offence with which he was ultimately charged (conspiracy to supply drugs). Second, the accused must account 'for a specific state of fact' and not merely refer to 'other states of fact, from which it can be inferred what his account might be'. Thus, when D1 was re-interviewed and provided 'no comment' responses following the detection of heroin on the substantial amount of money found at his address, his statement at an earlier interview (prior to the discovery of the contamination) to the effect that his wife was a heroin addict and he had received the money from his father, a known dealer, meant that he had not accounted for the presence of heroin on the money. Third, a relevant response from the accused will not necessarily prevent an adverse inference being drawn. D2, in whose safe the contaminated sum of £30,000 was found, had responded to questions relating to the contamination by stating that he was a heroin addict. It was held that he had not accounted for the presence of heroin on the money by this bare assertion that he used heroin. Finally, with regard to the direction to be given if the accused gave a 'no comment' interview following legal advice, the Court of Appeal held that the judgment in *R* v. *Betts* [2001] 2 Cr App R 257 (CA) on directions under s. 34 was also relevant to the judge's task under s. 36. The jury must be told that they can hold the accused's failure to give an explanation against him only if they are sure that he had no reasonable explanation to offer: they have 'to be sure *both* that the solicitor's advice was not an adequate explanation for the silence *and* that there was no innocent explanation' (see now *R* v. *Howell* [2003] EWCA Crim 1, 9.2.2.1 *ante*).

Section 37 allows inferences to be drawn from the failure of the accused to explain his presence at a particular place (defined in s. 38(1)) at or about the time of the offence. The provision is very similar to s. 36: the accused must have been arrested, the arresting or investigating officer must have reasonably believed his presence at that place and at that time was possibly attributable to his participation in the commission of the offence, the accused must have been informed of the officer's belief and asked to account for his presence, and he must have failed or refused to give an explanation. If these conditions are satisfied such inferences as appear proper may be drawn from the accused's silence. Again, any inference may be taken into account by the tribunal of fact in determining whether the accused is guilty (s. 37(2)(*d*)) or by the court when determining whether there is a case to answer (s. 37(2)(*c*)); but neither of these decisions may be reached solely on the basis of the inference (s. 38(3)).

Sections 36 and 37 allow inferences to be drawn from silence in a variety of situations whether or not the accused gives an innocent explanation at his trial. An example would be where the accused failed to explain his presence near the scene of a pub 'glassing' soon after the offence was committed (s. 37) and/or failed to explain the blood and shards of glass on his clothes (s. 36). The tribunal of fact will of course need to consider all the circumstances before drawing an adverse inference, particularly the accused's explanation; but there is no requirement in either section that the accused should reasonably have been expected to explain the object or mark, or his presence, before an inference can be drawn. Where the prosecution seek to rely on these provisions the jury will be invited to conclude that the accused had no innocent explanation to give the police. They will then be entitled to infer that he is more likely to be guilty of the offence charged.

9.2.4 Other Provisions

The accused's failure to provide a 'defence statement' to the prosecution prior to trial on indictment, in accordance with the requirements of s. 5 of the Criminal Procedure and Investigations Act 1996, allows the jury to draw an adverse inference when deciding whether he is guilty (s. 11). Adverse inferences may also be drawn if the accused's defence at trial is inconsistent with that disclosed in his statement, or where he relies on an alibi at trial which was not disclosed in his statement (see generally 13.1.2 *post*). The Police and Criminal Evidence Act 1984 allows the police to take an intimate sample (defined in s. 65) so long as the accused has given his consent, but if the accused refuses to give such consent without good cause the tribunal of fact may draw 'such inferences from the refusal as appear proper' in determining whether he is guilty of the offence charged (s. 62(10)(*b*)). An adverse inference may also be drawn in determining whether there is a case to answer (s. 62(10)(*a*)(ii)). In civil proceedings, s. 23(1) of the Family Law Reform Act 1969 provides that, where the court gives a direction under s. 20(1)(*b*) for the taking of a bodily sample from a person to determine parentage, and that person fails to take any step required of him for the purpose of giving effect to that direction, the court may draw from his failure 'such inferences ... as appear proper in the circumstances'.

9.3 Silence During the Trial

Over the last century or so there has been a marked change in attitude towards the accused's absence from the witness box in criminal proceedings. Before 1898 the accused did not enjoy the general right to testify in his own defence. This was altered by s. 1 of the Criminal Evidence Act 1898 which made him competent, but not compellable, raising the issue of what (if anything) could be inferred from his refusal to testify and what (if any) comments could legitimately be made by the trial judge. (The prosecution were prohibited from commenting by s. 1(*b*) of the 1898 Act.) Section 35 of the Criminal Justice and Public Order Act 1994 now expressly permits the tribunal of fact to draw adverse inferences from the accused's failure to testify; and s. 1(*b*) of the 1898 Act has been repealed. The position in civil proceedings continues to be governed by the common law.

9.3.1 The Position at Common Law

In civil proceedings the failure of the defendant to testify or call evidence to rebut a *prima facie* case established by the claimant allows the tribunal of fact to draw an inference strengthening the claimant's case. A recent example is provided by *Francisco* v. *Diedrick* (1998) *The Times* 3.4.98 (QBD), where the plaintiff established a *prima facie* case that the defendant had committed a tort on her daughter – that he had assaulted and killed her – but the defendant refused to give evidence in his own defence. Alliott J held that the effect of the defendant's refusal to testify was to turn the *prima facie* case into a very strong case against him.

In an appropriate case the trial judge in criminal proceedings may comment on the accused's failure to call a material witness in support of his defence, certainly if that witness could not have been called by the prosecution and there is no good reason for his absence. In *R* v. *Khan* [2001] EWCA Crim 486 the Court of Appeal noted that, in the absence of guidance from the judge, the jury would inevitably speculate as to why a witness had not given evidence and as to the evidence the witness might have given, and recognised that there are situations where the jury would be entitled to ask themselves why a witness had not been called. (Examples are *R* v. *Gallagher* [1974] 1 WLR 1204 (CA), where the prosecution could not have known before the close of their case that the absent witness had relevant evidence to give, and *R* v. *Wilmot* (1988) 89 Cr App R 341 (CA), where the absent witness, the accused's solicitor, could not have been called by the prosecution to give evidence of what he had been told by the accused.) It was also noted, however, that an adverse comment on the accused's failure to call a witness might lead to injustice in some cases as there could be a good reason for the witness's absence. According to the Court, the dangers of making adverse comments and of failing to warn the jury not to speculate would usually be the paramount consideration; but it was also recognised that the case for permitting a comment on the accused's failure to call an available witness might be stronger now that adverse comments are permissible under s. 34 of the Criminal Justice and Public Order Act 1994 (9.2.2 *ante*) and s. 11 of the Criminal Procedure and Investigations Act 1996 (13.1.2 *post*). In the final analysis, 'much depends on the judge's sense of fairness in the particular situation', save that the judge should invite submissions from both parties in the absence of the jury before deciding whether to make an adverse comment; and if the judge does comment it would in some cases be appropriate to refer to the burden of proving the case remaining with the prosecution. These guidelines were approved by the Court of Appeal in *R* v. *G(R)* [2003] Crim LR 43.

The trial judge's entitlement to comment on the accused's failure to testify in his own defence is now governed by s. 35 of the Criminal Justice and Public Order Act 1994 (9.3.2 *post*); but even before the Act came into force the judge was entitled at common law to comment on the accused's failure to testify once he had become a competent witness (*R* v. *Rhodes* [1899] 1 QB 77 (CCCR)). In the light of the judge's comments, an appropriate inference strengthening the prosecution case could be drawn. The nature and degree of the judge's comments were regarded as matters within his discretion, so long as it was made clear that the accused was entitled not to give evidence and that guilt could not be assumed merely because he had exercised that right (see *R* v. *Martinez-Tobon* [1994] 1 WLR 388 (CA)). It has been noted above that the prosecution could not comment on the accused's failure to testify; but no such restriction operated against a co-accused (*R* v. *Wickham* (1971) 55 Cr App R 199

(CA)). Further, regardless of whether the judge or counsel for the co-accused commented on the accused's refusal to testify, there can be little doubt that the jury would often apply their collective common sense and draw an adverse inference in any event.

9.3.2 Section 35 of the Criminal Justice and Public Order Act 1994

Section 35, implementing a recommendation in the Criminal Law Revision Committee's Eleventh Report ((1972) Cmnd 4991 at pp. 68–70), provides a further evidential factor in support of the prosecution case where the accused either fails to testify or does testify but refuses to answer some of the questions put to him. The accused's common-law 'right of silence' remains, however, to the extent that he cannot be compelled to testify in his own defence (s. 35(4)). Section 35 is not a particularly radical departure from the position at common law, but it does give the judge a far wider discretion as to the comments he may properly make. Section 168(3) of the Act (and Schedule 11 thereto) repealed s. 1(*b*) of the Criminal Evidence Act 1898, which formerly prohibited the prosecution from commenting on the accused's failure to testify.

Subsections (1) and (3) provide that where an accused is on trial for a criminal offence then, unless his physical or mental condition makes it undesirable for him to give evidence, his failure to give evidence or his refusal without good cause to answer any question once sworn permits the tribunal of fact to 'draw such inferences as appear proper' from such failure or refusal when determining whether he is guilty of the offence. If the accused has been sworn and he refuses to answer any question, such refusal will be without good cause unless he is entitled to refuse on the ground of privilege or any enactment, or he is excused from answering the question by the court (s. 35(5)), or there is no issue calling for a factual explanation or answer from the accused (*R* v. *McManus* [2001] EWCA Crim 2455). (For the relevant procedural rules, see s. 35(2) and *Practice Direction (Criminal Proceedings: Consolidation)* [2002] 1 WLR 2870 (SC) at pp. 2902–3.) The court must satisfy itself that the accused is aware of his right to testify and the adverse consequences of failing to do so, even if he has voluntarily absconded (*R* v. *Gough* [2002] 2 Cr App R 121 (CA); see also *Radford* v. *Kent County Council* (1998) 162 JP 697 (DC)).

In *R* v. *Cowan* [1995] 3 WLR 818, the leading case on s. 35, the Court of Appeal held that apart from the mandatory exception in s. 35(1)(*b*) – where the accused's physical or mental condition makes it undesirable for him to give evidence – the judge has a 'broad discretion' as to whether and in what terms he should direct the jury, save that while it would generally be open to the judge to direct the jury against drawing an adverse inference, 'there would need either to be some evidential basis for doing so or some exceptional factors in the case making that a fair course to take'. (It is not permissible for the accused's advocate to give theoretical reasons for his silence in the absence of supporting evidence.) It was further held that the judge should explain in his summing-up that the accused is entitled not to testify and that an adverse inference can be drawn by the jury only if they are first satisfied that the prosecution have established a case to answer. If this is done and, in spite of any evidence relied upon by the accused to explain his silence, the jury conclude that his silence can only sensibly be attributed to his having no answer or none that would stand up to cross-examination, they may draw an adverse inference. It was stressed that so long as an adequate direction on the law is given, the Court of Appeal will not lightly interfere with the way the judge has exercised his discretion. The importance of an adequate direction, particularly in respect of the jury being satisfied that there is a case to answer before drawing an adverse inference, was reaffirmed by the Court of Appeal in *R* v. *Birchall* [1999] Crim LR 311 (96/2301/W5) where Lord Bingham CJ noted that 'logic demands that a jury should not start to consider whether they should draw inferences from a defendant's failure to give oral evidence at his trial until they have concluded that the Crown's case against him is sufficiently compelling to call for an answer by him'. If the accused were to be required to provide an explanation before a *prima facie* case has been established, he would in effect be under an obligation to prove his innocence in violation of Article 6(2) of the European Convention on Human Rights (*Telfner* v. *Austria* (2001) Application 33501/96 (ECtHR); see also *Murray* v. *United Kingdom* (1996) 22 EHRR 29 (ECtHR) at pp. 62–3). That said, a failure to provide any aspect of the s. 35 direction will not necessarily result in a successful appeal: if it is plain on the evidence, in the light of the directions which were given, that the conviction is safe, it will stand notwithstanding the judge's omission (*R* v. *Bromfield* [2002] EWCA Crim 195).

Where the accused is so mentally disturbed as to be unfit to plead, s. 35 is of course irrelevant. However, in the situation where a mentally subnormal accused *is* fit to stand trial, the judge must determine whether he falls within the s.35(1)(*b*) exception. A situation of this sort arose in *R* v. *Friend* [1997] 1 WLR 1433. The accused, who did not give evidence, was a 15-year-old boy with a mental age lower than that of a 10-year-old and an IQ lower than 70. These facts comprised the evidential basis for the defence submission that the accused's mental condition made it undesirable for him to give evidence and that no adverse inference should be drawn. The judge rejected the submission, having taken into account the accused's responses in his interviews with the police and a clinical psychologist, and expert evidence that the accused was less suggestible than average people, and directed the jury that they could draw an adverse inference. The Court of Appeal, dismissing the appeal, held that the judge had been entitled to consider not only the clinical psychologist's evidence and the other evidence in the case, but also the accused's conduct before and after the offence was committed and the answers he had given in his police interview. The judge's exercise of his discretion could be impugned only if it was '*Wednesbury* unreasonable', but in this case the judge had reached his conclusion in a balanced and proper manner, taking into account relevant matters and disregarding irrelevant matters. The Court did, however, give examples of when it might be undesirable for an accused to testify: 'A physical condition might include a risk of an epileptic attack; a mental condition, latent schizophrenia where the experience of giving evidence might trigger a florid state.' In *R* v. *Lee* [1998] CLY 320 (CC) the trial judge observed that it could be undesirable for an accused to testify if the act of giving evidence itself would be likely to cause his mental state to deteriorate or be likely to lead to embarrassing outbursts which could prejudice the jury against him.

The Court of Appeal has declined to give examples of what might prevent an adverse judicial comment on the accused's silence on the ground that each case must turn on its own facts. Any reason put forward for not drawing an inference must of course be relevant to the accused's failure to testify, but relevance will not necessarily guarantee that the judge's discretion will be exercised in the accused's favour. In *R* v. *Cowan* [1995] 3 WLR 818 the Court of Appeal rejected one of the most obvious reasons for not testifying when it stated that the risk of the accused being cross-examined on his bad character under s. 1(3)(ii) of the Criminal Evidence Act 1898 was not a sufficiently good reason for directing the jury against drawing an adverse inference. Moreover, Northern Ireland case-law suggests that neither the fact that the accused has made a statement to the police (*R* v. *Hamill* [1994] 5 BNIL 51 (NICA)) nor that the accused is afraid of having an adverse inference drawn under s. 34 of the Act (*R* v. *McAnoy* [1996] 6 BNIL 50 (NICA)) will prevent the court from applying s. 35 if he refuses to testify. If the accused is particularly inarticulate or nervous it may be possible to persuade the judge to rule that the accused falls within s. 35(1)(*b*) of the Act, but evidence will have to be adduced in the absence of the jury to support the submission. However, if the submission fails there is nothing to prevent the same evidence being adduced before the jury to support a closing speech explaining why the accused has failed to give evidence (*R* v. *A* [1997] Crim LR 883 (CA)). Needless to say, any purported reason for not drawing an adverse inference which has no logical bearing on the accused's failure to testify will get short shrift from the judge and the Court of Appeal. In *R* v. *Napper* (1995) 161 JP 16 (CA) the accused refused to testify at his trial in 1995 on the ground that the police had only questioned him in 1992 about one of the eight counts on the indictment and that it was now too late for him to remember clearly what had happened. This argument failed because the crucial issues in the trial involved matters which the accused would have been able to remember without difficulty, and in any event he could have prepared a memory-refreshing statement soon after being charged with the offences.

The judge is perhaps more likely to direct the jury that an adverse inference can be drawn from silence if there is a strong case against the accused. In other words, if the prosecution case is just sufficient to overcome a submission of no case to answer the judge may feel it would be inappropriate for any adverse inference to be drawn. If the judge does direct the jury that they are entitled to draw an adverse inference from the accused's failure to testify, the jury must consider whether they should draw such an inference and, if so, its nature. The only guidance provided by s. 35 is that the jury 'may draw such inferences as appear proper', but in *Murray* v. *DPP* [1994] 1 WLR 1 (HL), a Northern Ireland case, Lord Mustill said (at p. 5):

'[T]he fact-finder is entitled as a matter of common sense to draw his own conclusions if a defendant who is faced with evidence which does call for an answer fails to come forward and provide it ... It is, however, equally a matter of common sense that even where the prosecution has established a prima facie case ... it is not in every situation that an adverse inference can be drawn from silence .... Everything depends on the nature of the issue, the weight of the evidence adduced by the prosecution upon it ... and the extent to which the defendant should in the nature of things be able to give his own account of the particular matter in question. It is impossible to generalise, for dependent upon circumstances the failure of the defendant to give evidence may found no inference at all, or one which is for all practical purposes fatal.'

In the same case, Lord Slynn said (at p. 11):

'The accused cannot be compelled to give evidence but he must risk the consequences if he does not do so. Those consequences are not simply ... that specific inferences may be drawn from specific facts. They include in a proper case the drawing of an inference that the accused is guilty of the [offence] with which he is charged ... [I]f parts of the prosecution case had so little evidential value that they called for no answer, a failure to deal with those specific matters cannot justify an inference of guilt. On the other hand, if aspects of the evidence taken alone or in combination with other facts clearly call for an explanation which the accused ought to be in a position to give, if an explanation exists, then a failure to give any explanation may as a matter of common sense allow the drawing of an inference that there is no explanation and that the accused is guilty.'

If there is an evidential basis for not drawing an adverse inference, but the judge nonetheless decides to direct the jury that an adverse inference may be drawn, it will be incumbent on him to remind the jury of the defence's explanation (and supporting evidence) so they can take it into account when deciding whether or not to draw an inference. In the absence of any evidence the judge is under no obligation to suggest possible innocent reasons for the accused's failure to testify.

9.4   Silence and Article 6 of the European Convention on Human Rights

In *Murray* v. *United Kingdom* (1996) 22 EHRR 29, a case concerning Northern Ireland's silence provisions, the European Court of Human Rights held (at p. 60) that, while the right to remain silent under police questioning and the privilege against self-incrimination are generally recognised international standards which lie at the heart of the notion of fair procedure under Article 6 of the European Convention, providing protection against improper compulsion by the authorities, they are not absolute immunities. It was further held that, so long as the accused is not convicted solely or mainly on the basis of inferences drawn from his silence, and those inferences are used for the limited purpose of 'assessing the persuasiveness' of the prosecution evidence, the right to remain silent and the privilege against self-incrimination should not prevent the accused's silence in the face of police questioning, or his refusal to testify in his own defence, from being taken into account 'in situations which clearly call for an explanation from him'. The Court added that whether the drawing of adverse inferences from silence infringes Article 6 is a matter to be determined in the light of all the circumstances of the case, having particular regard to the situations where inferences may be drawn, the weight attached to them and the degree of compulsion inherent in the situation. In the instant case adverse inferences had been drawn from the applicant's refusal to answer police questions *and* his refusal to testify in his own defence, but there had been no infringement of Article 6(1) or 6(2). The applicant had been under no direct compulsion (on pain of punishment) to speak to the police or testify; he had been warned of the legal consequences of maintaining his silence; the prosecution had established a *prima facie* case against him on the basis of other evidence; the tribunal of fact, an experienced judge, had been entitled rather than obligated to draw an inference, had given his reasons for drawing inferences, and the exercise of his discretion could be reviewed by the appellate courts; and, finally, the only inferences which could be drawn were 'common sense inferences' arising from the adduction of evidence which was 'sufficiently strong to require an answer'.

Most of the safeguards referred to in *Murray* v. *United Kingdom* (1996) 22 EHRR 29 (ECtHR) apply equally to the silence provisions in ss. 34–37 of the Criminal Justice and Public Order Act 1994, although the impossibility of ascertaining what weight, if any, is given to the accused's silence by a jury, and the Court of Appeal's inability to review the jury's approach, meant there had been a violation of Article 6(1) in *Condron* v. *United Kingdom* (2000) 31 EHRR 1, where the trial judge had failed to give an appropriate direction on s. 34 of the Act (see 9.2.2.4 *ante*). According to the European Court of Human Rights in that case, the absence in England and Wales of these additional safeguards made it 'even more compelling' that the jury should be properly advised on how to address the accused's silence; and the trial judge's omission to restrict the jury's discretion was therefore 'incompatible with the exercise by the applicants of their right to silence at the police station'. The importance of a carefully framed direction to the jury when drawing an adverse inference from the accused's silence was reiterated by the European Court of Human Rights in *Beckles* v. *United Kingdom* (2002) Application No. 44652/98, and has been stressed by the Court of Appeal on a number of occasions (see, for example, *R* v. *Birchall* [1999] Crim LR 311 and *R* v. *Gill* [2001] 1 Cr App R 160).

In *Averill* v. *United Kingdom* (2000) 31 EHRR 839 the Strasbourg Court noted that an innocent person may not wish to make any statement before he has had the opportunity to consult a lawyer, and held that the absence of a solicitor during a suspect's interrogation by the police is a relevant factor to be weighed in the balance when assessing the fairness of a decision to draw an adverse inference from silence in that context. It was further held that, because the applicant had been denied access to his solicitor during the first 24 hours of his interrogation by the police, and an adverse inference could be (and indeed was) drawn from his silence during that period, there had been a violation of Article 6(1) and (3)(c) of the European Convention (see also *Murray* v. *United Kingdom* (1996) 22 EHRR 29 (ECtHR)). Accordingly, ss. 34(2A), 36(4A) and 37(3A) of the 1994 Act have been brought into force to prohibit the drawing of adverse inferences from pre-trial silence if the accused was at an authorised place of detention at the time of his failure or refusal and he had not been allowed an opportunity to consult a solicitor (see s. 58 of the Youth Justice and Criminal Evidence Act 1999 (and SI 2003 No. 707)).

9.5 The Right to Remain Silent

The suspect's right to remain silent in the face of police questioning and the accused's right not to testify in his own defence may be seen, in a broad sense, as two facets of a single privilege against self-incrimination (14.1 *post*). Alternatively, these specific entitlements and the privilege against self-incrimination may be regarded as separate facets of a general 'right of silence'. In *R* v. *Director of Serious Fraud Office ex parte Smith* [1992] 3 WLR 66 (HL) (at p. 74) Lord Mustill described the common-law 'right of silence' as a 'disparate group of immunities' comprising:

'(1) A general immunity, possessed by all persons and bodies, from being compelled on pain of punishment to answer questions posed by other persons or bodies. (2) A general immunity, possessed by all persons and bodies, from being compelled on pain of punishment to answer questions the answers to which may incriminate them. (3) A specific immunity, possessed by all persons under suspicion of criminal responsibility whilst being interviewed by police officers or others in similar positions of authority, from being compelled on pain of punishment to answer questions of any kind. (4) A specific immunity, possessed by accused persons undergoing trial, from being compelled to give evidence, and from being compelled to answer questions put to them in the dock. (5) A specific immunity, possessed by persons who have been charged with a criminal offence, from having questions material to the offence addressed to them by police officers or persons in a similar position of authority. (6) A specific immunity ... possessed by accused persons undergoing trial, from having adverse comment made on any failure (a) to answer questions before the trial, or (b) to give evidence at the trial.'

In this generic sense the common-law 'right of silence' continues to exist, save that some of its component immunities have been diminished or removed by legislation. An individual or suspect may be compelled to answer questions put to him by the police only in limited circumstances; and a self-incriminating answer may be used against him in a subsequent trial only if the permitting provision was enacted to achieve a legitimate objective and is a proportionate response to the aim which was sought to be achieved (see 14.1 *post*). In other respects, a suspect may still refuse to answer questions put to him during police interrogation in the knowledge that he will not thereby commit an offence; and the accused may still refuse to testify in his own defence in the knowledge that he will not be in contempt of court or charged with a further offence for that refusal (16.3.1 *post*).

As a general rule, then, the privilege against self-incrimination means that there can be no *direct* compulsion to answer questions put by the police or to testify. Nor, as a general rule, is a suspect under any *indirect* compulsion to answer police questions, in the sense that an adverse inference might be drawn from his refusal to co-operate should he subsequently be put on trial. Where neither ss. 36 nor 37 of the Criminal Justice and Public Order Act 1994 applies, an adverse inference from silence in the face of police interrogation may be drawn by a jury only if the strict requirements of s. 34(1) have been satisfied, although it is true to say that this possibility places the suspect under 'a certain level of indirect compulsion' to co-operate (*Murray* v. *United Kingdom* (1996) 22 EHRR 29 (ECtHR) at p. 61). The second aspect of Lord Mustill's sixth immunity has been removed, however. The accused is now indirectly compelled to testify in his own defence, for a failure to do so is likely to result in an adverse inference being drawn.

A suspect's pre-trial entitlement to refuse to co-operate with the police and, in particular, his entitlement not to incriminate himself, may be justified at three levels. First, every person has a right to privacy and to live his life free from the interference of others, at least to the extent set out in Article 8(1) of the European Convention on Human Rights. Accordingly, it is for the police to substantiate their allegation and ultimately for the prosecution to prove their case in accordance with Article 6(2) of the European Convention. It should not be for the suspect, who is presumed to be innocent, to disprove the allegation let alone provide evidence against himself, so as a matter of principle no adverse inference should be drawn from a suspect's refusal to respond to police questions. Second, a suspect should be protected from the possibility of brutal or oppressive police questioning by a right which not only reduces the likelihood of such tactics being adopted but also provides a legal justification for resisting them if they are. Third, since there may be a wide range of reasons for remaining silent in the face of police questioning, the jury may draw an erroneous inference from a suspect's refusal to co-operate and convict on a mistaken basis.

The first of these justifications does not prevent State interference in all aspects of citizens' private affairs, however; and, notwithstanding the presumption of innocence, it would be absurd if the right to privacy could prevent the fair questioning of suspects with a view to eliciting relevant evidence, particularly as there may be no other available source of information as to what happened (and the suspect may be willing to volunteer a confession if given the opportunity). It is to be noted that Article 8(2) of the European Convention expressly permits state interference in the right to have one's private life respected insofar as it is necessary in a democratic society for, *inter alia*, the prevention of disorder or crime or the protection of the rights and freedom of others (such as victims). The second justification now carries little weight, given the reforms introduced by the Police and Criminal Evidence Act 1984, its Codes of Practice and subsequent legislation. The suspect's right to have a solicitor (and, where relevant, an appropriate adult) present during his interview, the routine tape-recording of what is said and done, and the likelihood that any interview record will be excluded under ss. 76(2) or 78(1) of the 1984 Act if there is a breach of one of its provisions or Code C all militate against the risk of oppressive questioning or any other type of maltreatment. The third justification does nothing more than raise concerns about how silence should be approached as circumstantial evidence and the necessity of forensic safeguards such as an appropriate direction from the judge. It provides no argument for a blanket prohibition on the drawing of adverse inferences, for in some cases the nature of the inference will be apparent.

Ultimately, then, whether the accused's pre-trial silence should be used against him depends, first, on the nature of the inference which it is suggested should be drawn; second, on whether society's general interest in bringing criminals to justice is sufficient to override the individual's personal right to privacy to the extent proposed; and, third, on whether it is possible to put in place sufficient safeguards to ensure that the accused receives a fair trial. As interpreted by the judiciary, the relevant provisions of the Criminal Justice and Public Order Act 1994, including the most controversial provision, s. 34, strike the right balance. After all, s. 34 merely encourages a suspect to reveal any assertions he intends to rely on in his defence, should the matter proceed to trial, so that they can be investigated and tested and the jury can have the benefit of the prosecution's informed response (*R* v. *Betts* [2001] 2 Cr App R 257 (CA)), which is hardly a radical departure from the common law. Furthermore, adverse inferences may be drawn under ss. 34 and 36–37 only in very limited circumstances, due weight having been given by Parliament to the autonomy of the individual and the right to privacy. The prosecution must prove that the accused was warned by the police of the consequences of failing to co-operate; and the jury must be given a carefully framed direction to ensure that any inference drawn from the accused's silence is actually reliable, reflecting a *culpable* reason for his refusal to co-operate, and that the inference may be used only to *support* an already established *prima facie* case against him. A further body of safeguards is provided by the Police and Criminal Evidence Act 1984 and its Codes of Practice, for a significant breach of Code C may result in any record of the accused's interview being excluded under s. 78(1) of that Act, preventing an adverse inference from being drawn under s. 34(1)(*a*) of the

1994 Act. Moreover, in *R* v. *Dervish* [2002] 2 Cr App R 105 the Court of Appeal said that if the police acted in bad faith, deliberately breaching the safeguards in the 1984 Act and its Codes, so that the accused's interview record would be excluded under s. 78(1), 'it would be likely that the judge would not invite consideration of any adverse inference' under s. 34(1)(*b*) if the accused was also silent when charged.

In the light of the limited infringements of the right of silence under the 1994 Act, and the numerous safeguards against unfairness with which the provisions are hedged, the most cogent argument which may be directed against s. 34 is, in the words of Professor Di Birch, 'whether the game of drawing inferences from silence is worth the candle' ([1999] Crim LR 78). The provision has generated a vast body of case-law, the result being that juries must now be given a lengthy and somewhat complicated, if not confusing, direction (see 9.2.2.4 *ante* and the Judicial Studies Board specimen direction at www.jsboard.co.uk); and yet, as Professor Birch points out, the inference drawn often has little weight by comparison with other evidence before the jury. Indeed, given that the jury must be satisfied that there is a *prima facie* case against the accused before the provision can be utilised, any s. 34 adverse inference can have no more than a supporting or 'corroborative' role. A cost-benefit analysis of the provision has led Professor Birch to conclude that it is 'too expensive' and may need to be repealed (see Birch, 'Suffering in Silence' [1999] Crim LR 769).

By contrast, the accused's right not to testify – justified on the ground that the prosecution, bearing the legal burden of proof, should convince the jury of his guilt without his help – has generally been regarded as less fundamental than the pre-trial right of silence, primarily because there is little if any risk of impropriety in open court. Factors such as the presence of the judge, jury and public, the high standard of proof, pre-trial disclosure, the requirement of a case to answer, the availability of publicly-funded legal representation and the time available for preparation all make silence in court difficult to justify once a *prima facie* case has been established against the accused.

Chapter Summary

- At common law a party's pre-trial silence in the face of an allegation made against him may allow the inference to be drawn that he accepted the truth of the allegation if he and his accuser were on equal terms and it would have been reasonable to expect a denial from him in the circumstances.
- An adverse inference may also be drawn at common law from the accused's failure to explain himself when found in a compromising position. Sections 36–37 of the Criminal Justice and Public Order Act 1994 now allow adverse inferences to be drawn from the accused's failure to explain (when arrested) incriminating substances or marks or his presence at a particular place.
- Section 34 of the Criminal Justice and Public Order Act 1994 allows the jury or magistrates to draw an adverse inference from the accused's failure to mention to the police when interviewed a fact subsequently relied on by him in his defence, so long as the other evidence provides a *prima facie* case against him and it would

have been reasonable in the circumstances to expect him to mention the fact to the police when questioned.

- An adverse inference may also be drawn from the accused's pre-trial refusal to allow an intimate sample to be taken from him (s. 62(10)(*b*) of the Police and Criminal Evidence Act 1984); or from his refusal to provide a satisfactory defence statement before his trial on indictment (s. 11 of the Criminal Procedure and Investigations Act 1996).

- Section 35 of the of the Criminal Justice and Public Order Act 1994 provides that an adverse inference may be drawn from the accused's failure to testify, or to answer questions while testifying, if there is a *prima facie* case against him on the other evidence, unless the circumstances are such that the judge should direct the jury against drawing any such inference. An adverse inference may also be drawn in certain circumstances from the accused's failure to call a witness to testify on his behalf.

Further Reading

Criminal Law Revision Committee, 11th Report (1972) Cmnd 4991, pp. 16–34, 65–70

Greer, 'The Right to Silence: A Review of the Current Debate' (1990) 53 MLR 709

The Royal Commission on Criminal Justice Report (1993) Cm 2263, Chapter 4

Munday, 'Inferences from Silence and European Human Rights Law' [1996] Crim LR 370

Birch, 'Suffering in Silence' [1999] Crim LR 769

Home Office Research Study 199 (2000) (www.homeoffice.gov.uk/rds/pdfs/hors199.pdf)

Dennis, 'Silence in the Police Station' [2002] Crim LR 25

---

10   Evidence Obtained by Unlawful or Unfair Means

10.1 **The General Rule**

The admissibility of unlawfully obtained evidence was addressed by the Privy Council in the original leading case of *Kuruma* v. *R* [1955] 2 WLR 223. K had been searched by Kenyan police officers and, it was alleged, found to be in unlawful possession of two rounds of ammunition, a capital offence under the Emergency Regulations then in force. The law provided that only an officer of or above the rank of assistant inspector could lawfully search persons suspected of being in possession of ammunition, yet neither officer involved was of such rank. Consequently the evidence purportedly found on K had been obtained unlawfully and he appealed against his conviction on the ground that it should not have been admitted. Dismissing the appeal Lord Goddard CJ said (at pp. 226–7):

> 'In their Lordships' opinion the test to be applied in considering whether evidence is admissible is whether it is relevant to the matters in issue. If it is, it is admissible and the court is not concerned with how the evidence was obtained ... There can be no difference in principle for this purpose between a civil and a criminal case. No doubt in a criminal case the judge always has a discretion to disallow evidence if the strict rules of admissibility would operate unfairly against an accused ... If, for instance, some admission of some piece of evidence, e.g., a document, had been obtained from a defendant by a trick, no doubt the judge might properly rule it out.'

Thus, the unlawful search did not justify the exclusion of evidence, reaffirming the principle asserted by Crompton J in *R* v. *Leatham* (1861) 8 Cox CC 498 (DC) at p. 501: 'It matters not how you get it; if you steal it even, it would be admissible in evidence.' Yet according to Lord Goddard the ammunition might have been excluded if it had been obtained by mere trickery. This apparent paradox was reinforced by subsequent cases where unlawful conduct was held to be insufficient to justify exclusion, whereas lawful impropriety which had misled the accused into revealing evidence could justify its exclusion. An assurance made to the accused by the police before a medical examination, which the police subsequently reneged on prior to his trial, justified the exclusion of evidence obtained in consequence of that examination in *R* v. *Payne* [1963] 1 WLR 637 (CCA). The accused, having been involved in a road accident and charged with drink-driving, was induced to submit himself to the medical examination on the understanding that he would not be examined for the purpose of determining his fitness to drive. At the trial the doctor gave evidence, based on what he had observed during the examination, that the accused was under the influence of drink to such an extent as to be unfit to drive. His conviction was quashed as the judge ought to have exercised his discretion to exclude that evidence (see also *R* v. *Court* [1962] Crim LR 697 (CCA)). In *Jeffrey* v. *Black* [1977] 3 WLR 895 (DC), however, the fact that the accused's lodgings had been unlawfully searched by the police could not justify the exclusion of cannabis found during that search at his trial for unlawful possession of that drug. Evidence obtained in consequence of an unlawful search was admissible and there was no discretion to exclude it, save that Lord Widgery CJ felt able to recognise the existence of an exclusionary discretion in exceptional cases where the police 'have been guilty of trickery or they have misled someone, or they have been oppressive or they have been unfair, or in other respects they have behaved in a manner which is morally reprehensible'. A similar discretion had been recognised in *Callis* v. *Gunn* [1963] 3 WLR 931 (DC) where Lord Parker CJ suggested that prosecution evidence could be excluded if it was obtained in consequence of oppression, false representations, tricks, threats or bribes.

The apparent paradox was finally explained by the House of Lords in *R* v. *Sang* [1979] 3 WLR 263. S was charged with offences relating to counterfeit US dollar bank-notes and at his trial sought a ruling that there existed a judicial discretion to exclude evidence obtained as a result of incitement by an *agent provocateur* acting for the police. The judge ruled that he had no such discretion and consequently S decided to plead guilty to challenge the ruling on appeal. The House of Lords dismissed his appeal on the ground that, while a trial judge (or magistrates' court) had a discretion to exclude prosecution evidence if its admission would prevent the accused from receiving a fair trial – in particular because the unduly prejudicial effect of the evidence would outweigh its probative value – there was no broader discretion to exclude evidence just because it had been obtained by improper or unfair means (for example by an *agent provocateur*). However, a limited exclusionary discretion unrelated to trial fairness was recognised, explaining the decision in *R* v. *Payne* [1963] 1 WLR 637 (CCA) and the dicta in *Kuruma* v. *R* [1955] 2 WLR 223 (PC), *Jeffrey* v. *Black* [1977] 3 WLR 895 (DC) and *Callis* v. *Gunn* [1963] 3 WLR 931 (DC). There was a discretion to exclude confessions and analogous evidence tantamount to a self-incriminatory admission (such as fingerprints or medical evidence) which had been obtained unfairly or by trickery from the accused *after* the commission of the offence in violation of his privilege against self-incrimination ('*nemo tenetur se ipsum prodere*'). With regard to any other evidence the judge was not concerned with how the evidence had been obtained; the question was whether its use by the prosecution would prevent the accused from receiving a fair trial.

In *R* v. *Fox* [1985] 1 WLR 1126 the House of Lords considered the scope of the common-law discretion in the context of reliable evidence which might be regarded as analogous to a confession. Following a road accident in which the accused, as the driver of a vehicle, was involved, two police officers trespassed on his premises and asked him to provide a breath specimen. The accused refused to comply with their request, so he was arrested and taken to a police station where a sample was eventually obtained. The House of Lords held that as the result of the breath test had not been obtained by any 'inducement, threat ... trick or other impropriety', and as the police officers had been acting in good faith when committing their civil trespass, the evidence had been properly admitted by the magistrates even though it had been obtained unlawfully. The fact that the police officers had done nothing more than 'make a *bona fide* mistake as to their powers' meant that the evidence could not be said to fall within the scope of the *Sang* discretion.

Section 78(1) of the Police and Criminal Evidence Act 1984 ('PACE'), which came into force in 1986, now provides as follows:

> In any proceedings the court may refuse to allow evidence on which the prosecution proposes to rely to be given if it appears to the court that, having regard to all the circumstances, including the circumstances in which the evidence was obtained, the admission of the evidence would have such an adverse effect on the fairness of the proceedings that the court ought not to admit it.

By virtue of s. 82(3) the common-law basis for excluding admissible prosecution evidence remains unaffected. However, since the statutory discretion is 'at least as wide as that conferred by the common law' (*R* v. *Khan* [1996] 3 WLR 162 (HL) at p. 172) the *Sang* discretion has in effect been rendered otiose (save that, unlike s. 78(1), it may be applied to *withdraw* evidence from the jury's consideration if it has already been adduced). For present purposes the fundamental question is whether the statutory discretion is *wider* than the *Sang* discretion and, in particular, whether it is wide enough to exclude *reliable* evidence (in addition to confessions and analogous evidence) on the ground that it was obtained unlawfully or unfairly. A relevant consideration is whether a wider discretion is necessary to ensure compliance with the requirements of Article 6 of the European Convention on Human Rights.

The European Court of Human Rights has held that, since the question of admissibility is primarily a matter for regulation under national law it will not, as a matter of principle and in the abstract, regard evidence as inadmissible merely on the ground that it was obtained unlawfully; its role is limited to ascertaining whether the particular applicant's proceedings as whole were fair (*Schenk* v. *Switzerland* (1988) 13 EHRR 242 at pp. 265–6). Needless to say, if the impropriety in the way the evidence was obtained adversely affects its reliability, or prevents the accused from being able effectively to challenge its reliability, there is likely to be a breach of Article 6 if the evidence is admitted against the accused. But Article 6 is concerned not only with fairness of this sort (what might be called 'forensic fairness') but also with fairness at a more abstract level (what might be called 'visceral unfairness'). In the light of the judgment of the European Court of Human Rights in *Teixeira de Castro* v. *Portugal* (1998) 28 EHRR 101 (at p. 116) it is clear that there may be a breach of Article 6 regardless of the fact that the trial itself would be forensically fair if the impropriety gives rise to an instinctive (visceral) *feeling* of unfairness. Accordingly, when determining whether there has been a violation of Article 6 it is necessary to examine any unlawfulness by the police and, where there has been a violation of another Convention right, the nature of that violation (*Khan* v. *United Kingdom* (2000) 31 EHRR 1016 (ECtHR), *PG* v. *United Kingdom* (2001) Application No. 44787/98 (ECtHR), *Allan* v. *United Kingdom* (2002) Application No. 48539/99 (ECtHR)).

Confessions aside, relevant evidence obtained in consequence of breaches of the civil and/or criminal law remains *prima facie* admissible in England and Wales, even if there has also been a breach of Article 8 of the European Convention (*R* v. *Khan* [1996] 3 WLR 162 (HL), *R* v. *Sargent* [2000] 3 WLR 992 (HL), *R* v. *P* [2001] 2 WLR 463 (HL)). But it has been seen that evidence which is *reliable* and *prima facie* admissible can be *excluded* at common law and under s. 78(1) of PACE. In other words English law already recognises that visceral unfairness is a sufficient reason for excluding *some* admissible evidence, as demonstrated by the decision in *R* v. *Payne* [1963] 1 WLR 637 (CCA). The question is whether the need to avoid visceral unfairness for the purposes of Article 6 is wider than the equivalent common-law principle and, if so, whether exclusion is the most appropriate way of ensuring that the requirements of Article 6 are met.

It will be seen below that the response to visceral unfairness in England and Wales is not markedly different from the position in Strasbourg, save that the national courts have approached the problem from two different directions. Some types of police impropriety may be so egregious that it would be an abuse of the process of the court to allow the trial to proceed, regardless of how cogent or reliable the evidence against the accused might be. Visceral unfairness is obviated by preventing the trial from proceeding – the proceedings are 'stayed' as an 'abuse of process' (10.4 *post*). Less serious types of police misconduct will not justify a stay, in which case s. 78(1) may be applied to exclude improperly obtained evidence if the impropriety has rendered the evidence unreliable (or of unascertainable reliability) or of course if the visceral unfairness comes from a violation of the accused's privilege against self-incrimination (10.3 *post*). However, it will also be seen that the subsection is wide enough to exclude evidence on the basis that the defence's application under s. 78(1) is in effect a belated application that the proceedings be stayed as an abuse of process (10.5 *post*). Section 78(1) is therefore primarily (but not exclusively) concerned with forensic fairness, complementing the doctrine of abuse of process to ensure that the accused does *not* receive an *unfair* trial.

In the context of civil proceedings, there is no common-law discretion to exclude evidence merely because of the improper or unlawful way in which it was obtained. However r. 32.1 of the Civil Procedure Rules 1998 now provides the trial judge with the power to exclude admissible evidence, the only limitation being that it must be exercised in accordance with the 'overriding objective' in r. 1.1(1)–(2) to deal with cases justly (*Grobbelaar* v. *Sun Newspapers* (1999) *The Times* 12.8.99 (CA)). In *Jones* v. *University of Warwick* [2003] 1 WLR 954 (CA) it was held that an unlawful act by a party in the way evidence was obtained (such as a breach of Article 8 of the European Convention) is a relevant circumstance to be weighed in the balance by the judge when coming to a decision as to how he should properly exercise his discretion in making orders as to the management of the proceedings, but the fact that Article 8 has been breached does not require the judge to exclude the evidence for it would be 'artificial and undesirable' for relevant evidence not to be placed before the judge who has the task of trying the case. According to the Court, the judge may give effect to the overriding objective, take into account the wider interests of the administration of justice, deter improper conduct and do justice between the parties by admitting the evidence and making an order for costs against the malefactor.

10.2 Reasons for Excluding Illegally or Unfairly Obtained Evidence in Criminal Proceedings

There are several principles which might be relied on to justify the exclusion of evidence obtained as a result of police impropriety – the reliability principle, the disciplinary principle, the protective principle, the integrity principle and the self-incrimination (*'nemo tenetur'*) principle.

10.2.1 The Reliability Principle

If the method by which an item of evidence was obtained has adversely affected its reliability or, if admitted, would prevent the accused from being able to challenge its reliability, the evidence can be excluded to ensure forensic fairness. Conversely, the reliability principle militates against the exclusion of any demonstrably reliable evidence.

Any prosecution evidence may be excluded if its admission would deny the accused a forensically fair trial, on the basis that the evidence is manifestly unreliable or because in other respects its unduly prejudicial effect would outweigh its probative value. The general nature of this exclusionary discretion was not recognised until the decision of the House of Lords in *R* v. *Sang* [1979] 3 WLR 263. If it had been recognised earlier it would no doubt have been applied in *Kuruma* v. *R* [1955] 2 WLR 223 (10.1 *ante*) where there was a very real possibility that the ammunition found on K had been planted, as he had claimed. K had knowingly cycled into a road block when he could have taken an alternative route, three witnesses to the search were not called by the prosecution, and a knife allegedly found with the ammunition was not adduced in evidence (the police officers having claimed that it had been returned to K while he was still in custody). As Heydon points out, the reason the Emergency Regulations required searches to be conducted by a senior police officer was presumably to prevent the possibility of evidence being planted ('Illegally Obtained Evidence' [1973] Crim LR 603 at p. 607). However, despite the capital nature of the offence, the unreliability of the evidence and the recognition of a common-law discretion 'to disallow evidence if the strict rules of admissibility would operate unfairly against an accused' the Privy Council refused to hold that the evidence should have been excluded.

It might be argued that as real evidence exists independently of the impropriety which leads to its discovery, and as the *forensic* fairness of the trial cannot be affected by its admission, the interests of justice favour the admission of any real evidence found during an unlawful search (*R* v. *Collins* [1987] 1 SCR 265 (SCC) at p. 284, *R* v. *Grayson* [1997] 1 NZLR 399 (NZCA) at pp. 406 and 412). However, while there is force in this view if it is not disputed that the accused was actually in possession of the real evidence, it can hardly justify the admission of real evidence which the accused alleges was planted on him (as, for example, in *Kuruma* v. *R* [1955] 2 WLR 223).

10.2.2 The Disciplinary Principle

This principle could justify the exclusion of unlawfully obtained evidence on the ground that it would deter police officers from adopting the same tactics again. Its application is exemplified by the way the United States Supreme Court has dealt with violations of the Fourth Amendment to the US Constitution prohibiting unreasonable searches and seizures (see, for example, *United States* v. *Leon* (1984) 468 US 897 at p. 906 and *Arizona* v. *Evans* (1995) 514 US 1 at pp. 10–11).

The problem with this principle is its lack of practical utility. The risk of exclusion may be too remote to have a significant effect on the investigating officers and other factors may therefore override it, for example the need to obtain results quickly. In fact the officers' behaviour may never even be called into question by a court: the suspect may accept a caution or plead guilty without contesting the police action, particularly if there is other evidence suggesting his guilt or he has previous convictions which could be brought out during a trial. In any event the appellate courts of England and Wales have expressly stated on a number of occasions that it is *not* their business to discipline the police. In *R* v. *Sang* [1979] 3 WLR 263 (HL) Lord Diplock said (at p. 271):

'It is no part of a judge's function to exercise disciplinary powers over the police or prosecution as respects the way in which evidence to be used at the trial is obtained by them. If it was obtained illegally there will be a remedy in civil law; if it was obtained legally but in breach of the rules of conduct for the police, this is a matter for the appropriate disciplinary authority to deal with.'

The same point has also been made on several occasions since the enactment of s. 78(1) of PACE (for example *R* v. *Mason* [1988] 1 WLR 139 (CA) at p. 144, *R* v. *Delaney* (1988) 88 Cr App R 338 (CA) at p. 341, *R* v. *Keenan* [1989] 3 WLR 1193 (CA) at p. 1206 and *R* v. *Oliphant* [1992] Crim LR 40 (CA) at p. 41). The disciplinary principle may therefore be discounted as a factor to be taken into consideration when s. 78(1) or its common-law counterpart is applied. Nor is it a factor to be taken into consideration by the court when considering whether to stay a prosecution as an abuse of process, although it has been recognised that a stay may have this effect in practice (*R* v. *Looseley, Attorney General's Reference (No. 3 of 2000)* [2001] 1 WLR 2061 (HL) at pp. 2067 and 2073, *R* v. *Mullen* [1999] 3 WLR 777 (CA) at p. 789).

10.2.3 The Protective Principle

The protective principle demands respect for the suspect's fundamental human rights, militating against the admission of evidence obtained in a way which violates any such right. This principle, if applied, would also have the effect of deterring police misconduct; and would operate to exclude even demonstrably reliable evidence, trumping the competing reliability principle.

One can recognise the operation of this principle most clearly in a case such as *Lam Chi-Ming* v. *R* [1991] 2 WLR 1082 (7.1.3.7 *ante*) where demonstrably true confessions to murder were held to be inadmissible at common law because the prosecution had failed to prove that they had been provided voluntarily (see also *Timothy* v. *The State* [2000] 1 WLR 485 (PC)). The principle underpins s. 76(2)(*a*) of PACE but is also of relevance to s. 76(2)(*b*), for a confession can be inadmissible under either or both limbs of the subsection even if it is true (7.1.3.1–2 *ante*). The decision in *Lam Chi-Ming* v. *R* illustrates a problem with this rationale for excluding evidence, however. The persons against whom there was cogent evidence of complicity in a brutal murder walked free because of the need to give express recognition to, and provide protection for, the rights of detainees and suspects. The application of the protective principle may therefore fail adequately to protect the human rights of the victim, his family and other members of society, and may for that reason bring the law into disrepute.

The privilege against self-incrimination (the *nemo tenetur* principle) is a particular facet of the protective principle. The *nemo tenetur* principle was cited with approval by the majority of the House of Lords in *R* v. *Sang* [1979] 3 WLR 263 as the justification for the common-law discretion to exclude confessions and analogous evidence obtained by police trickery.

Given that the disciplinary principle has been expressly rejected as a relevant consideration when determining whether a prosecution should be stayed as an abuse of process, the protective principle also has a role to play in this aspect of procedural law. In *R* v. *Looseley, Attorney General's Reference (No. 3 of 2000)* [2001] 1 WLR 2061 (HL) (at p. 2063) Lord Nicholls explained that the doctrine is available to ensure that executive agents of the state do not misuse their powers and thereby oppress its citizens.

10.2.4 The Integrity Principle

This principle could operate to exclude unlawfully obtained evidence on the ground that the integrity of the criminal justice system would be brought into disrepute if such evidence were allowed to be admitted against the accused. Closely allied with this notion of judicial integrity is what Dennis refers to as the moral authority of the verdict, that is, the need to ensure that any verdict of guilt is morally as well as factually sound (Dennis, 'Reconstructing the Law of Criminal Evidence' (1989) 42 CLP 21 at pp. 34–40).

If integrity is to be regarded as a relevant consideration when deciding whether to exclude prosecution evidence it would, as a general rule, be necessary to weigh the nature of the unlawful conduct and the attitude of the state agents involved against the gravity of the alleged offence. Breaches of the criminal law by the police would be looked upon with particular disfavour, but other types of unlawful behaviour might equally justify the exclusion of evidence if the police acted in bad faith, for example by deliberately disregarding the PACE Codes of Practice.

The importance of the integrity principle as a factor justifying the exclusion of evidence has been expressly recognised in Canada (s. 24(2) of the Canadian Charter of Rights 1982, *R* v. *Collins* [1987] 1 SCR 265 (SCC) at pp. 280–8), Australia (*Bunning* v. *Cross* (1978) 141 CLR 54 (HCA), s. 138 of the Australian Evidence Act 1995), New Zealand (*R* v. *Shaheed* [2002] 2 NZLR 377 (NZCA)) and the USA (*Mapp* v. *Ohio* (1961) 367 US 643 (USSC)). In England and Wales it is a consideration to be weighed in the balance when deciding whether a prosecution ought to be stayed as an abuse of process (*R* v. *Latif* [1996] 1 WLR 104 (HL) at pp. 112–13, *R* v. *Looseley, Attorney General's Reference (No. 3 of 2000)* [2001] 1 WLR 2061 (HL) at pp. 2073 and 2091).

10.3 Section 78(1) of PACE

Section 78(1) of PACE provides trial judges (and magistrates) with a discretion to exclude any evidence on which the prosecution propose to rely if it appears, having regard to all the circumstances, including *the circumstances in which the evidence was obtained*, that the admission of the evidence would have such an adverse effect on the fairness of the proceedings that the court ought not to admit it. Proceedings means criminal proceedings (s. 82(1)).

There was until recently considerable uncertainty over the meaning of 'fairness' in this context. One interpretation was that the subsection was limited to forensic fairness, save that (in line with the common-law discretion) the reliability principle could be overridden by the *nemo tenetur* principle if the evidence was a confession (or analogous to a confession). Thus, in *R* v. *McCarthy* [1996] Crim LR 818 (CA) it was held that the discovery of real evidence during a search could not be excluded under s. 78(1) merely because the police had acted in breach of s. 2 of PACE. On this view, s. 78(1) was no more than a statutory restatement of the *Sang* discretion; and the term 'proceedings' rather than 'trial' had been used by Parliament to ensure that both aspects of that common-law discretion were covered. In *R* v. *Mason* [1988] 1 WLR 139 (CA) (at p. 144) it was said that s. 78(1) 'does no more than to re-state the power which judges had at common law'; and in *R* v. *Christou* [1992] 3 WLR 228 (CA) (at pp. 234–5) Lord Taylor CJ expressed the view that 'the criteria of unfairness are the same whether the trial judge is exercising his discretion at common law or under the statute'. Similarly, in *R* v. *Latif* [1996] 1 WLR 104 (at p. 113) the House of Lords would appear to have accepted that as the co-accused, a dealer in heroin, 'was not in any way prejudiced in the presentation of his defence' by the subterfuge used to get him to enter the UK to face trial, an argument based on s. 78(1) to exclude the evidence of prosecution witnesses involved in that operation could not succeed (see also *R* v. *Khan* [1996] 3 WLR 162 (HL)).

The alternative interpretation was that s. 78(1) allowed the criminal courts to consider fairness beyond the extent recognised in *R* v. *Sang* [1979] 3 WLR 263 (HL) and thus exclude prosecution evidence if there had been a violation of principles other than reliability or the privilege against self-incrimination. First, there were dicta to the effect that s. 78(1) was considerably broader in scope than the common-law discretion (*DPP* v. *McGladrigan* [1991] RTR 297 (DC) at p. 300, *R* v. *Cooke* [1995] 1 Cr App R 318 (CA) at p. 328); and in *R* v. *Horseferry Road Magistrates' Court, ex parte Bennett* [1993] 3 WLR 90 (HL) (at p. 103) Lord Griffiths was of the view that s. 78(1) 'enlarges a judge's discretion to exclude evidence obtained by unfair means'. Second, in *R* v. *Smurthwaite, R* v. *Gill* (1993) 98 Cr App R 437 the Court of Appeal expressed the view that the evidence of an undercover police officer could be excluded under s. 78(1) if he had acted as an *agent provocateur* and enticed the accused into committing an offence he would not otherwise have committed. Third, there were dicta suggesting that s. 78(1) could be applied to exclude confessions where there had been a breach of s. 58 of PACE and/or Code C of the PACE Codes of Practice associated with bad faith on the part of the police (*R* v. *Alladice* (1988) 87 Cr App R 380 (CA) at p. 386) or identification evidence where there had been a 'complete flouting' of Code D (*R* v. *Nagah* (1990) 92 Cr App R 344 (CA) at p. 348) or 'an abuse of process, e.g. because evidence has been obtained in deliberate breach of procedures laid down in an official code of practice' (*R* v. *Quinn* [1990] Crim LR 581 (CA) at p. 583).

The problem with the third argument, however, is that the cases referred to do not necessarily support the view that s. 78(1) is broader than the discretion available at common law. Confessions have always been treated as a special type of evidence, and it is difficult to draw any conclusions from the confession cases about the application of s. 78(1) at a more general level. Further, the fact that a confession could be excluded following a breach of s. 58 or Code C might just as easily be said to reaffirm the common-law principle that a confession should not be admitted if its reliability cannot be effectively challenged or the accused's privilege against self-incrimination has been violated. Similarly, while identification evidence may be excluded following a breach of Code D of the PACE Codes of Practice, it is likely that the breach will have affected the reliability (or the accused's ability to challenge the reliability) of that evidence.

Reliability is an important consideration when determining whether a confession ought to be excluded under s. 78(1) where there has been a breach of the Code C 'verballing' provisions or s. 58 of PACE, or if the confession was elicited during a covert operation (7.1.3.3 *ante*). Breaches of these provisions, or a failure to make a contemporaneous audio recording of what was said during a covert operation, take on a special significance because the accused may be prevented from challenging the admissibility of his confession under s. 76(2) of PACE. But even reliable confessions may be excluded if the accused has been tricked (or forced) into incriminating himself in contravention of his privilege against self-incrimination.

Similarly, a number of cases concerning drink-driving demonstrate that reliability is not the sole criterion for excluding evidence under s. 78(1) where the evidence is *analogous* to a confession. In *Matto* v. *Wolverhampton Crown Court* [1987] RTR 337 two police officers entered the accused's private land and requested a breath test from him even though they were aware they had no authority to make that request, having already been told to leave. The officers simply told the accused that he would be free to sue them for wrongful arrest if he felt aggrieved by their conduct. The accused therefore agreed to undergo a screening breath test which proved positive and he was arrested. At the police station a further test was administered and the positive result was used by the prosecution at his trial for driving with excess alcohol. He appealed to the Crown Court against his conviction in the magistrates' court and, though it was accepted that the police had acted in bad faith prior to the screening test, his application to have the results of the second test excluded under s. 78(1) failed. The Divisional Court quashed his conviction on the ground that, as the police had acted in bad faith and oppressively to obtain the screening test, it had been open to the Crown Court to exclude the result of the second test under s. 78(1) notwithstanding its reliability. Woolf LJ clearly had in mind the common-law discretion to exclude improperly obtained evidence tantamount to a confession, so this decision may be seen as a further example of the application of the *nemo tenetur* principle, as in *R* v. *Payne* [1963] 1 WLR 637 (CCA) (10.1 *ante*). In *R* v. *Fox* [1985] 1 WLR 1126 the House of Lords regarded the absence of bad faith on the part of the police as a relevant criterion at common law (and the Court of Appeal has since emphasised the relevance of bad faith when considering the application of s. 78(1) to confessions). It is true that in *DPP* v. *Godwin* [1991] RTR 303 the Divisional Court held that s. 78(1) could be applied to exclude the result of a breath test notwithstanding the absence of bad faith on the part of the police, but this decision is also in line with the approach taken in the context of confessions. While bad faith on the part of the police will certainly justify the exclusion of a confession where there has been a breach of s. 58 of PACE or Code C, this does not mean that the absence of bad faith will prevent a confession from being excluded where there has been such a breach. In *DPP* v. *Godwin* there had been a breach of s. 6(1) of the Road Traffic Act 1988, requiring reasonable cause to suspect the accused had been drinking, which is not dissimilar to an important aspect of Code C-10.1. A breach of Code C-10.1 will often result in the exclusion of a confession under s. 78(1) (see 7.1.3.3 *ante*).

The importance attached by the courts to the *nemo tenetur* principle also explains the decision of the Court of Appeal in *R* v. *Nathaniel* [1995] 2 Cr App R 565. The accused in that case was charged with raping two women in 1991 and consented to having a blood sample taken from him for the purpose of establishing his DNA profile, having been informed in advance that the sample would be destroyed following an acquittal. He was acquitted of those rapes following a trial in 1992 but the police failed to destroy the DNA profile obtained from his blood sample (in breach of what was then s. 64 of PACE and contrary to the assurances given to him), and that evidence was used by the prosecution at his trial in 1994 for the rape in 1989 of a different woman. The Court of Appeal quashed his conviction on the ground that the DNA evidence ought to have been excluded under s. 78(1), notwithstanding the trial judge's conclusion that there had been no bad faith on the part of the police, the very serious nature of the offence in question and the reliability of the evidence.

However, utilitarian considerations of what is in the public good, or what common sense requires, may occasionally be allowed to override the *nemo tenetur* principle, notwithstanding serious police impropriety, if the reliability of the evidence has not been affected and the exclusion of the evidence in question would lead to the acquittal of an obviously guilty person. In *R* v. *Cooke* [1995] 1 Cr App R 318 the DNA evidence relied on by the prosecution at the accused's trial for rape and kidnapping had been obtained by the police from samples of hair sheath taken from the hair plucked from his scalp following a threat that it would be taken by force if he did not comply with their request. This threat was reinforced by the presence of three police officers wearing riot gear. The Court of Appeal held that if the sample had not been taken in accordance with the procedural requirements of PACE – that is, even if the method of extraction had amounted to an assault – the judge had been right not to apply s. 78(1) to exclude the evidence as it was highly probative of the accused's guilt and its reliability had not been affected. Given the threat to use force, and the fact that this must have operated on the accused's mind, this is a somewhat surprising decision, particularly as the House of Lords was clearly of the view in *R* v. *Fox* [1985] 1 WLR 1126 that the use of a threat or other oppressive behaviour by the police to obtain a breath specimen might justify the exclusion of such evidence, and the Court of Appeal accepted that the statutory discretion was 'substantially wider' than that available at common law. The reason for the Court's approach would seem to lie in its view that 'the fairness of proceedings involves both fairness to the accused person and fairness to the public good', implying that the trial judge should enter into some kind of balancing exercise when considering whether to exclude prosecution evidence under s. 78(1). The desirability of ensuring that persons who are obviously guilty of serious offences are convicted would also seem to explain the decision in *R* v. *Apicella* (1985) 82 Cr App R 295. The accused in that case consented to a sample of gonorrhoea being taken from his penis by a consultant physician because he had been told by a prison officer that, as a prisoner, he had no choice. The doctor obtained the sample in good faith for a therapeutic purpose, assuming the accused had been freely consenting. The unusual strain of the disease he was suffering from matched the infections contracted by the three women he was alleged to have raped and the evidence was adduced at his trial. The Court of Appeal held that the judge was right not to have excluded the evidence (at common law) just because it was a bodily sample obtained without the accused's true consent, the justification being that 'the law of evidence should not stray too far from commonsense' and a sample could just as easily have been obtained by examining the accused's underpants or urine. The Court was willing to accept, however, that if the accused had been tricked into submitting to the medical examination (as in *R* v. *Payne* [1963] 1 WLR 637 (CCA)) the common-law discretion could have been applied to exclude the evidence.

In any event, not every type of police trickery after the commission of the offence is to be regarded as improper. Post-offence trickery which is considered to be a proportionate response by the police to the problems they face in combating crime will not lead to the exclusion of evidence obtained as a consequence even if it led to a degree of self-incrimination. In *R* v. *Christou* [1992] 3 WLR 228 the Court of Appeal gave as an example the blackmailer who is lured out and identified by the bait of marked money or by the victim's having arranged an appointment with him, and held that incriminating comments made to undercover police officers had been properly admitted even though the offences charged (burglary and handling in the alternative) had been committed prior to those conversations (see 7.1.3.3 *ante*). Nor will relatively minor impropriety or trickery by the police justify the exclusion of a reliable confession (or analogous evidence) if there has been no violation of the *nemo tenetur* principle. This is evident from the decision of the House of Lords in *R* v. *Khan* [1996] 3 WLR 162 where it was held that the accused's admissions, recorded by a listening device which had been attached to a suspect's home, could not be excluded under s. 78(1) as he had not been 'induced' to make them.

The importance attached to the reliability principle in cases such as *R* v. *Cooke* [1995] 1 Cr App R 318 (CA) and *R* v. *Apicella* (1985) 82 Cr App R 295 (CA) makes sense given the seriousness of the offences and the nature of the impropriety, although in the absence of any safeguards it might be seen as sanctioning a doctrine of 'the end justifies the means'. It has been noted that in *R* v. *Cooke* the Court of Appeal seemed to suggest that it was necessary to balance fairness to the accused against fairness to the public, and this same point has been made by the Court of Appeal on other occasions (see, for example, *R* v. *Smurthwaite*, *R* v. *Gill* (1993) 98 Cr App R 437 at p. 440). A balancing exercise would certainly provide a safeguard against a doctrine that *any* impropriety may be excused if the offence is sufficiently serious, but until recently the absence of any clear guidance as to what should be taken into consideration left judges and magistrates with nothing but their own subjective feeling of whether it would be 'fair' to allow the evidence to be adduced (see Hunter, 'Judicial Discretion: Section 78 in Practice' [1994] Crim LR 558). The only general guidance available to magistrates and trial judges was that s. 78(1) was at least as wide as the common-law exclusionary discretions recognised in *R* v. *Sang* [1979] 3 WLR 263 (HL) and that it was potentially available to exclude evidence obtained in the course of an entrapment operation (*R* v *Smurthwaite*, *R* v. *Gill*, 10.5 *post*) and/or where there had been an abuse of process (*R* v. *Quinn* [1990] Crim LR 581 (CA)).

The Court of Appeal could have recognised an explicit balancing of competing principles whenever s. 78(1) was being considered. In other words, the application of s. 78(1) could have been governed by a guided discretion whereby the reliability principle (reflecting the need to convict the guilty) was expressly weighed against the protective and integrity principles in the light of all the circumstances of the case (see *Bunning* v. *Cross* (1978) 141 CLR 54 (HCA) at pp. 72–80 and *R* v. *Shaheed* [2002] 2 NZLR 377 (NZCA) at pp. 419–21). Alternatively, the Court of Appeal could have held that fairness for the purposes of s. 78(1) was limited to forensic fairness with other types of unfairness (that is, breaches of principles other than the reliability principle) being rectified by the balancing exercise which is applied when determining whether a prosecution should be stayed as an abuse of process. In *R* v. *Chalkley* [1998] 3 WLR 146 the Court of Appeal adopted the latter alternative. The police suspected C of conspiring to commit robberies and so arrested him and his girlfriend in respect of unrelated matters in order to sneak into his home to plant a battery-powered bugging device. As a result the police were able to record C conspiring with his co-accused to commit robberies as well as their admissions relating to robberies they had already committed. The trial judge exercised his discretion under s. 78(1) by weighing in the balance a number of competing principles – including the seriousness of the crimes and danger to the public, the absence of any inducement by the police, the reliability of the evidence, the unlawful conduct of the police and the need to uphold the integrity of the criminal justice system – and concluded that in all the circumstances the evidence ought to be admitted. The judge's ruling was upheld on appeal, but the Court of Appeal held that the test which should have been applied was simply that of reliability and forensic fairness. According to Auld LJ (at pp. 169–71):

> 'The determination of the fairness or otherwise of admitting evidence under section 78 is distinct from the exercise of discretion in determining whether to stay criminal proceedings as an abuse of process. Depending on the circumstances, the latter may require consideration, not just of the potential fairness of the trial, but also of a balance of the possibly countervailing interests of prosecuting a criminal to conviction and discouraging abuse of power. However laudable the end, it may not justify any means to achieve it ...
>
> At first sight, the words in section 78 "the circumstances in which the evidence was obtained" might suggest that the means by which the

evidence was secured, even if they did not affect the fairness of admitting it, could entitle the court to exclude it as a result of a balancing exercise analogous to that when considering a stay for abuse of process. On that approach, the court could, even if it considered that the intrinsic nature of the evidence was not unfair to the accused, exclude it as a mark of disapproval of the way in which it had been obtained. That was certainly not the law before the Act of 1984. And we consider that the inclusion in section 78 of the words the circumstances in which the evidence was obtained was not intended to widen the common law rule in this respect as stated by Lord Diplock in *Reg. v. Sang* [1980] AC 402. That is that, save in the case of admissions and confessions and generally as to evidence obtained from the accused after the commission of the offence ... there is no discretion to exclude evidence unless its quality was or might have been affected by the way in which it was obtained ...

Because of our unease about the possible effect on the reasoning of the judge of his adoption of the balancing exercise appropriate to abuse of process cases, we consider that the proper course is to make our own decision about the fairness of admitting this evidence. We have no doubt whatever about the fairness of doing so. As we have said, there was no dispute as to its authenticity, content or effect; it was relevant, highly probative of the defendants' involvement in the conspiracy and otherwise admissible; it did not result from incitement, entrapment or inducement or any other conduct of that sort; and none of the unlawful conduct of the police or other of their conduct of which complaint is made affects the quality of the evidence.'

The broad distinction drawn by Auld LJ between the function and remit of s. 78(1) of PACE and the common-law doctrine of abuse of process was accepted as the correct approach by the Court of Appeal in *R* v. *Bray* (1998) unreported (98/04661), *R* v. *Shannon* [2001] 1 WLR 51 and *R* v. *Hardwicke* [2001] Crim LR 220 (99/06296/Z2), and has now been approved by the House of Lords (*R* v. *Looseley, Attorney General's Reference (No. 3 of 2000)* [2001] 1 WLR 2061, 10.5 *post*).

It is therefore now clear (in the context of evidence other than confessions and analogous evidence) that the primary purpose of s. 78(1) is to ensure *forensic* fairness in line with the scope of the general common-law discretion. Generally speaking the subsection should be applied to exclude improperly or unlawfully obtained evidence only if that impropriety has so affected the reliability of that evidence (or has so undermined the accused's ability to challenge its reliability) that its admission would prevent the accused from receiving a fair trial. It is not the appropriate mechanism for registering the court's disapproval of the techniques used by the police or protecting the rights of the state's citizens or upholding the integrity of the criminal justice system. If the executive agents of the State misuse their powers to such an extent that the criminal justice system would be brought into disrepute by allowing a trial to take place at all, the judge should stay the proceedings as an abuse of process.

That said, in *R* v. *Looseley, Attorney General's Reference (No. 3 of 2000)* [2001] 1 WLR 2061 the House of Lords accepted – explaining *R* v. *Smurthwaite, R* v. *Gill* (1993) 98 Cr App R 437 (CA) and approving the analysis of the Court of Appeal in *R* v. *Shannon* [2001] 1 WLR 51 – that evidence may properly be excluded under s. 78(1) if the behaviour of the police or prosecuting authority has been such as to justify a stay on the grounds of abuse of process. Accordingly, while the accused should usually apply to have the proceedings stayed at the beginning of the trial, s. 78(1) may be relied on subsequently if it amounts to a belated application to have the proceedings stayed, in which case the *Latif* balancing exercise appropriate to abuse of process cases should be conducted to determine whether the evidence ought to be excluded (10.4 *post*). In cases where the prosecution evidence has been obtained unlawfully or unfairly it is likely that the principal or only evidence of the accused's guilt will be that improperly obtained evidence; after all, covert operations are conducted because of the difficulty obtaining evidence by more conventional methods. The use of s. 78(1) to exclude the evidence will therefore result in the collapse of the prosecution case and a direction from the judge to acquit. In the unlikely event that there is some other cogent evidence against the accused which would justify a conviction at the end of the trial, the judge would be able to exclude *all* the prosecution evidence if the impropriety of the police is regarded as sufficiently grave to have justified a finding of abuse of process at the beginning of the trial.

The decisions in *R* v. *Cooke* [1995] 1 Cr App R 318 (CA) and *R* v. *Apicella* (1985) 82 Cr App R 295 (CA) would now seem to exemplify the new approach as applied to evidence which is analogous to a confession, where the degree to which the accused has been unfairly treated and the seriousness of the offence need to be balanced to achieve a result which is fair to the public and not contrary to common sense. In cases of this sort a successful application during the trial to exclude the evidence under s. 78(1) would amount (in effect) to a belated application to have the proceedings stayed as an abuse of process, given the absence of any other evidence against the accused. The court should therefore take into consideration the accused's privilege against self-incrimination, the nature of the police misconduct, the seriousness of the alleged offence and the reliability of the evidence. The importance of the last two factors is apparent from the decision of the House of Lords in *Attorney-General's Reference (No. 3 of 1999)* [2001] 2 WLR 56. That case concerned the interpretation of (what used to be) s. 64(3B)(*b*) of PACE, which provided that where DNA samples are required to be destroyed under (what was) s. 64(1) following the accused's acquittal, information derived from that sample 'shall not be used ... for the purposes of any investigation of an offence'. The accused (D) was arrested in respect of a burglary and a sample of his saliva was lawfully obtained from him. D was subsequently acquitted of that offence and the sample should have been destroyed under s. 64(1). It was not destroyed, however, and the DNA profile derived from it remained on the national DNA database. In contravention of s. 64(3B)(*b*) it was subsequently found that the DNA profile obtained from D's sample matched the profile of the man who had brutally raped a 66-year-old women in 1997 and D was arrested in relation to that offence. A non-intimate sample of plucked head hair was then lawfully taken from D and (unsurprisingly) the DNA profile obtained from it matched the DNA sample obtained from samples of semen left behind by the rapist. D was accordingly charged with that rape but, following submissions from counsel, the judge ruled that the evidence of the match between the DNA profile obtained from D's hair and the rapist's DNA profile was inadmissible. The prosecution case collapsed and the judge directed an acquittal. The Attorney-General referred the matter to the Court of Appeal, which upheld the trial judge's approach and quashed a conviction for murder in the conjoined appeal of *R* v. *Weir* ([2000] 2 Cr App R 416). The House of Lords had no hesitation in holding that the trial judge and Court of Appeal had erred in their interpretation of the provision. Evidence obtained in breach of s. 64(3B)(*b*) was not automatically inadmissible; rather, the judge had a discretion to exclude it under s. 78(1). In reaching this decision Lord Steyn, having noted that the purpose of the criminal law is to permit everyone to go about their daily lives without fear of harm to person or property, emphasised that there must be fairness to all sides and that this requires the court to consider a 'triangulation of interests' involving the position of the accused, the victim (and his or her family) and the public. The interpretation of the Court of Appeal and trial judge was not only in conflict with the plain words of the statute but had produced results which were contrary to good sense. Lords Cooke, Clyde and Hutton agreed with this analysis, with Lord Hutton stating that the interests of the victim and the public must be taken into account, as well as the interests of the accused, when the application of s. 78(1) is considered. (In the light of the decision of the Court of Appeal in the two cases before it Parliament has made substantial amendments to s. 64 of PACE.)

10.4 The Doctrine of Abuse of Process

The civil and criminal courts have an inherent jurisdiction to stay proceedings as an abuse of process. This common-law power (indeed duty) is part of the law of civil and criminal procedure rather than the law of evidence, but it is necessary to have an understanding of the doctrine on account of its increasing importance as a remedy for the accused in cases where prosecution evidence has been obtained unlawfully and the extent to which it overlaps with s. 78(1) of PACE.

In the context of criminal proceedings a prosecution will be stayed if the accused cannot receive a (forensically) fair trial or if it would be (viscerally) unfair for the accused to be tried at all (*R* v. *Horseferry Road Magistrates' Court, ex parte Bennett* [1993] 3 WLR 90 (HL), *R* v. *Beckford* [1996] 1 Cr App R 94 (CA)). In practice the two categories will often overlap. It is for the accused to prove on the balance of probabilities that he would suffer such serious prejudice that a fair trial cannot be held

(*Attorney-General's Reference (No. 1 of 1990)* (1992) 95 Cr App R 296 (CA)) or the factual circumstances which render the prosecution itself unfair (*R* v. *Mullen* [1999] 3 WLR 777 (CA)).

A trial should be stayed on the ground that a fair trial is not possible only in exceptional circumstances, for in most cases forensic fairness can be provided by the application of s. 78(1) and appropriate directions to the jury (*Attorney-General's Reference (No. 1 of 1990)* (1992) 95 Cr App R 296 (CA)); but both the Crown Court and magistrates' courts are empowered to stay a prosecution on this ground (*R* v. *Horseferry Road Magistrates' Court, ex parte Bennett* [1993] 3 WLR 90 (HL)). An example is provided by *R* v. *Birmingham* [1992] Crim LR 117 (CC) where, despite receiving specific requests for unused material, the police failed to provide the accused with the videotape from a closed-circuit television camera which was trained on the scene of the incident and would have contained matters of relevance to the accused. The judge stayed the case because the tape had disappeared by the time the matter came to be tried (see also *R (Ebrahim)* v. *Feltham Magistrates' Court* [2001] 1 WLR 1293 (DC)). Similarly, where there is adverse pre-trial publicity the prosecution will be stayed if, notwithstanding the safeguards inherent in the trial process and the measures the judge would take to ameliorate forensic unfairness, the risk of prejudice to the accused remains serious enough to render a fair trial impossible (*Montgomery* v. *HM Advocate* [2001] 2 WLR 779 (PC)). The same principle applies if the time which has elapsed between the commission of the alleged offence and the trial would so prejudice the accused that he would be unable to receive a fair trial (*Attorney-General's Reference (No. 1 of 1990)*; see also 11.10 *post*).

The second ground for staying a prosecution as an abuse of process is concerned not with the fairness of the trial itself but with the serious misconduct of agents of the executive, most obviously the police, customs officers and the CPS (though it may be that equivalent misconduct by an ordinary citizen will justify a stay in certain circumstances). Thus, regardless of whether the accused would actually receive a fair trial, a prosecution will be stayed if, for example, the police deliberately disregarded the accused's human rights and the state's international legal obligations by forcibly bringing the accused into the jurisdiction (*R* v. *Mullen* [1999] 3 WLR 777 (CA)) or the police brought about the commission of a crime which would not otherwise have been committed (*R* v. *Looseley, Attorney General's Reference (No. 3 of 2000)* [2001] 1 WLR 2061 (HL), 10.5 *post*). The Crown Court has jurisdiction to stay a prosecution as an abuse of process on this ground; but where the allegation involves an infraction of the rule of law outside the narrow confines of the actual trial or court process a magistrates' court should adjourn the case so that an application may be made to the Divisional Court for the issue to be addressed there (*R* v. *Belmarsh Magistrates' Court ex parte Watts* [1999] 2 Cr App R 188 (DC)). The rationale underlying this aspect of the doctrine is threefold. First, citizens should be protected from agents of the executive (such as police officers) who might abuse their executive power; second, agents of the executive should be discouraged from abusing their power; and, third, the courts must maintain the integrity of the criminal justice system by refusing to allow their coercive, law enforcement functions to be misused (see *R* v. *Horseferry Road Magistrates' Court, ex parte Bennett* [1993] 3 WLR 90 (HL) at pp. 104–5, *R* v. *Latif* [1996] 1 WLR 104 (HL) at p. 112, *R* v. *Looseley, Attorney General's Reference (No. 3 of 2000)* [2001] 1 WLR 2061 (HL) at pp. 2063, 2067, 2069, 2073–5, 2080 and 2090–1).

Where the accused argues that it would be 'unfair' (that is, inappropriate) to try him, even though a trial would be (forensically) fair, the judge must weigh countervailing considerations and determine whether the proceedings, if allowed to continue, would bring the administration of justice into disrepute. In *R* v. *Latif* [1996] 1 WLR 104, a case where it was submitted that the proceedings should be stayed (or the prosecution evidence excluded under s. 78(1) of PACE) on the ground that a customs officer and his informer had incited L's co-accused, S, to commit the offence of being knowingly involved in the fraudulent importation of heroin and had lured him into the jurisdiction, Lord Steyn explained the general approach which should be adopted (at pp. 112–13):

> 'The court has a discretion: it has to perform a balancing exercise. If the court concludes that a fair trial is not possible, it will stay the proceedings. That is not what the present case is concerned with ... In this case the issue is whether, despite the fact that a fair trial was possible, the judge ought to have stayed the criminal proceedings on broader considerations of the integrity of the criminal justice system. The law is settled. Weighing countervailing considerations of policy and justice, it is for the judge in the exercise of his discretion to decide whether there has been an abuse of process, which amounts to an affront to the public conscience and requires the criminal proceedings to be stayed ... General guidance as to how the discretion should be exercised in particular circumstances will not be useful. But it is possible to say that in a case such as the present the judge must weigh in the balance the public interest in ensuring that those that are charged with grave crimes should be tried and the competing public interest in not conveying the impression that the court will adopt the approach that the end justifies the means.'

The reference to grave crimes would appear to suggest that the seriousness of the offence is a relevant consideration. Indeed in *R* v. *Mullen* [1999] 3 WLR 777 the Court of Appeal held that 'great weight' must be attached to the fact that the accused was charged with a terrorist offence, and emphasised that there may be cases where the seriousness of the offence is so great relative to the nature of the abuse of process that it would nonetheless be a proper exercise of judicial discretion to permit the prosecution to proceed. This is no doubt the case where the impropriety is wholly extraneous to the commission of the offence, as in *R* v. *Mullen*, but it seems the seriousness of the offence will not be given much (if any) weight as a factor militating against a stay if the allegation of impropriety is that agents of the executive deliberately brought about that offence as *agents provocateurs* (*R* v. *Looseley, Attorney General's Reference (No. 3 of 2000)* at pp. 2070, 2079 and 2090).

Although the justification for the second ground in criminal proceedings turns on the need to control the agents of the state so that they do not violate the rights of its citizens, it may be that the balancing exercise is to be undertaken if the allegation is merely that an ordinary citizen instigated the commission of the offence, save that lawlessness of this sort is to be given less weight than executive lawlessness (see *R* v. *Hardwicke* [2001] Crim LR 220 (CA)). If this is a general principle it is one which is difficult to understand, unless of course the citizen is acting in league with agents of the executive as their stooge. A more appropriate solution would be to prosecute the *agent provocateur* for incitement or as an accessory in respect of the offence allegedly committed by the accused (the person incited), and to take into consideration the degree of incitement as a mitigating factor for the accused in the event that he is convicted.

Civil courts also have an inherent jurisdiction to stay proceedings as an abuse of process if it would be manifestly unfair to a party to allow the proceedings to continue or the proceedings would otherwise bring the administration of justice into disrepute among right-thinking people (*Hunter* v. *Chief Constable of the West Midlands Police* [1981] 3 WLR 906 (HL) at p. 909, *Re Barings (No. 2)* [1999] 1 All ER 311 (CA) at pp. 335–6 and 339; see also r. 3.4(2)(*b*) of the Civil Procedure Rules 1998). In *Arrow Nominees* v. *Blackledge* [2000] 2 BCLC 167 (CA) Chadwick LJ said (at pp. 193–4):

'where a litigant's conduct puts the fairness of the trial in jeopardy, where it is such that any judgment in favour of the litigant would have to be regarded as unsafe, or where it amounts to such an abuse of the process of the court as to render further proceedings unsatisfactory and to prevent the court from doing justice, the court is entitled, indeed ... bound, to refuse to allow that litigant to take further part in the proceedings and (where appropriate) to determine the proceedings against him.'

10.5 **Entrapment**

In *R* v. *Sang* [1979] 3 WLR 263 (HL) it was held there was no discretion at common law to exclude prosecution evidence merely because the accused had been incited to commit the offence by a police *agent provocateur*. Since there was no defence of entrapment in English law there could be no discretion to exclude such evidence as that would amount to the defence being made available through the back door. However, in *R* v. *Smurthwaite, R* v. *Gill* (1993) 98 Cr App R 437, two cases (consolidated on appeal) in which the prosecution depended on the evidence of undercover police officers who had posed as contract killers, the Court of Appeal recognised that s. 78(1) of PACE is available to exclude prosecution evidence obtained by police *agents provocateurs*, providing authority for the view that reliable evidence might fall within the exclusionary remit of that subsection. The Court listed some of the factors the trial judge ought to consider when deciding whether to apply s. 78(1) (at pp. 440–1):

> 'Was the officer acting as an *agent provocateur* in the sense that he was enticing the defendant to commit an offence he would not otherwise have committed? What was the nature of any entrapment? Does the evidence consist of admissions to a completed offence, or does it consist of the actual commission of an offence? How active or passive was the officer's role in obtaining the evidence? Is there an unassailable record of what occurred, or is it strongly corroborated? ... [Has the officer] abused his role to ask questions which ought properly to have been asked as a police officer and in accordance with the [PACE] Codes [?]'

In each of these two cases the accused had sought to hire a killer to murder his or her spouse, and they were both convicted on the evidence of what they had said to undercover police officers. S had offered an officer £20,000 to kill his wife and subsequently paid him £10,000 up front. He had approached the officer of his own volition and all the conversations had been recorded by concealed recording equipment. G had first telephoned an acquaintance and asked him to kill her husband, but prior to their meeting the acquaintance had contacted the police and was therefore accompanied by an undercover officer when he met her. The officer gave evidence that G had discussed the murder of her husband and although there was no recording of what was said (nor any independent confirmation from the acquaintance) their subsequent recorded meetings corroborated the officer's account of what had been said during their first meeting. In each case the officer had been a passive listener whom the accused had voluntarily approached and solicited. Neither officer could be described as an *agent provocateur* and, unsurprisingly, the Court of Appeal held that their evidence had been properly admitted (see also *R* v. *Mann* [1995] Crim LR 647 (CA)).

It is to be noted that some of the factors cited in *R* v. *Smurthwaite, R* v. *Gill* (1993) 98 Cr App R 437 (CA) are nothing other than well-established principles. The desirability of having an 'unassailable record' represents the continuing importance of the reliability principle; and the significance of the evidence consisting of 'admissions to a completed offence' lies in the importance attached to the privilege against self-incrimination. Nevertheless, the Court's observations represented a departure from the common-law discretion, as it was accepted that reliable evidence could be excluded under s. 78(1) if it related to an offence which had been incited by a police officer.

Prior to the decision in *R* v. *Looseley, Attorney General's Reference (No. 3 of 2000)* [2001] 1 WLR 2061 (HL) it was clear that if the police merely provided the accused with an opportunity to commit an offence the evidence obtained in consequence would not be excluded under s. 78(1). This was the approach adopted by the Divisional Court in *Williams* v. *DPP* (1993) 98 Cr App R 209, a case following a police 'manna from heaven' operation in which officers had parked an insecure and unattended van, containing what appeared to be a load of cigarette cartons, on a busy high street where there had been a high rate of vehicle crime. The police ensured that the cartons were visible to the general public through the partly-opened roller shutter at the rear of the van, and then withdrew to keep watch from a distance. A large number of pedestrians passed the van during the next hour without showing any interest in it or its contents, but a little later the two accused arrived and began to assess the situation. They removed some of the cartons about 10 minutes later and were subsequently arrested and charged. At their trial they argued that as they had not set out to commit the crime but had been tempted by the police, the evidence of the observing officers ought to be excluded under s. 78(1). This submission was rejected by the magistrates and the Divisional Court, the latter holding that the police had not acted as *agents provocateurs* as they had done nothing to force, persuade, encourage or coerce the accused to do what they had done. Rather, the accused had acted voluntarily in the absence of any pressure and with full understanding of their own dishonesty. Wright J drew an analogy with the situation where a policewoman dresses in plain clothes and walks around a particular neighbourhood to attract a molester thought to be operating in the area. Just as there would be no unfairness in admitting evidence that an alleged sex offender had been seen to attack an undercover policewoman, there was no unfairness in admitting the officers' evidence that the accused had removed cartons from the van. The problem with this analysis is that it failed to consider whether the accused would have committed the offence even without the police trickery. In fact there was nothing to suggest that they would have interfered with a vehicle if the trap had not been set for them, the implication being that the police were entitled to create crime in order to secure convictions. A particular locality is unlikely to have many sex offenders who are willing to attack women in public, but it is likely that many citizens will be tempted by an opportunity to commit petty theft; and, while theft is to be deprecated, one might question police tactics which are designed to encourage rather than prevent the commission of crime.

Thus, in the absence of active incitement there was an unwillingness to consider anything but the reliability principle when considering the application of s. 78(1). Another example is *DPP* v. *Marshall* [1988] 3 All ER 683 (DC), where it was held there had been nothing to justify the exclusion of the evidence of undercover police officers who had made a 'test purchase' of four cans of lager and a bottle of wine from the accused, causing him to be in breach of his licence to sell liquor by the case (see also *London Borough of Ealing* v. *Woolworths* [1995] Crim LR 58 (DC)).

The extent to which it is permissible for the police to obtain evidence by setting up an undercover operation in relation to prospective criminal conduct, where they become involved in the criminal conduct of the accused and then testify against him at his trial, was considered by the European Court of Human Rights in *Teixeira de Castro* v. *Portugal* (1998) 28 EHRR 101, a case which concerned an act of incitement by undercover police officers on a man who was previously unknown to them and who had no criminal record. Following a request for drugs by the officers the applicant obtained heroin for them and was subsequently charged and convicted on the basis of their evidence. The European Court of Human Rights held there had been a violation of Article 6 of the European Convention, notwithstanding the reliability of the evidence and the fact that the accused had had a trial which was (forensically) fair, as the officers had not acted pursuant to an authorised undercover operation and there had been no evidence that the applicant was predisposed to commit the offence. According to the Court (at pp. 115–16):

'The ... Government have not contended that the officers' intervention took place as part of an anti-drug-trafficking operation ordered and supervised by a judge. It does not appear either that the competent authorities had good reason to suspect that Mr Teixeira de Castro was a drug-trafficker; on the contrary, he had no criminal record and no preliminary investigation concerning him had been opened ... There is no evidence to support the Government's argument that the applicant was predisposed to commit offences. The necessary inference from these circumstances is that the two police officers did not confine themselves to investigating Mr Teixeira de Castro's criminal activity in an essentially passive manner, but exercised an influence such as to incite the commission of the offence ... [T]he Court concludes that the two police officers' actions went beyond those of undercover agents because they instigated the offence and there is nothing to suggest that without their intervention it would have been committed. That intervention and its use in the impugned criminal proceedings meant that, right from the outset, the applicant was definitively deprived of a fair trial.'

The judgment in *Teixeira de Castro* v. *Portugal* was considered by the Divisional Court in the 'test purchase' case of *Nottingham City Council* v. *Amin* [2000] 1 WLR 1071. D was in the centre of Nottingham driving a car which was licensed as a taxi, but not for that particular area. The car was fitted with a roof light, which was not lit, and hailed by two special constables in plain clothes. D took the constables to their destination and was paid his fare, following which he was spoken to by enforcement officers acting for Nottingham City Council and prosecuted for plying for hire without the appropriate licence. The stipendiary magistrate relied on *Teixeira de Castro* v. *Portugal* and s. 78(1) of PACE to exclude the constables' evidence on the ground that they had incited D to commit the offence, and the prosecution appealed by way of case stated. Allowing the appeal the Divisional Court held that, while it would be 'deeply offensive to ordinary notions of fairness' if a person were to be convicted of a crime which he committed only because he had been incited, D had not been persuaded to commit the offence. It was unobjectionable for law enforcement officers to provide an opportunity to break the law in circumstances where the accused would have behaved in the same way if the opportunity had been offered by anyone else, and the decision of the

European Court of Human Rights in *Teixeira de Castro* v. *Portugal* had to be understood in the context of the particular facts of that case. Accordingly, the stipendiary magistrate should not have excluded the evidence.

The degree to which undercover police officers might properly become involved in the commission of an offence, and the appropriate remedy for the accused if they went beyond what could be justified, was finally resolved by the House of Lords in *R* v. *Looseley, Attorney General's Reference (No. 3 of 2000)* [2001] 1 WLR 2061. The following principles may be derived from their Lordships' speeches.

First, while entrapment is not a substantive defence to criminal liability, it is nonetheless unacceptable for the state, through its agents, to lure or entrap its citizens into committing crimes and then to prosecute them for their criminal conduct. To allow such prosecutions to take place would be to condone the executive's abuse of its power, compromise the integrity of the criminal justice system, result in an abuse of the process of the court and possibly lead to a violation of Article 6 of the European Convention on Human Rights (as in *Teixeira de Castro* v. *Portugal*). Such prosecutions should therefore be stayed as an abuse of process, in line with the approach adopted by the Supreme Court of Canada in *R* v. *Mack* [1988] 2 SCR 903 and favoured by McHugh J in his dissenting judgment in *Ridgeway* v. *R* (1995) 184 CLR 19 (HCA) at pp. 91–2. The test to be applied is the balancing exercise identified by Lord Steyn in *R* v. *Latif* [1996] 1 WLR 104 (HL) at pp. 112–13 (10.4 *ante*) and reaffirmed by Lord Hutton at p. 2090: '[I]t is necessary to balance the competing requirements that those who commit crimes should be convicted and punished and that there should not be an abuse of process which would constitute an affront to the public conscience.' When ordering a stay on the ground of abuse of process the court is not disciplining the police, although it may have that effect in practice. The reason for the stay is to prevent any prosecution which would be an affront to the public conscience. In other words, the accused should not be tried if it would be (viscerally) unfair to do so, even though he would receive a (forensically) fair trial.

Second, s. 78(1) of PACE, being primarily concerned with forensic fairness, is an appropriate remedy where police impropriety is alleged in two situations: (i) where the admission of the evidence would lead to a (forensically) unfair trial; and, (ii) where the application to exclude evidence under s. 78(1) is in effect a belated application to have the proceedings stayed. Accordingly, it is permissible to exclude prosecution evidence under s. 78(1) if the behaviour of the police or prosecuting authority has been such as to justify a stay on grounds of abuse of process, in which case the *Latif* balancing exercise should be undertaken. In particular, it is permissible to exclude prosecution evidence (indeed all the prosecution evidence) under s. 78(1) in cases of entrapment (in line with *R* v. *Smurthwaite, R* v. *Gill* (1993) 98 Cr App R 437 (CA)), save that the grant of a stay on the ground of abuse of process should be the appropriate response in most cases.

Third, not every type of active involvement by the police (or similar agency) in the commission of a crime is to be regarded as unacceptable. In the context of regulatory offences, random test purchases from persons such as traders and taxi drivers fall within this category of permissible conduct, so long as the accused was approached in a way which is no different from the way in which any ordinary customer might have approached him (as, for example, in *Nottingham City Council* v. *Amin* [2000] 1 WLR 1071 (DC)). Proactive investigatory techniques are also permissible in relation to other types of crime, such as offences concerning the supply of drugs, so long as the conduct of the police does not amount to 'state-created crime'. Thus, if the accused already had the intention to commit an offence of the same or a similar kind to that ultimately committed, and the police merely provided him with the opportunity to put his intention into effect, an argument to stay the proceedings or exclude the prosecution evidence under s. 78(1) on the ground of entrapment would fail.

Fourth, state-created crime covers the sort of situation where the police implanted the intent in the accused's mind so that he committed a crime which would otherwise not have been committed. It would, for example, be objectionable for an undercover officer to coerce a vulnerable drug-addict into supplying drugs by repeatedly badgering him with offers of excessive and increasing amounts of money. This does not mean that the presence or absence of a predisposition to commit the crime is a criterion by which the acceptability of police conduct is to be assessed, however, for a predisposition to commit crime does not negative the misuse of state power. Accordingly, the appropriate test will generally be 'whether the police did no more than present the defendant with an unexceptional opportunity to commit a crime', that is, 'whether the police conduct preceding the commission of the offence was no more than might have been expected from others in the circumstances' (*per* Lord Nicholls at p. 2069). The following dictum of McHugh J was approved:

'The state can justify the use of entrapment techniques to induce the commission of an offence only when the inducement is consistent with the ordinary temptations and stratagems that are likely to be encountered in the course of criminal activity. That may mean that some degree of deception, importunity and even threats on the part of the authorities may be acceptable. But once the state goes beyond the ordinary, it is likely to increase the incidence of crime by artificial means.' (*Ridgeway* v. *R* (1995) 184 CLR 19 (HCA) at p. 92)

Accordingly, because a dealer will not voluntarily offer drugs to a stranger unless the stranger first makes an approach to him, and the stranger may need to persist in his request for drugs before they are supplied, a persistent request by an undercover officer for drugs may not amount to entrapment if the accused (supplier) already had the intention to supply.

Fifth, in some situations the proceedings should be stayed as an abuse of process (or the evidence excluded under s. 78(1)) even if the police merely provided the accused with an opportunity to commit the crime, if that crime was artificially created by the state. An example would be where a police officer seeks to increase his arrest rate by planting a wallet in an obvious location in a park with a view to arresting the person who steals it. A relevant factor is whether the officer concerned was acting in the course of an officially authorised investigation (*Teixeira de Castro* v. *Portugal*). Such unacceptable conduct should be contrasted with *bona fide*, authorised investigations where the police have reasonable grounds for suspecting that an individual is committing crime, or that crime is being committed in a certain place or area, and it is necessary to set a trap (in the form of an opportunity) to catch the offender. For example, it would be permissible to leave a handbag in a bus terminal where numerous thefts have recently taken place or an unattended van with cigarette cartons in the back in an area where thefts from vehicles is commonplace (as in *Williams* v. *DPP* (1993) 98 Cr App R 209 (DC)).

Sixth, ultimately the test for whether the proceedings should be stayed as an abuse of process (or s. 78(1) applied) is whether the conduct of the police or similar agency was so seriously improper as to bring the administration of justice into disrepute. To determine this a number of factors need to be brought into the *Latif* balancing exercise, the weight and importance of which will depend on the particular facts of the case. The judge should consider the nature of the offence (in the sense that proactive investigatory techniques are necessary); the reason for the operation (for example whether there are reasonable grounds for suspecting criminal activity, save that random testing may be the only practicable way of policing some activities); the intrusiveness of the investigatory technique used by the police (a factor which incorporates the Convention question of proportionality); whether the operation was *bona fide* and authorised; and the nature and extent of police participation in the crime, including the significance of any inducement (for which the accused's circumstances and vulnerability are relevant factors). It would not normally be objectionable for the police to behave like any ordinary customer of a (lawful or unlawful) trade being carried on by the accused. The accused's criminal record may be relevant as a factor giving rise to a reasonable suspicion that he is currently engaged in similar activity, but otherwise it should be disregarded. Nor in itself is the seriousness of the offence a relevant factor.

Seventh, Article 6 of the European Convention on Human Rights, as interpreted in *Teixeira de Castro* v. *Portugal*, includes the right not to be tried at all if the prosecution would amount to an abuse of state power. Accordingly there is no appreciable difference between the requirements of Article 6 and English law. Section 78(1) of PACE and the common-law doctrine of abuse of process are sufficient safeguards to ensure that the accused receives a fair trial and that he will be tried only when it is fair (that is, appropriate) to do so.

In *R* v. *Looseley* the police were concerned about the trade in class A drugs in their area and had reason to believe that a public house in Guildford was the focal point of the trade. They therefore set up an undercover operation involving an officer known as 'Rob' who spent time in that public house. While there, Rob was provided with the name and telephone number of a possible supplier. He called that person (who turned out to be L) and said, 'Hello, mate, can you sort us out a couple of bags?' L agreed and gave Rob directions to his flat. At the flat L agreed to provide Rob with some heroin for £30, and the two of them went to another flat where the heroin was obtained. On two further occasions Rob bought small quantities of heroin from L and ultimately L was charged with supplying or being concerned in the supplying to another of a class A controlled drug. Following a *voir dire* the judge rejected the application to stay the proceedings (or apply s. 78(1) to exclude Rob's evidence) and this ruling was upheld by the House of Lords. The covert operation had been authorised and supervised by a senior officer; there was reason to believe that L was involved in the heroin trade; Rob had presented himself to L as nothing other than a heroin addict and prospective customer; and Rob had not incited the commission of a crime (indeed there was evidence to suggest that L had encouraged Rob to take more heroin).

The facts in *R* v. *Looseley* were described by Lord Hoffmann as 'miles away' from what had happened in *Teixeira de Castro* v. *Portugal*, but the same cannot be said of the covert operation which led to the stay in *Attorney General's Reference (No. 3 of 2000)*. In that case the accused was approached by undercover officers and sold some purportedly contraband cigarettes. The officers subsequently asked him whether he could provide them with heroin, and he eventually obtained some for them, even though he had made it clear that he was not 'into' that drug. The House of Lords held that the judge had been entitled to exercise his discretion to stay the proceedings in the accused's favour, even if it had been an authorised operation. The accused, who had made it clear that he was not involved in the heroin trade, had been repeatedly offered (and supplied with) cut-price cigarettes as an inducement and he had felt obliged to return this favour by obtaining what the officers had asked for. In short, the officers had instigated an offence which the accused would not otherwise have committed. Only Lord Scott was of the view that the officers' conduct had not been sufficiently grave to amount to an abuse of process, although it was accepted that the trial judge's decision was one that he was entitled to reach on the facts.

Lord Hoffmann pointed out that while the court's inherent jurisdiction to stay proceedings is said to be on the ground that the proceedings are an abuse of process it would be more accurate to describe the jurisdiction more broadly as one to prevent abuse of executive power. It follows that if the accused was incited to commit the offence charged by an ordinary citizen, the submission that the proceedings should be stayed ought to fail. This would appear to have been accepted in *R* v. *Shannon* [2001] 1 WLR 51 where the accused was encouraged to supply drugs to an undercover newspaper reporter posing as an Arab sheikh. The Court of Appeal stated that an abuse of process argument was unavailable unless there was impropriety on the part of 'the police (or someone acting on behalf of or in league with the police) and/or the prosecuting authority'. However, in *R* v.

Hardwicke [2001] Crim LR 220 the Court of Appeal accepted that commercial unlawfulness might justify staying criminal proceedings as an abuse of process (in the absence of forensic unfairness); and in *R* v. *Marriner* [2002] EWCA Crim 2855 the Court of Appeal would appear to have assumed that journalistic entrapment could lead to a stay.

With regard to the way in which other common-law jurisdictions have addressed the problem of police entrapment, the approach consistently adopted by the US Supreme Court since its decision in *Sorrells* v. *United States* (1932) 287 US 435 is that it amounts to a substantive defence to an allegation of criminal liability (so long as the accused was not predisposed to commit the offence), save that sufficiently outrageous conduct by the police may justify a decision to halt the proceedings on 'due process principles' (*United States* v. *Russell* (1973) 411 US 423 (USSC) at pp. 431–2). In *Ridgeway* v. *R* (1995) 184 CLR 19 the majority of the High Court of Australia held that where the commission of the offence was procured by unlawful conduct, evidence of the accused's guilt could properly be excluded 'on public policy grounds' (applying or extending the general discretion to exclude unlawfully obtained evidence recognised in *Bunning* v. *Cross* (1978) 141 CLR 54 (HCA)). A discretion to exclude evidence in such circumstances 'to prevent an abuse of process by the avoidance of unfairness' has also been recognised in New Zealand (*Police* v. *Lavalle* [1979] 1 NZLR 45 (NZCA) at p. 48).

10.6 Exceptions to the General Rule

Although the general rule is that unlawfully or unfairly obtained evidence is *prima facie* admissible in any proceedings, whether civil or criminal, there are a number of exceptions, three of which are worth noting. First, a confession excluded in criminal proceedings by virtue of s. 76(2) of PACE is inadmissible as a matter of law (see 7.1.3.1–2 *ante*). Second, in civil proceedings where one party has by stealth or by trick taken possession of documents brought into court by his opponent he will not be able to adduce such evidence: the public interest which favours a litigant's freedom to bring documents into court safe in the knowledge that they will not be taken by his opponent outweighs the principle of free proof (*ITC Film Distributors* v. *Video Exchange* [1982] 1 Ch 431 (ChD)). Third, by virtue of s. 17 of the Regulation of Investigatory Powers Act 2000 (supplanting s. 9 of the Interception of Communications Act 1985) evidence which discloses any of the contents of an intercepted communication (that is, any communication intercepted in the course of its transmission by means of a postal service or telecommunication system) is generally inadmissible in civil or criminal proceedings, the rationale being the desirability of keeping the nature of such surveillance operations secret (see *R* v. *P* [2001] 2 WLR 463 (HL) at pp. 475–9). An intercepted communication does not include the recording of a telephone conversation by one party to the call (*R* v. *Hardy* [2003] 1 Cr App R 494 (CA)).

Chapter Summary

- As a general rule evidence which is admissible remains admissible if it has been obtained unlawfully or unfairly by the police or a party to civil proceedings.
- At common law and under s. 78(1) of the Police and Criminal Evidence Act 1984 the criminal courts may exclude prosecution evidence which has been unlawfully obtained if the manner in which it was obtained has adversely affected its reliability (or the accused's ability to test its reliability) or the evidence is analogous to a confession obtained by trickery in violation of the accused's privilege against self-incrimination.
- The criminal courts have a discretion to 'stay' proceedings as an abuse of process to maintain the integrity of the criminal justice system if the police acted unlawfully in obtaining the evidence against the accused, for example where the accused was incited by the police to commit an offence so that he could be prosecuted for it. The court will balance countervailing considerations of policy and justice to determine whether it is appropriate for the accused to be tried. An application to exclude prosecution evidence during the trial under s. 78(1) of the Police and Criminal Evidence Act 1984 may be treated as a belated application to stay the proceedings as an abuse of process.
- Civil courts have a discretion to stay proceedings as an abuse of process, and may exclude admissible evidence, but if evidence has been obtained unlawfully by one party it would be undesirable to exclude it for that reason.

Further Reading

Ashworth, 'Excluding Evidence as Protecting Rights' [1977] Crim LR 723

Dennis, 'Reconstructing the Law of Criminal Evidence' (1989) 42 CLP 21

Allen, 'Discretion and Security: Excluding Evidence under Section 78(1)' (1990) CLJ 80

Gelowitz, 'Section 78 of PACE' (1990) 106 LQR 327

The Royal Commission on Criminal Justice Report (1993) Cm 2263, pp. 172, 233–5

Robertson, 'Entrapment Evidence' [1994] Crim LR 805

Birch, 'Excluding Evidence from Entrapment' (1994) 47(2) CLP 73

Stone, 'Exclusion of Evidence under Section 78' [1995] 3 Web JCLI (http://webjcli.ncl.ac.uk)

Grevling, 'Fairness and Exclusion of Evidence under Section 78(1)' (1997) 113 LQR 667

Ashworth, 'Re-drawing the Boundaries of Entrapment' [2002] Crim LR 161

Ormerod and Roberts, 'The Trouble with *Teixeira*' (2002) 6 E & P 38

Ormerod, 'ECHR and the Exclusion of Evidence' [2003] Crim LR 61

11 Safeguards Against Unreliability and Error

It has been seen that hearsay evidence is generally inadmissible in criminal proceedings because it is not possible to cross-examine the person who made the statement to test the reliability of his evidence (5.2 *ante*). It has also been seen that there are exceptions to the hearsay rule, and that if a hearsay statement is admitted in criminal proceedings the judge will comment on the unavailability of the person who made it and point out any specific weaknesses in the evidence (6.3 *ante*). The need to give some form of direction or cautionary warning arises in respect of other types of evidence too, either on account of its inherent unreliability or because of some other risk associated with it; but, unlike hearsay evidence, no blanket exclusionary rule applies and the jury will usually be entitled to consider the evidence at the end of the trial.

It is difficult to generalise about the various types of evidence covered in this chapter, apart from the fact that there is a risk in each case that the jury might draw an erroneous inference if allowed to consider it in the absence of a safeguard. Unreliability may be an inherent and latent quality of the evidence, or may lie in the number of alternative inferences capable of being drawn from it; or there may be a danger associated with the evidence simply because of its complexity (and the risk that its true probative value will be misunderstood) or because of the possibility that a witness is lying. It should not be assumed, however, that *every* item of evidence falling within one of the categories covered here is inherently weak or unreliable. The potential for unreliability and error is a matter of degree, and some such evidence will in fact be *highly* reliable (and highly probative). Visual-identification evidence, the category covered here in most depth, is a good example. As a general rule evidence of this sort is notoriously unreliable, and has been the cause of a number of miscarriages of justice; but the risk of a mistaken identification (or recognition) will occasionally be negligible. For example, the victim of a kidnapping who has spent several weeks in close proximity to his captor may be able to give irrefutable eye-witness testimony identifying the accused as the perpetrator.

11.1 Visual-identification Evidence

If it is not in dispute that an offence has occurred, the only remaining issue at the trial will often be the identity of the perpetrator. The class of possible candidates may be narrowed down by drawing inferences from circumstantial evidence (such as fingerprints, footprints, DNA, handwriting, fibres, scent, motive, opportunity and so on) or, of course, by calling a witness to testify that he *saw* the accused committing the offence. There seems to be a general assumption by lay triers of fact that eye-witness testimony is one of the safest bases for any identification; there have certainly been convictions based on very weak visual-identification evidence (for example, *R* v. *Mattan (Deceased)* (1998) *The Times* 5.3.98 (97/6415/S2) (CA) and *R* v. *Ross* [1960] Crim LR 127 (CCA)). In fact visual-identification evidence is often unreliable, and is therefore a potentially hazardous way of connecting a person to an offence. The classic example is where a witness testifies that he saw the offence being committed by a stranger some distance away, for a relatively short period of time, in far from ideal conditions. But it is not just such 'fleeting glance' identification evidence which can lead to miscarriages of justice. Even what appears to be highly reliable recognition evidence may in fact be quite erroneous, and there is no better illustration of this than the tale of Mr Adolf Beck.

Adolf Beck lived in South America for many years towards the end of the nineteenth century, during which time a man, who called himself John Smith, and who resembled Beck, was convicted of a number of deception offences against women in London. In 1895, after Beck had returned to London and Smith had been released from prison, similar deceptions on women again began to occur. The offender would visit women in their homes, become intimate with them, gain their confidence and then defraud them of money and jewellery. Beck was identified as the culprit by one of the women and arrested. Subsequently he was positively identified by a further eleven women who had been defrauded and by two former police officers as the John Smith in whose case they had been involved in 1877. Beck was convicted and sentenced to seven years' imprisonment. In 1904, within three years of Beck's release, the same sort of offences once again began to be committed. Beck was arrested, identified by four women and again convicted. However, during the period while Beck was in custody further frauds were perpetrated and Smith was finally arrested. It subsequently became apparent that it was Smith who had committed the offences Beck had been convicted of; so, despite the numerous and apparently reliable visual identifications, Beck had been wrongly convicted on two occasions (see *The Trial of Adolf Beck, Notable British Trials* (1924)).

The Beck case is not an isolated example for there have been numerous other cases of mistaken identifications resulting in a conviction. For example, a Mr Oscar Slater spent almost two decades in prison, having been mistakenly identified by fourteen witnesses, before his conviction was quashed in 1928. A Committee of Inquiry set up following the Beck miscarriage concluded that identifications based on subjective personal impressions were inherently unreliable ((1904) Cd 2315). This view was endorsed by the Criminal Law Revision Committee in its Eleventh Report ((1972) Cmnd 4991, p. 116) which stated that 'the greatest cause of actual or possible wrongful convictions' was mistaken visual-identification evidence. There are a number of reasons why this is so.

First, the physical and psychological condition of the witness, as a fallible human being, militates against an accurate identification. To identify a suspect or the accused by sight as the same person seen on a previous occasion is, after all, no more than the witness's personal opinion based on his subjective perception of apparent similarities between two images on his retina. The reliability of the witness's opinion depends entirely on the reliability of the visible features of the first image which were actually seen and mentally recorded by him (which in turn depends on the extent to which he was paying attention, his physical and psychological powers of perception at that time and his memory) together with the reliability of his comparison of the stored image with the visible features of the second image.

Identifying witnesses may focus on broad impressions or features which stimulate their own subjective preferences rather than on the multitude of specific physical details, so markedly different facial characteristics between the offender and the accused may go unnoticed while vague similarities may be given undue weight. The problem becomes even more acute when the identifying witness and the identified person (the offender) are from different racial groups or generations. Another problem, which may arise in a case of purported *recognition*, is that of 'unconscious transference' where the witness confuses the offender with a different person seen in some other context. Conversely, if the witness claims never to have seen the offender before, the reliability of his identification is likely to decrease with time as his memory fades.

Second, the eye-witness may be honestly mistaken but sincerely convinced that his identification is correct. In *R* v. *Fergus* (1993) 98 Cr App R 313 (CA), for example, the sole prosecution witness was said to have felt an 'invincible conviction in the correctness of his identification' of the accused even though the witness had poor eyesight, did not take much notice of the offender's face and first described the offender as 5' 11" tall with a light complexion and stubble, when the accused was 5' 7" tall, dark-skinned and had not yet started shaving.

The conventional forensic tool for revealing weaknesses in testimony is cross-examination, but where visual-identification evidence is concerned this tool may be singularly ineffective and, ironically, may indirectly buttress the witness's testimony. In other words, a mistaken witness may become more convinced that he is right, and therefore appear even more convincing to the jury, the more his identification evidence is challenged (as indeed happened when Adolf Beck was tried). Alternatively, the witness may convince himself of the accuracy of his identification the more he thinks about it, or the more he discusses it with other individuals, particularly if those individuals also claim to have seen what happened and the witness is suggestible. The witness's memory may be distorted not only by the passage of time but by his having rehearsed the matter in his own mind, or in response to questions, or by his having been subconsciously influenced by the suggestions of other individuals.

Marcus Stone (*Proof of Fact in Criminal Trials* (1984), pp. 76–7) notes that errors in the witness's identification may become 'frozen' the more he recalls the incident he observed, with the witness recalling what he previously said or thought (rather than what he actually saw), becoming more confident about the accuracy of his identification on each subsequent occasion. Other factors include the tendency for evidence to become 'coherent, consistent and integrated over a period, so that doubts and gaps are eliminated and it becomes streamlined', and the witness's anxiety about the consequences of his being inconsistent. An example is provided by *R* v. *Johnson* [2001] 1 Cr App R 408, where the eye-witness's perception of the accuracy of her observation on 5 January varied from 'I don't think I would know him again' in her first statement to the police on the same date, to 'I'm not quite sure' at the identification parade on 2 March (when she picked out the accused), to 'I am quite certain that the man I picked out was the man I saw on January 5' in her statement of 6 March and 'I recognise the defendant Johnson as the driver ... I stared at the driver and he stared back at me' in her deposition of 29 March. The Court of Appeal noted that it is 'common experience that a witness who is perfectly honest can become more positive in their identification as time passes, when it is well-known that identification becomes more difficult after a lapse of time'.

Third, the circumstances and duration of the observation may adversely affect the reliability of the eye-witness's evidence. In addition to the problems associated with the witness's own physical and psychological ability (and willingness) to perceive, remember and compare, features may go unnoticed at the time of the identification because of extraneous factors such as movement, poor lighting, the distance involved and obstructions along the line of sight. A visual identification made over a lengthy period of time in conditions of good visibility is less likely to be unreliable but, even then, the possibility of mistake cannot always be discounted. It should be remembered that John Smith was seen at close quarters by all the women he defrauded, and yet sixteen of them were able to misidentify Adolf Beck as the offender.

The accused's advocate will of course focus on the circumstances of any visual identification to show that they were not conducive to accurate observation, but lay triers of fact will not necessarily be able to translate court-room descriptions into an accurate picture of the real circumstances. The problem can be overcome to some extent by having the jury visit the site as, for example, in *R* v. *Sawoniuk* [2000] 2 Cr App R 220 (CA), a recognition case where the court visited the scene of a wartime massacre of Jewish women in eastern Europe, but it will only rarely be possible to recreate the exact circumstances of the witness's observation, particularly as the description of the circumstances may depend on nothing more than the eye-witness's own recollection. Unless the circumstances were so poor as to make any purported identification patently absurd, there is always a risk that the jury or magistrates will instead rely on the demeanour and apparent self-confidence of the witness standing before them to determine whether his identification was accurate; but, as explained above, the witness's self-confidence may be no more than honest self-delusion. The Supreme Court of Victoria summarised the problems associated with visual-identification evidence in *R* v. *Dickson* [1983] 1 VR 227 (at p. 231):

> 'Jurors, who ... have not given thought to the way in which evidence of visual identification depends on the witness receiving, recording and recalling accurately a fairly subjective impression on the mind, are unlikely to be aware of the extent of the risk that honest and convincing witnesses may be mistaken, especially where their opportunities for observing a previously unknown offender were limited.'

In the mid-1970s further miscarriages of justice based on visual-identification evidence came to light, resulting in the formation of the Devlin Committee and its subsequent report on identification evidence in criminal trials ((1976) HC 338). The Devlin Report recommended that in all cases where the prosecution had to rely wholly or mainly on disputed visual-identification evidence the jury should be warned of its hazardous nature. Another recommendation was that convictions based on such evidence should be permissible only if the identification was supported by additional evidence, unless there were 'exceptional circumstances' to justify a conviction without supporting evidence, for example where the identification evidence comprised a recognition by someone who knew the accused well, or the accused admitted that he had been one of a small group at the scene of the offence and the prosecution could prove one of that group had committed the offence. The Devlin Committee gave as examples of additional evidence an identification by the witness of a distinctive feature on the offender or an inference drawn from the accused himself, and envisaged the introduction of legislation to implement its recommendations. However, within a few months of the Committee's findings being published Parliament was pre-empted by the Court of Appeal in *R* v. *Turnbull* [1976] 3 WLR 445. Cynics might suggest that the speed with which the Court of Appeal acted demonstrated its fear of Devlin-inspired legislation and its desire to introduce a watered-down version in its place.

11.1.1 The *Turnbull* Guidelines

The judgment of the five-member Court of Appeal in *R* v. *Turnbull* [1976] 3 WLR 445 (at pp. 447–9) represents one of the landmark decisions in the law of evidence. Lord Widgery CJ, giving the Court's judgment, suggested the following guidelines to prevent miscarriages of justice caused by unreliable visual-identification evidence:

> 'Firstly, whenever the case against an accused depends wholly or substantially on the correctness of one or more identifications of the accused which the defence alleges to be mistaken, the judge should warn the jury of the special need for caution before convicting the accused in reliance on the correctness of the identification or identifications. In addition he should instruct them as to the reason for the need for such a

warning and should make some reference to the possibility that a mistaken witness can be a convincing one and that a number of such witnesses can all be mistaken. Provided this is done in clear terms the judge need not use any particular form of words.

Secondly, the judge should direct the jury to examine closely the circumstances in which the identification by each witness came to be made. How long did the witness have the accused under observation? At what distance? In what light? Was the observation impeded in any way, as for example by passing traffic or a press of people? Had the witness ever seen the accused before? How often? If only occasionally, had he any special reason for remembering the accused? How long elapsed between the original observation and the subsequent identification to the police? Was there any material discrepancy between the description of the accused given to the police by the witness when first seen by them and his actual appearance? If in any case, whether it is being dealt with summarily or on indictment, the prosecution have reason to believe that there is such a material discrepancy they should supply the accused or his legal advisers with the particulars of the description the police were first given. In all cases if the accused asks to be given particulars of such descriptions, the prosecution should supply them. Finally, he should remind the jury of any specific weaknesses which had appeared in the identification evidence.

Recognition may be more reliable than identification of a stranger; but even when the witness is purporting to recognise someone whom he knows, the jury should be reminded that mistakes in recognition of close relatives and friends are sometimes made.

All these matters go to the quality of the identification evidence. If the quality is good and remains good at the close of the accused's case, the danger of mistaken identification is lessened; but the poorer the quality the greater the danger.

In our judgment when the quality is good, as for example when the identification is made after a long period of observation, or in satisfactory conditions by a relative, a neighbour, a close friend, a workmate and the like, the jury can safely be left to assess the value of the identifying evidence even though there is no other evidence to support it: provided always, however, that an adequate warning has been given about the special need for caution ...

When, in the judgment of the trial judge, the quality of the identifying evidence is poor, as for example when it depends solely on a fleeting glance or on a longer observation made in difficult conditions, the situation is very different. The judge should then withdraw the case from the jury and direct an acquittal unless there is other evidence which goes to support the correctness of the identification ... The trial judge should identify to the jury the evidence which he adjudges is capable of supporting the evidence of identification ...

A failure to follow these guidelines is likely to result in a conviction being quashed and will do so if in the judgment of this court on all the evidence the verdict is ... unsafe.'

The Court of Appeal departed from the Devlin recommendation that visual-identification evidence, upon which the prosecution were heavily dependent, should in all but exceptional circumstances be supported by other evidence, holding instead that a case would need to be withdrawn from the tribunal of fact only if the sole evidence against the accused comprised an unsupported poor-quality identification. The reason given for imposing a less onerous burden on the prosecution was to ensure that an offender could still be convicted on the basis of one eye-witness's good-quality identification evidence. The *Turnbull* guidelines therefore represent the judiciary's age-old attempt to reconcile two competing principles – the need on the one hand to admit evidence to ensure that the guilty are convicted (the principle of free proof); and the competing principle that unduly prejudicial evidence ought to be excluded to ensure that the innocent are acquitted.

The view of the Devlin Committee was that visual-identification evidence is, as a general rule, so unreliable and prejudicial that it should form the substance of the prosecution's case only in exceptional circumstances. The Court of Appeal in *R* v. *Turnbull* decided instead that evidence of this sort is to be regarded as unduly prejudicial only if it is of 'poor quality'. The Court's wider test is a significant improvement over its previous approach (in *R* v. *Long* (1973) 57 Cr App R 871 (CA)) but it is debatable whether the guidelines go far enough to prevent the innocent from being convicted following a misidentification. The quality of visual-identification evidence has been defined in terms of duration, lighting, distance and so on, but the most notorious miscarriages occurred notwithstanding such 'good-quality' evidence. Extraneous circumstances are of course relevant, but the inherent unreliability of visual-identification evidence stems from the fallibilities of the human mind. Trial judges have been given no guidance on whether or how this problem ought to be explained to the jury, although it has been recognised that one weakness which ought to be drawn to their attention is the extent to which the eye-witness was distracted at the time of the identification (*R* v. *Langley* [2000] All ER (D) 55 (99/2017/Z5) (CA)).

The problems associated with visual-identification evidence and 'similar fact evidence' are not dissimilar. Evidence of the accused's extraneous misconduct is generally inadmissible because its probative value in most cases is outweighed by the unduly prejudicial effect its admission would have on the accused and his defence (3.3 *ante*). Jurors and magistrates are thought to be unable to separate the probative wheat from the prejudicial chaff, so such evidence is admissible only exceptionally. Similarly, jurors and magistrates cannot be expected to ascertain the true probative value of visual-identification evidence because of its latent unreliability. There is a real risk that they will assume it to be of high probative value, even when it is unreliable, thereby prejudicing the accused's right to a fair trial. If this analogy is accepted then the appropriate test for the admissibility of visual-identification evidence should be similar to that proposed by the Devlin Committee: in cases where a visual identification comprises an important element of the prosecution case, the presumption of inherent unreliability would justify exclusion unless it could be rebutted by additional evidence supporting the identification or by the exceptional circumstances of the identification. A test along these lines is unlikely to be introduced, however, because numerous offenders would go unpunished. The *Turnbull* guidelines are the product of a cost-benefit analysis aimed at minimising (as opposed to eliminating) wrongful convictions while ensuring that the guilty are brought to account. In fact within a year of *R* v. *Turnbull* the Court of Appeal stated that its guidelines were 'intended primarily to deal with the ghastly risk run in cases of fleeting encounters' (*R* v. *Oakwell* [1978] 1 WLR 32). The 'fleeting glance' cases have been targeted for the obvious reason that the possibility of a wrongful conviction in such circumstances is very high. On the other hand the type of misidentification which led to Adolf Beck's convictions is regarded as highly improbable (see, for example, *R* v. *Ryan* [1990] Crim LR 50 (CA)). This improbability is considered to be incapable of justifying a change in the law which would seriously affect the ability of the criminal justice system to convict offenders. In the final analysis this is a utilitarian approach which accepts the occasional misidentification and wrongful conviction as the price society has to pay to guarantee its safety. This is perhaps why the Court of Appeal in *R* v. *Constantinou* (1989) 91 Cr App R 74 held that a photo-fit picture compiled from eye-witness descriptions of the offender, and admissible as real evidence at the accused's trial, did not warrant a *Turnbull* direction even though it clearly represented a form of visual-identification evidence.

In *R* v. *Forbes* [2001] 2 WLR 1 the House of Lords recognised that the Court of Appeal as constituted in *R* v. *Turnbull* [1976] 3 WLR 445 was 'of exceptional strength'; and the Privy Council has approved the *Turnbull* guidelines on a number of occasions, holding that a failure to give a *Turnbull* direction where the prosecution case has depended wholly or substantially on visual-identification evidence will in all but exceptional circumstances result in the conviction being quashed (see, for example, *Reid* v. *R* [1989] 3 WLR 771 and *Beckford* v. *R* (1993) 97 Cr App R 409; see also *Domican* v. *R* (1992) 173 CLR 555 (HCA)). Exceptional circumstances were found in *Freemantle* v. *R* [1994] 1 WLR 1437 (PC) and *Shand* v. *R* [1996] 1 WLR 67 (PC), though it is to be noted that in each case the jury had been entitled to find supporting evidence in the inculpatory words attributed to the accused. In *Freemantle* v. *R* the offender was recognised as the accused by two prosecution witnesses in bright moonlight, from less than 50 feet away and for between one and two minutes. Moreover, the offender's reaction when the accused's name was shouted out allowed an inference to be drawn that he had acknowledged the recognition to be correct (9.2.1 *ante*). The Privy Council considered the identification evidence to be 'exceptionally good' and upheld the conviction, despite the judge's failure to give a *Turnbull* direction, as the jury would inevitably have convicted even if the direction had been given. In *Shand* v. *R* two eye-witnesses recognised the accused in daylight from four and 30 feet away respectively and, though the Privy Council felt a *Turnbull* direction should have been given, the conviction was upheld. There was nothing to suggest that the witnesses had mistakenly identified the accused, and there was evidence before the jury that he had subsequently confessed his guilt.

The *Turnbull* direction is also necessary in cases where the identification evidence is a disputed recognition (*R* v. *Bowden* [1993] Crim LR 379 (CA), *R* v. *Rodrigues* [2001] EWCA Crim 444). However, because of the higher likelihood that recognition evidence is reliable, it was accepted in *Beckford* v. *R* (1993) 97 Cr App R 409 (PC) that there could be 'very rare' exceptions to this general rule. This is not surprising. In certain circumstances, where the possibility of mistake can be entirely discounted, the accused who disputes recognition evidence will be questioning nothing other than the witness's veracity. A *Turnbull* direction in such cases would be meaningless. Thus, although a direction of some sort is nearly always required, even in recognition cases, it should be tailored according to the facts of the case to prevent the jury being given unnecessary or irrelevant advice. As noted in *R* v. *Bentley* (1991) 99 Cr App R 342 (CA) (at p. 344):

> '[Visual identification] cases ... may vary from one extreme to another: from the fleeting sight of a stranger in a moving car in indifferent light on the one hand to the purported recognition of a familiar face which has taken place over a considerable period of time in perfectly good conditions of lighting and so on. The former will obviously require the full *Turnbull* direction. It contains all the classic identification pitfalls to which the human witness is susceptible. But, if the judge were to give that full *Turnbull* direction in the latter type of case, the jury would rightly wonder whether he, the judge, has taken leave of his senses, because most of the *Turnbull* direction would in those circumstances be quite unnecessary.'

In *R* v. *Taal* [2002] EWCA Crim 1953 the Court of Appeal reaffirmed that the judge should explain the dangers associated with recognition evidence but, noting that the judge was entitled to bring to the jury's attention that a recognition might be more reliable than an identification of a stranger, concluded that a failure to do so would not affect the safety of the conviction if the evidence was presented in a neutral way. Ultimately, the form and content of the summing-up in any case involving a visual-identification depends on the circumstances of the case (*R* v. *Qadir* [1998] Crim LR 828 (CA), *R* v. *Beckles* [1999] Crim LR 148 (CA)).

11.1.1.1 *Turnbull* and the Defence of 'Frame-up'
If the circumstances of a witness's recognition are such as to dispel any risk of mistake, the accused will have no option but to suggest that the witness is lying. In such cases it will not be necessary to give the jury a *Turnbull* direction. In *Beckford* v. *R* (1993) 97 Cr App R 409 the Privy Council gave the example of a witness conversing for half an hour, face to face, with a colleague known to him for 20 years. The only question for the jury would be whether to believe the witness, as there could be no question of a mistaken identification. In *R* v. *Cape* [1996] 1 Cr App R 191 an

incident of violent disorder in a public house was witnessed by the publican, and the prosecution case relied wholly on his testimony. There was no dispute that the publican knew each of the co-accused and that they had all been in his pub at the time; the defence case was that he was motivated by malice and lying on oath. The Court of Appeal held that as the sole issue had been the veracity of the publican, a *Turnbull* direction had been unnecessary (see also *R* v. *Courtnell* [1990] Crim LR 115 (CA)).

That said, where the defence comprises an attack on the eye-witness's veracity there will often be the secondary possibility, once the jury have accepted his truthfulness, that he could have made an honest mistake. In such cases it *is* necessary to give the *Turnbull* direction. A good example is *Beckford* v. *R* (1993) 97 Cr App R 409. The prosecution witness testified that from his hiding place by the road he had recognised the accused murdering a motorist. The accused sought to counter this by alleging that the witness was either a compulsive liar or susceptible to mental aberrations because of his past mental illness. The Privy Council held that a *Turnbull* direction should have been given.

11.1.1.2 *Turnbull* and Police Officers' Evidence

A *Turnbull* direction should be given even if the prosecution eye-witness is a police officer (*Reid* v. *R* [1989] 3 WLR 771 (PC), *R* v. *Bowden* [1993] Crim LR 379 (CA)). Police officers are not infallible observers and may, like any other witness, make honest mistakes. However they do differ from eye-witnesses generally in that their training and experience encourages them to be more observant and to focus on detail, and there is no reason why this should not be taken into account when assessing the reliability of their evidence (see *R* v. *Tyler* (1992) 96 Cr App R 332 (CA) at pp. 342–3). In *R* v. *Williams* (1994) *The Times* 7.10.94 (CA) a police officer made a conscious effort to remember the face of the person he was observing and, though he was able to watch the person for only a short while, the enhanced reliability of his evidence took it outside the fleeting-glance type of case (see also *R* v. *Ramsden* [1991] Crim LR 295 (CA)).

11.1.1.3 *Turnbull* and Undisputed Presence

The mere fact that the accused admits his presence along with others at the scene of a crime does not obviate the need for a *Turnbull* direction if he denies participating in the offence and the issue is mistaken identification. In *R* v. *Thornton* [1995] 1 Cr App R 578 several people attacked a man at a wedding reception and, though the accused admitted being there, he denied any involvement in the offence. The case against him comprised the disputed visual-identification evidence of two witnesses, but no *Turnbull* direction was given. The Court of Appeal quashed his conviction as the full *Turnbull* direction ought to have been given, including a reminder to the jury that several other people at the reception had been dressed like the accused (see also *R* v. *Suleiman* [2000] All ER (D) 1840 (CA)).

In *R* v. *Slater* [1995] 1 Cr App R 584 the Court of Appeal stated that whether a full *Turnbull* direction is necessary in cases of undisputed presence depends on all the circumstances and, in particular, on whether there was a possibility of one person being mistaken for another. S was a man of unusually large size who had allegedly inflicted grievous bodily harm on another person in a crowded nightclub. S admitted his presence in the nightclub but claimed he had not been involved in the assault. The Court of Appeal rejected the argument that a full *Turnbull* direction ought to have been given as S's unusual size and the absence of anyone else of similar build in the nightclub precluded the possibility of a mistaken identification. The judge had fairly summarised the circumstances of the identification and the possibility that the witness's judgment had been impaired through drink, and on the facts there had been no need for a reference to the possibility of an honest witness being mistaken and convincing (see also *R* v. *Oakwell* [1978] 1 WLR 32 (CA) and *R* v. *Curry* [1983] Crim LR 737 (CA)).

11.1.1.4 *Turnbull* and the Submission of No Case to Answer

The tribunal of law is obliged to accede to a submission of no case to answer at the end of the prosecution case if the prosecution have relied wholly or substantially on disputed visual-identification evidence of poor quality and there is no additional evidence supporting the correctness of that identification (*R* v. *Turnbull* [1976] 3 WLR 445 (CA), *R* v. *Weeder* (1980) 71 Cr App R 228 (CA)). On the other hand, if the visual-identification evidence is of good quality the tribunal of fact should be allowed to consider it even in the absence of supporting evidence. In determining whether the evidence is good or poor it is necessary to consider not only the circumstances of the original observation but also any subsequent factors, such as breaches of Code D-3 of the Police and Criminal Evidence Act 1984 Codes of Practice (11.1.2 *post*) which might have affected the reliability of the evidence (see *R* v. *Hutton* [1999] Crim LR 74 (CA)). There has been some reluctance to accept that recognition evidence can fall within the category of 'poor quality' evidence. In *R* v. *Ryan* [1990] Crim LR 50 the prosecution case relied entirely on a schoolgirl who testified that she had recognised the accused as a man she had seen outside her school on two or three previous occasions. The accused's submission of no case to answer failed and he was convicted. The Court of Appeal, dismissing his appeal, stated that it 'was rare for the court to feel concern about the rightness of a conviction based on evidence of recognition as opposed to that of identification of a stranger'.

In *Daley* v. *R* [1993] 3 WLR 666 the Privy Council sought to reconcile the decision in *R* v. *Turnbull* [1976] 3 WLR 445 with that of the Court of Appeal in *R* v. *Galbraith* [1981] 1 WLR 1039, the principal authority on submissions of no case to answer (16.7 *post*). The *Galbraith* guidelines are intended to ensure that the question of a witness's veracity will be left to the tribunal of fact. In cases of poor visual-identification evidence, the question is not one of veracity but of honest reliability, and the latent hazards associated with such evidence justify the judge's wider powers under the *Turnbull* guidelines.

11.1.1.5 The 'Reverse *Turnbull*' Direction

Just as a person may mistakenly identify the accused, a witness may mistakenly identify a person other than the accused at an identification parade. It seems that so long as the judge sums up fairly, and points out the weaknesses in the prosecution case, he is entitled to point out the circumstances surrounding the identification parade which could suggest to the jury that the witness made a mistake on that occasion (*R* v. *Trew* [1996] Crim LR 441 (CA)).

11.1.1.6 *Turnbull* and Vehicles

In *R* v. *Browning* (1991) 94 Cr App R 109 the Court of Appeal considered whether the *Turnbull* direction had to be given if the disputed visual identification related to a car as opposed to a person. Clearly there is a risk of misidentification, but different considerations must apply because of the important differences between cars and people. There are only so many types of car, their structures do not vary in the way human features and expressions can, and some people find it far easier than others to differentiate between the various models. Accordingly, the Court of Appeal held that trial judges ought to give some form of direction on the witness's opportunity to identify the car in question, and on his knowledge of different types of car and their characteristics, but the *Turnbull* direction itself was said to be unnecessary.

11.1.1.7 Photographic Evidence

If there is video or photographic evidence of the offender, the members of the tribunal of fact are entitled to act as the identifying witnesses, comparing the accused with the photographic image before them (*R* v. *Dodson* (1984) 79 Cr App R 220 (CA)). The accused is entitled to refuse to provide assistance to the tribunal of fact, and it would appear that no adverse inference may be drawn from this (*R* v. *McNamara* [1996] Crim LR 750 (CA)); but his refusal to assist may not prevent a comparison being made in practice. It would appear to be necessary for the trial judge to explain to the jury that they need to exercise particular care, and that there is a possibility of making a mistake, when comparing the accused with a photographic image of the offender (*R* v. *Blenkinsop* [1995] 1 Cr App R 7 (CA); *cf. R* v. *Downey* [1995] 1 Cr App R 547 (CA)). A witness who knows the accused is entitled to give evidence that he recognised him as the offender from a video recording, even though the photographic evidence is available and could instead be placed before the jury without the witness being called (*Attorney-General's Reference (No. 2 of 2002)* [2003] 1 Cr App R 321 (CA)).

In *R* v. *Clare* [1995] 2 Cr App R 333 the Court of Appeal held that a police officer who had studied the video evidence closely and analytically had properly been allowed to give an expert opinion on whether the recorded images showed the accused, as it would have been impracticable for the jury to conduct similar research during the trial (see also *R* v. *Breddick* (2001) *The Independent* 21.5.01 (CA)). Further, where a video image is alleged to be the accused in disguise, or the accused has changed his appearance since the commission of the offence, the expertise of a facial-mapping specialist may be called upon to provide the tribunal of fact with information and assistance (*R* v. *Stockwell* (1993) 97 Cr App R 260 (CA), *R* v. *Clarke* [1995] 2 Cr App R 425 (CA)). Indeed it has been held that the evidence of such an expert may be sufficient to justify a conviction even in the absence of any other evidence of the accused's guilt (see *R* v. *Hookway* [1999] Crim LR 750 (CA)).

11.1.1.8 Supporting Evidence
Supporting evidence must identify the accused as the offender and not merely show that an offence has been committed or demonstrate the identifying witness's honesty (which will rarely be in issue). In *R* v. *Turnbull* [1976] 3 WLR 445 the Court of Appeal gave some examples of what might amount to such evidence: (i) the accused's false alibi (11.6 *post*), (ii) unexplained 'odd coincidences' and (iii) the fact the offender was seen to run into the accused's father's house. It was also said that the accused's failure to testify could not amount to supporting evidence, but this must now be read in the light of s. 35 of the Criminal Justice and Public Order Act 1994. An inference drawn under ss. 34–37 of the 1994 Act is capable of providing supporting evidence (see Chapter 9). The mere fact that the witness testifies that the offender had a particular feature such as a spotty face, which the accused shares, will not support his identification if there is no independent evidence to show the offender actually had that feature and the witness was not mistaken (*R* v. *Willoughby* (1988) 88 Cr App R 91 (CA)).

Any sufficiently probative circumstantial evidence identifying the accused (such as fibres and fingerprints) will amount to supporting evidence. In *R* v. *Sadler* [2002] EWCA Crim 1722, for example, the fact that the accused's shirt was heavily stained with the blood of the person he had allegedly attacked supported that person's identification evidence; and in *R* v. *Walters* [2001] EWCA Crim 1261 the supporting evidence was provided by the accused's access to a car of the same type as that used by the murderer, and his telephonic communications with the hostel which the murderer had visited just before the victim was stabbed. The accused's confession will support a visual identification (*Freemantle* v. *R* [1994] 1 WLR 1437 (PC), *Shand* v. *R* [1996] 1 WLR 67 (PC)); and an identification by one witness may be supported by another witness's identification, so long as the judge emphasises to the jury that even several honest witnesses can be mistaken (*R* v. *Weeder* (1980) 71 Cr App R 228 (CA)). In *R* v. *George* [2002] EWCA Crim 1923 identification evidence of the accused as the person who shot and murdered a television personality was supported by other witnesses' description evidence and qualified identifications (11.1.4 *post*) together with circumstantial evidence comprising, *inter alia*, the accused's fascination with celebrities, his familiarity with firearms, a particle of firearm discharge residue found in his coat, and his admitted presence in the vicinity at the time the murder was committed.

Although the *Turnbull* guidelines include a requirement that the judge should identify to the jury the evidence which he adjudges is capable of supporting the evidence of identification, a conviction will not be regarded as unsafe if this was not done if an express reference to the supporting evidence would have strengthened the prosecution case (*R* v. *Barratt* (2000) unreported (00/3718/Z5) (CA)).

11.1.1.9 Circumstantial Description Evidence

No *Turnbull* direction is required if the evidence is not an identification of a particular person's facial features, but a description of the type of person seen and the clothes worn by him. In a case of this sort the witness would be unable to identify the offender again at an identification parade, but his description, when taken together with other evidence identifying the accused, might allow the tribunal of fact to infer that the person described was the accused. An example is provided by *R* v. *Gayle* [1999] 2 Cr App R 130 (CA). A handbag was stolen from a school during the afternoon, and the caretaker described a stranger he had seen on the premises at about 3 p.m. as a stocky black man, wearing a black bomber jacket bearing the logo 'Kangol' on the back, and walking towards a nearby public house. The accused, a black man, was subsequently seen by a cook at the public house to be acting suspiciously by the dustbins where the handbag was later found. His top was described as a black nylon jacket with a brightly coloured K on the back. The accused admitted that he was the person by the dustbins, but denied any involvement in the theft. He claimed that he had gone to the dustbins to urinate, had found the handbag and then disposed of it to avoid any trouble. As the caretaker had not purported to identify the accused, a *Turnbull* direction was unnecessary. The caretaker had done no more than provide a general description of the stranger he had seen on the premises and where he had been heading. This evidence made it more likely that the accused, who matched the description, was the burglar, but it was not evidence which had to be approached with any particular caution. As the caretaker was an independent witness who was either telling the truth or fabricating his testimony for no obvious reason, no special warning or direction was required (see also *R* v. *Oscar* [1991] Crim LR 778 (CA), *R* v. *Nicholson* [2000] 1 Cr App R 182 (CA) and *R* v. *Doldur* [2000] Crim LR 178 (CA)).

A different type of description evidence was considered in *R* v. *White* [2000] All ER (D) 602 (99/06964/Z2). The eye-witness recognised a youth (L) who was well known to her, with another youth who appeared to be his friend but whose identity she did not know. She saw the unknown youth attack the victim and was able to describe him. The unknown youth (allegedly the accused) admitted that he may have been at the scene with L, but denied any involvement in the attack. The Court of Appeal held that no *Turnbull* direction had been necessary in respect of the witness's recognition of L, as the defence had not challenged the evidence that he had been present (see also *R* v. *Bath* [1990] Crim LR 716 (CA)). Further, the witness's description of the offender, and her evidence that he was associated with L, was not relied on as identification evidence. It was circumstantial evidence which allowed the jury to infer that the accused was indeed the offender, supporting the visual-identification evidence of other witnesses.

11.1.1.10 Dock Identifications

It will usually be highly prejudicial for an accused to be identified by a witness for the first time while in the dock because of the real risk that he is being identified simply for being in that position. Accordingly a so-called 'dock identification' is not normally permissible (*R* v. *Cartwright* (1914) 10 Cr App R 219 (CCA), *R* v. *Johnson* [2001] 1 Cr App R 408 (CA), *R* v. *Conibeer* [2002] EWCA Crim 2059). In other words, while evidence of this sort is technically admissible, in most cases it will be excluded on the ground that its unduly prejudicial effect outweighs its limited probative value (*R* v. *Horsham Justices, ex parte Bukhari* (1981) 74 Cr App R 291 (DC)). Generally a controlled identification should take place prior to the trial, in accordance with Code D-3 of the Police and Criminal Evidence Act 1984 Codes of Practice (11.1.2 *post*) and only if this has been done should the witness be permitted to identify the accused in the dock.

A dock identification is exceptionally permissible in the Crown Court if it would not unduly prejudice the accused, such as where the accused is well known to the witness and the earlier out-of-court observation was a recognition as opposed to an identification of a stranger (*R* v. *Reid* [1994] Crim LR 442 (CA)). Dock identifications are also permissible in summary proceedings, at least in cases where the accused has failed to notify the prosecution prior to the trial that identification is in issue (*Barnes* v. *Chief Constable of Durham* [1997] 2 Cr App R 505 (DC), *Karia* v. *DPP* (2002) 166 JP 753 (QBD)).

11.1.2 Code D-3 of the PACE Codes of Practice

The provisions of Code D-3 (formerly Code D-2) of the Codes of Practice issued pursuant to s. 66 of the Police and Criminal Evidence Act 1984 ('PACE') complement the *Turnbull* direction by providing additional safeguards designed to ensure that any visual-identification evidence used by the prosecution is reliable. The purpose of Code D-3 and its Annexes is to ensure that identification evidence is obtained in a controlled environment, avoiding practices which might corrupt or devalue the evidence. The various procedures set out in the Code have been designed to test the ability of the witness to identify the person they saw on a previous occasion and to provide safeguards against mistaken identification (D-1.2).

The current version of Code D, which took effect on 1 April 2003, provides for the routine use of video identification parades to overcome the delays and abuses associated with traditional live identification parades (as, for example, in *R* v. *Perry* (2000) *The Times* 28.4.00 (CA), *Perry* v. *United Kingdom* (2002) Application No. 63737/00 (ECtHR), where the accused failed to attend identification parades over a period of several months). Code D-3.14 provides that a video identification parade will normally be more suitable than a live identification parade if it can be arranged and completed sooner; but this does not mean that expediency has overridden all other considerations. It is evidently in the interests of justice that an identification procedure should be held as soon as possible after the event which the witness observed, while matters are still fresh in his mind and any suspect appears much as he did at that time. Furthermore, there is evidence to suggest that video parades are actually a more effective mechanism for testing a witness's identification than live parades, as well as being less prejudicial for suspects and less stressful for witnesses (Roberts and Clover, 'The Government's Consultation Draft on PACE–Code D' [2002] Crim LR 873 at pp. 884–5; Tinsley, 'The Case for Reform of Identification Procedures' (2001) 5 E & P 99).

Code D-3 is divided into three principal parts: '(a) *Cases when the suspect's identity is not known*' (D-3.2 and D-3.3); '(b) *Cases when the suspect is known and available*' (D-3.4 to D-3.20); and '(c) *Cases when the suspect is known but not available*' (D-3.21 to D-3.24). In all cases the police are under a duty to record the description of the offender as first given by the eye-witness; and, where a suspect is known, and it is practicable to do so, to provide a copy of the description to the suspect or his solicitor before the witness's participation in an identification procedure under part (b) or part (c) (D-3.1). However, it is not necessary that the first description should set out the witness's opportunity to see the offender, such as the angle at which he saw the offender's face or the distance between them (*R v. Nolan* [2002] EWCA Crim 464).

Three alternative identification procedures are described in part (b) for the situation where the suspect's identity is known to the police and he is available. A suspect is 'known' if there is sufficient information to justify his arrest for suspected involvement in the offence; he is 'available' if he is (or soon will be) available to take part in one of the identification procedures and he is willing to participate (D-3.4). The witness must not be shown photographs, computerised or artist's composite likenesses or similar likenesses or pictures prior to the identification procedure (D-3.3). The three identification procedures are: first, the video identification parade, where the witness is shown moving images of the known suspect together with similar images of other people who resemble him (D-3.5, D-3.6 and Annex A); second, the live identification parade, where the witness sees the suspect in a line of other people who resemble him (D-3.7, D-3.8 and Annex B); and, third, the group identification, where the witness sees the suspect in an informal group of people (D-3.9, D-3.10 and Annex C), for example where the suspect is observed travelling on a public escalator with unsuspecting members of the public. (A fourth, less-desirable option is available under part (c), where the suspect is directly confronted by the witness.) The identification procedure must be arranged and conducted by an officer or member of the civilian support staff who is not involved in the investigation of the offence (D-3.11 and D-3.19).

If the suspect disputes an identification made (or purported to have been made) by an available witness, and it is practicable to hold an identification procedure, such a procedure *must* be held unless 'it would serve no useful purpose in proving or disproving whether the suspect was involved in committing the offence' – for example, where 'it is not disputed that the suspect is already well known to the witness' – or there is no reasonable chance that the witness would be able to identify the suspect (D-3.12). In other cases, an identification procedure *may* be held if the officer in charge of the investigation considers that it would be useful (D-3.13). The D-3.12 requirement to hold an identification procedure also applies if a dispute as to identity is not expressly raised by the suspect but may reasonably be anticipated (*R* v. *Rutherford* (1993) 98 Cr App R 191 (CA), *R* v. *Harris* [2003] EWCA Crim 174). A 'no comment' interview does not give rise to the reasonable anticipation that identity is in dispute (*R* v. *McCartney* [2003] EWCA Crim 1372).

The exception in D-3.12 for cases where the suspect is 'already well known to the witness' requires something more than mere recognition. In *R* v. *Harris* [2003] EWCA Crim 174 two 16-year-old boys were robbed by a group of youths, one of whom was purportedly identified by the boys as a youth ('T') who had previously been a student at their school. The police did not hold an identification procedure on the basis that it was a case of recognition, but this was held to be a breach of (what is now) D-3.12. The suspect (T) had disputed the claim that he was well known to the boys and, in any event, they had not seen him for about two years, a significant period of time for a developing teenager, so it was quite possible that one or both of the boys might not have picked him out if an identification procedure had been held. By way of contrast, in *Hawksley* v. *DPP* [2002] EWHC 852 Admin (QBD) it was held that an identification procedure had not been necessary as the witness, a police officer, had known the suspect for more than three years and had seen him with reasonable regularity around his housing estate. Similarly, in *H* v. *DPP* [2003] EWHC 133 Admin (QBD) there was no need for an identification procedure because the witness had known the suspect for 18 months and the assault had lasted for seven minutes.

Needless to say, where the issue is *not* one of mistaken identification it is unnecessary to comply with Code D-3. In *R* v. *Oscar* [1991] Crim LR 778 (CA) a witness was able to describe an individual offender by the distinctive clothes he was wearing and a man fitting that description was arrested near the scene of the offence. Because the witness had not purported to identify any individual person an identification parade would have served no useful purpose and had therefore been unnecessary (for other examples see *R* v. *Montgomery* [1996] Crim LR 507 (CA), *D* v. *DPP* (1998) *The Times* 7.8.98 (DC), *R* v. *Gayle* [1999] 2 Cr App R 130 (CA), *R* v. *Nicholson* [2000] 1 Cr App R 182 (CA) and *R* v. *White* [2000] All ER (D) 602 (CA)). Nor is an identification procedure necessary if there was continuity of vision, that is to say, if the witness continuously observed the same individual from the moment he committed the offence to the time when he was apprehended by the police (*R* v. *Akinyemi* [2001] EWCA Crim 1948). In *R* v. *Byron* (1999) *The Times* 10.3.99 (CA) it was held that evidence of a 'factually descriptive nature' was not necessarily identification evidence, so the fact that the prosecution had been unable to adduce identification evidence, because of a breach of Code D, did not mean they should also have been prevented from adducing evidence that a large tattoo had been seen on the assailant's upper left arm.

In cases where it is necessary or desirable to hold an identification procedure, the identification officer should consult the officer in charge of the investigation to determine which procedure should be used. There is now a presumption that the suspect will initially be offered a video identification or, if that would not be practicable, a live identification parade (D-3.11 and D-3.14), but a group identification may be offered if the officer in charge of the investigation considers that it would be the most satisfactory procedure in the circumstances (D-3.16). In any event, if there is to be an identification procedure it must be held 'as soon as practicable' (D-3.11). A suspect who refuses the identification procedure which is first offered may himself, or through his solicitor or appropriate adult, make representations as to why another procedure should be used, and an alternative procedure may be provided if it would be suitable and practicable (D-3.15). As a general rule the suspect must be told, in advance of the identification procedure, the information enumerated in D-3.17, including the fact that a refusal to consent in an identification procedure may be given in evidence – see *R* v. *Doyle* [2001] EWCA Crim 2883 (9.2.1 *ante*) – and that, if he refuses to consent, the police may in any event conduct a covert procedure or 'make other arrangements' to test whether a witness can identify him (that is, an arrangement under D-3.21). As a general rule the suspect must also be told that if he significantly alters his appearance before the identification procedure this may be given in evidence and, again, another arrangement may be considered. Under D-3.20, it is permissible in certain circumstances for the police to obtain an image of the suspect without complying with D-3.17. (Section 64A of PACE entitles the police to take photographs of suspects, in accordance with Code D-5, for, *inter alia*, the investigation of offences and the conduct of prosecutions, whether or not the suspect consents.)

Part (c) of Code D-3, which covers cases where the suspect is known but not (or no longer) available, such as where the suspect has deliberately failed to turn up for a live parade or has taken steps to prevent himself from being seen by a witness during such a parade, allows the police to proceed with an identification procedure in accordance with Annex A using moving or still images, including images of the suspect which have been obtained covertly, or a group identification in accordance with Annex C (D-3.21 and D-3.22). A non-forceful 'confrontation' may be arranged if no other alternative is practicable (D-3.23 and Annex D).

Part (a) of Code D-3 covers cases when the suspect's identity is *not* known. The procedures set out in these paragraphs are intended to cover two broad types of situation. The first (covered by D-3.2) is where an unknown person has been seen participating in an offence – for example, an attack outside a night club – and he may still be in the immediate vicinity. The witness will be taken round the neighbourhood, or to the place where a group of possible suspects is milling, to see whether he can informally identify any individual as the offender. Insofar as it is practicable, the principles applicable to formal identification procedures under Code D-3.5 to D-3.10 should be followed. In particular: a record should be made of any initial description given by the witness; care should be taken not to direct the witness's attention to any individual unless this cannot be avoided; every effort should be made to keep witnesses apart; and once there is sufficient information to justify the arrest of a particular individual for suspected involvement in the offence (for example, where one witness has made a positive identification) a formal identification procedure should be adopted for any other witnesses. The officer (or member of the civilian support staff) accompanying the witness must make a record in his pocket book of what is said and done. There is no breach of D-3.2 where a suspect willingly returns with the police to the site of the criminal activity and is in effect confronted by a witness before an orderly identification process can be arranged (*R* v. *O'Brien* [2003] EWCA Crim 1370). The second type of situation (covered by D-3.3 and Annex E) is where the witness has seen an unknown person participate in an offence and may be able to identify him from photographs, computerised or artist's composite likenesses or similar likenesses or pictures the police have in their possession. A situation involving the showing of photographs, but not covered by D-3.3, arose in *R* v. *Folan* [2003] EWCA Crim 908. In that case, the remains of the accused's wife were discovered in a shallow grave on a building site 17 years after her disappearance in 1981. There was already a body of circumstantial evidence suggesting that the accused had murdered his wife and, following the discovery of her remains, the police took steps to determine whether he had been working on the building site in 1981, which included showing a photograph of the accused from that period to persons involved with the construction company renovating the site at that time. Although (what are now) D-3.3 and Annex E did not apply, as the suspect's identity was known, the Court of Appeal was of the view that the procedures set out in the Annex should nonetheless have been followed as they provided valuable guidance.

The latest version of Code D has not addressed the problems which arose in *R* v. *Willoughby* [1999] 2 Cr App R 82, where one witness identified the suspect soon after the identification parade had ended and another altered her position from one of uncertainty to one of certainty that the man she had picked out was the offender. Although para. 20 of Annex B provides that, where a witness identifies the suspect after the parade has ended, the suspect and (if present) his solicitor should be informed, and that consideration should be given to allowing the witness a second opportunity to identify the suspect, there is no guidance as to when the suspect or his solicitor should be informed or what should be done if a witness's enhanced view as to the correctness of the identification follows information from another source that it was correct. The Court of Appeal provided the following observations. First, if a witness identifies the suspect after the parade has ended, or a witness modifies in any significant way the identification made on the identification parade, the suspect or his solicitor should be informed as soon as practicable. Second, a witness should not be told whether the suspect has or has not been picked out until that witness has made any further statement he may wish to make. Third, 'there would be the utmost ground for concern' if the police had nudged, prompted or encouraged a witness to make a more positive identification.

11.1.3 Breaches of Code D-3

A breach of any provision in Code D-3 or its five Annexes (A–E) may be taken into consideration at the trial (s. 67(11) of PACE), although whether the identification evidence will be excluded under s. 78(1) of the Act depends on whether the breach would have such an adverse effect on the fairness of the proceedings that it ought not to be admitted. The correct approach was summarised by the Court of Appeal in *R* v. *Quinn* [1995] 1 Cr App R 480 (at pp. 488–9):

'The fact that there have been breaches – even several breaches – of the Code is not conclusive as to whether or not the evidence should be admitted. The judge has a task, if there have been breaches, to consider whether those breaches, taken either singly or in the aggregate, are such as to make it requisite for him, pursuant to section 78, to exclude the evidence. He will only do so if he comes to the conclusion – it is a matter for his discretion – that to admit the evidence would have an adverse effect on the fairness of the proceedings ... Before this Court could reach the conclusion that the judge was wrong in that respect, we would have to be satisfied that no reasonable judge ... could have reached the conclusion that he did.'

In *R* v. *Forbes* [2001] 2 WLR 1 the House of Lords agreed with the view of the Court of Appeal in *R* v. *Popat* [1998] 2 Cr App R 208 that non-compliance with Code D will not inevitably lead to the evidence being excluded. Each case will turn on its own facts, but minor breaches are less likely to result in unfairness than more substantial breaches (*R* v. *Grannell* (1989) 90 Cr App R 149 (CA)); and even significant breaches, such as a failure to hold a video or identification parade, will not result in a successful appeal if no unfairness resulted. In *R* v. *Rutherford* (1993) 98 Cr App R 191 (CA), for example, the strength of the other evidence implicating the accused and the substance of the judge's summing-up meant the accused had not suffered any unfairness despite the breach of the Code (see also *R* v. *Kelly* (1998) 162 JP 231 (CA)).

In some cases, however, the breach will be sufficiently serious to warrant exclusion. In *R* v. *Conway* (1990) 91 Cr App R 143 (CA), for instance, the only identification procedure had been a 'dock identification' at the accused's committal proceedings. The failure to hold a formal parade was held to be a 'clear breach' of the Code, and the evidence should have been excluded. That was a case where there had been no satisfactory identification procedure at all, but identification evidence may be excluded where there has been a formal procedure which was not carried out in accordance with the Code or its Annexes. In *R* v. *Gall* (1989) 90 Cr App R 64 an identification parade was held but the investigating officer was present in breach of what is now D-3.8 (and para. 7 of Annex B) and had therefore been given the opportunity to talk to the witness. The Court of Appeal held that the identification evidence should have been excluded (see also *R* v. *Finley* [1993] Crim LR 50 (CA)). In *R* v. *Nagah* (1990) 92 Cr App R 344 (CA) the accused consented to an identification parade, which would have been practicable, but as he left the police station he was identified by the complainant whom the police had deliberately arranged to be there to have a look at him. This 'complete flouting of the Code' justified the exclusion of the complainant's identification, particularly as she had previously given a description of her assailant which did not match the accused. By contrast, in *R* v. *Penny* (1991) 94 Cr App R 345 the police failed to hold an identification parade, through what would appear to be inefficiency, opting instead for a group identification in a crowded street. The Court of Appeal accepted that even if there had been a breach of the Code the trial judge had been entitled to have regard to all the circumstances when exercising his discretion under s. 78(1) and, though the street identification had been less satisfactory than a parade, the police had not acted improperly. Accordingly the evidence had been properly admitted.

Where there has been a breach of Code D and the identification evidence is nonetheless admitted, the judge is obliged to explain the nature of the breach and invite the jury to consider its possible effect (*R* v. *Forbes* [2001] 2 WLR 1 (HL)). The jury should also be told that an identification procedure enables suspects to put the reliability of an eye-witness's identification to the test, that the suspect has lost the benefit of that safeguard, and that they should take account of that fact in their assessment of the whole case, giving it such weight as they think fit (*R* v. *Harris* [2003] EWCA Crim 174). If, however, the accused deliberately delayed putting identification in issue before the trial, so that the difficulties associated with the evidence would be compounded by the passage of time, the judge is entitled to add an appropriate comment to his '*Forbes* direction' to reflect what happened (*R* v. *McCartney* [2003] EWCA Crim 1372).

11.1.4 Qualified Identification Evidence

Where a witness is able to describe the offender's general appearance, or the clothes he was wearing, but is unable to describe the offender's face, the witness's description is admissible circumstantial evidence implicating the accused. Conversely, where a witness claims that he observed the offender's face, but was unable to pick out the accused at an identification procedure, the non-identification is admissible to support the defence's contention that a person other than the accused committed the offence (*R* v. *Graham* [1994] Crim LR 212 (CA)). However, the witness may still give oral evidence to describe the offender and, indeed, to explain the circumstances of the identification procedure (*R* v. *George* [2002] EWCA Crim 1923).

Another situation is where a witness is able to provide a description of the offender, but makes only a partial or qualified identification of the accused at the identification procedure. For example, the witness may state, following a video identification parade, that he 'thinks' a particular person is the offender but he cannot be 100 per cent sure. In *R* v. *George* [2002] EWCA Crim 1923, where the accused had grown a volume of facial hair during the period between the commission of the crime and the identification procedure, it was held that, while a conviction cannot be based on a qualified identification alone, such evidence may be admissible against the accused if it supports or is consistent with other evidence which indicates that he committed the offence (such as another witness's positive identification) or if the explanation for the qualified (or non-) identification places that qualified (or non-) identification in its proper context, for example by showing that the witness's other evidence, such as his initial description of the offender, might still be correct.

11.1.5 Police Photographs

Police photographs ('mug shots') may be used to help a witness identify an offender, but it is important that this initial means of identifying the accused is not revealed to the jury lest they infer that the accused has a criminal record (*R* v. *Lamb* (1980) 71 Cr App R 198 (CA)). However, this is not an absolute exclusionary rule for in some circumstances it may be appropriate to refer to such an identification, so long as the probative value of the evidence outweighs its unduly prejudicial effect. One such case was *R* v. *Bleakley* [1993] Crim LR 203 where the witness, a shopkeeper, first identified the accused from a police photograph and subsequently picked him out at an identification parade. The defence sought to explain why the accused had been picked out by suggesting that the witness had seen him when he had visited his shop the day before the parade. The prosecution were then permitted to rebut this suggestion by referring to the earlier identification. The Court of Appeal held that the judge had exercised his discretion properly for if the defence suggestion had not been rebutted by the adduction of such evidence the jury would have been misled. It is also permissible for a police officer to give evidence that he recognised the accused from a closed-circuit television recording of the offence being committed, even though the jury may infer that the accused has a criminal record (*R* v. *Caldwell* (1993) 99 Cr App R 73 (CA)).

11.2 Voice-identification Evidence

If there is a relevant audio recording of an individual's voice, the tape may be played before the jury (*R* v. *Bentum* (1989) 153 JP 538 (CA)). The jury will compare a recording of the offender's voice with a proven recording of the accused's voice or, where the accused has testified, his voice when giving evidence. In *R* v. *Robb* (1991) 93 Cr App R 161 (CA) it was held that expert opinion evidence is admissible to assist the jury in determining whether two recorded voices belong to the same individual. In that case the expert's opinion was based solely on a (subjective) auditory phonetic analysis of the two recordings, but it is doubtful whether this approach is still permissible. It is now accepted that the more reliable approach, in most cases at least, is to supplement any auditory analysis with a quantitative acoustic analysis (see *R* v. *O'Doherty* [2003] 1 Cr App R 77

(NICA) and generally Ormerod, 'Sounding Out Expert Voice Identification' [2002] Crim LR 771).

In the absence of a recording of the offender's voice, the principal question is likely to be whether the witness who heard the offender, and who subsequently relied on his memory to identify the accused as that person, is correct in his assertion. As with visual-identification evidence, however, there is the very real possibility of error on account of the circumstances surrounding the witness's initial perception of the offender's voice (and the medium through which it was heard), the witness's ability to remember the way the offender spoke and, in particular, his ability accurately to compare the offender's voice with that of the accused.

It was recognised by the New Zealand Court of Appeal in *R* v. *Waipouri* [1993] 2 NZLR 410 that voice-identification evidence is generally less reliable than visual-identification evidence and that even greater caution is required when relying on it. In *R* v. *Roberts* [2000] Crim LR 183 (99/0458/X3) the Court of Appeal received expert evidence to the effect that a voice identification is more likely to be wrong than a visual identification, that ordinary people are as willing to rely on identification by ear-witnesses as they are on identification by eye-witnesses and that the identification of a stranger's voice is a very difficult task, even if the opportunity to listen to the voice was relatively good. Accordingly, in cases where the prosecution are permitted to adduce such evidence the jury must be given a direction analogous to that established for visual-identification evidence in the case of *R* v. *Turnbull* [1976] 3 WLR 445 (*R* v. *Hersey* [1998] Crim LR 281 (CA), *R* v. *Gummerson* [1999] Crim LR 680 (CA), *R* v. *Chenia* [2003] 2 Cr App R 83 (CA)). Indeed it would seem that a more stringent direction is needed. In *R* v. *Erskine* [2001] EWCA Crim 2513 it was held that the jury should have been told 'that voice identification can be at least as problematical as visual identification, perhaps more so' and in *R* v. *Roberts* the Court of Appeal noted the view of an expert witness:

> '[T]he warning given to jurors of the danger of a miscarriage of justice in relation to witnesses who are identifying by voice should be even more stringent than that given to jurors in relation to the evidence of eye-witnesses. It should be brought home to jurors that there is an even greater danger in the first case of the witness believing himself or herself to be right and yet in fact mistaken.'

Further, by analogy with the position for visual-identification evidence where the jury compare a photographic image of the offender with the accused (11.1.1.7 *ante*), the jury should be given an appropriate warning when they are asked to compare a recording of the offender's voice with the accused's voice (*Bulejcik* v. *R* (1996) 185 CLR 375 (HCA), *R* v. *O'Doherty* [2003] 1 Cr App R 77 (NICA)).

As with visual-identification evidence, some voice identifications may be sufficiently reliable to justify a conviction even in the absence of any other identifying evidence, such as where a colleague or sibling's quite distinctive voice has been overheard and *recognised* in a context which rules out the possibility of a mistaken identification. Generally, however, it should not be possible to found a conviction if there is no identifying evidence other than a witness's voice identification, at least in cases where the offender was previously unknown to the witness. As noted above, there is the possibility of error associated with listening to, remembering and comparing two voices heard on different occasions; but even if the witness could clearly hear the offender's voice, accurately remember it and subsequently identify it as a voice similar to the accused's, and even if the possibility of distortion or disguise can be discounted, the voice is unlikely to be sufficiently distinctive to rule out the realistic possibility that the offender was some other person. The true value of (non-recognition) voice-identification evidence therefore lies in the inference which may be drawn that the offender belongs to a particular social category, such as a regional or ethnic group.

Code D of the Police and Criminal Evidence Act 1984 Codes of Practice does not cover voice-identification evidence. Accordingly, the police are not obliged to hold a voice-identification parade (*R* v. *Deenik* [1992] Crim LR 578 (CA), *R* v. *Gummerson* [1999] Crim LR 680 (CA)), although if such a parade is arranged, with the witness listening to recordings of several individuals including the suspect, the evidence of what happened is admissible (*R* v. *Hersey* [1998] Crim LR 281 (CA); see also *R* v. *Khan* (2002) *The Times* (news report) 5.12.02 (CCC)). Nor is there a formal requirement that a description of the offender's voice be taken by the police, although this is something which clearly ought to be done (if the witness is capable of describing the voice) if only to establish particulars such as the offender's age, sex, social class, regional identity or idiosyncratic vocabulary and pronunciation.

11.3 Olfactory-identification Evidence – Tracker Dogs

In *R* v. *Pieterson* [1995] 1 WLR 293 the Court of Appeal held that evidence of a tracker dog's actions in following a scent was admissible so long as the reliability of the dog was first proved to the satisfaction of the court. The dog's handler should therefore be called to give detailed evidence of its training and of its reactions over a period of time indicating its reliability. The judge should also alert the jury to the care needed when approaching such evidence, having regard to the fact that tracker dogs might not always be reliable and cannot be cross-examined (see also *R* v. *Sykes* [1997] Crim LR 752 (CA)).

11.4 Fingerprints, Palm-prints and Ear-prints

Fingerprint evidence has been admitted to prove guilt since 1902 when one Harry Jackson was convicted of a London burglary on the basis of a thumbprint left on a windowsill. Seven years later the Court of Criminal Appeal affirmed that fingerprint evidence is sufficient, without more, to justify a conviction (*R* v. *Castleton* (1909) 3 Cr App R 74).

Fingerprint (and palm-print) evidence is used primarily in criminal proceedings to identify the accused as the offender, although it may also be used to eliminate a suspect from the police's enquiries. Where fingerprint evidence is relied on to prove the accused's guilt, the prosecution will call an expert on the subject to give his opinion that the offender's 'latent' (and usually incomplete) print – which has been found on (and lifted from) an object associated with the crime – is the same as part of the complete 'rolled' print taken from the accused by the police (pursuant to their powers under ss. 27, 61 and 63A of the Police and Criminal Evidence Act 1984, in accordance with Code D-4 of the Codes of Practice). The pre-trial process has come to be known by the acronym 'ACE-V', representing four consecutive stages: the *analysis* by a fingerprint examiner of the latent print's distinctive patterns of loops, whorls, arches and deltas; his *comparison* of the latent print's patterns with those of the suspect's rolled print; his subjective *evaluation* to determine whether the prints are, or are not, impressions made by the same finger; and *verification* (or not, as the case may be) by one or more other examiners, having conducted the same three steps.

Two premises underpin the probative value of fingerprints as evidence of identification. The first is that no two individuals share the same combination of ridges and troughs which make up a fingerprint. The patterns which form on a foetus's fingers and palms during its pre-natal development are dependent on both genetic and environmental factors, so it is inherently unlikely that two individuals will share exactly the same print. There is, moreover, no evidence to suggest that two individuals have ever been found to share the same prints (although this does not *prove* that any particular individual's fingerprints are unique). Indeed the result of an algorithmic study conducted in the USA was that the probability of finding two persons with identical fingerprints was one in ten to the ninety-seventh power. The second premise is that an individual's fingerprints are permanent. Research on pre-natal development suggests that, once a foetus's fingerprints have developed, they do not change with time unless affected by a very deep wound. Given this evidence, Pollak J, a federal judge in the USA, recently took judicial notice of the uniqueness and permanence of fingerprints (*USA* v. *Plaza (No. 1)* (7 January, 2002) Cr No. 98-362-10; *USA* v. *Plaza (No. 2)* (13 March, 2002) Cr No. 98-362-10 (USDC, ED Pa)).

The problem with fingerprints as identifying evidence does not lie in the validity of these premises, which are universally accepted as valid. If a complete, good-quality latent print is found, and it matches the rolled print obtained from the accused, there can be no reasonable doubt that the latent print was left by the accused. The potential for unreliability, and therefore a mistaken identification, comes, first, from the incomplete nature of latent prints; second, from the distortion and smearing associated with such prints because of the way the underlying surface has been touched, the nature of the surface, and the properties of the medium used to lift them; and, third, from the possibility of an erroneous opinion following the evaluation stage, on account of the subjective nature of the test (and possibly the examiner's insufficient knowledge, ability or experience). In *R* v. *McNamee* (1998) unreported (97/4481/S2), for example, the Court of Appeal heard evidence over seven days from 14 fingerprint experts in relation to a single thumb print and, save for those who said that the print was unreadable, there was no unanimity amongst those experts, and very substantial areas of disagreement.

Given that a small number of ridge characteristics may be shared by a considerable number of individuals, the question the courts have had to answer is how the reliability of fingerprint evidence can be guaranteed when the discernable latent print may represent only a very small fraction of the offender's complete print. For many years a national fingerprint standard was in place, the consequence being that the prosecution would not seek to rely on fingerprint evidence unless at least 16 separate matching ridge characteristics could be identified.

More recently, however, a consensus has developed amongst experts in the field that fewer than 16 matching characteristics are needed to establish beyond any doubt that the latent print was left by the accused. Indeed, according to a study in the late 1980s, there is no scientific, logical or statistical basis for the retention of *any* numerical standard, let alone one requiring as many as 16 points of similarity (see *R* v. *Buckley* (1999) 163 JP 561 (CA) at p. 567). After all, a latent print may show only a small number of ridge characteristics, but be sufficiently clear to show fine detail such as the shapes of the ridges and the structure and location of sweat pores.

Fingerprint evidence showing fewer than 16 matches was tendered by the prosecution, and admitted by the judge, in *R* v. *Giles* (1998) unreported (97/5495/W2) (CA) and in *R* v. *Charles* (1998) unreported (98/0104/Z2) (CA). In the former case leave to appeal against conviction was refused; in the latter case, where the conviction was based on 12 matching ridge characteristics and the opinion of an expert of long experience and high standing, the appeal was dismissed. In *R* v. *Buckley* (1999) 163 JP 561 the judge allowed the prosecution to rely on fingerprint evidence showing a mere nine matching ridge characteristics (although this was not the only evidence of the accused's guilt). The accused was convicted and appealed on the ground that the fingerprint evidence ought not to have been admitted. Dismissing the appeal, the Court of Appeal held that there was nothing to suggest that, in exercising his discretion, the judge had erred. The Court explained the position in the following terms (at pp. 567–8):

'Fingerprint evidence, like any other evidence, is admissible as a matter of law if it tends to prove the guilt of the accused. It may so tend, even if there are only a few similar ridge characteristics, but it may, in such a case, have little weight. It may be excluded in the exercise of judicial discretion, if its prejudicial effect outweighs its probative value ... It may be that in the future, when sufficient new protocols have been established to maintain the integrity of fingerprint evidence, it will be properly receivable as a matter of discretion, without reference to any particular number of similar ridge characteristics. But, in the present state of knowledge of expertise in relation to fingerprints, we venture to proffer the following guidance ... If there are fewer than eight similar ridge characteristics, it is highly unlikely that a judge will exercise his discretion to admit such evidence and, save in wholly exceptional circumstances, the prosecution should not seek to adduce such evidence. if there are eight or more similar ridge characteristics, a judge may or may not exercise his or her discretion in favour of admitting the evidence. How the discretion is exercised will depend on all the circumstances of the case, including in particular (i) the experience and expertise of the witness; (ii) the number of similar ridge characteristics; (iii) whether there are dissimilar characteristics; (iv) the size of the print relied on, in that the same number of similar ridge characteristics may be more compelling in a fragment of print than in an entire print; and (v) the quality and clarity of the print on the item relied on, which may involve, for example, consideration of possible injury to the person who left the print, as well as factors such as smearing or contamination.'

The Government has recently announced that the current standard prescribed for fingerprint evidence is the 'non-numerical system which was introduced from 11 June 2001' (*Hansard* (HL) 25 February 2002, WA172). Furthermore, any fingerprint evidence presented in criminal proceedings will have gone through the ACE-V procedure, with verification being provided by two further experts (*Hansard* (HL) 11 March 2002, WA47). Fingerprint evidence showing fewer than eight matching ridge character-istics is *prima facie* admissible, subject to the judge's discretion to exclude it if it is insufficiently reliable. In exercising their discretion judges will continue to take into consideration the *Buckley* guidelines and warn the jury that the expert's opinion is not conclusive and that it is for them, the jury, to determine whether guilt is proved in the light of all the evidence (see *R* v. *Buckley* (1999) 163 JP 561 (CA) at p. 568 and, generally, 12.2.4–5 *post*).

Ear-print evidence is also *prima facie* admissible, although it is unclear whether the underlying premises of uniqueness and permanence are valid in this context (*R* v. *Dallagher* [2003] 1 Cr App R 195 (CA)). Ear-print evidence is therefore far more likely to be admitted in cases where it is not the only evidence identifying the accused as the offender.

11.5 DNA-profile Evidence

It may seem strange that DNA (deoxyribonucleic acid) evidence has been included in this chapter, for the public perception is that evidence of this sort provides an irrefutable way of identifying an offender. However, it is this perception which has on occasion given rise to problems. The techniques associated with the extraction and analysis of DNA are not free from the risk of human error; and, more important, the resulting DNA profile will not necessarily pinpoint the offender's identity with certainty. Yet the statistics involved, the possibility of drawing fallacious inferences from them, and the danger that the jury will be overwhelmed by their own perception of the evidence and its scientific 'stamp of approval' may give rise to problems if it is not handled, explained and interpreted correctly.

The problems to which the use of DNA evidence in criminal trials has given rise – principally the so-called 'prosecutor's fallacy' – are not unique to evidence of this sort. Any evidence involving a statistical evaluation may result in the possibility of an erroneous inference being drawn, if the probabilities involved are unusually small and explained with insufficient care (as, for example, in the 'cot deaths' case of *R* v. *Clark* (2000) unreported (1999/07459/Y3) (CA), *R* v. *Clark (No. 2)* [2003] EWCA Crim 1020). But it is the cases on DNA evidence which provide the best examples of the misuse of statistics in criminal proceedings. That said, DNA evidence has the potential to revolutionise criminal detection and, if used correctly, can be extremely probative either by exculpating a suspect or, particularly in the context of other circumstantial evidence, identifying the accused as the offender. It should also be noted that the dangers associated with misinterpreting the value of DNA evidence have recently fallen with the advent of a more sophisticated profiling technique (the 'SGM-plus' procedure).

Sufficient DNA for a profile can now be extracted from a single human cell left at the scene of a crime, and it is already possible to draw certain conclusions about an offender's ethnic appearance, hair colour and eye colour from a sample of his genetic material. Such information can allow the police to focus their search for likely suspects. Further, by obtaining a DNA profile from a suspect held in custody, or from the Forensic Science Service's National DNA Database, and comparing it with the offender's profile, it is possible to establish a statistical probability that the two samples came from the same individual. It is this probability, calculated by a Forensic Science Service expert, which will be relied on by the prosecution at the accused's trial.

The use of DNA as evidence involves three stages: the extraction and measuring stage, the statistical evaluation stage, and the inference drawing stage.

The first stage involves extracting a DNA sample from a number of the chromosomes in one or more human cells left at the scene of a crime (the 'crime stain') and a sample from the equivalent chromosome parts taken from the suspect's cells. The offender's sample is likely to come from the nuclei of cells taken from the root of one of his hairs or from a stain of blood, semen or saliva left behind by him, although it is now possible to extract and use DNA from cell mitochondria in, for example, hair shafts. (An important difference is that nucleus DNA is unique to any individual – or a pair of identical twins – whereas mitochondria DNA is inherited in its entirety from the individual's mother.) The suspect's sample will usually be obtained by taking a swab from his mouth or by plucking a follicle of his hair (see ss. 63, 63A(2) and 65 of the Police and Criminal Evidence Act 1984, and Code D-6 of the Codes of Practice).

The two samples are broken down into smaller fragments of DNA by the application of restriction enzymes, and each collection of fragments is separated according to molecular weight by a technique known as gel electrophoresis. This technique creates a pattern which is then transferred to a nylon membrane. Radioactive 'probes' (sequences of DNA bases taken from another source) are applied to the pattern on the membrane where they bind with regions of repeated sequences of DNA bases in the samples – it is the distribution of repeated sequences of bases which is used to identify an individual. An X-ray film is then applied to the membrane to produce an 'autoradiograph' of bands. The images of the two samples are analysed by a computer to produce the two individuals' DNA profiles which are then compared.

If there is an unexplained discrepancy between the two profiles then they are not from the same source and this may clear the suspect (depending on what other evidence is available and how many persons committed the offence). If a large number of the bands correspond exactly then there is a high probability that the two samples came from the same person: the higher the number of matching bands the higher the probability. Only minute samples of DNA are used in the profiling technique so the profile produced is unlikely to be unique to the individual from whom the sample was taken. A second stage is therefore called for and this involves a statistical evaluation of the match based on the number of matching bands and the frequency of such band matching in the racial group of the suspect (derived from a database of a sizeable number of persons drawn from that group).

The result of the first two stages is a figure – the match (or random occurrence) probability – representing the number of persons from the suspect's racial group and gender who might be *expected* to have the same number of corresponding bands. Like other identifying circumstantial evidence, DNA places the offender and the suspect in a smaller class of persons than society as a whole. What makes DNA evidence so highly probative is that the class of persons in which they are both placed is extremely small.

The third and final stage of the process is where the tribunal of fact draws an inference from the expert evidence that the offender and the suspect (now the accused) are both members of the same small class of persons. Standing alone this evidence may be insufficient to identify the accused as the offender, but in the context of some other credible prosecution evidence the tribunal of fact would be entitled to infer, as a virtual certainty, that the two persons are the same. For example, if the accused is a white male and, relatives aside, the probability of the match between his and the offender's profile is estimated to be one in a million, then out of a population of about 28 million white males in the United Kingdom (excluding, for the sake of argument, the possibility of an offender from overseas) there is a class of 28 men who could have committed the offence. This is not enough to prove the accused is guilty, but there is likely to be some other evidence linking him to the crime, such as his presence in the region, his accent and an untruthful alibi (as in *R* v.

Doheny [1997] 1 Cr App R 369 (CA)), or his admitted acquaintance with the complainant (as in *R* v. *Adams* [1997] 1 Cr App R 369 (CA)), or his suspicious behaviour and a visual identification (as in *R* v. *Gordon* [1995] 1 Cr App R 290 (CA)). The cumulative effect of the DNA evidence and the other evidence will be to narrow the class of possible offenders down to a single person, the accused. In *R* v. *Lashley* (2000) unreported (99/3890/Y3) it was estimated, taking into account the likely age of the offender, that a class of about five or six males in the UK could have been responsible for the offence, a robbery in Liverpool. In the absence of any other evidence linking the accused to the crime it was not possible to justify his conviction, but the Court of Appeal noted that the position would have been different if there had been evidence linking the accused to Liverpool at the time when the offence was committed.

Of course if the match probability is sufficiently low, for example one in 200 million, and there is nothing to suggest that the offender was not resident in the UK, the DNA evidence will entitle the jury to infer that the accused was that person, even in the absence of any other supporting evidence (see *R* v. *Adams* [1996] 2 Cr App R 467 (CA) and *R* v. *Adams (No. 2)* [1998] 1 Cr App R 377 (CA)). Indeed, given recent advances in the profiling techniques used by the Forensic Science Service (in particular, the SGM-plus procedure) match probabilities as low as one in a thousand million are now being established (*Hansard* (HC) 1 March 2001, Column 747W; *R* v. *Weir* (2000) unreported (99/4829/W2) (CA)). In *R* v. *Hanratty (Deceased)* [2002] 2 Cr App R 419, for example, the Court of Appeal felt able to state that 'the DNA evidence standing alone is certain proof of James Hanratty's guilt'. However, this does not mean that in all future cases where DNA evidence is available it will be unnecessary to rely on any other evidence linking the accused to the offence. The match probability may be considerably higher if the accused's close relatives are taken into account, and this will reduce the probative value of the matching DNA profiles (as, for example, in *R* v. *Watters* [2000] All ER (D) 1469 (99/6966/Y4) (CA)).

DNA evidence is therefore very probative (if not always conclusive) evidence of the accused's guilt, but there are dangers. First of all, things can go wrong during the process of extracting DNA from human cells at the scene of the crime and the subsequent processes that make up the first stage. For example, samples may be mixed up or contaminated by other DNA from bacteria, viruses, the victim or even laboratory staff; or errors may arise during the electrophoresis or comparison stage resulting in an erroneous match probability at the statistical evaluation stage. It is therefore imperative that the prosecution prove that the samples were properly obtained and analysed – a failure to do this resulted in a successful appeal in *R* v. *Loveridge* [2001] EWCA Crim 734. A further problem is that the ethnic database used for the statistical evaluation may not be appropriate for the accused's own ethnicity, again leading to an erroneous match probability. The likelihood of this problem arising should decrease, however, as the number and variety of ethnic databases increases.

Given the complexities associated with statistical evaluations, perhaps the greatest danger comes from the possibility that the jury will be encouraged by the prosecution to draw an erroneous inference from a correct match probability. The advent of the SGM-plus procedure has reduced the likelihood of an erroneous inference being drawn in many (if not most) cases, but the problem may still arise.

In the example given above the match probability was one in a million, leading to the expectation that the accused was one of a class of 28 males in the UK who could have committed the offence. This figure of one in a million is, however, capable of being twisted into a statement that the odds against the accused being innocent are a million to one. This fallacious and highly prejudicial reasoning (the 'prosecutor's fallacy') has been relied on in the past, resulting in several successful appeals against conviction (*R* v. *Deen* (1993) *The Times* 10.1.94 (CA), *R* v. *Doheny* [1997] 1 Cr App R 369 (CA), *Pringle* v. *R* [2003] UKPC 9). In *R* v. *Doheny*, Phillips LJ said (at pp. 373–4):

> 'The cogency of DNA evidence makes it particularly important that DNA testing is rigorously conducted so as to obviate the risk of error in the laboratory, that the method of DNA analysis and the basis of subsequent statistical calculation should – so far as possible – be transparent to the defence and that the true import of the resultant conclusion is accurately and fairly explained to the jury.'

11.6 The Accused's Lies

If the jury or magistrates are satisfied that the accused has lied about something relevant to the proceedings it is permissible for them to draw from it an inference adverse to the accused, whether the lie occurred before the trial or while the accused was in the witness box. The inference will amount to an item of evidence against the accused, but its relevance and weight will depend on the significance of the lie in the context of the case. Its probative value may be such that, without more, it establishes his guilt, such as where the jury reject his defence to a charge of handling stolen goods that he did not know or believe the goods were stolen. Alternatively, the lie may demonstrate the accused's consciousness of guilt and support other prosecution evidence. The inference may therefore support an eye-witness's identification for the test established in *R* v. *Turnbull* [1976] 3 WLR 445 (CA) (11.1.1.8 *ante*) or any suspect witness requiring a cautionary warning in accordance with *R* v. *Makanjuola* [1995] 1 WLR 1348 (CA) (11.8 *post*). Less significant lies may permit a weaker inference to be drawn, that is, one which merely undermines the accused's credibility without having a more direct bearing on the question of his guilt.

This section is concerned with the second type of lie, where the jury are being asked to infer, or might of their own volition infer, that the accused's dishonesty does not merely undermine his credibility but provides additional, more direct evidence of his guilt. The problem is that an erroneous inference of 'consciousness of guilt' might be drawn on the basis of a lie told for a quite different reason by a person who is not in fact guilty of the allegation. The accused might have lied about a relatively peripheral matter in the proceedings or given a false alibi for some entirely innocent reason. If the jury are not forewarned of this possibility they may draw an erroneous inference of guilt, jumping to the conclusion that the accused is guilty simply *because* of his lie, without paying due regard to possible alternative explanations. For example, a fabricated alibi could have been the only way for the accused to hide a true but embarrassing alibi (such as a visit to a brothel); or he might have felt that no-one would believe part of his story, leading him to fabricate something which he regarded as more plausible. In *R* v. *Middleton* [2001] Crim LR 251 (99/4593/W3) (CA) Judge LJ said:

> 'People do not always tell the truth. Laudable as it may be to do so, whatever' the circumstances, they do not, or cannot, always bring themselves to face up to reality. Innocent people sometimes tell lies even when by doing so they create or reinforce the suspicion of guilt. In short, therefore, while lying is often resorted to by the guilty to hide and conceal the truth, the innocent can sometimes misguidedly react to a problem, or postpone facing up to it, or attempt to deflect ill-founded suspicion, or fortify their defence by telling lies.'

In short, if the jury are not directed to consider innocent explanations before drawing an inference from the accused's lies there may be an erroneous finding of guilt. The jury must therefore be directed not to regard the accused's proven or admitted lie as evidence of his guilt *unless* they are sure that it was deliberate, that it related to a material issue and that it was told by the accused because of his realisation of guilt and fear of the truth as opposed to any innocent reason (*R* v. *Goodway* (1993) 98 Cr App R 11 (CA)). These three criteria can be traced back to the decision of the Court of Appeal in *R* v. *Lucas* [1981] 3 WLR 120, a case on whether out-of-court lies could amount to technical 'corroboration' under the old common-law rules (11.12 *post*). For this reason the warning on lies is still generally referred to as the '*Lucas* direction'. In *R* v. *Goodway* (1993) 98 Cr App R 11 (CA) it was said that the *Lucas* direction should be given when the prosecution have relied on the accused's lies (or the jury might of their own volition rely on his lies) as evidence of his *guilt* rather than as evidence merely reflecting adversely on his credibility. The jury should be reminded, in appropriate cases, that people sometimes lie in an attempt to bolster up a just cause, or out of shame, or out of a wish to conceal disgraceful behaviour from their family.

It is important to remember, however, that the *Lucas* direction is a safeguard for cases where there is a real possibility the jury might *erroneously* conclude that the accused is *guilty* just because he has lied about something material in the proceedings. The direction is aimed at preventing the jury from instinctively jumping to a wrong conclusion about the accused's guilt. Accordingly, in *R* v. *Burge* [1996] 1 Cr App R

163 the Court of Appeal explained that the *Lucas* direction does *not* have to be given in every trial just because the accused has lied, and that, where the direction *is* necessary, it should be tailored to meet the circumstances of the case. Generally a *Lucas* direction need only be given: (i) where the jury are advised to look for supporting evidence or are required to find technical 'corroboration'; or (ii) where there is a real possibility that the lie will be regarded by the jury as evidence of the accused's guilt; or (iii) where the defence is one of alibi. In other words, the direction is necessary only if the prosecution have suggested, or the jury might infer, that the accused's lie is a manifestation of his consciousness of guilt – an implied admission of guilt supporting the other prosecution evidence. In giving the judgment of the Court of Appeal in *R* v. *Middleton* [2001] Crim LR 251 (99/4593/W3), Judge LJ went on to say:

> 'The purpose of giving the *Lucas* direction ... is to avoid the risk that they may adopt ... forbidden reasoning ... that lying demonstrates, and is consistent only with, a desire to conceal guilt, or, putting it another way, to jump from the conclusion that the defendant has lied to the further conclusion that he must therefore be guilty ... [I]n order to avoid the prohibited reasoning, the jury will often need to be warned – perhaps more accurately, reminded – of the reality, namely that an innocent defendant may sometimes lie and that the inference of guilt does not automatically follow. Where, however, there is no risk that the jury may follow the prohibited line of reasoning, then a *Lucas* direction is unnecessary. On the whole, approaching the matter generally, it is inherently unlikely that such a direction will be appropriate in relation to lies which the jury conclude that the defendant must have told them in his evidence. In this situation, the consequence of the jury rejecting the defendant's evidence is usually covered by the general directions of law on the burden and standard of proof ...'

The type of case which demands a *Lucas* direction is illustrated by *R* v. *Ghilwan Abdullah* (1998) unreported (98/2542/Y2) (CA). The accused was charged with having wounded another man with a knife during the course of a street fight. It was not in issue that the accused had been in possession of the knife, but while the prosecution alleged that the accused had been the aggressor, it was his defence that he had brought out the knife towards the end of the fight in order to defend himself. When the police arrived at the accused's home about half an hour after the fight, he told them that he did not have a knife. However, the knife used in the fight was found under his bed shortly afterwards and, at his trial, it was conceded that he had lied to the officers, a fact relied on by the prosecution in their endeavours to persuade the jury of his guilt. The accused's explanation for the lie was that, although he had acted in self-defence, he was frightened and wanted to dissociate himself from the knife. This explanation might well have been true given the circumstances, and the jury should have been warned against reasoning that his admitted lie was consistent only with a desire to conceal guilt.

In *R* v. *Middleton* [2001] Crim LR 251 the accused was charged with burglary and aggravated vehicle-taking. A number of items were stolen from a house in west London, along with the occupant's BMW car. The accused was arrested in the BMW later the same day, having been pursued at speed by the police, and the other property was found in his mother's home. The accused's defence was one of alibi. He gave evidence to the effect that he had not been involved in the burglary; at the time it took place he was with a married woman; he had been paid by someone to drive the BMW to a garage outside London; and he had found the items of property in the car and left them at his mother's home. A *Lucas* direction was therefore unnecessary. If the jury concluded that the accused had lied to them when explaining his involvement with the car and property, the obvious inference was that he was lying to conceal his guilt and, according to the Court of Appeal, 'any attempt to embellish the summing-up with a *Lucas* direction would have served to confuse and complicate an essentially simple issue'. The guidance provided by Judge LJ in *R* v. *Middleton* [2001] Crim LR 251 was approved in *R* v. *Barnett* [2002] 2 Cr App R 168 (CA), where it was noted that it would be 'absurd' to suggest that every case of handling stolen goods should require a *Lucas* direction merely because the prosecution have asserted that the accused was lying when denying he knew or believed the goods in question were stolen.

Because the *Lucas* direction is unnecessary if there is no possibility of the jury's adopting the 'forbidden reasoning', a direction should not be given if the nature of the accused's defence is such that by rejecting it the jury are necessarily finding him guilty (*R* v. *Harron* [1996] 2 Cr App R 457 (CA), *R* v. *Quang Van Bui* [2001] EWCA Crim 1). If there is a direct and irreconcilable conflict between the prosecution witnesses and the accused as to the accused's involvement in the offence, an acceptance that the prosecution witnesses are telling the truth and not mistaken will necessarily mean the accused is lying and therefore guilty. As there is no distinction between the issue of guilt and the issue of lies the direction would serve only to confuse the jury. This might be the case where the accused has relied on an alibi and yet one or more credible eye-witnesses have testified that he was physically involved in the commission of the offence (as in *R* v. *Harron* [1996] 2 Cr App R 457 (CA) and *R* v. *Holden* (1999) unreported (99/2630/Y2) (CA)), or where the accused has changed his version of events as more scientific evidence has come to light (as in *R* v. *Hill* [1996] Crim LR 419 (CA)).

11.7 The Accused's Silence

It is permissible to draw inferences adverse to the accused from his pre-trial silence in certain circumstances and from his failure to testify in his own defence. However, because there are numerous possible reasons for remaining silent, the tribunal of fact must be directed to exclude the possibility of an innocent explanation before drawing an adverse inference. This topic is covered separately in Chapter 9.

11.8 **Unreliable Witnesses**

In an ideal world all witnesses would be disinterested, medically sound and dependable. In practice there will always be some witnesses who have either fabricated or embellished their evidence or who have in some other way given a distorted account of the circumstances in question. This may be through personal interest (such as self-preservation, revenge, spite or financial gain) or for a more innocent reason such as genuine confusion or error. One of the purposes of cross-examination is to flush out any improper motive, bias or innocent mistake, but as a forensic tool this is not always effective. The technique of cross-examination may make an honest but mistaken witness resentful and seemingly more reliable (as with visual-identification witnesses, 11.1 *ante*), it may provoke resentment in the tribunal of fact, or it may simply fail to penetrate the facade which has been erected by a dishonest witness.

At common law persons who fell within one of a number of classes of witness in criminal proceedings were deemed to be inherently unreliable and worthy of special attention by the trial judge in his summing-up. Where any complainant in a sexual case, or an accomplice, or a child gave testimony for the prosecution against an accused the judge was obliged, first, to give the jury a 'full corroboration warning' to the effect that it would be dangerous to convict the accused on the basis of the witness's uncorroborated testimony and, second, to explain to the jury what evidence could properly be regarded by them as 'corroborative' (according to the technical test adopted in *R* v. *Baskerville* [1916] 2 KB 658 (CCA), 11.12 *post*). The reason for this level of distrust stemmed from the belief that young children were inherently unreliable because of their youth, that complainants often brought false allegations of sexual abuse out of shame, spite, neurosis or fantasy, and that accomplices were keen to minimise their own role in the alleged offence at the accused's expense. It did not matter how reliable the witnesses actually seemed to be, or that there was no evidential basis for the presumption that a given witness was unreliable, the full corroboration warning was mandatory for any prosecution witness who fell within one of these categories.

A less rigid common-law rule of practice also developed for other witnesses, by analogy with the categories of presumed unreliability, where there was material to suggest that their evidence might be unreliable. This covered certain complainants in non-sexual cases who were unstable or resentful, and other witnesses (such as quasi-accomplices) having some purpose of their own to serve. In *R* v. *Beck* [1982] 1 WLR 461 the Court of Appeal recognised that there was an obligation upon a judge to advise a jury to proceed with caution where there was material to suggest that a witness's evidence might be tainted by an improper motive. The general proposition was that it was necessary to give a cautionary warning in respect of any witness whose reliability was thrown into doubt by some motive which rendered him biased against the accused. Thus, where a co-accused testified and implicated the accused, the judge did not have to give a full corroboration warning (though he had a discretion to do so) but he was obliged to warn the jury that the co-accused might have a purpose of his own to serve in giving such evidence (*R* v. *Knowlden* (1981) 77 Cr App R 94 (CA), *R* v. *Cheema* [1994] 1 WLR 147 (CA)). The question of unreliable complainants arose in *R* v. *Spencer* [1986] 3 WLR 348, where criminal inmates at a mental hospital alleged ill-treatment by the nursing staff. The trial judge had directed the jury to approach the inmates' evidence with great caution, had told them it would be wise to look for support for their evidence, and had explained the reasons for his warning. His direction, and the general proposition in *R* v. *Beck* [1982] 1 WLR 461 (CA), was approved by the House of Lords. The way in which the certified point of law was answered suggested that a full corroboration warning was obligatory, save that the word 'dangerous' was unnecessary. The better view is that the House of Lords recognised the need for a *Beck* 'cautionary warning' in cases where the complainant was unreliable, with the jury being additionally required to look for supporting evidence (as opposed to 'corroboration') to meet the justice of the particular case. Lord Ackner certainly deprecated the opening of a new category of presumed unreliability for mental patients with criminal convictions.

Section 34(2) of the Criminal Justice Act 1988 (and s. 32(3) of the Criminal Justice and Public Order Act 1994) abrogated the obligatory corroboration warning in respect of children. Children's evidence is often no less reliable than the evidence of adult witnesses generally, so while there will be cases where some warning is appropriate (such as where a particular child is unduly suggestible or imaginative) a blanket warning for all children was difficult to justify. The same is of course true for complainants in sexual cases and accomplices. Some such witnesses may warrant a warning but there can be no logical reason for assuming that every complainant in a sexual case is untruthful or that every accomplice has an axe to grind. The Law Commission (Law Com No. 202 (1991)) recommended the abolition of the two remaining categories, and this recommendation was effected by s. 32(1) of the 1994 Act.

The Court of Appeal addressed the impact of s. 32(1) in *R* v. *Makanjuola* [1995] 1 WLR 1348, where the general principles applicable to any witness were set out (at pp. 1351–2):

'The judge will often consider that no special warning is required at all. Where, however, the witness has been shown to be unreliable, [the judge] may consider it necessary to urge caution. In a more extreme case, if the witness is shown to have lied, to have made previous false complaints, or to bear the defendant some grudge, a stronger warning may be thought appropriate and the judge may suggest it would be wise to look for some supporting material before acting on the impugned witness's evidence. We stress that these observations are merely illustrative of some, not all, of the factors which judges may take into account in measuring where a witness stands in the scale of reliability and what response they should make at that level in their directions to the jury. We also stress that judges are not required to conform to any formula and this court would be slow to interfere with the exercise of discretion by a trial judge who has the advantage of assessing the manner of a witness's evidence as well as its content ...

It is a matter for the judge's discretion what, if any, warning he considers appropriate in respect of ... any ... witness in whatever type of case. Whether he chooses to give a warning and in what terms will depend on the circumstances of the case, the issues raised and the content and quality of the witness's evidence ... There will need to be an evidential basis for suggesting that the evidence of the witness may be unreliable. An evidential basis does not include mere suggestion by cross-examining counsel ... Where some warning is required, it will be for the judge to decide the strength and the terms of the warning.'

By stating that the *Makanjuola* guidelines apply in respect of any witness, in whatever type of case, the Court of Appeal made it clear that the mandatory cautionary warning established in cases such as *R* v. *Beck* and *R* v. *Knowlden* – and, indeed, in *R* v. *Spencer* – was also being abrogated, and this is now the established position (*R* v. *Muncaster* [1999] Crim LR 409 (CA), *R* v. *Causley* [1999] Crim LR 572 (CA)). However, the *Makanjuola* guidelines in no way affect the guidelines established in *R* v. *Turnbull* [1976] 3 WLR 445 (CA), which address the particular problem of *honest* unreliability in the context of visual-identification evidence (11.1.1 *ante*), or the warning which may need to be given if the accused has lied (11.6 *ante*).

Whether the jury ought to be given a *Makanjuola* direction and, if so, the nature of the direction, lie within the judge's discretion, guided by his duty to put the accused's case fairly and adequately. It was said in *R* v. *Makanjuola* that the judge's ruling would not be interfered with on appeal unless it was '*Wednesbury* unreasonable', a point which has been reaffirmed by the Court of Appeal on a number of occasions in recent years (for example *R* v. *Mountford* [1999] Crim LR 575 (98/2930/X4), *R* v. *Gregory* (2000) unreported (99/4313/Y3) and *R* v. *Whitehouse* [2001] EWCA Crim 1531). Nonetheless, the duty to put the accused's case fairly – described as the 'overriding rule' in *R* v. *Spencer* – does have the effect of restricting the otherwise broad scope of this judicial discretion. The purpose of the *Makanjuola* direction is to assist the jury to arrive at a safe verdict, so if there was evidence at the trial to suggest that a prosecution witness was unreliable, but the judge decided not to give a *Makanjuola* direction, this will be regarded as *Wednesbury* unreasonable if the effect was to deny the accused a fair trial. As noted in *R* v. *Hamill* [2001] EWCA Crim 1922, the accused's trial will not be fair if the judge exercises his discretion in an improper manner; and the question whether or not he exercised his discretion properly or improperly is determined by reference to *Wednesbury* principles.

Although there are no longer any formal categories of witness who are to be regarded as unreliable, and who might expect to be the subject of a

Makanjuola direction, it is possible to identify some obvious situations where a direction should be given (or where the judge ought at least to consider whether a direction should be given). In *R* v. *Makanjuola* Lord Taylor CJ referred to cases where a witness is shown to have lied, to have made previous false complaints, or to bear the accused a grudge. This non-exhaustive list includes the sexual complainant who has made and withdrawn false allegations of a similar type in the past (*R* v. *F* [1999] Crim LR 306 (98/893/X3) (CA)) or who has changed her story a number of times before the trial (*R* v. *Walker* [1996] Crim LR 742 (CA)). It also includes the witness who has an improper purpose of his own to serve (such as an 'axe to grind'); for example the sexual complainant who has an improper motive for seeing the accused convicted (*R* v. *B(MT)* [2000] Crim LR 181 (CA)) and the witness, whether or not a co-accused, whose interests are served by deflecting suspicion away from himself (*R* v. *Hempton* (2000) unreported (99/3835/X2) (CA), *R* v. *Porter* [2001] EWCA Crim 2699). Indeed, where an accomplice has given evidence for the prosecution, it will 'usually be necessary' for the judge to give the jury a specific warning about the care with which they should approach his evidence (*R* v. *Hunter* [2002] EWCA Crim 2693). However, where two co-accused have testified in their own defence against each other it is not appropriate for the judge to give, in respect of each witness, the 'normal' cautionary warning applicable to cases where a witness has a purpose of his own to serve, as this would require the jury to perform mental gymnastics; it is sufficient if the trial judge underlines the extreme care with which the jury should approach the allegations against each co-accused (*R* v. *Burrows* [2000] Crim LR 48 (CA)).

A cautionary *Makanjuola* direction will almost certainly be required if a central plank of the prosecution case is an unrecorded 'cell confession' purportedly made by the accused to another inmate while he was in prison awaiting his trial (*R* v. *Causley* [1999] Crim LR 572 (CA), *Pringle* v. *R* [2003] UKPC 9, *Benedetto* v. *R* [2003] 1 WLR 1545 (PC)). None of the safeguards in the Police and Criminal Evidence Act 1984 or its Codes of Practice applies to confessions of this sort, and there will usually be evidence that the prosecution witness is a dishonest reprobate or that he had an improper motive for assisting the authorities (or both). According to the Privy Council in *Pringle* v. *R*, if there is evidence to suggest that the witness wished to ingratiate himself with the authorities in the hope of receiving favourable treatment, the trial judge should draw the jury's attention to that evidence (which may be nothing more than the surrounding circumstances), explain its significance and then advise the jury to be cautious before accepting the witness's testimony. In *Benedetto* v. *R* the Privy Council expressed the view that, by analogy with the situation where the prosecution case depends wholly or substantially on the correctness of visual-identification evidence and a *Turnbull* direction is required, in cases where an untried prisoner claims that a fellow untried prisoner confessed his guilt, there is an acute problem 'which will always call for special attention'.

11.9 **Section 77 of PACE**

Any confession which the prosecution propose to rely on in criminal proceedings is inadmissible unless the prosecution can prove it was not made 'in consequence of anything said or done which was likely, in the circumstances existing at the time, to render unreliable any confession which might be made by him in consequence thereof' (s. 76(2)(*b*) of the Police and Criminal Evidence Act 1984, 7.1.3.2 *ante*). Section 77(1) of PACE provides, in addition, that where the prosecution case against a mentally-handicapped accused (as defined by s. 77(3)) depends wholly or substantially on a confession made by him in the absence of an independent person, the tribunal of fact must be warned of the 'special need for caution' before convicting in reliance on the confession and have the reasons explained to them (see also s. 77(2) for summary proceedings). A s. 77 warning need not be given if the prosecution case does not depend substantially on the confession, the test being whether the prosecution case would be 'substantially less strong' without it (*R* v. *Campbell* [1995] 1 Cr App R 522 (CA)). In *R* v. *Bailey* [1995] 2 Cr App R 262 (CA) Roch LJ said (at p. 275):

> 'What is required of a judge in a summing up in such cases, in our judgment, is a full and proper statement of the mentally handicapped defendant's case against the confessions being accepted by the jury as true and accurate. Because the defendant is significantly mentally handicapped, this duty will include a duty to see that points made on the defendant's behalf and other points which appear to the judge to be appropriate to his defence that the confessions are unreliable or untrue, are placed before the jury.'

11.10 **Delay in Child Sexual Offence Cases**

Where an adult complainant alleges that the accused sexually abused her when she was a child, it will usually be necessary for the judge to direct the jury on any prejudice caused to the accused on account of the delay between the time when the abuse allegedly occurred and the trial, in addition to the usual directions on the burden and standard of proof. An additional direction on the prejudicial effects of delay provides a 'control mechanism' to ensure that the accused who has to face old allegations receives a fair trial (*R* v. *Maybery* [2003] EWCA Crim 783). Thus, in *R* v. *MB* [2003] EWCA Crim 1204 where the allegation was of child-rape during a 1979 trip in the accused's lorry, the trial judge should have directed the jury on the ways in which the substantial delay might have affected the accused's ability to counter the allegations, with reference to the unavailability of any records relating to the movements of the accused's lorry on the date of the alleged rape and any medical evidence relating to the complainant's assertion that she had become pregnant and miscarried as a result. Another example is provided by *R* v. *Chapman* [2001] EWCA Crim 2434, where D's convictions were quashed as the trial judge had, *inter alia*, failed properly to direct the jury on the difficulties D had faced in trying to counter, a decade after the alleged incidents, the complainant's specific allegations. The Court of Appeal has made it clear on a number of occasions that the question whether a direction is necessary, and the substance of any direction which is given, depends on the particular facts of the case – although it has also been said that 'a clear warning will usually be desirable as to the impact which [the purported delay] may have had on the memories of witnesses and as to the difficulties which may have resulted for the defence' (*R* v. *M* [2000] 1 Cr App R 49 (CA); see also *R* v. *GY* [1999] Crim LR 825 (CA)).

Exceptionally, some cases which depend on nothing more than the complainant's oral allegation may relate to events which allegedly occurred so long ago that the accused would be unable to defend himself in any meaningful sense if he were to be tried. In a case of this sort, where a direction from the judge would be an insufficient safeguard, the proceedings will be permanently stayed as an abuse of process (see *R* v. *Jenkins* [1998] Crim LR 411 (CA) and 10.4 *ante*). In *R* v. *B* [2003] 2 Cr App R 197 the Court of Appeal stated that the best time to assess whether a case is fit to be left to the jury in cases of this sort is not before the trial has started but at the end, when the judge is in a position to take into account the evidence presented by the prosecution and the defence. Bizarrely, although the Court could find no fault with the trial judge's ruling on abuse of process (that is, a fair trial was possible) or with the trial process and summing-up (that is, the accused received a fair trial), D's convictions for alleged acts of indecency between 1969 and 1972 were quashed on the ground that there exists a 'residual discretion' to set aside a conviction which is felt to be unsafe or unfair. Given the dates when the incidents allegedly took place and the nature of the prosecution evidence (comprising nothing more than the complainant's allegations) the accused had been put in an impossible position to defend himself, for all that he could do was say that he had not committed the alleged acts. The Court therefore felt duty-bound to allow his appeal. In the light of this decision, it is doubtful whether any more cases involving inordinate delay will be tried.

11.11 Demeanour

The demeanour of a witness while giving evidence is regarded as a form of real evidence, which can be scrutinised to help the tribunal of fact decide whether the witness is telling the truth. Voluntary and involuntary facial expressions, changes in intonation and general body language can, it is assumed, give valuable clues to the veracity of the witness. Unfortunately there are reasons to believe that such evidence is not a particularly reliable indicator of credibility. First of all, because of cultural and/or social differences between the witness and the tribunal of fact the witness's non-verbal signals may be completely misunderstood. But even where there are no such differences, the artificial and controlled environment of the trial and the interrogative process between advocate and witness are likely to make the untrained witness feel ill at ease, giving a distorted impression of his character, particularly during cross-examination. Expressions or tremors which might be indicative of guilt in ordinary circumstances may be indicative of nothing more than an honest witness's nervousness if communicated from the witness box. Conversely, the practised liar may be able to appear self-confident and truthful giving an intentionally false impression of his credibility.

At present the relationship between a witness's demeanour and his credibility is left to the jury's common sense, with no cautionary warning necessary from the judge, but it would be well for jurors – and other triers of fact – to bear in mind the unreliability of this evidence. Lord Devlin (*The Judge* (1979) p. 63) expressed this view, when he adopted the following words of Mr Justice MacKenna:

'I doubt my own ability ... to discern from a witness's demeanour, or the tone of his voice, whether he is telling the truth. He speaks hesitantly. Is that the mark of a cautious man, whose statements are for that reason to be respected, or is he taking time to fabricate? Is the emphatic witness putting on an act to deceive me, or is he speaking from the fullness of his heart, knowing that he is right? Is he likely to be more truthful if he looks me straight in the face than if he casts his eyes on the ground perhaps from shyness or a natural timidity?'

11.12 **Supporting Evidence and 'Corroboration'**

Generally any judgment or verdict may be reached on the unsupported evidence of a solitary witness. There are, however, a few statutory exceptions to this rule; for example, it is not possible to be convicted of perjury solely on the evidence of one witness as to the falsity of the statement in question (s. 13 of the Perjury Act 1911) or of speeding solely on the opinion evidence of one witness as to the accused's speed (s. 89(2) of the Road Traffic Regulation Act 1984).

Before the abolition of the categories of presumed unreliability, the test for what could properly be regarded as 'corroborative evidence' was that established in *R* v. *Baskerville* [1916] 2 KB 658 (CCA): it had to be admissible 'independent ... evidence ... which confirms in some material respect not only the evidence that the crime has been committed, but also that the [accused] committed it'. The evidence also had to be credible (*DPP* v. *Kilbourne* [1973] 2 WLR 245 (HL) at p. 267). However, in the light of *R* v. *Makanjuola* [1995] 1 WLR 1348 (CA) (11.8 *ante*) it is clear that the *Baskerville* test is now to be relied on only in exceptional cases where a criminal provision has been interpreted to demand technical corroboration. In other words, if the jury are given a *Makanjuola* direction to the effect that it would be wise to look for some 'supporting material' before acting on an impugned witness's evidence, it is not necessary that the evidence should satisfy the *Baskerville* test. Although no definition of 'supporting material' was provided in *R* v. *Makanjuola*, the trial judge will nonetheless have to explain to the jury what evidence is capable of supporting the unreliable witness's testimony, and the jury will have to act in accordance with the guidance they are given (*R* v. *B(MT)* [2000] Crim LR 181 (CA)). It is of course a question of fact for the jury whether any such item of evidence should actually be regarded as supporting material.

The *Baskerville* test required evidence which came from a source other than the suspect witness. There is clear logic in this requirement, and judges should be reluctant to identify evidence as supporting if it is not independent. In particular, the self-serving nature of a suspect witness's repeated claim should prevent it from confirming the truth of his testimony. However, it would be wrong to prevent evidence from being supportive just because it is not *technically* independent of the suspect witness. For example, if an unreliable young child alleges indecent assault by the accused, the fact she and the accused both had gonorrhoea soon after the alleged incident should support her testimony (as in *R* v. *Gregg* (1932) 24 Cr App R 13 (CCA)).

Independent evidence which merely bolstered the credibility of the unreliable witness could not be technical corroboration, but there is no reason why sufficiently probative evidence of this sort should be excluded from the meaning of 'supporting material'. In *R* v. *McInnes* (1989) 90 Cr App R 99 (CA) the accused was charged with kidnapping and raping a seven-year-old girl. The girl had been picked up by a stranger, taken away in his car and then sexually assaulted. She was able to describe her assailant and the appearance and interior of the car (the interior was said to be littered with Fox's glacier mint sweet-wrappers, the base of the gear-lever was torn and the knob of the gear-lever was off-centre), and she was able to pick out both the car and the accused in identification parades. The interior of the accused's car was found to match the description given by the girl – the gear-lever and its knob were as described, and a Fox's glacier mint wrapper was found too. The accused denied the girl had been in his car, but she could hardly have known about the interior unless she had been inside it, so her *peculiar knowledge* showed her to be a truthful witness. Her knowledge amounted to circumstantial evidence, 'independent' of her identification of the accused, which supported that identification and amounted to corroboration in respect of the kidnapping charge. (This knowledge could not corroborate her evidence with regard to the rape, however, as it did not show any such offence had been committed by the accused as required by the *Baskerville* test.) Evidence of this sort will now be regarded as 'supporting material' for the purposes of the *Makanjuola* direction. In *R* v. *Causley* [1999] Crim LR 572 (97/393/X2) (CA) the veracity of an unreliable prosecution witness was capable of being supported, in respect of whether the accused had confessed to him in prison, by his peculiar knowledge of matters which, according to the prosecution case, could have come only from the accused.

A suspect complainant's distressed state following an alleged sexual assault should not be identified as potentially supportive evidence if the circumstances were such that the risk of fabrication cannot be excluded. If, however, the circumstances suggest that the distress was probably genuine the jury should be permitted to consider it even though the evidence is not independent of the complainant. This was the approach adopted under the old law on corroboration, but the Court of Appeal has recently accepted that it remains valid for the modern law on supporting evidence (*R* v. *Venn* [2003] EWCA Crim 236). In *R* v. *Chauhan* (1981) 73 Cr App R 232 (CA), for example, an independent witness gave evidence that the complainant had cried out and run away from the accused soon after the alleged indecent assault on her. The jury were entitled to regard it as corroborating the complainant's testimony so long as they first discounted the possibility that the distress had been feigned or had resulted from a misunderstanding (see also *R* v. *Redpath* (1962) 46 Cr App R 319 (CCA) where fabrication was improbable given the remoteness of the location and the unlikelihood of the complainant being observed by anyone).

Circumstantial evidence which is independent of the suspect witness and implicates the accused in the alleged offence should amount to supporting evidence if it is sufficiently probative of his guilt. This could include adverse inferences drawn from the accused's silence or his refusal to provide a body sample, or his lies, or admissible evidence of his disposition, or DNA evidence and so on. Before the jury can treat a lie by the accused as supporting evidence (or corroboration) they must be directed to be sure that the lie was deliberate, related to a material issue, was told by the accused because of his realisation of guilt and fear of the truth, and has been established as untrue from evidence other than that of the unreliable witness requiring support (*R* v. *Lucas* [1981] 3 WLR 120 (CA)). An innocuous item of circumstantial evidence may not of itself be probative enough to support a suspect witness, but several items of innocuous circumstantial evidence taken together may amount to supporting evidence if the cumulative probative value is sufficiently high (*R* v. *Hills* (1987) 86 Cr App R 26 (CA) at pp. 30–1). Express or implied admissions by the accused which have a bearing on the evidence requiring support should suffice, as should an independent witness's testimony. Medical evidence of injuries will support a complainant's allegation of an act of violence against her, although it may have nothing to say about the accused's involvement.

If the accused is tried on several counts in a single indictment and the evidence of several witnesses is ruled to be cross-admissible as similar fact evidence (3.3.10 *ante*), although the risk of collusion between the prosecution witnesses is not relevant to the determination of admissibility it was, under the old law, relevant to whether the witness's evidence could amount to corroboration. Unless the jury were satisfied that the witnesses' evidence was free from collusion it could not be regarded as corroborative or, indeed, relied on for any other purpose adverse to the accused (*R* v. *H* [1995] 2 WLR 737 (HL)). Although technical corroboration is no longer required, the position must be the same for supporting evidence.

Chapter Summary

- The police must gather visual-identification evidence in accordance with the provisions of Code D-3 of the Police and Criminal Evidence Act 1984 Codes of Practice. Breaches of the Code may result in the exclusion of the identification evidence under s. 78(1) of the Act.
- If the case against the accused depends wholly or substantially on the correctness of disputed visual-identification evidence, the judge should warn the jury of the special need for caution before convicting in reliance on it (the *Turnbull* direction). If the quality of the evidence is good the jury can be left to assess it even though there is no supporting evidence; but if its quality is poor the judge must withdraw the case from the jury unless there is other evidence to support the correctness of the identification. A direction analogous to the *Turnbull* direction should be given in cases where the prosecution rely on voice-identification evidence.
- If the accused can be shown to have lied and the prosecution have suggested, or the jury might infer, that it is a manifestation of his consciousness of guilt, but the inference of guilt does not automatically follow in the circumstances, it is necessary for the judge to warn the jury not to assume that the accused is guilty because of his lies (the *Lucas* direction).
- If there is evidence to suggest that a witness is unreliable, the judge may need to give the jury a cautionary warning and in some cases suggest that it would be wise to look for supporting evidence before acting on the witness's evidence (the *Makanjuola* direction).
- If the prosecution case against a mentally-handicapped accused depends wholly or substantially on a confession made by him in the absence of an independent person, the judge must warn the jury of the special need for caution before convicting in reliance on it (s. 77(1) of the Police and Criminal Evidence Act 1984).
- If it is alleged that the accused sexually abused the complainant many years before the trial, it will usually be necessary for the judge to direct the jury on the prejudice caused to the accused on account of the (alleged) delay.

Further Reading

Criminal Law Revision Committee, 11th Report (1972) Cmnd 4991, pp. 116–121
The Devlin Report (1976) HC 338
Williams, 'Evidence of Identification: The Devlin Report' [1976] Crim LR 407
Devlin, *The Judge* (OUP, 1979) pp. 188–198
Jackson, 'The Insufficiency of Identification Evidence' [1986] Crim LR 203
Tinsley, 'The Case for Reform of Identification Procedures' (2001) 5 E & P 99
Ormerod, 'Sounds Familiar? Voice Identification Evidence' [2001] Crim LR 595

Balding and Donnelly, 'The Prosecutor's Fallacy and DNA Evidence' [1994] Crim LR 711
Redmayne, 'Doubts and Burdens: DNA Evidence' [1995] Crim LR 464
Evett *et al*, 'DNA Profiling' [2000] Crim LR 341

Mirfield, '"Corroboration" After the 1994 Act' [1995] Crim LR 448
Birch, 'Corroboration: Goodbye to All That? [1995] Crim LR 524
Dein, 'Non Tape Recorded Cell Confession Evidence' [2002] Crim LR 630

Stone, 'Instant Lie Detection? Demeanour and Credibility' [1991] Crim LR 821

12   Opinion Evidence

In any trial it is necessary to determine a number of factual issues – sometimes referred to as the 'ultimate' or 'material' issues – upon which the final verdict or judgment will depend. In order to come to a decision on these issues the tribunal of fact is obliged to consider, and entitled to draw inferences from, all the available evidence, including the testimony of any witnesses who have been called. Witnesses are generally limited to testifying as to facts within their own personal knowledge. As a rule they have no right to give their own opinions on the ultimate issues, for the determination of the issues is the preserve of the tribunal of fact.

In most cases, then, witnesses' opinions are regarded as irrelevant and so inadmissible, but there are two important exceptions to this rule. First, it will often be impossible for witnesses to refrain from stating certain inferences of their own when describing facts directly perceived by them, at least if they are to give their oral evidence in a natural way. Witnesses, whether or not they are experts in any particular field, may therefore provide their evidence as if they were describing events in a less formal environment, even if this means that certain inferences they have drawn will be conveyed as incontrovertible facts. Second, experts in specialised fields are allowed to give their own opinions on matters falling within their expertise if the tribunal of fact would be unable properly to decide an issue without their help.

This chapter is primarily concerned with the admissibility of expert opinion evidence, but also explains the non-expert witness's limited right to give his own opinion. The last part of this chapter sets out the rules governing the admissibility of judgments from other proceedings. A judgment is, after all, nothing more than the opinion of the tribunal of fact in an earlier trial (see *Hui Chi-Ming* v. *R* [1991] 3 WLR 495 (PC)). Another type of admissible opinion evidence, which is not considered further here, is evidence of reputation, which may be given to establish or discredit character (3.4.1 and 3.4.5 *ante*, 16.5.4.3 *post*) or to prove pedigree or the existence of a public right (6.1.2.4–5 *ante*).

12.1   Non-expert Opinion Evidence

Any descriptive testimony such as 'she was a young schoolgirl' or 'the old man was rather upset' is actually a compendious way of summarising a number of inferences based on the witness's observations. If witnesses were prohibited from drawing any inferences of their own they would have to state each and every perceived fact which allowed the inference to be drawn. It would not be possible for a witness to say, for example, that the person he observed was a 'young girl' or an 'angry man', or that the weather that day was 'hot and humid'; he would instead have to list all the specific, perceived facts which allowed him to form his opinion. This would be unbearable for all concerned, as well as impracticable. Witnesses are therefore allowed to give opinions which are no more than a natural way of conveying to the court what they directly perceived. In the Northern Ireland case of *Sherrard* v. *Jacob* [1965] NI 151 (NICA) Lord MacDermott CJ gave some examples (at p. 156):

'(1) the identification of handwriting, persons and things; (2) apparent age; (3) the bodily plight or condition of a person, including death and illness; (4) the emotional state of a person – e.g. whether distressed, angry, aggressive, affectionate or depressed; (5) the condition of things – e.g. worn, shabby, used or new; (6) certain questions of value; and (7) estimates of speed and distance.'

The law also recognises, however, that some non-expert opinion evidence is inherently unreliable, and where the guilt of the accused depends on the accuracy of such evidence further considerations come into play. If the case against the accused depends wholly or substantially on the accuracy of a witness's visual identification of him the judge is obliged to give the jury a '*Turnbull* direction' on the dangers associated with such evidence (11.1.1 *ante*); and, although, by virtue of s. 8 of the Criminal Procedure Act 1865, non-expert opinion evidence is admissible to identify the author of disputed handwriting, juries must be given expert guidance in criminal trials (*R* v. *Harden* [1963] 1 QB 8 (CCA)). Similarly, if the accused is charged with driving a vehicle in excess of the speed limit he cannot be convicted solely on a single witness's opinion of the speed (s. 89(2) of the Road Traffic Regulation Act 1984); and it is permissible to give an opinion that the accused had been drinking alcohol only if the perceived facts upon which that opinion is based are also provided (*R* v. *Davies* [1962] 1 WLR 1111 (C-MAC)).

Section 3(2) of the Civil Evidence Act 1972 has placed the common law on non-expert opinions in civil proceedings on a statutory footing; and s. 3(3) of the Act makes it clear that non-expert opinions may also be given on any issue. In criminal trials non-expert witnesses are not supposed to give their opinion on an issue, although this rule is subject to exceptions and sometimes ignored in practice. In *R* v. *Beckett* (1913) 8 Cr App R 204 (CCA), for example, a witness was allowed to give his non-expert opinion on the cost of the damage done to a window; and in *R* v. *Johnson* [1994] Crim LR 376 (CA) a witness was permitted to say that she believed the complainant was genuinely distressed following admitted sexual intercourse with the accused, which was in effect an opinion on whether the complainant had indeed been raped as alleged. That such opinions are occasionally permitted is not surprising, for it may be impossible to enforce an absolute prohibition in some contexts. A visual identification of the accused is, after all, an opinion on the issue of the offender's identity; and to say that the accused had been drinking, when the charge is one of driving while unfit through drink, is again to give an opinion on one of the facts in issue. In *Sherrard* v. *Jacob* [1965] NI 151 (NICA) it was accepted that 'the non-expert witness is competent to give inferential, or opinion, evidence on certain matters which may very well be matters in issue and for decision'. However, it is *not* for a witness in criminal proceedings to give an opinion on whether the accused is guilty of the offence charged (*R* v. *Cleeland* [2002] EWCA Crim 293 at para. 128).

12.2 Expert Opinion Evidence

Specialised areas of knowledge need to be explained by experts to prevent erroneous inferences being drawn from certain types of evidence with which the tribunal of fact is unfamiliar. Witnesses having a relevant degree of expertise are therefore competent to give an opinion on matters which lie within their specialisation. Unlike the opinions of non-expert witnesses, which are regarded as superfluous and irrelevant, the opinion of an expert on the subject of his expertise has a significant degree of probative value warranting its admission as evidence. The problem the law has had to confront, particularly in the context of criminal proceedings, is the extent to which experts should be allowed to influence the tribunal of fact's decisions on the disputed issues. The principle of free proof justifies the admission of expert opinion evidence to ensure that difficult or unusual matters can be properly evaluated; and yet, by allowing such evidence to be given, there is a danger that the tribunal of fact's role will be usurped.

12.2.1 The Admissibility of Expert Opinion Evidence

An expert is entitled to give an opinion only on relevant matters which are, first, within his particular area of expertise and, second, outside the general knowledge and understanding of the tribunal of fact. This test ensures that superfluous evidence is not received, and enshrines the principle that questions of fact should be decided by the tribunal of fact to the standard imposed by law and not by witnesses according to their own subjective standards:

> '[O]ne purpose of jury trials is to bring into the jury box a body of men and women who are able to judge ordinary day-to-day questions by their own standards, that is, the standards in the eyes of the law of theoretically ordinary reasonable men and women ... Where the matters in issue go outside that experience and they are invited to deal with someone supposedly abnormal, for example, supposedly suffering from insanity or diminished responsibility, then plainly in such a case they are entitled to the benefit of expert evidence. But where, as in the present case, they are dealing with someone who by concession was on the medical evidence entirely normal, it seems to this Court abundantly clear ... that it is not permissible to call a witness, with whatever his personal experience, merely to tell the jury how he thinks an accused man's mind – assumedly a normal mind – operated at the time of the alleged crime with reference to the crucial question of what that man's intention was.' (*R* v. *Chard* (1971) 56 Cr App R 268 (CA) at pp. 270–1)

'An expert's opinion is admissible to furnish the court with ... information which is likely to be outside the experience and knowledge of a judge or jury. If on the proven facts a judge or jury can form their own conclusions without help, then the opinion of an expert is unnecessary ... The fact that an expert witness has impressive ... qualifications does not by that fact alone make his opinion on matters of human nature and behaviour within the limits of normality any more helpful than that of the jurors themselves; but there is a danger that they may think it does.' (*R* v. *Turner* [1975] 2 WLR 56 (CA) at p. 60)

Thus, while expert opinion evidence is admissible (and often necessary) on physical illnesses, abnormal mental conditions, science, technology, engineering, foreign law, business practices, art and any other matter which most people would be unfamiliar with, it is not admissible if the tribunal of fact has sufficient understanding to reach a decision on the issue without such assistance. For example in *R* v. *Hersey* [1998] Crim LR 281 (CA) an expert in voice identification could not explain the evident differences between a recording of the accused's voice and recordings of other voices (used on a voice-identification parade) as he would have done no more than point out differences which the jury could hear for themselves. Conversely, expert evidence is admissible on a matter which the tribunal of fact may assume is within their understanding if that assumption would be erroneous. In *R* v. *Woods* [2003] EWCA Crim 1147 it was held that the trial judge had been right to allow a medical doctor experienced in the field of alleged sexual offences to give evidence to the effect that a woman could experience an orgasm during sexual activity even if she was not consenting.

The opinion evidence of psychiatrists and psychologists deserves particular attention. The tribunal of fact would not be expected to resolve questions relating to a mental illness without the assistance of a suitably qualified expert. Expert medical (usually psychiatric) evidence may therefore be given on conditions such as automatism (*Bratty* v. *Attorney-General for Northern Ireland* [1961] 3 WLR 965 (HL)) and post-traumatic stress disorder (*R* v. *White* [1995] Crim LR 393 (CA)). Such evidence is *necessary* if diminished responsibility (*R* v. *Dix* (1981) 74 Cr App R 306 (CA)) or insanity (ss. 1 and 2 of the Criminal Procedure (Insanity and Unfitness to Plead) Act 1991) has been raised, or it has been alleged that a person has suffered a psychiatric injury for the purposes of the Offences Against the Person Act 1861 (*R* v. *Chan-Fook* (1993) 99 Cr App R 147 (CA)).

There is of course no definitive line separating extreme emotions from mild mental illnesses or the mentally normal from the mentally sub-normal, but the desirability of reserving questions of fact for the tribunal of fact, insofar as it is possible to do so, has led to the drawing of arbitrary lines. In *R* v. *Masih* [1986] Crim LR 395 the Court of Appeal held that the dividing line between the mentally normal and sub-normal was to be drawn at the IQ value of 70. According to this test, if the accused has an IQ below 70 the expert's opinion is deemed to be sufficiently probative to justify its admission even though this will necessarily undermine the jury's own fact-finding role. If, however, the accused has an IQ of 70 or above, the assistance which the jury could get from the expert's opinion is felt to be insufficiently probative to justify its admission – the principle which demands trial by jury rather than by witnesses takes precedence over the principle of free proof. M faced an allegation of rape and wished to call a psychiatrist to explain how his low IQ would have affected his ability to appreciate the absence of consent. This evidence was inadmissible because M had an IQ of 72, even though he was 'dull-normal', immature, docile and had a limited understanding of people. In *R* v. *Weightman* (1990) 92 Cr App R 291 (CA) the accused sought to call a psychiatrist to show that her confession was unreliable on account of her 'histrionic personality disorder'. This evidence was held to be inadmissible on the ground that she was neither suffering from a mental illness nor below normal intelligence. Her abnormal personality was regarded as something within the experience of normal, non-medical people.

Such an arbitrary and inflexible distinction can lead to injustice in borderline cases and a more flexible approach has now been adopted, at least where the reliability of a *confession* is in dispute. In *R* v. *Raghip* (1991) *The Times* 9.12.91 the accused was a young abnormally-suggestible man, with an IQ of 74 and a level of functioning equivalent to that of a 9-year-old child, who had been convicted of murdering a police officer on the basis of a confession. The Court of Appeal held that psychological and psychiatric evidence on the accused's mental condition should have been admitted on the issue of the reliability for the purposes of s. 76(2)(*b*) of the Police and Criminal Evidence Act 1984 (7.1.3.2 *ante*) and that, even if the judge had correctly ruled the confession to be admissible, the expert opinion should have been put before the jury to help them assess its reliability and probative value. The Court drew a distinction between the admissibility of psychiatric and psychological evidence going to the reliability of a confession – it is admissible if the jury would be 'assisted in assessing' the accused's mental condition – and the admissibility of such evidence in relation to the accused's *mens rea* (as in *R* v. *Masih* [1986] Crim LR 395 (CA)).

In *R* v. *Ward* [1993] 1 WLR 619 (at p. 690) the Court of Appeal expressed the view that the expert evidence of a psychiatrist or a psychologist could properly be admitted, in relation to whether the accused's confession was reliable, if it was to the effect that the accused was 'suffering from a condition not properly described as mental illness, but from a personality disorder so severe as properly to be categorised as mental disorder'. However, in *R* v. *Roberts* (1998) unreported (96/3953/ S1) (CA) it was held that the question is not whether the accused's personality disorder was so severe that it could be 'categorised' as a mental disorder, but whether the nature of the disorder might render his confession unreliable. Expert opinion evidence was therefore admissible on the accused's suggestible and compliant personality. The same approach was adopted in *R* v. *O'Brien* [2000] Crim LR 676 (CA), where it was held that admissibility is dependent on three conditions being satisfied. First, the disorder must be of a type which might render a confession unreliable; second, the accused's condition must show a very significant deviation from the norm; and, third, there must be independent evidence of a history of disorder pre-dating the making of the confession. One of three co-accused, H, had confessed to involvement in a robbery in which a newsagent had been killed and implicated O and S at their trial. The appeals were allowed on the ground that expert opinion evidence on H's mental disorder, a personality associated with those who make false confessions which, in his case, was particularly severe, should have been admitted. The Court of Appeal also expressed the view that the expert opinion evidence should have been admitted on the question whether H's *testimony* was reliable. In other words, if the accused confesses and implicates his co-accused, and the three *O'Brien* conditions are satisfied, the expert evidence is admissible not only on the reliability of his confession but also on his capacity to give reliable testimony against his co-accused.

Expert evidence is admissible to determine whether a would-be witness is competent to give evidence and, if so, whether he should give his evidence on oath (ss. 54(5) and 55(6) of the Youth Justice and Criminal Evidence Act 1999); and on whether a 'special measures direction' should be made, varied or discharged (r. 9 of the Crown Court (Special Measures Directions and Directions Prohibiting Cross-examination) Rules 2002 (SI 2002 No. 1688), r. 9 of the Magistrates' Courts (Special Measures Directions) Rules 2002 (SI 2002 No. 1687)). Expert evidence is also admissible to show that a witness, though competent, is suffering from a mental illness rendering him totally or substantially incapable of giving reliable evidence (*Toohey* v. *Metropolitan Police Commissioner* [1965] 2 WLR 439 (HL) at p. 447, *R* v. *Mackenney* (1981) 76 Cr App R 271 (CA), *R* v. *Smith* [2002] EWCA Crim 2074; see 16.5.4.4 *post*).

In *R* v. *Turner* [1975] 2 WLR 56 (CA) it was not possible for a psychiatrist to give his expert opinion on the accused's veracity as a witness. If a witness is mentally capable of giving reliable evidence it is for the jury, assisted by appropriate warnings from the judge and counsel, to decide whether the witness's evidence is in fact reliable (*R* v. *Mackenney* (1981) 76 Cr App R 271 (CA), *R* v. *Walsh* [2000] All ER (D) 2457 (CA), *R* v. *Burton* [2002] EWCA Crim 614). Similarly, it has been said that in civil proceedings it is for the judge to determine whether a child witness is credible without the assistance of an expert opinion on the question (*Re N (a Minor) (Sexual Abuse: Video Evidence)* [1997] 1 WLR 153 (CA)). In *Re M and R (Child Abuse: Evidence)* [1996] 2 FLR 195, however, the Court of Appeal suggested that in cases where a child complainant is alleging abuse, it *is* permissible for an expert to give his opinion on the accuracy or truthfulness of the child's evidence, the question for the judge being one of weight rather than admissibility.

Different considerations may apply in criminal proceedings if more than one accused is being tried for the same offence and they run 'cut-throat' defences. In *Lowery* v. *R* [1973] 3 WLR 235 two young men, L and K, were jointly charged with the brutal and sadistic murder of a

15-year-old girl in Australia for which they blamed each other. The Privy Council held that in the special circumstances of the case, and because L had already put his character in issue by giving evidence to show he was not the sort of person who would commit such an offence, it had been permissible for K to call a professional psychologist to give evidence as to their respective personalities, showing that L was the more aggressive and dominant of the two and supporting K's version of events. In *R* v. *Turner* [1975] 2 WLR 56 the Court of Appeal stated that the decision in *Lowery* v. *R* had been 'decided on its special facts' and did not set a precedent for the general admissibility of psychiatric or psychological evidence to prove the accused's veracity.

Another important aspect of the decision in *R* v. *Turner*, a case in which the accused's defence to a charge of murder was provocation, was that the psychiatrist called by the defence could not give his expert opinion on the accused's deep affection for the deceased or his profound grief following her death. According to Lawton LJ (at p. 61): 'Jurors do not need psychiatrists to tell them how ordinary folk who are not suffering from any mental illness are likely to react to the stresses and strains of life.' Human emotions such as depression, insecurity and grief must therefore be assessed without any expert assistance. In *R* v. *Browning (No. 2)* [1995] Crim LR 227 (CA) a professor of psychology could not give evidence on the deterioration of a prosecution witness's memory with time; in *R* v. *Loughran* [1999] Crim LR 404 (CA) a psychiatrist, if called, would not have been able to give his opinion on the accused's anxiety at the prospect of sexual intercourse; in *R* v. *Ugoh* [2001] EWCA Crim 1381 it was held that, while a psycho-pharmacologist could address the effect of the alcohol consumed by a rape complainant on her ability to give informed consent to sexual intercourse, he could not give his opinion on whether the accused had appreciated that she was unable to give such consent; and in *R* v. *Gilfoyle (No. 2)* [2001] 2 Cr App R 57 the Court of Appeal doubted whether assessing levels of happiness or unhappiness, in this case whether the deceased had been suicidal, was a matter which required the expert opinion of a psychologist. Psychiatric evidence has also been held to be inadmissible in respect of whether or not the accused could differentiate between reality and fantasy (*R* v. *Reynolds* [1989] Crim LR 220 (CA)) and on the likelihood of a suicide pact (*R* v. *Wood* [1990] Crim LR 264 (CA)).

What is a 'stress and strain' of life is also a matter of degree, however, and an inflexible rule is unlikely to be satisfactory, particularly where psychological conditions caused by stresses and strains are now coming to be understood as true medical conditions beyond the understanding of jurors. In *R* v. *Merry* (1993) 99 Cr App R 326 (CA) the accused and her boyfriend were jointly charged with offences of manslaughter and cruelty against her three-year-old child. The accused wished to call a psychologist and a psychiatrist to explain that the reason she had not prevented acts of cruelty on her child by her boyfriend was that she herself had been abused as a child and an adult, and was suffering psychological damage which had prevented her from acting as a normal person would have done in the circumstances. Farquharson LJ said (at p. 332):

'It is not suggested here that the appellant is suffering from a mental illness, but that is not in itself conclusive against the admission of this evidence. The law is in a state of development in this area. There may well be other mental conditions about which a jury might require expert assistance in order to understand and evaluate their effect on the issues in a case.'

In the similar case of *R* v. *Emery* (1992) 14 Cr App R (S) 394 the Court of Appeal felt that the trial judge had properly allowed experts to give evidence of the accused's condition of 'learned helplessness' ('battered woman syndrome') caused by the routine abuse she herself had suffered at the hands of her boyfriend (the co-accused) as the condition was 'complex ... not known by the public at large' and relevant to her defence of duress. Battered woman syndrome, a form of post-traumatic stress disorder, has now come to be recognised as a medical condition for the purposes of the *Turner* test, and is admissible if a woman has pleaded provocation as a partial defence to the murder of her alleged tormentor (*R* v. *Thornton (No. 2)* [1996] 2 Cr App R 108 (CA)). Expert evidence on psychological conditions other than battered woman syndrome is now admissible if provocation has been raised to show the accused's personality was affected at the time of the killing. In *R* v. *Humphreys* [1995] 4 All ER 1008 (CA), for example, the accused's 'attention-seeking traits' amounted to such a condition justifying a psychiatrist's expert opinion. Expert opinion evidence may also be admissible in respect of the accused's 'paranoid personality disorder' if he has raised self-defence and the disorder affected his perception of the danger he faced at the time the force was used or his defence to murder is diminished responsibility (see *R* v. *Martin* [2002] 2 WLR 1 (CA)).

It is questionable whether an arbitrary line between normality and abnormality in the context of psychological or personality disorders is conducive to the interests of justice. An alternative test would be to apply the general principles governing the admissibility of logically relevant evidence (3.1 *ante*). Admissibility would then be governed by an assessment of the probative value of the expert testimony in the context of the case when weighed against competing policy considerations such as the need to minimise delay, cost, unreliability, the risk of overburdening the jury, and so on. The desirability of preventing the jury's role from being usurped could be regarded as but one of several considerations militating against the admission of the expert's opinion. This discretionary approach would not be so straightforward to apply as the *Turner* test, but it would be more likely to guarantee the accused a fair trial. It would also be flexible enough to allow for the admission of different types of expert testimony as scientific (particularly psychological) knowledge increases.

Given the inherent unreliability of visual-identification evidence, and the guidelines which have been introduced to safeguard the accused (11.1.1 *ante*), it might be expected that the expert opinion evidence of psychologists would be admissible to explain the reasons for such unreliability. After all, the principal reason for the *Turnbull* direction is that the unreliability of visual-identification evidence is not within the experience and understanding of lay fact-finders. The question has not been addressed in England and Wales, but in Australia the evidence of a psychologist on the unreliability of identification evidence has been held to be inadmissible (*R* v. *Smith* [1987] VR 907 (VSC)). It remains to be seen whether English courts will adopt the same approach, but it is to be noted that expert opinion evidence is admissible in respect of other types of identification evidence, such as fingerprints, DNA profiles and voice comparisons.

Whether a publication is obscene for the purpose of ss. 1 and 2 of the Obscene Publications Act 1959 (that is, whether it tends to 'deprave and corrupt') is generally to be decided by the tribunal of fact without the assistance of expert opinion evidence from psychologists, doctors or sociologists (*R* v. *Anderson* [1971] 3 WLR 939 (CA), *DPP* v. *Jordan* [1976] 3 WLR 887 (HL)), although in the latter case Lord Wilberforce recognised a possible exception where the potential readers of such material comprised a 'special class' upon whom its likely impact would not, in the absence of expert assistance, be understood by the jury or magistrates. The only example to date of such a special class arose in *DPP* v. *A and BC Chewing Gum* [1967] 3 WLR 493. A chewing gum company had been marketing packets of gum containing cards showing battle scenes and was prosecuted under the 1959 Act, but the magistrates refused to hear a prosecution expert on child psychiatry who had been called to give his opinion on the likely effects of the cards on children. The Divisional Court held that the expert should have been allowed to give his opinion on the effect certain types of pictures (including some of the battle scenes) would be likely to have on the minds of children. It was said (at p. 497) that 'when you are dealing ... with children ... any jury and any magistrates need all the help they can get' (see also *R* v. *Skirving* [1985] 2 WLR 1001 (CA)). Section 4(1) of the 1959 Act provides a statutory defence of 'public good' to a charge of publishing obscene material contrary to s. 2, obliging the accused to show that the obscene material was justified 'in the interests of science, literature, art or learning, or of other objects of general concern'. Expert opinion evidence is admissible under s. 4(2) to prove such grounds.

Part 35 of the Civil Procedure Rules 1998 provides that expert evidence '*shall* be restricted to that which is reasonably required to resolve the proceedings' (r. 35.1). Accordingly, the court's leave is required in civil proceedings before an expert can be called to give evidence or an expert's report can be adduced in evidence (r. 35.4(1)). Rule 35.5(1) provides that expert evidence is to be given in a written report unless the court directs otherwise. This restriction on the admissibility of expert evidence was introduced to stem the disproportionate use of experts in civil proceedings and the associated expense and delay for the parties concerned. For example, in *Re B (Minors) (Care Proceedings: Practice)* [1999] 1 WLR 238 (FD) the parties sought to call 13 expert witnesses on the question whether a child had been shaken and, if so, by whom; and of those experts all seven medical specialists were in agreement on the specific questions requiring their expertise.

Civil courts also have the power to direct that evidence be given by a 'single joint expert' (see CPR 1998 r. 35.7(1) and para. 6 of Practice Direction 35). This is a wide discretion, but it would be inappropriate to order a single expert in some cases, most obviously where there is more than one school of thought on the issue (*Oxley* v. *Penwarden* [2001] Lloyd's Rep Med 347 (CA)).

12.2.2 The Competence of Expert Witnesses

Whether a person who purports to be an expert can properly be regarded as such is a question for the judge. It is the expertise itself which determines a witness's competence and not the route by which he came to have that expertise. As such it is not always necessary to have formal qualifications to be an expert, although in practice much will depend on the nature of the purported expertise. An amateur study of handwriting over several years may qualify a witness to give his opinion on the authorship of disputed handwriting (*R* v. *Silverlock* [1894] 2 QB 766 (CCCR)); a police officer's careful examination of a closed-circuit television film may qualify him to give an opinion on the identity of persons filmed (*R* v. *Clare* [1995] 2 Cr App R 333 (CA)); a police officer with no formal qualifications may be sufficiently experienced and knowledgeable to give an expert opinion on ear-print identification evidence (*R* v. *Dallagher* [2003] 1 Cr App R 195 (CA)) or on whether a particular quantity of drugs is too large to be for personal consumption (*R* v. *Hodges* [2003] 2 Cr App R 247 (CA)); and a professor of the history of architecture, though not a qualified architect, may have sufficient expertise to give an opinion on architectural questions, such as the design of the buildings at Auschwitz (*Irving* v. *Penguin Books* [2001] EWCA Civ 1197).

Amateur experience will be insufficient for some other fields of knowledge, however. In *R* v. *Robb* (1991) 93 Cr App R 161 (CA) Bingham LJ felt that the opinion evidence of an amateur psychologist would be inadmissible, but went on to hold that a specialist holding a minority view in his own field could still be regarded as an expert so long as he was not merely 'a quack, a charlatan or an enthusiastic amateur'. This must now be read in the light of *R* v. *Gilfoyle (No. 2)* [2001] 2 Cr App R 57, where the Court of Appeal held, in the context of evidence of psychological conditions, that 'evidence based on a developing new brand of science or medicine is not admissible until accepted by the scientific community as being able to provide accurate and reliable opinion'. According to this test, a would-be expert witness must furnish the court with a sufficient database and a substantial body of academic writing approving his methodology. In other words, there must be the necessary scientific criteria for testing the accuracy of an expert's conclusions, to enable the judge or jury to form their own independent judgment by the application of those criteria to the facts proved. However, a more flexible approach was adopted in *R* v. *Dallagher* [2003] 1 Cr App R 195 (CA), a case on the admissibility of ear-print evidence, where it was thought that the sole test for admissibility is whether the field of expertise is sufficiently well-established to pass the ordinary tests of relevance and reliability.

In the South Australian case of *R* v. *Bonython* (1984) 38 SASR 45 (SASC) (at pp. 46–7) King CJ broke down the test for determining the competence of a witness to give an expert opinion into three questions. First, is the subject matter of the opinion such that a person without instruction or experience in the area would be able to form a sound judgment without the assistance of a witness possessing special knowledge or experience in the area? Second, does the subject matter of the opinion form part of a body of knowledge or experience which is sufficiently organised or recognised to be accepted as a reliable body of knowledge or experience? Third, has the witness acquired by study or experience sufficient knowledge of the subject matter to render his opinion of value in resolving an issue before the court? This test was cited with approval in *Barings* v. *Cooper & Lybrand* [2001] PNLR 551 (ChD) and *Clarke* v. *Marlborough Fine Art (London) (No. 3)* [2002] EWHC 11 (ChD), and has been tacitly approved by the Court of Appeal (*R* v. *Woods* [2002] EWCA Crim 3189, *R* v. *Hodges* [2003] 2 Cr App R 247 (CA)). To the three *Bonython* criteria may be added a fourth. The expert must be able to provide an impartial, objective opinion on the matter within his expertise. If the expert is unable to discharge this duty he is not competent to give his opinion (*Field* v. *Leeds City Council* [2001] 2 CPLR 129 (CA)).

12.2.3 Primary and Secondary Facts

In formulating his opinion an expert will naturally have to rely on certain facts directly arising out of the case itself ('primary facts'), but to justify his opinion he will almost certainly have to refer to extraneous sources of information such as articles or data published in reputable journals and texts ('secondary facts'). The reliability of an expert's opinion depends to a large extent on the reliability of the primary facts upon which that opinion has been based. Primary facts, like any other evidence relied on in the proceedings, must be proved by admissible evidence, whether or not by the expert himself, so the court can ensure that the expert has not been misinformed or taken irrelevant facts into consideration (*R* v. *Turner* [1975] 2 WLR 56 (CA) at pp. 59–61). In *R* v. *Loveridge* [2001] EWCA Crim 734 the accused was charged with robbery on the basis of DNA evidence obtained from a balaclava helmet worn by one of the robbers. However, while there was a forensic scientist who was able to interpret DNA profiles, the prosecution failed to prove by admissible evidence the provenance of the two profiles she had before her. The Court of Appeal therefore concluded that there was 'no admissible evidence before the court to make the DNA evidence admissible' and quashed the conviction for robbery (see also *R* v. *Jackson* [1996] 2 Cr App R 420 (CA)).

Different considerations apply to secondary facts because they are unlikely to be unreliable. The information and data published in reputable journals will already have been scrutinised and commented upon by other specialists in the field, and the justifications for excluding hearsay generally do not apply to such evidence. For this reason secondary facts are not excluded by the hearsay rule. Such facts are not only admissible but *ought* to be admitted, once the primary facts have been proved, to demonstrate to the court how the expert reached his opinion. This was made clear in the leading case of *R* v. *Abadom* [1983] 1 WLR 126. The accused in that case was alleged to have been one of a group of masked robbers who had entered an office, broken a window and demanded money. The evidence identifying him as one of the offenders included the opinion of a forensic scientist who gave evidence that glass fragments found on the accused's shoes matched the broken glass at the scene of the crime, in that they shared the same refractive index, and that such glass was relatively uncommon. In formulating his opinion the expert had relied on unpublished Home Office statistics which showed that the refractive index of the glass in the two samples had been found in only 4 per cent of all glass samples analysed in various forensic laboratories over a number of years. The accused appealed on the ground that the scientist should not have been allowed to rely on the statistics which, it was submitted, were inadmissible hearsay. The Court of Appeal held that the exclusionary hearsay rule applied only to primary facts and not to any secondary facts. So long as the evidence of the refractive index of each of the two glass samples had been proved by the person who had analysed the sample in question, the secondary facts (that is, the Home Office data) had been properly relied on by the expert in reaching his opinion.

In *H* v. *Schering Chemicals* [1983] 1 WLR 143 (QBD) Bingham J suggested that where an expert refers to the results of research published by a reputable authority in a reputable journal the court would ordinarily regard those results as supporting inferences fairly to be drawn from them, unless or until a different approach was shown to be proper. The Home Office statistics in *R* v. *Abadom* had not been published, but this did not seem to trouble the Court of Appeal, suggesting that whether hearsay evidence will be ruled admissible as secondary facts is governed by a test of apparent reliability. In *R* v. *Edwards* [2001] EWCA Crim 2185 the accused, charged with possession of ecstasy with intent to supply, sought to call as an expert witness an employee of a drug advice charity to testify that some users of the drug took substantially more than 12 tablets during a 24-hour period, to support his defence that he was a heavy user and that the 29 tablets found in his possession were for his personal use. The problem for the accused was that the would-be expert's knowledge was based on what he had been told by drug addicts rather than on his own personal experience or academic materials. The basis of his knowledge was therefore unreliable hearsay falling outside the scope of the secondary facts exception. Indeed, because his knowledge had come from such an unreliable source, he could not even be regarded as an expert on ecstasy consumption (*cf. R* v. *Smart* [2002] EWCA Crim 772).

The secondary facts exception to the hearsay rule applies only to data relied on by an *expert*. If a non-expert witness wishes to rely on such data he will be able to do so only if there is a general exception to the hearsay rule which can be relied on. In *Dawson* v. *Lunn* [1986] RTR 234 the

Divisional Court held that the (non-expert) accused should not have been permitted to adduce an extract from the British Medical Journal in support of his defence to a charge of drink-driving without a properly-qualified witness being called to give the magistrates guidance on the information contained in it.

One remaining question is whether an expert who refers to privileged primary facts thereby waives his client's legal professional privilege in respect of them. In *Clough* v. *Tameside & Glossop Health Authority* [1998] 1 WLR 1478 (QBD), a medical negligence case decided under the old Rules of the Supreme Court, the defendant's disclosed expert report (Dr H's report) referred to another doctor's undisclosed, privileged report (Dr P's report) which Dr H had been sent and seen as part of the background documentation in the case. Bracewell J held that by disclosing Dr H's expert report, and referring in that report to Dr P's privileged report, the defendant had waived the privilege which had hitherto attached to Dr P's report, even though Dr H may not have relied on Dr P's report in reaching his expert opinion. The justification for this decision was that an expert is under a duty to make full disclosure of all facts considered by him when reaching his opinion so that the opposing party will be able to ascertain whether the opinion was based on a sound factual basis. Bracewell J said (at p. 1484):

'It is only by proper and full disclosure to all parties, that an expert's opinion can be tested in court, in order to ascertain whether all appropriate information was supplied and how the expert dealt with it ... Fairness dictates that a party should not be forced to meet a case pleaded or an expert opinion on the basis of documents he cannot see.'

In *Bourns* v. *Raychem* [1999] 3 All ER 154 (CA), however, it was held that mere reference to a document does not waive privilege in it; there must at least be reference to the contents and reliance on the document. Aldous LJ was not willing to accept Bracewell J's view of the law in *Clough* v. *Tameside & Glossop Health Authority* (although it was thought that the result in that case was probably correct); and Swinton Thomas LJ stated that he would wish to reserve for future consideration whether, even on its own facts, *Clough* v. *Tameside & Glossop Health Authority* had been correctly decided. The position in civil proceedings is now governed by the Civil Procedure Rules 1998. Rule 31.14(2) provides that, subject to r. 35.10(4), a party may apply for an order for inspection of any document mentioned in an expert's report which has not already been disclosed. An expert's report must state the substance of all written instructions on the basis of which the report was written (r. 35.10(3)) but, while the instructions are not privileged against disclosure, the court will not order disclosure of any specific document (or permit cross-examination in court) in relation to those instructions unless there are reasonable grounds to consider the statement of instructions to be inaccurate or incomplete (r. 35.10(4)). It remains to be seen whether the approach adopted in *Clough* v. *Tameside & Glossop Health Authority* applies in criminal proceedings. In *R* v. *Davies* (2002) 166 JP 243 the Court of Appeal left the question open, but noted that, even if it did apply, the court would be able to ameliorate any unfairness to the accused by applying s. 78(1) of the Police and Criminal Evidence Act 1984.

12.2.4 Expert Opinions on Ultimate Issues

At common law it has traditionally been unacceptable for an expert to give an opinion on any 'ultimate' issue. The view has been that issues of fact are ultimately for the tribunal of fact to decide according to the standard of proof determined by law; it is not for experts to usurp that fact-finding role by applying their own individual standard. Thus in *Haynes* v. *Doman* [1899] 2 Ch 13 (CA) it was not permissible for persons involved in a particular trade to give their opinion on the reasonableness of a restraint of trade clause in a contract of employment. Similarly, in *DPP* v. *A and BC Chewing Gum* [1967] 3 WLR 493 (DC) (12.2.1 *ante*) Lord Parker CJ felt that while an expert in child psychiatry was competent to give an expert opinion on the effect of battle scenes on children, it would be wrong for him to give his opinion on whether any of the defendant company's cards actually tended to corrupt or deprave 'because that final stage was a matter which was entirely for the justices' (see also *R* v. *Lupien* [1970] SCR 263 (SCC)).

The ultimate issues rule is unnecessary if its rationale is to prevent the usurpation of the tribunal of fact's role. As a general rule, the tribunal of fact has the right to ignore any expert opinion evidence (12.2.5 *post*). Perhaps the true justification is to prevent jurors from simply accepting expert opinions without question and abrogating their own responsibility to find the facts. This fear would seem to be implicit in Lawton LJ's dictum in *R* v. *Turner* [1975] 2 WLR 56 (CA) (12.2.1 *ante*), but it is an insufficient basis for the rule because any opposing party is able to call his own expert to give a conflicting opinion. In fact, given the adversarial system, there would seem to be no valid justification for the rule so long as experts confine their opinions to questions of fact. After all, experts are better qualified to draw appropriate inferences from evidence falling within their areas of expertise than lay triers of fact.

The ultimate issues rule has now been abolished for civil proceedings (s. 3(1) and 3(3) of the Civil Evidence Act 1972) and its formal abolition was recommended for criminal trials by the Criminal Law Revision Committee in its Eleventh Report (Cmnd 4991 (1972) at p. 155). The rule has often been disregarded in criminal proceedings anyway, as noted by Lord Parker CJ in *DPP* v. *A and BC Chewing Gum* [1967] 3 WLR 493 (DC) (at p. 497):

> 'Those who practise in the criminal courts see every day cases of experts being called on the question of diminished responsibility, and although technically the final question "Do you think he was suffering from diminished responsibility?" is strictly inadmissible, it is allowed time and time again without any objection.'

In *R* v. *Stockwell* (1993) 97 Cr App R 260 the Court of Appeal accepted that if there was a rule prohibiting experts from giving an opinion on an ultimate issue 'it has long been more honoured in the breach than the observance' and went on to hold (at p. 266):

'In our view an expert is called to give his opinion and he should be allowed to do so. It is, however, important that the judge should make clear to the jury that they are not bound by the expert's opinion, and that the issue is for them to decide.'

It is now beyond doubt that an expert is able to give his opinion on an 'ultimate issue' in criminal proceedings, so long as that opinion is within the area of his expertise and the judge makes it clear that it is for the jury to decide the issue (*R* v. *Gokal* (1999) unreported (97/04132/S2) (CA), *R* v. *Ugoh* [2001] EWCA Crim 1381, *R* v. *KL* [2002] EWCA Crim 2171).

12.2.5 The Status of Expert Opinion Evidence

As a general rule, it is open to the tribunal of fact to attach to an expert's opinion such weight as it thinks fit, or even disregard it, like any other item of evidence (*R* v. *Lanfear* [1968] 2 WLR 623 (CA), *R* v. *Stockwell* (1993) 97 Cr App R 260 (CA), *R* v. *Fitzpatrick* [1999] Crim LR 832 (CA)). In *R* v. *Rivett* (1950) 34 Cr App R 87 the Court of Criminal Appeal held that the issue of criminal insanity was a question to be determined by the jury and that there would be no interference with a finding of guilt merely because there had been evidence by medical men of the highest standing that the accused was insane at the time of the offence. This is not surprising because the defence of insanity is not simply a medical question; but in *R* v. *O'Brien* [2000] Crim LR 676 (98/06926/S1) the Court of Appeal held that where expert evidence of the accused's mental abnormality has been placed before the jury, they must be directed that they are not obliged to accept it. The same general principle applies in civil proceedings. For example, in *Fuller* v. *Strum* (2000) *The Times* 14.2.01 (ChD) the trial judge was able to reject the opinion of a handwriting expert, favouring instead the evidence of lay witnesses to the effect that a will had not been forged. As noted by the judge, a handwriting analyst's opinion is ultimately impressionistic, falling outside the 'purely scientific category' in respect of which the judge would be helpless without expert assistance. It was therefore permissible for the judge to draw his own inference from the differences between the disputed and genuine signatures and reject the opinion of the expert. Where the evidence is of a 'purely scientific' type, however, the judge will need to provide sound reasons for his decision to reject uncontroverted expert opinion evidence in favour of non-expert evidence (*Re B (a Minor)* [2000] 1 WLR 790 (CA)).

The principle that expert opinion evidence may be rejected is of general application, but there is an important exception. In *R* v. *Rivett* (1950) 34 Cr App R 87 the Court of Criminal Appeal recognised that a conviction could be quashed on appeal if it was a verdict no reasonable jury could have come to on the evidence before them, such as where the jury had rejected an opinion which the expert had been able to give with 'certainty, as in the case of a bodily disease, from specific symptoms such as a rash, a coma or other physical signs that a disease exists'. Similarly, in *R* v. *Matheson* [1958] 1 WLR 474 a five-member Court of Criminal Appeal held that juries were obliged to accept medical expert opinion evidence adduced by the defence if there was nothing in the other evidence to lead them to a different conclusion. Thus, in *R* v. *Smith* [1999] All ER (D) 1455 the Court of Appeal quashed a conviction for rape where the jury had rejected unchallenged medical evidence that the incident could not possibly have happened as described by the complainant. Although it was accepted that situations might arise where medical evidence was only part of the picture, and that there might therefore be a good reason why it was rejected by the jury, this was not such a case. The complainant had been two years from puberty at the time of the alleged incident, and the expert had been firmly of the view that the allegation of vigorous and prolonged intercourse could not possibly have occurred without injuring her. Similarly, in *R* v. *Bailey* (1961) 66 Cr App R 31 (CCA) the accused's conviction for murder was quashed as the jury had unreasonably rejected the uncontradicted expert evidence of three doctors that the accused had been suffering from an abnormality of the mind induced by disease such that his mental responsibility for the killing had been substantially impaired (in other words, diminished responsibility).

However, in *Walton* v. *R* [1977] 3 WLR 902 (PC) it was held that the jury had been entitled to disregard uncontradicted medical evidence. The quality and weight of the evidence in that case rendered it 'not entirely convincing' and the jury had also had before them other (non-medical) evidence which could have suggested the absence of any abnormality of the mind. A similar approach was adopted by the Court of Appeal in *R* v. *Eifinger* [2001] EWCA Crim 1855. The jury had been entitled to find the accused guilty of murder, notwithstanding the existence of uncontradicted medical evidence supporting his defence of diminished responsibility. The two psychiatrists who had given that evidence had based their opinions on nothing other than what the accused himself had told them, and the jury had had the opportunity to see the accused and assess for themselves the reliability of his evidence (see also *R* v. *Bradshaw* (1985) 82 Cr App R 79 (CA)). In *R* v. *Sanders* (1991) 93 Cr App R 245 (at p. 249) the Court of Appeal concluded that there were 'two clear principles' in cases of diminished responsibility:

> 'The first is that if there are no other circumstances to consider, unequivocal, uncontradicted medical evidence favourable to a defendant should be accepted by a jury and they should be so directed. The second is that where there are other circumstances to be considered the medical evidence, though it be unequivocal and uncontradicted, must be assessed in the light of the other circumstances.'

It is often the case that conflicting expert opinion evidence will be adduced by the opposing parties. In civil trials where the judge is the sole trier of fact he must resolve the conflict and give his reasons (*Sewell* v. *Electrolux* (1997) *The Times* 7.11.97 (CA)). In criminal trials if an expert is called by the prosecution to give an opinion on an issue which the prosecution must prove, the jury must be sure that his evidence is correct before they can rely on it (*R* v. *Platt* [1981] Crim LR 332 (CA)).

12.2.6 The Expert Witness's Duties

In *The Ikarian Reefer* [1993] 2 Lloyd's Rep 68 (QBD) (at pp. 81–2) Cresswell J set out the duties and responsibilities of expert witnesses in civil litigation. These guidelines have, in effect, been incorporated into the Civil Procedure Rules 1998 Practice Direction (PD 35) for experts and assessors. Expert evidence must be the independent product of the expert, uninfluenced by the pressures of litigation. An expert should assist the court by providing an objective, unbiased opinion on matters within his expertise, and should consider all material facts including those which might detract from his opinion. An expert should make it clear when a question or issue falls outside his expertise and when he is not able to reach a definite opinion because, for example, he has insufficient information; and, if after producing a report, he changes his view on any material matter, this should be communicated to all parties without delay. An expert should also set out in his written report: the details of any literature or other material relied on in preparing it; the substance of the material facts and instructions given to him; and which of the facts stated in the report are within his own knowledge (see also CPR 1998, r. 35.10(3)).

Rule 35.3 of the Civil Procedure Rules 1998 expressly provides that the expert's duty to help the court overrides any obligation to the person from whom he has received instructions or by whom he is paid. Further, the expert must include at the end of his written report a statement to the effect that he understands his duty to the court and that he has complied with it (CPR 1998, r. 35.10(2)). If an expert fails to comply with this requirement the court may exclude his evidence, notwithstanding its importance to the case (see *Stevens* v. *Gullis* [2000] 1 All ER 527 (CA)).

Cresswell J's summary of the expert witness's duties was cited with approval by the Court of Appeal in *The Ikarian Reefer* [1995] 1 Lloyd's Rep 455 (at p. 496) and by Otton LJ in *Stanton* v. *Callaghan* [1999] 2 WLR 745 (CA) (at p. 774) and would, therefore, appear to represent the position at common law. It follows that experts in criminal proceedings are, in effect, under the same duty as their counterparts in civil proceedings. Indeed, one of the successful grounds of appeal in *R* v. *Ward* [1993] 1 WLR 619 (CA) was the fact that government 'scientists' had deliberately withheld material experimental data in the belief that such data might damage the prosecution case, a breach of their 'clear duty' to assist the court in an impartial way.

12.3 Previous Judgments as Evidence

Sections 11 to 13 of the Civil Evidence Act 1968 and s. 74 of the Police and Criminal Evidence Act 1984 provide for the admissibility of previous judgments, a form of opinion evidence, in certain circumstances. The common-law rule is that previous convictions, and therefore previous civil judgments, are inadmissible in subsequent proceedings (*Hollington* v. *Hewthorn* [1943] 1 KB 587 (CA)).

12.3.1 Sections 11 to 13 of the Civil Evidence Act 1968

In civil proceedings a subsisting criminal conviction is admissible for the purpose of proving that the person convicted, whether or not a party to the civil proceedings, committed that offence (s. 11(1)). So, if cars driven by P and D were involved in a collision which damaged P's car and/or injured him, proof of D's conviction for careless driving arising out of that collision will be admissible to prove his negligence in the subsequent civil proceedings. This is to be expected because the standard of proof in criminal proceedings is higher than in civil proceedings: the fact that D's negligence has been proved beyond reasonable doubt, or that he has pleaded guilty, is highly probative evidence of his civil negligence. That said, the conviction is not conclusive of his civil liability. By virtue of s. 11(2)(*a*) the conviction raises a persuasive presumption that D committed the offence, so it is open to D to prove on the balance of probabilities that he did not commit it. Although it has been said that 'this is likely to be an uphill task' (*Hunter* v. *Chief Constable of the West Midlands Police* [1981] 3 WLR 906 (HL)) and that the burden is 'a heavy one' (*Cooper* v. *Pitcher* (1999) unreported (98/0574/2) (CA)), this should not be the case where the burden of proof was on D in the earlier criminal proceedings.

In *Stupple* v. *Royal Insurance* [1970] 3 WLR 217, a case where the plaintiff sought to disprove his conviction for robbery, there was a difference of opinion in the Court of Appeal as to the effect of a conviction adduced pursuant to s.11(1). Buckley LJ felt its value was limited to reversing the burden of proof, obliging the plaintiff to prove on the balance of probabilities that he did not commit the offence. Lord Denning MR went further, suggesting that a conviction also amounted to a 'weighty piece of evidence' in its own right to be considered by the judge when deciding whether the burden of proof had been discharged by the plaintiff, and the weight to be given to a previous conviction was, like any other evidence, a matter for the judge. According to Lord Denning, because the plaintiff had been convicted after a month-long trial by a jury who were unanimous, his conviction carried 'great weight' in his civil action.

In defamation trials proof that a person stands convicted of a criminal offence is conclusive evidence that he committed the offence (s. 13(1)). The policy behind this provision is to ensure that where a person's criminal offence has been reported it should not be open to that person to initiate a collateral attack on his conviction by commencing proceedings for defamation (*Hunter* v. *Chief Constable of the West Midlands Police* [1981] 3 WLR 906 (HL) at pp. 915–16). It also guarantees the freedom to report that a person has committed an offence once he has been convicted of it. Section 12 governs the admissibility of findings of adultery and paternity in subsequent civil proceedings, an exception to the general rule that civil judgments are not admissible as evidence in subsequent civil proceedings.

12.3.2 Section 74(1) of the Police and Criminal Evidence Act 1984

In criminal proceedings it may be necessary or desirable for the prosecution to prove that a crime has been committed by a person other than the accused in order to prove that the accused is guilty of the offence charged. An obvious example is where the accused faces a charge of handling stolen goods. The prosecution must prove the goods were stolen, and one way of doing this is to show that another person has already been convicted of stealing or handling them. Another example is provided by the facts of *R* v. *Gummerson* [1999] Crim LR 680 (97/08492/W2) (CA). D1 and D2 were recognised by the victim, on the basis of their voices, as two of the men who had robbed and assaulted him. D1 was convicted following a guilty plea, but D2 pleaded not guilty and was tried. The prosecution adduced D1's conviction to undermine D2's defence that the circumstances of the robbery would have prevented the victim from being able to identify any of the offenders (including D2) from their voices.

Section 74(1) of the Police and Criminal Evidence Act 1984 governs the admissibility of such convictions which have not been quashed on appeal (s. 75(4)). If a conviction is admissible under s. 74(1) there is a persuasive presumption that the offence was committed by the convicted person (s. 74(2)), so it is still open to the jury to find that he was not guilty (*R* v. *Pigram* [1995] Crim LR 808 (CA), *R* v. *Dixon* (2000) 164 JP 721 (CA)). If the judge rules that a conviction is relevant and admissible under s. 74(1), and ought not to be excluded by the application of s. 78(1), the contents of the relevant information, complaint, indictment or charge-sheet are admissible to identify the facts on which the conviction was based (s. 75(1)(*b*)). Section 75(1) does no more than specify the documents which are admissible for the purpose of identifying the facts on which a conviction is based, once the admissibility of the conviction itself has been established under s. 74(1) (*R* v. *Hinchcliffe* [2002] EWCA Crim 837).

In many cases the admission of a conviction under s. 74(1) will not unduly prejudice the accused, but where the offence the accused has been charged with is inextricably tied up with the offence committed by the other person the risk of undue prejudice must be addressed, and it may be appropriate in such cases for the judge to exclude a conviction which is *prima facie* admissible. The possibility of undue prejudice is a consequence of the Court of Appeal's broad interpretation of s. 74(1) in *R* v. *Robertson* [1987] 3 WLR 327 where it was held that the provision applied to 'any issue' in the proceedings and not just issues which were an essential ingredient of the offence charged.

If, for example, D is on trial for conspiring to commit an offence with G it is technically open to the prosecution to prove pursuant to ss. 74(1) and 75(1) that G has already pleaded guilty to *that* conspiracy. However, it has been held that in cases of this sort s. 78(1) should be applied to exclude G's conviction as it would imply that D is guilty unless he can prove the contrary (*R* v. *O'Connor* (1986) 85 Cr App R 298 (CA)). If s. 78(1) were not applied in such cases there would in effect be a reversal of the burden of proof, and the common-law principle established in *R* v. *Moore* (1956) 40 Cr App R 50 (CCA), that a plea of guilty by one co-accused is not evidence against another, would be significantly undermined. Accordingly in *R* v. *Curry* [1988] Crim LR 527 the Court of Appeal held that s. 74(1) should be sparingly used, particularly in relation to joint offences such as conspiracy and affray, and should not be used at all if the conviction would necessarily imply the accused's complicity. The Court of Appeal's reasoning is of general application; so in *R* v. *Mattison* [1990] Crim LR 117 (CA), where D was charged with an offence of gross indecency with G, contrary to s. 13 of the Sexual Offences Act 1956, G's conviction should have been excluded as it necessarily implied D's guilt.

Where, however, G's conviction does not necessarily imply D's guilt because of the nature of the offence, or the number of persons alleged to have been involved in the conspiracy, there may be no unfairness in allowing its admission simply to prove the commission of an offence. In *R* v. *Robertson* [1987] 3 WLR 327, D faced an allegation of conspiring with G1 and G2 to commit burglaries and the prosecution relied on s. 74(1) to prove that G1 and G2 had pleaded guilty to the substantive offences of burglary, and therefore that there had been a conspiracy. The Court of Appeal held that the judge had properly allowed evidence of the convictions to be admitted to prove the existence of a conspiracy as it did not necessarily imply D's involvement in it, particularly as D's name was absent from the counts to which G1 and G2 had pleaded guilty. In *R* v. *Lunnon* (1988) 88 Cr App R 71 four co-accused were charged with conspiracy to steal from shops, but one pleaded guilty on arraignment and her conviction was adduced pursuant to s. 74(1) at the trial of the other three. The Court of Appeal dismissed D's appeal against conviction as the judge had properly exercised his discretion under s. 78(1): G's guilty plea had been adduced simply as evidence of the first limb of the prosecution's case – the existence of a conspiracy – and the judge had made it quite clear in his summing-up that the jury had to be sure that each co-accused, including D, had actually been involved (the second limb of the prosecution case). Similarly, in *R* v. *Bennett* [1988] Crim LR 686, where D was charged with theft – a charge to which G had already pleaded guilty, in that as a supermarket cashier she had passed goods for less than their true price to D – the Court of Appeal held that G's conviction had been properly admitted simply to show there had been a theft. Whether or not D had been involved in the theft had been a matter for the jury. D could, for instance, have been ignorant of G's culpable conduct.

As already noted, it is always open to the trial judge to exercise his exclusionary discretion under s. 78(1) of PACE to prevent the prosecution from relying on s. 74(1) if the admission of a former co-accused's guilty plea would adversely affect the fairness of the accused's trial. A relevant consideration for the judge will be the strength of the case against the former co-accused and the fact that the remaining accused will be denied the opportunity of challenging the prosecution evidence upon which that conviction was based (*R* v. *Lee* [1996] Crim LR 825 (CA)). The judge should also take into account the fact that the former co-accused is not available to be cross-examined (*R* v. *Kempster* [1989] 1 WLR 1125 (CA)) – although this will be of no consequence if cross-examination would have been unlikely (*R* v. *Robertson* [1987] 3 WLR 327 (CA)). In *R* v. *Boyson* [1991] Crim LR 274 the Court of Appeal set out four principles governing the admissibility of convictions under s. 74(1):

> '(a) the conviction must be clearly relevant to an issue in the accused's trial; (b) section 74(1) must be sparingly used; (c) the judge should consider the question of fairness under section 78 of the Act and whether the probative value of the conviction outweighs its prejudicial [effect]; and (d) the judge must direct the jury clearly as to the issues to which the conviction is not relevant and also why the evidence is before them and to what issue it is directed.'

In *R* v. *Stewart* [1999] Crim LR 746, however, the Court of Appeal reaffirmed the principle that, when considering the application of s. 78(1), it is necessary to have regard not only to the interests of the accused but also to the interests of the prosecution and justice as a whole.

In some cases there may be a more fundamental objection to the admissibility of a conviction under s. 74(1). In *R* v. *Mahmood* [1997] 1 Cr App R 414, D, on trial for rape, admitted that he had had sexual intercourse with the complainant but contended that she had consented or, alternatively, that he had believed she was consenting. The case against him was that the complainant had been incapable of consent on account of being drunk. The prosecution therefore sought to adduce the fact that D's former co-accused (G) had already pleaded guilty on the ground that it was relevant to the issue of consent. The judge allowed G's conviction to be adduced and D was convicted. The Court of Appeal held that G's guilty plea had not been relevant to the issue of consent as G had had sex with the complainant some time after D, and it had not even been made clear on what basis G had pleaded guilty. Moreover, even if there had been any probative value in the conviction it had been 'wholly outweighed' by the prejudice caused to D. D's conviction was therefore quashed.

12.3.3 Section 74(3) of the Police and Criminal Evidence Act 1984

Section 74(3) provides that 'where evidence is admissible of the fact that the accused has committed an offence, in so far as that evidence is relevant to any matter in issue in the proceedings for a reason other than a tendency to show in the accused a disposition to commit the kind of offence with which he is charged, if the accused is proved to have been convicted of the offence ... he shall be taken to have committed that offence unless the contrary is proved'. This provision, unlike s. 74(1), presupposes that the accused's previous conviction is *already* admissible at common law or pursuant to a separate statutory provision (for example, s. 1(3) of the Criminal Evidence

Act 1898). The subsection does not itself render previous convictions admissible (*R* v. *Harris* [2001] Crim LR 227 (CA)).

The qualification in s.74(3) – 'in so far as that evidence is relevant to any matter in issue in the proceedings for a reason other than a tendency to show in the accused a disposition to commit the kind of offence with which he is charged' – is, in effect, a restatement of the old '*Makin* test' for the admissibility of similar fact evidence (3.3.4 *ante*). This suggests that similar fact evidence which is admissible by virtue of the test established in *DPP* v. *P* [1991] 3 WLR 161 (HL) (3.3.6 *ante*) falls within the scope of the subsection, and that inadmissible similar fact evidence remains inadmissible. On this view (which would appear to have been accepted by the Court of Appeal in *R* v. *Shanks* [2003] EWCA Crim 680) the accused is deemed to have committed the other similar fact offences of which he has been convicted, and it is for him to prove the contrary.

12.3.4 Acquittals as Evidence

An acquittal usually establishes nothing more than that the tribunal of fact was not satisfied beyond reasonable doubt of the accused's guilt, save that a defence which has been accepted may in certain circumstances amount to a specific finding of fact. Juries (and some lay magistrates) do not give reasons for their verdicts or explain their findings of fact, so in most cases an acquittal says nothing about any factual issue which had to be determined by them. For this reason acquittals are generally inadmissible as evidence for the determination of any issue in subsequent criminal or civil proceedings as 'the verdict reached by a different jury ... in the earlier trial [is] irrelevant' (*Hui Chi-Ming* v. *R* [1991] 3 WLR 495 (PC) at p. 500). Exceptionally, however, an acquittal may be admissible if it has sufficient probative value and its exclusion would be contrary to the interests of justice.

In *R* v. *Cooke* (1986) 84 Cr App R 286, for example, it was held that the circumstances of the trial at which A1 and A2 had been acquitted should have been admitted at D's trial. D, A1 and A2 were alleged to have made confessions over a short period of time, about the same series of events, to a particular police officer and there was a clear inference from the acquittals at the earlier trial of A1 and A2 that the officer had been disbelieved by the jury. The Court of Appeal provided the following analysis (at pp. 291–2):

'[W]here a police officer has allegedly obtained admissions on interviews about the same group of offences from different accused as part of a connected series of interviews over a short period, where those interviews are alleged to have been fabricated, and where the alleged admissions were the essential evidence against one or more of the accused who were nevertheless acquitted, justice demands that the jury should know this when they are considering a challenge by another accused to the truth of evidence of admissions said to have been made by him to the same officer at about the same time and about the same series of events.'

The same approach was adopted in *R* v. *Edwards* [1991] 1 WLR 207, where the Court of Appeal held that the test was whether the acquittal 'demonstrated' that the prosecution witness's evidence was disbelieved by the jury (see also 3.3.19 *ante*).

In *R* v. *Hay* (1983) 77 Cr App R 70 the accused was charged with burglary and the prosecution relied on the record of his police interview in which he had confessed to the burglary and an offence of arson. At the accused's (earlier) trial for arson the prosecution case had been based on an edited version of the same interview record, and the acquittal in that trial followed a defence in which it was alleged that the confession had been fabricated by the police. During the trial for burglary the accused insisted that the whole record of his interview should go before the jury, and sought to adduce evidence of the acquittal to support his defence that the confession to burglary had been fabricated. The trial judge refused the application and the accused was convicted. The Court of Appeal, relying on the decision in *Sambasivam* v. *Public Prosecutor of Malaya* [1950] AC 458 (PC), held that the jury should have been told that the accused had been acquitted of arson and that the acquittal was conclusive evidence that he was not guilty of arson and that his confession to that offence was untrue (see also *R* v. *Gall* (1989) 90 Cr App R 64 (CA)). In *Sambasivam* v. *Public Prosecutor of Malaya* Lord MacDermott had stated (at p. 479) that an acquittal not only prevented the accused from being tried again for the same offence but was also 'binding and conclusive in all subsequent proceedings between the parties to the adjudication'. In *R* v. *Z* [2000] 3 WLR 117, however, the House of Lords held that, so long as the accused is not placed in double jeopardy, evidence which is relevant in a subsequent trial is not inadmissible merely because it tends to show that the accused is guilty of an offence of which he has already been acquitted. Although Lord Hutton, who provided the leading speech, declined to give an opinion on whether *R* v. *Hay* had been correctly decided, it is clear that the second limb of Lord Macdermott's dictum (which was relied on in *R* v. *Hay*) is no longer the law. However, there can be little doubt that evidence of an acquittal in a case such as *R* v. *Hay* is still admissible to show that a confession may be unreliable, just as an acquittal is admissible if it shows that a police officer was disbelieved by another jury and is therefore an unreliable witness (3.3.19 *ante*). In other words, an acquittal is not conclusive evidence that the accused was not guilty of the earlier offence, or that his confession was fabricated, but it is evidence which the jury should take into consideration when deciding whether the accused's confession is reliable.

12.3.5 Section 73 of the Police and Criminal Evidence Act 1984

Section 73(1) provides that where the fact that a person has been convicted or acquitted of an offence is admissible in criminal proceedings, it may be proved by producing a certificate of conviction or acquittal. For convictions or acquittals following trial on indictment, the certificate must include the 'substance and effect ... of the indictment and of the conviction or acquittal' (s. 73(2)(*a*)). For convictions or acquittals following summary proceedings, the certificate must 'consist of a copy of the conviction or of the dismissal of the information' (s. 73(2)(*b*)). A duly signed document purporting to be a certificate of conviction or acquittal is to be considered such a certificate unless the contrary is proved (s. 73(2)).

Section 73(1) does not preclude the proof of convictions by other means, however (s. 73(4)). In *Moran* v. *CPS* (2000) 164 JP 562 (DC), for example, the accused, who was on trial for driving a vehicle on 8 April 1999 while disqualified, admitted that he had been disqualified by a magistrates' court on 3 February 1999 following a conviction.

Chapter Summary

- As a general rule, a witness is not entitled to give his opinion on any matter in the proceedings. There are two exceptions to this rule.
- Any witness is permitted to give his oral evidence in a natural way, even if this means that his testimony includes a number of inferences he has drawn from what he saw or heard.
- A competent expert witness is entitled to give his (expert) opinion on relevant matters outside the general knowledge and experience of the tribunal of fact, for example on psychiatric or psychological conditions (as opposed to normal human emotions and feelings). As a general rule the tribunal of fact may attach to an expert's opinion such weight as it thinks fit.
- Whether an expert is competent to give an opinion depends on whether his field of expertise is recognised by the court and he has sufficient expertise in that field. He must also be able to give an objective opinion on the matter calling for his expertise. An expert is entitled (indeed ought) to place before the court the data and information he has relied on in formulating his opinion.
- A subsisting conviction is admissible in civil proceedings under s. 11 of the Civil Evidence Act 1968 to prove that the convicted party committed that offence. In criminal proceedings the relevant conviction of a person other than the accused is admissible under s. 74(1) of the Police and Criminal Evidence Act 1984 to prove a disputed issue, save that the evidence may be excluded under s. 78(1) if its admission would unduly prejudice the accused. Acquittals are usually irrelevant and inadmissible, but it may exceptionally be permissible for the accused to rely on an acquittal in subsequent criminal proceedings if it has sufficient probative value.

Further Reading

Hand, 'Considerations Regarding Expert Testimony' (1901) 15 Harvard LR 40
Jackson, 'The Ultimate Issue Rule' [1984] Crim LR 75
Howard, 'The Neutral Expert' [1991] Crim LR 98
Spencer, 'The Neutral Expert' [1991] Crim LR 106
Mackay and Colman, 'Excluding Expert Evidence' [1991] Crim LR 800
Spencer, 'Court Experts and Expert Witnesses' (1992) 45(2) CLP 213
The Royal Commission on Criminal Justice Report (1993) Cm 2263, Chapter 9
Roberts, 'Forensic Science Evidence after Runciman' [1994] Crim LR 780

13 Disclosure and Public Interest Immunity

The first part of this chapter is concerned with the law governing pre-trial disclosure of admissible evidence and other relevant information, reflecting two aspects of the right to a fair hearing: first, that litigants should have the means by which to gain access to relevant material in advance of the trial so that they can effectively pursue their claim or defence; and, second, that litigants should not be 'ambushed' during the trial by evidence which they are in no position to challenge at short notice. The second part of this chapter describes an important countervailing consideration of public policy, a rule of secrecy which not only overrides the principle of 'openness' underlying pre-trial disclosure but may also prevent relevant evidence from being admitted during the trial itself.

13.1 Pre-trial Disclosure

It is in the public interest that the parties to a dispute – and for that matter third parties – should reveal all relevant evidence in their possession so that justice can be done and be seen to be done. If parties could withhold evidence which might assist their opponents, the number of miscarriages of justice would increase and this in turn would lead to a decrease in public confidence in the legal process. Parties to civil or criminal proceedings are therefore under an obligation to make some sort of pre-trial disclosure, and even third parties may be compelled to testify or produce relevant documentary evidence.

As a general rule the prosecution in a criminal trial, and the parties to civil proceedings, are duty-bound to reveal all relevant evidence in their possession, subject to a successful claim to public interest immunity (13.2 *post*) or privilege (14.1–3 *post*). In criminal proceedings, the accused has traditionally enjoyed a general right of non-disclosure on account of the presumption of innocence, but there has been a significant curtailment of this right in recent years.

13.1.1 Civil Proceedings

Part 31 of the Civil Procedure Rules 1998 sets out a two-stage process of disclosure and inspection, comprising a preliminary exchange of lists revealing the existence of relevant documents which are or have been in a party's control (the 'disclosure' stage), followed by production of those documents for inspection and copying (the 'inspection' stage). Rule 31.6, which applies where an order to give 'standard disclosure' has been made, provides that a party's list must include (a) the documents on which he relies; (b) the documents which (i) adversely affect his own case, (ii) adversely affect another party's case, or (iii) support another party's case; and (c) the documents which he is obliged to disclose by a relevant practice direction. Each party is under a duty to make a reasonable search for documents falling within categories (b) and (c) (r. 31.7(1)). For these purposes, a document is 'anything in which information of any description is recorded' and a copy is 'anything onto which information recorded in the document has been copied, by whatever means and whether directly or indirectly' (r. 31.4).

Subject to r. 31.3(2) on disproportionate inspection, all documents included in a disclosing party's list which are still in his control must be made available for the opposing party to inspect and copy (r. 31.15) unless the disclosing party 'has a right or duty' to withhold inspection (r. 31.3(1)). A party has a *right* not to produce a document if it is privileged (14.1–3 *post*); he has a *duty* not to produce a document for inspection if it is protected by public interest immunity (13.2 *post*). A disclosing party's *list* will include documents which are privileged, but will not include documents protected by public interest immunity if an order for non-disclosure on this ground has been made under r. 31.19(1) (13.2.1 *post*). A party may also inspect (and copy) a document mentioned in a statement of case, a witness statement, a witness summary or an affidavit (r. 31.14(1)). If it is believed that a disclosing party has not complied with his obligations to disclose and allow inspection, the court may make an order for 'specific disclosure' or 'specific inspection' under r. 31.12(1).

Under the Civil Procedure Rules 1998, parties to civil proceedings must also provide one another with copies of their experts' reports and witness statements prior to the trial. An expert's report may not be adduced in evidence without the leave of the court (r. 35.4(1)), so an order dealing with expert evidence and the exchange of reports will be made at any early stage in the pre-trial proceedings. A witness statement is a signed, written statement setting out the evidence the witness 'would be allowed to give orally' at the trial (r. 32.4(1)). Rule 32.4(2) provides that the court 'will order a party to serve on the other parties any witness statement of the oral evidence which the party serving the statement intends to rely on … at the trial'. If a witness statement is not served within the time specified by the court, the witness will not be able to give oral evidence at the trial unless the judge gives leave (r. 32.10). If a party serves a witness statement, but does not call the witness to give evidence at the trial or put the statement in as hearsay evidence, any other party may put the statement in as hearsay evidence (r. 32.5(5)). Rule 35.13 provides that a party who fails to disclose an expert's report may not, without the court's leave, use the report at the trial or call the expert to give oral evidence.

It should also be noted that a claimant (or prospective claimant) may exceptionally be granted a 'search order' under s. 7(1) of the Civil Procedure Act 1997 (and r. 25.1(1)(*h*) of the Civil Procedure Rules 1998) entitling his or another solicitor to search for and preserve evidence from the (intended) defendant's premises; and that in *Norwich Pharmacal* v.

Customs and Excise Commissioners [1973] 3 WLR 164 (HL) it was held that even third parties can be compelled to reveal relevant information in certain circumstances. (Note also ss. 33–34 of the Supreme Court Act 1981, ss. 52–53 of the County Courts Act 1984 and rr. 25.1(1)(*i*)–(*j*) and 31.17 of the Civil Procedure Rules 1998.)

13.1.2 Criminal Proceedings

Given the presumption of innocence and the right to a fair trial, it goes without saying that the accused should have advance disclosure of the nature of the allegation against him and the evidence on which the prosecution propose to rely. Without such disclosure the accused could be severely handicapped in the preparation his defence. Any person charged with an offence which is to be tried before a jury in the Crown Court is therefore entitled, by the time of committal proceedings, to receive the evidential basis of the case against him (ss. 5A–F of the Magistrates' Courts Act 1980, in particular s. 5B(2)(*c*)); and any person charged with an indictable offence which is 'triable either way' is entitled to pre-trial disclosure in the magistrates' court of copies of the prosecution's witness statements or a 'summary of the facts and matters of which the prosecutor proposes to adduce evidence' (r. 4 of the Magistrates' Courts (Advance Information) Rules 1985 (SI 1985 No. 601)). Although persons charged with a 'summary only' offence in a magistrates' court have no statutory or common-law entitlement to advance disclosure, in *R* v. *Stratford Justices ex parte Imbert* [1999] 2 Cr App R 276 the Divisional Court recommended that the prosecution should, as a general rule, furnish the accused with the evidence on which they propose to rely. Paragraph 43 of the Attorney-General's *Guidelines on Disclosure* (www.lslo.gov.uk) now directs that the accused be provided with 'all evidence upon which the Crown proposes to rely in a summary trial' (regardless of the nature of the offence) to 'allow the accused or their legal advisers sufficient time properly to consider the evidence before it is called'. The only caveat is that 'statements may be withheld for the protection of witnesses or to avoid interference with the course of justice'. In certain circumstances a suspect and his solicitor will be entitled to know something of the case against him at a much earlier stage in the proceedings, even before the suspect has been charged, where it is necessary for the solicitor to provide his client with informed legal advice on a matter such as whether he should provide answers during the course of his police interrogation (9.2.2 *ante*) or admit his guilt and receive a caution (*DPP* v. *Ara* [2002] 1 Cr App R 159 (DC)).

In addition to the evidence on which the prosecution propose to rely at the accused's trial, there will also be a body of material acquired by the police during the course of their criminal investigation – much of which may be regarded as irrelevant, superfluous or perhaps even damaging to their case – on which the prosecution will *not* wish to rely. The European Court of Human Rights has stated that 'according to the principle of equality of arms, as one of the features of the wider concept of a fair trial, each party must be afforded a reasonable opportunity to present his case in conditions that do not place him at a disadvantage *vis-à-vis* his opponent' (*Foucher* v. *France* (1997) 25 EHRR 234 at p. 247, *FR* v. *Switzerland* (2001) Application No. 37292/97). Given that the accused and his representatives will have neither the time nor the resources to conduct their own investigation into the alleged offence, and will in any event lack the powers available to the police's investigating officers, it is clearly appropriate that the accused should have access to any such 'unused' material which is (or which might be) relevant to his defence. More important, it is no part of the state's functions to secure a conviction at any cost. It is right *in principle* that the accused should have access to unused material which might assist him, for non-disclosure of relevant information, such as evidence which would undermine the credibility of a key prosecution witness, might well cause the jury to be misled and result in a wrongful conviction. Fairness under Article 6(1) of the European Convention therefore requires 'that the prosecution authorities disclose to the defence all material evidence *for or against* the accused' (*Edwards* v. *United Kingdom* (1992) 15 EHRR 417 (ECtHR) at pp. 431–2, *Dowsett* v. *United Kingdom* (2003) Application No. 39482/98 (ECtHR)).

The law governing the disclosure of unused material in criminal proceedings is now contained in the provisions of the Criminal Procedure and Investigations Act 1996, save that for cases which are to be tried on indictment pre-committal disclosure is still governed by the common law, the test being whether justice and fairness require immediate disclosure in the particular circumstances of the case (*R* v. *DPP ex parte Lee* [1999] 2 Cr App R 304 (DC) at p. 318, para. 34 of the Attorney-General's *Guidelines on Disclosure*). The provisions of the Act are supplemented by the Code of Practice on disclosure – which is admissible in evidence and 'shall be taken into account' if relevant to any question arising in the proceedings (s. 26(3)–(4)) – and by the *Guidelines on Disclosure*. Paragraphs 2 and 3 of the *Guidelines* state that the statutory scheme is designed to ensure that there is fair disclosure of unused material, to 'assist the accused in the timely preparation and presentation of [his] case and assist the court to focus on all the relevant issues', while protecting other interests, 'including those of victims and witnesses who might otherwise be exposed to harm'.

If the offence is to be tried on indictment the prosecution are obliged to comply with 'primary disclosure' under s. 3(1) as soon as is reasonably practicable after the accused has been committed for trial (s. 13(1)). This requires disclosure of any unused 'prosecution material ... which in the prosecutor's opinion might undermine the case for the prosecution against the accused' (s. 3(1)(*a*)) or a written statement that there is no such material to be disclosed (s. 3(1)(*b*)), save that material protected by public interest immunity (13.2.2 *post*) must not be disclosed (s. 3(6)). (The common law on public interest immunity is preserved by s. 21(2).) Section 3(2) defines prosecution material as material 'which is in the prosecutor's possession, and came into his possession in connection with the case for the prosecution against the accused' or which, in pursuance of the Code of Practice, the prosecutor 'has inspected in connection with the case for the prosecution against the accused'. If, however, the prosecution are aware of

material relating to an unconnected trial which has a material bearing on
the credibility of a prosecution witness in the instant case against the
accused, their general duty to act fairly means that this too should be
disclosed (*R* v. *Cucchiara* [2001] EWCA Crim 1529). Paragraph 2.1 of the
Code of Practice defines material as 'material of any kind, including
information and objects, which is obtained in the course of a criminal
investigation and which may be relevant to the investigation'; and para. 37
of the Attorney-General's *Guidelines* states that the prosecution should
pay particular attention to material which 'has potential to weaken the
prosecution case or is inconsistent with it', setting out the following six
examples: (i) any material casting doubt upon the accuracy of any
prosecution evidence; (ii) any material which may point to another person
having involvement in the commission of the offence; (iii) any material
which may cast doubt upon the reliability of a confession; (iv) any
material which might go to the credibility of a prosecution witness; (v) any
material which may support a defence which has either been raised or is
apparent from the prosecution papers; and (vi) any material which may
have a bearing on the admissibility of any prosecution evidence. This will
include material such as the accused's exculpatory comments, the
inconsistent statements or criminal records of prosecution witnesses, and
any prosecution eye-witness's initial description of the suspect.

The accused (to be tried on indictment) is then required to give a
'defence statement' to the court and the prosecution within 14 days of
primary disclosure having been made (s. 5(5) and reg. 2 of the Criminal
Procedure and Investigations Act 1996 (Defence Disclosure Time Limits)
Regulations 1997 (SI 1997 No. 684)), although it is possible to apply for
an extension of time before the deadline expires. Section 5(6) provides that
a defence statement is a written statement setting out in general terms
(*a*) the nature of the accused's defence, (*b*) the matters on which he takes
issue with the prosecution and (*c*) the reason why he takes issue with the
prosecution. If the defence statement discloses an alibi, the accused must
give particulars of it (s. 5(7); see also para. 27 of the Attorney-General's
Guidelines on Disclosure). In his *Review of the Criminal Courts* (October
2001, pp. 459–60), Lord Justice Auld expressed the view that there is a
sound need for a defence statement:

> 'A criminal trial is not a game under which a guilty defendant should be
> provided with a sporting chance. It is a search for truth in accordance
> with the twin principles that the prosecution must prove its case and
> that a defendant is not obliged to inculpate himself, the object being to
> convict the guilty and acquit the innocent. Requiring a defendant to
> indicate in advance what he disputes about the prosecution case offends
> neither of those principles.'

Section 11 of the Act provides that if the accused fails to give a defence
statement, or gives it late, or sets out inconsistent defences, or puts
forward a defence at his trial which differs from any defence therein, or
adduces evidence or calls witnesses in support of an alibi without having
given the necessary particulars, 'the court or, with the leave of the court,

any other party may make such comment as appears appropriate'
(s. 11(3)(*a*)) and 'the court or jury may draw such inferences as appear
proper in deciding whether the accused is guilty of the offence'
(s. 11(3)(*b*)). The accused cannot, however, be convicted of an offence
solely on the basis of any such inference (s. 11(5)). Where the accused's
defence at trial is inconsistent with his defence statement he may be cross-
examined without the court's leave on the differences, but leave is required
before the jury can be invited to draw an adverse inference under s. 11(3)(*b*)
(see s. 11(4) and *R* v. *Tibbs* [2000] 2 Cr App R 309 (CA)). Given the
powers in s. 11(3) and, in particular, the possibility of an adverse inference
being drawn from a sufficiently significant difference between the
accused's defence statement and his defence, it has been suggested that
the accused should personally sign his defence statement as an acknowledgement of its accuracy (*R* v. *Wheeler* [2001] 1 Cr App R 150 (CA)). If it
has not been signed, the judge is entitled to require the accused to satisfy
the court that he has actually complied with s. 5(5) of the Act and that the
document tendered really is his defence statement (*R (Sullivan)* v. *Crown
Court at Maidstone* [2002] 1 WLR 2747 (DC)).

Once the accused has served his defence statement the prosecution must
comply with their duty to make 'secondary disclosure' in accordance with
s. 7(2) of the Act as soon as is reasonably practicable (s. 13(7)). The
prosecution must (*a*) disclose to the accused any material which has not
previously been disclosed and 'which might reasonably be expected to
assist the accused's defence as disclosed by the defence statement' or (*b*)
give to the accused a written statement that there is no such material.
Again, material protected by public interest immunity must not be
disclosed (s. 7(5)). Paragraph 40 of the Attorney-General's *Guidelines on
Disclosure* sets out some of the types of material which might reasonably
be expected to be disclosed where it relates to the defence being put
forward: (i) recorded scientific or scene-of-crime findings; (ii) previous
descriptions of suspects (where identification may be in issue) together
with all records of identification procedures; (iii) information that any
prosecution witness has requested, been promised or received any
payment or reward in connection with the case; (iv) plans of crime scenes
or video recordings made by investigators of crime scenes; (v) names of
individuals who may have relevant information but who will not be
interviewed; and (vi) records of information provided by any individual.
In *R* v. *Cairns* [2003] 1 Cr App R 662 (CA) it was held that the prosecution
should have disclosed to the accused the defence statements provided by
her co-accused because, in the light of her own defence statement, those
statements might reasonably have been expected to assist her defence.

If the offence is to be tried summarily, the prosecution must comply
with primary disclosure under s. 3(1) as soon as is reasonably practicable
after the accused has entered a not guilty plea (s. 13(1)). Once primary
disclosure has been effected, the accused is *entitled* to give a defence
statement but need not do so (s. 6(2)). If the accused decides to serve a
defence statement the position in the magistrates' court is identical to that
which applies to trials on indictment. If he decides not to submit a defence

statement he will suffer no adverse consequences; but nor will he be entitled to secondary disclosure by the prosecution.

In any case where a defence statement has been served and the prosecution have purported to comply with secondary disclosure under s. 7, the accused may apply to the court for an order requiring the prosecution to disclose additional material if he has reasonable cause to believe undisclosed material exists which might reasonably be expected to assist his defence as disclosed in his defence statement (s. 8(2)). Section 8(2) does not apply to material which is subject to public interest immunity (s. 8(5)).

The Attorney General's *Guidelines on Disclosure* also set out a number of 'general principles' relating to disclosure by police officers and the prosecution. The guidelines for police officers are particularly important, given that they may have their own firm views on the guilt of the accused and be reluctant to disclose material which might render a conviction less likely (see, for example, *R* v. *Taylor* (1993) 98 Cr App R 361 (CA)). Accordingly, para. 5 expressly provides that investigators and disclosure officers must be 'fair and objective' and must work together with prosecutors to ensure that the disclosure obligations are met. Similarly, para. 13 directs prosecutors to do all that they can to facilitate proper disclosure in the interests of justice, as part of 'their general and personal professional responsibility to act fairly and impartially'. Moreover, disclosure officers must specifically draw material to the attention of the prosecutors for consideration where they have any doubt as to whether it might undermine the prosecution case or might reasonably be expected to assist the defence disclosed by the accused (para. 11); and, in deciding what material should be disclosed, prosecutors are directed by para. 20 to resolve any doubt they may have in favour of disclosure (unless the material is to be the subject of a public interest immunity application).

The statutory scheme was recently considered by Lord Justice Auld as part of his *Review of the Criminal Courts* (October 2001), and a number of recommendations for reform are set out at pp. 472–3 on the basis that the '1996 Act has not worked well'. The main concerns about the disclosure provisions of the 1996 Act are summarised at pp. 464–5:

'a lack of common understanding within the Crown Prosecution Service and among police forces of the extent of disclosure required, particularly at the primary stage; the conflict between the need for a disclosure officer sufficiently familiar with the case to make a proper evaluation of what is or may be disclosable and one sufficiently independent of the investigation to make an objective judgment about it; the consignment of the responsibility to relatively junior officers who are poorly trained for the task; general lack of staffing and training for the task in the police or the Crown Prosecution Service for what is an increasingly onerous and sophisticated exercise; in consequence, frequent inadequate and late provision by the prosecution of primary disclosure; failure by defendants and their legal representatives to comply with the Act's requirements for giving the court and the prosecutor adequate and/or timely defence statements and lack of effective means of enforcement of those requirements; seemingly and confusingly different tests for primary and secondary disclosure; and the whole scheme, whether operated efficiently or otherwise, is time consuming and otherwise expensive for all involved.'

Under the Crown Court (Advance Notice of Expert Evidence) Rules 1987 (SI 1987 No. 716) and the Magistrates' Courts (Advance Notice of Expert Evidence) Rules 1997 (SI 1997 No. 705), both the accused and the prosecution must disclose in advance of the trial any expert evidence on which they propose to rely. Furthermore, where material evidence is in the control of a third party who refuses to allow access to it, an application may be made under ss. 2–2A of the Criminal Procedure (Attendance of Witnesses) Act 1965 or s. 97 of the Magistrates' Courts Act 1980 for a witness summons compelling him to produce it.

13.2 Public Interest Immunity

The public interest in the administration of justice, which requires, in accordance with the principle of free proof, the disclosure of all relevant evidence so that trials can be conducted fairly, may on occasion need to be overridden by the public interest in preserving the secrecy of certain sensitive information, the disclosure of which might adversely affect the interests of the state or the administration of justice in a wider sense. Where the public interest favouring non-disclosure prevails, any documentary or oral evidence of the information must be withheld on the ground of public interest immunity ('PII').

13.2.1 Civil Proceedings

To understand the modern law on PII it is useful to know something of its historical development. In *Duncan* v. *Cammell Laird* [1942] AC 624 the House of Lords held that there were two possible claims to what was then known as 'Crown privilege': *class* claims and *contents* claims. A contents claim was one based on the sensitive nature of the information itself, such as military secrets. A class claim was one based on the category of correspondence involved, such as the communications between Cabinet ministers, regardless of the content of the document in question. Class claims were thought necessary so that ministers and civil servants would feel able to communicate candidly with one another (the so-called 'candour' justification). It was open to the executive to claim Crown privilege for either reason, and once a claim had been made in the proper form the courts were obliged to give effect to it and order that the information be withheld from production. Government ministers were thus recognised as the final arbiters of what ought or ought not to be produced, even though they might be motivated by little more than political expediency.

In *Conway* v. *Rimmer* [1968] 2 WLR 998, which concerned an action for malicious prosecution by a former probationary police officer against his erstwhile superintendent, the House of Lords took the opportunity to reconsider the question of Crown privilege. During the course of pre-trial discovery the defendant disclosed a list of documents which included four reports made by him about the plaintiff as a probationary officer and a further report he had made to the Chief Constable relating to a theft the plaintiff was alleged to have committed and which, following his acquittal, had given rise to the instant civil proceedings. The Home Secretary objected to disclosure, claiming that none of the five documents could be produced as they each fell within one or other of two privileged classes, namely confidential reports by police officers relating to the fitness for employment of officers under their command and reports by police officers concerning criminal investigations.

Overruling *Duncan* v. *Cammell Laird* [1942] AC 624 (HL), the House of Lords held that whether the Crown could withhold information on the ground of public interest was ultimately a question of law to be determined by the courts and not by government ministers, though it was also recognised that certain types of document should never be disclosed. While a claim for non-disclosure could be made on the basis of the contents of a particular document or on the ground that the document belonged to a particular class, class claims were of two different types. The first type covered documents requiring absolute protection regardless of their content. However, the justification for this class was not the old argument based on candour, but rather the risk that disclosure 'would create or fan ill-informed or captious public or political criticism' (*per* Lord Reid at p. 1015) and that it would be 'entirely inimical to the proper functioning of the public service if the public were to learn of these high level communications' (*per* Lord Upjohn at p. 1050). Documents falling within this class included Cabinet minutes and correspondence, documents concerned with policy making within government departments, high-level inter-departmental minutes and communications, dispatches from ambassadors abroad, correspondence and documents pertaining to the administration of the armed forces or the security of the state, and correspondence and reports concerning the promotion or transfer of reasonably high-level personnel in the service of the Crown. Such documents 'ought not to be disclosed whatever their contents may be' (*per* Lord Reid at p. 1015); they required 'absolute protection' (*per* Lord Hodson at p. 1033), and their 'production would never be ordered' (*per* Lord Pearce at p. 1044). The second type of class claim was based, as it was in the instant case, on a vague assertion by a minister that the documents fell within a class which ought to be withheld in the public interest. Documents falling within a low-level class were of a more routine or trivial nature and were therefore not to be afforded the same sort of protection. Such documents were to be produced if the trial judge determined, having inspected them, that the public interest favouring concealment was outweighed by the public interest favouring the disclosure of all relevant information to the litigants. Non-disclosure would be justified only if it was 'really necessary for the proper functioning of the public service' (*per* Lord Reid p. 1015). It was stressed, however, that full weight would be given to the minister's view in every case, and if the reasons given were of a character which judicial experience was not competent to weigh then the minister's view would have to prevail. This was not the case with regard to the superintendent's reports and, once Lord Reid had inspected them, the House of Lords ordered that they be made available to the plaintiff. With regard to contents claims, it was felt that while it would rarely be proper to question the view of a minister that it would be contrary to the public interest to make public the contents of a particular document, as a matter of law the judge would be entitled to inspect the documents and balance the public interests in the same way as for low-level class claims.

Non-disclosure in the public interest is not a privilege for the Crown to claim or waive but ultimately a question of law for the judiciary to determine (see 13.2.3 *post*). This is one reason why the term 'Crown privilege' is no longer used. Another reason is that, while a minister will often be the most appropriate person to raise the question of non-disclosure in the public interest, this is not a necessary requirement. The question may be raised by any person, including the judge (*R* v. *Lewes Justices ex parte Secretary of State for the Home Department* [1972] 3 WLR 279 (HL)). It is not even necessary that the relevant document should have emanated from a government department. For example, in *D* v. *NSPCC* [1977] 2 WLR 201 the House of Lords held that it was not in the public interest for certain confidential information possessed by a charity to be revealed; in *Gaskin* v. *Liverpool City Council* [1980] 1 WLR 1549 the Court of Appeal upheld a local authority's PII claim in respect of documents in the possession of its child care service; in *Buckley* v. *Law Society (No. 2)* [1984] 1 WLR 1101 (ChD) it was held that PII attached to documents in the possession of the Law Society; and in *Roylance* v. *General Medical Council* (1999) *The Times* 27.1.99 the Privy Council held that PII attached to the *in camera* deliberations of the GMC's professional conduct committee. There is, however, no general duty to weigh in the balance *any* public interest favouring non-disclosure against the competing public interest that the administration of justice should not be frustrated. In *D* v. *NSPCC* [1977] 2 WLR 201 (HL) it was felt that the law could develop only by analogy with heads of public interest which had already been recognised, a view subsequently endorsed by the House of Lords in *Leyland Cars* v. *Vyas* [1979] 3 WLR 762 where it was held that PII could not be raised to prevent the disclosure of confidential records on persons who had been interviewed for a job in an industrial concern.

If a legitimate question of PII does arise in civil proceedings, the public interest favouring disclosure requires the judge to consider the private interests of the litigants themselves, bearing in mind Article 6(1) of the European Convention on Human Rights, the general public interest that justice should be seen to be done, and the importance of the particular litigation to the public at large. Decided cases identify the heads of public interest which have justified the non-disclosure of evidence in the past, but ultimately the conclusion the judge reaches will depend on all the circumstances of the case before him. Indeed, notwithstanding the dicta in *Conway* v. *Rimmer* [1968] 2 WLR 998 (HL) suggesting that high-level class claims to PII can never be challenged, it is now clear that there is no absolute immunity for all documents falling within such classes. The judge is entitled to inspect even high-level documents in respect of which a class claim to PII has been made, and thereafter determine whether the balance of public interest lies in their production or concealment. In *Burmah Oil* v. *Bank of England* [1979] 3 WLR 722 the House of Lords ordered that documents relating to the formulation of government policy should be made available to their Lordships for inspection. Lord Keith said (at pp. 749–50):

> '[T]he nature of the litigation and the apparent importance to it of the documents in question may in extreme cases demand production even of the most sensitive communications at the highest level ... The courts are ... concerned with the consideration that it is in the public interest that justice should be done and should be publicly recognised as having been done. This may demand, though no doubt only in a very limited number of cases, that the inner workings of government should be exposed to public gaze, and there may be some who would regard this as likely to lead, not to captious or ill-informed criticism, but to criticism calculated to improve the nature of that working as affecting the individual citizen.'

Thus, in *Williams* v. *Home Office* [1981] 1 All ER 1151 (QBD) McNeill J ordered the production of documents relating to the formulation of government policy on an experimental prison 'control unit' even though the documents contained communications between ministers and senior civil servants; and in *Air Canada* v. *Secretary of State for Trade* [1983] 2 WLR 494 (HL) Lord Fraser expressed the view (at p. 523) that even Cabinet minutes were not completely immune from disclosure, though his Lordship added that such documents were entitled to a high degree of protection. Where, however, the claim to PII is made in relation to documents affecting national security or diplomatic relations, matters on which the executive have far greater knowledge and experience, the minister's objection to disclosure will almost certainly prevail (*R* v. *Lewes Justices ex parte Secretary of State for the Home Department* [1972] 3 WLR 279 (HL) at p. 294; see also *Balfour* v. *Foreign and Commonwealth Office* [1994] 2 All ER 588 (CA) at p. 596).

The same cannot be said for other interests, however. Prior to the coming into force of the Human Rights Act 1998, the courts demonstrated a willingness to dispense with the balancing exercise and grant blanket immunity to certain classes of information in order to facilitate the fight against crime and other social evils, regardless of the adverse effect this would have on the party seeking disclosure. In *Marks* v. *Beyfus* (1890) 25 QBD 494 the Court of Appeal held there was a rule of law that the names of police informants should never be revealed in civil proceedings, the reasons being, first, that informants should be protected from possible reprisals and, second, that other persons should not be discouraged from providing information. This class of PII was extended in *D* v. *NSPCC* [1977] 2 WLR 201 (HL) to cover the identity of informants who provide confidential information on child abuse to the National Society for the Prevention of Cruelty to Children. Similarly, in *R* v. *Lewes Justices ex parte Secretary of State for the Home Department* [1972] 3 WLR 279 (HL) it was held that any information provided to the Gaming Board in confidence should not be produced, for otherwise prospective informants might withhold the sort of information which was necessary for the Board to perform its statutory duty to identify and prevent undesirable persons from obtaining gaming licences. The balancing exercise was also dispensed with in *Gaskin* v. *Liverpool City Council* [1980] 1 WLR 1549 (CA), a case where a local authority had claimed PII in respect of documents relating to the treatment of children in its care on the ground that if such documents could be produced social workers and doctors would be inhibited from freely expressing their views on such children. However, now that the European Convention on Human Rights must be taken into consideration, a more 'case-specific' approach has been adopted, in line with the position in criminal proceedings (13.2.2 *post*). In *Chief Constable of Greater Manchester Police* v. *McNally* [2002] 2 Cr App R 617, a claim for malicious prosecution and false imprisonment, the Court of Appeal held that the claimant's Article 6(1) right to a fair hearing could override a police informer's own rights under Article 2 and Article 8 of the Convention. In other words, as 'part of a wider jurisprudential move away from near absolute protection of various categories of public interest in non-disclosure' there is no longer an absolute prohibition on disclosing an informer's identity in civil proceedings. If the informer's identity is relevant to the claimant's claim, the public interest in protecting his identity will be balanced against the public interest in ensuring that justice is done in the particular case. In appropriate cases disclosure may be justified.

This wider jurisprudential move away from blanket immunity is also exemplified by the approach adopted in *R* v. *Chief Constable of the West Midlands Police ex parte Wiley* [1994] 3 WLR 433 where the House of Lords felt there would need to be 'clear and compelling evidence' before any new class-based claim to PII is recognised by the courts, and held that there was no general class of immunity covering all documents created in the course of an investigation into alleged police misconduct. (Reports made by the investigating officers are covered by PII as a class, however, because of the need for candour: *Taylor* v. *Anderton* [1995] 1 WLR 447 (CA).) Further, where a claim to PII is successful there would now seem to be an obligation on the part of the protected litigant to mitigate the adverse effect of the ruling on the opposing party's ability to put his case. As Lord Woolf noted in *ex parte Wiley* (at p. 460), it might be possible for some information to be provided without producing the actual documents, or to disclose a part of the document or a document on a restricted basis: 'There is usually a spectrum of action which can be taken if the parties are sensible which will mean that any prejudice due to non-disclosure of the documents is reduced to a minimum.'

A claim to PII in civil proceedings is made under r. 31.19 of the Civil Procedure Rules 1998. Unlike a claim to privilege, where the party is obliged to reveal ('disclose') the existence of the relevant documents but is entitled to withhold the documents from inspection, the party or other individual claiming PII may apply under r. 31.19(1), without notice, for a court order permitting him to withhold disclosure. The opposing party will not know that the application is being made and, if the application is successful, will often have no knowledge that the applicant has the documents: r. 31.19(2) provides that, unless the court orders otherwise, the order must not be served on any other person. There is also provision under r. 31.19(3)–(4) to claim a 'duty to withhold inspection' of a document in the list in which the document is disclosed, in which case a party may apply to the court to determine whether the claim should be upheld. Where an application is made under r. 31.19 the court may require the person claiming PII to produce the document to the court; and the court may invite any person, whether or not a party, to make representations (r. 31.19(6)). It is important to note, however, that the case-law of the European Court of Human Rights suggests that, if the affected party is denied the opportunity to make representations in respect of a PII claim, and a judge other than the trial judge determines the question, that party may be denied the fair hearing to which he is entitled under Article 6(1) of the European Convention (13.2.2 *post*).

13.2.2 Criminal Proceedings

In *R* v. *Governor of Brixton Prison ex parte Osman* (1990) 93 Cr App R 202 (DC) Mann LJ said (at p. 208):

> 'The seminal cases in regard to public interest immunity do not refer to criminal proceedings at all. The principles are expressed in quite general terms. Asking myself why those general expositions should not apply to criminal proceedings, I can see no reason but that they do. It seems correct in principle that they should apply. The reasons for the development of the doctrine seem equally applicable to criminal as to civil proceedings.'

Although the law on PII in the context of civil proceedings may, at one level, be said to apply equally to criminal proceedings, there is an important difference. The public interest in ensuring that the innocent should not be convicted is of such importance that it will invariably outweigh the public interest justifying non-disclosure. Thus, although there may be a balancing exercise in theory, in practice a PII application will fail if disclosure might help the accused to secure an acquittal. In other words: 'If ... there is material which might assist the defence, then the necessity for the defendant to have a fair trial outweighs the other interests in the case and the prosecution must either produce the undisclosed material or discontinue the prosecution' (*R* v. *Dervish* [2002] 2 Cr App R 105 (CA) at p. 111). Accordingly, the relevant documents should be inspected by the judge as a matter of course following the prosecution's application (*R* v. *K* (1992) 97 Cr App R 342 (CA), *R* v. *Keane* [1994] 1 WLR 746 (CA)). If the prosecution are successful, no evidence may be adduced and no questions may be asked which might reveal the withheld information. (It may be possible, however, to provide the defence with other material in the document containing the withheld information by serving the document in an edited form or producing a separate summary.)

Many PII claims in criminal proceedings concern the identity of police informers and surveillance techniques, or, where the allegation is one of child abuse, records held by social services or the local authority relating to the child in question (but see also para. 6.12 of the Code of Practice issued under the Criminal Procedure and Investigations Act 1996, which lists other examples of sensitive material for which a claim might be thought necessary). In *R* v. *Hallett* [1986] Crim LR 462 (CA) Lord Lane CJ explained the application of the exclusionary presumption in *Marks* v. *Beyfus* (1890) 25 QBD 494 (CA) (13.2.1 *ante*) to criminal proceedings:

'[I]t is a rule which excludes evidence as to the identity of informants, unless the judge comes to the conclusion that it is necessary to override the rule and to admit the evidence in order to prevent a miscarriage of justice, and in order to prevent the possibility that a man may, by reason of the exclusion, be deprived of the opportunity of casting doubt upon the case against him ... The result is, on [counsel's] submission, that if the judge does come to the conclusion that the lack of information as to the identity of the informer is going to cause a miscarriage of justice, then he is under a duty to admit the evidence. We would respectfully agree with that view.'

In *R* v. *Keane* [1994] 1 WLR 746 (CA) Lord Taylor CJ, referring to evidence of this type, said that if 'the disputed material may prove [*sic*] the defendant's innocence or avoid a miscarriage of justice, then the balance comes down resoundingly in favour of disclosing it'. In other words, the accused's right to a fair trial under Article 6 of the European Convention on Human Rights is of such importance that it will invariably override the informer's own Article 8 right to have his privacy respected and even his Article 2 right to life, an outcome explicitly recognised by the Court of Appeal (Civil Division) in *Chief Constable of Greater Manchester Police* v. *McNally* [2002] 2 Cr App R 617 (13.2.1 *ante*). So long as the accused has a tenable defence which might realistically be assisted by knowledge of the informer's identity he will be entitled to that information. It will also be necessary to disclose the fact that a prosecution witness was an informer and participant in the matter with which the trial is concerned if non-disclosure might cause the jury to be misled by his testimony (*R* v. *Patel* [2002] Crim LR 304 (CA)). If, however, the accused's defence is 'manifestly frivolous and doomed to failure' the judge will be entitled to refuse disclosure (*R* v. *Agar* (1989) 90 Cr App R 318 (CA)). It goes without saying that a claim for PII will be upheld if the accused's defence *is* tenable but the information would provide him with no assistance. This was the position in *R* v. *Slowcombe* [1991] Crim LR 198 (CA) where the identity of an informer who had tipped off the police about a planned robbery could not have assisted the accused's defence that he had merely been involved in a conspiracy to steal (see also *R* v. *Menga* [1998] Crim LR 58 (CA) and *R* v. *Dervish* [2002] 2 Cr App R 105 (CA)).

The procedures governing PII applications were laid down by the Court of Appeal in *R* v. *Davis* [1993] 1 WLR 613 (at p. 617), and are now to be found in the Crown Court (Criminal Procedure and Investigations Act 1996) (Disclosure) Rules 1997 (SI 1997 No. 698) (and the Magistrates' Courts (Criminal Procedure and Investigations Act 1996) (Disclosure) Rules 1997 (SI 1997 No. 703)). The prosecution will make their application to the court under the Criminal Procedure and Investigations Act 1996 (ss. 3(6), 7(5), 8(5) or 9(8)) and, as a general rule, will notify the defence, specifying the 'nature of the material' they wish to withhold. The application will then be made in the presence of the defence and both parties will be permitted to make representations to the judge. Where, however, the prosecution have reason to believe that to disclose the nature of the material would have the effect of revealing the information which they contend should not be disclosed, the application will be made in the absence of the defence (the *ex parte* procedure) and the defence will be told only that an application is to be made. (The judge will, however, be aware of the defence case from the accused's defence statement, or any other details provided by his representatives, so that an informed decision can be made on the relevance and value of the withheld information.) Given the absence of the defence, the prosecution are under a duty to be 'scrupulously accurate' in the information they provide during their application (*R* v. *Jackson* [2000] Crim LR 377 (CA); see also para. 42 of the Attorney-General's *Guidelines on Disclosure*). Exceptionally, where the prosecution have reason to believe that the mere knowledge that an *ex parte* PII application is to be made would have the effect of revealing the information which they contend should not be disclosed, the application may be made without notifying the defence (the 'exceptional' *ex parte* procedure).

The role of the judge is twofold. First of all he must assess the credibility of the accused's defence. Then, having inspected the withheld information for himself, and taken any other relevant material into account – which need not be admissible evidence (*R* v. *Law* (1996) *The Times* 15.8.96 (CA)) – he must determine whether the information might further that defence. In *R* v. *Turner* [1995] 1 WLR 265 the Court of Appeal expressed concern about defences being fabricated to obtain the identity of an informer, and stated that applications for disclosure should be scrutinised with 'very great care'. It follows that the accused is in effect obliged to give full and specific details of his defence and the issues likely to be raised during the trial for otherwise the judge will be unable to determine the value of the withheld information to his case (see *R* v. *Keane* [1994] 1 WLR 746 (CA) at p. 752). If the judge rules in favour of non-disclosure he must nevertheless continue to monitor the issue during the trial as new issues emerge, and may subsequently need to review his original decision (see s. 15(3) of the Criminal Procedure and Investigations Act 1996 and, at

common law, *R* v. *Davis* [1993] 1 WLR 613 (CA) at p. 618). By virtue of
ss. 14(2) and 15(4) of the Act, the defence may apply for a review before
the end of the summary or Crown Court trial.

The *ex parte* PII procedure was considered by the European Court of
Human Rights in *Jasper* v. *United Kingdom* (2000) 30 EHRR 441 and *Fitt*
v. *United Kingdom* (2000) 30 EHRR 480. In each case a bare majority of
the Court held that there had been no violation of Article 6 of the
Convention. Although Article 6 requires that the prosecution should
disclose to the defence all material evidence in their possession, this is not
an absolute right. Competing interests such as national security and the
need to protect witnesses (and preserve their human rights) must be
weighed against the rights of the accused. In some cases, therefore, it is
permissible to withhold certain evidence from the accused, so long as the
measures restricting the accused's rights are strictly necessary and any
difficulties caused to the defence are sufficiently counterbalanced by
procedures designed to ensure that the accused receives a fair trial. In each
case before the Court the applicant had received a fair trial, notwithstanding the non-disclosure of certain material (which had not formed
part of the prosecution case). Important considerations were the fact that
the defence had been able to make representations to the trial judge
outlining the nature of their case, the test adopted by the judge following
the *ex parte* application and the further safeguard provided by the judge's
having monitored the need for disclosure during the course of the trial. In
the light of these judgments, the Court of Appeal has expressed its view
that the *ex parte* PII procedure is not 'by definition or in principle' a
procedure which violates the accused's right to a fair trial under Article 6
(*R* v. *Lawrence* [2001] EWCA Crim 1829). Indeed, the approach adopted
by the majority in *Jasper* v. *United Kingdom* and *Fitt* v. *United Kingdom*
was unanimously approved by the European Court of Human Rights in
PG v. *United Kingdom* (2001) Application No. 44787/98. It is to be noted,
however, that the 'exceptional' *ex parte* procedure, where the accused
receives no notice of the prosecution's application, has not been
considered; and, in the light of the foregoing, it is doubtful whether this
procedure would be regarded as compatible with the accused's right to a
fair trial. A scheme which would allow a 'special independent counsel' to
be instructed by the court to represent the accused's interests would
overcome this problem (see Lord Justice Auld's *Review of the Criminal
Courts* (October 2001) at pp. 476–8).

The public interest justifying the anonymity of police informers applies
with equal force to any business premises or private accommodation used
by the police for surveillance operations; but, as with the identity of
informers, the judge must order disclosure if the information might help
the accused to secure an acquittal (*R* v. *Rankine* [1986] 2 WLR 1075 (CA)).
If, for instance, the accused claims in his defence that he has been
mistakenly identified from the observation post, and this is indeed a
realistic possibility, the judge ought to disclose the location of the premises
so that the identification evidence can be properly tested in cross-
examination. If, however, there is no real risk of a mistaken identification,

the judge will rule in favour of non-disclosure even though the accused's ability to cross-examine the observing officers will to some extent be hampered as a result. In *R* v. *Johnson* [1988] 1 WLR 1377 the accused faced several counts of supplying cannabis and cocaine on a street in London. His defence was that he had been buying rather than selling drugs and requested the identity of the addresses from which the police officers had made their observations in order to ascertain whether there had been any obstacles which would have obstructed their view. The judge ruled that the prosecution should disclose no more than the maximum distance involved and the accused was convicted. The Court of Appeal dismissed his appeal on the ground that, although there had been some restraints placed upon the conduct of the defence by the judge's ruling, the jury had been made aware of those restraints and the judge had given safeguarding directions during his summing-up. However, the Court went on to hold that PII applications in such cases would need to be supported by evidence from the sergeant in charge of the surveillance operation to the effect that he had spoken to the occupants prior to the operation and ascertained their attitude to the use of the premises and the possible disclosure thereafter of facts which could lead to the identification of the premises, and, further, by evidence from a senior officer (that is, a chief inspector or above) to the effect that he had spoken to the occupants just prior to the trial to ascertain their attitude to disclosure. If the judge rules in favour of non-disclosure he must also explain the effect of his ruling to the jury. In *R* v. *Brown* (1987) 87 Cr App R 52 (CA) it was held that the public interest which justifies the non-disclosure of information identifying static observation posts cannot apply to mobile posts such as unmarked police cars as they have no occupant in need of protection. It was felt, however, that there might be an additional ground for claiming PII based on the need to ensure that the methods used by the police to combat crime should not be revealed.

PII claims are also often made in respect of confidential records held by social services or a local authority relating to the child the accused has allegedly abused. In such cases the judge must conduct a balancing exercise to determine 'whether the public interest in maintaining the confidentiality of those documents and the public interest in seeing that justice is done, particularly in a criminal case involving the liberty of the subject, requires either that the documents be withheld or ... disclosed' (*R* v. *Higgins* [1996] 1 FLR 137 (CA) at p. 140, followed in *R* v. *Brushett* [2001] Crim LR 471 (CA)). Where the material might assist the accused in securing an acquittal, on the basis that it undermines the reliability of the child's evidence, the prosecution will be ordered to disclose it.

13.2.3 Duty, Waiver and Secondary Evidence

Echoing the view of Lord Simon in *R* v. *Lewes Justices ex parte Secretary of State for the Home Department* [1972] 3 WLR 279 (HL) (at p. 289), in *Air Canada* v. *Secretary of State for Trade* [1983] 2 WLR 494 (HL) Lord Fraser said (at p. 526): 'Public interest immunity is not a privilege which may be waived by the Crown or by any party.' A similar point was made by Bingham LJ in *Makanjuola* v. *Commissioner of Police of the Metropolis* [1992] 3 All ER 617 (CA) (at p. 623):

> 'Where a litigant asserts that documents are immune from production or disclosure on public interest grounds he is not (if the claim is well founded) claiming a right but observing a duty. Public interest immunity is not a trump card vouchsafed to certain privileged players to play when and as they wish. It is an exclusionary rule, imposed on parties in certain circumstances, even where it is to their disadvantage in the litigation.'

As to whether a party is under a duty to claim PII, in *R* v. *Chief Constable of the West Midlands Police ex parte Wiley* [1994] 3 WLR 433 the House of Lords recognised that the relevant Secretary of State (as opposed to an ordinary litigant) is competent to conduct the PII balancing exercise and should voluntarily disclose the relevant documents once he has concluded, after due consideration, that the public interest in disclosing them for the purposes of the litigation outweighs the public interest favouring non-disclosure. In other words, documents which might be the subject of a contents claim – it will be seen below that the present Labour Government is not making class claims – may be assessed by the relevant minister with a view to determining whether a PII application should be made. If the minister comes to the conclusion that the public interest is best served by revealing the information, there will be no application. (The question is not, therefore, whether PII is being 'waived' but whether there are actually grounds for making a valid claim in the first place.) By contrast, a minister who concludes that the balance of public interest comes down in favour of non-disclosure is under a duty to claim PII (*R* v. *Lewes Justices ex parte Secretary of State for the Home Department* [1972] 3 WLR 279 (HL) at p. 294). Similarly, in criminal proceedings the prosecution should voluntarily disclose documents in respect of which a claim to PII might be made if the Treasury Solicitor is satisfied that the balance of public interest falls clearly in favour of disclosure (*R* v. *Horseferry Road Magistrates' Court ex parte Bennett (No.2)* (1993) 99 Cr App R 123 (DC)); but if the balance falls the other way the prosecution must make an application to withhold the evidence.

In *Savage* v. *Chief Constable of Hampshire* [1997] 1 WLR 1061 (CA) it was held that a police informer's willingness to waive anonymity was not determinative of the issue whether a PII claim should be upheld – it was for the judge to determine whether there was still a significant public interest, extraneous to the informer and his own personal safety, which would be damaged if the informer were allowed to reveal his identity and role. The informer does not have a personal privilege which he is entitled to claim or waive as he thinks fit. Where, however, a class-claim to PII has been recognised for the purpose of protecting a particular body of individuals, such as informers or the occupants of premises used for a surveillance operation, the willingness of the protected individual to waive his anonymity is clearly a relevant factor for the judge to take into consideration when undertaking the balancing exercise, simply because the primary justification for the PII claim has now disappeared (*Savage* v. *Chief Constable of Hampshire* at p. 1067; see also *R* v. *Johnson* [1988] 1 WLR 1377 (CA), 13.2.2 *ante*, and *R* v. *Chief Constable of the West Midlands Police ex parte Wiley* [1994] 3 WLR 433 (HL) at p. 453).

As noted above, the present Government has accepted that it should no longer make class claims to PII. In a written answer to the House of Commons on 11 July 1997 (*Hansard* (HC), vol. 297, cols. 616–17) the Attorney-General said:

> '[P]ublic interest immunity will not be asserted by the Government unless the relevant Minister believes that disclosure of a document or piece of information will cause real damage to the public interest. The test will be applied rigorously. Where public interest immunity applies, Ministers will nevertheless make voluntary disclosure if they consider that the interests of justice outweigh the public interest in withholding the document or information in question. In all cases, a Minister's claim for public interest immunity is subject to the Court's power to order disclosure. The approach will be followed in both criminal and civil cases.'

This statement of policy does not prevent local authorities or other organisations such as the police from asserting a class-based claim to PII. Indeed, it would seem that where information in the possession of a non-governmental body falls within a protected class a PII claim must be made so that the question can be determined by the judge. That a local authority is under a duty to claim PII was explicitly recognised by the Court of Appeal in *R* v. *Higgins* [1996] 1 FLR 137; and in *R* v. *Chief Constable of the West Midlands Police ex parte Wiley* Lord Woolf expressed the view (at pp. 451–2) that litigants other than government departments should make a class-claim so that the cases where disclosure occurs can be restricted by the courts to situations where it is necessary.

Finally, where a document is protected by PII, it is not permissible to rely on secondary evidence (such as a copy of the document) to prove the protected information (*Hennessy* v. *Wright* (1888) 21 QBD 509 (DC), *Chatterton* v. *Secretary of State for India* [1895] 2 QB 189 (CA), *R* v. *Lewes Justices ex parte Secretary of State for the Home Department* [1972] 3 WLR 279 (HL)).

Chapter Summary

- As a general rule the parties to a civil dispute, and the prosecution in criminal proceedings, are under a legal duty to disclose and produce the evidence upon which they intend to rely at the trial along with the (possibly) relevant evidence which they do not intend to rely upon. The accused is under a limited duty of pre-trial disclosure. He must provide the prosecution with the expert evidence upon which he intends to rely and (if he is to be tried on indictment) he must provide the court and prosecution with a 'defence statement' setting out his defence and the matters on which he takes issue with the prosecution.

- If a party to civil proceedings has evidence in respect of which a valid claim to public interest immunity might be made then, as a general rule, the claim must be made so that the court can determine whether the evidence ought to be withheld or disclosed. To determine the issue the court will balance the public interest favouring disclosure against the public interest favouring non-disclosure, bearing in mind the rights of the parties and other affected individuals under the European Convention on Human Rights. The relevant Secretary of State is competent to conduct the balancing exercise and should make an application to the court on public interest immunity grounds only if he concludes that (or is unsure whether) the public interest is best served by non-disclosure.
- If the Treasury Solicitor is satisfied that evidence which might justify a public interest immunity claim should be disclosed in criminal proceedings then the prosecution may voluntarily disclose that evidence, otherwise a public interest immunity application must be made to the court. If the court concludes that the evidence might assist the accused's defence then the prosecution must either disclose it to the accused or discontinue their prosecution.

Further Reading

The Royal Commission on Criminal Justice Report (1993) Cm 2263, pp. 91–100, 221–3

Ganz, '*Matrix Churchill* and Public Interest Immunity' (1993) 56 MLR 564, (1995) 58 MLR 417

Tomkins, 'Public Interest Immunity after *Matrix Churchill*' (1993) PL 650

Brown, 'Public Interest Immunity' (1994) PL 579

Zuckerman, 'Public Interest Immunity' (1994) 57 MLR 703

Scott, 'The Acceptable and Unacceptable Use of Public Interest Immunity' (1996) PL 427

Forsyth, 'Public Interest Immunity: Recent and Future Developments' (1997) CLJ 51

Sharpe, 'Disclosure, Immunity and Fair Trials' (1999) 63 JCL 67

Taylor, 'In the Public Interest: PII and Police Informants' (2001) 65 JCL 435

Temkin, 'Digging the Dirt: Disclosure of Records in Sexual Assault Cases' (2002) CLJ 126

Zander, 'Advance Disclosure' (2002) 146 SJ 824

Ormerod, 'Improving the Disclosure Regime' (2003) 7 E & P 102

Criminal Justice Bill (2003), Part 5
and Explanatory Note (www.publications.parliament.uk)

14   Privilege

In the previous chapter it was seen that the principle of free proof in respect of some evidence may have to give way to a policy consideration favouring non-disclosure, not because the evidence is unreliable or likely to prejudice the tribunal of fact against a party, but because the public interest militating against disclosure outweighs the public interest in the due administration of justice. Highly probative and reliable evidence may also be withheld on the ground of 'privilege'. There are, however, two important differences between the exercise of a privilege and the operation of public interest immunity. First, if evidence falls within the scope of a recognised privilege the party in whose favour it operates is *entitled* to claim it but is under no obligation to do so. Privilege is no more than a personal *right* which a party may claim or waive as he thinks fit, allowing him to refuse to produce certain documents for inspection and to refuse to answer certain questions in the witness box (even if he has been compelled to testify). He will suffer no sanction as a result of his exercising that right; nor can any adverse inference be drawn from his silence or refusal to produce evidence. Second, unlike public interest immunity, privilege entitles the person in whom it is vested not to reveal certain information, but it does not prevent that information from being adduced by an opponent if he has secondary evidence of it, for example because he has managed to obtain a copy of a privileged document or has overheard a privileged conversation.

14.1 The Privilege Against Self-incrimination

The common-law privilege against self-incrimination is the personal right of any person not to answer any question or produce any evidence which would tend to expose him 'to any criminal charge, penalty or forfeiture [of property]' (*Blunt* v. *Park Lane Hotel* [1942] 2 KB 253 (CA)), save that it cannot be relied on if the charge, penalty or forfeiture arises under foreign law (*Brannigan* v. *Davison* [1996] 3 WLR 859 (PC), *Attorney-General for Gibralter* v. *May* [1999] 1 WLR 998 (CA)). The position in civil proceedings is now governed by statute. By virtue of ss. 14(1) and 16(1)(*a*) of the Civil Evidence Act 1968, the privilege may be relied on by a person in respect of possible proceedings for an offence or penalty under UK law, entitling him 'to refuse to answer any question or produce any document or thing' which would tend to expose him (or his spouse) to such proceedings, including proceedings for civil contempt (*Memory Corporation* v. *Sidhu* [2000] 2 WLR 1106 (ChD)). If a party to litigation successfully invokes the privilege he cannot be punished or made the subject of a court order to do the act which he has objected to (*Versailles Trade Finance* v. *Clough* (2001) *The Times* 1.11.01 (CA)).

398   *Evidence*

The privilege against self-incrimination may be seen as one of the 'disparate group of immunities' collectively known as the 'right of silence' (*R* v. *Director of Serious Fraud Office ex parte Smith* [1992] 3 WLR 66 (HL) at p. 74). In a broad sense the suspect's right to remain silent in the face of police questioning and the accused's right not to testify in his own defence may be regarded as two facets of a single privilege against self-incrimination. In a narrow sense the privilege has been seen to exist independently of, but in association with, these common-law rights of silence. In *Saunders* v. *United Kingdom* (1996) 23 EHRR 313 (at p. 337) the privilege, in both senses, was described by the European Court of Human Rights as a generally recognised international standard lying at the heart of the notion of a fair procedure under Article 6 of the European Convention on Human Rights. It was also noted that the right not to incriminate oneself:

> 'presupposes that the prosecution in a criminal case seek to prove their case against the accused without resort to evidence obtained through methods of coercion or oppression in defiance of the will of the accused. In this sense the right is closely linked to the presumption of innocence contained in Article 6(2) of the Convention.'

The traditional view is that the privilege against self-incrimination – the '*nemo tenetur* principle' (10.1 *ante*) – came to be recognised as part of the common law in the seventeenth century in response to the horrors of the Star Chamber (see, for example, *Bishopsgate Investment Management* v. *Maxwell* [1992] 2 WLR 991 (CA) at p. 1001). However, recent research suggests that it evolved during the late eighteenth and early nineteenth centuries as the criminal trial process changed from an inquisitorial approach to adversarial proceedings, and that it did not become firmly established until the middle of the nineteenth century (see *Azzopardi* v. *R* (2001) 179 ALR 349 (HCA) at pp. 378–88). The privilege is usually justified on the ground that it discourages the ill-treatment of suspects and the production of dubious confessions (*AT & T Istel* v. *Tully* [1992] 3 WLR 344 (HL) at p. 350; *R* v. *Hertfordshire County Council ex parte Green Environmental Industries* [2000] 2 WLR 373 (HL) at pp. 377–8). Perhaps a more valid justification for the twenty-first century is that it encourages witnesses to provide relevant evidence and discourages perjury. If a witness could be compelled to give self-incriminating evidence he would be far less willing to come forward to reveal what he knows; and the apprehension he would suffer in the witness box might affect the way he gives his evidence, undermining his apparent credibility and inhibiting his willingness to reveal his knowledge about the facts in issue. Furthermore, if he were to be asked a specific question requiring a self-incriminating answer he would have three choices, each resulting in a possible adverse consequence. He could lie and commit perjury; he could tell the truth and incriminate himself; or he could remain silent and be punished for contempt of court. It would be unfair to put a witness in that position.

Notwithstanding the importance attached to the principle at common law, the privilege against self-incrimination has been overridden by a number of statutory provisions designed to compel unresponsive individuals to reveal information required by the state. The compulsion may be direct in that there will be a sanction for non-compliance, or indirect in that an adverse inference may be drawn from the non-compliance at a subsequent criminal trial. Furthermore, until relatively recently a considerable number of statutory provisions imposed an obligation to respond to questions *and* permitted a self-incriminating answer to be used by the prosecution as an admission in subsequent criminal proceedings. Provisions of this sort – namely, ss. 434 and 436 of the Companies Act 1985 – were considered by the European Court of Human Rights in *Saunders* v. *United Kingdom* (1996) 23 EHRR 313. Section 434(1) and (2) provided that questions put by Department of Trade and Industry (DTI) inspectors investigating corporate fraud had to be answered by any officer or agent of the company under investigation. A refusal to co-operate could be punished as contempt of court (s. 436(3)). Section 434(5) provided that answers could be used in subsequent criminal proceedings. S was convicted of a number of offences relating to his conduct in an unlawful share support operation during a corporate take-over bid in 1986 on the basis of, *inter alia*, self-incriminating answers he had given to the DTI inspectors during the course of seven lengthy interviews. The trial judge had ruled that the transcripts containing S's answers should not be excluded under s. 78(1) of the Police and Criminal Evidence Act 1984, a decision which was upheld by the Court of Appeal. However, the European Court of Human Rights held that the prosecution's use of incriminating answers which S had been legally compelled to provide, and which formed 'a significant part' of the case against him, had violated his right to a fair trial under Article 6(1) of the European Convention, even though some of his answers, if true, would have been exculpatory. According to the Court (at pp. 337–40):

'The right not to incriminate oneself is primarily concerned ... with respecting the will of an accused person to remain silent. As commonly understood in the legal systems of the Contracting Parties to the Convention and elsewhere, it does not extend to the use in criminal proceedings of material which may be obtained from the accused through the use of compulsory powers but which has an existence independent of the will of the suspect such as, *inter alia*, documents acquired pursuant to a warrant, breath, blood and urine samples and bodily tissue for the purpose of DNA testing ... [S]ome of the applicant's answers were ... of an incriminating nature in the sense that they contained admissions to knowledge of information which tended to incriminate him. In any event, bearing in mind the concept of fairness in Article 6, the right not to incriminate oneself cannot reasonably be confined to statements of admission of wrongdoing or to remarks which are directly incriminating. Testimony obtained under compulsion which appears on its face to be of a non-incriminating nature ... may later be deployed in criminal proceedings in support of the prosecution case, for example to contradict or cast doubt upon other statements of the accused or evidence given by him during the trial or to otherwise undermine his credibility ... [T]he general requirements of fairness contained in Article 6, including the right not to incriminate oneself, apply to criminal proceedings in respect of all types of criminal offences without distinction, from the most simple to the most complex. The public interest cannot be invoked to justify the use of answers compulsorily obtained in a non-judicial investigation to incriminate the accused during the trial proceedings.'

As an interim measure following this judgment, the Attorney-General instructed prosecutors to avoid using answers obtained in consequence of any compulsory powers during the accused's trial, whether as part of their case against the accused or during cross-examination (*General Note for Prosecutors* (1998) 148 NLJ 208). Since then, s. 59 of the Youth Justice and Criminal Evidence Act 1999 and Schedule 3 thereto have amended a number of provisions (including s. 434 of the Companies Act 1985) to prohibit the use in a criminal trial of answers provided by the accused under legal compulsion during a preceding non-judicial investigation. (Some provisions, such as s. 31 of the Theft Act 1968, s. 9 of the Criminal Damage Act 1971, s. 72 of the Supreme Court Act 1981 and s. 98 of the Children Act 1989, already provided for the inadmissibility in criminal proceedings of answers given under legal compulsion.)

However, not all statutory provisions which affect the privilege against self-incrimination have been, or need to be, amended. First, the Strasbourg Court was concerned solely with the use of the accused's statements (obtained under legal compulsion) as *evidence* against him at his criminal trial. The Court did not address the propriety of provisions which compel a response from someone who is being investigated, even if he faces a criminal sanction for refusing to co-operate. Indeed it is now clear that the privilege 'does not per se prohibit the use of compulsory powers to require persons to provide information about their financial or company affairs' (*Allen* v. *United Kingdom* (2002) Application No. 76574/01 (ECtHR)). Second, it is implicit in the Court's use of the expression 'unjustifiable infringement of the right' (at p. 338) that some infringements may be permissible; in other words the privilege against self-incrimination is *not* absolute (see, for example, *Heaney* v. *Ireland* (2000) 33 EHRR 264 at p. 280). Accordingly, where there is no statutory bar the prosecution may still adduce self-incriminating answers obtained under legal compulsion without violating Article 6(1) of the Convention, so long as the infringing provision was enacted to achieve a legitimate objective and is a proportionate response to the problem it was intended to address. Third, it is clear from the Court's judgment that there is no prohibition on the use, even in a criminal trial, of 'material which may be obtained from the accused through the use of compulsory powers but which has an existence independent of the will of the suspect' (see also *Heaney* v. *Ireland*

(2000) 33 EHRR 264 (ECtHR) at p. 278 and *L* v. *United Kingdom* [2000] 2 FLR 322 (ECtHR) at p. 331).

One provision which may have the effect of infringing the privilege against self-incrimination, and provide the prosecution with a self-incriminating response to use as evidence against the accused at his criminal trial, is s. 172(2)(*a*) of the Road Traffic Act 1988, which provides that, where the driver of a vehicle is alleged to be guilty of an offence to which the section applies, such as driving under the influence of alcohol, the keeper of the vehicle 'shall give such information as to the identity of the driver as he may be required to give'. A keeper who fails to comply with this requirement is guilty of an offence (s. 172(3)) and liable to a maximum fine of £1000 and possible disqualification. In *Brown* v. *Stott* [2001] 2 WLR 817 the accused was confronted by the police in an apparently intoxicated state at a 24-hour superstore in Dunfermline, Scotland. Asked how she had come to the store, she replied that she had travelled by car and pointed to a vehicle in the car park which she said was hers. At the police station the keys to the car were found in the accused's handbag and, pursuant to s. 172(2)(*a*), the police required her (as the keeper of the vehicle) to say who had been driving the car at the time when she would have been travelling in it to the store. She replied, 'It was me' and subsequently provided a specimen of breath which proved that she had been under the influence of alcohol at that time. On appeal from the Scottish High Court of Justiciary, the question for the Privy Council was whether the prosecution would be able to rely at her trial on the admission which she had been compelled to make. Concluding that the right not to incriminate oneself is an implied right within Article 6(1) of the European Convention, but not an absolute right, the Privy Council held that the provision, as a limited infringement reasonably directed towards a clear and proper public objective, was acceptable and that the accused's admission, if admitted, would not prevent her from receiving a fair trial.

It was not in dispute that the high incidence of death and injury on the roads caused by the misuse of motor vehicles is a serious social problem which needs to be addressed. That is to say, there is a clear public interest in subjecting the use of motor vehicles to a regime of regulatory rules and in being able to enforce the relevant legislation. The question for the Privy Council was whether s. 172(2)(*a*), properly applied, was a necessary and proportionate response to this problem, bearing in mind the need to balance the general interests of the individual (and her Convention rights) against the interests of the community (and their Convention rights). This question was answered in the affirmative for a number of reasons. First, the provision allows one simple question to be put by the police, and the answer given will not necessarily incriminate the keeper as it is not an offence to drive a car (so long as the driver holds a valid licence). Second, insofar as the privilege against self-incrimination is infringed, it is a relatively narrow interference, allowing the police to go no further than demand the name of the driver at a particular time. Third, the police are not entitled to use any overbearing methods to elicit a response. Fourth, the penalty for refusing to answer is moderate and non-custodial. Fifth, people who own and drive cars know that they are subjecting themselves to a regulatory regime of which s. 172(2)(*a*) is a part – the keeper of a car must be taken to have accepted responsibility for its use and the corresponding obligation to provide information when required to do so. Finally it was noted that, under Scottish law, it is necessary for a confession to be corroborated.

The decision in *Brown* v. *Stott* was approved in *DPP* v. *Wilson* (2001) 165 JP 715 (DC) and applied to the similar provision (for non-keepers) in s. 172(2)(*b*) of the Act in relation to the offence of speeding. Moreover, according to the Court no caution is necessary if s. 172(2) is being relied on to elicit self-incriminating information from a suspect, notwithstanding para. C-10.1 of the PACE Code of Practice (7.1.3.3 *ante*). The existence of the offence under s. 172(3) of the Act means that a caution 'would, at best, cause confusion ... and, at worst, undermine the clear statutory purpose' underlying the section. Furthermore, although confessions do not need to be corroborated in England and Wales, a sufficient safeguard is provided in this jurisdiction by the fact that a confession is inadmissible if the prosecution are unable to discharge their burden of proof under s. 76(2) of the Police and Criminal Evidence Act 1984. (The exclusionary discretions under ss. 78(1) of the 1984 Act and 12(1) of the Road Traffic Offenders Act 1988 Act provide an additional safeguard for the accused.) It has also been held that the use of s. 172(2) for the offence of going through a red light is a proportionate response to the problem of maintaining road safety (*Charlebois* v. *DPP* [2003] EWHC 54 Admin (QBD)).

The question whether a provision which compels a person under pain of penalty to provide information infringes his right to a fair trial, should he fail to comply with the demand and be tried for the offence thereby committed, was considered by the European Court of Human Rights in *Heaney* v. *Ireland* (2000) 33 EHRR 264 and *JB* v. *Switzerland* (2001) Application No. 31827/96. In *Heaney* v. *Ireland* the applicant had been arrested and interrogated by the police about his suspected involvement in a recent terrorist attack and asked to account for his movements at the relevant time, a failure to provide such an account being an offence under s. 52 of Ireland's Offences Against the State Act 1939. The applicant refused to provide the requested information and he was tried and convicted of the s. 52 offence. The Strasbourg Court held that the applicant's privilege against self-incrimination and pre-trial right of silence had in effect been extinguished by the degree of compulsion used and that there had therefore been a violation of Article 6(1) of the Convention. A relevant consideration was that an account of the applicant's movements, if provided in response to the s. 52 request, could have been used in evidence against him in criminal proceedings for the terrorist offence. The Court recognised that the privilege against self-incrimination is not an absolute right, but concluded that s. 52 could not be regarded as a proportionate response to the threat of terrorism. In *JB* v. *Switzerland* the Court held that there had been a breach of Article 6(1) in relation to proceedings in which the applicant had been fined for refusing to provide the Swiss tax authorities with documents relating to his investments. The factor which led the Court to conclude that there had been a violation of the applicant's privilege against self-incrimination was that proceedings had already been commenced against him for the offence of tax evasion and the authorities had been trying to compel him to provide evidence which could have been used against him in those separate proceedings.

A provision which compels a person under pain of penalty to provide information was recently considered by the Court of Appeal in *R* v. *Kearns* [2003] 1 Cr App R 111. In that case, K, a bankrupt, was charged with having committed an offence contrary to s. 354(3)(*a*) of the Insolvency Act 1986, carrying a maximum sentence of two years' imprisonment, in that he had failed without reasonable excuse to account for the loss of part of his property having been required to do so by the Official Receiver. If K had provided the information it could not have been used against him in a subsequent trial for some *other* offence because of amendments to s. 433 of the 1986 Act introduced by s. 59 of the Youth Justice and Criminal Evidence Act 1999 and Schedule 3 thereto. Nevertheless, K submitted that s. 354(3)(*a*) of the 1986 Act violated his privilege against self-incrimination and therefore his right to a fair trial under Article 6(1) of the European Convention. The argument was rejected by the Court of Appeal. The demand for information under s. 354(3)(*a*) was made in the course of an extra-judicial procedure to investigate his estate rather than to obtain evidence to prove a case against him in subsequent criminal proceedings. He was not charged with any other offence when the demand was made, and there was no possibility that any information obtained as a result of the statutory demand could be used against him in subsequent criminal proceedings. The judgments in *Heaney* v. *Ireland* (2000) 33 EHRR 264 and *JB* v. *Switzerland* (2001) Application No. 31827/96 offered no support for K's submission, for in those cases the purpose in obtaining information from the applicants had been to provide evidence for other charges. Further, even if it could be said that s. 354(3)(*a*) had infringed K's privilege against self-incrimination, there had been no violation of Article 6(1). The privilege against self-incrimination is not absolute and, according to the Court of Appeal, the provision was a proportionate legislative response to the problem of administering and investigating bankrupt estates.

In *Allen* v. *United Kingdom* (2002) Application No. 76574/01 the European Court of Human Rights held that the requirement to make a declaration of assets to the Inland Revenue raises no issue under Article 6(1), even though a penalty is attached to non-compliance with the Revenue's request for information. In that case, D had been served with a notice under s. 20(1) of the Taxes Management Act 1970 to provide the Inland Revenue with a statement of his assets and liabilities. Following his failure to comply, and the presentation to him of a '*Hansard* warning' to the effect that his co-operation would be a relevant factor when deciding whether he should be prosecuted for fraud, D delivered a false schedule of assets. He was subsequently charged with and convicted of cheating the Inland Revenue and, following an unsuccessful appeal to the House of Lords (*R* v. *Allen* [2001] 3 WLR 843) applied to Strasbourg on the basis that he had been compelled to provide a schedule which was used in evidence against him at his trial. The Court gave D's argument short shrift. The obligation to make disclosure of income and capital for the purposes of assessing tax was said to be a common feature of the taxation systems of contracting states and, in any event, he had been charged with and convicted of the offence of making a false declaration. He had not been placed under compulsion to incriminate himself in relation to an offence which he had already committed.

It will be remembered that in *Saunders* v. *United Kingdom* (1996) 23 EHRR 313 (ECtHR) it was said that the privilege against self-incrimination cannot be relied on in respect of 'material which may be obtained from the accused through the use of compulsory powers but which has an existence independent of the will of the suspect'. Thus, in *PG* v. *United Kingdom* (2001) Application No. 44787/98 (ECtHR) it was held that the underhand way in which the police had obtained samples of the accused's voice had not infringed his privilege against self-incrimination as 'the voice samples, which did not include any incriminating statements, may be regarded as akin to blood, hair or other physical or objective specimens used in forensic analysis and to which the privilege against self-incrimination does not apply'. Provisions which entitle the police to take samples from a suspect cannot therefore be challenged in Strasbourg on the ground that their use by the prosecution at his subsequent trial violated Article 6(1), even though the accused may have been compelled to reveal what was *not* already in existence. (As Lord Bingham pointed out in *Brown* v. *Stott* [2001] 2 WLR 817 (PC) (at p. 837) the whole purpose of requiring a driver to blow into a breathalyser, on pain of a criminal penalty if he refuses, is to obtain evidence which is not yet available and which could be enough to convict him of an offence.) In the present context it is to be noted that ss. 6(4) and 7(6) of the Road Traffic Act 1988 provide that it is an offence (in certain circumstances) to refuse without reasonable excuse to provide a specimen of breath, blood or urine; and that fingerprints and non-intimate body samples may be taken from a suspect without his consent under ss. 61 and 63 of the Police and Criminal Evidence Act 1984 (in accordance with Code D-4 and D-6 of the PACE Codes of Practice). Samples or specimens obtained from a suspect during an investigation into an offence may be used in evidence against him at his trial.

In *Attorney-General's Reference (No. 7 of 2000)* [2001] 1 WLR 1879 the accused, a bankrupt, was legally obliged to deliver up to the official receiver his books, papers and other records relating to his estate and affairs by virtue of s. 291(1)(*b*) of the Insolvency Act 1986 (supported by a contempt sanction in s. 291(6)). He was charged with having committed an offence under s. 362(1)(*a*) of the Act (of having materially contributed to, or increased the extent of, his insolvency by gambling) and, following a defence application in the Crown Court, the judge ruled that the admission of documentary evidence (including a betting file, bank statements, cheque stubs and gambling statements) would violate the accused's right to a fair trial and directed the jury to acquit. The Court of Appeal held that the trial judge had erred. Approving the analysis of La Forest J in *Thomson Newspapers* v. *Director of Investigation and Research* [1990] 1 SCR 425 (SCC), it was held that the distinction drawn in *Saunders* v. *United Kingdom* between statements made by the accused and other pre-existing material was 'jurisprudentially sound' and, accordingly, that the documents had been admissible, subject to the judge's discretion to exclude them under s. 78(1) of the Police and Criminal Evidence Act 1984. This approach accords, in the context of civil proceedings, with the view of Lord Templeman in *AT & T Istel* v. *Tully* [1992] 3 WLR 344 (HL) (at p. 350) that it was 'difficult to see any reason why ... the privilege against self-incrimination should be exercisable so as to enable a litigant to refuse relevant and even vital documents which are in his possession or power and which speak for themselves'. That said, the European Court of Human Rights has held that there can be a violation of the accused's privilege against self-incrimination in respect of his pre-existing documents if the authorities tried to obtain them from him 'by means of coercion and in defiance of the will' with a view to their being used as evidence against him in separate criminal proceedings (*JB* v. *Switzerland* (2001) Application No. 31827/96; see also *Funke* v. *France* (1993) 16 EHRR 297 (ECtHR) at p. 326).

Some provisions impose no liability for an offence should a person refuse to comply with a request, but provide that non-compliance will allow an adverse inference to be drawn at that person's subsequent trial. In particular, s. 11(3)(*b*) of the Criminal Procedure and Investigations Act 1996 provides that the accused's failure to give notice of his defence to the prosecution and court prior to his trial on indictment allows the jury to 'draw such inferences as appear proper in deciding whether the accused is guilty of the offence concerned'; ss. 34, 36 and 37 of the Criminal Justice and Public Order Act 1994 allow adverse inferences to be drawn (in certain circumstances) from the accused's failure to respond to police questions; and s. 62(10)(*b*) of the Police and Criminal Evidence Act 1984 permits an adverse inference to be drawn from the accused's failure without good cause to allow an intimate body sample to be taken from him.

In the absence of a statutory exception, a witness may claim the privilege against self-incrimination in relation to any evidence on which a prosecuting authority might wish to rely in establishing guilt or in deciding whether or not to prosecute (*Den Norske Bank* v. *Antonatos* [1998] 3 WLR 711 (CA) at p. 727). Whether a witness will be permitted to refrain from answering a question on the ground of self-incrimination depends, first, on whether his response would incriminate him and, second, on the likelihood that he would be prosecuted for the offence in question. These are questions for the judge to answer, but he is under no legal obligation to explain the existence of the privilege to the witness for every person is presumed to be aware of it (*R* v. *Coote* (1873) LR 4 PC 599 (PC)). The first question will occasionally give rise to a dilemma for the witness because he may have to disclose his self-incriminating answer to the judge (perhaps *in camera*) so that it can be decided whether he should have to repeat it in the trial. With regard to the second question, the privilege may be claimed only if the trial judge is of the opinion that a criminal charge is 'reasonably likely' to be preferred against him (*Blunt* v. *Park Lane Hotel* [1942] 2 KB 253 (CA)) or, at least, that it is a realistic possibility (*Khan* v. *Khan* [1982] 1 WLR 513 (CA), *Renworth* v. *Stephansen* [1996] 3 All ER 244 (CA)). This will depend on a number of factors, including the gravity of the offence in question, how long ago it was committed and any undertakings given by the prosecuting authority. If the CPS undertake not to use the incriminating material or to prosecute there will be no justification for allowing the witness to rely on the privilege (see *AT & T Istel* v. *Tully* [1992] 3 WLR 344 (HL)).

If a witness validly asserts the privilege and refuses to answer a question, no inference of guilt may be drawn from his silence 'or the privilege would be at once destroyed' (*Wentworth* v. *Lloyd* (1864) 10 HLC 589 (HL) at p. 590). At common law if a witness was entitled to claim the privilege, but was wrongly compelled to answer, the compulsion rendered his admission involuntary and therefore inadmissible at his subsequent trial for the offence (*R* v. *Garbett* (1847) 1 Den 236 (CCCR)). Should the same situation occur today the admission would presumably have to be ruled inadmissible under s. 76(2)(*a*) of the Police and Criminal Evidence Act 1984 on the ground of 'oppression' (or excluded by the mandatory application of s. 78(1) of the Act).

If the accused testifies, then, subject to s. 1(3) of the Criminal Evidence Act 1898, he may be asked 'any question in cross-examination notwithstanding that it would tend to criminate him as to any offence with which he is charged in the proceedings' (s. 1(2)). The accused has no privilege against self-incrimination in respect of an offence he is on trial for and must answer any such question (*Maxwell* v. *DPP* [1935] AC 309 (HL) at p. 318). If the accused has retained his s. 1(3) 'shield' against cross-examination on his bad character he 'shall not be asked, and if asked shall not be required to answer' any question relating to his possible involvement in any other offence. No adverse inference may be drawn from his silence in the face of any such impermissible question (s. 35(5)(*a*) of the Criminal Justice and Public Order Act 1994). However, if an exception to the s. 1(3) shield applies, the accused may be asked, and required to answer, questions relating to other offences he has committed even if he has not yet been convicted of them.

14.2 **Legal Professional Privilege**

The public interest in the due administration of justice outweighs the desirability of upholding most guarantees of confidentiality; so, as a general rule, it is not possible to claim that privilege attaches to information merely because it has been communicated in confidence. However, an important exception to this rule has been recognised for confidential legal advice ('advice privilege') and certain confidential communications made in contemplation of legal proceedings ('litigation privilege'). Advice privilege and litigation privilege are two aspects of 'legal professional privilege', but this term is misleading. The privilege is the personal right of the client (or litigant) and his to claim or waive regardless of the wishes of his lawyer or anyone else. A lawyer is bound by his client's wishes and may not disclose privileged information unless authorised to do so.

14.2.1 The Scope of the Privilege

Regardless of whether legal proceedings are contemplated, advice privilege attaches to confidential communications passing between a professional legal adviser and his client (or his client's agent) where the dominant purpose is to seek and receive legal advice. Legal advice means advice on what the law is and 'advice as to what should prudently and sensibly be done in the relevant legal context' (*Balabel* v. *Air India* [1988] 2 WLR 1036 (CA)). The privilege would also seem to cover confidential documents the client intended to send to his legal adviser, but which were never received (because, for example, they were lost or the client died before they could be posted); but it does not attach to confidential documents prepared by other individuals as raw material in respect of which the client would subsequently seek advice, even if those preparatory documents were sent to the legal adviser (*Three Rivers District Council* v. *Governor & Company of the Bank of England (No. 5)* [2003] 3 WLR 667 (CA)). Nor does the privilege protect information or communications such as the record of a client's attendance contained in his solicitor's appointments diary (*R* v. *Manchester Crown Court ex parte Rogers* [1999] 1 WLR 832 (DC)) or a client's address and contact details (*R (on the application of Miller Gardner Solicitors)* v. *Minshull Street Crown Court* [2002] EWHC 3077 Admin (DC)) or a solicitor's response to a request for a quote regarding possible conveyancing work (*C* v. *C* [2001] 3 WLR 446 (CA)).

Litigation privilege attaches to confidential communications between (i) the professional legal adviser and the client (or his agent), (ii) the professional legal adviser and a third party and (iii) the client (or his agent) and a third party, so long as the communications are made for the purpose of pending or contemplated legal proceedings (*Wheeler* v. *Le Marchant* (1881) 17 ChD 675 (CA)). In practice the third party will often be an expert witness. Litigation privilege is also governed by a 'dominant purpose' test. In *Waugh* v. *British Railways Board* [1979] 3 WLR 150 a train driver had been fatally crushed in a collision at work and his wife sought compensation from the defendant, alleging that the collision had been caused by their negligence. She wished to inspect reports prepared for the defendant soon after the accident, but the defendant withheld them on the ground that they had been prepared not only for the purpose of assessing how to avoid future accidents but also for their lawyers to use in any litigation arising out of the collision. The House of Lords ordered the production of the reports for inspection. Litigation privilege did not attach to the reports because the 'dominant purpose' for which they had been brought into existence was not that they should be used in litigation; the need to prevent the recurrence of similar accidents had been an equally important reason for their creation.

Section 10(1) of the Police and Criminal Evidence Act 1984, which restates the position at common law, sets out the meaning of 'items subject to legal privilege' for the purposes of the entry, search and seizure provisions of the Act. Advice privilege covers 'communications between a professional legal adviser and his client or any person representing his client made in connection with the giving of legal advice to the client' (s. 10(1)(*a*)). Litigation privilege covers 'communications between a professional legal adviser and his client or any person representing his client or between such an adviser or his client or any such representative and any other person made in connection with or in contemplation of legal proceedings and for the purposes of such proceedings' (s. 10(1)(*b*)).

Legal professional privilege also attaches to items enclosed with or referred to in privileged communications, if the items are in the possession of a person who is entitled to possession, so long as the items were brought into existence in connection with the giving of legal advice or in connection with (or in contemplation of) legal proceedings and for the purposes of such proceedings (see s. 10(1)(*c*) of the Police and Criminal Evidence Act 1984). Examples include a sample of blood taken from the accused pursuant to a request by his solicitor and the subsequent report prepared by an expert following his analysis of that sample (*R* v. *R* [1995] 1 Cr App R 183 (CA)). Moreover, where in criminal proceedings an expert has based his opinion on privileged information or items, the expert's opinion, as well as his written report, is privileged (*R* v. *Davies* (2002) 166 JP 243 (CA)). However, no privilege attaches to any pre-existing items the client has sent his legal adviser, so in *R* v. *King* [1983] 1 WLR 411 (CA) pre-existing documents which the accused's solicitor had sent to a handwriting expert for analysis were not protected.

A professional legal adviser need not be in private practice for legal professional privilege to arise. Communications between in-house lawyers and their employers are also privileged (*Alfred Crompton Amusement Machines* v. *Customs and Excise Commissioners (No. 2)* [1972] 2 WLR 835 (CA)) as are communications with foreign advisers (*Re Duncan* [1968] 2 WLR 1479 (PD)). A communication with a solicitor's clerk, acting on the solicitor's behalf, is also privileged (*Taylor* v. *Forster* (1825) 2 C & P 195 (CCP), *Wheeler* v. *Le Marchant* (1881) 17 ChD 675 (CA)). In *R (Bozkurt)* v. *Thames Magistrates' Court* [2002] RTR 246 the Divisional Court held (following *Du Barré* v. *Livette* (1791) Peake 108 (KB)) that the interpreter who was present during a solicitor's interview with his client was bound by the client's privilege to the same extent as the solicitor. Furthermore, a number of statutory provisions have now extended the scope of the privilege to communications with individuals such as licensed conveyancers, trade mark agents and persons providing advocacy or litigation services.

14.2.2 The Justification for the Privilege

It is for reasons of public policy that communications between a professional legal adviser and his client may be withheld at the behest of the client, notwithstanding the public interest in the due administration of justice. In *R* v. *Derby Magistrates' Court ex parte B* [1995] 3 WLR 681 (HL) Lord Taylor CJ justified the privilege in the following terms (at p. 695):

> '[A] man must be able to consult his lawyer in confidence, since otherwise he might hold back half the truth. The client must be sure that what he tells his lawyer in confidence will never be revealed without his consent. Legal professional privilege is thus much more than an ordinary rule of evidence, limited in its application to the facts of a particular case. It is a fundamental condition on which the administration of justice as a whole rests.'

The necessity of advice privilege has been recognised since the sixteenth century to ensure that a client will speak candidly with his legal adviser and thereby obtain the most appropriate advice and representation. Litigation privilege is a more recent development. It has its roots in the adversarial system as it was practised in the nineteenth century – just as each party was entitled to conceal his case until the trial, so he was entitled to conceal all the evidence upon which his case was based. However, this justification is hardly a valid reason in the twenty-first century for withholding evidence. Civil litigants are now required to disclose their evidence in advance of the trial, and even in criminal proceedings the accused is under a pre-trial obligation to disclose the nature of his defence and any expert evidence he wishes to rely on. That said, it is clearly important that the litigant, his lawyer and third parties such as expert witnesses should be able to speak candidly with one another while preparing for the trial; so while the historical justification for litigation privilege has disappeared, the justification for advice privilege provides a valid reason for its continued existence.

The justification for either privilege disappears, however, once the relevant evidence has come into the opponent's possession. If this has happened the public interest favouring the adduction of all relevant evidence stands uncontradicted and, in the absence of any further policy consideration justifying its exclusion, the evidence will be admissible. As a matter of law the same is true whether the information has come into the opponent's possession innocently or been obtained through theft or trickery; so, subject to the judge's exclusionary discretion under r. 32.1 of the Civil Procedure Rules 1998, privileged documents or copies of such documents which have been obtained by the opposing party may be adduced in civil proceedings even if the originals or copies were stolen (*Calcraft* v. *Guest* [1898] 1 QB 759 (CA), *Waugh* v. *British Railways Board* [1979] 3 WLR 150 (HL) at p. 159). In criminal proceedings prosecution evidence which has been stolen or obtained by trickery from the accused may be excluded by the application of s. 78(1) of the Police and Criminal

Evidence Act 1984 (or the prosecution itself may be halted as an abuse of process) but if the evidence has come into the hands of the prosecution innocently there is no rule of law to prevent their using it. In *R* v. *Tompkins* (1977) 67 Cr App R 181 a privileged note the accused had written and given to his barrister during the trial was found on the floor of the court-room and handed to the prosecuting barrister. The Court of Appeal held that the prosecution had been entitled to cross-examine the accused on its content.

In civil proceedings it may be possible for a person who has had his privileged information taken by some improper means to obtain an injunction to prevent any use being made of it (*Lord Ashburton* v. *Pape* [1913] 2 Ch 469 (CA), *Goddard* v. *Nationwide Building Society* [1986] 3 WLR 734 (CA)). (This equitable remedy is not available to prevent the Crown from relying on admissible evidence in criminal proceedings: *Butler* v. *Board of Trade* [1970] 3 WLR 822 (ChD).) Subject to the judge's power under r. 32.1 of the Civil Procedure Rules 1998, the question of admissibility in a civil trial turns on relevance; but if an equitable remedy is sought before the question of admissibility arises, the way in which the information was obtained is itself relevant to whether the remedy ought to be granted. In *Guinness Peat Properties* v. *Fitzroy Robinson Partnership* [1987] 1 WLR 1027 (CA) it was accepted that an injunction could be granted even if the privileged information had been obtained as a result of an obvious but honest mistake.

Rule 31.20 of the Civil Procedure Rules 1998 now provides that a privileged document which has been 'inadvertently' produced for inspection may not be relied on by the opposing party unless the judge permits it, but the Court of Appeal has held that the pre-CPR principles have not been affected. In other words, the inspecting party is entitled to assume that privilege has been waived, but injunctive relief *may* be granted to prevent him from using the evidence if there has been fraud or an obvious mistake (*Breeze* v. *John Stacey* (1999) *The Times* 8.7.99 (CA), *Al Fayed* v. *Commissioner of Police of the Metropolis* [2002] EWCA Civ 780).

In *R* v. *Derby Magistrates' Court ex parte B* [1995] 3 WLR 681 the majority of the House of Lords came down firmly in favour of the view that *advice* privilege is absolute in nature regardless of any unfairness this approach might cause in individual cases. In 1978 a 16-year-old girl was murdered and B, having confessed to the murder, was charged with the offence. Before his trial B changed his story and alleged instead that his stepfather had been responsible, and in reliance on this second version of events he managed to secure an acquittal. His stepfather was subsequently charged with the girl's murder and at his committal proceedings B was called as a prosecution witness. Not surprisingly, the accused wished to obtain the documentary record of B's instructions to his solicitor before the date when he had changed his story. It could be assumed that B's first version of events would be inconsistent with the evidence he would give at the accused's trial, and if the defence was equipped with that information B could be cross-examined on it for the purpose of undermining the value of his evidence (see 16.5.3 *post*). The House of Lords held that there could never be the sort of balancing exercise which was permissible in cases where a claim to public interest immunity was asserted and that the accused was not entitled to the requested material unless B was willing to waive his privilege. Lord Taylor CJ, in a speech with which Lords Keith, Mustill and Lloyd agreed, said (at pp. 696–7):

> '[O]nce any exception to the general rule is allowed, the client's confidence is necessarily lost. The solicitor, instead of being able to tell his client that anything which the client might say would never in any circumstances be revealed without his consent, would have to qualify his assurance ... But it is not for the sake of the applicant alone that the privilege must be upheld. It is in the wider interests of all those hereafter who might otherwise be deterred from telling the whole truth to their solicitors. For this reason I am of the opinion that no exception should be allowed to the absolute nature of legal professional privilege, once established.'

Lord Lloyd added (at p. 697):

> 'There may be cases where the principle will work hardship on a third party seeking to assert his innocence. But in the overall interests of the administration of justice it is better that the principle should be preserved intact.'

The same utilitarian approach was adopted by the majority of the High Court of Australia in *Carter* v. *Northmore Hale Davy & Leake* (1995) 183 CLR 121; and in *General Mediterranean Holdings* v. *Patel* [2000] 1 WLR 272 (QBD) Toulson J opined (at p. 296) that the accused who was denied access to another person's privileged material would still receive a fair trial within the meaning of Article 6 of the European Convention on Human Rights. However, it is difficult to see how this view, as a general proposition, can be sustained. Although a balancing exercise is permitted when determining what is meant by a 'fair trial' (2.9 *ante*), there can be little doubt that to deny the accused access to cogent (and otherwise admissible) evidence of his innocence on the ground that it is privileged material will on occasion result in a violation of Article 6(1). It is true that the importance of lawyer-client confidentiality as an aspect of the Article 8(1) right to have one's private life respected has been recognised by the European Court of Human Rights (*Campbell* v. *United Kingdom* (1992) 15 EHRR 137, *Foxley* v. *United Kingdom* (2000) 31 EHRR 637), but there is nothing in the Strasbourg jurisprudence to suggest that the privilege can be allowed to override all other considerations whatever the circumstances. Where privileged material would demonstrate the accused's innocence (or give rise to a reasonable doubt as to his innocence) the privilege must give way to the requirements of Article 6(1). This was recently recognised by the Supreme Court of Canada in *R* v. *McClure* [2001] 1 SCR 445, where it was accepted that, while lawyer-client privilege 'must be as close to absolute as possible' it would have to yield if reliance on it would prevent the accused from establishing his innocence. A two-stage 'innocence at stake' exception to the privilege was set out to be applied in cases where the accused cannot raise a reasonable doubt as to his guilt in any other way and the privileged information is not available from any other source:

> The first stage ... requires production of the material to the trial judge for review ... The trial judge must ask: '*Is there some evidentiary basis for the claim that a solicitor-client communication exists that could raise a reasonable doubt about the guilt of the accused?*' ... The evidence sought should be considered in conjunction with other available evidence in order to determine its importance ... Once the first stage ... has been met, the trial judge must examine the record ... The trial judge must ask herself the following question: '*Is there something in the solicitor-client communication that is likely to raise a reasonable doubt about the accused's guilt?*'

Subject to any intervention by Parliament or relevant decision in Strasbourg, it would appear that advice privilege is to maintain its status in England and Wales as an absolute common-law right, notwithstanding the changes introduced by the Human Rights Act 1998 (see *R (Morgan Grenfell)* v. *Special Commissioner of Income Tax* [2002] 2 WLR 1299 (HL) at pp. 1304 and 1310). Accordingly, if there is a case where non-disclosure of privileged evidence would prevent the accused from receiving the fair trial to which he is entitled under Article 6, it will be necessary to argue that the proceedings should be stayed as an abuse of the court's process (10.4 *ante*). This approach to the problem, if adopted, might be addressed by a two-stage test similar to that established in *JC* v. *R* (2001) 195 DLR (4th) 513, although the outcome would of course be quite different. (There is authority for the view that a person's advice privilege would not be infringed by disclosure to the judge for such a limited purpose: *Parry-Jones* v. *Law Society* [1968] 2 WLR 397 (CA), *R (Morgan Grenfell)* v. *Special Commissioner of Income Tax* [2002] 2 WLR 1299 (HL) at p. 1307.)

It is to be noted, however, that the stepfather in *R* v. *Derby Magistrates' Court ex parte B* [1995] 3 WLR 681 submitted at his trial for murder that the proceedings should be stayed or, alternatively, that the evidence of his stepson, the principal prosecution witness, should be excluded in its entirety under s. 78(1) of the Police and Criminal Evidence Act 1984 by virtue of his refusal to waive advice privilege. These submissions were rejected by the trial judge on the basis that the stepfather's position was adequately protected by his counsel's freedom to comment on the information which was probably in the privileged documents and explore the stepson's reasons for asserting his privilege. The judge's rulings were upheld on appeal following the stepfather's conviction (*R* v. *Brookes* (1998) unreported (96/5986/X2) (CA)).

The present nature of advice privilege means that it may be removed only by legislation, where the statute expressly overrides the right of confidentiality or overrides it by necessary implication. An example of the latter type of provision is s. 33(3)(*f*) of the Limitation Act 1980, which directs the court to have regard to the nature of the legal advice received by the claimant when deciding whether to grant him leave to bring an action out of time (see *Jones* v. *G D Searle* [1979] 1 WLR 101 (CA)).

Litigation privilege is *not* absolute, however. In *Re L (a Minor)* [1996] 2 WLR 395 the majority of the House of Lords held that litigation privilege does not apply to proceedings under Part IV of the Children Act 1989 which are non-adversarial in nature and place the welfare of the child as the primary consideration.

14.2.3 Duration and Waiver

Once legal professional privilege has arisen it can be lost only if the client waives that right. Subject to waiver, a privileged communication is privileged for all time and in all circumstances – 'once privileged always privileged' (*Calcraft* v. *Guest* [1898] 1 QB 759 (CA) at p. 761). Indeed both the privilege and the right to waive it survive the death of the client in favour of his personal representative or successors-in-title (*R* v. *Molloy* [1997] 2 Cr App R 283 (CA)). As with the privilege against self-incrimination, no adverse inference may be drawn if a person refuses to waive his legal professional privilege (*Wentworth* v. *Lloyd* (1864) 10 HLC 589 (HL), *Sayers* v. *Clarke Walker* [2002] EWCA Civ 910).

Although the right of waiver, like the privilege itself, is that of the client, the legal adviser is deemed to act with his client's authority in the conduct of the litigation and may therefore waive the privilege on his client's behalf, even if he (the legal adviser) has acted inadvertently and contrary to his client's interests. This is apparent from the Court of Appeal's decision in *Great Atlantic Insurance* v. *Home Insurance* [1981] 1 WLR 529, where it was held that waiver in respect of part of the information in a privileged document amounts to waiver in respect of all the privileged information therein, unless the nature of the subject-matter is sufficiently dissimilar to justify severance. (It is possible, however, to withhold – by blanking out – the privileged parts of a document containing privileged and non-privileged material; see *The Sagheera* [1997] 1 Lloyd's Rep 160 (QBD) at p. 170.) According to the Court of Appeal in *Al Fayed* v. *Commissioner of Police of the Metropolis* [2002] EWCA Civ 780, where a party or his solicitor has inadvertently permitted another party to inspect documents, the inspecting party 'is in general entitled to assume' that any privilege which might have been claimed for the documents has been waived. As a general rule it will be too late for the privilege to be claimed by obtaining injunctive relief, although, as explained above, such relief may be granted if the documents were procured for inspection by fraud or made available for inspection as a result of an obvious mistake. If, however, a lawyer *intentionally* reveals privileged information to the other side it will not be possible to argue subsequently that privilege was not waived. In *R* v. *Cottrill* [1997] Crim LR 56 (CA) the accused's written statement was sent to the CPS, without his knowledge or consent, in an attempt by his solicitor to persuade the CPS to drop the case. The prosecution were therefore entitled to cross-examine the accused on the inconsistencies between his testimony and his written statement.

A former client who sues his solicitor impliedly waives his privilege in respect of any relevant communications between them (*Paragon Finance* v. *Freshfields* [1999] 1 WLR 1183 (CA)).

14.2.4 Iniquity

Communications between a client and his legal adviser which were intended by the client or the adviser, or indeed both of them, to facilitate a crime or fraud are not covered by legal professional privilege (*R* v. *Cox* (1884) 14 QBD 153 (CCCR)). Communications which are 'criminal in themselves' also fall outside the scope of the privilege, for example where a client threatens to commit murder or makes an obscene telephone call (*C* v. *C* [2001] 3 WLR 446 (CA)). The iniquity rule does not apply, however, if the legal adviser simply volunteered advice to his client warning him that if he persisted in a particular course of conduct he could be prosecuted (*Butler* v. *Board of Trade* [1970] 3 WLR 822 (ChD)).

Fraud has a broad meaning in this context and includes 'all forms of fraud and dishonesty such as fraudulent breach of trust, fraudulent conspiracy, trickery and sham contrivances' (*Crescent Farm (Sidcup) Sports* v. *Sterling Offices* [1972] 2 WLR 91 (ChD) at p. 100). Indeed, it now seems that any sufficiently iniquitous purpose will prevent the privilege from attaching, the test being objective. In *Barclays Bank* v. *Eustice* [1995] 1 WLR 1238 the Court of Appeal held that entering into transactions at an undervalue for the purpose of prejudicing the interests of a creditor was 'sufficiently iniquitous' for the communications between the transferor and his solicitor relating to those transactions not to be privileged, and that it did not matter whether the client or the solicitor shared that view. In *Dubai Aluminium* v. *Al Alawi* [1999] 1 All ER 703 (QBD) private investigators employed by the plaintiff's solicitors had obtained information about the defendant's finances and assets by means of false representation and impersonation amounting to a criminal offence under what was then s. 5(6) of the Data Protection Act 1984. This conduct was held to fall within the scope of the 'crime, fraud or iniquity' doctrine thereby preventing litigation privilege from attaching to the reports and documents relating to the investigation.

The rule in *R* v. *Cox* (1884) 14 QBD 153 is not an exception to the absolute nature of advice privilege. Rather it is a situation where, for reasons of public policy, the privilege does not attach. This limitation can be justified on two grounds. First, a person with fraudulent intentions cannot legitimately expect the communications between himself and his legal adviser to be privileged. Second, the innocent legal adviser should be free to explain what transpired so that he can disassociate himself from his client's criminal or fraudulent conduct. If a party wishes to displace another party's claim to privilege under this rule, a *prima facie* case of iniquity must be established (*O'Rourke* v. *Darbishire* [1920] AC 581 (HL)).

Section 10(2) of the Police and Criminal Evidence Act 1984 provides that items held with the intention of furthering a criminal purpose are not subject to legal professional privilege. In *R* v. *Central Criminal Court ex parte Francis* [1988] 3 WLR 989 the majority of the House of Lords held that the intention in question need not be that of the person holding the items (in most cases the legal adviser) but could be the intention of any person.

14.3 'Without Prejudice' Communications

Written or oral communications made by parties to litigation in the course of a genuine attempt to settle their dispute are privileged. If the parties fail to reach a compromise their various offers, counter-offers and concessions may not be disclosed at the trial as evidence of the strength or weakness of their respective cases. Generally such correspondence is expressly asserted to be on a 'without prejudice' basis, but these words are not strictly necessary for the privilege to attach so long as the communication is genuinely aimed at reaching a settlement (*Rush & Tompkins* v. *Greater London Council* [1988] 3 WLR 939 (HL)). Conversely, the mere addition of the words 'without prejudice' to other types of correspondence will not give rise to the privilege (*Buckinghamshire County Council* v. *Moran* [1989] 3 WLR 152 (CA)).

Two justifications have been given for the 'without prejudice' rule. First, and most important, it is in the public interest that parties to litigation should not proceed to trial. In other words, public policy dictates that parties should be encouraged to reach a settlement (*Rush & Tompkins* v. *Greater London Council* [1988] 3 WLR 939 (HL) at p. 942). The exclusionary rule performs this function by allowing parties to negotiate without running the risk that their communications, usually express or implied admissions, will be used against them. Indeed, the strength of the public interest underlying the rule is such that it will not be displaced for the benefit of one party merely because the other party, who wishes to rely on it, is putting forward an implausible or inconsistent case (*WH Smith* v. *Colman* [2001] FSR 91 (CA)). The second justification is that the parties may be said to have agreed that their 'without prejudice' communications should not be used as evidence against them should their dispute proceed to trial (*South Shropshire District Council* v. *Amos* [1986] 1 WLR 1271 (CA) at p. 1277, *Unilever* v. *Procter & Gamble* [2000] 1 WLR 2436 (CA) at p. 2442).

The exclusionary rule is not absolute, however, for 'the veil imposed by public policy may have to be pulled aside, even so as to disclose admissions, in cases where the protection afforded by the rule has been unequivocally abused' (*Unilever* v. *Procter & Gamble* [2000] 1 WLR 2436 (CA) at p. 2449). In that case, eight exceptions to the rule were enumerated, each of which permits communications to be adduced in civil proceedings regardless of the fact that they were made during the course of 'without prejudice' negotiations. Furthermore, in *Prudential Assurance Co* v. *Prudential Insurance Co of America* [2002] EWHC 2809 (ChD) it was held that the 'without prejudice' rule does not apply in respect of communications during negotiations aimed at *preventing* a dispute from arising, the reason being that the rule should be applied with restraint, in accordance with the public interest considerations which underlie it, to ensure that relevant evidence is not excluded without good reason. However, the privilege does attach to communications which were aimed at resolving an existing dispute, even though legal proceedings had not been commenced at the time the negotiations took place (*Rabin* v. *Mendoza* [1954] 1 WLR 271 (CA)).

In *Rush & Tompkins* v. *Greater London Council* [1988] 3 WLR 939 (HL) it was held that the public policy which applies to protect genuine negotiations from being admissible in evidence should extend to protect those negotiations from being discoverable to third parties. As the privilege belongs to both parties it may be waived only if they both consent.

14.4 **Other Confidential Communications**

Generally speaking, the mere fact that a communication was made as a result of an assurance of confidentiality will not protect it from being revealed in court (or during pre-trial discovery). If a witness has been told something in confidence he can be compelled to reveal that information and will be in contempt of court if he refuses to comply. To this there are some well-established exceptions, but they are few in number and confidentiality is not a separate head of privilege or public interest immunity. If it were, 'the law would operate erratically and capriciously according to whether or not a particular communication was made confidentially' (*D* v. *NSPCC* [1977] 2 WLR 201 (HL) at p. 226). In *Attorney-General* v. *Mulholland* [1963] 2 WLR 658 (CA) Lord Denning MR said (at p. 665):

> 'The only profession that I know which is given a privilege from disclosing information to a court of law is the legal profession, and then it is not the privilege of the lawyer but of his client. Take the clergyman, the banker or the medical man. None of these is entitled to refuse to answer when directed to by a judge.'

Confidential communications to priests are not protected (*Wheeler* v. *Le Marchant* (1881) 17 ChD 675 (CA) at p. 681, *Du Barré* v. *Livette* (1791) Peake 108 (KB) at pp. 109–10). Medical doctors too may be compelled to reveal what their patients have told them in confidence (*Hunter* v. *Mann* [1974] 2 WLR 742 (DC)); and bankers may be compelled to disclose the details of their books (if an order has been made under s. 7 of the Bankers' Books Evidence Act 1879). Close friends and family members are also obliged to reveal what they have been told in confidence (*Wheeler* v. *Le Marchant* (1881) 17 ChD 675 (CA) at p. 681); and, although spouses are compellable to testify only in certain situations (16.3.2 *post*), once they have taken the oath they must answer any question like any other witness (*R* v. *Pitt* [1982] 3 WLR 359 (CA)). However, because of the importance attached in democratic societies to the freedom of the press, and the concomitant need to ensure that journalists' sources are not deterred from disclosing information which ought to be in the public domain, journalists are obliged to reveal their sources only if it is necessary in the interests of justice or national security or for the prevention of disorder or crime (see s. 10 of the Contempt of Court Act 1981 and Article 10 of the European Convention on Human Rights). In other words, a disclosure order should be made only if it is justified by an overriding requirement in the public interest (*Goodwin* v. *United Kingdom* (1996) 22 EHRR 123 (ECtHR), *Ashworth Hospital Authority* v. *MGN* [2002] 1 WLR 2033 (HL)).

There are dicta, however, to the effect that trial judges possess a discretion as to whether a witness should be compelled to reveal a confidential communication. For example, in *British Steel* v. *Granada Television* [1980] 3 WLR 774 (HL) Lord Wilberforce said (at p. 821):

> '[A]s to information obtained in confidence, and the legal duty, which may arise, to disclose it to a court of justice, the position is clear. Courts have an inherent wish to respect this confidence, whether it arises between doctor and patient, priest and penitent, banker and customer, between persons giving testimonials to employees, or in other relationships ... But in all these cases the court may have to decide, in particular circumstances, that the interest in preserving this confidence is outweighed by other interests to which the law attaches importance.'

Similarly, in *D* v. *NSPCC* [1977] 2 WLR 201 (HL) (at p. 232) Lord Edmund-Davies recognised a discretion in civil proceedings to uphold a refusal to disclose relevant evidence if 'disclosure would be in breach of some ethical or social value' and 'on balance the public interest would be better served by excluding such evidence'. Whether a witness should be compelled to breach a confidence will depend 'largely on the importance of the potential answer to the issues being tried' (*Hunter* v. *Mann* [1974] 2 WLR 742 (DC) at p. 748). In other words, the question is governed by the judge's discretion to exclude logically relevant evidence on the basis that countervailing considerations – in this case confidentiality – outweigh the importance of the evidence to the resolution of one or more issues in the trial (*Vernon* v. *Bosley* [1994] PIQR 337 (CA) at p. 340; see generally 3.1.3 *ante*). This might explain the decision in *R* v. *Griffin* (1853) 6 Cox CC 219 (CCC) where it was considered inappropriate to allow a chaplain to reveal what the accused had told him in confidence.

Chapter Summary

- The privilege against self-incrimination is the personal right of any person not to answer any question or produce any evidence which would, *inter alia*, tend to expose him to a criminal charge. It is, however, subject to a number of infringing statutory provisions which place unresponsive individuals under a degree of legal compulsion to provide information. A failure to respond may result in a penalty or an adverse inference being drawn from the individual's silence. A provision may even allow the prosecution to rely on a self-incriminating answer provided under legal compulsion as evidence against the individual at his trial for an offence

which has already been committed, but only if the provision in question was enacted to achieve a legitimate objective and is a proportionate response to the problem it was intended to address.
- There are two types of legal professional privilege. Advice privilege is the personal right of a legal adviser's client to withhold the confidential communications between them, so long as the (dominant) purpose of the communications was to seek and receive legal advice. It is an absolute right at common law Litigation privilege, which is not absolute at common law, is the personal right of the client to withhold communications between him and his legal adviser (and any third party) if their communications were made for the (dominant) purpose of pending or contemplated legal proceedings. Privilege also attaches to items enclosed with or referred to in privileged communications if they were brought into existence in connection with the provision of legal advice or in connection with (and for the purpose of) legal proceedings. Legal professional privilege does not extend to communications which were intended to facilitate a crime, fraud or some other sufficiently iniquitous conduct.
- As a general rule, 'without prejudice' communications between parties to litigation in the course of a genuine attempt to settle their dispute are privileged.
- Other confidential communications are not protected by privilege (or public interest immunity), but the judge has a discretion to prevent the disclosure of confidential information if, in the circumstances of the particular case, countervailing considerations of policy outweigh the principle of free proof.

Further Reading

Macnair, 'Development of the Privilege Against Self-Incrimination' (1990) 10 OJLS 66
Dennis, 'Reassessing the Privilege Against Self-Incrimination' (1995) CLJ 342

Newbold, 'The Crime/Fraud Exception to Legal Professional Privilege (1990) 53 MLR 472
Tapper, 'Prosecution and Privilege' (1996) 1 E & P 5
Pattenden, 'Litigation Privilege' (2000) 4 E & P 213
Murphy, 'The Innocence at Stake Test' [2001] Crim LR 728

15   The Mechanics of Proof

The purpose of the trial is to resolve disputed issues of fact to the satisfaction of the court by the adduction of admissible evidence. The law of evidence sets out the principles and rules which determine whether evidence is admissible and, if so, whether it ought to be admitted, but it is also concerned with the process of *proof*. For a trial to function effectively it is necessary to understand: which party has to prove any disputed issue of fact ('discharge the burden of proof'); what is meant by 'proof' in this context; what happens when there is no evidence in support of or against a particular factual proposition; and to what extent the tribunal of fact may rely on its own knowledge.

15.1 **The Burden and Standard of Proof**

The legal burden of proof (sometimes known as the 'persuasive' or 'probative' burden) is the obligation the law imposes on a party to prove a fact in issue. In effect it is no more than a risk-allocation mechanism: the party who bears the legal burden on an issue carries the risk of losing on that issue if the evidence relevant to it is evenly balanced or non-existent. It is for that party to adduce sufficient evidence to persuade the tribunal of fact that his version of events is correct. In *Rhesa Shipping* v. *Edmunds* [1985] 1 WLR 948 (HL) (at pp. 955–6) Lord Brandon said of the tribunal of fact in civil proceedings:

> 'The ... judge is not bound always to make a finding one way or the other with regard to the facts averred by the parties. He has open to him the third alternative of saying that the party on whom the burden of proof lies in relation to any averment made by him has failed to discharge that burden. No judge likes to decide cases on burden of proof if he can legitimately avoid having to do so. There are cases, however, in which, owing to the unsatisfactory state of the evidence or otherwise, deciding on the burden of proof is the only just course for him to take.'

The claimant who alleges negligence must prove that the defendant's conduct amounted to a breach of duty and that he suffered a consequential loss; if the evidence is evenly balanced on either issue the claimant's claim will fail. In *Wakelin* v. *London & South Western Railway* (1886) 12 App Cas 41 (HL) it was alleged that the defendant railway company's negligence had caused the death of the plaintiff's husband. The deceased had been found on a railway crossing following a collision between him and one of the defendant's trains, but there were no witnesses to what had happened. There was nothing to show whether it was the defendant or the deceased who had been negligent; and even if it was assumed that the defendant had been negligent there was no evidence to suggest that it had caused the deceased's death. The legal burden lay with the plaintiff to prove both facts in issue and as she had been unable to do this her claim could not succeed. The 'third alternative' is not always an available option for the tribunal of fact, however, for it has been held that it may not be relied on where there is a clash of medical opinion (*Sewell* v. *Electrolux* (1997) *The Times* 7.11.97 (CA)).

If the claimant is unable to discharge the legal burden he bears on any fact in issue in relation to his case, the whole of that case will collapse. For this reason it is sometimes said that he bears a specific legal burden on each of the facts in issue he is obliged to prove and an 'ultimate burden' to prove his case as a whole. By contrast, if the defendant bears the legal burden on an issue, for example because he has responded to the claimant's allegation of negligence with his own counter-allegation of contributory negligence, his failure to discharge that burden will not necessarily mean he will lose his case. He may fail to prove contributory negligence, but if the claimant fails to prove any of the facts in issue which comprise his allegation of negligence it is the claimant who will ultimately lose, for the defendant will not be found liable to any extent.

Generally the party who makes an assertion of fact must prove it ('he who asserts must prove'), although this principle occasionally has to give way to a weightier principle such as the accused's right not to be convicted of a crime he has not committed. Thus, in criminal proceedings the prosecution generally have to prove each of the elements of the offence charged (that is, that the accused committed the *actus reus* of the offence with the requisite *mens rea*) and also disprove any affirmative defence raised by the accused. If the accused is charged with murder and testifies that he acted in self-defence the prosecution must prove that he killed the deceased with malice aforethought and that he did *not* act in self-defence. If the prosecution fail to prove any of these specific facts in issue the accused must be acquitted. This is the general position, but it is subject to a number of exceptions where policy has dictated that the accused should bear the legal burden of proving his defence (and therefore his innocence) in certain situations.

The legal burden of proof has to be distinguished from the 'evidential burden'. The evidential burden is not a burden of *proof* as such but rather an obligation to demonstrate that sufficient evidence has been adduced or elicited in support of an assertion of fact so that it can become a live issue. Whether the legal burden has been discharged, in respect of any fact in issue, is determined by the tribunal of fact at the end of the trial in the light of all the evidence adduced by both parties. However, the tribunal of fact is entitled to adjudicate on any such issue only if the tribunal of law has decided that there is sufficient evidence in support of that assertion of fact. For example, it is for the judge to say whether fault can *legitimately* be inferred, but for the jury to determine whether it *ought* to be inferred (*Metropolitan Railway* v. *Jackson* (1877) 3 App Cas 193 (HL) at p. 200). For this reason the evidential burden is sometimes known as 'the duty of passing the judge'. If the party bearing an evidential burden fails to discharge it the issue is withheld or withdrawn from the tribunal of fact and that party will therefore lose on that issue (see, for example, *Alexander* v. *Arts Council of Wales* [2001] 1 WLR 1840 (CA)).

As a general rule, the party bearing the legal burden of proof on a fact in issue also bears the evidential burden to make it a live issue. If insufficient evidence has been adduced by the close of P's case to support an assertion of fact made against D the tribunal of law will hold that the asserted fact is not to be considered by the tribunal of fact. The consequence is that P will lose on that issue and the case against D will fail. The tribunal of law may come to such a ruling of its own volition, but in practice it will usually follow a submission by D that there is 'no case to answer' (16.7 *post*). If the evidential burden in respect of each element of an allegation has been discharged there is said to be a *prima facie* case against the opposing party. In criminal proceedings it will be a case against the accused. In civil proceedings the claimant will have a claim against the defendant, but it is also possible for the defendant to bring a counterclaim against the claimant. (For example, where there has been a road accident involving a collision between two motorists it is not uncommon for each motorist to allege negligence against the other by way of a claim and counterclaim.) Thus, if the claimant alleges negligence and adduces insufficient evidence by the end of his case for a reasonable tribunal of fact to be able to conclude at the end of the trial, taking the evidence at its highest, that the defendant was in breach of his duty of care to the claimant, the defendant will succeed on a submission of no case to answer and the claimant's case will collapse. Likewise, if the prosecution allege murder and are unable to adduce sufficient evidence by the end of their case that the accused killed the deceased, the case against the accused will be dismissed for want of evidence.

In criminal proceedings there is an exception to the general rule that the party with the legal burden of proof on an issue also carries the evidential burden. If the accused raises a defence which the prosecution are obliged to disprove, there must be sufficient evidence to support that defence by the end of the trial or the tribunal of law will withdraw the issue from the tribunal of fact. Thus, if the prosecution have discharged their evidential burden in respect of all the elements of murder – that is, they have adduced sufficient evidence which if believed, and in the absence of evidence to the contrary, would enable a reasonable and properly directed jury to find the accused guilty of murder – and the accused raises self-defence, the accused will have to show there is some admissible evidence in support of his defence or the judge will not allow the jury to consider it. This will usually mean the accused will have to adduce evidence of his own, for example by testifying or calling witnesses on his behalf. However, if evidence of self-defence has come out during the prosecution case, for example because a prosecution witness has revealed something to that effect while being cross-examined, the judge will allow the jury to consider the defence even if the accused has adduced no evidence of his own (*R* v. *Gill* [1963] 1 WLR 841 (CCA), *Bullard* v. *R* [1957] 3 WLR 656 (PC)).

Whether the evidential burden has been discharged is a question of law for the judge, and neither the question itself nor the judge's ruling on it should be mentioned to the jury. The judge must, however, direct the jury on the incidence of the legal burden of proof, and on the standard of proof required, so that they can determine whether that burden has been discharged (*R* v. *Gibson* (1983) 77 Cr App R 151 (CA)).

If the party bearing an evidential burden on an issue manages to discharge it this is said to place on his opponent a 'tactical' or 'provisional' burden to adduce evidence in rebuttal. The tribunal of law's ruling means that sufficient evidence has been adduced on the issue for the tribunal of fact to find, at the end of the trial, that it has been proved. If the opponent fails to adduce evidence to show the contrary it is quite possible that the issue will be proved against him. It would therefore be to the opponent's advantage to adduce evidence in rebuttal rather than simply hope the tribunal of fact does not find in the proponent's favour: he is obliged, in a *tactical* sense, to adduce evidence of his own. If the prosecution have established a *prima facie* case against the accused it is not incumbent on him to adduce evidence of his own, for the jury may decide in his favour anyway. However, that might be a very risky approach to take, particularly as the jury are entitled to draw an adverse inference from the accused's refusal to testify (9.3.2 *ante*).

For the tribunal of fact to be able to determine whether the legal burden of proof has been discharged by the party bearing it there must be a standard (a degree of probability) against which the likelihood of his version being true can be compared. This is known as the 'standard of proof'. Common sense dictates that very little, if anything, can be known with certainty, particularly in the adversarial context of criminal and civil proceedings where there is so much scope for falsehood and error, so the standard must be lower than 100 per cent. It is also meaningless to talk of an issue being 'proved' (at least in the conventional sense of the word) if an alternative explanation is equally or more likely, so the standard of proof must be greater than a probability of 50 per cent. Where the standard is set between these limits in civil and criminal proceedings is governed by considerations of policy. This is subject to the power of the judiciary, or indeed Parliament, to attribute to the word 'proof' a meaning which does not accord with conventional usage, and set a standard which is lower than 50 per cent, obliging the party bearing the legal burden to establish a possibility (or a reasonable possibility) rather than a likelihood. Thus, if a claim for asylum has been rejected by the Home Office, at the subsequent appeal hearing (the trial process) the claimant need only establish that there is a 'reasonable degree of likelihood' that he has a 'well-founded fear of persecution' because of the serious consequences which might befall him should a legitimate claim be rejected (*R* v. *Secretary of State for the Home Department ex parte Sivakumaran* [1988] 2 WLR 92 (HL) at pp. 98–9). Furthermore, in the context of criminal proceedings, it is now clear that the word 'prove' will be interpreted to mean no more than an obligation to discharge an evidential burden if its conventional meaning would amount to a disproportionate interference with the presumption of innocence guaranteed by Article 6(2) of the European Convention on Human Rights (see 15.2.2.1 *post*).

It would appear that neither the defence nor the prosecution bear an evidential burden or the legal burden of proof in relation to whether the trial judge (or magistrates) should exercise their power under s. 78(1) of the Police and Criminal Evidence Act 1984 to exclude prosecution evidence, and that no particular standard of proof applies in respect of the facts relevant to the exercise of this power (*R (Saifi)* v. *Governor of Brixton Prison* [2001] 1 WLR 1134 (DC)).

Finally it should be noted that when determining whether a party has discharged the burden of proof to the requisite standard of probability the tribunal of fact will not apply a theoretical or statistical approach, particularly if a jury is evaluating the evidence. The question must be determined 'not by means of a formula, mathematical or otherwise, but by the joint application of [the jury's] individual common sense and knowledge of the world to the evidence before them' (*R* v. *Adams* [1996] 2 Cr App R 467 (CA) at p. 481). That said, the cogency of certain *types* of circumstantial evidence, such as DNA and fingerprint evidence, can only properly be evaluated at a statistical level (see 11.4–5 *ante*).

15.2 The Burden of Proof in Criminal Proceedings

15.2.1 The 'Golden Thread'

The starting point for any discussion on the incidence of the legal burden of proof in criminal proceedings is the landmark case of *Woolmington* v. *DPP* [1935] AC 462 (HL). Reginald Woolmington's wife, Violet, left him to live with her mother just a couple of months after their marriage and on 10 December 1934 he cycled round to their house in an attempt to induce her to return to him. The next-door neighbour, a Mrs Smith, heard the sound of a gun at about 9.30 a.m. and, upon looking out of her front window, saw Woolmington mount his bicycle and ride away. Mrs Smith entered her neighbour's home to find Violet lying on the floor. She had been shot through the heart and was dead. A note was later found in Woolmington's coat pocket which suggested that he had intended to kill his wife and then himself. At his trial for murder, Woolmington admitted that he had cycled round to Violet's house armed with a loaded sawn-off shotgun but said that he had merely intended to frighten her into returning with him by threatening suicide and that the gun had gone off accidentally. The trial judge directed the jury, in accordance with the law as it was generally understood to be, that once it had been proved by the prosecution that Woolmington had killed his wife a presumption of murder arose and it was for him to prove that he had not intended to kill her. Woolmington was convicted of murder and appealed unsuccessfully to the Court of Criminal Appeal, and then finally to the House of Lords. The House of Lords quashed his conviction, and in a speech with which all their Lordships concurred Viscount Sankey LC said (at pp. 481–2):

'Throughout the web of the English Criminal Law one golden thread is always to be seen, that it is the duty of the prosecution to prove the prisoner's guilt subject to what I have already said as to the defence of insanity and subject also to any statutory exception ... No matter what the charge or where the trial, the principle that the prosecution must prove the guilt of the prisoner is part of the common law of England and no attempt to whittle it down can be entertained.'

The consequence is that, as a general rule, the prosecution are obliged (i) to prove that the accused committed the *actus reus* of the offence with the requisite *mens rea* and (ii) to disprove any defence (in respect of which the accused has discharged a mere evidential burden). Viscount Sankey referred to the common-law defence of insanity and certain statutory exceptions, demonstrating that while the presumption of innocence is fundamental it is *not* an absolute right immune from derogation; but such exceptions aside, the burden rests with the prosecution to disprove any defence which the judge has allowed the jury to consider, and the judge must make this clear in his summing-up. As Lord Bingham CJ stated in *R* v. *Bentley (Deceased)* [2001] 1 Cr App R 307 (CA) (at p. 326):

'The jury must be clearly and unambiguously instructed that the burden of proving the guilt of the accused lies and lies only on the Crown, that (subject to exceptions not here relevant) there is no burden on the accused to prove anything and that if, on reviewing all the evidence, the jury are unsure of or are left in any reasonable doubt as to the guilt of the accused that doubt must be resolved in favour of the accused.'

Even though the presumption of innocence is regarded as a fundamental part of the law of criminal evidence, it is a surprisingly recent development. The judge presiding over Woolmington's trial applied the law as it was understood to be in 1935 and the Court of Criminal Appeal agreed (*R* v. *Woolmington* (1935) 25 Cr App R 72 at pp. 75–9). So, although Viscount Sankey spoke of the presumption of innocence being 'part of the common law', it was actually a departure from the historical position which had required the alleged murderer to prove his killing was not murder (see *Jayasena* v. *R* [1970] 2 WLR 448 (PC) at p. 453).

The principle which underlies the 'golden thread' is the self-evident truth that people have a *right* not to be convicted of offences they have not committed. This is reflected in Article 6(2) of the European Convention on Human Rights which provides that everyone charged with a criminal offence 'shall be presumed innocent until proved guilty according to law'. The importance attached to this principle is reinforced by the very high standard of proof the prosecution must attain to secure a conviction (15.4.1 *post*), but the desirability of acquitting the innocent is not the only justification for the presumption of innocence. Other considerations, such as the dignity of the individual, and the individual's right to privacy and liberty, which may be violated as a result of any decision to prosecute, demand that prosecutions should be commenced and continued only when there is cogent evidence to justify such course of action. The point was eloquently made in the Supreme Court of Canada in *R* v. *Oakes* [1986] 1 SCR 103 (at pp. 119–20):

'The presumption of innocence is a hallowed principle lying at the very heart of criminal law. ... [It] protects the fundamental liberty and human dignity of any and every person accused by the State of criminal conduct. An individual charged with a criminal offence faces grave social and personal consequences, including potential loss of physical liberty, subjection to social stigma and ostracism from the community, as well as other social, psychological and economic harms. In light of the gravity of these consequences, the presumption of innocence is crucial. It ensures that until the State proves an accused's guilt beyond all reasonable doubt he or she is innocent. This is essential in a society committed to fairness and social justice.'

The presumption of innocence and the concomitant high standard of proof which the prosecution must satisfy act as a bulwark against unwarranted intrusions into the private life of the individual and minimise the possibility that innocent persons will be convicted. A corollary of this is that the presumption serves 'to maintain public confidence in the enduring integrity and security of the legal system' (*State* v. *Coetzee* (1997) (4) BCLR 437 (SACC) at p. 522).

The prosecution therefore have to *disprove* the defences of provocation (*Mancini* v. *DPP* [1942] AC 1 (HL)), self-defence (*R* v. *Lobell* [1957] 2 WLR 524 (CCA)), mechanical defect (*R* v. *Spurge* [1961] 3 WLR 23 (CCA)), duress (*R* v. *Gill* [1963] 1 WLR 841 (CCA)) and non-insane automatism (*Bratty* v. *Attorney-General for Northern Ireland* [1961] 3 WLR 965 (HL)) to list but some of the principal examples. However, it would be intolerable if the prosecution had to anticipate and then disprove any such defence in the absence of evidence to suggest the possibility of its being true. The accused therefore bears an evidential burden in respect of these defences, and this must be discharged for the defence to be left to the tribunal of fact as a live issue. The standard of disproof for the prosecution is 'beyond reasonable doubt' (15.4.1 *post*) so in a trial on indictment the accused's evidential burden will be discharged if the judge is of the view that there is enough evidence for the jury to be able to accept the truth of his defence as a *reasonable possibility*. If the judge accepts that the evidential burden has been discharged the jury will be directed to consider the defence and told that it is for the prosecution to disprove it beyond reasonable doubt.

It is interesting to note that the accused bears an evidential burden whether his defence is one which operates by trumping his proven *actus reus* and *mens rea*, for example the defence of duress, or is simply a denial of his having committed the *actus reus* with the requisite *mens rea*, for example the defences of self-defence and non-insane automatism. Although in principle the accused should not have to bear an evidential burden in respect of the absence of an element of the offence charged, this is overridden by the need to ensure that the prosecution are not unduly disadvantaged by having to prove what in essence (if not in theory) amounts to an affirmative defence when there is no evidence to support it. For this reason it would seem that the accused bears an evidential burden if his defence is one of accident (*Bratty* v. *Attorney-General for Northern Ireland* [1961] 3 WLR 965 (HL) at p. 975 (*obiter*)) or alibi (*R* v. *Johnson* [1961] 1 WLR 1478 (CCA) at p. 1479 (*obiter*)), although this would be more acceptable in relation to the latter defence than the former as an averment of alibi entails something more than a mere denial of presence. In any event the prosecution are obliged to prove the falsity of the defences of alibi (*R* v. *Helliwell* [1995] Crim LR 79 (CA)) and accident (*Woolmington* v. *DPP* [1935] AC 462 (HL)). Similarly, while the accused bears an evidential burden on the defence of consent to a charge of indecent assault, it is for the prosecution to disprove the defence (*R* v. *May* [1912] 3 KB 572 (CCA), *R* v. *Donovan* [1934] 2 KB 498 (CCA)).

The absence of consent forms part of the statutory definition of the *actus reus* of rape (s. 1(2)(*a*) of the Sexual Offences Act 1956) and, according to the majority of the House of Lords in *DPP* v. *Morgan* [1975] 2 WLR 913, the prosecution bear both the evidential burden and the legal burden of proof on that issue. It is also implicit in their Lordships' speeches that the accused bears no more than a tactical burden in relation to the 'defence' that he mistakenly believed the complainant was consenting. However, this is subject to the principle that the jury should not be subjected to unnecessary and irrelevant directions, so if there is no evidence to suggest the possibility that the accused was mistaken there is no requirement that the judge should direct the jury to consider the question (*R* v. *Adkins* [2000] 2 All ER 185 (CA)). In effect, then, the accused bears an evidential burden to make the question of mistaken belief a live issue for the jury to consider. Similarly, if the offence charged is one which requires proof that the accused intended a particular consequence, and his defence is that he was so drunk that he did not have that specific intent, he will have to discharge an evidential burden in relation to that issue (*R* v. *McKnight* (2000) *The Times* 5.5.00 (CA)).

15.2.2 Proving Innocence – Insanity and Reverse Onus Provisions

In *Woolmington* v. *DPP* [1935] AC 462 (HL) Viscount Sankey recognised that while the legal burden of proof generally lies with the prosecution there was the one common-law exception of insanity and a number of statutory exceptions to this rule. In all cases where the accused bears the legal burden of proof on an issue the standard which has to be met is proof on the 'balance of probabilities' (15.4.1 *post*). An obligation to prove a defence also entails an obligation to discharge an evidential burden in relation to it (*R* v. *Windle* [1952] 2 QB 826 (CCA) at p. 831). For an evidential burden of this sort to be discharged, the judge must be of the view that there is enough evidence in support of the defence for a properly directed jury to be able to conclude (at the end of the trial) that the issue has been proved to the requisite standard.

15.2.2.1 Article 6(2) of the European Convention

By imposing a burden of proof on the accused in respect of a defence he wishes to rely on, and obliging him to prove that defence on the balance of probabilities, the jury may convict him even though they feel there is a reasonable doubt as to his guilt. That is, the jury may accept that it is reasonably possible (but not probable) that his defence is true and that he is not guilty. Moreover, as there is no logical distinction between the definitional elements of a statutory offence and any linked statutory defence the so-called defence may in fact oblige the accused to *disprove his presumed moral culpability*, the 'gravamen' of the offence. As Lord Steyn recently noted: 'there are ... cases where the defence is so closely linked with *mens rea* and moral blameworthiness that it would derogate from the presumption [of innocence] to transfer the legal burden to the accused' (*R* v. *Lambert* [2001] 3 WLR 206 (HL) at p. 220).

Consider, for instance, ss. 5(3) and 28(3) of the Misuse of Drugs Act 1971. Section 5(3) provides that, subject to s. 28, it is an offence for a person to have a controlled drug in his possession with the intent to supply it to another. Section 28(3) provides a defence if the accused 'proves that he neither believed nor suspected nor had reason to suspect that the substance or product in question was a controlled drug' (see s. 28(3)(*b*)(i)). The traditional interpretation of these provisions was that the prosecution had only to prove that the accused had possession of an item, in the sense that he had control over it and knew of its existence, and that that item was in fact a controlled drug. There was no obligation on the prosecution to prove that the accused *knew* the item was a controlled drug, for s. 28(3) raised a rebuttable presumption of knowledge – once the prosecution had proved those two facts beyond reasonable doubt it was for the accused to prove on the balance of probabilities that he neither believed nor suspected nor had reason to suspect that the item was a controlled drug (*R* v. *McNamara* (1988) 87 Cr App R 246 (CA)). The effect of the provisions was to give rise to a presumption that the accused had the requisite culpable state of mind and oblige him to rebut that presumption – in effect to place on the accused an obligation to prove the absence of *mens rea*, albeit framed as a defence. Thus, if the accused picked up a bag from one acquaintance to be delivered to another, and the bag contained an item which the accused believed to be pornography, and the police searched the bag and found that the item was a controlled drug, it would be for the accused to prove (on the balance of probabilities) that he had no reason to suspect that the item was a controlled drug; and if the jury accepted that it was reasonably possible that this was the case (that is, they accepted there was a reasonable doubt as to whether he had the requisite culpable state of mind), but were not satisfied that his defence was more likely than not to be true, he would be convicted of the very serious s. 5(3) offence. A separate provision in s. 28 raises a similar rebuttable presumption of knowledge by providing that 'it shall be a defence for the accused to prove that he neither knew of nor suspected nor had reason to suspect the existence of some fact alleged by the prosecution which it is necessary for the prosecution to prove if he is to be convicted' (s. 28(2)), and the traditional view has been that this too places a legal burden on the accused (see *R* v. *Champ* (1981) 73 Cr App R 367 (CA)). This would provide the accused with a defence in the sort of situation where he is found to have a controlled drug in the bag in his possession, raising the presumption that the accused was (knowingly) in possession of its contents, his defence being that he neither knew nor suspected nor had reason to suspect that that item was in his bag. (In *Salmon* v. *HM Advocate* (1999) JC 67 (HCJ) (at pp. 73–4) it is suggested that s. 28(3) applies only to the situation where the accused knows he has a substance such as powder or pills in his possession and his defence is that he was ignorant of the nature of that substance as a controlled drug.)

A factual scenario of this type, albeit one in which the accused asserted that he believed his bag contained 'scrap jewellery', arose in the case of *R* v. *Lambert* [2001] 3 WLR 206 (HL) where the accused was convicted of possessing two kilograms of cocaine with intent to supply, for which he received a sentence of seven years' imprisonment. He appealed to the Court of Appeal (*R* v. *Lambert* [2001] 2 WLR 211) and then to the House of Lords on the ground that the onus he bore to prove his non-culpable state of mind on the balance of probabilities for the purposes of s. 28(2)–(3) conflicted with the presumption of innocence. The appeal was dismissed by the House of Lords because his trial had taken place before the Human Rights Act 1998 came into force, and the Act did not apply retrospectively. Nevertheless, their Lordships took the opportunity to express their (*obiter*) views on his ground of appeal.

The question for the House of Lords was whether the defences in s. 28(2)–(3) of the 1971 Act, given their ordinary meaning (that is, without recourse to s. 3(1) of the Human Rights Act 1998) were compatible with Article 6(2), given that the right protected is not absolute and not every reverse onus provision will be incompatible with the Convention. The European Court of Human Rights has accepted that reverse onus provisions (and for that matter strict liability offences) can be reconciled with Article 6(2) so long as they are confined 'within reasonable limits which take into account the importance of what is at stake and maintain the rights of the defence' (*Salabiaku* v. *France* (1988) 13 EHRR 379 at p. 388, *Hoang* v. *France* (1992) 16 EHRR 53 at p. 78). Accordingly, whether a reverse onus provision breaches the Convention depends on whether the modification or limitation of the right protected by Article 6(2) pursues a legitimate aim and satisfies the principle of proportionality. As Lord Hope said (at p. 237):

'It is now well settled that the principle which is to be applied requires a balance to be struck between the general interest of the community and the protection of the fundamental rights of the individual. This will not be achieved if the reverse onus provision goes beyond what is necessary to accomplish the objective of the statute.'

Thus, the mere fact that a provision places the legal burden of proof on the accused in respect of a particular issue, and may therefore result in his being convicted where there is a reasonable doubt as to his guilt, does *not* of itself determine the question of compatibility. It is first necessary to determine whether the interference with the presumption of innocence is directed towards a legitimate public objective: 'What is the nature of the threat faced by society which the provision is designed to combat?' (*R* v. *DPP ex parte Kebilene* [1999] 3 WLR 972 (HL) at pp. 998–9). Further, a degree of deference will be paid to the view of Parliament as to what is in the interest of the public generally; as Lord Hope explained in *R* v. *DPP ex parte Kebilene* (at p. 994): '[i]n some circumstances it will be appropriate for the courts to recognise that there is an area of judgment within which the judiciary will defer, on democratic grounds, to the considered opinion of the elected body'. If the reverse onus provision *is* directed at a legitimate objective, it is then necessary to consider the issue of proportionality, that is, whether the provision is a reasonable measure to take to achieve that legitimate objective, a measure which does not go beyond what is strictly necessary to accomplish it. Relevant factors include, first, what it is that the prosecution have to prove for the presumption to arise and, second, the nature of the burden on the accused: 'does it relate to something which is likely to be difficult for him to prove, or does it relate to something which is likely to be within his knowledge or ... to which he readily has access?' (*R* v. *DPP ex parte Kebilene* at p. 998). However, in the absence of exceptional circumstances it is doubtful that much weight will be attached to the 'within his knowledge' criterion where the offence is serious, as it would justify placing an obligation on the accused to prove anything which only he could be aware of (such as whether or not he had the requisite *mens rea* for murder). A third factor is whether the legitimate objective could just as effectively be achieved by placing on the accused nothing more than an *evidential* burden (which would be far less likely to lead to a contravention of Article 6(2)). If, for instance, the legal burden has been placed on the accused to prevent an unmeritorious defence being raised frivolously, and an evidential burden would serve just as well, the imposition of the legal burden would go beyond what is strictly necessary to achieve the legitimate objective.

This approach to the question of compatibility is evident in the way the Privy Council determined whether two reverse onus provisions were compatible with the presumption of innocence enshrined in Article 11(1) of Hong Kong's Bill of Rights in *Attorney-General of Hong Kong* v. *Lee Kwong-Kut* [1993] 3 WLR 329. Lord Woolf said (at p. 341):

'This implicit flexibility allows a balance to be drawn between the interest of the person charged and the state. There are situations where it is clearly sensible and reasonable that deviations should be allowed from the strict applications of the principle that the prosecution must prove the defendant's guilt beyond reasonable doubt ... Some exceptions will be justifiable, others will not. Whether they are justifiable will in the end depend upon whether it remains primarily the responsibility of the prosecution to prove the guilt of an accused to the required standard and whether the exception is reasonably imposed

... If the prosecution retains responsibility for proving the essential ingredients of the offence, the less likely it is that an exception will be regarded as unacceptable. In deciding what are the essential ingredients, the language of the relevant statutory provision will be important. However, what will be decisive will be the substance and reality of the language creating the offence rather than its form.'

Applying this test, the Privy Council held that a provision obliging the accused to prove that money found in his possession had not been stolen or obtained unlawfully was inconsistent with the presumption of innocence, as the accused bore the legal burden of proof in respect of the most significant element in the definition of the offence, the onus on the prosecution being limited to the 'formality' of proving possession and certain facts from which a reasonable suspicion could be inferred that the property had been unlawfully obtained. The second provision was upheld, however. The prosecution had to prove, first, that the accused was involved in a transaction involving another person's proceeds of drug trafficking and, second, that the accused knew or had reasonable grounds to believe that the other person carried on or had carried on (or had benefited from) drug trafficking. Only then was the accused obliged to prove that he had not known or suspected that the involvement in question related to any person's proceeds of drug trafficking, a 'manifestly reasonable' provision in the view of the Privy Council given the context of the war against drug trafficking and the difficulty the prosecution would face if they had to prove the accused had taken steps necessary to ensure that he did not have the relevant knowledge or suspicion.

Two aspects of the approach adopted in *Attorney-General of Hong Kong* v. *Lee Kwong-Kut* require further consideration. First, the Privy Council referred to 'the substance and reality of the language creating the offence rather than its form', making the important point that a reverse onus provision may be the gravamen of the offence, the very issue which determines moral blameworthiness. Lord Steyn made the same point in *R* v. *Lambert* [2001] 3 WLR 206 (HL) (at pp. 219–20) when he said that the 'distinction between constituent elements of the crime and defensive issues will sometimes be unprincipled and arbitrary' and that it was 'sometimes simply a matter of which drafting technique is adopted: a true constituent element can be removed from the definition of the crime and cast as a defensive issue'. The second point is that the Privy Council accepted that the 'war against drug trafficking' was a legitimate public objective, which might suggest that the serious nature of the criminal activity is a relevant consideration when determining where the balance is to be drawn (see also *R* v. *Lambert* [2001] 2 WLR 211 (CA) at p. 221). However, as noted by Lord Steyn in *R* v. *Lambert* (HL) (at p. 218), repeating the dictum of Sachs J in *State* v. *Coetzee* (1997) (4) BCLR 437 (SACC) (at p. 522): 'the more serious the crime and the greater the public interest in securing convictions of the guilty, the more important do constitutional protections of the accused become'. The general interest of the community in suppressing crime *is* relevant, but it 'will not justify a state in riding roughshod over the rights of a criminal defendant' (*McIntosh* v. *Lord Advocate* [2001] 3 WLR 107 (PC) at p. 119).

The House of Lords in *R* v. *Lambert* recognised that it was clearly in the public interest to discourage the 'grave social evil' of trafficking in drugs and that there were sound practical reasons for the reverse onus provisions in s. 28 of the Misuse of Drugs Act 1971. However, the majority view was that the imposition of the legal burden of proof on the accused by those provisions could not be justified as a proportionate measure given the gravity of the consequences which would follow a conviction (with a sentence of life imprisonment in the most serious cases), the rights of the accused and the express recognition in the 1971 Act that it was wrong to penalise an individual who neither believed nor suspected nor had reason to suspect that the item in his possession was a controlled drug (s. 28(3)) or who neither knew of nor suspected nor had reason to suspect the existence of some essential fact alleged by the prosecution (s. 28(2)). The reverse onus could therefore result in a lengthy custodial sentence when there was a reasonable doubt as to whether the accused had the specified culpable state of mind, and 'if any error is to be made in the weighing of the scales of justice it should be to the effect that the guilty should go free rather than that an innocent person should be wrongly convicted' (*per* Lord Clyde at p. 258). According to Lords Slynn, Steyn, Hope and Clyde, the words 'if he proves' in s. 28(3)(*b*)(i), and the words 'for the accused to prove' in the defence provided by s. 28(2), in effect obliging the accused to prove absence of *mens rea*, would be incompatible with Article 6(2) unless 'read down' by virtue of s. 3(1) of the Human Rights Act 1998 to impose on the accused no more than an evidential burden, with the prosecution being obliged to prove the accused's culpable state of mind beyond reasonable doubt. Only Lord Hutton felt that the reverse onus provisions in question were a proportionate measure striking a fair balance between the general interest of the community and the personal rights of the individual, the threat to society being sufficiently grave and the difficulty of proving the accused's state of mind sufficiently great to justify a rebuttable presumption of *mens rea* for persons found to be in possession of drugs. His Lordship suggested that the imposition of a mere evidential burden would not be adequate to deal with the problem with which the reverse onus provisions were intended to deal, such as where it is proved that the accused was in possession of a bag containing a controlled drug and he says that he thought the bag contained a video, as it would be very difficult for the prosecution to disprove a defence of this sort beyond a reasonable doubt.

Any express (or implied) reverse onus provision may now be challenged on the ground that it is incompatible with the European Convention. This does not mean that every such provision *will* be held to be incompatible with Article 6(2), of course, for there can be little doubt that exceptions which impose an obligation in relation to regulatory offences of a relatively trivial or quasi-criminal nature, where the accused may be obliged to do nothing more than present evidence that he is licensed to do a particular activity, will be considered reasonable infringements of the presumption of innocence. But there are many reverse onus provisions which are not so trivial, which in effect place on the accused the burden of proving that he was not *morally* culpable at the time the offence was allegedly committed. These are all now open to challenge, and there will be a considerable degree of uncertainty in the law until each and every such provision has been adjudicated upon. It is also quite clear that different judges will have very different opinions on how the balance between the interests of the community and the protection of the rights of the individual should be struck, as starkly demonstrated by the differences of opinion in the Court of Appeal and House of Lords in *R* v. *Lambert*. Indeed, in *Sheldrake* v. *DPP* [2003] 2 WLR 1629 the original two-judge Divisional Court could not agree on the approach to be taken with s. 5(2) of the Road Traffic Act 1988 and the matter had to be reheard by a differently constituted three-judge Court, which was also divided.

Needless to say, it has since been held by the Court of Appeal that the defences in s. 28(2)–(3) of the Misuse of Drugs Act 1971 place only an evidential burden on the accused (*R* v. *Lang* [2002] EWCA Crim 298, *R* v. *Carrera* [2002] EWCA Crim 2527). The same conclusion was reached in *R* v. *Carass* [2002] 2 Cr App R 77 (CA) in respect of s. 206(4) of the Insolvency Act 1986, which provides a defence to a charge under s. 206(1)(*a*) if the accused can 'prove that he had no intent to defraud', the Court of Appeal being of the view that there was insufficient justification in the ease-of-proof argument for imposing the legal burden on the accused in relation to what was clearly 'an important element of the offence' (see also *R* v. *Daniel* [2003] 1 Cr App R 99 (CA)). Similarly, in *Sheldrake* v. *DPP* [2003] 2 WLR 1629 the Divisional Court held that s. 5(2) of the Road Traffic Act 1988, which had hitherto placed the legal burden on the accused to prove 'no likelihood of his driving' if the accused had been found drunk in charge of a motor vehicle (for the purposes of the s. 5(1)(*b*) offence) should be read down to impose no more than an evidential burden.

However, in *L* v. *DPP* [2002] 3 WLR 863 the Divisional Court upheld the reverse onus in s. 139(4) of the Criminal Justice Act 1988, which obliges the accused 'to prove that he had a good reason or lawful authority' as a defence to a charge of having a bladed article in his possession in a public place, contrary to s. 139(1) of the Act. In reaching its conclusion, and distinguishing the provisions considered by the House of Lords in *R* v. *Lambert*, it was noted that the prosecution had to prove possession, including knowledge on the part of the accused that he had the relevant article; that there was a strong public interest in bladed articles not being carried in public without good reason; that the accused was obliged to prove something within his own knowledge; and that respect should be given to the way in which Parliament had sought to strike the right balance between the demands of the community and the protection of the rights of the individual. *L* v. *DPP* was followed in *R* v. *Matthews* [2003] 3 WLR 693, in respect of s. 139(4) and (5) of the 1988 Act, where the Court of Appeal opined that the two subsections 'strike a fair balance between the general interest of the community in the realisation of a legitimate legislative aim and the protection of the fundamental rights of the individual and go no further than is necessary to accomplish Parliament's objective in protecting the public from the menace posed by persons having bladed articles in public places without good reason'. In *R* v. *Ali*, *R* v. *Jordan* [2001] 2 WLR 211 (CA) it was held that s. 2(2) of the Homicide Act 1957 continues to place the legal burden on the accused to prove diminished responsibility on the ground that it is a defence unconnected to the elements of murder which is of benefit to those who are in a position to take advantage of it, and which would be difficult for the prosecution to disprove if the accused was unwilling to be examined by a doctor. Furthermore, the reverse onus in s. 15(3) of the Road Traffic Act 1988 (the so-called 'hip-flask defence' to drink-driving) was upheld in *R* v. *Drummond* [2002] 2 Cr App R 352 (CA); the reverse onus in s. 92(5) of the Trade Marks Act 1994 (reasonable grounds for believing there was no trade mark infringement) was upheld in *R* v. *S* [2003] 1 Cr App R 602 (CA) and *R* v. *Johnstone* [2003] 1 WLR 1736 (HL); the reverse onus in s. 40 of the Health and Safety at Work Act 1974 was upheld in *R* v. *Davies* [2002] EWCA Crim 2949; and the reverse onus in s. 11(2) of the Terrorism Act 2000 (a defence to the s. 11(1) offence of belonging to a proscribed organisation) was upheld in *Attorney-General's Reference (No. 4 of 2002)* [2003] 2 Cr App R 346 (CA).

Now that the Human Rights Act 1998 is in force, Parliament has begun to introduce statutory defences which, though framed in terms which suggest that the accused bears the legal burden of proof, must, by virtue of an express provision, be interpreted to place on the accused no more than an evidential burden. The Terrorism Act 2000 contains a number of express defences which the accused is obliged to 'prove', but by virtue of s. 118(1)–(2) the accused has to discharge no more than an evidential burden if the defence is included in s. 118(5). There are, however, other defences in the Act, such as s. 11(2) (above), which do not benefit from s. 118, and which the accused *is* obliged to prove on the balance of probabilities, subject of course to any contrary view the courts may have on the matter.

Section 57(2) of the Terrorism Act 2000 deserves special mention because its predecessor, a reverse onus provision in s. 16A(3) of the Prevention of Terrorism (Temporary Provisions) Act 1989 (now repealed), was the subject of some scrutiny in the Divisional Court and House of Lords just before the Human Rights Act 1998 came into force (*R* v. *DPP ex parte Kebilene* [1999] 3 WLR 175 (DC), [1999] 3 WLR 972 (HL)). The Divisional Court was of the view that, by placing the legal burden of proof on the accused, ss. 16A(3) and 16B(1) undermined the presumption of innocence 'in a blatant and obvious way'. The House of Lords, though reversing the decision of the Divisional Court on an unrelated issue, expressed its own opinions on s. 16A(3). Lords Slynn, Steyn, Hobhouse and Hope each felt that the issue of incompatibility remained arguable, Lords Hope and Hobhouse making the point that the Divisional Court had considered only *prima facie* incompatibility and not gone on to address the necessary balancing exercise. Lord Cooke was minded to agree with the Divisional Court's view, but felt that it might be permissible to infringe Article 6(2) in the particular context of the threat posed to society by terrorism, a view which Lord Hope seemed to support when pointing out that in *Murray* v. *United Kingdom* (1994) 19 EHRR 193 (at p. 222) the European Court of Human Rights expressly recognised that 'due account will be taken of the special nature of terrorist crime, the threat which it poses to democratic society and the exigencies of dealing with it'. Clearly concerned by the possibility of a successful argument on incompatibility, Parliament decided to include s. 57(2) of the Terrorism Act 2000 within s. 118(5) and, accordingly, the accused now bears only an evidential burden in relation to that defence.

Whether terrorism is to be regarded as an exceptional category of crime remains to be seen but, if so, it might be justified on the ground that crimes of this sort threaten the very fabric of the free and democratic societies in which human rights are valued and upheld. The argument would be that a certain reduction in these freedoms is necessary to save liberties and democracy at a more general level.

15.2.2.2 Insanity

As the law stands, if the accused wishes to rely on the common-law defence of insanity he bears the legal burden of proving it (*R* v. *Smith* (1910) 6 Cr App R 19 (CCA)) and, of course, the evidential burden too (*R* v. *Windle* [1952] 2 QB 826 (CCA) at p. 831). By virtue of ss. 1(1) and 6(1) of the Criminal Procedure (Insanity and Unfitness to Plead) Act 1991, for the evidential (and legal) burden to be discharged there must be expert opinion evidence in support of the defence from two or more registered medical practitioners (at least one of whom must be 'duly approved' as having special experience in the diagnosis or treatment of mental disorder).

The incidence of the burden of proof for insanity dates back to the *M'Naghten* Rules of 1843 (*M'Naghten's Case* (1843) 10 Cl & F 200 at p. 210) and was so clearly established as part of the common law that the House of Lords in *Woolmington* v. *DPP* [1935] AC 462 was clearly not prepared to overturn it. Although there is no generally accepted rationale for this reverse burden it would appear to be a policy-driven decision predicated on the desirability of convicting persons who have committed serious offences. No doubt an apprehension that the defence might easily be faked (and be difficult for the prosecution to disprove), a distrust of psychiatric evidence (or the jury's ability to assess it), and an awareness that the vast majority of individuals who stand trial are sane, have to some extent contributed to the retention of this rebuttable 'presumption of sanity'. The consequence is of course that, contrary to principle, 'a verdict of guilty [can] be properly returned if the jury entertain a reasonable doubt as to the existence of a fact which is essential to guilt, namely, the capacity in law of the accused to commit that crime' (*Davis* v. *United States* (1895) 160 US 469 (USSC) at p. 488).

The insanity exception was recently considered by the Supreme Court of

Canada in *R* v. *Chaulk* [1990] 3 SCR 1303. (The Canadian two-stage test means that the question of proportionality is considered only after an infringement of the presumption of innocence has been identified, a strict approach being adopted in relation to the preliminary issue.) The majority view was that the reverse onus insanity provision in the Criminal Code violated the presumption of innocence guaranteed by s. 11(*d*) of the Canadian Charter of Rights and Freedoms (as it permitted a conviction notwithstanding a reasonable doubt in the mind of the tribunal of fact as to the accused's guilt) but that it was nonetheless a reasonable and proportionate limitation given the desirability of convicting sane offenders and the 'impossibly onerous burden' which the prosecution would bear if sanity had to be proved beyond reasonable doubt once the accused had discharged a mere evidential burden. An alternative view was adopted by Wilson J who, having agreed with the majority that the reverse onus provision violated the presumption of innocence, felt that the requirement of proving insanity on the balance of probabilities could not be justified – an evidential burden would suffice, in line with the position adopted by the United States Supreme Court in *Davis* v. *United States* (1895) 160 US 469, on the ground that the prosecution would have to do no more than address the doubt engendered by the accused's evidence, and there was nothing to suggest that this had placed an unduly onerous burden on the prosecution in the US federal courts and the State jurisdictions which had adopted this approach. A third view was that the reverse onus provision did not contravene the presumption of innocence at all. Insanity could not properly be regarded as a 'true' defence as it resulted in no more than a formal acquittal, followed by the imposition of alternative coercive measures (namely, detention and treatment). In other words, the prosecution were still obliged to prove all the elements of the offence and disprove any 'true' defence raised on the evidence, so there was no violation of s. 11(*d*) of the Charter.

In *Attorney-General of Hong Kong* v. *Lee Kwong-Kut* [1993] 3 WLR 329 (at p. 341) the Privy Council, comprising five Law Lords, inclined towards the majority view in *Chaulk* v. *R* as 'common sense'. The European Commission of Human Rights considered the question in *H* v. *United Kingdom* (1990) Application 15023/89, and in dismissing the applicant's submission that the insanity exception contravened Article 6(2) as manifestly ill-founded, formed the view that the rule did 'not concern the presumption of innocence, as such, but the presumption of sanity' and that it could not be said to be unreasonable or arbitrary. Lord Hope would appear to have been reflecting this view when suggesting that the presumption was 'one of sanity, not responsibility' and that it was for the prosecution to prove *mens rea* (*R* v. *DPP ex parte Kebilene* [1999] 3 WLR 972 (HL) at p. 991). However, as *Smith & Hogan, Criminal Law* (10th edn, 2002, pp. 226–7) points out, if the accused relies on the *first* limb of the test in the *M'Naghten* Rules (that is, that he did not know the nature and quality of his act) he is in effect obliged to prove absence of *mens rea*, and if he is to bear the legal burden of proof on that issue a different rationale must be found.

If the accused raises the defence of diminished responsibility to a charge of murder, the prosecution may counter by alleging that he was insane, in which case the burden of proving insanity rests with them (see s. 6 of the Criminal Procedure (Insanity) Act 1964).

15.2.2.3   Express Statutory Exceptions

It has been seen that statutory offences may expressly provide the accused with an exception which he must prove on the balance of probabilities, subject of course to any such provision being read down under s. 3(1) of the Human Rights Act 1998 so as to place no more than an evidential burden on him. The following examples illustrate the different types of formula used by Parliament. 'Any person who without lawful authority or reasonable excuse, *the proof whereof shall lie on him*, has with him in any public place any offensive weapon shall be guilty of an offence' (s. 1(1) of the Prevention of Crime Act 1953; see also s. 139(4) of the Criminal Justice Act 1988). 'In any proceedings for an offence under this Act it shall ... be a *defence for the person charged to prove* ...' (s. 24(1) of the Trade Descriptions Act 1968). 'On a charge of murder, it shall be *for the defence to prove* that the person charged is by virtue of this section not liable to be convicted of murder' (s. 2(2) of the Homicide Act 1957: diminished responsibility). 'Where in any of the foregoing sections the description of an offence is expressed to be subject to exceptions mentioned in the section, *proof of the exception is to lie on the person relying on it*' (s. 47 of the Sexual Offences Act 1956). 'Where in any proceedings against a person for an offence ... it is proved that any money, gift or other consideration has been paid or given to or received by a person in the employment of His Majesty or any Government Department or a public body by or from a person, or agent of a person, holding or seeking to obtain a contract ... the money, gift or consideration shall be deemed to have been paid or given and received corruptly ... *unless the contrary is proved*' (s. 2 of the Prevention of Corruption Act 1916).

Until the Human Rights Act 1998 was passed, the courts consistently held that exceptions to statutory offences which expressly impose a requirement of proof on the accused place a *legal* burden upon him. Thus, in *R* v. *Hunt* [1986] 3 WLR 1115 (HL) Lord Ackner said (at p. 1137): 'It is accepted that when Parliament by express words provides that the proof of the excuse shall lie upon the accused, the legal burden of proof ... is placed upon the defendant, and that is discharged on the balance of probabilities'. This is now true only of such provisions which (i) are not subject to an express interpretation clause placing a mere evidential burden on the accused (such as s. 118(2) of the Terrorism Act 2000) *and* (ii) have been (or will be) upheld by the courts.

As the law stands, the accused bears the legal burden of proof in respect of, *inter alia*, diminished responsibility (*R* v. *Dunbar* [1957] 3 WLR 330 (CCA), *R* v. *Ali, R* v. *Jordan* [2001] 2 WLR 211 (CA)); lawful authority or reasonable excuse for s. 1(1) of the Prevention of Crime Act 1953 (*R* v. *Brown* (1971) 55 Cr App R 478 (CA)); that money (etc.) was not paid or given and received corruptly for s. 2 of the Prevention of Corruption Act

1916 (*R* v. *Braithwaite* [1983] 1 WLR 385 (CA)); good reason or lawful authority for s. 139(4) of the Criminal Justice Act 1988 (*L* v. *DPP* [2002] 3 WLR 863 (DC)); the 'hip-flask defence' in s. 15(3) of the Road Traffic Act 1988 (*R* v. *Drummond* [2002] 2 Cr App R 352 (CA)); the defence to trade mark infringement in s. 92(5) of the Trade Marks Act 1994 (*R* v. *S* [2003] 1 Cr App R 602 (CA)); the defence of 'not reasonably practicable' in s. 40 of the Health and Safety at Work Act 1974 (*R* v. *Davies* [2002] EWCA Crim 2949); and the defence of marital coercion in s. 47 of the Criminal Justice Act 1925 (*R* v. *Cairns* [2003] 1 Cr App R 662 (CA)).

15.2.2.4 Implied Statutory Exceptions

Since 1848 there has been a provision which, while not expressly placing any specific legal burden on the accused, provides that where the accused in summary proceedings wishes to rely on an exception to a statutory offence he bears the burden of proving it. The present incarnation of this provision is now found in s. 101 of the Magistrates' Courts Act 1980:

> Where the defendant to an information or complaint relies for his defence on any exception, exemption, proviso, excuse or qualification, whether or not it accompanies the description of the offence or matter of complaint in the enactment creating the offence or on which the complaint is founded, the burden of proving the exception, exemption, proviso, excuse or qualification shall be on him ...

This provision was originally enacted as s. 14 of the Summary Jurisdiction Act 1848. It was subsequently amended and re-enacted as s. 39(2) of the Summary Jurisdiction Act 1879, and then as s. 81 of the Magistrates' Courts Act 1952. Viscount Sankey therefore almost certainly had the provision in mind when referring to 'any statutory exception' in *Woolmington* v. *DPP* [1935] AC 462 (HL) (15.2.1 *ante*). Thus, subject to any ruling on incompatibility with Article 6(2) of the European Convention, s. 101 of the Magistrates' Courts Act 1980 places the legal burden on the accused to *prove* any 'exception' to the statutory offence he has been charged with in a magistrates' court. This was the view taken in *Gatland* v. *Metropolitan Police Commissioner* [1968] 2 WLR 1263 where the accused faced a charge under s. 140(1) of the Highways Act 1959 arising out of his having deposited a builders' skip on a road in Croydon. Section 140(1) provided that it was an offence if a person 'without lawful authority or excuse, deposits any thing whatsoever on a highway'. The Divisional Court, applying s. 81 of the Magistrates' Courts Act 1952, held that it was for the accused to prove 'lawful authority or excuse' (see also *Baker* v. *Sweet* [1966] Crim LR 51 (DC) and *Guyll* v. *Bright* (1986) 84 Cr App R 260 (DC)).

If s. 101 were uniformly applied, so as to place the legal burden of proof on the accused in respect of any expressly stated exception to a summary offence, it could be justified, albeit with reservations. Statutory summary offences which are qualified by an express proviso or exception tend to be relatively minor and regulatory rather than truly criminal. Indeed, given the large number of summary offences of strict liability, statutory offences qualified by an exception, which at least give the accused a chance of avoiding criminal liability, could be seen as something of a concession to the defence. The problem with s. 101 is that it has not been applied consistently by the courts, resulting in considerable uncertainty in the law, and its scope has (in effect) been extended to cover offences which are triable on indictment (although this latter problem may be of no more than historical interest now that the Human Rights Act 1998 is in force).

The first comment to make about s. 101, then, is not so much a criticism of the provision itself but of the way in which it has, or has not, been applied. There has been little consistency in the approach adopted by the Divisional Court, with the legal burden being placed on the accused in respect of some excuses and on the prosecution in respect of others. Thus, unless a particular provision has already been interpreted by the Divisional Court the accused will not know in advance of his trial whether or not he will be obliged to prove his defence. Take, for instance, the case of *Nagy* v. *Weston* [1965] 1 All ER 78. The accused faced a charge under s. 121(1) of the Highways Act 1959 which provided that it was an offence if a person 'without lawful authority or excuse, in any way wilfully obstructs the free passage along a highway'. The offence was qualified with an exception, and its similarities with s. 140(1) are obvious, yet the Divisional Court failed to mention s. 81 of the Magistrates' Courts Act 1952 and held that it was for the prosecution to prove that there was no lawful authority and that the accused's use of the highway was unreasonable (that is, that he had no excuse). Even if this was an oversight on the part of the Divisional Court, the decision was applied in *Hirst* v. *Chief Constable of West Yorkshire* (1986) 85 Cr App R 143 (DC) to the identical provision now found in s. 137(1) of the Highways Act 1980. In this latter case, which concerned the reasonableness of a protest by animal rights supporters outside a furrier's shop, Otton J recognised the constitutional importance of the right to protest on issues of public concern. However, as s. 101 of the Magistrates' Courts Act was not mentioned in the judgment it is unclear whether it was deliberately ignored, because of the importance attached to freedom of speech, or simply overlooked. In any event, whatever the justification for the interpretation of what is now s. 137(1) of the Highways Act 1980, s. 101 has also been ignored or overlooked in a variety of other contexts. It is an offence under s. 7(6) of the Road Traffic Act 1988 to fail 'without reasonable excuse' to provide a specimen of breath, blood or urine for analysis; yet it has been held that once the accused has discharged a mere evidential burden the prosecution must disprove the defence (*DPP* v. *Ambrose* [1992] RTR 285 (DC)). Similarly, an offence under s. 1(1) of the Criminal Damage Act 1971 is not committed if the accused acted with 'lawful excuse', two examples of which are set out in s. 5(2); however, in *Jaggard* v. *Dickinson* [1981] 2 WLR 118 the Divisional Court held that it was for the prosecution to disprove a statutory lawful excuse.

Section 101 applies only to offences tried in magistrates' courts, with the common-law position governing trials on indictment. This means that if the accused is charged with an offence which is triable either way, and there is an exception he may be able to rely on, he will bear the legal burden of proof on that issue in the magistrates' court (subject to the provision actually being applied) but will bear only an evidential burden in the Crown Court unless there is an equivalent common-law exception. Until 1974 there was considerable authority, dating back to the case of *R* v. *Turner* (1816) 5 M & S 206 (KBD), for the view that statutory provisions were to be interpreted so as to place the legal burden of proof on the accused where he sought to rely on facts peculiarly within his own knowledge in cases where the prosecution alleged that the accused was not qualified to do (or possess) what he had done (or had in his possession). So, for example, in *R* v. *Scott* (1921) 86 JP 69 it was held by Swift J at first instance that the accused had to prove he was licensed to supply cocaine; in *R* v. *Oliver* [1944] 1 KB 68 (CCA) the accused had to prove that he had the requisite war-time licence to supply sugar; and in *R* v. *Ewens* [1966] 2 WLR 1372 (CCA) the accused had to prove he had been issued a valid prescription for the drinnamyl tablets found in his possession. The same approach to the interpretation of statutory offences was also adopted in summary proceedings: in *John* v. *Humphreys* [1955] 1 WLR 325 (DC) the accused charged with driving without a licence had to prove he had a current driving licence, and in *Philcox* v. *Carberry* [1960] Crim LR 563 (DC) the accused charged with driving without insurance had to prove he was covered by an appropriate policy. In neither case was s. 81 of the Magistrates' Courts Act 1952 applied.

In *R* v. *Edwards* [1974] 3 WLR 285 the accused faced a charge of selling intoxicating liquor without a justices' licence contrary to s. 160(1)(*a*) of the Licensing Act 1964. At his trial (on indictment) he failed to show he had a licence and was convicted. He appealed on the ground that it had been for the prosecution to prove he did not have a licence as the prosecution's access to the register of licences meant it was not a fact peculiarly within his own knowledge. The Court of Appeal dismissed his appeal and held that as the provision first enacted as s. 14 of the Summary Jurisdiction Act 1848 had then reflected the common law, so s. 81 of the Magistrates' Courts Act 1952 represented the common law as it stood in 1974. Giving the judgment of the Court, Lawton LJ said (at pp. 295–6):

'In our judgment ... the common law, as a result of experience and the need to ensure that justice is done both to the community and to defendants, has evolved an exception to the fundamental rule of our criminal law that the prosecution must prove every element of the offence charged ... It is limited to offences arising under enactments which prohibit the doing of an act save in specified circumstances or by persons of specified classes or with specified qualifications or with the licence or permission of specified authorities. Whenever the prosecution seeks to rely on this exception, the court must construe the enactment under which the charge is laid. If the true construction is that the enactment prohibits the doing of acts, subject to provisos, exemptions and the like, then the prosecution can rely upon the exception. In our judgment its application does not depend upon either the fact, or the presumption, that the defendant has peculiar knowledge enabling him to prove the positive of any negative averment ...

Two consequences follow from the view we have taken as to the evolution and nature of this exception. First, as it comes into operation upon an enactment being construed in a particular way, there is no need for the prosecution to prove a prima facie case of lack of excuse, qualification or the like; and secondly, what shifts is the onus: it is for the defendant to prove that he was entitled to do the prohibited act. What rests on him is the legal or, as it is sometimes called, the persuasive burden of proof. It is not the evidential burden.'

While it makes sense that the incidence of the legal burden of proof should not be determined by the venue of the accused's trial, the decision in *R* v. *Edwards* gives rise to a number of problems. In *Woolmington* v. *DPP* [1935] AC 462 (HL) the obligation on the prosecution to prove the accused's guilt was held to be subject to only one common-law exception, the defence of insanity. If this is correct, the enactment of 1848 had not put the common law on a statutory footing but had created a new exception applicable only to summary proceedings. Even if this is not accepted, s. 101 does not even reflect what was originally in the 1848 Act as the relevant provision in that Act was re-enacted in an amended form in 1879. To say that what is now s. 101 of the 1980 Act reflects the common law applicable to trials on indictment would also seem to conflict with the decision in *R* v. *Curgerwen* (1865) LR 1 CCR 1 (CCCR), where it was held that a statutory proviso to the offence of bigamy in s. 57 of the Offences Against the Person Act 1861 (that is, that the first spouse had been absent for seven years and was not known by the accused to be alive during that period) had to be disproved by the prosecution. Further, if the common-law position is and always has been as set out in s. 101 it is difficult to understand why Parliament has enacted so many provisions which expressly place the legal burden of proof on the accused. In effect the Court of Appeal in *R* v. *Edwards* created a new exception to the 'fundamental rule' in *Woolmington* v. *DPP*. So long as the 'true construction' of the provision in question was that it prohibited the doing of an act, subject to a 'proviso' or 'exception' (and the like), then the accused was obliged to prove that the proviso or exception covered his situation. That said, the Court of Appeal has on occasion adopted the approach of the Divisional Court and either ignored this common-law rule or shown itself to be entirely ignorant of its existence. In *R* v. *Burke* (1978) 67 Cr App R 220 (CA) it was held that the prosecution had to disprove the 'antique firearm' exemption in s. 58(2) of the Firearms Act 1968 to an offence under s. 1(1); and in *R* v. *Cousins* [1982] 2 WLR 621 (CA) it was held that the prosecution had to disprove 'lawful excuse' in s. 16 of the Offences Against the Person Act 1861. In neither case was *R* v. *Edwards* referred to.

The issue came before the House of Lords in *R* v. *Hunt* [1986] 3 WLR 1115. A number of police officers had raided H's home in 1984 and found a paper fold containing white powder which was subsequently analysed and found to contain morphine. H was charged under s. 5(2) of the Misuse of Drugs Act 1971 with unlawful possession of a controlled drug in contravention of s. 5(1) of the Act, and at his trial the analyst's report was adduced in evidence by the prosecution. This report listed the ingredients of the white powder ('morphine mixed with caffeine and atropine') but failed to specify the actual proportion of morphine. Possession of a preparation 'containing ... not more than 0.2 per cent of morphine' was not unlawful for the purposes of s. 5(1) of the 1971 Act (by virtue of reg. 4(1) of the Misuse of Drugs Regulations 1973 and para. 3 of Schedule 1 thereto) and at the trial a submission of no case to answer was made on the ground that the prosecution had failed to prove that the white powder contained more than 0.2 per cent morphine. Following the judge's ruling against that submission H pleaded guilty and appealed, at first unsuccessfully to the Court of Appeal and then to the House of Lords. The questions which had to be answered were, first, whether the Court of Appeal had been correct in *R* v. *Edwards* [1974] 3 WLR 285; and, if so, whether the proportion of morphine in a preparation was to be regarded as an element of the definition of the offence, which had to be proved by the prosecution, or whether there was an 'exception' to a charge of possessing morphine where the preparation contained no more than 0.2 per cent of the drug, which the accused was obliged to prove. Lord Griffiths, in a speech with which Lords Keith and Mackay agreed, expressed the view that as the decision in *Woolmington* v. *DPP* (15.2.1 *ante*) had been solely concerned with the defence of accident to a charge of murder (that is, everything else said by Viscount Sankey in that case had been *obiter*) and had cast no doubt on cases decided before 1935, Viscount Sankey's reference to 'any statutory exception' could not be interpreted to exclude implied statutory exceptions. Lord Griffiths summarised the position (at pp. 1127–8):

'*Woolmington* ... did not lay down a rule that the burden of proving a statutory defence only lay upon the defendant if the statute specifically so provided: that a statute can, on its true construction, place a burden of proof on the defendant although it does not do so expressly: that if a burden of proof is placed on the defendant it is the same burden whether the case be tried summarily or on indictment, namely, a burden that has to be discharged on the balance of probabilities. The real difficulty in these cases lies in determining upon whom Parliament intended to place the burden of proof when the statute has not expressly so provided. It presents particularly difficult problems of construction when what might be regarded as a matter of defence appears in a clause creating the offence rather than in some subsequent proviso from which it may more readily be inferred that it was intended to provide for a separate defence which a defendant must set up and prove if he wishes to avail himself of it ...

However [in *Nimmo* v. *Alexander Cowan & Sons* [1967] 3 WLR 1169 (HL)] their Lordships were in agreement that if the linguistic construction of the statute did not clearly indicate upon whom the burden should lie the court should look to other considerations to determine the intention of Parliament such as the mischief at which the Act was aimed and practical considerations affecting the burden of proof and, in particular, the ease or difficulty that the respective parties would encounter in discharging the burden. I regard this last consideration as one of great importance for surely Parliament can never lightly be taken to have intended to impose an onerous duty on a defendant to prove his innocence in a criminal case, and a court should be very slow to draw any such inference from the language of a statute. When all the cases are analysed, those in which the courts have held that the burden lies on the defendant are cases in which the burden can be easily discharged.'

Accordingly, *R* v. *Edwards* [1974] 3 WLR 285 (CA) was held to have been correctly decided, save that Lawton LJ's definition of the scope of this exception to the rule in *Woolmington* v. *DPP* was considered to be no more than a guide to construction: 'In the final analysis each case must turn upon the construction of the particular legislation to determine whether the defence is an exception within the meaning of section 101 of the Act of 1980 which the Court of Appeal rightly decided reflects the rule for trials on indictment' (*per* Lord Griffiths at p. 1129). Lord Ackner also approved the approach taken by the House of Lords in *Nimmo* v. *Alexander Cowan & Sons* [1967] 3 WLR 1169 and said (at pp. 1133 and 1135):

'Where Parliament has made no express provision as to the burden of proof, the court must construe the enactment under which the charge is laid. But the court is not confined to the language of the statute. It must look at the substance and the effect of the enactment ... The Court of Appeal, in construing the relevant statutory provisions in order to ascertain where the burden of proof lay, rightly concluded, relying on the decision of your Lordships' House in *Nimmo* v. *Alexander Cowan & Sons* ..., that they were not restricted to the form or wording of the statutory provisions but were entitled to have regard to matters of policy.'

The House of Lords unanimously agreed that H's conviction should be quashed as it had been for the prosecution to prove as an essential element of the offence that his preparation of morphine was of the prohibited type. Lord Griffiths suggested that in a practical sense it would be far easier for the prosecution to discharge the burden in such cases because the accused would no longer have access to the drugs once they had been seized. A further consideration was the seriousness of the offence, which required any ambiguity to be resolved in favour of the accused. Lord Ackner pointed out that where Parliament had made its intention known, either expressly or by necessary implication, the courts were bound to give effect to what Parliament had provided. This deference to Parliament, together with the desirability of ensuring that the incidence of the burden of proof should not vary depending on whether the accused is tried summarily or on indictment, led the House of Lords to follow the decision in *R* v. *Edwards* [1974] 3 WLR 285 (CA). The policy consideration favouring the adoption of a uniform approach in all criminal courts won the day, the trade-off being the absence of any consistent approach to the incidence of the legal burden of proof where a defence is relied on: if it is a common-law defence (other than insanity) the accused bears a mere evidential burden; if it is a statutory defence then the common-law equivalent of s. 101 provides that the accused should bear the legal burden of proving it. Lord Griffiths dismissed the recommendation of the Criminal Law Revision Committee's Eleventh Report (Cmnd 4991 (1972) at pp. 87–91) that the accused should generally bear only an evidential burden: that was a matter for Parliament. In a similar vein Lord Ackner said (at pp. 1137–8):

> 'The hypothesis is that by necessary implication Parliament has provided in a statute that proof of a particular exculpatory matter shall lie on the accused. However, the discharge of an evidential burden proves nothing – it merely raises an issue. Accordingly, the mere raising of an issue by the defence would not satisfy the obligation which Parliament has imposed.'

However, what was more worrying about this decision was the extent to which the exception to the general rule in *Woolmington* v. *DPP* [1935] AC 462 (HL) had been enlarged. The distinction between an offence and an exception to it is in many respects artificial, for it is the cumulative effect of the offence elements *and* any exception which defines the parameters of what is permissible and what is not. As a matter of logic there is no difference between the proposition that 'driving without a licence is an offence' and the proposition that 'driving is an offence, except where the driver holds a licence'. The *actus reus* of rape is defined as sexual intercourse with a person who does not consent, but logically it could be said that sexual intercourse is a criminal offence, save that there is an exception if the parties consent. The distinction between the offence and any exception to it is devoid of substance, for any definitional element of an offence may be removed and turned on its head to become an exception to the remaining definitional elements. Indeed, with the demise of the 'peculiar knowledge' approach to statutory interpretation (according to the Court of Appeal in *R* v. *Edwards* [1974] 3 WLR 285) cases such as *John* v. *Humphreys* [1955] 1 WLR 325 (DC) suggest that driving *is* the offence, qualified by an exception for anyone who holds a valid licence. (In *DPP* v. *Kavaz* [1999] RTR 40, however, the Divisional Court opined that it was unnecessary to consider s. 101 of the Magistrates' Courts Act 1980 on the ground that there was 'overwhelming' authority to the effect that the 'peculiar knowledge' rule obliged the accused to prove he had an MOT certificate for his car.)

Following the decision of the House of Lords in *R* v. *Hunt* the courts were no longer limited to finding exceptions and provisos which were linguistically described as such. Trial judges could make reference to 'other considerations' such as the mischief at which the Act was aimed, practical factors such as ease of proof, and any relevant considerations of policy. In other words, judges were given a discretion, justified by policy, to create exceptions to statutory offences and thereby shift the legal burden of proof from the prosecution to the accused. So, in theory at least, judges were entitled to pick out an element of a statutory offence, turn it on its head, classify it as an exception and thereby impose a legal burden on the accused to prove his innocence. It is true that Lord Griffiths sought to distinguish between 'statutory defences' and the 'essential ingredients' of the offence, but this might be no more than a semantic distinction (at least in respect of any element which is not patently the gravamen of a very serious offence). Take, for instance, s. 170(3) of the Road Traffic Act 1988 which provides that it is an offence for a driver involved in a road accident to fail to report it. Although the accused must know he was involved in an accident to be liable, it is for him to prove that he did not have that knowledge (*Selby* v. *Chief Constable of Avon* [1988] RTR 216 (DC)). The accused's state of mind, usually regarded as the *mens rea* and therefore an 'essential ingredient' if not the gravamen of the offence, has been held to be a defence which the accused himself must prove.

It will be remembered that the House of Lords was particularly influenced by the decision in *Nimmo* v. *Alexander Cowan & Sons* [1967] 3 WLR 1169. That case was an appeal from Scotland concerning the interpretation of s. 29(1) of the Factories Act 1961 and, though the case concerned a civil action, a breach of s. 29(1) can lead to criminal liability (s. 155(1)). Section 29(1) provides that workplaces 'shall, so far as is reasonably practicable, be . . . kept safe for any person working there'. The question for the House of Lords was whether it was for the plaintiff, a workman, to prove it had been reasonably practicable for the defendant company to keep the workplace safe or for the defendant to prove it had not been reasonably practicable. The majority of the House of Lords held that the burden of proof lay with the defendant, thereby implying that if a prosecution were to be brought under s. 155(1) the offence would be defined as not keeping a workplace safe (which would need to be proved by the prosecution) but this would be subject to an exception which the accused would have to prove, namely that it was not reasonably practicable to keep the workplace safe.

The foregoing must now of course be read in the light of the Human Rights Act 1998. In *R* v. *Lambert* [2001] 3 WLR 206 (HL) (at p. 233) Lord Hope explained that there were three distinct questions which would now need to be addressed in respect of any provision of the sort considered in *R* v. *Edwards* [1974] 3 WLR 285 (CA) and *R* v. *Hunt* [1986] 3 WLR 1115 (HL). First, whether on the proper construction of the enactment the defence relied on is actually an exception of this type; second, whether the language used by parliament, according to its ordinary meaning, has indeed placed the legal burden of proof on the accused; and, third, whether the provision is compatible with Article 6(2) of the European Convention by reference to the general test applicable to express reverse onus provisions (15.2.2.1 *ante*), replacing the 'considerations of policy' test formulated in *R* v. *Hunt*. Accordingly, there will now need to be an expressly stated justification in terms of proportionality for placing the legal burden of proof on the accused, bearing in mind the ease with which he would be able to discharge it or the difficulty he would encounter (as the case may be) and the obligations borne by the prosecution. In other words, the only real difference between the test formulated in *R* v. *Hunt* and that described in *R* v. *Lambert* is that the courts must now consider whether the legitimate objective could just as effectively be achieved by placing on the accused an evidential burden rather than the legal burden of proof. The continuing relevance of factors such as 'ease of proof' and 'accessibility' means that where the accused is obliged by s. 101 of the Magistrates' Courts Act 1980 (or its common-law equivalent) to show he was licensed to do a particular activity, or to possess a particular item, he will still bear the legal burden of proof in relation to that issue. Thus, in *R (on the application of Grundy & Co Excavations)* v. *Halton Division Magistrates' Court* (2003) 167 JP 387 (DC) it was held that the accused bore the legal burden of proving he had a felling licence (or that a licence was not required) for the purposes of ss. 9 and 17 of the Forestry Act 1967; and in *McNamara* v. *Television Licensing Region* [2002] EWHC 2798 Admin (QBD) Rose LJ accepted that the user of a television set had to prove that he held the requisite licence to avoid liability under s. 1(1) of the Wireless Telegraphy Act 1949. It may even be that the continuing relevance of the accused's 'peculiar knowledge' to the question of ease of proof will justify retaining the rule in *Selby* v. *Chief Constable of Avon* [1988] RTR 216 (DC) that the accused must prove that he was unaware of the road accident he was involved in if charged with an offence under s. 170(3) of the Road Traffic Act 1988; and no doubt the maxim 'it is easier to prove a positive than a negative' will also have a continuing role to play in helping judges and magistrates determine the incidence of the legal burden. (This maxim might explain why in *R* v. *Curgerwen* (1865) LR 1 CCR 1 (CCCR) the legal burden of proof was placed on the prosecution to disprove the bigamy proviso. It would be truly onerous for the accused to have to prove that he did not know his spouse was alive at any time during a seven-year period.)

The principal problem with this area of the law is that much of it is uncertain and will remain so until all the express and implied reverse onus provisions have been definitively addressed by the appellate courts. For the time being trial judges and magistrates are themselves under an onerous burden in that they must consider the mischief at which the relevant offence and defence were aimed, any considerations of policy, the issue of proportionality; and then determine whether the accused ought to bear the legal burden of proof or merely an evidential burden. With so many considerations to weigh in the balance it may also be impossible for the parties to know in advance of the trial who will have to prove or disprove the relevant provision.

15.2.3 The Burden of Proving the Admissibility of Evidence

The party who wishes to adduce evidence is obliged to prove any preliminary collateral facts upon which the admissibility of that evidence is dependent. The tribunal of law is the tribunal of fact for these purposes, the question of admissibility being one of law (*R* v. *Yacoob* (1981) 72 Cr App R 313 (CA)). Generally speaking the standard borne by the prosecution is beyond reasonable doubt while the accused need only discharge his burden on the balance of probabilities. However, the balance of probabilities test applies when determining the competence of any witness to give evidence (s. 54(2) of the Youth Justice and Criminal Evidence Act 1999).

Thus, the prosecution must prove beyond reasonable doubt that the accused's confession was not obtained in the ways set out in s. 76(2) of the Police and Criminal Evidence Act 1984, that the maker of a hearsay statement tendered pursuant to s. 23 of the Criminal Justice Act 1988 is unable to attend court to give oral evidence for one of the reasons specified in that section, and that a sample of the accused's handwriting was actually written by him (*R* v. *Ewing* [1983] 3 WLR 1 (CA)). If the prosecution cannot discharge their burden to the requisite standard of proof in relation to any such collateral fact the evidence which depends on it is inadmissible, for as noted in *R* v. *Ewing* (at p. 7) a case cannot be said to be proved beyond reasonable doubt if the prosecution merely satisfy the judge on the balance of probabilities that their allegedly genuine samples of the accused's handwriting are in fact genuine. It would seem, however, that where the question is whether a document tendered by the prosecution is authentic, something which the jury will need to decide for themselves at the end of the trial as a question of fact, the judge need only be satisfied of its authenticity on the balance of probabilities, for otherwise the jury's role might be usurped (*R* v. *Robson* [1972] 1 WLR 651 (CCC)).

15.3 **The Burden of Proof in Civil Proceedings**

The incidence of the burden of proof is a matter of substantive law established by statute or precedent, but generally it lies with the party asserting an affirmative proposition to prove it: 'he who asserts must prove'. In *Joseph Constantine Steamship Line* v. *Imperial Smelting Corpn* [1942] AC 154 (HL) Lord Maugham said (at p. 174) that this was a general rule 'founded on considerations of good sense [which] should not be departed from without strong reasons'. It would perhaps be more apt to describe it as a cogent guiding *principle*. Lord Maugham also pointed out that the incidence of the legal burden 'depends on the circumstances in which the claim arises' which suggests that a more flexible approach is adopted in civil proceedings. This should not be surprising. The 'golden thread', which acts to protect the reputation and liberty of the individual in criminal proceedings, does not warrant such reverence in other contexts, where the parties are equal (at least in theory) and the question of punishment rarely arises. Having said that, as an underlying principle it does have a counterpart in civil proceedings, and Lord Wright expressly referred to the 'presumption of innocence' in *Joseph Constantine*

Steamship Line v. *Imperial Smelting* as a justification for placing the legal burden of proof upon the party alleging fault.

The principle that the legal burden lies with the party asserting an affirmative proposition does not mean that whenever the claimant's assertion is capable of being described as a negative the burden will lie with the defendant. If a proposition has been described in negative terms but is substantially affirmative in nature it will still fall upon the party asserting it to prove it. In *Soward* v. *Leggatt* (1836) 7 C & P 613 (CE), for example, it was for the landlord to prove his assertion that the tenant 'did not repair' his premises, in breach of a term of the lease, as the 'substance and effect' of the assertion was affirmative in nature notwithstanding the linguistic formula used in the pleadings. It follows that where the claimant's assertion is deemed to be an essential element of the claim, the mere form of words used will not affect the incidence of the legal burden of proof. A claimant alleging negligence must prove the defendant's breach of duty ('D's conduct was not reasonably competent') and his own consequential loss; and a claimant alleging breach of contract must prove the existence of the contract, its terms and the defendant's breach ('D did not perform his obligations'). If the defendant has a counterclaim against the claimant he will have to prove his assertions in the same way.

The principle that a party should have to prove any proposition essential to his case makes sense. It is just that the person who institutes proceedings, and thereby creates expense and trouble for the defendant, should have to justify his conduct and prove his case. In effect it is a different way of stating that the presumption of innocence applies to civil proceedings, but (unlike the golden thread) it works both ways. The defendant will often raise a counterclaim against the claimant so the claimant too is entitled to be protected by the presumption and it is for the defendant to prove any such assertion. The civil presumption of innocence is also less imposing than its criminal counterpart. If a party raises an affirmative defence to a claim or counterclaim it is for him to prove that defence.

However, while the 'he who asserts must prove' principle protects individuals from having to defend themselves against vexatious and unmeritorious allegations, many claims are justifiable demands for compensation. The principle, if afforded too much respect, could lead to unfairness in cases where the claimant is in the worst position to prove a fact in issue. For this reason, to give effect to the policy that proceedings should be fair to all parties, it may be appropriate to place the legal burden on the party who is in the best position to discharge it; while in other situations even wider considerations of policy may be brought into play to ensure a just result is reached more often than not in a particular type of claim.

Contractual disputes often cause problems in practice because of the exemption clauses and provisos included amongst the terms of the parties' agreement. If the parties have expressly stated where the burden of proof lies the judge will give effect to their intentions. Similarly, if a standard form commercial contract has been used it may be possible to find a precedent to demonstrate how it should be interpreted. In all other cases it is for the judge to determine the incidence of the legal burden in a way which will be fair to both parties in the circumstances of the particular case. The principle that the legal burden rests with the party making the assertion is the obvious place to start.

In *Munro, Brice & Co* v. *War Risks Association* [1918] 2 KB 78 (KBD) it was necessary to determine whether the assured shipowners or the marine risks underwriters should bear the legal burden in respect of an exclusion clause in a policy of marine insurance. The policy covered losses caused by perils of the sea, but excluded losses caused by 'hostilities or warlike operations'. The ship had disappeared without trace in 1917 and the owners sought to recover under their policy. There had been no communication from the ship prior to her disappearance, and all that was known was that submarines had been operating in the area and that the ship might have encountered stormy weather. Bailhache J held that it was for the underwriters to prove that the exclusion clause applied and, as they were unable to prove the ship had been sunk by the enemy, the shipowners were entitled to claim under the policy. (A seaworthy ship which has disappeared without trace is presumed to have been lost as a result of the perils of the sea.) Bailhache J's decision accords with the view of the Court of Appeal in *The Glendarroch* [1894] P 226, a case which was concerned with exclusion clauses in a bill of lading. The plaintiffs' cargo of cement had been carried on the defendants' ship and rendered worthless by an influx of water following the ship's collision with a rock. The cargo was never delivered and the plaintiffs sought to recover their loss from the defendants under the contract of carriage. The Court of Appeal held that once the plaintiffs had proved the existence of the contract and the fact that their goods had not been delivered, the defendants were obliged to prove the applicability of the exclusion clause which exempted them from liability for loss by perils of the sea. It had then been for the plaintiffs to prove that the facts actually fell within the scope of a proviso to that clause which would prevent the defendants from avoiding liability for any loss caused by their negligence. By contrast, in *Hurst* v. *Evans* [1917] 1 KB 352 (KBD) it was held that the applicability of an exclusion clause in a policy of insurance which benefited the defendant insurance company had to be disproved by the assured. The plaintiff, a jeweller, had obtained a policy of insurance from the defendant which covered his property, save that an exclusion clause provided that the defendant would not be liable for any loss caused by the theft or dishonesty of any of the plaintiff's employees. The plaintiff sought to recover part of his loss under the policy following a theft from his safe. However, as it was held that the plaintiff bore the burden of proving his employees had not been involved, and there was evidence which suggested one of them might have been, he was unable to recover under the policy. It is implicit in the judgment of the court that Lush J wished to place the burden of proof on the party who was best placed to discharge it, but it is not clear that the assured in a case such as this will always be that party. An assured employer will need to prove that each and every one of his employees was not involved in the theft and it is difficult to see how he will be able to discharge that burden.

Ease of proof is certainly a consideration which may be relied on when deciding who should bear the legal burden of proof on civil proceedings. This is clear from the decision of the House of Lords in *Joseph Constantine Steamship Line* v. *Imperial Smelting Corpn* [1942] AC 154. Charterers had entered into a contract with the owners of a ship to carry a cargo of ore from South Australia to Europe, but while the ship was waiting for a loading berth an explosion occurred on board which disabled her and rendered the voyage impossible. The charterers claimed damages from the shipowners for their breach of contract and the shipowners responded by arguing that the contract had been frustrated as a result of the explosion. The charterers contended that frustration could not be relied on if the explosion had been caused by the shipowners' negligence and that it was for the shipowners to prove they had not been negligent. The shipowners in turn submitted that it was for the charterers to prove that they (the shipowners) had been negligent. The cause of the explosion was unknown so the incidence of the legal burden of proof became decisive to the outcome of the proceedings. The House of Lords unanimously held that it was for the party denying frustration (the charterers) to prove that the party relying on the defence (the shipowners) had been negligent. Several considerations were advanced to justify this decision: the difficulty shipowners would face if obliged to prove a negative (that is, to prove the absence of negligence on their part) was cited by Lords Simon, Maugham, Russell and Wright; the presumption of innocence was cited by Lords Wright and Porter, with Lord Maugham applying the general rule that he who asserts an affirmative must prove it; and the desirability of achieving a just and reasonable result was cited by Lords Maugham and Wright. Viscount Simon said (at p. 161):

> 'Suppose that a vessel while on the high seas disappears completely during a storm. Can it be that the defence of frustration of the adventure depends on the owner's ability to prove that all his servants on board were navigating the ship with adequate skill and that there was no default which brought about the catastrophe?'

But in a situation such as this it would be equally difficult for anyone else to prove the crew had been at fault. Julius Stone ((1944) 60 LQR 262 at p. 278) has pointed out that in the great majority of frustration cases there is no fault on the part of either party, so if it is impossible to establish what has happened a rule requiring the defendant pleading frustration to prove the absence of fault would do injustice to the great majority of defendants, while a rule requiring the claimant to prove fault would do injustice to only a small minority of claimants. Moreover, even if it is not impossible to establish what has happened, there will be fewer cases of injustice through failure of proof among claimants obliged to prove an affirmative than there would be among defendants obliged to prove a negative. This analysis suggests that the considerations referred to by the House of Lords were applied to minimise the number of miscarriages of justice in cases where frustration is pleaded. In this sense policy is brought into play to give effect to the principle that miscarriages of justice should be kept to a minimum.

However, there is no absolute rule that a party should not be obliged to prove a negative. If goods are deposited with a bailee for safe keeping and he subsequently fails to return them to the bailor, the bailee can avoid liability only if he is able to prove he was not at fault (*Brook's Wharf & Bull Wharf* v. *Goodman Brothers* [1937] 1 KB 534 (CA), *Coldman* v. *Hill* [1919] 1 KB 443 (CA)). In *Joseph Constantine Steamship Line* v. *Imperial Smelting* Lord Wright explained this obligation on the bailee to prove absence of fault as a rule which had arisen in ancient times from the custom of the realm, but the underlying rationale would appear to be that the bailee is best placed to prove what happened to the goods while they were in his possession (see *Levison* v. *Patent Steam Carpet Cleaning* [1977] 3 WLR 90 (CA), *Easson* v. *LNER* [1944] 1 KB 421 (CA) at p. 423 and, in the context of lost travellers' cheques, *Braithwaite* v. *Thomas Cook Cheques Ltd* [1989] 3 WLR 212 (QBD) at p. 217).

The party bearing the legal burden of proof on an issue usually bears the evidential burden on it too, although the operation of an evidential presumption can affect this general position (see 15.5.3 *post*). Thus, the claimant will bear the legal and evidential burden on a number of specific issues and by the close of his case he must adduce sufficient evidence in respect of each one to prevent a successful submission of no case to answer. The claimant must therefore establish a *prima facie* case against the defendant by the close of his case. The judge has to decide whether the tribunal of fact would be able to find in the claimant's favour if his evidence, as it stands, were believed. If this test is satisfied the trial will proceed to the defendant's case. Technically the defendant is under no more than a tactical burden to adduce evidence in rebuttal, but this understates the true position. If the claimant has adduced cogent and credible evidence in support of his claim then at the end of the trial the judge, as the tribunal of fact, will inevitably find in his favour if no evidence has been adduced in rebuttal. Indeed an inference strengthening the claimant's case is almost certain to be drawn from the defendant's failure to call any evidence (9.3.1 *ante*). In this situation the defendant is effectively under an evidential burden to adduce evidence in rebuttal for otherwise it is inevitable that he will lose. If the defendant were to win without adducing evidence in rebuttal, judgment against the claimant would be appealable on the ground that it was a perverse decision unsupported by the evidence. Whether the defendant is under a tactical or evidential burden is therefore a question of degree which depends upon the cogency of the claimant's evidence.

15.4 The Standard of Proof

15.4.1 Criminal Proceedings

The standard of proof to be attained for the legal burden to be discharged depends on whom the burden rests. In *R* v. *Carr-Briant* [1943] 1 KB 607 the Court of Criminal Appeal held that if it is the accused who bears the legal burden the standard is simply the 'balance of probabilities' and the jury must be directed accordingly (see also *Sodeman* v. *R* [1936] 2 All ER 1138 (PC)). This is the same standard as that applied in civil proceedings and simply means that the fact in issue will be proved if the accused's version is considered more probable than any other alternative. It has therefore been suggested that the jury should be directed to be satisfied that it is 'more likely than not' or 'more probable than not' that the fact has been made out (*R* v. *Swaysland* (1987) *The Times* 15.4.87 (CA)).

If (as is usually the case) the legal burden rests with the prosecution, the standard is 'proof beyond reasonable doubt': 'If, at the end of and on the whole of the case, there is a reasonable doubt ... the prosecution has not made out the case and the prisoner is entitled to an acquittal' (*Woolmington* v. *DPP* [1935] AC 462 (HL) at p. 481). The policy which justifies this high standard is inextricably tied up with the golden thread, that is, the need to give effect to the fundamental principle that the accused should not be convicted of an offence he has not committed. As Brennan J said in *Re Winship* (1970) 397 US 358 (USSC) (at pp. 363–4):

'The accused during a criminal trial has at stake interests of immense importance, both because of the possibility that he may lose his liberty upon conviction and because of the certainty that he would be stigmatized by the conviction. Accordingly, a society that values the good name and freedom of every individual should not condemn a man for commission of a crime when there is a reasonable doubt about his guilt ... Moreover, use of the reasonable-doubt standard is indispensable to command the respect and confidence of the community in applications of the criminal law. It is critical that the moral force of the criminal law not be diluted by a standard of proof that leaves people in doubt whether innocent men are being condemned.'

Absolute certainty of guilt is rarely possible and if such a standard were to be set for the prosecution few persons would ever be convicted of a criminal offence. There will often be the possibility of a mistaken conviction and the law seeks to reduce that possibility to a minimum while leaving enough scope for the guilty to be convicted. The 'beyond reasonable doubt' formula is thought to strike the right balance between these two competing public interests. In *Miller* v. *Minister of Pensions* [1947] 2 All ER 372 (KBD) Denning J said (at p. 373):

'Proof beyond reasonable doubt does not mean proof beyond a shadow of a doubt. The law would fail to protect the community if it admitted fanciful possibilities to deflect the course of justice. If the evidence is so strong against a man as to leave only a remote possibility in his favour which can be dismissed with the sentence of course it is possible, but not in the least probable, the case is proved beyond reasonable doubt, but nothing short of that will suffice.'

The high standard of proof in criminal proceedings means, of course, that many persons who are guilty of the offence charged will inevitably slip through the net and escape conviction, but this type of miscarriage of justice is generally regarded as a lesser evil than the alternative. A lower standard of proof would make the conviction of the innocent far more likely, amount to a violation of the human rights of a large number of law-abiding citizens and undermine public confidence in the criminal justice system. That said, it is worth noting the view expressed by Denning LJ in *Bater* v. *Bater* [1951] P 36 (CA) (at pp. 36–7):

> 'In criminal cases the charge must be proved beyond reasonable doubt, but there may be degrees of proof within that standard. As ... many ... great judges have said, in proportion as the crime is enormous, so ought the proof to be clear.'

Whether juries and magistrates consciously or subconsciously adopt a lower standard of proof (or a lower requirement of cogency in relation to the evidence which will satisfy them of the accused's guilt) in cases where the allegation is relatively minor is something which remains unclear. The theory, at least, is that the same high standard applies across the board, whether the allegation is murder or one of the most trivial motoring offences.

The 'beyond reasonable doubt' formula would seem to be clear enough for juries to understand, if they are directed in accordance with Denning J's explanation in *Miller* v. *Minister of Pensions*, but this was not the view of Lord Goddard CJ who criticised this phrase on a number of occasions and established what has now become an acceptable and widely-used alternative. In *R* v. *Summers* [1952] 1 All ER 1059 (CCA) his Lordship said (at p. 1060):

> 'I have never yet heard any court give a real definition of what is a reasonable doubt, and it would be very much better if that expression was not used ... The jury should be told that it is not for the prisoner to prove his innocence, but for the prosecution to prove his guilt, and that it is their duty to regard the evidence and see if it satisfies them so that they can feel sure, when they give their verdict, that it is a right one.'

In *R* v. *Hepworth* [1955] 3 WLR 331 the 'sure' test was preferred over two others which met with the approval of the Court of Criminal Appeal (those alternatives comprising 'completely satisfied' and 'satisfied beyond reasonable doubt'), although a test of being 'satisfied' was held to be insufficient as it suggested too low a standard. The 'sure' test is now well established as an acceptable way of directing the jury (*R* v. *Wickramaratne* [1998] Crim LR 565 (CA)) but, in spite of Lord Goddard's disapproval, the 'beyond reasonable doubt' test is still in favour (see *McGreevy* v. *DPP* [1973] 1 WLR 276 (HL), *Ferguson* v. *R* [1979] 1 WLR 94 (PC), *R* v. *Sang* [1979] 3 WLR 263 (HL), *R* v. *Bentley (Deceased)* [2001] 1 Cr App R 307 (CA) and s. 76(2) of the Police and Criminal Evidence Act 1984). It has also been said that it is not the particular formula which matters but the effect of the summing-up on the jury hearing the case (*Walters* v. *R* [1969] 2 WLR 60 (PC)). However, for obvious reasons trial judges will prefer to stay within the limits of what has been expressly approved.

In recent years the Court of Appeal has recommended that judges should keep their direction on the standard of proof 'short and clear' (*R* v. *Penny* (1991) 94 Cr App R 345) and not try to attempt any gloss upon the terms 'sure' or 'reasonable doubt' by, for example, the use of analogies (*R* v. *Yap Chuan Ching* (1976) 63 Cr App R 7). In the latter case the trial judge had given an explanation that a reasonable doubt was one which might influence a person considering some business matter such as a mortgage over his house. Although the Court of Appeal dismissed the appeal because the effect of the summing-up as a whole had been satisfactory, it was made clear that such analogies were not to be used. In *R* v. *Gray* (1973) 58 Cr App R 177 the Court of Appeal felt a direction in terms of what might 'affect the mind of a person in the conduct of important affairs' would have been acceptable; but the use of the phrase 'everyday affairs' by the trial judge had set the standard of proof too low.

An unembellished version of the 'sure' test is now recommended by the Judicial Studies Board in their specimen direction for Crown Court judges (www.jsboard.co.uk); but, while this test has the attraction of being 'short and clear' it also begs the question, for the jury may not understand what 'sure' means in the context of criminal proceedings. In *R* v. *Stephens* [2002] EWCA Crim 1529 the trial judge described 'sure' as 'less than being certain', an explanation which did not find favour in the Court of Appeal on the ground that most people would find it difficult to discern any real difference between being sure of guilt and being certain of guilt. According to the Court, the trial judge faced with a query from the jury should simply remind them 'that they had to be sure of guilt before they could convict, indicating, if he felt it necessary, that that was the limit of the help which he could give them'. This simplistic approach is to be contrasted with the position adopted in *R* v. *Lifchus* [1997] 3 SCR 320. In that case the Supreme Court of Canada recognised that there 'cannot be a fair trial if jurors do not clearly understand the basic and fundamentally important concept of the standard of proof that the Crown must meet in order to obtain a conviction' and held that the judge should therefore give a direction in line with the following 'suggested form' (at para. 39):

'The accused enters these proceedings presumed to be innocent. That presumption of innocence remains throughout the case until such time as the Crown has on the evidence put before you satisfied you beyond a reasonable doubt that the accused is guilty ... A reasonable doubt is not an imaginary or frivolous doubt. It must not be based upon sympathy or prejudice. Rather, it is based on reason and common sense. It is logically derived from the evidence or absence of evidence. Even if you believe the accused is probably guilty or likely guilty, that is not sufficient. In those circumstances you must give the benefit of the doubt to the accused and acquit because the Crown has failed to satisfy you of the guilt of the accused beyond a reasonable doubt. On the other hand you must remember that it is virtually impossible to prove anything to an absolute certainty and the Crown is not required to do so. Such a standard of proof is impossibly high.'

For the prosecution to discharge their evidential burden and prevent a successful submission of no case to answer at 'half time' they must adduce enough evidence in respect of each and every issue they are obliged to prove for the judge to be satisfied that a reasonable and properly directed jury would be able to find the accused guilty beyond reasonable doubt (16.7 *post*). Where the accused bears an evidential burden (but not the legal burden) he must show there is sufficient evidence in support of his defence for the judge to be satisfied that a reasonable jury would be able to conclude that there is a reasonable doubt as to his guilt; but where he bears both an evidential and the legal burden of proof in relation to his defence the judge must be of the view that there is enough evidence for the jury to be able to determine that that defence has been proved on the balance of probabilities. In each case the judge will assume the evidence will be believed and not contradicted by evidence from the opposing party when deciding whether the evidential burden has been discharged.

15.4.2 Civil Proceedings

Generally, the degree of cogency required to discharge a legal burden of proof in a civil case is proof on the 'balance of probabilities'. According to Denning J in *Miller* v. *Minister of Pensions* [1947] 2 All ER 372 (KBD) at p. 374: 'If the evidence is such that the tribunal can say: we think it more probable than not, the burden is discharged, but, if the probabilities are equal, it is not.' The test is not whether one party's version is more probable than the other party's for it may be that neither version of events is credible (*Rhesa Shipping* v. *Edmunds* [1985] 1 WLR 948 (HL)). The party bearing the burden will discharge it only if the tribunal of fact is satisfied that his version of events is more probable than any alternative version. However, the 'balance of probabilities' test says nothing about how far above 50 per cent the probability should be that his version of events is correct. One theory holds that *anything* over 50 per cent suffices, no matter what the nature of the allegation (the so-called '51 per cent test', see *Davies* v. *Taylor* [1972] 3 WLR 801 (HL) at p. 810). According to this view there is a single standard of proof but as serious impropriety is less likely to have occurred than something relatively trivial a serious allegation requires highly cogent evidence to overcome that inherent unlikelihood and bring the probability of its occurrence over the 50 per cent watershed. In *Hornal* v. *Neuberger Products* [1956] 3 WLR 1034 (CA) Morris LJ said (at p. 1048):

'The phrase "balance of probabilities" is often employed as a convenient phrase to express the basis upon which civil issues are decided ... Though no court and no jury would give less careful attention to issues lacking gravity than to those marked by it, the very elements of gravity become a part of the whole range of circumstances which have to be weighed in the scale when deciding as to the balance of probabilities ... In English law the citizen is regarded as being a free man of good repute. Issues may be raised in a civil action which affect character and reputation, and these will not be forgotten by judges and juries when considering the probabilities in regard to whatever misconduct is alleged.'

This approach was recently approved by the House of Lords in *Re H (Minors) (Sexual Abuse: Standard of Proof)* [1996] 2 WLR 8 where the issue was the standard which had to be met in order to prove that young girls were at risk of being sexually abused by their mother's partner. Lord Nicholls, in a speech with which Lords Goff and Mustill agreed, said (at pp. 23–4):

'The balance of probability standard means that a court is satisfied an event occurred if the court considers that, on the evidence, the occurrence of the event was more likely than not. When assessing the probabilities the courts will have in mind as a factor, to whatever extent is appropriate in the particular case, that the more serious the allegation the less likely it is that the event occurred and, hence, the stronger should be the evidence before the court concludes that the allegation is established on the balance of probability. Fraud is usually less likely than negligence. Deliberate physical injury is usually less likely than accidental physical injury. A stepfather is usually less likely to have repeatedly raped and had non-consensual oral sex with his under-age stepdaughter than on some occasion to have lost his temper and slapped her. Built into the preponderance of probability standard is a generous degree of flexibility in respect of the seriousness of the offence. Although the result is much the same, this does not mean that where a serious allegation is in issue the standard of proof required is higher. It means only that the inherent probability or improbability of an event is itself a matter to be taken into account when weighing the probabilities and deciding whether, on balance, the event occurred. The more improbable the event, the stronger must be the evidence that it did occur before, on the balance of probability, its occurrence will be established.'

This reflects the approach adopted by the majority of the High Court of Australia in *Neat Holdings* v. *Karajan Holdings* (1992) 110 ALR 449 (and now incorporated into s. 140 of the Evidence Act 1995). The alternative theory is that the 'balance of probabilities' standard is a sliding scale ranging from just over 50 per cent up to proof beyond reasonable doubt. According to this view the more serious the allegation the greater the probability required for the civil standard to be met. The standard in civil proceedings is a flexible one, commensurate with the gravity of the allegation made. In *Bater* v. *Bater* [1951] P 36 (CA) Denning LJ said (at p. 37):

'[I]n civil cases, the case must be proved by a preponderance of probability, but there may be degrees of probability within that standard. The degree depends on the subject-matter. A civil court, when considering a charge of fraud, will naturally require for itself a higher degree of probability than that which it would require when asking if negligence is established. It does not adopt so high a degree as a criminal court, even when it is considering a charge of a criminal nature; but still it does require a degree of probability which is commensurate with the occasion.'

However, in *Re H (Minors)* [1996] 2 WLR 8 (HL) Lord Nicholls went on to say (at p. 24):

'If the balance of probability standard were departed from, and a third standard were substituted in some civil cases, it would be necessary to identify what the standard is and when it applies. Herein lies a difficulty. If the standard were to be higher than the balance of probability but lower than the criminal standard of proof beyond reasonable doubt, what would it be? The only alternative which suggests itself is that the standard should be commensurate with the gravity of the allegation and the seriousness of its consequences. A formula to this effect has its attractions. But I doubt whether in practice it would add much to the present test in civil cases, and it would cause confusion and uncertainty.'

According to this view there is no 'sliding scale' or 'third standard' in English civil proceedings and, subject to one or two specific exceptions, the 'balance of probabilities' standard is *the* test, no matter how serious the allegation. In *S-T (Formerly J)* v. *J* [1997] 3 WLR 1287 (CA) (at p. 1308), Ward LJ expressed the view that, since the decision in *Re H (Minors)*, 'the standard of proof in all civil proceedings is the ordinary civil standard of a balance of probabilities'; and in *Re G (a child) (non-accidental injury: standard of proof)* [2001] 1 FCR 97 (CA) (at p. 102) it was said that the principles developed in *Re H (Minors)* 'are applied equally in civil and in family law cases' and have 'become the basis of the approach by judges at all levels in dealing with family cases' (see also *Springsteen* v. *Masquerade Music* [2001] EWCA Civ 563). Similarly, whereas in *Halford* v. *Brookes* (1991) *The Times* 3.10.91 (QBD) it was said that the standard of proof for a civil allegation of murder was proof beyond reasonable doubt, it has since been said that the test is the balance of probabilities (*Francisco* v. *Diedrick* (1998) *The Times* 3.4.98 (QBD)). If allegations as serious as these are to be governed by the conventional civil standard it is difficult to see how a third standard can be expressly justified or applied in respect of any other type of allegation, but in *Heinl* v. *Jyske Bank* [1999] Lloyd's Rep Bank 511 the majority of the Court of Appeal felt that a third standard of proof, requiring 'a high level of probability', lying somewhere between the conventional civil and criminal standards, applied when dishonesty was being alleged. Presumably the court had in mind a test similar to the 'clear and convincing' standard which applies in relation to certain types of allegation in the USA (*Addington* v. *State of Texas* (1979) 441 US 418 (USSC)).

The position remains unsettled, then, save that there *is* a well-established exception to the 'balance of probabilities' test in civil proceedings which has been recognised for obvious reasons of policy (and indeed was recognised by the House of Lords in *Re H (Minors)*). If an order is sought in civil proceedings to commit a person to prison, the proceedings, being in effect criminal in nature with an individual's liberty at stake, require that the standard of 'proof beyond reasonable doubt' be applied (*Re Bramblevale* [1970] Ch 128 (CA) (contempt of court); *Mubarak* v. *Mubarak* [2001] 1 FLR 698 (CA) (judgment summons application under the Debtors Act 1869)). The criminal standard (rather than the *Re H (Minors)* approach) is also applied by magistrates when an application is made to them in civil proceedings for an anti-social behaviour order under s. 1 of the Crime and Disorder Act 1998, following allegations of criminal or quasi-criminal conduct, for the pragmatic reason that this standard is easier for magistrates to understand and apply (*R (McCann)* v. *Crown Court at Manchester* [2002] 3 WLR 1313 (HL) at p. 1329; see also *B* v. *Chief Constable of Avon and Somerset Constabulary* [2001] 1 WLR 340 (DC) in respect of applications for sex offender orders under s. 2 of the Act).

With regard to the evidential burden in civil proceedings, if it rests with the party bearing the legal burden it is discharged by adducing enough evidence for the judge to be satisfied that a reasonable tribunal of fact would be able find the issue proved on the balance of probabilities. If the evidential burden rests with the party who does not bear the legal burden of proof on the issue, it is discharged by adducing enough evidence for the judge to be satisfied that a reasonable tribunal of fact might find the legal burden has not been discharged by that party's opponent.

15.5 **Presumptions**

Confusingly, the word 'presumption' is used in the law of evidence to describe a number of different concepts which have little in common. In one sense the word is used to mean no more than that one particular party bears the legal burden of proving an issue to the satisfaction of the court. In criminal proceedings one talks of the 'presumption of innocence' as a shorthand description of the prosecution's obligation to prove the accused's guilt. Similarly, the 'presumption of sanity' is often used to mean no more than that the accused bears the legal burden of proving his insanity should he raise that defence. Such presumptions could be described as 'presumptions without basic facts'. They arise without the need to prove any preliminary (or 'basic') fact in advance. By contrast, all the other types of presumption require the initial proof or admission of some other basic fact for the presumption to arise. Presumptions requiring the proof of a basic fact are traditionally divided into three classes – 'presumptions of fact', 'irrebuttable presumptions of law' and 'rebuttable presumptions of law' – but the requirement of proof or admission of a basic fact is the only thing they have in common.

An irrebuttable presumption of law (or 'conclusive presumption') is simply a rule of the substantive law couched in the language of presumptions. Such presumptions fall outside the scope of the law of evidence for, as their name suggests, no evidence is admissible to rebut them. A presumption of fact (or 'provisional presumption') is no more than an example of commonly occurring circumstantial evidence from which a common-sense inference has been drawn in the past and might be drawn again for the same reason. The effect of such evidence is simply to cast upon the opposing party a tactical burden to adduce evidence to the contrary, for if this is not done the tribunal of fact may (but need not) draw that inference. Rebuttable presumptions of law are of two types: 'persuasive presumptions' and 'evidential presumptions'. Rebuttable presumptions comprise a mechanism for allocating the legal burden of proof (persuasive presumptions) or an evidential burden (evidential presumptions) in situations where logic and/or policy dictate that this should be so.

15.5.1 Presumptions of Fact (Provisional Presumptions)

To say a presumption of fact has arisen is simply to state that as a matter of common sense it would be permissible to draw an inference from a proven or admitted basic fact. If a jewellery shop has been broken into and the accused is found in the vicinity soon after with a bag full of the proprietor's goods, common sense would suggest that he was probably involved in the burglary and, in the absence of a plausible explanation from the defence, it will be open to the jury to draw that inference at his trial. There is no fundamental difference between evidence of such 'recent possession' and any other evidence from which an inference might logically be drawn, yet a presumption of fact – 'the presumption of guilty mind' – is said to arise from being found in possession of stolen goods in such circumstances simply because evidence of this sort has often been adduced for the purpose of persuading the jury to draw that inference. In fact any item of evidence from which an inference might reasonably be drawn could quite properly be said to give rise to a presumption of fact, but the widespread use of the label is not to be encouraged. The better approach would be to abandon the label entirely as it falsely implies that some types of evidence are inherently more probative than others and obscures the reasoning process undertaken by the tribunal of fact. There is no better example of this than the way the presumption of guilty mind came to be known as 'the *doctrine* of recent possession', a label which suggested a rule of law rather than the logical possibility of an inference being drawn. Presumptions of fact say nothing about the incidence of the legal burden of proof; nor do they give rise to an evidential burden. Once a basic fact has been proved or admitted the tribunal of fact *may* (but need not) infer another fact, the presumed fact, in the absence of any or any sufficient evidence to the contrary.

The presumption of guilty mind has been referred to in the context of a burglary, although in practice it is more likely to be relied on if the allegation is one of handling stolen goods. If the prosecution have managed to prove that the alleged handler was found in possession of recently stolen goods and he has failed to provide any or any satisfactory explanation as to how he came to acquire them, that basic fact gives rise to the permissible inference – the presumed fact – that he knew or believed the goods were stolen when they came into his possession. It is not an

inference which must be drawn, but the tribunal of fact is entitled to draw
it. Although the example given here is one of receiving stolen goods, the
presumption applies equally to any other type of handling (*R* v. *Ball* [1983]
1 WLR 801 (CA)). In *R* v. *Raviraj* (1986) 85 Cr App R 93 (CA) Stocker LJ
said (at p. 103):

> 'The [presumption] is only a particular aspect of the general proposition
> that where suspicious circumstances appear to demand an explanation,
> and no explanation or an entirely incredible explanation is given, the
> lack of explanation may warrant an inference of guilty knowledge in the
> defendant. This again is only part of a wider proposition that guilt may
> be inferred from unreasonable behaviour of a defendant when
> confronted with facts which seem to accuse.'

Proof or admission of the basic fact of recent possession is
circumstantial evidence that the accused is guilty of handling but it is no
more than that. The accused does not bear any legal or evidential burden
to prevent the inference being drawn, although in a practical sense he
bears a tactical burden to provide a plausible alternative explanation. If
the period between the theft and the accused's being found in possession is
sufficiently short the accused may face a charge of theft (or a charge which
incorporates theft as an ingredient), in which case the presumption may
similarly be relied on as circumstantial evidence that he stole the goods. At
common law the inference of guilty knowledge could only be drawn from
the accused's refusal to give an explanation prior to his being cautioned,
imposing upon him a tactical burden to testify or adduce other evidence at
his trial to justify his pre-trial silence. The scope of the presumption has
now been increased by ss. 34 to 36 of the Criminal Justice and Public
Order Act 1994 (9.2.2–3 *ante*). The 'general proposition' referred to by
Stocker LJ also explains the presumption that the person driving a car at
any given time is its owner. If an adequate explanation to suggest the
contrary is not forthcoming at the trial, the tribunal of fact will be entitled
to draw that inference (*Elliot* v. *Loake* [1983] Crim LR 36 (CA)).

   The presumption of continuance is another example of a presumption
of fact. If it is proved that a certain state of affairs existed at a particular
time it may be possible to draw an inference that the same state continued
to exist some time later or earlier, although much will depend on the
nature of the state of affairs in question and the interval involved. Thus, in
Beresford v. *Justices of St Albans* (1905) 22 TLR 1 (DC) as it had been
proved that the accused was in the driving seat of his car at the third
milestone from St Albans, in the absence of any evidence to the contrary
the magistrates had been entitled to infer that he had also been driving the
car when it passed the seventh milestone eight and a half minutes earlier.
Similarly, if a man is given a lift into town during the daytime and
expresses his intention to 'get a ride tonight one way or the other' his state
of mind during the journey can be presumed to have continued until later
that night when he is alleged to have raped a woman in a park (*R* v.
Valentine [1996] 2 Cr App R 213 (CA)). The intention to rape is likely to
be fairly transitory so, logically, it will not be possible to infer its

continuance for more than a relatively short time. A religious, irreligious or political belief on the other hand is likely to last for some considerable time and an inference as to its continuing existence will be possible, in the absence of evidence to the contrary, for as much as several years after it was expressed. In *Attorney General* v. *Bradlaugh* (1885) 14 QBD 667 (CA) (at p. 711) it was said by Cotton LJ that if there was evidence that a person disbelieved in God in 1880 it would be possible to infer that he had the same disbelief in 1884. The same is true of a person's character or habits, which is why 'similar fact evidence' of a party's disposition may be admissible in criminal or civil proceedings (see 3.2–3 *ante*).

The question of continuance often arises when the issue is whether a person was alive on a particular date. Needless to say, whether it would be proper to infer that a person was alive on one date just because he was known to be alive on an earlier date depends on all the circumstances, including his age, health, lifestyle and the duration of the intervening period, as explained in *Axon* v. *Axon* (1937) 59 CLR 395 (HCA) (at pp. 404–5):

'The greater the length of time the weaker the support for the inference. If it appears that there were circumstances of danger to the life in question, such as illness, enlistment for active service or participation in a perilous enterprise, the presumption will be overturned, at all events when reasonable inquiries have been made into the man's fate or whereabouts and without result. The presumption of life is but a deduction from probabilities and must always depend on the accompanying facts.'

Thus, if it is proved that a man was alive and in good health on one day the inference that he was also alive on the next day will be 'almost irresistible', whereas proof that he was in a dying condition is unlikely to justify drawing any such inference (*R* v. *Lumley* (1869) LR 1 CCR 196 (CCCR)). In *MacDarmaid* v. *Attorney-General* [1950] P 218 (PD) the fact that a normal 27-year-old woman had been seen roller-skating in 1891 allowed the trial judge to infer that she had lived for a further three years; and in *Chard* v. *Chard* [1956] P 259 (PD) the trial judge was willing to infer that a 28-year-old woman of normal health had lived for a further 16 years.

A presumption which is particularly important in criminal proceedings is based on the generalisation that people intend the natural and probable consequences of their conduct. If, for example, the accused is charged with the murder of his former employer by caving his skull in with a hammer the inference is likely to be irresistible that the accused had the *mens rea* for murder, but there is no obligation on the jury to draw that inference because the presumption of intention is one of fact and not law (see s. 8 of the Criminal Justice Act 1967).

15.5.2 Irrebuttable Presumptions of Law (Conclusive Presumptions)

An irrebuttable presumption is simply a rule of law. Once a basic fact has been proved or admitted the presumed fact *must* be presumed and no evidence in rebuttal is admissible. Thus, it is 'conclusively presumed' that no child under the age of 10 can be guilty of any offence (s. 50 of the Children and Young Persons Act 1933); and in an action for libel or slander in which the question whether a person did or did not commit an offence is relevant to an issue, proof that that person stands convicted of that offence 'shall be conclusive evidence' that he committed it (s. 13(1) of the Civil Evidence Act 1968). The irrebuttable presumption in s. 15(2) of the Road Traffic Offenders Act 1988 – that, subject to an exception in s. 15(3), 'it *shall be assumed* that the proportion of alcohol in the accused's breath, blood or urine at the time of the alleged offence was not less than in the specimen' provided by the accused at the police station – has been held by the Divisional Court to be compatible with Article 6(2) of the European Convention on Human Rights (*Parker* v. *DPP* (2000) 165 JP 213). However, the s. 15(2) presumption will arise in the case of a breath specimen only if the magistrates are satisfied that the approved device used to obtain the specimen at the police station was reliable, and the presumption that any such device is reliable *is* rebuttable (see *DPP* v. *Brown, DPP* v. *Teixeira* (2001) 166 JP 1 (DC), *Cracknell* v. *Willis* [1987] 3 WLR 1082 (HL) and 15.5.3.4 *post*).

15.5.3 Rebuttable Presumptions of Law

Persuasive and evidential presumptions of law function as a risk-allocation mechanism where there is little or no evidence (or readily available evidence) on a particular issue. It should not be surprising therefore that the rationale underlying their existence is an amalgam of logic and policy.

A persuasive presumption is effectively a rule which places the legal burden of proof on a particular party once certain basic facts have been proved or admitted. The basic facts give rise to the presumed fact, and it is for the opposing party to prove the contrary. The presumed fact has no evidential value of its own but merely lays down the rule as to the incidence of the legal burden of proof. However, the basic facts which give rise to the rule may have evidential value, at least where the presumption has a logical basis, and this will need to be weighed in the balance at the end of the trial to see whether the opposing party has adduced sufficient evidence to discharge the legal burden. If no or no sufficient evidence is adduced by the opposing party to discharge the burden of proof (that is, to rebut the presumption) the tribunal of fact must accept the truth of the presumed fact.

An evidential presumption does not affect the incidence of the legal burden of proof but places an evidential burden upon the opposing party once certain basic facts have been proved or admitted. The party relying on the presumption still bears the legal burden of proving the presumed fact but this burden will be deemed to have been discharged, and the tribunal of fact will be obliged to accept its truth, if the opposing party has failed to adduce sufficient evidence to suggest the contrary. If the evidential burden has been discharged, the tribunal of fact will have to weigh in the balance the probative value of the evidence adduced by the opposing party against that of the basic facts and any other evidence adduced by the party bearing the legal burden, in order to determine whether the legal burden has been discharged.

If a presumption is persuasive the opposing party in civil proceedings bears a legal burden of disproof on the balance of probabilities. In criminal proceedings the prosecution will have to disprove the presumption beyond reasonable doubt, but it is highly unlikely any such presumption would be held to impose a legal burden of disproof upon the accused if the prosecution were to rely on it. (At common law the accused bears the legal burden of proof only on the issue of insanity (*Woolmington* v. *DPP* [1935] AC 462 (HL)) and this is unlikely to be overridden by any presumption developed in the context of civil proceedings.) If a presumption is evidential the opposing party will rebut it by adducing sufficient evidence for the tribunal of fact to find the presumed fact not to have been proved on the balance of probabilities.

15.5.3.1 The Presumption of Legitimacy

Generally, if the basic fact is proved that a child was born or conceived during lawful wedlock a persuasive presumption arises that the child is the legitimate offspring of the parties to the marriage. Thus, in *Maturin* v. *Attorney-General* [1938] 2 All ER 214 (PD) the presumption arose in respect of a child born 10 days after the dissolution of the marriage upon the decree absolute; and in the Scottish case of *Gardner* v. *Gardner* (1877) 2 App Cas 723 (HL), where the parties had got married just seven weeks before the child's birth, Lord Cairns LC accepted that the presumption would have arisen under English law. In *Re Overbury* [1955] Ch 122 (ChD) the child was conceived during one marriage and born two months into the mother's second marriage following the death of her first husband. The presumption that the child was the legitimate daughter of her mother's (first) husband at the time of conception was held to prevail over the presumption that she was the legitimate daughter of her mother's (second) husband at the time of her birth. Where, however, the parties are separated pursuant to a judicial order there is a presumption that sexual intercourse between them has stopped and the presumption of legitimacy does not arise; indeed a child conceived during such period will be presumed to be illegitimate (*Hetherington* v. *Hetherington* (1887) 12 PD 112 (PD)). In all other situations the presumption arises, even where the parties are living separately by agreement (*Ettenfield* v. *Ettenfield* [1940] P 96 (CA)) or the decree *nisi* has been granted prior to the ultimate dissolution of their marriage (*Knowles* v. *Knowles* [1962] P 161 (PD)).

In civil proceedings the party who wishes to rebut the presumption of legitimacy must prove on the balance of probabilities that the child is illegitimate (s. 26 of the Family Law Reform Act 1969). The presumption itself carries no probative value but simply determines which of the parties bears the legal burden of proof, so even weak evidence against legitimacy must prevail if there is no other evidence to counterbalance it (*S* v. *S* [1970] 3 WLR 366 (HL), *T* v. *T* [1971] 1 WLR 429 (PD)). The presumption is therefore a mechanism to ensure that children are not held to be illegitimate unless that fact can be proved to the satisfaction of the court; and it is this policy rather than logic which explains decisions such as *Ettenfield* v. *Ettenfield* [1940] P 96 (CA) and *Knowles* v. *Knowles* [1962] P 161 (PD). However, that is not to say that logic does not also underlie the presumption. As a matter of common sense a child born or conceived during lawful wedlock is far more likely to be the legitimate offspring of the parties to that marriage than the child of another man, so it is sensible that the child should be presumed legitimate in the absence of evidence to the contrary. The sort of evidence which might be relied on to rebut the presumption could include evidence of the husband's impotence or non-access, testimony as to the absence of sexual intercourse between the parties, the results from blood or DNA tests (as in *Leeds Teaching Hospitals NHS Trust* v. *Mr A* [2003] EWHC 259 (QBD)), a refusal to provide a blood sample (as in *F* v. *Child Support Agency* [1999] 2 FLR 244 (QBD)), the appearance of the child (such as its race), a third party's admission of paternity and so on. However, the fact the mother was having sexual intercourse with men other than her husband around the time of conception will not rebut the presumption if the husband was also having sexual intercourse with her around that time (*Gordon* v. *Gordon* [1903] P 141 (PD)).

It is doubtful, however, whether the presumption of legitimacy will survive for much longer. It has been said on a number of occasions that it is in the best interests of the child that paternity doubts should be resolved on the best evidence, and in *Re H and A (Paternity: Blood Tests)* [2002] 1 FLR 1145 Thorpe LJ, giving the judgment of the Court of Appeal, said (at p. 1154):

> 'In the nineteenth century, when science had nothing to offer and illegitimacy was a social stigma as well as a depriver of rights, the presumption was a necessary tool, the use of which required no justification ... But as science has hastened on and as more and more children are born out of marriage it seems to me that the paternity of any child is to be established by science and not by legal presumption or inference.'

15.5.3.2 The Presumptions of Marriage

Three presumptions of marriage developed at common law for reasons of policy and common sense. If it is proved that the parties to a purported marriage went through a ceremony capable of giving rise to a valid marriage under the domestic law of the country, a persuasive presumption arises – the presumption of formal validity – that all the necessary formalities were complied with and that the marriage is formally valid. Thus, in *Piers* v. *Piers* (1849) 2 HL Cas 331 (HL) it was presumed a marriage ceremony in a private house was formally valid despite the absence of any evidence that the necessary special licence had been granted. There is authority to suggest the standard of proof in civil proceedings is beyond reasonable doubt (*Mahadervan* v. *Mahadervan*

[1964] P 233 (DC)), but the trend has been to recognise that the conventional civil standard of proof is now of general application in civil proceedings (*Blyth* v. *Blyth* [1966] 2 WLR 634 (HL), *Re H (Minors)* [1996] 2 WLR 8 (HL)) so the standard required to rebut the presumption is now likely to be proof on the balance of probabilities. The basic facts which give rise to the presumption of formal validity also give rise to the presumption of essential validity, that is, that the parties to the marriage had the capacity to marry and that they validly consented to it. It may be that the presumption of essential validity is evidential rather than persuasive. If this is so the difference between it and the presumption of formal validity presumably lies in the importance the law attaches to the competence and consent of the parties over and above compliance with formalities, together with the unlikelihood that any necessary formalities have not actually been complied with. In *Tweney* v. *Tweney* [1946] P 180 (PD) it was felt that the presumption of essential validity would stand 'until some evidence is given which leads the court to doubt that fact' (see also *Re Peete* [1952] 2 All ER 599 (ChD)). A third presumption of marriage has been recognised to arise from the basic fact that a man and woman have been living together and holding themselves out as a married couple with that reputation in their neighbourhood. The presumption has traditionally been seen as a persuasive one requiring cogent evidence to rebut it (*Re Taylor* [1961] 1 WLR 9 (CA)), and this was recently reaffirmed in *Chief Adjudication Officer* v. *Bath* [2000] 1 FLR 8 where, having noted the underlying policy that the validity of marriages entered into in good faith should be upheld wherever possible, the Court of Appeal held that even evidence that the marriage ceremony had been irregular and invalid was insufficient to rebut the presumption of marriage arising from a couple's 37 years' cohabitation as man and wife.

15.5.3.3 The Presumption of Death

If a person has been missing for some considerable time but there is no positive evidence of his death it makes sense that a presumption of death should arise at some stage. As a matter of logic a person who has failed to contact his friends and relatives for a lengthy period of time has either died or become a recluse, and as a matter of policy the question should not be allowed to hang unanswered until such time that it can be said with absolute conviction that he must be dead. Matters of title will need to be resolved so that those entitled to his property will be able to inherit it during their own lifetime; and the missing person's spouse should not be required to remain single indefinitely but permitted to re-marry and enjoy family life again. For these reasons, at common law a person's death is presumed if four conditions (the basic facts) have been proved: (i) there is no acceptable affirmative evidence that he was alive at some time during a continuous period of seven years or more; (ii) there are persons who would be likely to have heard from him during that period; (iii) those persons have not heard from him; and (iv) all due inquiries have been made appropriate to the circumstances (*Chard* v. *Chard* [1956] P 259 (PD) at p. 272). A degree of logic underlies all four conditions to the extent that their cumulative effect is to suggest death rather than some other reason for the missing person's absence. Of course the actual period of seven years is purely arbitrary and cannot be justified on any logical ground; but it is sufficiently lengthy to suggest the possibility of death rather than some other reason for the disappearance – and a line has to be drawn somewhere. The seven-year period is significant for it is only after such time that the presumption arises as a matter of law; the inference of death must be drawn. Before seven years have elapsed the tribunal of fact may, but need not, draw the inference that the missing person has died.

Because of the nature of the basic facts which need to be proved, the common-law presumption of death does not fit easily into the classification which divides rebuttable presumptions of law into those which are persuasive and those which are evidential. If there is any credible evidence that the missing person is alive the first condition is not satisfied and the presumption will not even arise. The presumption could therefore be said to be evidential, though it would be wrong to speak of the evidence rebutting the presumption. The evidence would simply prevent the presumption from arising in the first place. Whether the evidence that the missing person is alive is sufficient to prevent the presumption arising is a question for the tribunal of fact (*Prudential Assurance* v. *Edmonds* (1877) 2 AC 487 (HL)). In the Australian case of *Axon* v. *Axon* (1937) 59 CLR 395 (HCA) the presumption could not be relied on by a woman in respect of the husband who had deserted her because he would have had every reason for not making his continued existence known to her, not least because she was seeking maintenance from him.

Once the presumption has arisen the missing person is merely presumed to have died at some time during the seven-year period but not at any particular time; the time of death must be proved by the adduction of evidence (*Re Phené's Trusts* (1870) 5 LR Ch App 139 (CA)). In *Lal Chand Marwari* v. *Mahant Ramrup Gir* (1925) 42 TLR 159 (PC) it was felt that the presumption of death could arise only on the date the issue was raised in the proceedings, with the seven-year period running back from then. Other authorities suggest that death may be presumed to have occurred seven years after the missing person first disappeared (see, for example, *Chipchase* v. *Chipchase* [1939] P 391 (DC)).

In addition to the common-law presumption of death, there are several statutory provisions which allow the presumption to be drawn. Section 19(3) of the Matrimonial Causes Act 1973 provides that where a married person petitions the court under s. 19(1) for a decree of presumption of death and dissolution of the marriage, 'the fact that for a period of seven years or more the other party to the marriage has been continually absent from the petitioner and the petitioner has no reason to believe that the other party has been living within that time shall be evidence that the other party is dead until the contrary is proved'. It is a defence to a charge of bigamy if the accused's first spouse was absent for the seven years preceding the second marriage and not known by the accused to be living within that period (s. 57 of the Offences Against the Person Act 1861). Section 184 of the Law of Property Act 1925 provides that where two or more persons have died in circumstances rendering it uncertain which of them survived the other or others, their deaths shall, for all purposes affecting the title to property, be presumed to have occurred in the order of seniority, and accordingly the younger shall be deemed to have survived the elder. This presumption has no logical basis but can be justified on grounds of policy and expediency to ensure that property can be distributed where there is no evidence to suggest who in fact died first. In *Hickman* v. *Peacey* [1945] AC 304 the majority of the House of Lords concluded that the presumption applied to the 'practically simultaneous' deaths caused by a German bomb, which destroyed the house in which the deceased had been staying during the Battle of Britain, as it was 'uncertain' who had died first following the explosion. Thus, although the legal burden is on the party challenging the presumption to prove that the younger did not survive the elder, if there is *any* uncertainty as to who died first the presumption is irrebuttable.

15.5.3.4 The Presumption of Regularity
The vast majority of persons in official positions have been properly appointed so common sense dictates that it should be for the opposing party to adduce evidence that any person acting in an official capacity was not entitled to perform that function. Thus, if the basic fact is proved or admitted that an act was performed by a person acting in an official capacity a rebuttable presumption arises that the person was properly appointed. The presumption is generally thought to impose upon the opposing party no more than an evidential burden, although in truth the question has not been satisfactorily resolved and there is authority for the view that the presumption is persuasive.

If, for example, it is proved that a person was acting as a police officer it is to be presumed, in the absence of sufficient evidence to the contrary, that he was properly acting as such (*R* v. *Gordon* (1789) 1 Leach 515 (CEC)). In *Cooper* v. *Rowlands* [1971] RTR 291 the Divisional Court held that a police officer who was on duty as a motor patrol officer could be presumed to have been in uniform at the time. Some other cases where the presumption has been applied include *R* v. *Roberts* (1878) 14 Cox CC 101 (CCCR) (a deputy county court judge), *Campbell* v. *Wallsend Slipway & Engineering* [1978] ICR 1015 (DC) (an inspector for the Health and Safety Executive) and *TC Coombs* v. *IRC* [1991] 3 All ER 623 (HL) (a tax inspector). In *R* v. *Cresswell* (1876) 1 QBD 446 (CCCR) it was presumed that the chamber adjacent to a church had been duly licensed for the purpose of a marriage ceremony as divine service had been celebrated there on a number of previous occasions; and in *Gibbins* v. *Skinner* [1951] 2 KB 379 (DC) the fact that a speed-limit sign had been erected gave rise to the presumption that the local authority had complied with its statutory duties and properly authorised its erection (*cf. Swift* v. *Barrett* (1940) 163 LT 154 (DC)). However, it may be that in criminal proceedings the prosecution are not able to rely on the presumption to establish facts which are central to the offence charged. This was certainly the view of the

Divisional Court in *Scott* v. *Baker* [1968] 3 WLR 796, where it was held that it could not be presumed that a breathalyser had been approved by the Secretary of State merely because it had been issued to the police, and the Privy Council in *Dillon* v. *R* [1982] 2 WLR 538. The latter case concerned an allegation that a police officer had negligently permitted the escape of two persons, the issue on appeal being whether it had been permissible for the prosecution to rely on the presumption of regularity to prove they had been in the officer's lawful custody. According to the Privy Council (at p. 541):

'The lawfulness of the detention was a necessary pre-condition for the offence of permitting escape, and it is well established that the courts will not presume the existence of facts which are central to an offence ... Moreover, this particular offence is one which touches the liberty of the subject, and on which there is, for that reason alone, no room for presumptions in favour of the Crown ... It has to be remembered that in every case where a police officer commits the offence of negligently permitting a prisoner to escape from lawful custody, the prisoner himself commits an offence by escaping, and it would be contrary to fundamental principles of law that the onus should be upon a prisoner to rebut a presumption that he was being lawfully detained which he could only do by the (notoriously difficult) process of proving a negative.'

The Privy Council assumed that the presumption of regularity imposes a legal burden of proof upon the party wishing to rebut it and no doubt this influenced its decision (see also *R* v. *Verelst* (1813) 3 Camp 432 (KBD) at p. 435: 'the presumption ... stands till the contrary is proved'). There is, however, recent authority for the view that the presumption is evidential (*Campbell* v. *Wallsend Slipway & Engineering* [1978] ICR 1015 (DC) at pp. 1024–5). Given the number of cases where the prosecution have been allowed to rely on the presumption the better view is that the presumption is evidential. The accused need only adduce sufficient evidence to raise a reasonable doubt as to the existence of the presumed fact for the prosecution to be put to proof.

There is also an evidential presumption that mechanical devices of a kind which are usually working properly are working properly at any particular time. This presumption is in many respects analogous to the presumption of regularity, although it is unnecessary to prove the basic fact of general reliability because judicial notice can be taken of it. Thus, in *Nicholas* v. *Penny* [1950] 2 KB 466 (DC) the speedometer in a police car was presumed to have been working properly while the accused's car was being followed; and in *Tingle Jacobs* v. *Kennedy* [1964] 1 WLR 638 (CA) Lord Denning MR accepted that traffic lights could be presumed to be in proper working order in the absence of evidence to the contrary. If the device is of a type which is not generally known to be working properly the presumption cannot arise and evidence will need to be adduced to prove the fact.

15.5.3.5 *Res Ipsa Loquitur*

In cases where negligence is alleged by the claimant he may rely on the maxim *res ipsa loquitur* ('the thing speaks for itself') to raise a *prima facie* case against the defendant. Once it has been proved or admitted that the relevant matter was under the management of the defendant or his employees, and the accident was such that in the ordinary course of things it would not have happened if proper care had been taken by those persons, then in the absence of evidence to the contrary a presumption of negligence arises (*Scott* v. *The London and St Katherine Docks* (1865) 3 H & C 596 (CEC)). Although there is authority to suggest the presumption shifts the legal burden of proof, it is now clear that once the basic facts have been established the presumption which arises is evidential (*Ng Chun Pui* v. *Lee Chuen Tat* [1988] RTR 298 (PC), *Ratcliffe* v. *Plymouth & Torbay Health Authority* [1998] Lloyd's Rep Med 162 (CA), *Royal Bank of Scotland* v. *Etridge (No. 2)* [2001] 3 WLR 1021 (HL)). On this basis the claimant will establish a *prima facie* case against the defendant at 'half time', following which the defendant is under an evidential burden to adduce sufficient evidence to the contrary; if the defendant cannot discharge his evidential burden the judge will be obliged to reach a finding of negligence at the end of the trial. However, the legal burden ultimately remains with the claimant to prove his allegation of negligence on the balance of probabilities. Thus, in *Widdowson* v. *Newgate Meat Corporation* (1997) *The Times* 4.12.97, a case of alleged negligence arising out of a road accident in which the plaintiff had been injured by one of the defendant's vehicles, the Court of Appeal held that the presumption had given rise to a *prima facie* case of negligence, so the trial judge should not have dismissed the claim following a submission of no case to answer simply because the plaintiff had adduced no other evidence.

In *Royal Bank of Scotland* v. *Etridge (No. 2)* [2001] 3 WLR 1021 the House of Lords compared the operation of the equitable doctrine of undue influence with the way in which *res ipsa loquitur* is invoked to prove negligence. Whether a transaction was brought about by the exercise of undue influence is a question of fact to be proved by the party asserting it and, in the absence of satisfactory evidence to the contrary, the burden of proof will be discharged if it is proved (i) that the complainant (C) placed trust and confidence in another person (T) in relation to the management of C's financial affairs and (ii) that the transaction in question is one which is not readily explicable by the relationship of C and T. In other words, once these two issues of fact have been proved there is a *prima facie* case of undue influence – an evidential presumption of undue influence arises – which the other party, for example a bank (B), will need to rebut by the adduction of evidence to the contrary. B in effect bears an evidential burden, for unless B is able to adduce evidence in rebuttal C's claim that the transaction was procured by undue influence will succeed. C will not need to adduce evidence to prove the first of these issues of fact, however, if the relationship between C and T can be proved to be one of the special types of relationship where it is irrebuttably presumed that C reposed trust and confidence in T (such as the relationship between solicitor and client).

The relationship between husband and wife is not one of these special types, so a wife (C) must prove that she actually placed trust and confidence in her husband (T) if she wishes to rely on the doctrine.

An alternative view as to how *res ipsa loquitur* operates is that proof or admission of the basic facts gives rise to a presumption of fact, the weight of which depends on the circumstances of the case. According to this interpretation, in some cases the circumstances will allow an inference of negligence to be drawn which will be insufficient, in the absence of supporting evidence, to allow the claimant to discharge his own evidential burden by 'half time'; in other cases the circumstances may be such that a reasonable tribunal of fact would be entitled to infer negligence and the judge will rule that there is a *prima facie* case; while in other cases the inference will be so strong that it would be perverse for the judge to rule that a *prima facie* case has not been made out, and perverse of the tribunal of fact not to find against the defendant should he fail to adduce any or any sufficient evidence to the contrary (see *Easson* v. *LNER* [1944] 1 KB 421 (CA) at p. 425).

A similar presumption of negligence has also been recognised in criminal cases where the allegation is one of careless driving, although the maxim *res ipsa loquitur* has been avoided because of the historical uncertainty over whether or not it casts upon the civil defendant – and therefore the accused – the legal burden of proof. Nonetheless, if the accused's vehicle was involved in an accident of a type which can leave no reasonable doubt in the mind of the magistrates that the accused was negligent then it will be permissible to convict him in the absence of evidence suggesting the contrary (*Wright* v. *Wenlock* [1971] RTR 228 (DC), *Rabjohns* v. *Burgar* [1971] RTR 234 (DC)).

15.5.3.6 Other Examples

There are numerous other rebuttable presumptions of law, and just a few examples are given here. There is an evidential presumption that the person in possession of property is its owner (*Robertson* v. *French* (1803) 4 East 130 (KBD)) and a persuasive presumption that a deceased person did not commit suicide (*Re Williams* [1969] Crim LR 158 (DC)). There is also a statutory persuasive presumption that an engagement ring is given absolutely (s. 3(2) of the Law Reform (Miscellaneous Provisions) Act 1970); and a statutory evidential presumption that an accident in the course of a person's employment arose out of it (s. 94(3) of the Social Security Contributions and Benefits Act 1992). There was, until recently, a persuasive presumption that a child between the age of 10 and 14 was incapable of committing a crime, imposing a legal burden on the prosecution to prove beyond reasonable doubt that the child knew that what he was doing was seriously wrong and not just naughty. This presumption was abolished by s. 34 of the Crime and Disorder Act 1998.

The effect of the 'reverse onus' provisions in the law of criminal evidence is to give rise to a persuasive presumption in respect of an element of the offence which would otherwise have to be proved by the prosecution. The accused will rebut the presumption if he is able to prove his statutory 'defence' on the balance of probabilities, save that if the provision in question is interpreted to place on the accused no more than an evidential burden the presumption too is evidential (see 15.2.2 *ante*). For example, the effect of s. 30(2) of the Sexual Offences Act 1956, which provides, *inter alia*, that 'a man who lives with or is habitually in the company of a prostitute ... shall be *presumed* to be knowingly living on the earnings of prostitution, *unless he proves the contrary*', is to give rise to a persuasive presumption that the accused was living on the earnings of prostitution for the purposes of the s. 30(1) offence. The accused will need to prove the contrary on the balance of probabilities (*R* v. *Ptohopoulos* (1967) 52 Cr App R 47 (CA), *R* v. *Wilson* (1983) 78 Cr App R 247 (CA)). It is unlikely that this provision will now be read down under s. 3(1) of the Human Rights Act 1998 so as to impose no more than an evidential burden on the accused, given that the European Commission of Human Rights held that this reverse onus provision was compatible with Article 6(2) of the European Convention in *X* v. *United Kingdom* (1972) Application 5124/71.

15.6 Proof Without Evidence

Some factual matters are deemed to be proved, notwithstanding the absence of any evidence adduced in support thereof, either because 'judicial notice' has been taken of them or they have been 'formally admitted' by the party whose case is thereby undermined.

15.6.1 Judicial Notice

For the more efficient use of court time and to ensure consistency of approach, the doctrine of judicial notice allows certain facts to be regarded as proved, even though no evidence in support has been adduced, if the facts are so well known by people generally (or in the general locality) that it would be pointless to call evidence. In Crown Court and civil jury trials it is for the judge to take judicial notice of any such 'notorious facts' and direct the jury to find that they exist. For example it would not be necessary to adduce evidence to prove that watching television is a normal part of everyday life, or that Christmas falls on 25 December. These are incontrovertible facts known by the vast majority of people and as such may be judicially noted. Once judicial notice has been taken of a fact its indisputable nature means a party cannot adduce evidence to rebut it.

An example is provided by human gestation. It is widely known that a human foetus normally takes about nine months to develop in the uterus but that some women give birth after a shorter or longer period of time; as such it is possible to take judicial notice of both these facts (*Preston-Jones* v. *Preston-Jones* [1951] AC 391 (HL)). However, where the period in question is said to fall either side of the norm it will not generally be appropriate to take judicial notice of its impossibility unless the period is so short or so long that it can be taken for granted. Thus in *R* v. *Luffe* (1807) 8 East 193 (KBD) judicial notice could be taken of the fact that a gestation period of two weeks was impossible, whereas in *Preston-Jones* v. *Preston-Jones* the House of Lords was not willing to accept that judicial notice could be taken of the impossibility of a period of 360 days. In the latter case the husband petitioned for divorce on the ground of his wife's alleged adultery. He had been out of the country for six months but his wife gave birth to a normal child weighing over eight pounds just six months after his return, meaning that he could have been the father only if the gestation period had lasted either 6 months or a year. While it was accepted that judicial notice could be taken of the impossibility of a six-month period for that baby the House of Lords refused to hold that such notice could be taken of the longer period, although it was recognised that a year might be close to the upper limit after which judicial notice would be acceptable. Other examples of judicially-noted facts include: the fact that the writing on a postcard is not concealed (*Huth* v. *Huth* [1915] 3 KB 32 (CA)); that Britain was at war on 1 January 1916 (*Commonwealth Shipping Representative* v. *P & O Branch Service* [1923] AC 191 (HL)); that the streets of London are full of traffic (*Dennis* v. *A J White* [1916] 2 KB 1 (CA)); that cats are ordinarily kept for domestic purposes (*Nye* v. *Niblett* [1918] 1 KB 23 (DC)); that Elvis Presley was resident in the USA (*RCA Corp* v. *Pollard* [1982] 2 All ER 468 (ChD)); and that 'cocaine hydrochloride' is a form of cocaine (*Attorney General for the Cayman Islands* v. *Roberts* [2002] 1 WLR 1842 (PC)). In *R* v. *Jones* [1970] 1 WLR 16 (CA) it was held that judicial notice could be taken of the fact that the 'Alcotest R80' breathalyser was a device approved by the Secretary of State on account of the large number of widely-reported decisions to that effect.

The doctrine of judicial notice helps to keep the length and cost of trials to a minimum, but it also ensures that different decisions are not reached on the same general questions of fact by different courts. This is a particularly important consideration in criminal proceedings where certainty in the law is essential. For this reason it is permissible to take judicial notice of the fact that certain types of knife, such as flick-knives (*R* v. *Simpson* (1983) 78 Cr App R 115 (CA)) and butterfly knives (*DPP* v. *Hynde* (1997) 161 JP 671 (DC)) are manufactured for the purpose of causing injury to the person. However, while the original first-instance decisions were examples of judicial notice being taken, the appellate courts' stamp of authority means that future decisions are not so much examples of the doctrine being re-applied but compliance with the separate doctrine of binding precedent. A similar point may be made in relation to the statutory provisions which impose an obligation to take judicial notice, such as s. 3 of the Interpretation Act 1978 (which provides that all Acts passed by Parliament since 1850 are to be judicially noticed as such) and s. 3(2) of the European Communities Act 1972 (which provides that judicial notice shall be taken of, *inter alia*, the decisions of the European Court of Justice and the EC Treaties), save that the relevant doctrine here is the supremacy of Parliament.

A court may also take judicial notice of indisputable facts 'after inquiry'. Unlike judicial notice without inquiry, the judge or magistrates will first refer to appropriate sources of information in order to decide the issue. Although such facts are not sufficiently 'notorious' to allow the court to take judicial notice without inquiry, this procedure is permitted on the ground that certain works of reference are so reliable and authoritative that it would be absurd to expect evidence to be adduced to prove the indisputable facts contained within them. An obvious example would be to refer to a calendar to find out which day of the week it was on a certain date; another would be to look at a map to find out the distance between two places. It is also permissible for the judge (or magistrates) to receive expert opinion evidence before determining a question of this sort, as for example in *McQuaker* v. *Goddard* [1940] 1 KB 687 (CA) where it was necessary to determine whether camels were wild or tame animals. It is also permissible for experts to be consulted if it is necessary for the court to determine the nature of a professional practice or custom.

Finally, where the question to be determined is political in nature, such as the status of an overseas territory or government, it will be necessary to refer to the appropriate government minister in order to avoid the risk of a conflict between the judiciary and the executive. The minister's response to such a request is conclusive (see *Duff Development Co Ltd* v. *Government of Kelantan* [1924] AC 797 (HL)).

15.6.2 The Local and Particular Knowledge of the Tribunal of Fact

Judges, jurors and magistrates are all permitted to rely on their 'local knowledge' – that is, matters generally known by people in the locality – because it amounts to no more than a localised form of judicial notice. Indeed one of the benefits of the lay magistracy is that as magistrates are drawn from the surrounding area they are likely to be familiar with local conditions and, in particular, the geography of the region. Thus, in *Paul* v. *DPP* (1989) 90 Cr App R 173 (DC), a case of 'kerb-crawling', magistrates in Luton could rely on the local knowledge that a particular area in that town was frequented by prostitutes; and in *Clift* v. *Long* [1961] Crim LR 121 (DC) magistrates in Felixstowe could rely on the local knowledge that a car park was a public place. (For other examples see *Ingram* v. *Percival* [1968] 3 WLR 663 (DC) and *Borthwick* v. *Vickers* [1973] Crim LR 317 (DC).)

In *Bowman* v. *DPP* [1991] RTR 263 the Divisional Court felt that the prosecution and defence should have been allowed to comment on the magistrates' use of local knowledge regarding the status of a car park in Portsmouth. Watkins LJ said (at pp. 269–70):

'It is always wise of justices to make the fact that local knowledge is going to be used known to the defence and the prosecution so as to give those representing those parties the opportunity of commenting upon the knowledge which the justice or justices claim to have and which they aim to use for the purpose of aiding them in reaching a determination

... It must be recognised in cases of this kind which involve local knowledge that justices simply cannot turn out of their minds knowledge which they acquire locally nor is it desirable that they should. Providing they take special care to keep within proper bounds and inform a defendant especially of that locally acquired knowledge and the use to which they may seek to put it, the justices act perfectly properly and rightly.'

As a general principle this is a sensible safeguard to ensure that magistrates rely on matters which *are* generally known in the locality and do not determine questions which might be in dispute and in respect of which either or both parties might wish to adduce evidence. *Bowman* v. *DPP* [1991] RTR 263 was followed in *Norbrook Laboratories (GB)* v. *Health and Safety Executive* (1998) *The Times* 23.2.98 (DC) where a conviction was quashed because the magistrates had not made it clear to the parties that they were relying on their local knowledge. Local professional judges, for example district judges in the county courts, also share the regional population's general knowledge and may rely on it in the same way (*Keane* v. *Mount Vernon Colliery* [1933] AC 309 (HL), *Reynolds* v. *Llanelly Associated Tinplate* [1948] 1 All ER 140 (CA)).

Different considerations ought to apply, however, where the knowledge is not local but particular to an individual trier of fact. Particular knowledge, unlike notorious facts, may be open to dispute and, as noted above, the issue ought to be resolved by the adduction of admissible evidence by either or both parties in the normal way.

15.6.2.1 The Particular Knowledge of Judges

In *Reynolds* v. *Llanelly Associated Tinplate* [1948] 1 All ER 140 the Court of Appeal held that a county court arbitrator had been wrong to use his own particular knowledge of the local employment prospects of a man of the applicant's age and experience. The knowledge relied on had not fallen within the common knowledge of the people in the locality so evidence ought to have been received on the issue. The Court of Appeal went further in *Owen* v. *Nicholl* [1948] 1 All ER 707 where it was held that a county court arbitrator could neither rely on the particular knowledge he had picked up from adjudicating in earlier proceedings concerning third parties nor refer to the court file relating to those earlier proceedings if the file had not been adduced in evidence. Similarly, in *Jarvis* v. *DPP* [1996] RTR 192 the Divisional Court held that 'it was wrong in principle' for a stipendiary magistrate to use evidence that he had heard in other cases to supplement the evidence in the case before him.

However, it seems professional judges may now have a wider discretion to rely on their own personal knowledge *after* judgment has been entered, at least in the county court. In *Mullen* v. *Hackney LBC* [1997] 1 WLR 1103 a county court judge imposed a fine of £5,000 on Hackney Council for being in breach of an undertaking to carry out repair work at one of their properties. The severity of the fine was justified on the ground that the Council had been in breach of numerous other undertakings to the court, yet no evidence was called to this effect. Despite the absence of any evidence, or indeed any indication as to the source of the judge's knowledge, the Court of Appeal upheld his decision. The judge had been entitled to rely on his knowledge of the Council's previous breaches as it could be assumed he had derived it from any one of three acceptable sources, namely: his personal experience or the records of the local county courts or his local knowledge. It is very doubtful whether the same approach would be permitted in a criminal court following a conviction.

15.6.2.2 The Particular Knowledge of Jurors

A number of nineteenth century cases suggest that if a juror has particular knowledge about a disputed issue in the trial he should give evidence on it in open court like any other witness (see, for example, *R* v. *Rosser* (1836) 7 C & P 648 (CCC)). While this procedure would ensure that the juror's knowledge is tested by cross-examination and revealed to all the other jurors, it is possible to envisage difficulties arising, for example if the juror's evidence is inadmissible. A more recent authority is *R* v. *Blick* (1966) 50 Cr App R 280 (CCA), a case in which a juror passed a note to the judge explaining that his own knowledge relating to a public lavatory contradicted the accused's testimony that it had been open and used by him at the time of the alleged robbery. The approach adopted by the trial judge, and upheld on appeal, was to allow the prosecution to call evidence relating to the matters in the note which could then be tested by cross-examination in the normal way. The juror himself was not required to give evidence. If it comes to the judge's attention that a juror has communicated his particular knowledge to the other jurors during their deliberations, and a strong direction to concentrate only on the evidence given during the trial would not sufficiently address the problem, the jury should be discharged from reaching a verdict (*R* v. *Fricker* (1999) *The Times* 13.7.99 (CA)).

15.6.2.3 The Particular Knowledge of Magistrates

Magistrates are allowed to rely on their own particular knowledge relating to the issues in dispute before them even though it is not concerned with their locality, the simple reason being that they are probably unable to exclude such matters from their minds. Perhaps the most famous example is *R* v. *Field and Others (Justices) ex parte White* (1895) 64 LJMC 158 (DC). A lay bench comprising three men who had served in the Royal Navy dismissed an allegation relating to the sale of adulterated cocoa on the ground that their experience in the Navy had made them experts in the field and they knew that cocoa could not be consumed in its pure state but had to contain other ingredients. Wills J said (at pp. 159–60):

'I do not say that the Justices pursued an altogether prudent course; and perhaps if the occasion arose again they would be wiser to hear evidence, and keep themselves technically right. However, they decided the case as they did upon their own knowledge; and in the nature of things, no one in determining a case of this kind can discard his own particular knowledge of a subject of this kind. I might as well be asked to decide a question as to the sufficiency of an Alpine rope without bringing my personal knowledge into play.'

The final sentence of this extract is of interest because it suggests that professional judges may find it just as difficult as lay magistrates to ignore their personal knowledge when trying a case (although this is not the official line).

In *Wetherall* v. *Harrison* [1976] 2 WLR 168 (DC) the accused was charged with failing to provide a sample of blood contrary to s. 9(3) of the Road Traffic Act 1972 and relied on the defence of reasonable excuse on the ground that he had had 'a sort of fit' at the time the sample was requested. The prosecution called the doctor who had seen the accused and he gave his expert opinion that the fit had been simulated. The accused did not call any medical evidence in rebuttal but the magistrates dismissed the charge, relying on their own knowledge of the fear that inoculations could cause and the professional opinion of one of their number, a medical practitioner. Dismissing an appeal by the prosecution, Lord Widgery CJ said (at pp. 172–3):

'If you have a judge sitting alone, trying a civil case, it is perfectly feasible and sensible that he should be instructed and trained to exclude certain factors from his consideration of the problem. Justices are not so trained ... Laymen (by which I mean non-lawyers) sitting as justices considering a case ... lack the ability to put out of their minds certain features of the case. In particular, if the justice is a specialist, be he a doctor, or an engineer or an accountant, or what you will, it is not possible for him to approach the decision in the case as though he had not got that training ... So ... it is not improper for a justice who has special knowledge of the circumstances forming the background to a particular case to draw on that special knowledge in interpretation of the evidence which he has heard ... He is not there to give evidence to himself, still more is he not there to give evidence to other justices; but that he can employ his basic knowledge in considering, weighing up and assessing the evidence given before the court is I think beyond doubt ... He can explain the evidence they have heard: he can give his views as to how the case should go and how it should be decided; but he should not be giving evidence himself behind closed doors which is not available to the parties.'

The position would therefore seem to be that while a specialist magistrate may give his own expert opinion on the evidence behind closed doors, he should not give evidence behind closed doors. Needless to say, this distinction is rather difficult to comprehend. In magistrates' courts it now seems that controvertible evidence may be given in the retiring room, untested by the parties, simply on the ground of expediency. The better solution would be for experts in the field to discharge themselves from hearing the case, so that it can be decided wholly on the evidence which has been adduced in court and openly scrutinised by the parties' own experts. That said, if the Divisional Court is of the view that the line between 'employing basic knowledge to assess evidence' and 'giving evidence' has been crossed there will be a remedy for the aggrieved party. In *Carter* v. *Eastbourne Borough Council* (2000) 164 JP 273 (DC) it was held that the magistrates had been wrong to judge for themselves the ages of a number of trees, as these questions were 'properly the subject matter of evidence and not of personal undisclosed belief on the part of the tribunal'.

15.6.3 Formal Admissions

An issue of fact may be formally admitted by a party. If this is done the fact is no longer in issue and the opposing party need not adduce evidence to prove it.

15.6.3.1 Criminal Proceedings
Any fact may be formally admitted by or on behalf of the accused or the prosecution; once this has been done the admission is, as against the party making it, conclusive evidence of the fact admitted (s. 10(1) of the Criminal Justice Act 1967). Any such admission may, however, be withdrawn with the leave of the court (s. 10(4)), but if the admission was made with the benefit of legal advice the judge is unlikely to give permission for it to be withdrawn unless there is cogent evidence that it was made on the basis of a mistake or misunderstanding (*R* v. *Kolton* [2000] Crim LR 761 (CA)).

Although the accused's legal representative may make a formal admission on his behalf, only the accused himself may enter a plea of guilty to the charge in court (*R* v. *Ellis* (1973) 57 Cr App R 571 (CA)). Once the accused has voluntarily entered a plea of guilty to an offence the prosecution are no longer obliged to prove their case, save that where there is some dispute over the facts it may be necessary to hold a '*Newton* hearing' to determine how the offence was committed (*R* v. *Newton* (1982) 77 Cr App R 13 (CA)). Once the facts have been established in this way the judge will know the seriousness of the offence and be able to pass the appropriate sentence. The court has a discretion to allow the accused to withdraw his guilty plea at any time prior to sentencing (*R* v. *Dodd* (1981) 74 Cr App R 50 (CA)).

15.6.3.2 Civil Proceedings
A party to civil proceedings may make a formal admission in a number of ways. The most obvious way is expressly to admit a fact in the party's statement of case (r. 14.1(2) of the Civil Procedure Rules 1998), but such admissions may also be made by the defendant's failure to respond to an allegation in the claimant's statement of case (CPR r. 16.5(5), *cf.* r. 16.7(2)), by expressly admitting a fact in answer to a 'notice to admit facts' (CPR r. 32.18(3)), by voluntarily serving a written admission on the opposing party (CPR r. 14.1(2)), or of course by admitting the fact at the trial.

Chapter Summary

- The burden of proof is the obligation on a party to prove a fact in issue to the standard (the degree of probability) required by law. In criminal proceedings the prosecution bear the burden of proof on the various issues which comprise their allegation against the accused *and* the burden of disproof on the accused's defence(s), save that the accused bears the burden of proof in respect of insanity and a number of statutory defences. In civil proceedings the party who makes a particular factual assertion usually has to prove it. A 'persuasive presumption' places the burden of proof on a particular party once preliminary facts have been proved or admitted.

- Whether a fact in issue has been proved to the requisite standard is determined by the tribunal of fact at the end of the trial. (A party may, however, have to discharge the burden of proof during the course of the trial in respect of a collateral fact on which the admissibility of an item of his evidence depends. The judge will determine whether the collateral fact has been proved.)

- The standard of proof for the prosecution in respect of a fact in issue on which they bear the burden of proof is 'beyond reasonable doubt'. For the accused it is 'on the balance of probabilities' (more probable than any other alternative) which is also the standard of proof in civil proceedings.

- If a party bears an evidential burden on an issue he must be able to show that sufficient evidence has been adduced or elicited in support of the issue for it to be considered by the tribunal of fact at the end of the trial. As a general rule the party bearing the burden of proof on an issue also bears an evidential burden on it. However, in criminal proceedings the accused will bear an evidential burden on an affirmative defence which the prosecution are obliged to disprove. An 'evidential presumption' places an evidential burden on a party once preliminary facts have been proved or admitted.

- Whether an evidential burden has been discharged is a question of law for the judge. If the prosecution bear an evidential burden on a fact in issue they must adduce sufficient evidence by the close of their case for the judge to be satisfied that a reasonable jury would be able to find that issue proved beyond reasonable doubt. If the accused bears an evidential burden in respect of a defence on which the prosecution bear the burden of disproof he must be able to show by the close of his case that there is sufficient evidence for the judge to be satisfied that a reasonable jury would be able to conclude that there is a reasonable doubt as to his guilt (that is, that there is a reasonable possibility that his defence is true). If the accused bears the burden of proof on his defence he must be able to show there is sufficient evidence for the judge to be satisfied that a reasonable jury would be able to find his defence proved on the balance of probabilities.

- Some facts are so well known that they do not need to be proved by the adduction of admissible evidence. Judicial notice may be taken of such 'notorious facts' without enquiry. Judicial notice may also be taken of other facts after enquiry (for example, where the court refers to an authoritative source of information to determine the question). The tribunal of fact is also entitled to use its own 'local knowledge', and lay magistrates are entitled to rely on their own particular knowledge in respect of the issues before them.

- A factual issue which is 'formally admitted' by the party who does not bear the burden of proof on it is no longer in issue between him and the party who would otherwise have borne the burden of proof.

Further Reading

Williams, 'The Evidential Burden: Some Common Misapprehensions' (1977) 127 NLJ 156

Williams, 'Evidential Burdens on the Defence' (1977) 127 NLJ 182

Healy, 'Proof and Policy: No Golden Threads' [1987] Crim LR 355

Birch, 'Hunting the Snark: the Elusive Statutory Exception' [1988] Crim LR 221

Smith, 'The Presumption of Innocence' (1987) 38 NILQ 223

Williams, 'The Logic of "Exceptions"' (1988) CLJ 261

Roberts, 'Taking the Burden of Proof Seriously' [1995] Crim LR 783

16   The Trial

16.1 **The Course of the Trial**

The trial process is broadly similar in criminal and civil proceedings, although there are significant procedural differences between jury and non-jury trials. The claimant or prosecution ('P') will give an opening speech outlining his case against the accused or civil defendant ('D') and identifying the factual issues which will need to be resolved. P will call his witnesses and adduce any other admissible evidence in support of his case. Each witness will be questioned by P with a view to eliciting favourable testimony ('examination-in-chief'); then questioned by D for the purpose of testing that witness's 'evidence in chief' ('cross-examination'); and then perhaps re-questioned by P on any matters which were raised in cross-examination ('re-examination'). At the close of P's case ('half time') D may make a submission to the court that P has not been able to establish a *prima facie* case against him. If D's 'submission of no case to answer' fails, D may adduce evidence in support of his defence (and, in civil proceedings, any counterclaim he might have). D may make an opening speech (subject to a restriction in criminal trials imposed by s. 2 of the Criminal Evidence Act 1898) and will then call his witnesses and adduce his admissible evidence. In criminal proceedings the accused will usually have to give his evidence before any other defence witness to the facts (s. 79 of the Police and Criminal Evidence Act 1984). In civil trials D and P will each finish off by making a closing speech and any necessary submissions on the law. In criminal trials P will make his closing speech before D makes his, so that D has the final word. (In summary trials D has no right to make a closing speech if he has already made an opening speech, and P has no right to make a closing speech at all.) Submissions on the law will often be made during the course of the trial, interrupting the flow of events, and in civil proceedings the judge may allow a witness's written statement to stand as his evidence in chief so that his account need not be elicited by time-consuming questioning. In jury trials the judge will summarise the facts for the jury at the end of the trial and direct them on the law ('the summing-up'), following which the jury will retire to consider the case and decide whether the facts in issue have been proved to the requisite standard.

If the accused is tried in the Crown Court on indictment, submissions on the admissibility and possible exclusion of evidence are made in the absence of the jury so that they will not hear any evidence which the judge excludes. Occasionally it is necessary for preliminary questions of fact to be determined by the judge so that he can decide whether or not an item of evidence ought to be admitted. This is done by holding a trial-within-the-trial (a 'hearing on the *voir dire*' or a '*voir dire*') in the absence of the jury. The judge may have to decide, for example, whether the prosecution have proved that the accused's confession was not obtained by oppression.

The accused in criminal proceedings has the right to be present during his trial; but he has no right to expect the proceedings to be adjourned or halted if he chooses not to attend. In cases where the accused is of full age and sound mind, and is fully aware of his forthcoming trial, the trial judge (or magistrates) may proceed in his absence if he voluntarily absconds, so long as a fair trial would still be possible; but if the accused's absence is attributable to involuntary illness or incapacity, it would not be appropriate to proceed unless he is legally represented and has asked that the trial should commence (*R* v. *Jones* [2002] 2 WLR 524 (HL)). Thus, in *R (on the application of R)* v. *Thames Youth Court* [2002] EWHC Admin 1670 (QBD) it was held that a juvenile, who had been prevented from attending court by virtue of his being under arrest for an unrelated matter, should not have been tried in his absence.

16.2 The Tribunals of Fact and Law

If a case is being tried before a judge and jury, the jury are the ultimate arbiters of fact and it is for them to decide, after the judge's summing-up, what facts in issue have or have not been proved. The judge has no part to play in these deliberations, although he is entitled to comment on the facts during his summing-up. The only fact-finding role the judge has in a jury trial arises when he sits as the tribunal of fact and law to determine a question of admissibility (which may follow a hearing on the *voir dire* in criminal proceedings). All questions of substantive and procedural law are for the judge, so the jury are obliged to follow the judge's directions on such matters, subject to their overriding constitutional right in criminal proceedings to follow their own conscience and *acquit* in spite of the law and evidence (*Bushell's Case* (1670) Vaugh 135 (CCP)). However, a criminal jury's decision to *convict* may be challenged on appeal on the ground that the verdict is unsafe; and in civil proceedings any verdict of a jury may be set aside if it is 'plainly wrong' (see *Grobbelaar* v. *News Group Newspapers* [2002] 1 WLR 3024 (HL) at pp. 3051–3).

In summary proceedings lay magistrates and district judges (formerly stipendiary magistrates) are the tribunal of fact and law, save that lay magistrates are expected to accept their clerk's advice on the law. One of the principal criticisms levelled against summary trials is the absence of any distinction between the tribunals of fact and law, for while magistrates may exclude relevant evidence in their role as the tribunal of law they will, as the tribunal of fact, still be aware of (and therefore perhaps influenced by) that material. In non-jury civil trials the judge is also the tribunal of fact and law, but the nature of the proceedings, and the judge's experience as a professional lawyer, means that this fusion of roles is less objectionable than in criminal proceedings.

16.3 **The Competence and Compellability of Witnesses**

A person who is lawfully permitted to give oral evidence in civil or criminal proceedings is said to be 'competent'. As a general rule all persons are competent, but this was not always the case. At common law no person having an interest in the outcome of a civil or criminal trial was competent to testify in those proceedings. Interested persons were recognised as competent by the Evidence Act 1843, and parties and their spouses became competent in civil proceedings soon after, by virtue of the Evidence Act 1851 and the Evidence Amendment Act 1853; but it was not until the Criminal Evidence Act 1898 came into force that the general prohibition was removed in criminal proceedings, allowing the accused to testify in his own defence. Section 53(1) of the Youth Justice and Criminal Evidence Act 1999 now sets out the general rule that 'in criminal proceedings all persons are (whatever their age) competent to give evidence'.

Any competent person who may lawfully be ordered to appear in court to give evidence is said to be 'compellable'; and, as a general rule, anyone who is competent is also compellable (*Hoskyn* v. *Metropolitan Police Commissioner* [1978] 2 WLR 695 (HL)). If a compellable witness refuses to comply with an order to testify he will be in contempt of court; and if a competent witness gives evidence, but refuses to answer a legitimate question, he too will be in contempt unless, exceptionally, he is legally entitled or under a legal duty to refrain from answering.

As a general rule, oral evidence given in court (or through a live television link) must be given on oath or on affirmation. A number of different oaths are available to suit various religious beliefs (see ss. 1 to 6 of the Oaths Act 1978). The oath and affirmation give rise to the possibility of a sanction – liability for perjury – which is meant to encourage truthful testimony. In cases where a witness has affirmed, and the ground is properly laid for an expectation that he would normally take the oath on a holy book relevant to his religious belief, the judge may allow the reason why the witness did not take the oath to be explored in cross-examination (*R* v. *Mehrban* [2002] 1 Cr App R 561 (CA)). Young children may be sufficiently intelligent and intelligible to give valuable testimony while not necessarily understanding the nature of the oath or the duty imposed by it, so provision has been made for child witnesses to give unsworn evidence in both civil and criminal proceedings. Indeed, no child under the age of 14 may give sworn evidence in criminal proceedings (but a penalty may be imposed for wilfully giving false unsworn evidence). In civil proceedings, evidence need not be taken on oath if the case has been allocated to the 'small claims track', where the strict rules of evidence do not apply (r. 27.8(4) of the Civil Procedure Rules 1998).

16.3.1 **The Accused**

The accused in criminal proceedings is competent to testify in his own defence and for a co-accused, but he is not competent to testify for the prosecution against himself or his co-accused (s. 53(4) of the Youth Justice and Criminal Evidence Act 1999). Insofar as the accused is competent, he cannot be compelled to give oral evidence (s. 1(1) of the Criminal Evidence Act 1898 Act; s. 35(4) of the Criminal Justice and Public Order Act 1994). If the accused pleads guilty, or the charges against him are dropped, or the judge rules that he and his co-accused should be tried separately, he becomes competent and compellable for the prosecution against his erstwhile co-accused (s. 53(5) of the 1999 Act). There is, however, a rule of practice to the effect that a person who is still to be tried for his alleged involvement in an offence should not be called to give evidence for the prosecution at the trial of his alleged accomplice (*R* v. *Pipe* (1966) 51 Cr App R 17 (CA)).

16.3.2 The Accused's Spouse

In criminal proceedings there are restrictions on the compellability (but not the competence) of the accused's husband or wife, which are now to be found in s. 80 of the Police and Criminal Evidence Act 1984. These restrictions do not encompass any other member of the accused's family, however, so his (or her) longstanding unmarried partner or child may be compelled to give oral evidence for the prosecution like any other person (*R* v. *Pearce* [2002] 1 WLR 1553 (CA)), as indeed may be the accused's former spouse (s. 80(5)) or the purported spouse of void bigamous 'marriage' (see *R* v. *Khan* (1986) 84 Cr App R 44 (CA)). In cases where the accused's spouse is competent but not compellable for the prosecution, and she is called to testify against him, she should generally be warned, in the absence of the jury and before being sworn, that she need not give evidence but that once she has taken the oath she will be treated like any ordinary witness (*R* v. *Pitt* [1982] 3 WLR 359 (CA)). The failure of the accused's spouse to give evidence cannot be commented upon by the prosecution (s. 80A), and any comments by the judge should be made with 'a great deal of circumspection' (*R* v. *Naudeer* [1984] 3 All ER 1036 (CA); see also *R* v. *Whitton* [1998] Crim LR 492 (CA)).

Subject in all cases to s. 80(4) of the Act – which affirms that no person who is charged in the instant proceedings is compellable – the accused's spouse is compellable to give evidence on behalf of the accused (s. 80(2)); and/or on behalf of a co-accused in respect of any 'specified offence' with which that person is charged (s. 80(2A)(*a*)); or for the prosecution in respect of any 'specified offence' with which any person is charged (s. 80(2A)(*b*)). Section 80(3) provides that an offence is a 'specified offence' if: (*a*) it involves an assault on, or injury or a threat of injury to, the spouse or a person who was at the material time under the age of 16; (*b*) it is a sexual offence (defined in s. 80(7)) alleged to have been committed in respect of a person who was at the material time under that age; or (*c*) it consists of attempting or conspiring to commit, or of aiding, abetting, counselling, procuring or inciting the commission of, an offence falling within (*a*) or (*b*).

Before s. 80 of the Act came into force, the accused's spouse was only exceptionally competent and never compellable for the prosecution

(*Hoskyn* v. *Metropolitan Police Commissioner* [1978] 2 WLR 695 (HL)). Although there has always been a public interest in ensuring that persons who commit crimes are convicted, this was considered to be subservient to the public interest in upholding the sanctity of marriage. Spouses were regarded as one and the same person with a unity of interest and affection; and the privilege against self-incrimination, the danger of perjury and the likelihood of public disquiet were thought to militate against a law which would allow or, even worse, compel a person to testify against his or her spouse. Section 80 reflects the greater importance now attached to convicting offenders, at least in respect of certain types of offence. The exception for the s. 80(3) offences, covering, *inter alia*, sexual and violent assaults in the home, can be justified on the basis of their seriousness and the unavailability of witnesses other than the spouse; but it is to be noted that the subsection has been framed in a way which would allow the spouse to be compelled in respect of relatively minor offences falling outside the context of domestic assaults, and some very serious offences are omitted. For example, a wife may be compelled to give evidence against her husband where it is alleged that he drove his car carelessly and injured a 15-year-old passer-by in the street; but it would not be possible to compel her to give evidence for the prosecution in respect of her husband's alleged murder of a 16-year-old boy. Perhaps a more sensible approach would be to abolish the general rule, which is now somewhat anachronistic, and allow the judge to determine in the exercise of a general discretion whether the accused's spouse should be compellable for a co-accused or the prosecution, taking into account the seriousness of the offence, the availability of other witnesses and evidence, and the genuineness, strength and duration of the marriage. Admittedly it might be difficult to ascertain the true status of the accused's marriage in some cases, but a discretionary approach would certainly be fairer from the point of view of a co-accused, who may only exceptionally compel the accused's spouse to testify on his behalf, regardless of how weak or, it seems, contrived their marriage might be.

16.3.3 Children and Mentally Defective Adults

In civil proceedings a child under the age of 18 is competent to give sworn evidence so long as he understands the nature of the oath in accordance with the test established in *R* v. *Hayes* [1977] 1 WLR 234 (CA). The test is whether the child has a sufficient appreciation of the solemnity of the occasion and the added responsibility to tell the truth, which is involved in taking the oath, over and above the duty to tell the truth which is an ordinary duty of normal social conduct. If the child does not understand the nature of the oath he may nonetheless be competent to give unsworn evidence, so long as he understands the duty to speak the truth and has sufficient understanding to justify his evidence being heard (s. 96(1)–(2) of the Children Act 1989). Adults who are mentally defective, to the extent that they do not understand the nature of the oath, are not competent to give sworn evidence; but, unlike children, they may not give unsworn evidence.

In criminal proceedings all persons, whatever their age, are competent to give evidence by virtue of s. 53(1) of the Youth Justice and Criminal Evidence Act 1999, save that a person is not competent if he is unable to understand questions put to him as a witness or give intelligible answers (s. 53(3)). If the question of a witness's competence arises, it is for the party calling him to satisfy the court, on the balance of probabilities, that he is competent (s. 54(2)). The question whether or not a competent witness should give *sworn* evidence is governed by s. 55 of the Act which provides, *inter alia*, that a witness may not be sworn unless he has attained the age of 14 and 'has a sufficient appreciation of the solemnity of the occasion and of the particular responsibility to tell the truth which is involved in taking an oath' (s. 55(2)). A witness is presumed to have a sufficient appreciation of those matters if he is able to give intelligible testimony, but if there is evidence to show the contrary it is for the party seeking to have the witness sworn to satisfy the court, on the balance of probabilities, that the conditions in s. 55(2) are satisfied (s. 55(3)–(4)). By virtue of s. 56 of the Act, any person (including the accused) who is competent to give evidence but unable to satisfy the conditions set out in s. 55(2) must give his evidence *unsworn*, either orally or in a written deposition; but, either way, it is an offence wilfully to give false unsworn evidence (s. 57). In *DPP* v. *M* [1998] 2 WLR 604 the Divisional Court accepted that the unsworn evidence of a four-year-old could be admissible if it was intelligible; and there is research to suggest that some children as young as three may be competent (see Jones, 'The Evidence of a Three-Year-Old Child' [1987] Crim LR 677).

It is doubtful whether a question of competence arises in respect of the maker of a hearsay statement tendered under ss. 23 or 24 of the Criminal Justice Act 1988, but the judge will take into consideration the maker's poor mental condition, bearing in mind the test in s. 53(3) of the 1999 Act, when deciding (under s. 26 of the 1988 Act) whether the statement ought to be admitted in the interests of justice (*R* v. *D* [2002] 3 WLR 997 (CA)).

16.3.4 Other Special Cases

A judge is competent to give evidence on matters of which he has become aware as a result of, and relating to, the performance of his judicial functions, but he is not compellable to give such evidence (*Warren* v. *Warren* [1996] 3 WLR 1129 (CA)). The Sovereign, ambassadors, High Commissioners (and certain other diplomatic staff) are also competent but not compellable.

16.4 The Examination-in-chief of Witnesses

A witness is examined 'in-chief' when he is questioned in court for the first time by the party who has called upon him to testify. The purpose of examination-in-chief is to elicit from the witness everything he knows which is relevant to the matters in dispute and *favourable* to the case of the party examining him. The witness must be permitted to give his own account of the events in question, so he cannot be asked questions in a way which suggests particular answers or assumes the existence of facts which have yet to be established. This rule against 'leading questions' is not absolute, however. Preliminary matters, such as the witness's name and address, as well as other undisputed facts, may be elicited in this way.

Examination-in-chief raises a number of problems, particularly in criminal proceedings, and has given rise to a body of rules governing matters such as whether (and, if so, in what circumstances) a witness may refer to an earlier statement to refresh his memory, or rely on a previous consistent statement to bolster his credibility, or have his previous inconsistent statement elicited (by the party who called him) to contradict the adverse evidence in chief he has given. These and other issues are addressed in the following paragraphs. Such problems are less likely to arise in civil proceedings, where there is a presumption that a witness's written statement should stand as his evidence in chief; but even a witness in civil proceedings may be given leave to expand upon his statement if there is good reason not to confine his evidence to its contents (r. 32.5(2)–(4) of the Civil Procedure Rules 1998).

16.4.1 Memory-refreshing Notes

Trials frequently take place some considerable time after the incident in question occurred, so it makes sense to allow witnesses to refer to written notes made by them soon after the incident when the facts were remembered more clearly. Similarly there is nothing objectionable about a witness watching a closed-circuit television recording of an incident (*R* v. *Roberts* (1998) 162 JP 691 (CA)) or listening to an audio recording of a conversation (*R* v. *Bailey* [2001] EWCA Crim 733) to refresh his memory as to what happened or was said on that earlier occasion.

Written notes used to refresh the memory are not regarded as admissible evidence. They merely serve to refresh or elicit what is supposedly already in the minds of the witnesses so that they can give more reliable testimony. Indeed, because memory-refreshing notes are not evidence it is not permissible for a witness to read his notes verbatim in court for he would then be no more than a medium transforming inadmissible hearsay into admissible testimony. That said, if a witness has no present recollection of what happened, but has a documentary record of the incident – 'past recollection recorded' – and is able to verify the accuracy of that record, he may nonetheless use it to 'refresh his memory' (*Maugham* v. *Hubbard* (1828) 8 B & C 14 (KB), *R* v. *Bryant* (1946) 31 Cr App R 146 (CCA)). Thus a witness who has entirely forgotten what happened may still 'refresh his memory' from a written note of the incident even though he is in effect channelling hearsay into court, albeit restated in different words. If, however, the witness admits that he has forgotten everything, and also admits that he cannot verify the accuracy of the note or (where he can verify its accuracy) admits that it makes no difference to his understanding of what happened, he cannot rely on the note.

Until relatively recently the courts drew a firm distinction between notes made shortly after the incident in question (contemporaneous notes) and notes made later on (non-contemporaneous notes). Only contemporaneous notes could be used to refresh the witness's memory while he was in the witness box; non-contemporaneous notes could be read only before the witness was called into court to testify (*R* v. *Richardson* [1971] 2 WLR 889 (CA)). This rather illogical distinction has now largely been abandoned. In *R* v. *Da Silva* [1990] 1 WLR 31 a prosecution witness started to give evidence about an incident a year earlier but could not remember what had happened. He was allowed by the trial judge to withdraw from the witness box and refer to a non-contemporaneous statement he had made about a month after the incident. The Court of Appeal held that the trial judge had a discretion to allow a witness to refresh his memory from a non-contemporaneous note, and he could refer to it while still in the witness box or outside the court-room so long as four criteria were satisfied: first, the witness could no longer remember the details of the events because of the lapse of time; second, he had made a statement much closer in time to the events which represented his recollection at that time; third, he had not read his statement before entering the witness box; and, fourth, he wished to read his statement before giving further evidence. It was also held, however, that a non-contemporaneous note (unlike a contemporaneous note) could not be used by a witness to refresh his memory during the course of his giving testimony. However, in *R* v. *South Ribble Magistrates ex parte Cochrane* [1996] 2 Cr App R 544 the Divisional Court emphasised that any decision on allowing a witness to refresh his memory in court from a non-contemporaneous note was a matter within the judge's 'genuine strong discretion' which would rarely be interfered with on appeal. The *Da Silva* criteria were said to be no more than a guide for the judge and, accordingly, it was held that a stipendiary magistrate had exercised his discretion properly by allowing a witness to refresh his memory from a statement which he had already read before going into court. The wide ambit of the trial judge's discretion was recently reaffirmed in *R* v. *Gordon* [2002] EWCA Crim 1, where no fault could be found in a decision to allow a functionally-illiterate prosecution witness to be taken through his witness statement by counsel, in the absence of the jury, for the purpose of refreshing his memory as to the substance of a confession which had been made to him by the accused. According to the Court of Appeal, there are no 'fixed and immutable rules which must be followed before a witness may refresh his memory by a document prepared by him when his memory was clearer'.

There is much to be said for removing the distinction between contemporaneous and non-contemporaneous notes, for a witness cannot be prevented from surreptitiously using a non-contemporaneous note before the trial. If any such note has been relied on by a witness to refresh his memory this should be made known so that it can be taken into consideration when the reliability of his testimony is assessed. The weight to be attached to a witness's testimony is a question of fact and degree contingent upon how well the witness is likely to have remembered the matter in question when he noted it down. This in turn depends on the nature of the matter recorded (for example, its complexity and uniqueness), how soon after the incident the note was made, and the personality and memory of the particular witness. If a witness testifies that the accused confessed his guilt to him, it would not matter that a note of the gist of what was confessed was made some days or even several weeks after the confession, for the uniqueness of the event and the generality of what was said will probably have remained in the witness's memory until the note was made. The situation would be quite different, however, if a witness were to testify in respect of something far more complex. He would need to have made a note very soon after the incident, for any delay would severely undermine the reliability of what was noted and therefore his evidence. These are all factors the judge should take into account when exercising his discretion. For example, a forgetful witness should not be allowed to refresh his memory from a note if it relates to a nondescript car registration number recorded some weeks after the incident. The reliability and probative value of his testimony would be too low. In less extreme cases, however, it might be appropriate to allow the witness to refresh his memory and then to give the jury an appropriate direction at the end of the trial on the factors they ought to take into consideration when assessing the weight of his evidence. For these reasons the second guiding criterion suggested in *R* v. *Da Silva* [1990] 1 WLR 31 (CA) should be reframed. The issue is not so much whether the witness's note 'represented his recollection at the time' but whether the incident was at that time 'still fresh in the witness's memory' (*Attorney-General's Reference (No. 3 of 1979)* (1979) 69 Cr App R 411 (CA) at p. 414).

If a witness wishes to rely on a note to refresh his memory, that note must have been written by the witness himself or, if written by a third party, personally verified by the witness while the incident was still clear in his mind so as to become his own note by adoption. If this is not done the witness will be unable to rely on the note to refresh his memory; and the note itself will be inadmissible on account of the exclusionary hearsay rule. In *R* v. *Eleftheriou* [1993] Crim LR 947, for example, a number of customs officers dictated observations to their colleagues for compilation in a log but they neither read the entries nor had them read back to them. The Court of Appeal therefore held that the officers should not have been allowed to use the logs as memory-refreshing documents (see also *Jones* v. *Metcalfe* [1967] 1 WLR 1286 (DC) and *R* v. *McLean* (1967) 52 Cr App R 80 (CA)). By contrast, in *R* v. *Kelsey* (1981) 74 Cr App R 213 a witness dictated the registration number of a car to a police officer who then read back what he had written down. The witness confirmed that the note was correct, although he did not actually read it. The Court of Appeal held that it had been permissible for the witness to refresh his memory from the note because he had aurally verified its content. Similarly, in *Anderson* v.

Whalley (1852) 3 C & K 54 (CCP) a ship's captain was able to refresh his memory from the mate's log as he (the captain) had visually verified the log within a week of the entry having been made, while the matters referred to were still fresh in his mind.

It is not uncommon for a person who has made brief jottings or rough notes to write them up subsequently in a more coherent way. A neat copy of the original note may be used as a memory-refreshing document so long as it is substantially the same as the original (*R* v. *Kwok Si Cheng* (1976) 63 Cr App R 20 (CA)); but where the copy represents an embellished version of the original, the additional material must have been added while the incident was still fresh in the witness's memory (*Attorney-General's Reference (No. 3 of 1979)* (1979) 69 Cr App R 411 (CA)). It seems, however, that the original itself, if it is still available, must be used as the memory-refreshing document in 'past recollection recorded' cases. In *R* v. *Harvey* (1869) 11 Cox CC 546 (Assizes) the bank clerk who entered the numbers of bank notes in a ledger when cheques were cashed was called to show that the accused had cashed a forged cheque at his bank. The clerk sought to refresh his memory in court from a memorandum of the numbers, copied by him from the original ledger, but as he had not been able to remember the incident at the time the copy was made he could not rely on it. However, if the original is no longer available it is permissible for the witness to rely on an accurate copy (*Topham* v. *M'Gregor* (1844) 1 C & K 320 (Assizes)). The decision in *R* v. *Chisnell* [1992] Crim LR 507 would appear to be a recent application of this principle. The Court of Appeal upheld the trial judge's decision to allow a police officer to refresh his memory from a statement accurately compiled from a (since lost) original contemporaneous note of an interview some nine months after it took place.

The mere use of a memory-refreshing document does not make its content admissible evidence, but if the opposing party, having inspected the document as he is entitled to do, cross-examines the witness on parts which were not relied on by the witness to refresh his memory, then the party who called the witness is entitled to have the document admitted (*Senat* v. *Senat* [1965] 2 WLR 981 (PD)). In criminal proceedings a document admitted in this way is not admissible hearsay, but it may be relied on to bolster the credibility of the witness by showing his consistency (*R* v. *Virgo* (1978) 67 Cr App R 323 (CA), *R* v. *Britton* [1987] 1 WLR 539 (CA)). In civil proceedings, however, any such document is not only evidence of the witness's consistency but also evidence of the truth of the matters stated (ss. 1(1) and 6(4)–(5) of the Civil Evidence Act 1995). The same rules on disclosure and cross-examination apply whether the witness has refreshed his memory before being called to testify or while in the witness box (*Owen* v. *Edwards* (1983) 77 Cr App R 191 (DC)).

The Law Commission has suggested reforming the law on memory-refreshing notes, recognising that valuable testimony is lost where there has been a failure to verify a note made by a third party or where the witness cannot remember the incident in spite of his notes (see Law Com

No. 245 (1997) at pp. 159–64). The suggestion is that if a witness does not (and cannot reasonably be expected to) remember a matter well enough to be able to give oral evidence of it, and he has previously made a statement of that matter when it was fresh in his memory, it should be admissible as evidence of the truth of the matters stated.

16.4.2 The Rule Against Previous Consistent Statements

A witness's earlier out-of-court statement, being consistent with his present testimony, may be inadmissible for two separate reasons. If it is tendered to prove the truth of the matters stated it will fall foul of the exclusionary hearsay rule (5.1 *ante*). If it is tendered simply to prove that the statement was made, suggesting that the witness has been consistent and that his testimony is therefore more likely to be true, it will fall foul of the 'rule against previous consistent statements' (also known as the 'rule against narrative'). The rule has evolved to exclude self-serving, superfluous evidence of little probative value which could easily have been manufactured by the witness to bolster his credibility. Thus, in *R* v. *Roberts* (1942) 28 Cr App R 102 (CCA) the accused, whose defence to murder was that his rifle had gone off accidentally, could not adduce evidence of an earlier statement he had made to his father to the effect that the death had been accidental; and in *Jones* v. *South-Eastern and Chatham Railway Co* [1918] 87 LJKB 775 (CA) the plaintiff's evidence that she had pricked her thumb on a nail at work could not be bolstered by evidence that she had made similar statements before the trial (see also *Corke* v. *Corke* [1958] P 93 (CA) and *R* v. *Jarvis* [1991] Crim LR 374 (CA)). However, the rule does not apply to prevent the accused from eliciting from a prosecution witness during *cross-examination* previous consistent statements made by that witness with a view to bolstering his credibility where his testimony has been favourable to the accused's defence (*R* v. *Evans* [2001] EWCA Crim 730).

The rule against narrative is just one facet of a more general prohibition on credibility-bolstering evidence. Although in criminal proceedings the accused is entitled to have his good character considered by the jury when assessing his credibility and determining the likelihood that he committed the offence charged (3.4.2 *ante*), other witnesses are presumed to be of good character and, as a general rule, evidence which might bolster their credibility (such as the absence of previous convictions) is deemed to be irrelevant and inadmissible.

However, evidence of a witness's general reputation for truthfulness may be adduced to *rebut* evidence of his general reputation for untruthfulness, and any witness may state his occupation notwithstanding the bearing this may have on the jury's view of his testimony (*R* v. *Hamilton* (1998) *The Times* 25.7.98 (97/6511/W2) (CA), *R* v. *Beard* [1998] Crim LR 585 (CA), *R* v. *DS* [1999] Crim LR 911 (CA)). Furthermore, although it has been said that 'on general principles' the prosecution cannot in any criminal case lead evidence to support the credibility of their witnesses (*R* v. *Keast* [1998] Crim LR 748 (CA)), there is an exception if the good character of a prosecution witness is deemed to be relevant to an *issue*. In *R* v. *Amado-Taylor (No. 2)* [2001] EWCA Crim 1898, a case of alleged rape where the sole issue was consent and the accused was almost a stranger to the complainant, it was held that evidence of the complainant's virginity and her strong religious objection to pre-marital sexual intercourse had been properly admitted on the ground that in sexual offence cases where consent is in issue the complainant's disposition not to engage in sexual intercourse is relevant to the determination of that issue (an exception to the general exclusionary rule which might be inferred from s. 41(5)(*a*) of the Youth Justice and Criminal Evidence Act 1999, 17.4 *post*). This approach was followed in *R* v. *Tobin* [2003] Crim LR 408 (CA), a case of alleged indecent assault involving forced oral sex where, again, the sole issue was consent. The Court of Appeal held that the trial judge had been correct to admit evidence that the complainant was, *inter alia*, very polite and respectful as her character was relevant to the issue of consent *and* the collateral question of her credibility. Reliance was placed on the decision in *R* v. *Funderburk* [1990] 1 WLR 587 (CA) (16.5.2 *post*), where it was said that 'where the disputed issue is a sexual one between two persons in private the difference between questions going to credit and questions going to the issue is reduced to vanishing point'. In *R* v. *G(R)* [2003] Crim LR 43 the Court of Appeal was willing to assume that, in a case where the accused is charged with murder and his defence is that he disarmed the deceased and stabbed him in self-defence, the deceased's friends would be able to give a negative answer to the prosecution's question 'have you ever known [the deceased] to carry a knife?', so long as their answers would satisfy the test of sufficiency of probative value.

Although previous consistent statements are generally inadmissible, the common law has come to recognise a number of exceptions where the circumstances are such that the possibility of fabrication is likely to be lower than usual, or it is otherwise expedient to admit the evidence. If an exception applies, the earlier statement is admissible evidence of the witness's consistency and therefore his credibility; but, unless the statement also falls within an exception to the rule against hearsay, it cannot be relied on as evidence of the truth of the matters stated. In civil proceedings the common-law exceptions have largely been replaced by an inclusionary discretion (s. 6(2)(*a*) of the Civil Evidence Act 1995); and, by virtue of ss. 1(1) and 6(5) of the 1995 Act, an admissible previous consistent statement is evidence of the witness's consistency *and* the truth of the matters stated.

16.4.2.1 Previous Statements used to Refresh the Memory
Memory-refreshing statements may become admissible evidence of consistency in criminal trials and of consistency and the truth of the matters stated in civil trials (see 16.4.1 *ante*).

16.4.2.2 Previous Statements of Complainants in Sexual Offence Cases
If the accused is on trial for a sexual offence, the complainant is permitted to bolster her testimony by referring to a voluntary complaint made by her

to a third party within a reasonable period after the alleged offence. The exception applies whether the complainant is male or female (*R* v. *Camelleri* [1922] 2 KB 122 (CCA)). The modern justification for this exception seems to be that, because many sexual offences occur in private, the credibility of the complainant is of more importance in proceedings of this sort than in other proceedings (see *R* v. *Jarvis* [1991] Crim LR 374 (CA)); but it has also been said that such evidence should be admitted 'as a matter of common sense' (*R* v. *Churchill* [1999] Crim LR 664 (CA)). If the exception is a concession to the complainant in sexual offence cases because of the unavailability of other evidence, logically it should be extended to cover any offence where there is little or no independent evidence. The exception has also been criticised on the ground that it perpetuates an assumption that genuine victims of sexual offences are likely to complain very soon after their attack, implying that complainants who have not acted in this way are more likely to be lying. In fact the exception has its historical roots in the doubt attached to the veracity of any woman alleging rape who had not immediately afterwards raised a 'hue and cry' about it (*R* v. *Osborne* [1905] 1 KB 551 (CCCR)).

The modern rule was established in *R* v. *Lillyman* [1896] 2 QB 167 (CCCR), where it was held that the person to whom the complaint was made could be called to give evidence of what was said, including the full particulars, so long as the complaint was made 'as speedily after the acts complained of as could reasonably be expected'. To determine whether the complaint was made within a reasonable time, the trial judge will look at all the circumstances, including the character of the complainant and whether a suitable or trustworthy third party was available. As noted in *R* v. *Valentine* [1996] 2 Cr App R 213 (CA), where an overnight delay was regarded as reasonable, 'some victims will find it impossible to complain to anyone other than a parent or member of their family whereas others may feel it quite impossible to tell their parents or members of their family' (see also *R* v. *Cummings* [1948] 1 All ER 551 (CCA) and *R* v. *Adams* [1997] 1 Cr App R 369 (CA)). Decided cases can provide guidance on the sort of factors which might make a delay reasonable but, because each case turns on its own facts, it would be pointless to try to reconcile the various decisions. For example in *R* v. *Hedges* (1909) 3 Cr App R 262 (CCA) a week's delay was considered reasonable, whereas in *R* v. *Rush* (1896) 60 JP 777 (CCC) a day's delay was regarded as unreasonable.

It may be that the concept of reasonable time has been extended for cases where the allegation of sexual abuse relates to events which occurred many years before the trial, at a time when the complainant was a young child who might have misunderstood what was happening or been too frightened to speak out. In *R* v. *NK* [1999] Crim LR 980 (98/7601/Y3) the Court of Appeal would appear to have accepted that a written complaint, contained in an unsent letter from the (then) 17-year-old complainant to her boyfriend, had been properly admitted as a recent complaint regardless of the considerable period of time between the occurrence of the alleged offences (the mid-1980s) and the occasion when the letter was written (1997). The appeal was allowed, not because this complaint (or an earlier, oral complaint) had actually been admitted, but because the judge had failed properly to direct the jury on its evidential value. The same reasoning would appear to underlie the (somewhat confused) decision of the Court of Appeal in *R* v. *GBL* (2000) unreported (00/1697/Z1), where the complainant's unsent letter to an 'agony aunt', written when she was 16, was admitted in respect of childhood abuse which allegedly took place until she was 14. Moreover, in *R* v. *Milner* [2000] All ER (D) 1163 (99/ 7320/Z2) the Court of Appeal held that an unsent letter written in 1988 by the (then) 16-year-old complainant, describing the sexual abuse she had suffered at the hands of her father from 1983 until 1987, had been admissible as a recent complaint at her father's trial in 1999. None of these cases was referred to by counsel in *R* v. *Birks* [2003] 2 Cr App R 122, however, where the complaint was made up to a year after the final incident of alleged abuse, some 12 or 13 years before the trial. Relying on the cases which did not concern allegations of historical abuse, the Court of Appeal reluctantly held that the complaint had been wrongly admitted.

In *R* v. *Osborne* [1905] 1 KB 551 the 12-year-old complainant's friend and sister asked her why she had not waited for them at the accused's chip shop, to which she replied that the accused had indecently assaulted her. According to the Court for Crown Cases Reserved, a recent complaint is admissible only if it has been made voluntarily, but the mere fact it has been made in response to a question does not necessarily render it involuntary. If, as in the instant case, the questioning was not suggestive or leading in character – such as 'What is the matter?' or 'Why are you crying?' – the reply would still be voluntary and admissible. If, however, the questions were suggestive – such as 'Did [the accused] assault you?' or 'Did [the accused] do this and that to you?' – the complaint would be inadmissible. To determine whether a complaint was given voluntarily in accordance with this test, the judge will consider all the circumstances of the case, including the nature of any question put and the relationship between the questioner and the complainant. In *R* v. *Norcott* [1917] 1 KB 347 (CCA) a complaint was regarded as sufficiently voluntary and spontaneous to be admissible even though the complainant had been pressed to speak out by a questioner who had said, 'I won't let you go until you do tell me' (see also *R* v. *Wilbourne* (1917) 12 Cr App R 280 (CCA)).

Recent complaints are admissible as an exception to the rule against narrative to show the complainant's consistency as a witness. If there is no testimonial evidence from the complainant her recent complaint will be inadmissible, as in *R* v. *Wallwork* (1958) 42 Cr App R 153 (CCA) where the complainant was too afraid to testify (see also *R* v. *Wright* (1987) 90 Cr App R 91 (CA)). A recent complaint is admissible, however, if the complainant's (admissible) hearsay evidence has been placed before the jury, even though she has not given live oral evidence from the witness box (*R* v. *Archibald* [2002] EWCA Crim 858, where the complainant's evidence was given in the form of a pre-recorded video tape pursuant to ss. 23 and 26 of the Criminal Justice Act 1988). In *R* v. *Islam* [1999] 1 Cr App R 23 the Court of Appeal held that a recent complaint is 'not evidence of the facts complained of' and that the jury must be directed that its value is limited to helping them decide whether the complainant is telling the truth, a point recently reaffirmed in *R* v. *Croad* [2001] EWCA Crim 644 and *R* v. *Hussain* [2002] EWCA Crim 2617.

In *R* v. *Lillyman* [1896] 2 QB 167 the Court for Crown Cases Reserved recognised that a recent complaint was not evidence of the truth of the matters stated, but added that it was relevant to the issue of consent. It now seems to be clear, however, that a recent complaint is not admissible hearsay in relation to the issue of consent; rather, it supports the complainant's testimonial evidence that she did not consent when the alleged offence took place (*R* v. *Archibald* [2002] EWCA Crim 858; see also *Papakosmas* v. *R* (1999) 196 CLR 297 (HCA) at p. 305).

If the complaint was communicated orally to a third party its terms must be proved by that person otherwise the complainant's own testimony that she made the complaint will be disregarded (*White* v. *R* [1998] 3 WLR 992 (PC)). However, a *written* complaint does not need to have been communicated to any third party to be admissible, so long as it is 'in form a complaint' and not 'mere narrative' (*R* v. *Milner* [2000] All ER (D) 1163 (CA)). It should also be noted that a recent complaint will not necessarily be excluded just because the complainant made an even earlier complaint to some other person (*R* v. *Lee* (1911) 7 Cr App R 31 (CCA), *R* v. *Wilbourne* (1917) 12 Cr App R 280 (CCA), *R* v. *Valentine* [1996] 2 Cr App R 213 (CA)).

The trial judge is best placed to decide whether a recent complaint satisfies the test for admissibility, so the Court of Appeal will not lightly interfere with his ruling (*R* v. *Valentine* [1996] 2 Cr App R 213 (CA)).

16.4.2.3 Previous Statements to Rebut an Allegation of Recent
         Fabrication

If during cross-examination a witness's testimony is challenged as being a recent invention, it is permissible to adduce rebuttal evidence of an out-of-court statement made by the witness which is consistent with his present testimony (*Fox* v. *General Medical Council* [1960] 1 WLR 1017 (PC), *R* v. *Oyesiku* (1971) 56 Cr App R 240 (CA)). In this context an allegation of 'recent' fabrication means an allegation that the witness's account of what happened was fabricated after a particular incident or date (*R* v. *Sekhon* (1986) 85 Cr App R 19 (CA), *R* v. *Okai* [1987] Crim LR 259 (CA)). In other words, if an allegation of fabrication has been made, the previous statement is admissible to show that the witness's version of events before that incident or date is the same as the version given by him during the trial. Accordingly, a previous statement cannot be admitted under this exception just because it has been alleged that the witness's testimony is false or because the witness has been cross-examined on a previous inconsistent statement (*R* v. *Beattie* (1989) 89 Cr App R 302 (CA), *R* v. *P* [1998] Crim LR 663 (CA)).

The trial judge must first of all decide whether there has been an allegation of recent fabrication and then determine, taking into consideration the time and relevant circumstances, whether the statement actually rebuts the allegation. This is a matter of judicial discretion and as such the Court of Appeal will be reluctant to reach a different conclusion (*R* v. *Oyesiku* (1971) 56 Cr App R 240 (CA)). In *Flanagan* v. *Fahy* [1918] 2 IR 361 (CAI)), for example, it was alleged in cross-examination that a witness had fabricated his evidence against the plaintiff because of their mutual hostility. It was therefore permissible to adduce evidence that the witness had told his employer the same story on an occasion prior to the cause of that hostility. In *R* v. *Tyndale* [1999] Crim LR 320 (CA) it was put to the complainant's mother in cross-examination that she had incited the complainant to make her allegation of sexual abuse against the accused because she (the mother) had discovered he was having an affair and was out for revenge. The prosecution were therefore allowed to adduce the complainant's previous consistent statement, made prior to the mother's discovery of the affair, to rebut that allegation. By way of contrast, in *R* v. *Williams* [1998] Crim LR 494 (CA) the prosecution case was that the accused's version of events had been fabricated from the outset, so it was not possible for the accused to rely on a consistent statement made at an early stage in the proceedings because it in no way rebutted the allegation of fabrication (see also *R* v. *Y* [1995] Crim LR 155 (CA)).

If the accused relies on a defence which he did not mention when questioned by the police, the jury may be invited to infer that it has since been fabricated (see 9.2.2 *ante*). To prevent this inference being drawn, the accused may call a third party to give evidence that he communicated his defence to him at or about the time of the interview. If the accused calls his solicitor to give such evidence he does not thereby waive the legal professional privilege which protects their communications (*R* v. *Condron* [1997] 1 WLR 827 (CA), *R* v. *Bowden* [1999] 1 WLR 823 (CA)).

In criminal proceedings a previous consistent statement adduced to rebut an allegation of recent fabrication is evidence of the witness's consistency; it is not evidence of the truth of the matters stated (*R* v. *Benjamin* (1913) 8 Cr App R 146 (CCA), *R* v. *M* (1999) unreported (97/4138/X3) (CA)). In civil proceedings, however, a statement of this sort, admissible under s. 6(2)(*b*) of the Civil Evidence Act 1995, is also admissible hearsay (see ss. 1(1) and 6(5)).

Finally, in *R* v. *L* [2001] EWCA Crim 1425 it was held that in cases of historical sexual abuse where it is alleged that the complainant was sexually abused as a child, many years before the police were approached, the complainant may give evidence in chief that she raised the abuse with a third party during the intervening period as part of the history of the case, 'to explain the delay wholly or in part without waiting to see whether the allegation of recent fabrication is put in terms'. If the evidence is admitted on this limited basis it is not permissible for the complainant to explain what she said; and the fact of the complaint is not evidence of the complainant's consistency as a witness.

16.4.2.4   Exculpatory Statements made in Response to a Criminal Allegation

The accused's wholly or partly inculpatory out-of-court statement is admissible against him under the 'confessions' exception to the hearsay rule (7.1.1 *ante*). A purely exculpatory (self-serving) statement made in reply to an allegation that he has committed a criminal offence may also be admissible at his trial for that offence, not under an exception to the hearsay rule but as evidence of his attitude at an early stage in the investigation. In *R* v. *Storey* (1968) 52 Cr App R 334 (CA) it was felt that an exculpatory statement made 'when first taxed with incriminating facts', though inadmissible to prove the truth of the matters stated, was admissible to show the accused's reaction at that time. The exception was extended in *R* v. *Pearce* (1979) 69 Cr App R 365 (CA) to cover exculpatory statements made on subsequent encounters with the police, save that a statement made when 'first taxed' would be likely to carry more weight. This does not mean that an exculpatory statement made at any stage in the pre-trial proceedings will be admissible, however, for if its weight is negligible it may be excluded on the ground of irrelevance. Indeed a written statement carefully prepared in advance and presented to the police with a view to its being adduced as part of the prosecution case is not to be admitted under this exception (*R* v. *Pearce* (1979) 69 Cr App R 365 (CA), *R* v. *Newsome* (1980) 71 Cr App R 325 (CA), *R* v. *Hutton* (1988) *The Times* 27.10.88 (CA)). If the statement is not inadmissible for that reason, the judge has a discretion as to whether it should be admitted. In other words, the judge will allow the statement to be admitted if it is sufficiently probative of the accused's consistency, considering the degree of spontaneity involved, and not superfluous (*R* v. *Tooke* (1989) 90 Cr App R 417 (CA)).

It would appear that the question of admissibility is not dependent on the accused actually giving oral evidence (*R* v. *McCarthy* (1980) 71 Cr App R 142 (CA); *cf. R* v. *Barbery* (1975) 62 Cr App R 248 (CA)). If the accused does not testify in his own defence the question of his consistency as a *witness* does not arise, so the value of the statement in such cases (if admitted) must be to show the consistency of his denial of guilt and, where his affirmative defence (if any) is the same as that mentioned by him to the police, the consistency of the basis for that denial.

16.4.2.5 Previous Statements of Identification
There is a well-established exception to the rule against narrative which allows a criminal court to hear that a witness identified the accused on an occasion before the trial, for example at an identification parade. Evidence of the out-of-court statement of identification may be given by the identifying witness himself or by a third party who witnessed the identification. In *R* v. *Christie* [1914] AC 545 (HL) the accused, who was alleged to have indecently assaulted a boy, was identified by the boy during the trial. It was held that the boy's mother and a police officer had been entitled to give evidence that the boy had gone up to the accused soon after the alleged incident and said, 'That is the man'. The evidence was admissible to show the boy's consistency: 'to exclude the idea that the identification of the prisoner in the dock was an afterthought or mistake'.

If the evidence of a previous identification goes only to the question of consistency and there has been no identification by the witness during the trial, then, logically, the previous identification should be inadmissible. To admit an earlier identification in the absence of any identification in court would amount to a new exception to the rule against hearsay, for the relevance of the out-of-court statement would lie solely in its being accepted as evidence of the truth of the matters stated. The decision in *R* v. *Osbourne* [1973] 2 WLR 209 suggests that the present exception to the rule against narrative has indeed been widened to become an exception to the rule against hearsay too. In that case two witnesses, Mrs B and Mrs H, were called at the trial to identify the accused, and they were each asked whether they could pick out from those in the dock the men they had identified at an identification parade some eight months earlier. Mrs B replied that she could not remember having picked out anyone at the parade; Mrs H was very nervous in the witness box and said the man she had picked out was not in the dock. As a result, the officer in charge of the parade was called and gave evidence of the witnesses' earlier identifications. The Court of Appeal held that there was 'no reason at all in principle why evidence of that kind should not be admitted'. The hearsay problem was expressly addressed, however, in the similar case of *R* v. *McCay* [1990] 1 WLR 645 (CA). The witness in that case could not remember whom he had identified at the identification parade three months earlier, so a police officer was called to give evidence that the witness had identified the accused by saying, 'It is number eight'. The admissibility of this evidence was justified on the ground that it fell within the *res gestae* exception to the rule against hearsay as a statement explaining a contemporaneous act (see 6.1.1.4 *ante*).

It has also been held that evidence such as a photofit or sketch prepared by a police officer or artist from an eye-witness's description does not amount to a statement. This sort of evidence is admissible as real evidence (like photographs). It is not covered by the hearsay rule or the rule against narrative (*R* v. *Cook* [1987] 2 WLR 775 (CA), *R* v. *Constantinou* (1989) 91 Cr App R 74 (CA)). In reality, of course, a photofit or sketch is nothing more than a compilation of descriptive statements made by the identifying witness and, as such, ought logically to be covered by both rules unless an exception applies.

16.4.2.6 Previous Statements Forming Part of the *Res Gestae*

A number of common-law exceptions to the hearsay rule allow out-of-court statements to be admitted if they formed part of the *res gestae* (see 6.1 *ante*). It is not strictly necessary for the declarant to be unavailable for any such exception to apply, so a previous consistent statement forming part of the *res gestae*, if tendered to prove the truth of the matters stated, will also stand as evidence of the declarant's consistency if he does give evidence (*R* v. *Shickle* (1997) unreported (97/1947/W4) (CA)).

16.4.2.7 A Closed List of Exceptions

It has been seen that the test in criminal proceedings for admitting the accused's exculpatory statement (16.4.2.4 *ante*) is in effect the same as the general test governing the determination of 'relevance'. There would seem to be no good reason why the admissibility of *any* previous consistent statement should not be governed by the same test, dependent on the probative value of the evidence in question and the strength of competing policy considerations (such as the desirability of excluding superfluous evidence) rather than on whether a recognised exception applies. However, as the law stands if a previous consistent statement cannot be brought within one of the established exceptions it must be excluded. An example is provided by *Fennell* v. *Jerome Property* (1986) *The Times* 26.11.86 (QBD), where it was held that out-of-court statements obtained by way of truth drugs, lie detectors or hypnosis were inadmissible (see also *R* v. *Béland* [1987] 2 SCR 398 (SCC) and *R* v. *McKay* [1967] NZLR 139 (NZCA)).

16.4.2.8 Reforming the Law on Previous Consistent Statements

The Law Commission has suggested reforms which would allow previous consistent statements to be admissible hearsay in circumstances where such statements are likely to be of better quality than the testimony available at trial (Law Com No. 245 (1997) at pp. 144–58). The present law is criticised for its illogicality, arbitrary scope and capacity to prejudice the accused; and for the fact that lay tribunals of fact are unlikely to be able to differentiate between the evidential value of out-of-court statements going only to credit and out-of-court statements which are admissible under an exception to the hearsay rule. The Commission has therefore recommended that a witness's previous statement should be admissible evidence of both his consistency and the truth of the matters stated in three situations: (i) where the witness is alleged to have recently fabricated his testimony, (ii) where the witness has made a prior identification and (iii) where the witness has made a recent complaint (in any type of case).

16.4.3 Unfavourable and Hostile Witnesses

In *R* v. *Honeyghon* [1999] Crim LR 221 (97/4136/X4) (CA), Beldam LJ said:

> 'The investigation of serious offences is increasingly rendered difficult or even impossible by the reluctance of witnesses to come forward to assist the police. In some instances witnesses who have given information resile from their statements, declining to testify or suffering inexplicable amnesia. Other witnesses change their testimony, refuting earlier statements and even inconsistently support the defence.'

If a party calls a witness, and that witness turns out to be *unfavourable* in that he does not say what was expected of him for some innocent reason, such as forgetfulness, it is not permissible for that party to question him on a previous statement, whether to elicit a more favourable response or to discredit him (*The Filiatra Legacy* [1991] 2 Lloyd's Rep 337 (CA) at p. 361). (Nor is it permissible to discredit any such witness by adducing evidence of his bad character: s. 3 of the Criminal Procedure Act

1865.) The solution to the problem is to allow the unfavourable witness to refresh his memory from an earlier statement made or verified by him (16.4.1 *ante*).

If a witness takes the oath and then either refuses to say anything or adopts an adverse attitude with no intention of speaking the truth, the judge may rule the witness to be *hostile*. The witness's motive for not wishing to speak the truth is irrelevant; he may be regarded as hostile even if he favours the party calling him but, for example, fears the consequences of testifying against the other party. In *R* v. *Prefas* (1986) 86 Cr App R 111 the Court of Appeal accepted that a witness could be regarded as hostile simply on the ground that he was 'not desirous of telling the truth ... at the instance of the party calling him'. A non-compellable individual (such as a spouse) may be treated as a hostile witness, like any other witness, once he has been sworn (*R* v. *Pitt* [1982] 3 WLR 359 (CA)).

At common law a witness who is 'decidedly adverse' to the party calling him may, with the leave of the judge, be cross-examined by that party as a hostile witness. This was confirmed in *R* v. *Thompson* (1976) 64 Cr App R 96, a case in which the accused was charged with incest and a prosecution witness, his 16-year-old daughter, pointedly refused to give any evidence once sworn. The Court of Appeal held that the judge had properly allowed the prosecution to cross-examine her on the written statement she had made to the police before the trial. In addition to this common-law rule, s. 3 of the Criminal Procedure Act 1865 (which applies to both civil and criminal proceedings) provides that once the judge has ruled a witness to be 'adverse' (that is, hostile) the party calling him may contradict him by other evidence or, with the judge's leave, prove that the witness has previously made a 'statement inconsistent with his present testimony' so long as the witness is first told the circumstances of the statement and asked whether or not he made it. (In *R* v. *Thompson* the witness gave no oral evidence – her written statement was not 'inconsistent' with any 'present testimony' – so the common law was applied.) In *R* v. *Prefas* (1986) 86 Cr App R 111, a case of arson, a prosecution witness, K, was treated as hostile as he had deliberately refrained from telling the truth by testifying that he did not recognise the accused as the person to whom he had given certain containers found at the scene of the fire. The prosecution were permitted to cross-examine K and then to call two police witnesses to give evidence that he had told them prior to the trial that he had identified the accused at an identification parade but had refrained from saying so at the time because he was frightened for his family's safety. The Court of Appeal held that the trial judge had been correct to treat K as hostile and to allow the police witnesses to give evidence of K's oral statement to them. Curiously, the Court did not refer to s. 3 of the 1865 Act but based its judgment on the common law as set out by Stephen in Article 147 of his *Digest of the Law of Evidence*, even though this was a case where the hostile witness had testified in a way which was inconsistent with an earlier statement.

The common law prior to what is now s. 3 of the 1865 Act also allowed an *unfavourable* witness to be contradicted by the adduction of additional evidence (*Ewer* v. *Ambrose* (1825) 3 B & C 746 (KB)). Section 3 could be said to suggest that only a hostile witness can now be contradicted by other evidence, but the provision has not been so interpreted and the common-law position survives (*Greenough* v. *Eccles* (1859) 5 CB(NS) 786 (CCP), *The Filiatra Legacy* [1991] 2 Lloyd's Rep 337 (CA)).

There is still some confusion over the extent to which a hostile witness may be cross-examined by the party calling him. It may be that the prohibition in s. 3 on impeaching the credit of a party's own witness by 'general evidence of bad character' applies even if the witness is ruled to be hostile, preventing cross-examination as to credit as well as the adduction of bad-character evidence. Yet Stephen's view of the common law, which was relied on by the Court of Appeal in *R* v. *Prefas* (1986) 86 Cr App R 111, would permit 'cross-examination [of a hostile witness] to the extent to which the judge considers necessary for the purpose of doing justice' including cross-examination as to 'factors affecting his accuracy, veracity or credibility'. If this is correct it would seem a hostile witness may be cross-examined at common law to the same extent as an opposing party's witness, which suggests that the same must be true for s. 3 of the 1865 Act. The problem is that Stephen's *Digest* was not referred to by the Court of Appeal in the common-law case of *R* v. *Thompson* (1976) 64 Cr App R 96, where it was assumed that a hostile witness could be cross-examined only to the extent that he could be asked leading questions. It is difficult to appreciate why a hostile witness – particularly a hostile witness who provides overt support for the opposing party's case – should not be cross-examined as to credit. It would therefore make sense if Article 147 of Stephen's *Digest* were to be recognised as representing both the common law and the correct interpretation of s. 3. The judge would then have a discretion to allow cross-examination as to credit where 'necessary for the purpose of doing justice' in the case before him. The most recent pronouncement on the position at common law was in *R* v. *Honeyghon* [1999] Crim LR 221 (97/4136/X4) (CA), where it was said that the party may 'ask leading questions of the witness and if necessary cross-examine him'.

The question of hostility is determined by the trial judge on the basis of the answers (if any) given by the witness during the trial, his demeanour in court and any out-of-court statements made by him which have been placed before the judge (*R* v. *Fraser* (1956) 40 Cr App R 160 (CCA), *R* v. *Darby* [1989] Crim LR 817 (CA)). However, in cases where it is not immediately evident that the witness is displaying hostility, the judge should first consider the 'intermediate step' of inviting the witness to refresh his memory from his previous statement (*R* v. *Maw* [1994] Crim LR 841 (CA)). Because the judge is best placed to reach a decision on hostility, any such ruling is treated as an exercise of judicial discretion and, as such, an appeal based on a determination of hostility is unlikely to prove successful (*R* v. *Manning* [1968] Crim LR 675 (CA)). In *R* v. *Dat* [1998] Crim LR 488 a prosecution witness had made two inconsistent written statements and, when examined in-chief, she gave evidence in accordance with her second (unfavourable) statement. The trial judge allowed the prosecution to treat her as hostile and she was cross-examined on her first (favourable) statement. The Court of Appeal held that the judge had been entitled to exercise his discretion in that way.

The evidential value of a hostile witness's testimony and any previous statement proved under s. 3 of the 1865 Act (or the common law) depends on the nature of the proceedings. If a hostile witness in a criminal trial refuses to accept the truth of an earlier statement, that statement does not become evidence of the truth of the matters stated. Its value is limited to showing the witness's lack of credibility and the jury must be told this (*R* v. *Golder* [1960] 1 WLR 1169 (CCA), *R* v. *Oliva* [1965] 1 WLR 1028 (CCA)). (The jury should not be allowed to retire with such a written statement lest they misconstrue its evidential value (*R* v. *Darby* [1989] Crim LR 817 (CA)).) In practical terms, the effect of a previous inconsistent statement will be to nullify the hostile witness's adverse testimony, but that is not to say that his testimony should be totally disregarded. Although in *R* v. *Golder* [1960] 1 WLR 1169 it was felt that the jury ought to be directed that a hostile witness's evidence should be regarded as unreliable, a more flexible approach has now been adopted. In *R* v. *Pestano* [1981] Crim LR 397 the Court of Appeal felt that it was for the jury to decide which parts of a hostile witness's testimony were true or untrue, guided by a warning from the judge on the weight, if any, to be attached to it (see also *R* v. *Goodway* (1993) 98 Cr App R 11 (CA) and *R* v. *Governor of Pentonville Prison ex parte Alves* [1992] 3 WLR 844 (HL) at pp. 849–50).

If in criminal proceedings a hostile witness accepts that some or all of his out-of-court statement (rather than his present testimony) represents the truth, and the judge concludes that he is sufficiently creditworthy for his evidence to be considered by the jury, his subsequent testimony may be relied on by them, guided by a suitable warning relating to the witness's purported reasons for being inconsistent and how that inconsistency might affect his credibility and the weight of his evidence (*R* v. *Maw* [1994] Crim LR 841 (CA)). Similarly, where a witness has been treated as hostile on account of his refusal to answer questions in the witness box, and has accepted his out-of-court statement as a result of that ruling, the jury should be told to bear that fact in mind when assessing the weight of his evidence (*R* v. *Ugorji* [1999] All ER (D) 603 (CA)). Where the judge decides to adjourn the trial so that a potentially hostile witness can refresh his memory from his out-of-court statement, and the witness subsequently testifies in accordance with that statement, the jury should be given a summing-up on the sequence of events and a direction 'akin to a hostile witness direction' (*R* v. *Corcoran* [2003] EWCA Crim 43).

In civil proceedings an out-of-court statement proved against a hostile witness will similarly form part of the witness's subsequent testimony if its truth is accepted by him. But even if the truth of the statement is not accepted, it will still stand as evidence of the truth of the matters stated (that is, as admissible hearsay) by virtue of ss. 1(1) and 6(5) of the Civil Evidence Act 1995.

If a person has provided a written statement to the police but is subsequently unwilling to attend court, the prosecution may compel the attendance of that person in the hope that he will give evidence once sworn, and apply to have him treated as a hostile witness if he refuses to provide assistance. This is an acceptable practice so long as the prosecution have an open mind as to how the witness's evidence will come out at trial (see *R* v. *Mann* (1972) 56 Cr App R 750 (CA)).

16.4.4 Vulnerable and Intimidated Witnesses

The traditional criminal trial, occurring many months after the alleged offence, with its intimidating formality and the stresses associated with the requirement that witnesses give their oral evidence and (in particular) face cross-examination in open court, may adversely affect the quality of some witnesses' testimony. Until recently the criminal courts could overcome this problem to some extent by utilising their inherent jurisdiction to control the proceedings or the limited statutory powers available in respect of child witnesses, but Chapter I of Part II of the Youth Justice and Criminal Evidence Act 1999 has now introduced a range of measures designed to improve the quality of evidence given by any vulnerable or intimidated witness (other than the accused) in criminal proceedings. The relevant provisions are extremely convoluted but, in short, ss. 23 to 30 describe the 'special measures' which certain witness may be able to benefit from, ss. 16 to 18 explain who those witnesses are, and ss. 19 to 22 set out the rules on 'special measures directions'. Most of these provisions are now in force (the exceptions being ss. 28 and 29) save that, by virtue of s. 18(2)(*a*), a special measure cannot be taken to be available until the court has been notified by the Home Office that relevant arrangements may be made available in its area.

Sections 16(1)–(2) and 18(1)(*a*) provide that a witness (other than the accused) is eligible for a special measures direction under ss. 23 to 30 if he is under the age of 17 (a 'child witness', by virtue of s. 21(1)(*a*)); *or* the quality of his evidence is likely to be diminished by reason of mental disorder (or a significant impairment of intelligence and social functioning) or a physical disability or disorder. In this context, the quality of a witness's evidence means its quality in terms of 'completeness, coherence and accuracy' (s. 16(5)). Sections 17(1)–(2) and 18(1)(*b*) provide that a witness (other than the accused) is eligible for a special measures direction under ss. 23 to 28 if the quality of his evidence is likely to be diminished 'by reason of fear or distress . . . in connection with testifying', considering, in particular, the nature and alleged circumstances of the offence; the witness's age; his (relevant) background, ethnicity, domestic and employment circumstances, religious beliefs and political opinions (if any); and any behaviour towards the witness on the part of the accused, the accused's family or associates or any other person who is likely to be on trial or a witness in the proceedings. The complainant who intends to give evidence in respect of an alleged sexual offence (defined in s. 62) is automatically eligible for a special measures direction under ss. 23 to 28 (s. 17(4)).

By virtue of s. 19(2)–(3), once the eligibility of a witness has been established under ss. 16 or 17, the court must determine whether any (or any combination) of the applicable special measures would be likely to improve the quality of his evidence and, if so, which of those measures, or combination of measures, would be likely to maximise the quality, having taken into consideration all the circumstances of the case including, in particular, the witness's views and whether the measure(s) might tend to inhibit his evidence being effectively tested. The court will then give a 'special measures direction' providing for the measure(s) so determined to apply to the evidence given by him. Subject to s. 21(8)–(9), a special measures direction will remain in force until the end of the proceedings, unless the interests of justice demand that it be discharged or varied (s. 20(1)–(2)).

The possible special measures which may be made in respect of a witness's evidence are: screening the witness from the accused (s. 23); allowing the witness to give evidence by means of a live television link or similar arrangement (s. 24); providing for the exclusion of specified persons (other than the accused, legal representatives or any person appointed to assist the witness) in cases where the proceedings relate to a sexual offence (defined in s. 62) or there are reasonable grounds for believing that a person other than the accused has sought, or will seek, to intimidate the witness (s. 25); providing for the wearing of wigs and gowns to be dispensed with (s. 26); providing for a video recording of an interview with the witness to be admitted as the witness's evidence in chief, unless the interests of justice demand that it should not be admitted (s. 27); and providing the witness with a device to enable questions or answers to be communicated to or by him (s. 30). Section 28 will enable the court to provide for the witness's cross-examination and re-examination to be recorded by means of a video recording and admitted (if a s. 27 direction provides for the admission of a recording as his evidence in chief). Section 29 will enable the court to provide for any examination of the witness to be conducted through an interpreter or other approved intermediary who will 'explain' the questions or answers. For a recording to be admitted under s. 27 the witness must be called to attend for cross-examination by the party tendering the recording unless a special measures direction provides for his evidence on cross-examination to be given 'otherwise than by testimony in court', or the parties have agreed that he need not be available (s. 27(5)(*a*)). If the witness is unavailable, and s. 27 cannot be relied on, the party tendering the recording may have to fall back on the hearsay exceptions in ss. 23 or 24 of the Criminal Justice Act 1988.

Section 21(2) provides that, in making a determination for the purposes of s. 19(2) in respect of a 'child witness', the court must first have regard to s. 21(3)–(7). Section 21(3) sets out the 'primary rule' that a special measures direction must be given which provides, first, for the admission under s. 27 of a video recording of an interview with the child, which was made with a view to its being admitted as his evidence in chief (a 'relevant recording'); and, second, for the child's live evidence in the proceedings to be given by means of a live link in accordance with s. 24. However, the primary rule is subject to s. 21(4)–(5), which provides, *inter alia*, that it does not apply if compliance with it would not be likely to maximise the quality of the child's evidence, unless the offence (or any of the offences) to which the proceedings relate is one falling within s. 35(3)(*a*)–(*d*), in which case the child is 'in need of special protection' (s. 21(1)(*b*)). Where a child is in need of special protection because the accused is charged with a (sexual) offence in s. 35(3)(*a*), any special measures direction must provide for the special measures available under s. 28 (when it is in force) to apply in relation to his cross-examination and re-examination (s. 21(6)), unless the child informs the court that he does not want that measure to apply (s. 21(7)(*b*)). Section 22 provides that, in relation to a witness (a 'qualifying witness') who was under the age of 17 when a relevant recording was made, but is no longer an eligible witness at the time it falls for the court to make a determination on special measures, then: s. 21(2)–(4) applies in relation to the admission of the relevant recording; s. 21(5) applies if the qualifying witness is in need of special protection; and s. 21(6)–(7) applies if the need for special protection arises because the offence falls within s. 35(3)(*a*).

Where a child witness is eligible by reason only of his age, any special measure direction ceases once he reaches the age of 17 unless he has already begun to give evidence in the proceedings (s. 21(8)), save that a direction which provides for a video recording to be admitted under s. 27, or for a s. 28 measure to apply, shall continue to have effect (in respect of those measures) when the witness attains the age of 17 if he was still under that age when the video recording was made (s. 21(9)).

Section 31 provides that a statement made by a witness which (in accordance with a special measures direction) is not made in direct oral testimony in court is to be treated as testimony. Section 32 requires the trial judge to give the jury such warning (if any) as he considers necessary to ensure that the accused is not prejudiced by that fact that a witness's evidence has been given in accordance with a special measures direction.

Although witnesses excluded by the eligibility provisions cannot benefit from a statutory special measures direction, a direction may still be made by the court 'in the exercise of its inherent jurisdiction or otherwise' (s. 19(6)). Thus, a non-eligible prosecution witness may be given leave to testify from behind a screen, so long as the jury are warned not to draw an inference adverse to the accused (*R* v. *X* (1989) 91 Cr App R 36 (CA), *R* v. *Cooper* [1994] Crim LR 531 (CA), *R* v. *Foster* [1995] Crim LR 333 (CA)); or the witness may be allowed the assistance of an interpreter (*R* v. *O'Brien* (1845) 1 Cox CC 185 (Assizes), *R* v. *Duffy* [1998] 3 WLR 1060 (CA)); or, exceptionally, the judge may exclude certain individuals from court while a witness is giving evidence if the administration of justice would otherwise be frustrated or rendered impracticable (*Attorney-General* v. *Leveller Magazine* [1979] 2 WLR 247 (HL) at p. 252, *R* v. *Richards* (1998) 163 JP 246 (CA); see also s. 37(1) of the Children and

Young Persons Act 1933 and *Practice Direction (Criminal Proceedings: Consolidation)* [2002] 1 WLR 2870 (SC) at pp. 2895–6). The judge can also require advocates to rephrase their questions, particularly those put in cross-examination, to ensure that they are fully understood by the witness (*R* v. *Mitchell* [2003] EWCA Crim 907).

The accused's exclusion from the statutory scheme is difficult to justify or understand, given the presumption of innocence. The court's inherent power to control the conduct of proceedings is not wide enough completely to redress the imbalance created by the accused's exclusion, so the compatibility of this part of the Act with Article 6 of the European Convention on Human Rights will almost certainly be challenged. In this context it is to be noted that Article 6(3)(d) of the Convention provides that the accused has the right 'to examine or have examined witnesses against him and to obtain the attendance and examination of witnesses on his behalf *under the same conditions as witnesses against him*'; and that the European Court of Human Rights has held it to be 'essential that a child charged with an offence is dealt with in a manner which takes full account of his age, level of maturity and intellectual and emotional capacities, and that steps are taken to promote his ability to understand and participate in the proceedings' (*V* v. *United Kingdom* (1999) 30 EHRR 121 at p. 179).

Notwithstanding the accused's exclusion, the courts can be expected to do everything within their present powers to accommodate his special needs, insofar as those needs affect his understanding of the proceedings or his ability to give evidence. In *R* v. *H* [2003] EWCA Crim 1208, for instance, guidelines were laid down for cases where the accused has learning difficulties: the accused may be permitted the services of 'the equivalent of an interpreter' while giving evidence; a detailed defence statement may be read to the jury if there is concern about the accused's ability to recall everything that he wants to say; and the accused may be permitted to recall matters by way of reference to a past coherent account of events he has given, in response to leading questions from his advocate if necessary.

The use of special measures for prosecution witnesses will not necessarily prevent the accused from having a fair trial, for the purposes of Article 6(1) and (3)(d) of the European Convention. It has been held that 'principles of fair trial also require that in appropriate cases the interests of the defence are balanced against those of witnesses or victims called upon to testify' and that criminal proceedings should be organised so that the interests of (prosecution) witnesses 'are not unjustifiably imperilled' (*Doorson* v. *Netherlands* (1996) 22 EHRR 330 (ECtHR) at p. 358). Thus, so long as the special measures for vulnerable witnesses do not go beyond what is necessary to accomplish the objective of eliciting the best evidence from them, and the accused is afforded an opportunity effectively to challenge their evidence, the accused's Article 6(1) right to a fair trial will not be infringed.

The 1999 Act preserves the accused's right to have the relevant witnesses' evidence challenged by cross-examination, and requires that the jury be warned, where necessary, against drawing an inference against the accused if a special measure has been used, so it is difficult to see how an effective challenge on the fairness of the trial can be made if the sole argument is that there has been an infringement of Article 6(3)(d). Indeed, the validity of the policy considerations underlying the use of pre-recorded evidence in chief and live television links for child witnesses (under earlier legislation) was recognised in *R (DPP)* v. *Redbridge Youth Court* [2001] 2 Cr App R 458 where, relying on *Doorson* v. *Netherlands* (1996) 22 EHRR 330, the Divisional Court held that protection of this sort for a vulnerable child witness 'cannot result in unfairness to a defendant provided always that [he] is given a fair opportunity both to test that evidence and to answer it'. More important, in *R (on the application of D)* v. *Camberwell Green Youth Court* (2003) 167 JP 210 the Divisional Court held that s. 21(5) of the 1999 Act, which provides that the s. 21(3) 'primary rule' requiring special measures directions under ss. 24 and 27 for child witnesses applies in any case where the child is in need of special protection, was compatible with the accused's Article 6(1) right to a fair trial because of the safeguards in ss. 20(2) and 24(3) and the court's uninhibited common-law power to prevent unfairness (and, the Court might have added, s. 27(2)). With regard to Article 6(3)(d), Rose LJ said (at p. 222): 'Neither live link, nor a video recording of evidence in chief, in my view infringes that right, provided, as here, the defendant's lawyers can see as well as hear the witness and can cross-examine.'

The most radical provision in the package of reforms (indeed, the only real innovation) is the removal of the accused's entitlement to have a vulnerable witness cross-examined live during the course of the trial. When s. 28 comes into force the cross-examination in some cases will take place in advance of the trial, and be admitted in the form of a pre-recorded video tape for the jury to watch along with the witness's pre-recorded evidence in chief (s. 27). The Strasbourg jurisprudence does not require that the accused should be able to challenge the evidence of prosecution witnesses during the trial itself, or even that the witness should actually attend; but it is desirable (if not always necessary) that the accused should have an opportunity to make an effective challenge at some stage in the proceedings (6.2.5 *ante*). In *PS* v. *Germany* (2001) 36 EHRR 1139 the European Court of Human Rights said (at pp. 1143–4):

'All the evidence must normally be produced at a public hearing, in the presence of the accused, with a view to adversarial argument. There are exceptions to this principle, but they must not infringe the rights of the defence. As a general rule, the accused must be given an adequate and proper opportunity to challenge and question a witness against him, either when he makes his statement or at a later stage ... In appropriate cases, principles of fair trial require that the interests of the defence are balanced against those of witnesses or victims called upon to testify, in particular where life, liberty or security of person are at stake, or interests coming generally within the ambit of Article 8 of the Convention ... However, only such measures restricting the rights of the defence which are strictly necessary are permissible under Article 6.

Moreover, in order to ensure that the accused receives a fair trial, any difficulties caused to the defence by a limitation on its rights must be sufficiently counterbalanced by the procedures followed by the judicial authorities ...'

In *SN* v. *Sweden* (2002) Application No. 34209/96 the European Court of Human Rights held that the applicant had received a fair trial in respect of an allegation of sexual abuse against a 10-year-old boy, even though the boy (who had been available) had not been called by the prosecution to give live evidence and neither the accused nor his legal representative had questioned him (or even seen him being questioned) before the trial. Nor did it matter that the boy's pre-recorded evidence in chief – a video recording of an initial interview conducted by a police officer – had been the only evidence that the applicant had abused him. According to the Court, 'in criminal proceedings concerning sexual abuse certain measures may be taken for the purposes of protecting the [complainant], provided that such measures can be reconciled with an adequate and effective exercise of the rights of the defence'; and, in the instant case, the applicant's right to challenge the boy's evidence and credibility had been sufficiently protected by the admission at his trial of the transcript (and the admission, on appeal, of the audio recording) of a second interview between the officer and the boy during which that officer had asked the questions to which the defence required answers.

The safeguards in s. 28(2) of the 1999 Act should ensure that the accused is able effectively to challenge the witness's evidence in chief, so s. 28, like s. 27, will no doubt be held to comply with the requirements of Article 6. The use of an intermediary during the trial itself should also be acceptable, given the safeguards in s. 29(3)–(7) of the Act. The other special measures are equally unlikely to provide the accused with an effective challenge on human rights grounds. It is to be noted that the European Commission of Human Rights accepted that it was legitimate in some cases to screen a prosecution witness from the accused and the public (*AM* v. *United Kingdom* (1992) Application No. 20657/92); and Article 6(1) of the Convention expressly provides that 'the press and public may be excluded from all or part of the trial ... where the interests of juveniles or the protection of the private life of the parties so require, or to the extent strictly necessary ... in special circumstances where publicity would prejudice the interests of justice'.

An interview with a child or mentally-disabled witness which is recorded with a view to its being admitted under s. 27(1) of the 1999 Act should be conducted by a skilled interviewer in accordance with Home Office guidelines – formerly the *Memorandum of Good Practice*, now *Achieving Best Evidence in Criminal Proceedings: Guidance for Vulnerable or Intimidated Witnesses, Including Children* – to ensure that the witness is not expressly or impliedly led into giving particular answers and that his evidence is reliable. Section 27(2) provides that a pre-recorded video of the witness's evidence should not be admitted if the court is of the opinion, having regard to all the circumstances of the case, that its admission would not be in the interests of justice. A relevant factor for this test is whether the witness's evidence is likely to be reliable. Under the old statutory regime governing the admission of pre-recorded evidence of children in criminal proceedings, an important consideration for the court when assessing reliability was the extent to which the *Memorandum of Good Practice* had been complied with (*G* v. *DPP* [1998] 2 WLR 609 (DC)). In *R* v. *P* [1998] Crim LR 663 (CA), for example, a video-recording was excluded because the way in which the interview had been conducted presumed the accused's guilt. It was also held that the judge could allow the jury to refer to a transcript of the recording while it is being played to them if it would be likely to help them follow the child's evidence, but that they should not normally be permitted to retire with it in case its value is over-emphasised (*R* v. *Welstead* [1996] 1 Cr App R 59 (CA), *R* v. *Morris* [1998] Crim LR 416 (CA)).

Pre-recorded interviews with children will normally be admitted in civil (family) proceedings concerned with the welfare of a child under s. 96(3) and (5)(*a*) of the Children Act 1989 and the Children (Admissibility of Hearsay Evidence) Order 1993 (SI 1993 No. 621). As a general rule, adults will be expected to give live oral evidence (*Re D (Sexual Abuse Allegations: Evidence of Adult Victim)* [2002] 1 FLR 723 (FD)). As with interviews conducted for criminal proceedings, where there is an allegation of sexual abuse against a child the interviewer should have reference to the guidance provided by the Home Office to ensure that the child's evidence is reliable (*Re D (Child Abuse: Interviews)* [1998] 2 FLR 10 (CA)).

16.4.5 Live Television Links

In addition to the special measure available under s. 24 of the Youth Justice and Criminal Evidence Act 1999 (16.4.4 *ante*), s. 32(1)(*a*) of the Criminal Justice Act 1988 Act (read with SI 1990 No. 2084) may be relied on in criminal proceedings for homicide or serious fraud to allow a witness outside the United Kingdom (other than the accused) to give his evidence through a live television link. Evidence given by way of a live television link under s. 24 of the Youth Justice and Criminal Evidence Act 1999 or s. 32(1) of the Criminal Justice Act 1988 is regarded as oral evidence given in the proceedings (see s. 31(1)–(2) of the 1999 Act and s. 32(3) of the 1988 Act). Accordingly, unless exempt, a witness who is to be examined in chief or cross-examined in this way must first take the oath or affirm (*R* v. *Sharman* [1998] 1 Cr App R 406 (CA)).

In civil proceedings, r. 32.3 of the Civil Procedure Rules 1998 provides that the court 'may allow a witness to give evidence through a video link or by other means'. Guidance on the use of video conferencing has been annexed to the practice direction which supplements Part 32 of the Rules. In *Rowland* v. *Bock* [2002] 4 All ER 370 (QBD) it was held that no defined limit or set of circumstances should be placed on the judicial discretion to permit video link evidence, save that 'costs, time, inconvenience and so forth' are relevant considerations, as is an overseas witness's reason for being unable to attend court in England. In that case the reason for the claimant's refusal to attend court to testify was the risk that he would be placed under arrest if he entered England. According to Newman J, however, 'full access to the court for justice in a civil matter should not, save in exceptional circumstances, be at a price of the litigant losing his liberty and facing criminal proceedings'.

16.5 The Cross-examination of Witnesses

'Human evidence shares the frailties of those who give it. It is subject to many cross-currents such as partiality, prejudice, self-interest and, above all, imagination and inaccuracy. Those are matters with which the jury, helped by cross-examination and common sense, must do their best.' (*Toohey* v. *Metropolitan Police Commissioner* [1965] 2 WLR 439 (HL) at p. 446)

Cross-examination has been described as 'a powerful and valuable weapon for the purpose of testing the veracity of a witness and the accuracy and completeness of his story' (*Mechanical and General Inventions* v. *Austin* [1935] AC 346 (HL) at p. 359). A witness may be cross-examined by any party to the proceedings other than the party who called him (unless the witness is 'hostile') the purpose being to elicit from the witness any evidence which may undermine the case of the party who called him and/or support the case of the party for whose benefit the cross-examination is being conducted. Once a witness has entered the witness-box and (where necessary) been sworn, he may be cross-examined regardless of whether he actually gave any evidence in chief (*R* v. *Bingham* [1999] 1 WLR 598 (HL)); and, in civil proceedings, a witness may be cross-examined on his witness statement regardless of whether any part of it was referred to during the course of his examination-in-chief (r. 32.11 of the Civil Procedure Rules 1998). If it is not possible to elicit anything favourable from the witness, the cross-examiner may have no choice but to cross-examine him 'as to credit'; that is to say, the cross-examiner will seek to undermine the weight of the witness's adverse evidence by attacking his credibility. He may try to show that the witness ought not to be believed on oath because of his past conduct, his previous convictions, his close relationship with the party who called him (or the alleged victim), his poor relationship with the cross-examining party, his relevant mental or physical condition or disability, or the fact that he has made statements which are inconsistent with his present testimony. Although there are certain common-law and statutory limits on the permissibility of cross-examination as to credit (16.5.1 *post*), as a general rule witnesses are under a legal obligation to answer any questions put to them during cross-examination.

During the course of cross-examination, the cross-examining party's version of events should be put to the witness so that he has an opportunity to comment on any differences between their respective stories. If any aspect of the witness's version is not questioned in this way the cross-examining party may be deemed to have accepted that version as correct and may therefore be unable to assert anything to the contrary later (*Browne* v. *Dunn* (1893) 6 R 67 (HL), *R* v. *Hart* (1932) 23 Cr App R 202 (CCA)). In *R* v. *Bircham* [1972] Crim LR 430 (CA), for example, the accused could not suggest that the co-accused or a prosecution witness had been involved in the offence because such allegations had not been put to them in cross-examination. The rule in *Browne* v. *Dunn* does not apply in summary proceedings (*O'Connell* v. *Adams* [1973] RTR 150 (DC)), so in *Wilkinson* v. *DPP* [2003] EWHC 865 Admin (QBD) a district judge was entitled to reject the accused's evidence, even though the prosecution had failed to cross-examine her.

The cross-examiner, unlike the examiner-in-chief, is entitled to ask the witness leading questions which suggest a particular (desired) answer. Indeed this is the sort of questioning which is most likely to be adopted, so that the cross-examining advocate can exercise full control over what the witness says. If, however, the cross-examining party has the same interest as the party who called the witness (for example, where the accused's witness is being cross-examined by a friendly co-accused) the answers elicited by leading questions are unlikely to carry much weight with the tribunal of fact. Moreover, it would be improper to question a favourable witness in this way.

16.5.1 Limits on Cross-examination

There are a number of common-law and statutory limits on cross-examination. In civil proceedings, r. 32.1(3) of the Civil Procedure Rules 1998 expressly provides that cross-examination may be limited, in accordance with the overriding objective of dealing with cases justly (r. 1.1(1)). Cross-examination may also be limited during the hearing of a small claim (r. 27.8(5)) In criminal proceedings, the accused is given a degree of protection from cross-examination on his bad character by s. 1(3) of the Criminal Evidence Act 1898 (4.3–7 *ante*) and the prosecution should not seek to elicit answers from him in cross-examination which would lose him that protection (*R* v. *Baldwin* (1925) 18 Cr App R 175 (CCA)). In proceedings for a sexual offence, ss. 41 to 43 of the Youth Justice and Criminal Evidence Act 1999 limit the extent to which the complainant may be cross-examined on her other sexual experiences (see 17.4 *post*). Furthermore, by virtue of ss. 34 to 36 of the 1999 Act, it is not permissible for the accused *himself* to cross-examine the complainant in proceedings for a sexual offence (defined in s. 62) or a 'protected witness' (child complainant or child witness) where the alleged offence falls within s. 35(3) or any witness in respect of whom a specific direction has been made (under s. 36). However, if the accused is prevented from cross-examining a witness in person, he will be permitted (and may be required) to have a legal representative to do it for him (s. 38); and the jury may need to be warned against drawing a prejudicial inference against him (s. 39). It would be difficult to support an argument that this prohibition on cross-examination in person denies the accused a fair trial, even though

Article 6(3)(c) of the European Convention on Human Rights expressly provides, *inter alia*, that the accused has the right 'to defend himself in person or through legal assistance of his own choosing'. The 'principles of fair trial also require that in appropriate cases the interests of the defence are balanced against those of witnesses or victims called upon to testify' (*Doorson* v. *Netherlands* (1996) 22 EHRR 330 (ECtHR) at p. 358). Thus in *Croissant* v. *Germany* (1992) 16 EHRR 135 (ECtHR) a provision requiring that the accused be legally represented in any case before the German Regional Court was held to be compatible with Article 6.

It is inappropriate in any proceedings to cross-examine a witness as to credit on trivial matters, or matters from long ago or of such a nature that they would not materially affect his credibility; nor should matters be raised which would severely affect the witness's character if his evidence is not particularly important (see *Hobbs* v. *Tinling* [1929] 2 KB 1 (CA) at p. 51 and *R* v. *Meads* [1996] Crim LR 519 (CA)). In *R* v. *Sweet-Escott* (1971) 55 Cr App R 316 (Assizes), Lawton J stated that since 'the purpose of cross-examination as to credit is to show that the witness ought not to be believed on oath, the matters about which he is questioned must relate to his likely standing after cross-examination with the tribunal which is trying him' and suggested, as an example, that it would be inappropriate to cross-examine an elderly witness about his having been caned as a schoolboy for petty theft from a class-mate. This test was applied by the Court of Appeal in *R* v. *Funderburk* [1990] 1 WLR 587 and, for civil proceedings, in *Watson* v. *Chief Constable of Cleveland Police* [2001] EWCA Civ 1547. Cross-examination should not be protracted, and it is 'indefensible' to cross-examine a witness in a discourteous manner (*Mechanical and General Inventions* v. *Austin* [1935] AC 346 (HL) at p. 360; see also *R* v. *Kalia* [1975] Crim LR 181 (CA)). Nor should questions be asked if the intention is to vilify, insult or annoy the witness or any other person. In *R* v. *Brown* [1998] 2 Cr App R 364 (CA) it was held that the trial judge should do everything he could, consistent with giving the accused a fair trial, to minimise the trauma suffered by other participants in the proceedings.

It goes without saying that a witness should not be asked questions in cross-examination about irrelevant or otherwise inadmissible evidence (*R* v. *Treacy* [1944] 2 All ER 229 (CCA)). If, however, a witness is handed and asked to read to himself a document written by a third party, his acceptance of the substance of the document allows it to become admissible hearsay evidence and he may then be questioned about it; but if he does not accept the truth of the document it remains inadmissible and cross-examination on it is prohibited (*R* v. *Gillespie* (1967) 51 Cr App R 172 (CA), *R* v. *Cross* (1990) 91 Cr App R 115 (CA)).

It has recently been held that if the accused's defence is that the allegation against him is a complete fabrication, the prosecution are entitled to ask him in cross-examination whether he knows of anything which might explain why the complainant has given false evidence against him, even if the prosecution anticipate a negative answer. In *R* v. *Brook* [2003] EWCA Crim 951 the Court of Appeal held that the question is relevant and so permissible for if there is anything known to the accused which would provide a reason for the complainant to lie, this would undermine the complainant's credibility as a witness, and the fact that a negative answer is anticipated cannot determine admissibility. According to the Court, moreover, a question of this sort does not invite speculation, or seek to elicit inadmissible opinion evidence from the accused, because it is directed at establishing the state of his *knowledge*. Nevertheless, this is a controversial decision for the accused may feel obliged to provide an explanation, and may therefore appear evasive in the witness box as he tries to come up with something which might satisfy the jury. In other words, the accused may feel obliged to speculate, even though, as a presumptively innocent person, he is under no burden to provide an explanation.

16.5.2 The Rule on the Finality of Answers on Collateral Matters

As a general rule, if a witness is cross-examined about a *collateral* matter his answer is said to be 'final', meaning that while the cross-examiner is not obliged to accept the truth of the answer, and may pursue the point with further questioning, he is not permitted to adduce evidence to show the contrary (*Attorney-General* v. *Hitchcock* (1847) 1 Exch 91 (CE), *Hobbs* v. *Tinling* [1929] 2 KB 1 (CA)). This prohibition on the adduction of evidence in rebuttal arose at common law to ensure that jurors would not be overburdened or confused by a morass of peripheral matters which would distract them from the essential issues (see *Toohey* v. *Metropolitan Police Commissioner* [1965] 2 WLR 439 (HL) at p. 446).

The rule on the finality of answers does not apply to cross-examination on matters which are *directly relevant to an issue* in the proceedings, though of course the distinction between collateral relevance and direct relevance is somewhat artificial, for collateral facts also have a bearing on the determination of the issues in dispute. The rule is therefore one 'of convenience, and not of principle' (*R* v. *Burke* (1858) 8 Cox CC 44 (CCAI) at p. 53, *R* v. *Neale* [1998] Crim LR 737 (CA)). If the judge rules that a question relates solely to a collateral matter, and that matter does not fall within an exception to the general exclusionary rule, it is not permissible for the cross-examining party to rebut the witness's answer by the adduction of additional evidence, even if that evidence would show that the witness is lying or mistaken on a matter of some importance. The utility of this rule is demonstrated by the facts of *R* v. *Colwill* [2002] EWCA Crim 1320, which concerned an allegation of rape where the only issue was whether or not the complainant consented. To undermine the complainant's assertion of non-consensual intercourse, counsel for the defence sought to undermine her credibility, and would have sought to question a prosecution witness (G) about her negative view of the complainant's credibility following a possibly false allegation the complainant had made against her (concerning the way G had been treating her children). The Court of Appeal held that the complainant herself could have been cross-examined on the allegations made by her but, as she would have asserted her belief in the truth of those allegations, the rule on the finality of answers on collateral matters would have prevented the defence from seeking to elicit evidence from G as to the falsity of the allegations. The truth or falsity of the allegations was 'truly collateral' to the issue of consent, notwithstanding the importance of the complainant's credibility to the determination of that issue:

> 'Sensible investigation of the truth or falsity of [the complainant's] telephone complaints to the police would have involved calling the two children, the investigating police officers and the representative of the Social Services Department as to the injuries ... Otherwise it would have been impossible for the jury to draw any real conclusion about those matters. It would have involved the further question whether, notwithstanding that the substance of [her] telephone complaints was untrue, she honestly believed them to be justified from all that which she saw and heard. It would have involved the jury embarking on an extremely difficult and complex task and ... would have overwhelmed the evidence ... on the real issue in the case.'

In *Attorney-General* v. *Hitchcock* (1847) 1 Exch 91 (CE) it was said that the test for determining whether evidence could be adduced to rebut an answer given in cross-examination was whether that evidence would be admissible in chief as part of the cross-examining party's case. In *Piddington* v. *Bennett* (1940) 63 CLR 533, which concerned a personal injury claim arising out of a road accident in Australia, one of the plaintiff's witnesses said he had seen the accident while returning from a bank, having done some business for a Mr J. The defendant cross-examined the witness about his presence at the scene and was later allowed to call the bank manager to say that there had been no transaction in respect of Mr J on that day. The majority of the High Court of Australia held that the bank manager should not have been called to give evidence in rebuttal as the witness's answer had related solely to a collateral matter (that is, the witness's memory or veracity). Although the manager's evidence was of some importance, suggesting that the plaintiff's witness had not actually been at the scene of the accident, it was not a matter the defendant would have sought to adduce as part of his defence if it had not arisen in cross-examination. Similarly, in *R* v. *Burke* (1858) 8 Cox CC 44 (CCAI), where the accused's witness was cross-examined on his purported inability to speak English, it was held that prosecution witnesses should not have been called to testify that he could speak English. The witness's knowledge or ignorance of English was relevant to nothing other than his credibility.

Thus, if a witness denies an allegation which relates solely to his credibility then, as a general rule, the cross-examining party will not be able to adduce evidence in rebuttal. This rule is subject to two broad qualifications, however. First, there are several specific exceptions to the exclusionary rule which allow evidence to be adduced in rebuttal even though the witness's answer relates to nothing other than his credibility

(16.5.4 *post*). Second, the witness's credibility may be so important in the context of the case that evidence undermining it may be regarded by the judge as directly relevant to an issue, in which case the rule on the finality of answers does not apply. An example is where the accused is on trial for rape, and his defence is that he and the complainant engaged in consensual sexual intercourse. Whether the jury find the accused guilty will depend heavily on the view they take of the complainant's testimony, which will of course depend on their assessment of her credibility as a witness. The complainant's credibility is therefore inextricably connected with the central (indeed the only) issue in the trial, so any evidence which would undermine her credibility may be said to have a direct bearing on that issue. The Court of Appeal acknowledged as much in *R* v. *Funderburk* [1990] 1 WLR 587 (at p. 597) where it was said that 'where the disputed issue is a sexual one between two persons in private the difference between questions going to credit and questions going to the issue is reduced to vanishing point'. The importance of any particular witness's credibility, and whether it might properly be said to have a direct bearing on an issue in the proceedings, is a matter of degree. For this reason the Court of Appeal has now accepted that the trial judge has a 'wide ambit of discretion' which allows him to determine whether the matter on which a witness's credibility is being tested may be said to have a direct bearing on an issue, bearing in mind the justifications for the exclusionary rule (*R* v. *Somers* [1999] Crim LR 744, following the approach of the Federal Court of Australia in *Natta* v. *Canham* (1991) 104 ALR 143). Relevant considerations include the importance of the witness's credibility to the issue, the importance of the evidence to that witness's credibility and 'the necessity in the interests of justice to avoid multiplicity of issues where possible' (*R* v. *Colwill* [2002] EWCA Crim 1320). In other words, the judge should 'have in mind questions of practicality, in the sense of trying to ensure that, while maintaining fairness, the trial [does] not get out of hand, nor the jury become confused by evidence and dispute on matters which were essentially collateral' (*R* v. *James* (1998) unreported (97/2785/Y4) (CA), referring with approval to *R* v. *S* [1992] Crim LR 307 (CA), 16.5.3 *post*).

16.5.3 Previous Inconsistent Statements

An effective way of undermining a witness's testimony is to cross-examine him on an earlier statement made by him which contradicts the version of events he has just given in chief. The *admissibility* of such statements is governed by ss. 4 and 5 of the Criminal Procedure Act 1865, which apply to civil as well as criminal proceedings.

Section 5 of the Act covers 'previous statements made by [the witness] in writing, or reduced into writing, relative to the subject matter of the indictment or proceeding'. For a statement of this sort to be admissible, the witness must first be allowed to see those parts which will be used to contradict him. If the witness is cross-examined only on certain parts of his previous statement, the judge has a discretion as to whether the jury should be permitted to see the entire statement or just those parts (*R* v. *Beattie* (1989) 89 Cr App R 302 (CA)). Section 4 covers 'any former statement made by [the witness] relative to the subject matter of the indictment or proceeding, and inconsistent with his present testimony' and provides that if the witness 'does not distinctly admit that he has made such statement, proof may be given that he did in fact make it', so long as he is first told about the circumstances of the statement and asked whether or not he made it. In *R* v. *Derby Magistrates' Court ex parte B* [1995] 3 WLR 681 (HL) (at pp. 687–8) it was felt that s. 4 allows proof of both oral and written statements which a witness does not distinctly admit, whereas s. 5 additionally permits the admission of a written statement even if the witness admits that he made it but adheres to evidence inconsistent with it.

It is important to appreciate that these two sections apply only to statements which are 'relative to the subject matter of the indictment or proceeding'. In other words, the inconsistencies must be relevant to an *issue* in the trial as opposed to a collateral matter (the witness's credibility) in line with the general common-law rule on the finality of answers on collateral matters. In *R* v. *Funderburk* [1990] 1 WLR 587 the accused was charged with unlawful sexual intercourse with a 13-year-old girl. She gave evidence which strongly suggested that the accused had taken her virginity and described in detail the alleged acts of intercourse. The accused denied the allegation and sought leave to cross-examine her on a statement she had made in conversation with a Miss P to the effect that the complainant had had sexual intercourse with two other men prior to the alleged offence. The accused also sought leave to adduce, if necessary, evidence in rebuttal by calling Miss P to testify. The Court of Appeal held that the accused should have been permitted to cross-examine the complainant on her previous inconsistent statement. Furthermore, he should, if necessary, have been permitted to rely on s. 4 of the 1865 Act to call Miss P to rebut the complainant's denial. Given the nature and circumstances of the allegation, the complainant's conflicting statements had been relevant to whether the accused had actually had sex with her.

In *R* v. *Nagrecha* [1997] 2 Cr App R 401, a case of alleged indecent assault, the Court of Appeal went further. The accused was permitted to cross-examine the complainant on a previous allegation of sexual impropriety she had made against her former manager. The complainant denied having made such an allegation, but admitted that she had complained about the manager's 'aggressive behaviour'. The accused was not permitted to call the manager to give evidence of the nature of her allegation as a previous inconsistent statement, and he was convicted. According to the Court of Appeal, the manager's evidence should have been admitted as it 'went not merely to credit, but to the heart of the case, in that it bore on the crucial issue as to whether or not there had been any indecent assault'. This test (which was approved by the Privy Council in *Tiwari* v. *The State* [2002] UKPC 29) suggests that where a case turns on the respective credibility of a prosecution witness and the accused, any evidence which would significantly undermine that witness's credibility may also be regarded as relevant to an issue, allowing the rule on the finality of answers to be side-stepped (see also *R* v. *Ellis* [1998] Crim LR 661 (CA)).

It should be remembered, however, that relevance is just one part of the equation; the judge should also consider any countervailing questions of practicality (see 16.5.2 and, generally, 3.1.3 *ante*). In *R* v. *S* [1992] Crim LR 307 the trial judge ruled that the complainant's previous complaint against a third party went only to her credibility, so the accused could not call that person to rebut her assertion that the previous complaint had been true. The Court of Appeal upheld the judge's ruling on the basis that criminal trials have to be kept within bounds and the jury should not be distracted from the issues in dispute by collateral matters, although it was accepted that, if the third party had been abroad at the time of the alleged incident, it would have been permissible to adduce evidence of that 'single and distinct fact'. This would seem to be the more sensible approach from a practical point of view, for otherwise there would need to be a collateral trial for the determination of whether there was an offence by the third party, in addition to the trial of the accused himself. This could lead to further collateral matters arising as the third party is cross-examined, and perhaps the prosecution would feel obliged to adduce further evidence in rebuttal. These matters would serve only to confuse the jury and distract them from the principal issues. That said, a third party's evidence may be highly probative of the complainant's credibility, particularly if the extraneous allegation is similar to that which has been made against the accused. In the final analysis, so long as it is understood that the distinction between 'relevance to an issue' and 'relevance to credit' is a matter of degree, with each case turning on its own facts, it will be appreciated that where the line is drawn must depend on the importance of the prosecution witness's evidence and the significance of the evidence which would show that witness to be untruthful. In practice this may turn out to depend on what the court perceives to be 'fair play rather than any philosophic or analytical process' (*R* v. *Funderburk* [1990] 1 WLR 587 (CA) at p. 598). In other words, it is a matter which the judge ought to be allowed to determine in accordance with the broad discretion recognised by the Court of Appeal in *R* v. *Somers* [1999] Crim LR 744.

If a previous inconsistent statement is admissible in criminal proceedings pursuant to ss. 4 or 5 of the 1865 Act, its evidential value (in cases where the witness does not adopt it as part of his testimony) is limited to undermining the witness's credibility and the jury must be told this (*R* v. *Askew* [1981] Crim LR 398 (CA), *R* v. *Jarvis* [1991] Crim LR 374 (CA)). In civil proceedings a previous inconsistent statement is also admissible to prove the truth of the matters stated, as an exception to the rule against hearsay (ss. 1(1) and 6(5) of the Civil Evidence Act 1995).

16.5.4 Exceptions to the Rule on the Finality of Answers on Collateral Matters

In *R* v. *Funderburk* [1990] 1 WLR 587 (CA) Henry J explained that the exceptions to the rule on the finality of answers 'demonstrate the obvious proposition that a general rule designed to serve the interests of justice should not be used where so far from serving those interests it might defeat them'. There are at present four recognised exceptions which may be relied on in criminal or civil proceedings to undermine a witness's credibility. Three of these provide for the adduction of evidence suggesting untruthfulness (that is, evidence of previous convictions, bias and dishonesty); the fourth permits the adduction of evidence of honest unreliability (that is, evidence of a relevant physical or mental disability). A further exception, which is discussed elsewhere, may be relied on only in criminal proceedings (see 6.2.4 *ante*).

The rules of evidence apply equally to evidence tendered in rebuttal, so the cross-examining party cannot adduce any evidence of dishonesty or honest unreliability if it is inadmissible. Moreover, if a witness is called to give evidence in rebuttal (for example, to show that the cross-examined witness is biased), the rebutting witness will also have to face cross-examination; and if he denies an allegation which falls within one of the exceptions (for example, having a reputation for dishonesty) a further witness may be called to rebut his evidence. In practice this is uncommon because there are few recognised exceptions, but the way in which a multiplicity of collateral matters can arise demonstrates why the general rule on the finality of answers was established.

16.5.4.1 Evidence of Previous Convictions

If it is put to a witness in civil or criminal proceedings that he has previous convictions, and he denies that he was so convicted (or he remains silent), then evidence of those convictions may be adduced under s. 6 of the Criminal Procedure Act 1865 (in accordance with s. 6(1) of the Act in civil proceedings and s. 73 of the Police and Criminal Evidence Act 1984 in criminal proceedings, 12.3.5 *ante*). This power must be read in the light of a number of other statutory provisions and the judge's common-law power to limit cross-examination which would have no bearing on the witness's credibility (*R* v. *Sweet-Escott* (1971) 55 Cr App R 316 (Assizes), *R* v. *Funderburk* [1990] 1 WLR 587 (CA), 16.5.1 *ante*).

With regard to other provisions, the accused in criminal proceedings may be cross-examined on his previous convictions only if he has lost the 'shield' provided by s. 1(3) of the Criminal Evidence Act 1898 (4.3–7 *ante*); and s. 16(2) of the Children and Young Persons Act 1963 provides that, if the accused is over 21, his convictions dating from when he was under the age of 14 are inadmissible and he must not be asked about them, even if he has lost his s. 1(3) shield.

Furthermore, s. 4(1) of the Rehabilitation of Offenders Act 1974 provides that a 'rehabilitated person' is generally to be treated as 'a person who has not committed or been charged with or prosecuted for or convicted of or sentenced for the offence or offences which were the subject of that conviction'. Such convictions are said to be 'spent', the rehabilitation period for a given offence being dependent on the sentence received (see s. 5). Section 4(1) is subject to a number of exceptions, however, the most important of which is found in s. 7(2)(*a*) which excludes criminal proceedings from its scope, although *Practice Direction (Criminal Proceedings: Consolidation)* [2002] 1 WLR 2870 (SC) recommends that no reference should be made to a spent conviction if it can be reasonably avoided and that no-one should refer in open court to a spent conviction without the authority of the judge. The *Practice Direction* could be regarded as invalid, insofar as it might be said to contradict the express will of Parliament, but in reality it does little more than restate the judge's common-law power to restrict cross-examination on matters which have little if any bearing on a witness's present credibility. In other words, although a spent conviction is *prima facie* admissible in criminal proceedings by virtue of s. 7(2)(*a*) of the Act, the judge may exclude such evidence on the ground that it has insufficient probative value to be regarded as 'relevant' (a point acknowledged by the Court of Appeal in *R* v. *Lawler* (1999) unreported (98/6952/W3)). Spent convictions may be admitted in civil proceedings if justice cannot otherwise be done in the case (see s. 7(3) of the Act and *Thomas* v. *Commissioner of Police* [1997] 2 WLR 593 (CA)).

Trial judges have a wide discretion over the admissibility of spent convictions in criminal proceedings (*R* v. *Lawrence* [1995] Crim LR 815 (CA)), but in an appropriate case a ruling which prevents the accused from cross-examining a prosecution witness on his spent convictions can lead to a successful appeal. One such case was *R* v. *Evans* (1991) 156 JP 539, where there was a direct conflict between the accused and the complainant over what had happened between them in private during a 'domestic' fight. His defence was that the complainant had tried to stab him and that he had fought her off in self-defence, but he was prevented from being able to cross-examine her on her spent convictions which included convictions for offences of dishonesty, possessing an offensive weapon and attempting to stab a police officer. The Court of Appeal held that, because of the direct conflict of testimony, the jury had been entitled to know about her criminal record in order to evaluate her credibility. This approach was followed in *R* v. *Harrington* [2001] EWCA Crim 2096 (in respect of police cautions which would have been spent under the 1974 Act had they been convictions).

16.5.4.2 Evidence of Bias

If a witness denies being biased, it is permissible to adduce evidence to rebut that denial. In *R* v. *Mendy* (1976) 64 Cr App R 4 it was put to a defence witness that he had been talking to a person who had been taking notes during the prosecution case. The witness denied the allegation, so a police officer was called to give evidence of what he had seen going on outside the court-room. The Court of Appeal held that the prosecution had been entitled to call that evidence in rebuttal as it showed the witness was 'prepared to cheat in order to deceive the jury and help the defendant'. An earlier example is provided by *Thomas* v. *David* (1836) 7 C & P 350 (Assizes) where evidence was admissible to rebut a witness's denial that she was sexually involved with the party who had called her (see also *R* v. *Shaw* (1888) 16 Cox CC 503 (Assizes)).

Where the evidence is relevant to an *issue* it is of course unnecessary to invoke the bias exception. Thus, in *R* v. *Whelan* [1996] Crim LR 423 (CA), a case of unlawful wounding, evidence that the complainant had made threatening telephone calls to the accused prior to their fight was admissible 'not merely on the ground of the exception of bias' but because, as original evidence relevant to the accused's fearful state of mind, it was relevant to the issue of self-defence. *R* v. *Phillips* (1936) 26 Cr App R 17 is a more difficult case. The accused in that case was charged with incest against his children, his defence being that the girls had been coached by their mother to give false evidence against him. In cross-examination each girl denied admitting to a woman that she had fabricated her evidence at her mother's instigation at the accused's earlier trial for indecent assault. The Court of Criminal Appeal held that the accused should have been permitted to call the two women to give evidence that the children had made such admissions to them, as the evidence went not to the question of the children's credibility but to the 'very foundation' of the accused's defence. The problem with this decision is that the children's out-of-court admissions to the women were hearsay and therefore inadmissible for the purpose of proving that they had been coached by their mother in the past to lie on oath, but this seems to be the reason why it was felt the women's evidence was admissible. Even if the bias exception had been expressly applied by the Court, the accused would still have been relying on hearsay evidence to prove that the children were biased. Perhaps the decision can best be explained as an application of s. 4 of the Criminal Procedure Act 1865 (16.5.3 *ante*) with the women's evidence of what the girls told them being admissible as a previous inconsistent statement 'relative to the subject matter of the indictment'. If under cross-examination the children had said they were not influenced by their mother, by denying that they had made inconsistent statements to the women, the women's evidence would have been admissible not as hearsay (that is, not to prove the truth of the girls' out-of-court admissions) but merely to show the girls had said something inconsistent with their answers in cross-examination.

One type of bias which has attracted interest in recent years is that of police officers who have fabricated evidence or gone to improper lengths to secure a conviction. In *R* v. *Busby* (1981) 75 Cr App R 79, for example, police officers were cross-examined to the effect that one of them had threatened a potential witness, Mr W, to prevent him from testifying for the accused. The officers denied the allegation. The Court of Appeal held that Mr W should have been allowed to give evidence that he had been threatened, by analogy with the decisions in *R* v. *Mendy* (1976) 64 Cr App R 4 (CA) and *R* v. *Phillips* (1936) 26 Cr App R 17 (CCA). However, it was felt that the evidence of impropriety went beyond the question of credibility to an issue in the trial. It was part of the accused's case that the officers had fabricated admissions attributed to him, so the evidence of their impropriety against him in other respects would have made his defence more credible. In *R* v. *Edwards* [1991] 1 WLR 207 the Court of Appeal accepted that an allegation of police impropriety in cross-examination fell within the bias exception to the rule on the finality of answers, but was unwilling to recognise the existence of a general exception based on police misconduct against third parties (see also 3.3.19 *ante*).

16.5.4.3 Evidence of Dishonesty

In *R* v. *Richardson* [1968] 3 WLR 15 the Court of Appeal summarised this exception in the following terms (at p. 19):

'1. A witness may be asked whether he has knowledge of the impugned witness's general reputation for veracity and whether (from such knowledge) he would believe the impugned witness's sworn testimony. 2. The witness called to impeach the credibility of a previous witness may also express his individual opinion (based upon his personal knowledge) as to whether the latter is to be believed upon his oath and is not confined to giving evidence merely of general reputation. 3. But whether his opinion as to the impugned witness's credibility be based simply upon the latter's general reputation for veracity or upon his personal knowledge, the witness cannot be permitted to indicate during his examination-in-chief the particular facts, circumstances or incidents which formed the basis of his opinion, although he may be cross-examined as to them.'

Given the general rule on the inadmissibility of opinions, it is curious that opinion evidence of untruthfulness, based on little more than rumour and gossip, should be admissible. Opinion evidence based on personal knowledge of specific incidents or circumstances is less objectionable, but it is difficult to understand why the foundation facts upon which that opinion is based should not be elicited during the witness's examination-in-chief.

Although the impeaching witness may be cross-examined on the reasons for his opinion, this can lead to real difficulties for the party who called the impugned witness. He is unlikely to know the reasons for the impeaching witness's opinion, and to cross-examine a witness and have those unknown reasons revealed is very risky (and contrary to one of the golden rules of advocacy). But it is equally dangerous to allow an impeaching witness's evidence to stand unchallenged. Furthermore, if the impeaching witness's reasons are revealed it is not permissible to adduce evidence to contradict him (*R* v. *Gunewardene* [1951] 2 KB 600 (CCA)). However, the impugned witness's character may be re-established by calling witnesses to testify as to his general reputation for *truthfulness* (*R* v. *Hamilton* (1998) *The Times* 25.7.98 (CA), *R* v. *Beard* [1998] Crim LR 585 (CA), *R* v. *DS* [1999] Crim LR 911 (CA)). (In *R* v. *Hamilton* the Court of Appeal doubted *R* v. *O'Connor* (1996) unreported (96/6365/Y4) (CA) where it was held that the trial judge has a discretion as to whether the prosecution may elicit from their police officer witnesses that they have no convictions or adverse disciplinary findings, following cross-examination on allegations of previous misconduct.)

Needless to say, if an impeaching witness is called to give his individual opinion based upon his personal knowledge as to whether the impugned witness ought to be believed, that personal knowledge must relate to the impugned witness's *present* character. In *R* v. *N* [2002] EWCA Crim 1595 one of the reasons why the father of a woman in her mid-thirties could not testify as to her untruthful character was that his personal knowledge related solely to her dishonest behaviour as a child.

16.5.4.4 Evidence of Physical or Mental Incapacity

A witness's reliability may be challenged by the adduction of evidence of a relevant mental or physical condition. In *Toohey* v. *Metropolitan Police Commissioner* [1965] 2 WLR 439 (HL) Lord Pearce said (at pp. 446–7):

> 'If a witness purported to give evidence of something which he believed that he had seen at a distance of 50 yards, it must surely be possible to call the evidence of an oculist to the effect that the witness could not possibly see anything at a greater distance than 20 yards ... So, too, must it be allowable to call medical evidence of mental illness which makes a witness incapable of giving reliable evidence, whether through the existence of delusions or otherwise.'

For example, in *R* v. *Eades* [1972] Crim LR 99 (Assizes), a case of causing death by dangerous driving, the trial judge ruled that a psychiatrist could be called by the prosecution to give his opinion on the unlikelihood that the accused had had a sudden recollection of the circumstances of the road accident. If, as will usually be the case, the witness's condition requires an expert medical opinion, that expert may give his diagnosis and evidence of 'all the matters necessary to show, not only the foundation of and reason for the diagnosis, but also the extent to which the credibility of the witness is affected' (*Toohey* v. *Metropolitan Police Commissioner* at p. 447).

16.5.4.5 Calling Evidence in Rebuttal

A party is expected to adduce all his evidence before the close of his case. Additional evidence may be adduced, however, if that party is relying on an exception to the rule on the finality of answers. In criminal proceedings the prosecution may be given leave to adduce further evidence after the close of their case in other circumstances, the question being one for the judge (or magistrates) to determine in the exercise of a general discretion rather than in accordance with a narrow list of specific exceptions to a general exclusionary rule (*R* v. *Francis* (1990) 91 Cr App R 271 (CA), *Jolly* v. *DPP* [2000] Crim LR 471 (DC), *Cook* v. *DPP* [2001] Crim LR 321 (DC), *R* v. *Hinchcliffe* [2002] EWCA Crim 837).

16.5.4.6 A New Approach

The general rule on the finality of answers is a rule of convenience and not of principle, apparently predicated on the assumption that evidence undermining a witness's credibility has less probative value than evidence which is deemed to be more directly relevant to an issue. That this assumption is incorrect is demonstrated by the exceptions. An eye-witness's poor eyesight or biased disposition is a collateral matter, but it may have a very significant bearing on the value of his testimony and the determination of any issue which depends on it. It is therefore illogical to adopt an artificial distinction between relevance to credit and relevance to an issue, with admissibility being determined on that basis subject to an immutable collection of recognised exceptions. This approach can lead to the exclusion of highly probative evidence, as demonstrated by the Australian case of *Piddington* v. *Bennett* (1940) 63 CLR 533 (HCA) (16.5.2 *ante*).

In *R* v. *Funderburk* [1990] 1 WLR 587 (CA) Henry J recognised that the exceptions exist to serve the interest of justice and stated that it 'may be that the categories of exception ... are not closed'; and in *R* v. *S* [1992] Crim LR 307 the Court of Appeal was willing to accept that it would be permissible to rebut an answer on a collateral question if the matter could be reduced to a 'single and distinct fact' such as whether a witness had been abroad at a certain time. Building upon these developments the Court of Appeal has now recognised that the trial judge has a broad discretion to hold that a particular witness's credibility is directly relevant to an issue in the trial, allowing the rule on the finality of answers on collateral matters to be side-stepped in cases where this would not result in an unduly complex trial (*R* v. *James* (1998) unreported (97/2785/Y4), *R* v. *Somers* [1999] Crim LR 744).

16.5.5 Reforming the Law on Previous Inconsistent Statements

The Law Commission has suggested that previous inconsistent statements admitted under ss. 3–5 of the Criminal Procedure Act 1865 should be admissible as evidence of the matters stated in any proceedings, save that the tribunal of fact in criminal proceedings should not be allowed to retire with evidence of this sort (Law Com No. 245 (1997) at pp. 165–9).

16.6 The Re-examination of Witnesses

Once a witness has been cross-examined, the party who called him is entitled to try to repair any damage done to his evidence in chief by asking further questions on the matters which arose during cross-examination. The leave of the court is required before other questions can be put. The rules applicable to examination-in-chief apply equally to re-examination.

16.7 The Submission of No Case to Answer

Unless the proceedings are an abuse of process or otherwise oppressive or vexatious, a criminal trial cannot be halted before the close of the prosecution case (*Attorney-General's Reference (No. 2 of 2000)* [2001] 1 Cr App R 503 (CA)). However, at the close of the prosecution case a 'half-time' submission may be made to the judge or magistrates that the prosecution's evidential burden has not been discharged in respect of a fact (or facts) in issue, and that the accused ought therefore to be acquitted. For trials on indictment, a submission of no case to answer will succeed if the prosecution evidence taken at its highest is such that a properly directed jury would be unable properly to convict on it; but it will fail if, on one possible view of the evidence, the jury could properly find the accused guilty (*R* v. *Galbraith* [1981] 1 WLR 1039 (CA)). However, taking the prosecution evidence at its highest does not mean 'picking out the plums and leaving the duff behind', so the case against the accused will be withdrawn if the jury *could* find the accused guilty (on one possible view of the evidence) but *would not properly* find him guilty, such as where the prosecution witnesses have been discredited as a result of cross-examination or the accused's confession is manifestly unreliable (*R* v. *Shippey* [1988] Crim LR 767 (CC), *R* v. *Mackenzie* (1992) 96 Cr App R 98 (CA), *R* v. *Shire* [2001] EWCA Crim 2800). If the prosecution fail to discharge their evidential burden, but the judge nonetheless rejects the accused's submission of no case to answer and allows the trial to proceed, the Court of Appeal will quash the subsequent conviction on the ground that the trial should have been halted, even if the accused admitted his guilt from the witness box (*R* v. *Smith* [1999] 2 Cr App R 238 (CA), *R* v. *Davis* [2001] 1 Cr App R 115 (CA)).

The judge need not withdraw the case from the jury in any case dependent on circumstantial evidence just because some inference other than guilt could reasonably be drawn from the evidentiary facts proved, save that there may be an exception for cases where the prosecution are seeking to prove the accused's guilt on the basis of an inference drawn from just one item of circumstantial evidence (*R* v. *Van Bokkum* (2000) unreported (99/0333/Z3) (CA)).

If the accused is tried on indictment the submission is made to the judge in the absence of the jury; and if the judge rules that there *is* a case to answer, this should not be mentioned to the jury (*R* v. *Smith* (1986) 85 Cr App R 197 (CA)). The judge is under a continuing duty to keep the matter under review, however, and may raise it with counsel and, having heard submissions, withdraw the case from the jury at any stage during (or at the close of) the defence case, regardless of whether a submission was made at 'half time' (*R* v. *Brown (Jamie)* [1998] Crim LR 196 (CA), *R* v. *Anderson* (1998) *The Independent* 13.7.98 (CA), *R* v. *Brown (Davina)* [2002] 1 Cr App R 46 (CA)). In summary proceedings, magistrates have the power to dismiss a case of their own motion so long as they first invite submissions from the prosecution (*R* v. *Barking and Dagenham Justices ex parte DPP* (1995) 159 JP 373 (DC)).

In civil proceedings, if the judge is trying the case without a jury the general position is that a submission of no case to answer should be heard and ruled on only if the defendant has elected not to call any evidence, although the judge retains a discretion (for use in rare cases) to entertain such a submission without requiring any election (*Alexander* v. *Rayson* [1936] 1 KB 169 (CA), *Boyce* v. *Wyatt Engineering* [2001] EWCA Civ 692). If the defendant elects to call no evidence and makes a submission, the judge should consider whether the claimant's case is made out on the balance of probabilities; but if a submission is entertained without the defendant having been put to his election, the standard is whether the claimant's case has any reasonable prospect of success (*Miller (t/a Waterloo Plan)* v. *Crawley* [2002] EWCA Civ 1100). In jury trials the judge may hear and rule on a submission of no case to answer without the defendant having to give any such undertaking (*Young* v. *Rank* [1950] 2 KB 510 (KBD)). By analogy with criminal trials on indictment, if the judge concludes that the claimant's evidence, taken at its highest, is such that a properly directed jury could not properly reach a necessary factual conclusion on an issue which the claimant has to prove, he must withdraw that issue from them (*Alexander* v. *Arts Council of Wales* [2001] 1 WLR 1840 (CA)).

16.8 The Trial Judge's Role

In addition to being the tribunal of law, ruling on questions of admissibility, the judge is supposed to act as an impartial 'umpire' controlling the proceedings to ensure matters are dealt with efficiently, fairly and courteously. The analogy should not be taken too far, however, for the judge also has the right to adopt a more proactive and inquisitorial role and, in criminal trials, may question and even call witnesses of his own volition (*R* v. *Roberts* (1984) 80 Cr App R 89 (CA); see also *R* v. *Haringey Justices ex parte DPP* [1996] 2 WLR 114 (DC)). In civil trials, it has been held that the parties' consent is required before the judge can call further witnesses (*Re Enoch & Zaretzky* [1910] 1 KB 327 (CA)), but r. 32.1(1) of the Civil Procedure Rules 1998 now provides that the court 'may control the evidence by giving directions as to ... the nature of the evidence which it requires ... and the way in which the evidence is to be placed before the court'.

In criminal proceedings the judge is entitled to question any witness, but he is expected to exercise restraint, particularly when it is the accused who is testifying (*R* v. *Marsh* (1993) *The Times* 6.7.93 (CA)). The judge may even take over the cross-examination of a child complainant in a rape case if she refuses to answer the questions put by defence counsel (*R* v. *Cameron* [2001] Crim LR 587 (CA)). According to the Court of Appeal in *R* v. *Mitchell* [2003] EWCA Crim 907, the judge may 'put questions to clarify matters and to intervene to prevent repetition, discursiveness or oppression of witnesses and to ensure that irrelevant matters are not pursued' but:

'he must be careful not to appear to enter the arena or to give the impression to the jury that he thinks little or nothing of the defendant's case or is promoting a witness as one whom he thinks the jury ought to believe. And the defendant must be permitted to give his evidence so that his case, however implausible the judge may think it to be, is properly put before the jury and he is not thrown off course by judicial interruptions.'

The judge's excessive intervention may be a ground for appealing against conviction as it undermines the adversarial system, but the number of interventions is not of itself determinative; the critical aspect of the investigation is the quality of the interventions as they relate to the attitude of the judge before the jury and the effect of those interventions upon 'the orderly, proper and lucid deployment of the case for the defendant by his advocate or upon the efficacy of the attack to be made on the defendant's behalf upon vital prosecution witnesses by cross-examination' (*R* v. *Matthews* (1983) 78 Cr App R 23 (CA) at p. 32, *R* v. *Hardwick* [2002] EWCA Crim 2379, *R* v. *Mitchell* [2003] EWCA Crim 907). In *R* v. *Frixou* [1998] Crim LR 352 (CA), for example, a conviction was quashed because the judge had taken over the questioning during what was supposed to be the accused's examination-in-chief, cross-examining him in a hostile, sarcastic and peremptory manner, thereby depriving him of the opportunity he should have had to put his case before the jury in an ordered and structured form; and in *R* v. *Gunning* (1980) 98 Cr App R 303 (CA), where there was no such hostility or sarcasm, the 165 questions put by the judge during the accused's examination-in-chief nonetheless prevented him from being able properly to give his evidence in chief and may have given the impression that the judge did not believe a word he was saying. The European Court of Human Rights has accepted that the nature and frequency of the judge's interventions may render a criminal trial unfair for the purposes of Article 6(1) of the European Convention, but particular weight is attached to the Court of Appeal's assessment because of its knowledge and experience of jury trials (*CG* v. *United Kingdom* (2001) 34 EHRR 789).

In *R* v. *Curtin* (1996) unreported (93/6847/Y3) the Court of Appeal stated that it was the trial judge's duty when summing up 'to give directions about the relevant law, to refer to the salient pieces of evidence, to identify and focus attention upon the issues, and in each of those respects to do so as succinctly as the case permits.' The judge must therefore explain the respective roles of judge and jury, direct the jury on the substantive law and on the burden and standard of proof, give any necessary warnings or directions on the evidence and the inferences which may properly be drawn from it, and explain the value of the various items of evidence. This last point would include directing the jury on the evidential value of an admissible out-of-court statement (that is, whether it is evidence of the truth of the facts stated or relevant only to the maker's consistency as a witness) and the relevance of the accused's good or bad character.

If the trial has gone on for a few days or more, the judge must give the jury an impartial review of the evidence; the factual issues not in dispute should be summarised, and where there is a significant dispute as to material facts the items of evidence which are in conflict should be succinctly identified so that the jury's attention is focused on the issues they have to resolve (*R* v. *Farr* (1998) 163 JP 193 (CA), *R* v. *Amado-Taylor (No. 1)* [2000] 2 Cr App R 189 (CA)). In particular, the judge must give a full and proper direction on any defence relied on by the accused and, indeed, on any other defence which is a reasonably possible (as opposed to a fanciful) issue in the light of the evidence adduced or elicited during the trial, such as self-defence where the accused has relied on 'accident' (*R* v. *Phillips* [1999] All ER (D) 1372 (CA), *Von Starck* v. *R* [2000] 1 WLR 1270 (PC)).

In *R* v. *Marr* (1989) 90 Cr App R 154 (CA) Lord Lane CJ said: 'It is ... an inherent principle of our system of trial that however distasteful the offence, however repulsive the defendant, however laughable his defence, he is nevertheless entitled to have his case fairly presented to the jury both by counsel and by the judge.' Further, according to the Court of Appeal in *R* v. *Reid* (1999) *The Times* 17.8.99 (98/8082/W3), where the case against the accused is strong, and his defence correspondingly weak, the judge must be scrupulous to ensure that the defence is presented in an even-handed and impartial manner, for justice 'is best served by a constant striving to give the accused what is his absolute right, that is a fair trial by an impartial tribunal, guided and directed by an impartial judge'. However, this does not mean that the accused is entitled to have his defence rehearsed blandly and uncritically by the judge in his summing-up. According to Simon Brown LJ in *R* v. *Nelson* [1997] Crim LR 234 (95/5258/W5) (CA):

'[T]he judge must remain impartial. But if common sense and reason demonstrate that a given defence is riddled with implausibilities, inconsistencies and illogicalities ... there is no reason for the judge to withhold from the jury the benefit of his own powers of logic and analysis ... Impartiality means no more and no less than that the judge shall fairly state and analyse the case for both sides. Justice moreover requires that he assists the jury to reach a logical and reasoned conclusion on the evidence.'

The judge may therefore comment on the evidence and its weight during the course of his summing-up, and may even express his own view in strong terms. This is acceptable practice so long as he reminds the jury that all questions of fact are for them alone to decide and his comments do not have the effect of undermining the jury's freedom to decide those questions for themselves. For obvious reasons the jury should be told that they may disregard the judge's own view of the facts *before* he gives his opinion, that is, at the beginning of his summing-up (*R* v. *Everett* [1995] Crim LR 76 (CA)). If the judge's summing-up is fundamentally unbalanced, however, the mere repetition of a direction that questions of fact are for the jury will not remedy that unfairness (*Mears* v. *R* [1993] 1 WLR 818 (PC), *R* v. *Wood* [1996] 1 Cr App R 207 (CA)).

The judge's summing-up went beyond the proper bounds of judicial comment, resulting in a successful appeal, in *R* v. *Winn-Pope* [1996] Crim LR 521 (CA), where the judge referred to the accused as a 'con man' who always had a 'ready answer'; and in *R* v. *Langford* (2000) *The Times* 12.01.01 (00/1697/Z1) the Court of Appeal quashed a conviction because, *inter alia*, the judge had usurped the role of the jury, in effect directing them to accept the complainant's evidence as truthful. Perhaps the most notorious example of an unfair summing-up in recent history was that

given in the case of *R* v. *Bentley (Deceased)* [2001] 1 Cr App R 307.
Bentley's conviction for murder in 1952, for which he was hanged about
six weeks later, was quashed by the Court of Appeal in 1998 on the
ground, *inter alia*, that the trial judge, Lord Goddard CJ, had failed
adequately to put his defence to the jury and his summing-up was such as
to deny him 'that fair trial which is the birthright of every British citizen'.
The summing-up was criticised for being 'a highly rhetorical and strongly
worded denunciation' of Bentley and his defence which 'must ... have
driven the jury to conclude that they had little choice but to convict'.
Another aspect of the summing-up which was criticised was Lord
Goddard's treatment of the evidence of the police officers who had
testified that Bentley had encouraged murder by shouting 'Let him have
it'. The police officers were commended for their 'highest gallantry and
resolution' and 'devotion to duty', whereas Bentley's evidence that he had
not spoken those words was dismissed as 'the denial of a man in grievous
peril'. The Court of Appeal noted that in recent years the courts have
deprecated judicial comments which suggest that police officers will be
professionally ruined if the accused is acquitted or which place police
officers in a different position from other witnesses; and that Lord
Goddard had fallen into the pitfall of inviting the jury 'to approach the
evidence on the assumption that police officers, because they are police
officers, are likely to be accurate and reliable witnesses and defendants,
because they are defendants, likely to be inaccurate and unreliable' (see
also *R* v. *Culbertson* (1970) 54 Cr App R 310 (CA), *R* v. *Harris* [1986] Crim
LR 123 (CA) and *R* v. *Beycan* [1990] Crim LR 185 (CA)). Just as police
officers should not be treated as a special type of witness, the judge should
not expressly state that he disbelieves a witness for the defence, even if his
evidence warrants incredulity (*R* v. *Iroegbu* (1988) *The Times* 2.8.88 (CA)).

The accused's trial must not only be fair but be seen to be fair, so it is
important that any judicial rebuke to the accused's advocate in the
presence of the jury is delivered in measured tones, and that the judge does
nothing which might lead the jury to conclude that he is unfairly
prejudiced against him (*R* v. *Kartal* (1999) unreported (98/4147/X5) (CA)).
In *R* v. *Wood* [2002] EWCA Crim 832 the accused was denied a fair trial
because of the way the judge had undermined his counsel in the eyes of the
jury and the knock-on effect this had had on the substance of his defence.

Finally, although the judge is entitled to direct the jury to acquit the
accused, he may not direct them to convict, even if the accused has in
effect admitted his guilt during the course of his testimony, unless
(perhaps) the accused has made 'something in the nature of a formal
admission of guilt' (*R* v. *Gent* (1989) 89 Cr App R 247 (CA)).

16.9 **The Jury's Deliberations**

Once the jury have retired to consider their verdict no further evidence or
equipment is admissible to assist them in their deliberations, although they
may ask the judge to *repeat* evidence they have already heard or seen

during the trial (*R* v. *Davis* (1975) 62 Cr App R 194 (CA)). In *R* v. *Stewart* (1989) 89 Cr App R 273 (CA), for example, a conviction was quashed on the ground that the jury had been given weighing scales with which to conduct experiments in the jury room. The reason for the bar on equipment is to prevent speculative re-enactments by the jury in private which counsel and the judge would be unable to comment on and from which the jury might draw erroneous inferences. Indeed, if the jury indicate that they are considering a re-enactment the judge is obliged to warn them of the dangers involved in such an exercise and to try to dissuade them from conducting it (*R* v. *Crees* [1996] Crim LR 830 (CA)). That said, the jury are entitled to ask for the sort of equipment which any juror might reasonably be expected to have on his own person, such as a magnifying glass, ruler or tape measure (*R* v. *Maggs* (1990) 91 Cr App R 243 (CA)).

Although a conviction is likely to be quashed if it is apparent that the jury conducted an experiment or re-enactment, in practice s. 8(1) of the Contempt of Court Act 1981 (which prohibits the disclosure of what occurred during the jury's deliberations) means that juries could be secretly conducting experiments on a regular basis without anyone knowing. In *R* v. *Young* [1995] 2 WLR 430 the accused was convicted of two counts of murder following the use by several jurors of a ouija board to contact the deceased. This came to light when a juror reported the matter to a solicitor, but the Court of Appeal nonetheless felt that s. 8(1) would have prohibited any inquiry into this irregularity if it had occurred during the jury's formal deliberations. As it was, the ouija board had been used by only four of the jurors during their overnight detention in a hotel, so it was not regarded as part of the deliberations and evidence of what had happened could be received.

The European Court of Human Rights has recognised that 'the rule governing the secrecy of jury deliberations is a crucial and legitimate feature of English trial law which serves to reinforce the jury's role as the ultimate arbiter of fact and to guarantee open and frank deliberations among jurors on the evidence which they have heard' (*Gregory* v. *United Kingdom* (1997) 25 EHRR 577 at p. 594). This rule has the effect of prohibiting an appeal against conviction based on a post-verdict complaint of alleged irregularities in the jury's deliberations, notwithstanding Article 6(1) of the European Convention (*R* v. *Qureshi* [2002] 1 WLR 518 (CA), *R* v. *Osmanioglu* [2002] EWCA Crim 930, *R* v. *Mirza* [2002] Crim LR 921 (CA)). However, it does not prevent the judge from investigating irregularities during the course of the trial (for example, where there is an allegation of bias on the part of one or more jurors within the confines of their room) if the irregularity can be established without undertaking an investigation into the jury's private deliberations. If a real danger of bias is established the judge may discharge up to three jurors or the entire jury. According to the European Court of Human Rights, this may be the only viable course of action in some cases if the accused is to have a fair trial (*Sander* v. *United Kingdom* (2000) 31 EHRR 1003 at p. 1010). In other cases a firm direction to try the accused on the evidence may be sufficient.

Chapter Summary

- As a general rule all individuals are competent to give (sworn or unsworn) evidence, and all competent individuals are compellable. However, in criminal proceedings the accused is not compellable for the defence (and not competent for the prosecution); the accused's spouse is only exceptionally compellable for the prosecution or a co-accused; and no individual (child or adult) is competent if he cannot understand the questions put to him or provide intelligible answers. In civil proceedings a child is competent so long as he understands the duty to speak the truth and has sufficient understanding to justify his evidence being heard, but adults are competent only if they understand the nature of the oath. A number of special measures are now available in criminal proceedings to improve the quality of the evidence given by vulnerable witnesses (other than the accused). There is an inherent jurisdiction to provide special measures in other cases.

- As a general rule a witness is not entitled to have his credibility bolstered by evidence of his good character (for example it is not permissible for a witness's credibility to be supported by evidence that he has made an out-of-court statement consistent with his present testimony). There are a number of exceptions to this rule. First, the accused is entitled to have evidence of his good character placed before the jury, on the ground that it is relevant to his credibility and disposition. Second, if it is alleged that the accused committed a sexual offence against the complainant and the issue is consent, evidence of the complainant's good character is admissible to prove that she did not consent and to bolster her credibility. Third, if evidence is adduced to show that a witness has a reputation for dishonesty, evidence may be adduced to prove the contrary. Fourth, there are a number of exceptions to the rule against the admission of previous consistent statements which permit the following types of statement to be adduced – the complainant's 'recent complaint' in a sexual offence case; a statement which rebuts an allegation of recent fabrication; the accused's exculpatory statement when the police made their allegation against him; statements of out-of-court identification; *res gestae* statements; and statements in (admissible) memory-refreshing documents.

- A witness who turns out to be 'hostile' to the party who called him may be cross-examined by that party on a previous inconsistent statement at common law or under s. 3 of the Criminal Procedure Act 1865 (which allows the statement to be proved).

- The rule on the finality of answers on collateral matters prevents the cross-examining party from adducing evidence to rebut an answer given by the witness which is relevant only to a collateral matter such as his credibility. However, if the resolution of a disputed issue is heavily dependent on that witness's credibility the rule will not be applied (and it will therefore be possible to adduce evidence of a previous inconsistent statement made by that witness under ss. 4 or 5 of the Criminal Procedure Act 1865). If the rule on the finality of answers does apply it is subject to exceptions which allow the cross-examining party to adduce (where relevant) evidence of the witness's: previous convictions, bias, reputation for dishonesty, and physical or mental incapacity.

- At the end of the trial the judge will give the jury directions on the relevant law and review the issues and evidence for them. The judge may comment, within limits, on the evidence and its weight, but he must remind the jury that the questions of fact are ultimately for them to decide.

Further Reading

Pattenden, 'The Character of Victims and Third Parties' [1986] Crim LR 367
Elliott, 'Video Tape Evidence: the Risk of Over-Persuasion' [1998] Crim LR 159
Birch, 'A Better Deal for Vulnerable Witnesses?' [2000] Crim LR 223
Hoyano, 'Special Measures Directions for Child Witnesses' [2000] Crim LR 250
McEwan, 'In Defence of Vulnerable Witnesses' (2000) 4 E & P 1
Law Commission Report, Law Com No. 273 (2001), *Evidence of Bad Character*,
    Part IX
Auld, *Review of the Criminal Courts* (2001), pp. 514–523, 546–556

Criminal Justice Bill (2003), Part 8; Part 11, Chapters 1–3
and Explanatory Note (www.publications.parliament.uk)

17   Sexual Behaviour as Evidence

17.1 Introduction

It will be remembered that for any item of evidence to be admissible it must be logically relevant to a fact in issue or a collateral fact (or contribute to an explanation of the 'background'). To determine whether evidence is logically relevant to a matter requiring proof the judge must formulate a generalisation from his own experience and what he understands to be conventional wisdom. There is a problem with this approach, however, for some aspects of human life are more widely understood than others, and what is thought to be a valid generalisation may in fact be no more than a vague stereotype. Moreover, conventional wisdom itself may be suspect because different cultural groups (including different generations) are unlikely to view the world in the same way or share the same values. What might appear to be a valid generalisation to one generation might well be considered absurd by another. Problems such as these have bedevilled the law governing the admissibility of the complainant's sexual experience in cases where the accused is alleged to have committed rape or some other sexual offence against her.

Depending on the generalisation relied on, evidence of the complainant's sexual experience may be considered logically relevant to her credibility or an issue in the proceedings or both. The judiciary's approach to evidence of this sort has altered with the changing moral values of English society, but even if the question of sexual morality is put to one side, as it now is, evidence of the complainant's sexual experience is quite capable of supporting the accused's defence. It is equally apparent, however, that if such evidence is adduced or elicited in cross-examination the complainant is likely to suffer a great deal of distress. This may have the knock-on effect of deterring genuine victims from coming forward to testify against men who have raped or otherwise sexually abused them. In other words, there is a clear conflict between the interests of the accused and the interests of the complainant (and society as a whole).

The accused has a considerable number of rights, both at common law and under the European Convention on Human Rights. In particular, he is presumed to be innocent (Article 6(2)) and is entitled to a fair trial (Article 6(1)). To this end he should in principle be entitled to adduce or elicit any evidence relevant to his defence to ensure that he is not convicted of an offence he did not commit. Certainly he should be able to have the evidence and credibility of his accuser challenged, and this is reflected in Article 6(3)(d) of the Convention which affirms the accused's 'minimum right' 'to examine or have examined witnesses against him'. These rights apply in any trial of course, but they take on particular significance in cases where the allegation is one of sexual impropriety, *a fortiori* if the allegation is that the accused raped the complainant. A convicted rapist faces many years in prison, segregated from other offenders and universally despised and detested. For an innocent man to be convicted of and punished for rape is perhaps the greatest injustice the criminal justice system can now deliver. And it is important to understand that men *are* sometimes falsely accused of rape by mendacious complainants.

The researchers Jessica Harris and Sharon Grace found that out of a sample of nearly 500 incidents initially recorded by the police as rape in 1996 some 25 per cent were 'no-crimed' by the police, the most common reason being the conclusion that the complainant was lying or malicious (see 'A question of evidence? Investigating and prosecuting rape in the 1990s', Home Office Research Study 196). But not every false allegation is filtered out before the trial. It is clear that innocent men have been (and no doubt are still being) wrongly convicted of rape on the basis of fabricated allegations. For example, in April 2000 a man who was sentenced in 1986 to a term of life imprisonment for rape and buggery, and who had served nearly 15 years of his sentence, was freed when the Court of Appeal concluded that the offences 'almost certainly never happened at all' (*R* v. *Burnett* (2000) unreported (99/4959/Z4)); and in December 2001 a man who had spent three years in prison out of a nine-year sentence had his convictions for rape and attempted rape quashed when the complainant admitted that she had lied to get her mother's attention (*R* v. *Beardmore* (2001) unreported (01/2705/Y5) (CA); see also *R* v. *Smith* [1999] All ER (D) 1455 (CA)). Various reasons have been put forward to explain why some complainants fabricate their allegations. These include a desire for revenge following the collapse of a relationship, guilt, fear and mental instability. A complainant may even bring a false allegation motivated by nothing more than financial gain (*R* v. *Milroy-Sloan* (2003) *The Times* (news report) 17.5.03 (CCC)).

A particularly interesting finding of the Home Office research study was that only 12 per cent of the sample involved allegations of 'stranger rape' (the other 88 per cent comprising allegations made against 'acquaintances' (45 per cent) and 'intimates' (43 per cent)) and that almost 25 per cent of complainants had had a prior sexual relationship with the alleged rapist. It follows that the evidence in a large proportion of the rape cases which reach court comprise nothing more than the protagonists' diametrically opposing views as to what happened in private between them, with the complainant alleging rape and the accused countering that there was no sex between them at all or that there was consensual sex and/or that he genuinely believed the complainant was consenting. In the first and second of these scenarios the outcome will turn on the jury's assessment of the credibility of both protagonists, and (given the presumption of innocence) the presumption has to be that the complainant is lying. In such cases there is *no rape* and *no victim* until the jury conclude at the end of the trial that the accused is actually guilty. The presumption of fabrication must stand unless the jury can be convinced beyond reasonable doubt that the complainant is actually telling the truth. As Lord Bingham CJ pointed out in *R* v. *Brown* [1998] 2 Cr App R 364 (CA) (at p. 370):

'Where . . . a defendant is accused of rape, the trial cannot be conducted on the assumption that he is a rapist and the complainant a victim, since the whole purpose of the proceeding is to establish whether that is so or not.'

The presumption that the complainant is lying is a natural consequence of the importance attached by a rights-based democratic society to the acquittal of its innocent citizens, even if some perpetrators of very serious offences are able to escape liability as a result. That said, rape is a most cowardly and brutal crime, and can profoundly affect a genuine victim's quality of life. Society has an interest in ensuring that men who do rape or sexually abuse women (or indeed other men) are tried and convicted, and it is reasonable to assume that the risk of being cross-examined on their (relevant) sexual experience will deter some victims from pursuing their complaints up to and including the trial process. If the complainant has indeed been raped by the accused then a trial in which she faces cross-examination on her most intimate private behaviour can only worsen what must have been a horrendous ordeal. Complainants, as witnesses, also have rights. Cross-examination on extraneous sexual experience which has little probative value may even amount to a violation of the complainant's right under Article 8 of the European Convention to have her private life respected. The point was made by the European Court of Human Rights (albeit in a different context) in *Doorson* v. *Netherlands* (1996) 22 EHRR 330 (at p. 358):

'It is true that Article 6 does not explicitly require the interests of witnesses in general, and those of victims called upon to testify in particular, to be taken into consideration. However, their life, liberty or security of person may be at stake, as may interests coming generally within the ambit of Article 8 of the Convention . . . Contracting States should organise their criminal proceedings in such a way that those interests are not unjustifiably imperilled. Against this background, principles of fair trial also require that in appropriate cases the interests of the defence are balanced against those of witnesses or victims called upon to testify.'

The decision in *Doorson* v. *Netherlands* was referred to with approval in *Oyston* v. *United Kingdom* (2002) Application No. 42011/98 (ECtHR), an admissibility decision on s. 2 of the Sexual Offences (Amendment) Act 1976 (17.3 *post*).

The crux of the problem, then, is that the law must try to reconcile what is perhaps irreconcilable. The accused is presumed to be innocent and the complainant will in many cases be presumed to be lying. To undermine this presumption of fabrication would be to undermine the presumption of innocence and run the risk of violating Article 6(1) of the European Convention. If the complainant's sexual experience is indeed relevant to an issue in the trial – which in the context of sexual intercourse in private may be no more than her credibility (16.5.2 *ante*) – the accused should be entitled to cross-examine her on it. Any evidence which can help the jury decide who is telling the truth ought to be admitted. But if the accused is permitted to cross-examine the complainant on any logically relevant sexual experience, regardless of how much or how little probative value that evidence has, there is a real risk that the complainant's own rights will be violated and that genuine rape victims will be deterred from pursuing their complaints. This would allow many rapists to re-offend with impunity. Accordingly it is necessary to try to strike some kind of balance between the interests of the accused and those of the complainant, insofar as it is possible to do so without denying the accused his right to defend himself in an effective manner.

The focus must therefore be on the *probative value* of the evidence. The exclusion of aspects of the complainant's sexual behaviour which are unlikely to assist the jury in any meaningful sense – and which might distract the jury from other evidence or cause them to attach less weight to the complainant's testimony for an illegitimate reason or cause her unnecessary distress – could be justified on the ground of 'irrelevance' (3.1.2–3 *ante*). Ultimately a test along these lines can be the only acceptable way of reconciling the accused's right to a fair trial with the complainant's right to have her private life respected; and if there is any doubt as to whether the evidence ought to be adduced or elicited it should be resolved in the accused's favour. Any reformative measure which seeks to assist complainants and increase the number of convictions for rape must ensure that the presumption of innocence and the accused's right to a fair trial in other respects are not undermined. Parliament has twice introduced legislation to shift the emphasis towards the protection of the complainant, but (inevitably) both attempts have resulted in a reversion to a test based on relevance and sufficiency of probative value.

Finally, while it is often reported that fewer than ten per cent of rape allegations end in a conviction, this should not be read as an indictment of the law of evidence, although no doubt some genuine victims are deterred from testifying by the nature of the questions they assume will be asked. It has already been mentioned that 25 per cent of all alleged rapes are 'no-crimed' by the police; and there is a continuing process of attrition thereafter. The Home Office research study reports that of the accused who are actually brought before the Crown Court for trial, 28 per cent are convicted of rape and 38 per cent are convicted of some other offence. Fewer than one in four (23 per cent) are acquitted of all charges. (The remaining 11 per cent are 'not known', 'case discharged' and 'case to lie on file'.)

17.2 The Relevance of the Complainant's Sexual Experience

Evidence of a complainant's sexual experience could be elicited in cross-examination at common law as it was deemed to be relevant to her general credibility as a witness. Unchaste women, supposedly lacking in general moral credibility, were thought to be more capable of deception than chaste women; so a complainant could be cross-examined on her sexual acts with other men as a way of undermining the value of her testimony (*R* v. *Holmes* (1871) LR1 CCR 334 (CCCR)). The purported connection between a witness's sexual experience and credibility was occasionally applied in other types of proceedings, but if the complainant's allegation was one of sexual abuse, such as rape or indecent assault, her sexual experience was elicited as a matter of course. There were two reasons for this. First, it was hoped the jury would despise the moral character of the complainant and therefore attach little weight to her evidence. Second, it was hoped the jury would realise that the accused deserved to be acquitted, *despite* the evidence against him, because of the complainant's character.

The belief that the complainant's sexual history was relevant to her veracity was not surprising given the moral climate until a few decades ago. If a woman had acted immorally in one way her entire moral credibility was tarnished, the assumption being that a woman who was willing to fornicate would also be willing to fabricate allegations and lie on oath. But there are two fundamental problems with the view that a woman's sexual experience is relevant to her credibility. First, in England and Wales pre-marital sexual relations are, as a general rule, no longer regarded as morally disreputable and so cannot be brought within the class of activities which might be referred to as objectively immoral. As such it is difficult to justify the view that evidence of this sort has any bearing on the complainant's moral credibility and therefore her veracity as a witness. Second, a woman who has freely consented to sexual activities with other men is perhaps *less* likely than a chaste woman to raise a false allegation of sexual abuse. Reasons why complainants lie include the desire for revenge, the need to protect their reputation and self-denial through shame; but the last two of these reasons are unlikely to arise if the complainant is sexually experienced. (It is pertinent to note that Home Office Research Study 196 (1999) reports a finding that those involved in the criminal justice system perceive prostitutes as convincing witnesses on the ground that, given the nature of their work, they are unlikely to 'cry rape'.)

Interestingly, at common law the complainant's sexual experience was regarded as irrelevant to any *issue* in the proceedings, although there were a few exceptions to this general rule. The sexual experience of certain types of complainant was considered relevant to the issue of consent, but only if the evidence showed the complainant to be notoriously sexually immoral (*R* v. *Greatbanks* [1959] Crim LR 450 (CCC)) or a prostitute (*R* v. *Bashir* [1969] 1 WLR 1303 (Assizes)) or it was evidence that the complainant had consented to sexual activity with the accused on some other occasion (*R* v. *Riley* (1887) 18 QBD 481 (CCCR)). In such cases, if the complainant denied what was put to her in cross-examination, evidence could be adduced in rebuttal. Such evidence could also be adduced in chief as part of the accused's case. In all other cases the complainant's sexual experience was regarded as relevant only to the collateral question of her credibility, so if she denied the allegation put to her in cross-examination the accused was bound by the rule on the finality of answers on collateral matters (16.5.2 *ante*) and unable to adduce evidence to show that she was lying (*R* v. *Holmes* (1871) LR1 CCR 334 (CCCR), *R* v. *Cargill* [1913] 2 KB 271 (CCA)).

Much of the common-law approach to relevance has now been abandoned as untenable, but there is clear logic in the view that the complainant's consensual sexual relationship with the accused himself can have a bearing on whether his defence is true. First, common sense dictates that a woman is unlikely to consent to sex with a man who has *already* raped her. Second, depending on the circumstances, a lengthy consensual sexual relationship prior to the alleged offence may allow the inference to be drawn that the alleged rape was also consensual sex or that the accused *believed* the complainant was consenting (the 'defence' of no *mens rea*). Certainly the defence of mistaken belief in consent where the allegation is one of indecent assault is far more likely to be true if the accused and complainant were involved in a lengthy sexual relationship prior to the incident, and it would be absurd to keep the jury (or magistrates) in the dark about that relationship. Alternatively, the turbulent nature of the protagonists' previous sexual relationship, or the way in which their relationship ended, might provide a motive supporting the accused's defence that the complainant has fabricated the allegation against him.

It is also clear, moreover, that the complainant's sexual experience with *other* persons may be logically relevant to an issue in the trial, particularly as her credibility will very often be inseparable from the issue whether sexual intercourse occurred or, if intercourse is admitted, whether she consented. Where the sole issue is consent and the complainant lies on oath, suggesting she would never have consented to sex in the circumstances of the admitted intercourse, the accused should be entitled to cross-examine her on any sexual experience which contradicts her testimony on the basis that it will undermine her credibility as a witness and therefore her testimony that she was raped. If, for example, it is alleged that the accused raped the complainant in her room while her child was sleeping near by, and the complainant testifies that she would never have consented to sex in those circumstances, it should be permissible to cross-examine her on the consensual sex she has had with boyfriends in her room while her child was sleeping there (see *R* v. *Riley* [1991] Crim LR 460 (CA)). Similarly, if the complainant testifies that prior to the alleged rape she was a virgin, and the accused is so unappealing that the jury would find it hard to believe that she would have consented to her first act of sex with him, evidence that she was in fact sexually experienced with other unappealing men would not only undermine her credibility as a witness (and therefore her evidence that she did not consent) but would also suggest to the jury that she might have been more willing to consent to sex in those circumstances (*cf. R* v. *SMS* [1992] Crim LR 310 (CA)).

Conversely, the complainant's sexual experience with other men may support the accused's defence of consent in a more direct way, undermining her credibility as a collateral consequence. If the accused's defence to rape is that the complainant consented to sex but then demanded payment and 'cried rape' when he refused to comply, evidence that she conducted herself in precisely the same way with other men would logically support the accused's defence, not on the ground that it directly contradicts her testimony but because of the probative value in the 'striking similarity' of her behaviour on different occasions (*cf. R* v. *Krausz* (1973) 57 Cr App R 466 (CA)). In other words, a pattern of peculiar conduct may allow an inference to be drawn that the complainant acted in the same way at the time of the alleged offence. For example, if the complainant alleges that she was raped by her personal fitness trainer, and his defence is that she threw herself at him and had consensual sex, after which she took umbrage at his decision not to pursue the relationship, evidence of consensual sexual relationships with a string of other personal fitness trainers in the preceding year, in which the complainant took the initiative, would materially support his version of events and increase the likelihood that she is not telling the truth.

As a matter of strict logic, if the allegation is one of vaginal rape outside marriage, evidence of any previous consensual extramarital sex by the complainant will be relevant to the issue of consent on the ground that it places the complainant in a particular category of woman (that is, women who are not absolutely opposed to fornication). The probative value of such evidence will of course be *extremely* low in the vast majority of cases and ought to be excluded on the ground of 'irrelevance' (3.1.3 *ante*). But the mere fact of extraneous consensual sex may have significant probative value in certain circumstances, particularly if the sexual acts are closely connected with the alleged rape. If, for example, the complainant was indulging in consensual sex with a stranger just a couple of hours after the alleged rape this would suggest that sex with the accused was also consensual, the generalisation being that women who have just been raped are unlikely to have casual sex so soon afterwards.

The complainant's extraneous sexual behaviour may also have a bearing on an issue other than consent. The accused may deny that he had sex with the complainant, and if she supports her allegation of rape with medical evidence of intercourse, evidence that she had sex with another man at about the same time as the alleged rape would logically undermine the prosecution case. Similarly, evidence of the complainant's sexual relationship with a man suffering from a sexually-transmitted disease would undermine her allegation that it was the accused, carrying no such disease, who raped and infected her. Alternatively, the accused's defence may be that he genuinely believed the complainant was consenting, even if it subsequently transpires that she was not. If the complainant says that she put up a fight during the alleged rape, evidence that she habitually pretended to put up a fight when having consensual sex with other men (and that the accused was aware of this) would materially support his defence.

In short, the complainant's extraneous sexual conduct may be logically relevant to her credibility as a witness or to an issue in the trial (or both) but it should *not* be regarded as relevant to her credibility on the basis that a sexually active woman is somehow inherently less trustworthy as a witness than a woman who is chaste. Nor in general should it be permissible to argue that the sexually promiscuous disposition of the complainant renders it more likely that she consented to sex with the accused. The 'moral credibility' argument has no basis in logic and any such evidence or line of questioning should be barred for that reason. The 'disposition' argument has some basis in logic, but the principle of free proof will in most cases carry insufficient weight when compared with countervailing considerations, such as the desirability of preventing prejudicial evidence from being placed before the jury (which might distract them or otherwise adversely affect their ability to consider the material evidence in a disinterested fashion), the need to respect the private life of the complainant (and prevent her from being unnecessarily distressed) and the public interest in encouraging genuine victims to bring their cases to court. *Any* evidence may be excluded on the ground of 'irrelevance' if its probative value is outweighed by competing policy considerations, a point noted by the Supreme Court of Canada in *R* v. *Darrach* [2000] 2 SCR 443 (at p. 467): 'An accused has never had a right to adduce irrelevant evidence. Nor does he have the right to adduce misleading evidence to support illegitimate inferences: the accused is not permitted to distort the truth-seeking function of the trial process.'

The common-law test for determining 'relevance', requiring an assessment of the probative value of the evidence (in the context of the issues and the factual matrix of the case) and any countervailing considerations of policy, is a sufficient basis for determining whether evidence of the complainant's extraneous sexual behaviour should be adduced or elicited, and statutory control over the admissibility of such evidence is necessary only insofar as it provides the judge with *guidance* on how his discretion ought to be exercised and the sort of policy considerations which need to be taken into account. In other words, because every case is factually unique and probative value cannot be determined in a vacuum, the test for admissibility should be one of guided discretion. This was recognised by the majority of the Supreme Court of Canada in *R* v. *Seaboyer* [1991] 2 SCR 577. It is certainly true that statutory provisions prohibiting the admission of the complainant's sexual experience may have a symbolic importance, but the desirability of appeasing political lobbyists is hardly an appropriate justification for enacting legislation which might exclude evidence of the accused's innocence in proceedings for very serious offences.

17.3 The Sexual Offences (Amendment) Act 1976

The common-law approach to relevance was significantly altered by s. 2 of the Sexual Offences (Amendment) Act 1976, the first statutory shield against intrusive questioning on the complainant's sexual history, which discarded the assumption that the complainant's sexual experience was always relevant to her credibility. Although this provision has now been repealed and supplanted by s. 41 of the Youth Justice and Criminal Evidence Act 1999 (17.4 *post*), the case-law to which it gave rise provides a number of examples of how a complainant's sexual experience may be relevant (and indeed highly probative) evidence of the accused's innocence.

Section 2 had its origins in the Heilbron Report (the Report of the Advisory Group on the Law of Rape, Cmnd 6352 (1975)). The Advisory Group felt that evidence of the complainant's sexual experience with persons other than the accused should be admissible only in exceptional circumstances on the ground that it was irrelevant to the complainant's credibility and would only rarely be relevant to any issue. The suggestion was that such evidence should be admissible only if it satisfied a similar facts test of 'striking similarity' analogous to the test established in *DPP* v. *Boardman* [1974] 3 WLR 673 (HL) (3.3.5 *ante*). This test did not become law as it was felt by Parliament to be unduly narrow. The need for reform was unquestionable, however, and the approach adopted in s. 2, although wider than the Heilbron proposal, was far more restrictive than the traditional common-law position, prohibiting cross-examination which amounted to no more than an attack on the sexual morality of the complainant as a way of suggesting that she was unlikely to be a truthful witness (*R* v. *Viola* [1982] 1 WLR 1138 (CA) at pp. 1142–3).

In most cases the mere fact that a complainant has had consensual sex with other persons will have little if any probative value with regard to whether she consented to sex with the accused on the occasion in question, but there may be circumstances where the probative value of her conduct is particularly high. In fact because the evidence under consideration is not directly associated with the facts of the allegation, its probative value can be determined by applying the same sort of reasoning which is used to determine the probative value of similar fact evidence (3.3.1 *ante*). The crucial difference is that because the accused is on trial (and is presumed to be innocent) the evidence of *his* past misconduct must be extremely probative of his guilt before its admission can be justified, on account of the risk that his defence will be unduly prejudiced. The complainant in a case of rape is in an entirely different category. The probative value of her sexual experience will be determined in the same way, but the risk of undue prejudice against her as a prosecution witness pales into insignificance when weighed against the need to ensure that an innocent man is not convicted of a serious offence. The Heilbron view that admissibility should be determined on the basis of a 'striking similarity' test was flawed for two reasons. First, past conduct can be highly probative in the absence of striking similarity (3.3.5 *ante*). Second, the strict test for the admissibility of similar fact evidence against the accused has developed in criminal trials so that the accused will get a fair trial. The Heilbron approach would have undermined that right.

Section 2(1) of the 1976 Act provided that no evidence could be adduced or elicited in cross-examination (by or on behalf of the accused) about the sexual experience of the complainant with any person other than the accused unless the judge gave leave. The judge was permitted to give leave under s. 2(2) only if it would be unfair to the accused to refuse to allow the evidence to be adduced or elicited. The judge had to apply a two-stage test which entailed first determining whether the evidence was relevant and then deciding whether it would be unfair to the accused to prevent the introduction of that evidence.

Although s. 2 applied only to 'rape offences', it was held that the spirit of the legislation should be applied to sexual offences generally (*R* v. *Funderburk* [1990] 1 WLR 587 (CA)). The provision did not, however, cover the complainant's other sexual acts with the accused himself or with things other than a person. Nor did it provide any guidance on how to determine the relevance of the complainant's sexual experience or the question of unfairness. It was for the judge in each case to look at the issues and evidence and apply his own judgment to determine whether the evidence was logically relevant to the accused's defence. If the relevance lay solely in attempting to undermine the complainant's broad moral credibility the questions would not be allowed. Generally, then, the accused had to show that the complainant's sexual experience was relevant to an issue in the trial; but because the question of the accused's guilt would often turn on whether the jury believed the accused or the complainant, her credibility would in practice be inextricably tied up with the credibility of the accused's defence. Accordingly leave to cross-examine under s. 2(2) could be obtained to attack the complainant's specific credibility, her veracity as a witness, so long as the resolution of an issue depended on whom the jury believed. If consent was in issue and there was no independent evidence to show what took place, any sexual experience which threw doubt on the complainant's veracity would be relevant to that issue and cross-examination on it was likely to be permitted – so long of course as its relevance did not depend on the discredited argument which had previously allowed juries to reason from promiscuity to untruthfulness.

Thus, it was *not* unfair to prevent the accused from cross-examining the complainant on her promiscuity if the sole argument was that her willingness freely to consent to sex with others made it more likely that she consented to sex with the accused (*R* v. *Brown* (1988) 89 Cr App R 97 (CA)); but promiscuity which was very proximate to the alleged rape could be sufficiently probative of consent to make its exclusion unfair to the accused. In *R* v. *Viola* [1982] 1 WLR 1138 the Court of Appeal was of the view that the accused should have been allowed to cross-examine the complainant on her sexual advances to other male acquaintances less than two hours before the alleged rape, and also on the fact that a naked man had been found lying on her sofa eight or nine hours after the alleged rape. This evidence was relevant to the issue of consent and sufficiently probative of the accused's innocence to be admitted.

In *R* v. *Cox* (1986) 84 Cr App R 132 the complainant had told her boyfriend that the accused had raped her the day before, when the boyfriend had been in police custody. The accused's defence was consent, and he sought leave to cross-examine the complainant on an earlier occasion when she had had sex with another man while her boyfriend was away and then made a false allegation of rape when the boyfriend had found out. The judge did not give leave and the accused was convicted. The Court of Appeal held that the cross-examination should have been permitted as it went to her credibility and the jury might well have come to a different conclusion if they had been allowed to hear it. The purpose of the intended cross-examination was not to attack the complainant's moral credibility as a promiscuous woman, but to attack her credibility in the legitimate sense of revealing to the jury that she was the sort of person who would have consensual intercourse and then fabricate an allegation of rape. Similarly, in *R* v. *Cleland* [1995] Crim LR 742, where the complainant claimed she had not had unprotected sex with her boyfriend and attributed her pregnancy to the alleged rape, the Court of Appeal held she should have been cross-examined on an abortion she had had before the alleged rape (and on the fact that she had menstruated after the alleged rape). In *R* v. *Redguard* [1991] Crim LR 213 the Court of Appeal held that cross-examination on the complainant's sexual experience should have been permitted as it went both to her credibility and to the issue of consent. The allegation was that the accused had raped the complainant in her flat. His defence was consent. The complainant testified that she would not have allowed anyone but her boyfriend to stay in her flat, let alone have sex with her there. The accused was prevented from cross-examining her about a consensual sexual encounter she had had with another man in her flat some weeks after the alleged rape. His appeal was allowed on the ground that the cross-examination could have shown the complainant was willing to lie on oath and that it was more likely she had consented to sex with the accused.

The variety of factual situations where the complainant's sexual experience can be relevant to her veracity and an issue is apparent. In the final analysis the (albeit vague) test of unfairness to the accused in s. 2(2) recognised this, relying on the trial judge to ascertain whether the evidence was logically relevant in the context of the case and whether it was sufficiently probative for its admission to be justified. Although the 1976 Act was not wholly satisfactory (applying only to 'rape offences' as opposed to all sexual offences) it prevented *improper* attacks on the dignity of the complainant while recognising the significant probative value the complainant's sexual experience could have in respect of her credibility (in a legitimate sense) and an issue in the proceedings. It therefore recognised the importance of the presumption of innocence and the concomitant desirability of allowing the accused to bring out evidence which undermined the case against him. The accused's rights were protected, as were the complainant's insofar as it was no longer permissible to cross-examine her with a view to tarnishing her moral credibility.

However, in 1998 a Home Office-led interdepartmental working group, citing one source of data which suggested that 'sexual history evidence is introduced in up to 75% of applications for the admission of [such] evidence in rape trials' (but providing no indication of the percentage of cases in which an 'application' is actually made) came to the firm conclusion that evidence of this sort was being used 'in an attempt to discredit the victim's [*sic*] character in the eyes of the jury' and that 'there is overwhelming evidence that the present practice in the courts is unsatisfactory' (Home Office report, *Speaking up for Justice* (1998) at p. 69). If this was the case (and the argument put forward in the report is anything but convincing) it could only have been the fault of trial judges for not applying their discretion to admit sexual experience evidence in accordance with the terms of the Act and the guidance provided by the Court of Appeal in *R* v. *Viola* [1982] 1 WLR 1138.

The test established by the Act was as satisfactory as it could be. In other words, while it would have been appropriate to provide the judiciary with better training or guidance on how probative value was to be determined, and on the nature and significance of factors militating against admitting the evidence, there was hardly a pressing need for root and branch reform. Indeed, the introduction of the Human Rights Act 1998, and with it an express reaffirmation of the principle that the accused is presumed to be innocent and entitled to a fair trial, militated against any significant change in the test for admissibility. Nevertheless, s. 2 of the 1976 Act was repealed and replaced by s. 41 of the Youth Justice and Criminal Evidence Act 1999 with effect from 4 December 2000.

17.4 The Youth Justice and Criminal Evidence Act 1999

In the case of *R* v. *Seaboyer* [1991] 2 SCR 577 the majority of the Supreme Court of Canada held that s. 276 of the Canadian Criminal Code, a provision prohibiting the admission of evidence of the complainant's extraneous sexual experience with persons other than the accused, had to be struck down as unconstitutional, the reason being that it comprised a blanket rule of exclusion subject to just three specific exceptions. If the section had been upheld, logically relevant evidence which supported the accused's defence would have been inadmissible (regardless of its probative value) if it could not be brought within one of the three categories of relevance. There was no facility for the trial judge to balance probative value against competing considerations so, while the provision ensured that evidence of sexual experience could not be used for illegitimate purposes, it also prevented the accused from being able to rely on such evidence when it would be legitimate to do so. Accordingly, s. 276 violated the accused's right not to be deprived of his liberty except in accordance with the principles of fundamental justice and his right to a fair trial (respectively ss. 7 and 11(*d*) of the Canadian Charter of Rights and Freedoms) and failed the proportionality test under s. 1 of the Charter as to what could be justified in a free and democratic society. The majority of the Court noted that provisions such as s. 276, comprising a mandatory rule of exclusion subject to specific exceptions (the so-called 'Michigan model'), were fundamentally flawed. Specific categories of relevance can never anticipate the multitude of circumstances which may arise in practice, and the trial judge was given no latitude to determine relevance and probative value in the case before him. It was noted that the 'category of relevance' approach had been rejected as an inappropriate basis for determining the admissibility of 'similar fact evidence' (3.3.4 *ante*) and, for similar reasons, it could not form the test for admitting evidence of the complainant's sexual experience. Importantly the Court also noted that in jurisdictions using the Michigan model the courts had circumvented the blanket prohibition by 'reading down' and 'constitutional exemption'. Section 276 was therefore held to be of no force and the judiciary were provided with guidelines explaining how the common-law exclusionary discretion should be applied. These guidelines were subsequently incorporated into a new version of s. 276 (see *R* v. *Darrach* [2000] 2 SCR 443 (SCC)). In the light of the Canadian experience, and given the enactment of the Human Rights Act 1998, it is difficult to understand why a Michigan-type model was thought to be an appropriate replacement for s. 2 of the Sexual Offences (Amendment) Act 1976.

Section 41(1) of the Youth Justice and Criminal Evidence Act 1999 provides that, in the absence of leave, the accused and his advocate are prohibited from adducing or seeking to elicit in cross-examination evidence relating to 'any sexual behaviour of the complainant' if the accused is charged with a 'sexual offence'. Sexual behaviour covers 'any sexual behaviour or other sexual experience, whether or not involving any accused or other person, but excluding ... anything alleged to have taken place as part of the event which is the subject matter of the charge against the accused' (s. 42(1)(*c*)). The relevant sexual offences are set out in s. 62 of the Act and include rape, burglary with intent to rape, indecent assault and unlawful intercourse. Thus, unlike the 1976 Act, the prohibition applies to sexual behaviour with the accused himself, to sexual behaviour with inanimate objects and in relation to allegations other than 'rape offences'.

The court *may* give leave under s. 41(2), but only if it is satisfied that s. 41(3) or (5) applies *and* a refusal of leave might have the result of rendering unsafe a conclusion on any relevant issue in the case. Further, by virtue of s. 41(6), the evidence or question must relate to one or more specific instances of alleged sexual behaviour on the part of the complainant (as opposed to evidence of reputation); and, for the purposes of s. 41(3) leave will not be given if it is reasonable to assume that the purpose (or main purpose) for which the evidence would be adduced or elicited is to impugn the credibility of the complainant as a witness (s. 41(4)). Any application for leave must be heard in private and in the absence of the complainant (s. 43(1)).

Section 41(5) applies if the evidence or question would enable the accused to explain or rebut 'any evidence adduced by the prosecution about any sexual behaviour of the complainant'. This would presumably allow the complainant to be cross-examined on the sort of evidence which was in issue in *R* v. *Cleland* [1995] Crim LR 742 (CA) (17.3 *ante*). A literal interpretation of the subsection suggests that, if the complainant were to state on oath that she was a virgin until the alleged assault, the defence would be unable to rebut that evidence as it would not fall within the meaning of 'any sexual behaviour' (as defined in s. 42(1)(*c*)). In *R* v.

Rooney [2001] EWCA Crim 2844 the Court of Appeal therefore held, following a concession from the Crown, that defence counsel should have been permitted to cross-examine the complainant under s. 41(5) on whether she had performed oral sex on a youth in the summer of 1996, following her testimony that she had 'never had a sexual experience before' an incident alleged to have occurred with the accused in 1997. Presumably, then, if the complainant testifies that she would *not* have consented to sex with the accused in the circumstances of the alleged offence, it will be permissible to rebut that assertion with evidence that she had previously consented to sex in such circumstances (as in *R* v. *Riley* [1991] Crim LR 460 (CA), 17.2 *ante*); and if the complainant testifies that she would never have consented to a man as physically unappealing as the accused, it would be permissible to cross-examine her on her consensual sexual involvement with even less attractive men. Subsection (5), unlike subsection (3), is not subject to the credibility prohibition in subsection (4), the reason being that the adduction of evidence to rebut the complainant's testimony is done for the purpose of undermining her credibility as a witness in a legitimate sense (rather than impugning her general moral credibility).

Section 41(3) applies if the evidence or question 'relates to a relevant issue in the case' and: (*a*) that issue is not an issue of consent; or (*b*) it is an issue of consent and the sexual behaviour is alleged to have taken place 'at or about the same time as the event which is the subject matter of the charge'; or (*c*) it is an issue of consent and the sexual behaviour 'is alleged to have been, in any respect, so similar (i) to any sexual behaviour of the complainant which ... took place as part of the event which is the subject matter of the charge ..., or (ii) to any other sexual behaviour of the complainant which ... took place at or about the same time as that event, that the similarity cannot reasonably be explained as a coincidence'.

Importantly for the accused, 'issue of consent' in s. 41(3)(*a*) does not include any issue as to the *belief* of the accused that the complainant consented, so the defence will be able to adduce or elicit from the complainant evidence of her previous sexual behaviour (of which he was aware) if it has a bearing on whether the accused mistakenly believed that she was consenting, so long as the judge is satisfied that to refuse leave might render unsafe a finding on that issue (s. 41(2)(*b*)) and the evidence or questioning is not prohibited by subsection (4) or (6). Accordingly, it is not permissible to cross-examine the complainant on her reputation or general character as a sexually promiscuous woman (s. 41(6)). In *R* v. *A (No. 2)* [2001] 2 WLR 1546 (HL) (at p. 1573) Lord Hope opined that s. 41(3)(*a*) would also permit cross-examination to show that the complainant was biased against the accused, that there is an alternative explanation for the physical conditions on which the prosecution rely to establish that sexual intercourse with the accused took place, and that the detail of a young complainant's account could have come from sexual activity with a person other than the accused. If s. 41(3)(*a*) does indeed permit cross-examination of the complainant on other sexual behaviour to show bias (that is, her motive for lying), there can be little doubt that the questioning will be prohibited if that motive can just as easily be shown without reference to her sexual behaviour (*R* v. *Mokrecovas* [2002] 1 Cr App R 226 (CA)).

The trial judge has a discretion as to whether the evidence of extraneous sexual experience should be admitted under s. 41(3)(*a*) (where the issue is not consent) and under s. 43(5) (where the evidence is aimed at impugning the complainant's credibility in a legitimate way), the governing criterion in each case being whether exclusion might lead to an unsafe conviction (s. 41(2)(*b*)). The problem with the scope of s. 41 lies in the test to be applied in cases where the issue *is* consent, as it is most likely to be in practice, for the only routes available to the accused are those provided by paragraphs (*b*) and (*c*) of s. 41(3).

Paragraph (*b*) is unlikely to be utilised much in practice, given the very narrow window provided by the phrase 'at or about the same time' as the alleged sexual assault. The explanatory notes provided by the Home Office suggest that this should be interpreted 'no more widely than 24 hours before or after the [alleged] offence' (in line with the wording used in the original Bill). This *res gestae* exception would permit cross-examination on, for example, the complainant's consensual sexual activity with another man soon after the alleged assault (as in *R* v. *Viola* [1982] 1 WLR 1138 (CA), 17.3 *ante*) or her consensual foreplay with the accused himself just prior to the alleged assault. However, it would not permit the admission of evidence such as that the accused and complainant had consensual sex a few days *after* the alleged offence or a lengthy sexual relationship prior to the alleged offence (if the last relevant act occurred a few days before the alleged offence) even though such evidence would have a logical bearing on whether the complainant consented during the incident in question. (In the latter case cross-examination might be permissible under s. 41(3)(*a*) if the accused is able to run a concurrent defence of mistaken belief in consent.) Read literally the exception in paragraph (*c*) is also very narrowly drawn, representing a resurrection of the sort of 'striking similarity' test originally proposed in the Heilbron Report (17.3 *ante*). It permits questioning on extraneous sexual behaviour only if that behaviour is so similar to any sexual behaviour which 'took place as part of' or 'at or about the same time as' the incident which gave rise to the allegation – but only if that similarity cannot reasonably be explained as a coincidence. This exception was not included in the original Bill, but was incorporated during its passage through Parliament following concerns that there was no provision permitting cross-examination on the complainant's peculiarly similar behaviour (such as re-enacting the balcony scene from *Romeo and Juliet* prior to intercourse).

In short, paragraphs (*b*) and (*c*) recognise that the complainant's extraneous sexual behaviour may indeed be logically relevant to the issue of consent, but (read literally) limit the test of relevance to two extremely narrow categories which apply even if the behaviour in question was with the accused himself. The only safeguard provided by s. 41 is that where the accused is also able to run the defence of mistaken belief in consent the evidence will be admissible for that purpose under s. 41(3)(*a*). Thus, if the accused is charged with indecently assaulting the complainant it will be permissible (subject to s. 41(2)(*b*)) to adduce or elicit evidence of their lengthy relationship involving consensual sex to show it was reasonably possible that he mistakenly *believed* she was consenting but not to show that she was *actually* consenting. It should not be assumed that it will always be possible to run the two defences concurrently, however, for the complainant may allege that she was violently raped and the accused's defence may be that it was nothing other than straightforward consensual intercourse during which the complainant took the initiative.

Section 41 was considered by the House of Lords in the case of *R* v. *A (No. 2)* [2001] 2 WLR 1546. The allegation against the accused was that he had raped the complainant, and the issue was whether she had consented to the admitted sexual intercourse with him or, in the alternative, whether he had believed that she was consenting. To this end counsel for the accused had wished to adduce or elicit evidence of the consensual sexual relationship between them, which had ceased about a week before the incident forming the subject of the allegation. The trial judge ruled against the accused on the ground that the evidence fell within none of the three categories of relevance in subsection (3) and was therefore absolutely prohibited. The Court of Appeal, following a concession from the Crown, held that the evidence was admissible under s. 41(3)(*a*) in relation to the issue of mistaken belief in consent but not the issue of consent itself, noting in the course of its judgment that the direction to the jury would 'have more of a flavour of Lewis Carroll than a rehearsal of the matters of jurisprudence'. It was also felt that, as a matter of common sense, a person who had previously had sexual intercourse with the accused might, on the occasion in dispute, have consented to sexual intercourse with him (see *R* v. *Y* (2001) *The Times* 13.2.01 (CA)). In the House of Lords it was also accepted that a prior consensual sexual relationship between a complainant and the accused himself might well be logically relevant to the issue of consent in situations not covered by (a literal reading of) paragraphs (*b*) and (*c*) of s. 41(3) for, as Lord Steyn noted (at p. 1557), what 'one has been engaged on in the past may influence what choice one makes on a future occasion'. Lords Steyn, Slynn, and Hutton concluded that, if read literally, s. 41 was incompatible with Article 6(1) of the European Convention on Human Rights, but felt that it was possible to construe s. 41(3)(*c*), in accordance with the interpretative obligation under s. 3(1) of the Human Rights Act 1998, so that it would permit evidence of the complainant's extraneous sexual experience to be adduced or elicited if its probative value was sufficiently high in relation to the issue of consent that the accused would be denied a fair trial if it was excluded. Although the appeal before the House of Lords was concerned with the relevance of sexual activity between the accused himself and the complainant, as a matter of logic and fairness the same interpretation must apply in relation to logically probative evidence of the complainant's behaviour with persons other than the accused. Section 41(3)(*c*) has therefore been judicially rewritten to represent the general common-law rule that the accused may adduce or elicit any evidence which is relevant to his defence unless its probative value is insufficiently high when weighed against competing considerations, the most important of which in this context is the importance of protecting the complainant from indignity and preventing the accused from misleading the jury.

Although there is nothing in s. 41 to suggest that the accused is able to cross-examine the complainant on whether she has previously fabricated an allegation of sexual assault, in *R* v. *T*, *R* v. *H* [2002] 1 WLR 632 the Court of Appeal held that questions or evidence about the complainant's false allegations of sexual assault (or about her failure to complain about the offence allegedly committed by the accused when complaining about sexual offences allegedly committed by other persons) would normally be admissible at common law on the ground that such evidence or questions would not be 'about any sexual behaviour of the complainant' for the purposes of s. 41(1), but there must be a proper evidential basis to support an assertion of this sort. One further point is whether it would be permissible to cross-examine the complainant on the alleged sexual acts if she denies the falsity of her allegations. The rule on the finality of answers on collateral matters will not necessarily apply given that the complainant's credibility may be inseparable from an issue in the trial (*R* v. *Nagrecha* [1997] 2 Cr App R 401 (CA), 16.5.3 *ante*), so it might be possible for the accused to rely on s. 41(3)(*a*) if the issue is not consent and on (the judicially rewritten) s. 41(3)(*c*) if the issue is consent. The problem here is that s. 41(4) (as it stands) would prohibit cross-examination along these lines, and the subsection may therefore need to be given a restrictive interpretation under s. 3(1) of the Human Rights Act 1998 if its application would deny the accused a fair trial. Support for this approach lies in Lord Hope's view in *R* v. *A (No. 2)* [2001] 2 WLR 1546 (HL) that s. 41(3)(*a*) would permit cross-examination to show that the complainant was biased against the accused, notwithstanding the *prima facie* exclusionary rule in s. 41(4). It should be noted, however, that in *R* v. *Mokrecovas* [2002] 1 Cr App R 226 the Court of Appeal felt that s. 41(4) reflected a desirable policy and expressed concern that s. 41(3)(*a*) might be misused to ride a coach and horses through it; and in *R* v. *Darnell* [2003] EWCA Crim 176 the Court of Appeal had difficulty reconciling Lord Hope's observations with the clear terms of the prohibition in s. 41(4).

Whether the rule on the finality of answers to questions on collateral matters is applied (in cases where the complainant's credibility is inseparable from an issue) would now seem to be governed by a somewhat pragmatic test (see 16.5.3 *ante*). If the complainant has made a previous complaint of sexual assault against a person other than the accused, and the accused's advocate wishes to cross-examine her on it with a view to demonstrating that it was a false allegation, in the first instance the questioning must be limited to whether the allegation was made and whether it was true. If the complainant maintains that she was indeed abused by that other person the judge will have to determine whether the rule on the finality of answers should be applied to prevent further cross-examination aimed at showing that the allegation was false, and this will depend on whether the falsity can be easily demonstrated or whether it will in effect necessitate an additional trial within the present one. In *R* v. *Brownlow* [2001] EWCA Crim 3042 the Court of Appeal, relying on the decision in *R* v. *T, R* v. *H* [2002] 1 WLR 632, held that the accused's counsel should have been permitted to cross-examine the complainant on whether she had made a complaint of sexual abuse against a man other than the accused, but further held that, if the complainant had maintained that the allegation was true, any further questioning could only have extended to whether the other man had ever been charged as a result of that allegation.

The prohibition on cross-examination as to credit in s. 41(4) of the Act was relied on in *R* v. *Singh (No. 2)* [2003] EWCA Crim 485 – which concerned very similar allegations by two teenage girls of stranger rape by the accused in 1997 – to prevent cross-examination on the fact that one of the complainants (C2) had lied on oath about her sexual experience. C2 alleged that D had raped her in December 1997, when she was 16 years old, and D was convicted following a trial in 1999. His conviction was quashed on appeal, however, when it transpired that C2's evidence that she had been a virgin prior to the alleged rape was false. At the retrial in 2001, where no such assertion of virginity was made, D's counsel applied to cross-examine C2 on the fact that she had lied on oath during the first trial, as it went 'to the issue of whether she gave truthful evidence' (that is, her credibility as a witness). The judge refused to give leave and D was again convicted. The Court of Appeal upheld the judge's ruling because of the prohibition in s. 41(4). It was therefore argued that the trial judge should have allowed the cross-examination on the alternative ground that C2's earlier act of intercourse was relevant to the issue 'whether or not the Defendant had had sexual intercourse ... with the ... complainant', his defence being that they had engaged in consensual sexual activity short of intercourse, and that the doctor who had examined her, if questioned on the matter, might have given an opinion that she had been penetrated on no more than one occasion. This argument was also rejected, because of the speculation involved and, further, because it was regarded as nothing more than another argument that the cross-examination should have been permitted to impugn C2's credibility. Given the nature of the case and the totality of the prosecution evidence against D, this was not a surprising outcome. The decision does not mean that s. 41(4) will always prevent cross-examination on lies involving sexual activity. If, unlike the instant case, an allegation depends solely on the credibility of the complainant, because there is no medical evidence of forced intercourse or other violence, no evidence of distress, and the only issue is whether she consented, the accused will almost certainly be permitted to cross-examine the complainant on her perjury even though it relates to her extraneous sexual behaviour.

Chapter Summary

- The complainant's extraneous sexual behaviour may be logically relevant to the accused's defence to an allegation of sexual abuse by tending to show that someone other than the accused committed the offence or that the complainant consented to the (admitted) activity with the accused or that the accused genuinely believed that the complainant was consenting or that her testimony is not worthy of belief. The relevance of the evidence is not based on the argument that complainants who have other sexual relationships are more likely to be untruthful. Nor is it based on the argument that a complainant who has been sexually involved with other persons is more likely to have consented to sexual relations with the accused at the material time.
- Section 41 of the Youth Justice and Criminal Evidence Act 1999 provides that if the accused is charged with a sexual offence against the complainant the court may give the accused's advocate leave to adduce or seek to elicit evidence of the complainant's extraneous sexual behaviour (whether or not it involved the accused) only if the evidence relates to specific instances of her sexual behaviour and refusal of leave might result in the jury's reaching an unsafe conclusion and:
  - the evidence would enable the accused to rebut prosecution evidence about the complainant's sexual behaviour (or the complainant's claim to have had no other sexual behaviour); or
  - the evidence relates to an issue and the purpose is not to use it to impugn the complainant's credibility and:– the issue is not (actual) consent; or the issue *is* consent and the evidence comprises *res gestae* evidence of sexual behaviour or the probative value of the evidence is sufficiently high in relation to consent that the accused would be denied a fair trial if it were to be excluded.

Further Reading

Berger, 'Man's Trial, Woman's Tribulation' (1977) 77 Columbia LR 1
Elliott, 'Rape Complainants' Sexual Experience with Third Parties' [1984] Crim LR 4
McColgan, 'Common Law and the Relevance of Sexual History Evidence' (1996) 16 OJLS 275
Durston, 'Cross-Examination of Rape Complainants' (1998) 62 JCL 91
Ellison, 'Cross-Examination in Rape Trials' [1998] Crim LR 605
Kibble, 'The Sexual History Provisions' [2000] Crim LR 274
Birch, 'Rethinking Sexual History Evidence' [2002] Crim LR 531
Temkin, 'Sexual History Evidence – Beware the Backlash' [2003] Crim LR 217
Birch, 'Untangling Sexual History Evidence' [2003] Crim LR 370
Redmayne, 'Myths, Relationships and Coincidences' (2003) 7 E & P 75

Index